The Sociological Eye

The Sociological Eye

Selected papers

Everett C. Hughes

ALDINE·ATHERTON
Chicago & New York

First published 1971 by
Aldine • Atherton, Inc.
529 South Wabash Avenue
Chicago, Illinois 60605

Library of Congress Catalog Card Number 73-140009
ISBN 202-30097-8, cloth; 202-30195-0, paper, vol. I;
202-30196-0, paper, vol. II.
Printed in the United States of America

Preface

The first of these fifty-eight papers was written in the fall of 1927 at the invitation of my teacher, Robert E. Park; the last in the summer of 1969 at the invitation of Edward Gross, a former student. A number of those in between were written at the request of some person or organization for a particular occasion; thus a representative of the American Nurses' Association asked me to write "Studying the Nurse's Work" to promote interest in a program of research. Others were written after a striking experience; I heard the Brown Shirts in the streets of Nuremberg in 1930 singing, "The true German youth is never so happy as when Jewish blood spurts from his knife;" I wrote "Good People and Dirty Work" and used it as a special lecture at McGill University where in the 1930's I taught a course on Social Movements that came to be known as "Hughes on the Nazis." Still others were written about some subject that was on my mind at the time; thus, I wrote "Dilemmas and Contradictions of Status" at a time when I was teaching and doing research (with a large and able group of graduate students back from the War) on race relations and on various kinds of work in and outside industry. The title seemed a broader yet more specific formulation of the term *marginal man,* making it useful in study of any situation where one identifying characteristic of a person contradicts other traits.

The papers are not presented in the order in which they were written, but according to a scheme worked out by Howard S. Becker. At first I didn't like the scheme, but as I read the papers in this order, it seemed fair to the basic emphasis of most of the items. It also became clear that the titles did not always indicate the contents of the papers. I have tried to remedy this by putting phrases in the table of contents that are meant

v

both to specify the contents and to indicate the more general sociological reference of the given article.

Although the items were not written to be collected and constitute neither treatise nor textbook, there are themes that run through the lot. In my first paper I speak of human ecology and the division of labor, of professions, of professional and lay culture, of initiation into an occupation; I hint at ethnic division of labor and at kinds of careers in various occupations. Indeed, a stranger came to me after I read that paper at a meeting of the American Sociological Society and warned me not to put so many ideas into one paper again. Having put them all in, I fear that I have kept at work on the same general ideas and problems, although the concrete subject and the occasion have varied. My own research and that of colleagues and students have led to restatement and enrichment of the same ideas and reformulation of the same problems.

In my work I have relied a great deal on free association, sometimes on a freedom of association that could seem outrageous to the defenders of some established interest or cherished sentiment. Wright Mills must be given credit for the phrase *the sociological imagination*. The essence of the sociological imagination is free association, guided but not hampered by a frame of reference internalized not quite into the unconscious. It must work even in one's dreams but be where it can be called up at will. When people say of my work, as they often do, that it shows insight, I cannot think what they could mean other than whatever quality may have been produced by intensity of observation and a turning of the wheels to find a new combination of the old concepts, or even a new concept. I think I even do my reading by free association: "Didn't Simmel, or Durkheim, Weber, Mead, Marshall, or someone say something on that point?" I do a good deal of my reading by starting with the index.

Observation and imagination must start somewhere. Leaving out earlier experiences, my significant education started in the Department of Sociology and Anthropology of the University of Chicago in the fall of 1923. Albion W. Small, Ellsworth Faris, Ernest Burgess and especially Robert E. Park were my teachers. My only problem was that I had no problem, no mission. So far as I know, unanalyzed as I am, I had no deep trauma. I was on the right side of most social causes. I gave up the teetotalism on which I had been reared without the least struggle. I was ready for a new father, but saw no need of liquidating my old one; some of my ideas and actions distressed my father, but he followed my career with interest and pride. There are some very sociological passages in the diary he left me.

It took me the better part of a term to begin to sense what Park was talking about. Then it turned out to be theories and ideas. One moment he talked in a newsy way and next in a very abstract way; he talked of social forces, races and nationalities, crowds and social movements, public opin-ion and the newspaper, cities, and finally, about human communities and human ecology. Whatever his course in a given term, I took it. I wrote term papers about the press agent, city land values, real estate agents who wanted to become professional, the Florida land boom, Pullman and other industrial model towns—sectarian Utopias, and the great commodity and money markets of the world, and the systems of communication and risk-spreading that made them possible. A very radical young woman and Robert Redfield and I wrote, for Professor Faris's course on social psy-chology, a paper on revolutionary movements in various civilizations and epochs.

While the substance of the courses was new and interesting, it was the point of view that took hold of me. Society is interaction. Interaction involves sensitivity to others, but to some others more than other others. Sects control their young by isolating them from interaction with dangerous others. "Even that which appears solid and fixed, such as the table on which my hands are resting, is a product of the mad interaction of particles. It could blow up" said Park in class one morning.

The most striking new thing was human ecology, which Park was then thinking and talking about. He had been interested in various movements to restore community life; from there he moved to study of the nature of communities. This led him to the concept of the plant community, developed by botantists, and to the human geographers, active at that time in France. One got the notion that every social nucleus, every module of human interaction was part of some larger scheme; it was a matter of finding the connections. Park at one time talked a good deal about "closed systems," but it seemed to him and seems to me now that the closure is never complete in human affairs. Human ecology was to be a view of things that would keep one on the lookout for the frontiers of any system of things and beyond the frontiers for remote connections with other orders of happenings. While any human phenomenon is worth studying closely, if at all, it is never to be completely understood in terms of itself. Its peripheries must be explored.

As a matter of fact, I had a good deal more contact with Park after I went to teach at McGill University than before. In the 1930's he was working on human ecology, and in his paper of that title[1] he speaks of the worldwide division of labor." The summer he wrote the paper we travelled and camped together through the Quebec countryside and together looked for signs of the ecological relations of the French and English. Thus the study of the effects of industrialization on the relations of French and

1. *American Journal of Sociology,* XLII, July, 1936, pp. 1-15.

English became a study of the ethnic division of labor, of demography and social structure. That study was reported in *French Canada in Transition*,[2] but a number of the papers in this collection deal with multi-ethnic societies. All of them are implicitly ecological, although not to the exclusion of more directly social interest.

My first paper grew out of study of an institution, ("The Growth of an Institution: The Chicago Real Estate Board"), one of whose aims came to be to turn a business into a profession. It turned out that this was a characteristic aim of occupations both new and old. I found myself looking for the dimensions along which occupations can be compared. Many of the students who came to my courses took up that interest. I became involved in study of work dramas and the roles to be played in them, but I did not settle down to study of any one occupation as my special interest. It was the patterns of interaction, not the particular occupation, that held my interest. In this, as in study of race relations, it is not the substance, but—as Simmel would have said—the recurring form and its many variations that catches my interest. The papers on the problems of work are thus, I trust, something of a contribution to the battery of concepts to be used in research and analysis.

Not all would agree with my definition of institutions. Cooley says an institution is simply a definite and established phase of the public mind. MacIver and others distinguish institutions from associations. But definitions are made for sociological man, not man for definitions. In any society there are certain mobilizations of people for expression or action. They are "going concerns;" some people keep them going. Other people get moved by them or to them from time to time and they also keep them going. When one studies that great ineffable phase of the public mind called religion, he eventually comes across parishes, congregations, and Norman Vincent Peale's and Oral Roberts' radio broadcasts. *Association* seems hardly the word. If we are to study human society, we must attend to the going concerns, which are subject to moral, social, and ecological contingencies. It is thus that institutions are discussed in these papers as enterprises that mobilize people into various offices and capacities,—and sometimes suddenly fail to do so.

Some say that sociology is a normative science. If they mean that social norms are one of its main objects of study, I agree. If they mean anything else, I do not agreee. Many branches of human learning have suffered from taking norms too seriously. Departments of language in universities are often so normative that they kill and pin up their delicate moths of poetry and stuff their beasts of powerful living prose before letting students exam-

2. University of Chicago Press, 1943, 1963.

ine them. Language, as living communication, is one of the promising fields of study; it is not quite the same as the study of languages. Men constantly make and break norms; there is never a moment when the norms are fixed and unchanging. If they do appear to remain unchanged for some time in some place, that, too, is to be accounted for as much as change itself.

Certainly I have never sat down to write systematically about how to study society. I am suspicious of any method said to be the one and only. But among the methods I would recommend is the intensive, penetrating look with an imagination as lively and as sociological as it can be made. One of my basic assumptions is that if one quite clearly sees something happen once, it is almost certain to have happened again and again. The burden of proof is on those who claim a thing once seen is an exception; if they look hard, they may find it everywhere, although with some interesting differences in each case.

CONTENTS

Book One — Institutions and Race

Book Two — Work, Self, and the Study of Society

Part III — Work and Self

Contents   xvii

Institutions and Race

Institutions

ONE

The Ecological Aspect
of Institutions

The only idea common to all usages of the term institution is that of some sort of establishment of relative permanence of a distinctly social sort. On this point even those agree who, like Allport, admit the reality of institutions only long enough to "find individuals to study who are behaving institutionally."[1] Some let this idea stand as a sufficient definition, thus allowing the simplest folkways and the most elaborate "culture-complexes" to fall under the category. Psychologists incline toward such inclusive usage as would make institutions merely the social aspect of the behavior which they describe. Sociologists are more likely to restrict usage of the term, by distinguishing institutions from simpler units of socially established behavior. Sumner, for instance, puts them over against the folkways and mores.[2]

Another idea fundamental to the study of human life, that of collective behavior, grows out of the fact that human beings so obviously behave in response to the behavior of each other that what the individual does can be understood only by using the collectivity as a point of reference. Institutions are sometimes defined by distinguishing them from such ele-

Read at the American Sociological Society, 1935. *Amerian Sociological Review,* Vol. 1, April, 1936. It was written at the request of R. D. McKenzie who prepared for the same meeting his paper on the Ecology of Institutions. See Amos H. Hawley (ed.), *Roderick D. McKenzie on Human Ecology,* Chicago, University of Chicago Press, 1968, pp. 102–117.

1. F. H. Allport, *Institutional Behavior,* Chapel Hill, University of North Carolina Press, 1933, p. 24.

2. W. G. Sumner, *The Folkways,* Boston, Ginn and Co., 1906, par. 63.

mentary forms of collective behavior as the crowd and the primary group, whose peculiar feature is social interaction not mediated by established forms.[3]

There is an order of social phenomena in which the feature of establishment and that of collective behavior meet in a particular way; namely, so that the very form taken by the collective behavior is something socially established. Phenomena of this order are called institutions in this paper.

Only where human effort is formally integrated are there institutions in our sense. Such formal integration takes place with reference to some functionary or group of functionaries, acting in recognized social offices. It is in the character of an office not only that it cannot exist or be carried on without the appropriate recognition and responses of other people, but also that the person who fills it may be succeeded by another.

The permanence which is generally thought of as a cardinal feature of a social institution is closely involved with the fact that persons do succeed one another in offices, and that other people continue to behave with reference to these succeeding persons in certain ways which are established as social expectations. It is usual to attribute this relative permanence to the alleged filling of some elemental human want by the institution. It should, however, be obvious that an institution does not fill wants in their generic and eternal aspects, but in their particularly defined and culturally peculiar aspects. The survival of an institution, therefore, represents the persistence of particular definitions of wants and of corporate ways of satisfying them. The passing on of these wants to succeeding generations is another of the processes involved in the survival of institutions.

The persistence of an effective want, and of an institution, is subject to a great number of contingent factors. The study of institutions is as much a matter of discovering these contingencies as of discovering their roots in human nature. The contingencies arise out of the inevitable relations of social phenomena with other social phenomena and with phenomena that are not social at all. Indeed, one might say that the scientific study of institutions does not have to do with their essential nature, but merely puts institutions into some orderly and understood relations with other phenomena upon which they are contingent. One studies, in short, the conditions of their survival, for all of the attributes of institutions (save that collective

3. C. H. Cooley, *Social Organization,* N.Y., Charles Scribner's Sons, 1921, pp. 30 and 319, *et passim.* See also E. Faris, "The Primary Group: Essence and Accident," *Amer. Jour. of Sociol.,* 38, July, 1932, pp. 41–50. Simmel, in his *Soziologie,* pp. 14–15, complained that social science had paid attention only to "those societal phenomena in which the interaction had already been crystallized out of its bearers," and had neglected the more immediate, intimate and passing forms of interaction. That is, attention had been given only to the larger, more formal and institutional aspects of social life.

nature which they share with less formal phenomena) are matters of their survival in relation to other social and nonsocial phenomena.

The isolated tribal community may be thought of as a single corporate unit. So closely are the activities of its members integrated that tradition can quite easily and apparently does assign to each person his place in the corporate whole. In such a community the survival of any institution is subject to essentially the same contingencies as that of the community as a whole. These contingencies are, in theory at least, quite simple. To quote from Radcliffe-Brown:

> The continuity of a corporation such as the Australian horde is dependent upon the continuity of its estate. In the first place, there is continuity of possession of the territory. Secondly, there is a continuity which transcends the space of a human life by the fact that as the group loses some members by death it acquires new members by the birth of children and the initiation of boys into the status of men.[4]

The succession of persons to status and to office proceeds by the "natural processes of generation." One can, in such a case, work out in detail, as does Radcliffe-Brown in the paper just quoted from, a sort of geometry or mechanics of transmission of rights and status by which the form of the society is maintained, subject only to the contingencies which arise from its exploitation of the territory from which it lives and from acts of God.

There is, in effect, no competition of institutions within such a community. Competitive relationships can be studied in terms of the community as a whole rather than in terms of its parts. The communication and transportation, both of men and of goods, which are an unfailing characteristic of civilizations, complicate this picture. Institutions, in communities where there is mobility, survive subject to contingencies which arise out of mobility.

McKenzie, in an unpublished paper on "The Ecology of Institutions," develops the idea that with elaboration of our producing techniques and the machinery required for them, with the increase in the quantity and range of transportation and communication, the institutional structure of communities is increased in complexity. That is to say, institutions are increased in number, and more specialized as to function. They have likewise become discrete entities, each with its locus in space. Since participation in the life of the community becomes increasingly a matter of participating in some way in institutional activities, the institution becomes the crucial unit for study of the underlying competitive processes with which ecology is especially concerned.

4. "Patrilinear and Matrilineal Succession," *Iowa Law Review,* 20, Jan., 1935, p. 289.

In complicated civilized communities the survival of institutions cannot be significantly described in the simple terms of the succession of natural generations. One must turn to succession in space, the movements of people and the bearing of such movements on the corporate units through which collective wants are satisfied, remembering at the same time that these movements are related to institutions both as cause and effect. Where mobility is great, the term institutional generation has little significance. Participation in institutional activity may become almost completely casual. While this may be more especially true of business institutions, even the more sacred ones are subject in some measure to contingencies arising from mobility.

One corollary of mobility and opportunist participation is that, in contrast to simpler and more homogeneous communities, most institutions have only a part of the community's population among their adherents. Each person, in turn, participates in some fashion in a complement of institutions corresponding to his peculiar wants and his status in the community. His complement of institutions will correspond at some points with that of other persons, but by no means at all points.

The features of modern institutions which we have been emphasizing amount to a sort of fiscal separateness, which may be seen in the fact that institutional units are established, survive for a longer or shorter time, and disappear while the community as a whole goes on. It is their fiscal separateness and the consequent precariousness of their existence that make institutions, perforce, enterprises. The entrepreneur is one who undertakes to coordinate the activities of others; he makes decisions and meets contingencies. This function, although performed in a rudimentary way even in simple tribal communities, becomes a crucial feature of institutions in a society where the mores, whatever else they may do, do not foreordain that the individual shall stay put and remain within the framework of given corporate units throughout his life.[5]

Enterprise is ordinarily associated with business. That is probably because business consists, by definition, of those activities which are freest from traditional control. The lack of such control allows enterprise to operate freely, which is another way of saying that competition is unhampered. Park and Burgess have said of competition "that it tends to create an impersonal order in which each individual, being free to pursue his own profit, and, in a sense, compelled to do so, makes every other individual a

---

5. It is of interest, in this connection, that the entrepreneur and business enterprise were somewhat neglected by the "chess-game" classical economics, but have become the special interest of institutional economics. The works of Werner Sombart, for example, are above all devoted to the study of the forms of economic enterprise and to the types of entrepreneur characteristic of capitalism. See also Paul T. Homan, "Economics: The Institutional School," and Maurice Dobb, "Entrepreneur," in the *Ency. of Soc. Scs.*

means to that end."[6] Even where profit, in the monetary sense, is not involved, the function of enterprise appears in an institution in the measure that it survives by the conscious mobilization of people, through their wants and sentiments, by some active agent.[7]

The point of all this is that in our society, free enterprise is, if not a quantitatively constant, at least an ever-present feature of our institutions. It is for this very reason that there is need of a method for study of the circumstances under which, given enterprise and given our mores, certain institutional forms survive.

It is at this point that it becomes appropriate to say that institutions in our world are not only separate enterprises, but are also spatially separate. They are not necessarily mutually exclusive in space, but have separate and observable seats or focal points of activity. The distribution of their adherents may be entwined with that of numerous other institutions. It is, indeed, precisely their seats of activity that meet the eye. The movements of people to and from them and their underlying connections with other institutions have, in each case, to be discovered. When discovered and related to similar data on other units, they furnish clues to the functional relations of institutions. Just as the institutional connections of the individual reveal the "complement" of institutional services and activities which make up his economy of life, or, if one likes, his standard of living, so the lines of interdependence between institutions reveal the complement of institutions which make up communities.

The question now arises whether and under what circumstances spatial relations reflect the competitive processes pertinent to the survival of institutions. Simmel, in a chapter devoted to the spatial aspect of social forms, notes that it is movement around great fixed centers or focal points (*Drehpunkte*) which distinguishes civilization from tribal life.[8] In the latter, small closed groups wander as a whole, though actually within a small range. Civilization is characterized not only by the fixity of certain focal points (cities), but by a great range and freedom of movement. These centers take on an intertribal character, and institutions of control on a territorial basis grow up at the expense of kinship or other closed groups. Civilization may be said to begin where some aspect of life is reorganized with reference to some point external to the local tribal community; that is,

6. *Introduction to the Science of Sociology*, Chicago, University of Chicago Press, 1921, 1969, p. 508.
7. Recent studies made by Chas. S. Johnson and E. Franklin Frazier seem to show that the Negro family is much more likely to survive where ownership of property or the status of a profession give an incentive for keeping the family together. That is, not automatic operation of the mores, but disciplined enterprise keeps the family going.
8. Georg Simmel, *Soziologie*, München: Duncker & Humblot, 1908, 1923, chap. IX.

with the rise of intertribal centers, of which shrines and trade centers are the prototypes.[9]

These centers are socially established as symbols which dominate the sentiments of people over a wide area and through long periods of time. They are also focal points of transportation, travel, and communication. They do not so much occupy space as integrate and dominate movement within it. This, it seems to be, is characteristic of our major institutions, as well as of cities. That is to say, our larger institutions are more open as to the space which they dominate, and yet more fixed as to seat, than perhaps those of any epoch.

Simmel, in this connection, suggests a fundamental distinction as to the manner in which social structures occupy space. Some, he says, are mutually exclusive in space; others occupy the same space.[10] States, for example, collide in space; they maintain sovereignity over individuals irrespective of their clan, racial, religious, or other affiliations. Max Weber says, in a similar vein, that the state exists finally in the effective monopoly of the use of force in a given territory.[11]

Other institutions share the feature of closed space. The racket, for instance, operates by using force to maintain a monopoly of some function within a territory. Both the state and the racket engage in armed conflict over territorial boundaries, as against other units of the same order. For such institutions, the maintenance of boundaries is crucial.

Most institutions cannot be bounded in any such mutually exclusive way. Their seats can be located and their constituencies plotted with reference to them. But their space is, so to speak, open. Institutions which have a clientele, a group of people for whom they perform some specialized service, may draw from the same territory as other institutions which perform a similar service for other people, or some other service for the same people.

Such institutions may compete for individual patronage; the persons who support them may be regarded somewhat as customers. "Customer" in-

9. See articles on "Holy Places," "Caliphate," and "Papacy" in *Ency. of Soc. Scs.*; on "Mecca" and "Lhasa," in *Ency. Brit.,* 11th Ed. A significant feature of imperialistic expansion is just this reorientation of local life toward outside centers. Even within the Western world this process goes on in drawing the more provincial regions into the main currents of industrial life. In French Canada, for instance, the social changes brought about by the development of industry initiated by English-speaking people do not take the form of individual defection from French life to English life, but proceed by the integration of an increasing number of phases of life about institutions whose focal point is the city of Montreal. Newspapers, trade and labor organizations, fraternal orders, as well as business and industry, are a few of the institutions in terms of which this reorientation may be gauged.

10. *op. cit.,* p. 462.

11. "Politik als Beruf," *Gesammelte Politische Schriften,* p. 397.

stitutions tend to be located with reference to the probable movements of population, and also with reference to their competitors, in the struggle to be equally accessible to the people whose wants they exploit.

If two institutions draw upon the same people, either they are in competition, or else the services which they offer are somehow different. Even in the latter case they may compete in some measure, for people have but a limited amount of time, effort and money to expend. To survive, an institution must find a place in the standards of living of people, as well as in their sentiments. There is some reason to believe that, at this point, there is some competition even between the church and the motion picture house, and that spatial accessibility may play some part in the issue.

Moreover, there is a tendency for even open institutions to approach a monopoly over some aspect of behavior; this amounts to saying that they too tend to establish a territorial monopoly of a function. Marketing institutions, for instance, form cartels, and in so doing make of their services a sort of public utility within a closed territory.

Even the Protestant churches are coming to look on the exclusive territorial parish as the ideal. It can be achieved only by standardizing religion, so that in a given area a church can be established which will so nearly satisfy all Protestants who live there that no competing church will grow up.

The Catholic church can, in a purely Catholic country, achieve this ideal, because no one wants any other kind of religious service. Religion becomes a public utility available to all through a monopoly. The parish can, in such a case, survive a good deal of mobility of population. Even so, there are class differences which make parishes differ from one another in style of preaching and details of parish organization and function. When cultural and language differences are introduced by succession, even the Catholic parish church finds a problem of survival and of parish boundaries on its hands.

Thus far we have been speaking of institutions which survive by "serving" a clientele to which they must be accessible. Such institutions are especially subject to contingencies arising from spatial movement of population. Their spatial relations seem to be a function of movements which they do not themselves produce or control. Some institutions, on the contrary, seem to determine the nature of the communities in which they are situated. These McKenzie calls basic institutions. They may be, in general, fixed in place by the heavy capital goods which they require, as well as by some intricate set of relationships to a larger region, and even by tradition. Their specific and significant feature is, however, that they tend to attract a configuration of other institutions about them so that they create a community of a certain kind. About a great university, for example, there grows up a seat of learning; about a great industry there grows up, in like manner, a community bearing its peculiar stamp.

It is with reference to basic institutions, in this sense, that the ecological method of using spatial configurations as indices of functional relationships has been most intensively applied.[12] Usually the method has been applied to communities in which the basic institutions are of the most secular sort, namely, marketing institutions and those which produce for a market. Such institutions tend to occupy their space in the freest way and to be highly sensitive to changes in the methods of transportation and communication; yet they do create about themselves typical constellations of other institutions, from large to small. Some of them invariably dirty their own nests, and perhaps bring on their own undoing.

It may be that business institutions are the basic ones in most communities. If they are not so originally, they may become so. Certainly in a community such as Sainte Anne de Beaupré, the shrine takes on a certain business character, and the welfare of all other institutions, down to the last family, is affected by the number of pilgrims who come. Likewise, a small university town takes a business-like attitude toward its university.

Ecology has likewise dealt with the basic institutional forms which grow up at the frontiers of the western commercial and industrial world, such as the plantation, which exploits native labor to produce goods for the world market. While the plantation may be a political institution, as Thompson suggested, in a paper read before the Society last year, it is also the crucial form of business enterprise in reorientation of tribal life toward the larger world.

Of less commercial institutions, the Protestant churches have received most study by the ecological method. In this case, the recent work has been done by people interested in making the Protestant churches efficient enterprises. They tacitly admit that this is to be done by adapting the church to the community; they seem to entertain no thought that the church is a basic institution. Charles Booth anticipated them in suggesting the hypothesis that the churches of London seem to vary significantly in character from area to area without much regard for denomination. He maintained that the religious institutions which exploit the peculiar combination of sentimental orthodoxy and a hopeless bent to sinning of the London poor are the same in form no matter what the denomination they belong to or the doctrine they preach. All must resort to the same devices to survive. He also related religious, as well as other institutions, to the

12. See R. D. McKenzie, *The Metropolitan Community*, New York, McGraw-Hill, 1933, and various articles by the same author.

standard of living. Such a hypothesis, since it has to do with the church in its competitive or survival, rather than its spiritual aspect, implies the ecological point of view.[13]

Certain studies of the family, such as Frazier's work on the Negro family in Chicago, and Charles S. Johnson's work on rural Negro families, might be called ecological. They constitute studies of the conditions under which, in the given state of the mores, the family will survive as a cooperative enterprise.

And that, it seems to me, is precisely the ecological aspect of institutions. It disregards the social-psychological aspect of collective behavior. In the case of marketing and industrial institutions in a free world such as ours, it seems quite justifiable to do so, for the element of enterprise is fairly constant and the restraints of tradition minimal. Even the more sacred institutions are subject to the necessity of competing, in some measure, to survive. Every institution, as an ongoing affair, has a secular aspect. The more sacred may respond less quickly to changes in the surrounding world. If they respond at all, they are subject to some such treatment.

The ecological method does not and cannot deal with those institutions which are completely indifferent to spatial contingencies. One may well doubt whether there are such, although certain sectarian institutions may be relatively so.

It has also paid no attention to spatially closed institutions, especially the state, although states are undoubtedly contingent in many ways upon the processes which ecology describes. The relation between political phenomena and ecological processes has not yet received the attention it deserves.

It might well be asked whether in some sort of planned society competitive processes might not be so rationally controlled that the survival of institutions would no longer be subject to the contingencies here discussed. Since planning seems to mean such coordination of enterprise with respect to given functions within a closed territory as would make public utilities of the institutions concerned, its success may depend upon a proper understanding of the competitive processes and relationships which set the limits within which such coordination may be accomplished.

13. Charles Booth, *Life and Labour of the People of London,* London, Macmillan, 1902, 3rd series, "Religious Influences," Vol. 7, "Summary." See also H. Paul Douglass, *Church Comity,* N. Y., 1929. Douglass recognizes that churches reflect the standards of living of people (p. 2); hence any movement of population which entails a change of standard of living in an area threatens the existing churches.

The Study of Institutions

A large proportion of the people in our society live together in families, who carry on a life which, though constrained within limits set by the mores and by law, reflects the peculiarities of their members and the contingencies to which their times and surroundings subject them. Likewise, people go to work in factories; they study, teach, and play in schools, or at least, as citizens, are taxed for their upkeep. If they are residents of Latin American villages, they will engage once a year in a great fiesta; if they live in the rural Middle West, they might possibly be annually mobilized by a county fair.

In all these instances people are mobilized to take their places—important or minor, casual or regular, voluntary or involuntary—in a collective enterprise carried on in a somewhat established and expected way. The things I have named—and many others as well—have been called institutions. Some of the other things which have been called by the same name are of quite different orders. It is not my purpose to explore the limits of a concept. I rest the case by saying that I conceive the study of institutions to be part of the study of society in action. The center of the field lies where the action takes place within forms which are somewhat firmly established. The student of institutions will, however, be interested also in seeing how social forms become established, how they bend and yield under pressure, how they give place to new, and what functions they perform. He will, if his interest is in the structure and functioning of society, be only incidentally concerned to answer categorically, the ques-

Read before the Mid-West Sociological Society, April 1941. Reprinted by permission of the publisher from *Social Forces,* Vol. 20, No. 3, March, 1942. Copyright 1942, University of North Carolina Press.

tion whether the newspaper, the beer parlor, the Republican Party or property is an institution at a given moment.

It is obvious that many people other than sociologists have been and are interested in institutions. That being so, what is the place of sociology in their study?

Sociology is that one of the social sciences which is especially and peculiarly, by intent and not by accident, a science of social institutions. In our branch of social science there have been developed concepts for analysis of social control and collective behavior. Following Sumner, we have been particularly aware of the nonlogical aspects of social behavior; following Cooley, as well as Sumner, we have taken account of the distinction between the informal pressures of primary group life and of the unthinking following of custom, on the one hand, and the formal and rationalized procedures of institutions, on the other. Sociologists have developed a frame of reference for describing the processes by which social movements arise and by which, under certain circumstances, they leave a residue of new forms of expected and routine action in the structure of a society. Our equipment includes—or should do so—the rich body of concepts developed by Max Weber for description of the ways in which the prophet becomes the priest, the political sect becomes the legitimate and highly structured mechanism of the state, disciples become a bureaucracy, and for similar processes by which the unusual, the illegitimate, and the romantic forms of collective behavior or even rational business enterprises become imbedded in society as legitimate and traditional routine. These concepts are part and parcel of sociological discourse. In no other field has an adequate parallel set of concepts been developed.

It does not follow that sociologists—by whom I mean people who use these concepts and are interested in these processes—know more about social institutions than other social scientists. In fact, sociological investigation has been generally limited to a few institutions. The most extensive work is that relating to the family. Meanwhile certain institutions have become the peculiar interest of students in other fields. Incidentally, one of the besetting sins of us sociologists has become what unkind critics call "sociologizing" about institutions we have not particularly studied.

This brings us to consideration of the investigation of social institutions by the other branches of social science. Each branch, in so far as it has scientific pretentions, has its own frame of reference for discovering facts, a sort of lens which hauls certain problems and facts into focus. Each of them has also a conventional content, arising partly from the practical problems with whose solution earlier students in the field were concerned, partly from the penchant of humans to see and be concerned about the general setting within which their special problems occur.

This point and its bearing for the study of institutions may be illustrated by reference to economics. Economics is not ordinarily conceived to be a method of studying economic institutions. Its peculiar concepts are those which have arisen in the attempt to predict the quantities of goods which people will produce, buy and sell at various prices under certain given conditions, of which the most important are rather free competition and single-minded, rational bargaining. In order to make this kind of analysis, it would not strictly be necessary for the economist to know about the corporate organization of production, finance, and market institutions; about labor movements, and consumers' cooperatives; about the troubles which employers have in getting employees to put forth full efforts; about the relations of politics to business, and about the history of economic institutions. Yet some economists and their partially accepted colleagues in schools of commerce have studied all of these things. Some of these are things which rise up to destroy or at least to limit the free competition necessary to the sensitivity of price. They are the disturbing and distracting creatures biting at the innocent bug which the economist has under his microscope. Or perhaps they are the things he is really interested in.

Whatever the reasons, it is the economist who, among academic people, knows the "news" about certain institutions. He may not, as did his colleagues Sumner, Weber, and Pareto, turn aside to develop a systematic method for study of the distracting institutional periphery of the market. He may, as did the authors of a bulletin of the Bureau of Economic Research on *Incomes from Independent Professional Practice,* strain his economic method of analysis to fit a situation not well-adapted to it. Or he may develop some method ad hoc, for better or for worse. It is done for the better by the authors of *The Structure of the American Economy,* a report issued by the National Resources Committee.[1] The latter, impressed by the fact that "market controls"—the control of supply and demand in the market—are less important than they once were, attempt to classify the various kinds of control found in producing and distributing institutions; the control of employer over employee, of investment bank over the producing industry, of financial "groups" over a series of related corporations, or government over the indebted farmer, etc. These forms of control they recognize as being about what the political scientists call "power."

A similar situation is found in the other theoretical and applied fields of social science. The political scientist knows political lore, news, and history. His attention has gone far afield from his original study of political constitutions, in the narrow sense. In addition to political parties, he has

1. Part I. Washington, 1939. Cf. the chapter on the "Structure of Controls."

studied the lobbying mechanisms developed by interest groups, trade associations, and even local political clubs which in another aspect have been studied as sports clubs, ethnic social clubs, or even as gangs. We find that the specialists in the more practical fields of education, social work and business—whatever their theoretical interests—know a great deal about schools, social agencies and business organizations, respectively, as well as about the events which affect them. Some, at least, of the people at work in these fields would not mind being called experts rather than scientists. Their primary concern is with the operation of certain institutions; theoretical questions may and do arise and are dealt with, but the operating institution is their first interest.

Whether the starting point be theoretical or practical, each social science has become, in fact, the depository of a great lot of "knowledge about" and the clearinghouse for news of some set of related institutions. The most significant exception is anthropology. The anthropologist, in so far as he has remained an observer of primitive societies, has studied all the institutions he could find. Circumstances favored him in this; for his society is usually small and he is generally alone in the field. At any rate, his preoccupation has been with the place of the parts within the whole, rather than with a specialized part of his society considered in relation to some assumed or real central function of each.

The situation which we find in social science is far from the logically ideal, but probably unrealizable, one in which each branch of social science would have its own methods which it would follow whither they led. It may be approaching, but has not reached the more effective state in which the students who find themselves familiar with the goings-on in one kind of institution compare notes, concepts, and methods with those who are studying other kinds. One can, of course, point out certain shining examples of such coordination of work; for example, the collaboration of an agricultural expert, Kimball, and a social anthropologist, Arensberg, in their study of the rural family in Ireland.[2] The collaboration of physiologists, psychiatrists, social anthropologists, and hard-headed industrial executives in the studies of work relations in industry undertaken by the Harvard Business School are an equally outstanding case.[3]

Generally, however, when we get into the literature on institutions we find a great confusion of problems and methods of attacking them, and often no systematic method at all. One of the difficulties seems to be that

2. Kimball and Arensberg, *Family and Community in Ireland* (Harvard University Press, 1941).

3. Cf. Elton Mayo, *The Human Problems of an Industrial Civilization* (New York: Macmillan Co., 1933); Roethlisberger and Dickson, *Management and the Worker* (Harvard University Press, 1939); Chester Barnard, *The Functions of the Executive* (Harvard University Press, 1938).

the person who has the intimate knowledge of some institution and sees fit to make some investigation for publication suffers — because of his point of view or perhaps because of his position with reference to the institution itself — from a certain bias.

A common bias of this sort is over emphasis upon some one function of the institution, which results either in not seeing other important functions or in impatience with those features which are out of accord with the investigators' conception of its function. For instance, Mr. George Counts has studied the social composition of school boards.[4] He means the occupations and economic standing of members. Others have noted that members of school boards are not invariably the best-educated citizens of the community. This information is generally given in a spirit of outrage. The investigators do not think of going on to inquire why this is so, whether it is something of a constant to be found in many institutions, or whether a school run entirely by the people most fanatically devoted to education would retain the confidence of the community. Perhaps it would not even be a nice school to teach in, as suggested by a remark recently made by a very practical superintendent of schools: "God pity the teacher if his Board of Education is made up of former school teachers and fond parents."

It is quite natural that people professionally and keenly interested in education should be impatient with the apparently obstructive features of schools; many of them, of course, have contributed to our understanding of these stubborn and annoying aspects of the school system. The contribution of the sociologist, as a comparative student of various institutions, might be to ask whether the things found true of school board members might not be true of a whole range of institutions. Any observant student of Catholic parishes would soon note that, although all members of the parish believe in the church and want to support it, the church wardens are not often the most ardently pious parishioners, although they are among the more respected and stable. The hypothesis might even occur to him that one of the functions of religious or educational institutions is to keep religion and education within the bounds of cost, intensity, and kind that the community — given its other characteristics — can stand and will support. I expect that it is characteristic of human societies almost everywhere that they want education, religion, and patriotism quite honestly, but that in ordinary times they don't want to be plagued to death by them, and that they will invent devices to keep in check the very people they hire to give them these valued things. The rather simple point I have to make on this score is that the comparative student of institutions might relax the in-

4. George Counts, *The Social Composition of Boards of Education* (Chicago: The University of Chicago Press, 1927).

tensity of focus upon a single feature of an institution, thus correcting the "institutional bias." He would expect that the selection of personnel of the functioning parts of any institution would reflect other factors than devotion and technical excellence, that there would be some interaction between the specialized institution and other features of the society. Likewise he would assume that one of the functions of an institution is to control as well as to provide the community with some service or other; therein lies the difference between a sect or a reform movement and an institution.

A case somewhat similar to this is found in studies of the institutions which offer medical services to the community. Such studies may be written to instruct candidates for the various healing professions, or they may be undertaken in connection with a program of action to reduce the cost of these services, or otherwise to make them available to a greater proportion of the population. In neither case do they investigate some of the most crucial relationships involved. For instance, it has been shown fairly definitely that the difference between the doctor of somewhat better than average income and the one who gets even more than that lies not in the kind of service he gives, but in the class of people to whom he gives it. The young physician must feel terrific anxiety on just this matter of who his patients are to be in terms of social class, influence and ability to pay. The patients make the doctor. Yet beyond a little polemics and apologetics the people who write either for or against existing systems of getting medical service distributed have contributed very little to this problem. We have no study of the manner in which a doctor gets his clientele. In this case, the people who know most about the institutions concerned are—by nature of their interests—not equipped with a system of concepts which would enable them to handle facts of this order, nor are they generally disposed to disclose the pertinent information.

This brings us to another problem of the sociologist. It is impossible to make an analysis of an institution without having access to the data which will reveal its inner workings. Such data cannot be got without the confidence of people to whom the data are known, either as matters of record or merely as things which they experience. The people who have these data may know that they are of importance, but may not trust others with them; perhaps even more commonly they have suppressed or even repressed them until they are out of sight. The people of a profession develop something very like a collective unconscious which keeps certain matters out of mind. The sociologist who would study any institution must sense these things, and get some kind of effective access to the pertinent data. In so far as we engage in field work at all, we have got into certain ruts. We have not got effective access to many institutions. When we do, it will have to be in some participant-observer role which can be made intelligible and acceptable to the people who guard the secrets of the temple. In studying many of our larger and more specialized institutions the people from whom pertinent information must be got—information about their own place in the institution, not mere records from the books—are as sophisticated and have as much or more social prestige than the investigator. Now it is strange but true that such a person may encourage a study, and yet be unwilling to give the information most pertinent to the very study he wants made. I speak, of course, not of our fellow social scientists, but of persons in authority in institutions. In such a case, the job of the investigator becomes that of skillful social manipulation. It sounds horribly as if he might have to be something of a salesman.

In summary it might be said that:

1. There has been developed in sociology a set of concepts very useful for analyzing the processes involved in the rise and functioning of social institutions.

2. Every social science has, in fact, become a sort of clearinghouse for knowledge about some set of institutions, but not necessarily of systematic and comparative analysis of these institutions.

3. The sociologist—the person with the sociological point of view and concepts—can make studies of institutions—any institutions—more valuable by introducing comparisons and the conception of "function" which will free the observer from several kinds of biases which limit observation.

And last, a point which I have not analyzed as much as it might be, that none of this is of any account unless the sociologist gets to know the institution thoroughly.

THREE

The Impact of War
on American Institutions

A war is total to the extent that it spares no established thing in mobilizing people and resources. Now institutions are precisely the established ways of doing things. In them people follow the round of life and have their being and their vested interests. Total war is thus a threat to institutions. On the other hand, the rationale of this war—and not merely its rationale but the moving faith of such as have faith—is that it is a struggle to preserve our institutions. If then we accept total war and its rationale, we must be willing to lose our institutions that we may save them.

It would be idle to believe that all Americans are in this frame of mind. Like most absolute ideas, that of total war turns out to be relative when one compares the various meanings given it by different people. The reluctance of the government to disrupt families—even *ad hoc* families— to get needed manpower amply illustrates the relativity of the idea in practice. Men are reluctant to leave their families, partly because of the pain of separation but perhaps not less so because of a concern over the standards of living which embody the conception which a family has of itself. Honest anxieties of this kind come to the surface or lie hidden just below it with each proposal to make the war more nearly total. Measures which seem likely to impair other institutions give rise to similar anxieties among those to whom the activities of these institutions are dear in relation to their personal careers and their vested interests. Of course, certain kinds of people who find that the existing framework of society frustrates their aspirations may welcome the break in the ordinary routine and balance of things in the hope that their lot will improve. At the opposite end of the scale are those who make the argument that the war is being fought to preserve our social system an excuse for opposing even war-time measures. In the middle are those whose attitude was expressed in a question recently put to Charles S. Johnson, an eminent sociologist and a Negro, in a public meeting: "What concessions must we make to you Negroes to get national unity for the duration of the war?"

Whatever the state of mind of individuals, the war will go on and will become more nearly total. It is a matter of vital concern to Americans to consider which among their institutions will weather the crisis. The answer to the question will lie to some extent in government policy. But, whatever choices the government may make within the limits of possibility and necessity, the fate of any given institution will depend upon other factors as well. Among such are the point which the institution has reached in its inward evolution, the state of faith of the various kinds of people concerned with it, and its functional position in relation to other features and trends of American society. Other papers in this volume consider particular institutions from this and related points of view. I shall forego continuing this survey and be content to point out certain characteristics of American institutions — characteristics which make them particularly vulnerable to a "total" diversion of attention, energy, and money to the end of military victory.

The American structure for social action of various kinds has been magnificently and notoriously voluntary. People have established new collective instruments at will, participated in them at will, and abandoned them at will. We are not the only people to have fought for freedom of association, but, of all people, we have made greatest use of the right and have applied it to the widest range of affairs. If we have looked upon private initiative and free enterprise as a fundamental feature of economic life, we have no less relied upon voluntary association — which is a kind of free enterprise — in our noneconomic activities. A century ago a French aristocrat, de Tocqueville, noted our penchant for voluntary association and considered it a necessary condition of individualistic democracy.[1]

1. Alexis de Tocqueville, *Democracy in America,* trans. Henry Reeve (New York: Colonial Press, 1899), Vol. II, Chap. v: "The Use Which the Americans Make of Public Associations in Civil Life." "Thus the most democratic country on the face of the earth is that in which men have in our time carried to the highest perfection the art of pursuing in common the object of their common desires, and have applied this new science to the greatest number of purposes . . . In aristocratic countries men do not need to combine in order to act, because they are strongly held together. Every wealthy and powerful citizen constitutes the head of a

Early in this century Max Weber emphasized the importance of voluntary associations in modern Germany, and especially in America, the country of their extreme development. He defined such associations as all that lie between the politically recognized powers—state, municipality, and established church—and the natural community of the family. But he had to add that in America even the churches are voluntary associations and that the Protestant churches are their very prototype.[2]

A corollary of the voluntary character of a social organization is the necessity of a high development of the spirit of enterprise; for, if it is an open question whether people will support a collective effort, their support must be actively sought. Now we customarily think of enterprise as a term applicable chiefly to business. Business offers its goods and services to takers in direct proportion to what each pays. No one, in theory at least, pays for what another receives. Enterprise is shown both in producing and offering what individuals will want and pay for and in making them want what is offered. It has been our way to allow a maximum of freedom to individuals or groups of them to engage in such enterprise.

But there are services whose nature is such that each taker does not, and some cannot, pay in exact proportion to what he receives. What one gets from the services of a church does not depend upon the size of his contributions. The student or his family pay part of the cost of a college education, but the return varies even though tuition is the same for all; in addition, a large part of the cost is met by other people. In a hospital one may pay much or little; the comforts will vary somewhat with the fees, but the whole requires subsidy. Physicians' services are not supposed to vary in quantity and quality with the fee which the various patients pay but rather in accordance with their needs. In fact, the real competition among physicians is for patients who can pay such large fees that the physician can afford to work at low cost or free for other patients. Obviously, charitable institutions are not paid for by the people who receive their services.

While some of these noncommercial or less-than-commercial services have been supplied for some or all of the population by government agencies, and while we have had our share of informal giving of them, the characteristic development in these fields has been the voluntary organi-

---

permanent and compulsory association, composed of all those who are dependent upon him, or whom he makes subservient to the execution of his designs. Amongst democratic nations, on the contrary, all the citizens are independent and feeble; they can do hardly anything by themselves, and none of them can oblige his fellow-men to lend him their assistance. They all, therefore, fall into a state of incapacity, if they do not learn voluntarily to help each other." (p. 115).

2. Max Weber, "Geschäftsbericht," J.C.B. Mohr, *Verhandlungen des ersten Deutschen Soziologentages* (Tübingen, 1911), pp. 52-60.

zation supported entirely or in part by voluntary contributions. Generally speaking, any person or group who wished could try to establish agencies to carry on such activities. Sometimes they have had a mandate from some larger body, as does the denominational college, mission, or hospital. Even so, the mandate was often of the individual's or the group's own making, and competing colleges of the same denomination have not been unknown. The history of social agencies usually begins with some group of devoted or enthusiastic individuals who started an enterprise on their own recognizances and only later received something like a mandate through interagency councils which are likewise voluntary bodies. The effect of these councils has been to give existing agencies something like public recognition and a near monopoly over solicitation of funds for the given purposes. The trend has most certainly been toward fewer foundings of voluntary agencies to carry out activities that require subsidy and toward greater control over those in existence. But the role of the voluntarily supported organization is still paramount in many fields of semipublic service.

In the past many such agencies were very much like enterprises, in that they were the concern of a few individuals and in that they were maintained only by a constant effort to keep the supporting public "sold" on the proposition that the given organization was not only worthy, but specifically worthy, of support in competition with others. Of recent years, the selling has had to be done not merely to individual donors but to foundations, community councils, accrediting associations, and other such critical bodies. The necessity of energetic promotion of the agencies which carry on many of our communal services has led to the development of a type of office, and corresponding type of man, which is characteristically American: the university president, the executive secretary of the social agency, the active heads of reform organizations, of church and mission boards, etc. Their enterprising spirit has carried over, perhaps of necessity, into state-supported schools and agencies. Of recent years, the presidents of state normal schools, for example, have carried on vigorous campaigns to be permitted to give the same courses and degrees as the state universities — which are supported from the same state budget — and to retain something like monopoly over teachers' training as well. These executive officers feel compelled to put promotion on a par with, or even above, administration in their economy of effort. Such men are not only enterprising; many of them have a strong sense of mission. And these two individualizing characteristics — enterprise and sense of mission — are in reality often difficult to distinguish. It makes a Cecil Rhodes and a General William Booth, a John D. Rockefeller and a William Rainey Harper, mutually admiring partners.

Out of all this has come an institutional structure which is remarkably the same in a great variety of organizations—a typically American form. It consists of a board (generally self-perpetuating or nearly so), an enterprising promotional and administrative officer, a professional staff, and two other categories of people—those who subsidize the organization and those who receive its services. These different parts articulate in some measure the social and economic structure of American society. This form is a by-product of voluntary founding and voluntary financial support in a prosperous, expanding, individualistic society. It differs from the form of organization of business in that the boards are trustees rather than owners and in that the receivers of the services pay for only part of what they receive. The financial liability is perhaps less, and the sense of public trust generally greater. But such organizations and their boards have enjoyed much of the freedom of business and much of the leeway allowed by Americans to individuals or groups with a "cause."

This war may very likely bring to a boil a long-stewing crisis in this fundamental complex of free founding, enterprising promotion, and voluntary support of institutions which deal with education, religion, and social welfare.

With or without inflation there will be less money to give. Inflation allows the government, but not individuals, to make great expenditures. If inflation is controlled, taxation will become a major item in the budgets not only of the rich but of the people of moderate means, who are good givers. Certain problems dealt with by voluntary giving in the last war have already reached such proportion that they have had to be taken over by the government. The depression was the "John the Baptist" of this change; and the problems of demobilization bid fair not to decrease but to increase the magnitude of public concerns which we will have to finance by taxation. In the last war we were asked to give until it hurt; in this one we will certainly be taxed until it hurts.

But the crisis is not and will not simply be a matter of money. It will involve the temper and beliefs of the people and of the whole American social structure.

Let us deal first with the beliefs, taking colleges as an example. A great many of our colleges were founded with quite specific purposes, believed in ardently by some group of people. The college of a given denomination was founded to give the young people not merely an education but an education in a particular religious atmosphere. The normal school was founded to train teachers for elementary schools; the agricultural college, to improve farming. So long as the belief in its peculiar purpose was unquestioned, such a college was not in competition with others. Its donors and its clientele were of undivided loyalty. But in course of the process of emancipation which followed the period of the burgeoning of peculiar faiths and causes, there arose an increasing number of people who wanted education but were not so particular about the religious atmosphere. Some of the colleges acquired traditions and family loyalties which served to bind their students and alumni, but not their larger donors, to them. Some even became "class" colleges, although few can become "classy" enough to hold the children of those alumni who attain the ultimate in social prestige. Meanwhile, those who have been emancipated less rapidly turn to more conservative colleges for proper religious training; or even turn to the Bible, and desert learning. The colleges, having lost their peculiar mission, have not the backing and the following from all ranks of society to do without one.

The other kinds of colleges — normal schools and agricultural colleges especially — have in the same period not only expanded in size but have reinterpreted their purposes. They offer Bachelors' and Masters' degrees in the same subjects as the denominational and other private colleges. The presidents of normal schools get the names of their institutions changed to obscure the original function and lobby for appropriations on the grounds they are the only college in the western, northern, or other section of the state. Each type of college, in short, becomes more like the others and actively seeks to compete with them while yet attempting to retain a special advantage in its original field. That which was strong when belief in a peculiar purpose was strong must, when the belief is weaker, actively seek new activities and new purposes in order to survive in competition.

Similar processes occur in other types of institutions. Many of our organizations which grew out of the voluntary effort of people who wanted to perform some peculiar service have not merely once, but several times, changed their conception of what the peculiar mission is.[3] It sometimes becomes a harried scramble to find one sufficiently like others, yet sufficiently different, to make claims for support; and there is no sorrier spectacle than a man, or an institution, seeking a mission. It is only sorry if the seekers have something to offer and have not the perspicacity and courage to discover and proclaim it. It is sinister if, sensing that they have nothing very valuable to offer, they seek, by attaching to themselves the current catchwords, to build sentimental fences around their vested interests.

At any rate, we may expect that the people of this country will be faced

3. A book was recently published on *The Purposes of Church-related Colleges* ("Contributions to Education") No. 783 (New York: Teachers College, Columbia University, 1940), by L.K. Patton. The author with straight and serious mien made a statistical analysis of the stated purposes of such institutions. At least they were numerous enough to be submitted to such treatment.

with the problem of strictly measuring much-reduced funds for voluntary giving against their faith in a great many of the enterprises which, in a day of freer money and deeper faith, they so freely founded.

In so far as the future subsidy of these services comes from taxation, the question will arise as to which of the existing structures shall be chosen for survival. The choice might be simply to keep alive those already so supported; it might be made on the basis of present solvency, or some other kind of expediency rather than because of past contribution and present discoverable valuable functions. However made, there will remain the even more crucial problem of determining the functions which are to be performed by government. With the outlet of voluntary organizations closed for those who want special types of education, charity, etc., we may expect an intensification of the struggle for the control of state-supported institutions. Finally, it will be a major problem to satisfy the American's craving to have his support and participation in collective effort be something of his own choice. Certainly many of us will be hurt by the double loss: loss of the choice to give money and moral support or not and loss of the choice of the causes and organizations which we shall support. Our minds and the economy of our emotions will undoubtedly have to become adjusted to less apparent freedom than we have become accustomed to.

With the decline of the voluntary type of organization, the form to which we alluded above will likewise undergo some sort of change. There has been some criticism of the social selection of the trustees of our foundations, colleges, and charitable bodies and especially of the fact that the terms of their mandate and even the definition of the people to whom their responsibilities are oriented have been vague. This social selection is almost certain to change, as will also the terms of the mandates of the governing and policy-making bodies. The point of greatest enterprise may also be changed from the executive officer of the individual organization, where it tends to be at present; it might find its center somewhere in the higher planning and integrating bodies of government.

Another feature of institutions which will be thrown into relief by the war is the essentially delicate balance of forces which has allowed many of them to develop and be maintained in the peculiar form in which we know them. We are inclined to think of our institutions as eternal, in spite of their essential volatility; indeed, one of our most familiar devices for inflating our egos is the invention of a fiction of great age or even of eternity for the institutions in which we are particularly interested. The modern commercial newspaper grew by the application of individual enterprise in a certain balance between literacy of the masses, the subsidies by cheap postal rates, the growth of advertising, and quick transportation and communication. Competition, it is said, made the press free. The competition came, at least in part, from the smallness of the capital required to start a paper.

Other institutions have taken form in their own matrices of social forces and conditions, have run their courses along with American society, and face this particular crisis at particular phases of their careers. The American Legion, for instance, may find that this war will create a new crop of veterans, of different temper and at just the time to rob the Legion of the glorious old age enjoyed by the Grand Army of the Republic. A labor union may find that the war came too soon to allow it the experience in industrial conflict that may be necessary to vigor and solidarity. A university may have developed its reputation to a point of great promise but not have had time to gather ivy, the loyalty of rich alumni, and solid endowments. It is the vague sensing of these vagaries of time and circumstance that gives rise to much of the anxiety of people concerning the effects of the war upon the particular institutions in which they are interested. Perhaps our fear is really that total war will spare the solidly established more than the not-yet-established. In any case, a crucial factor will remain the soundness of the rocks of faith against which the strong waves of war beat.

How Colleges Differ

The difference between an American and an Englishman is that the American pretends to work harder than he does, while the Englishman works harder than he pretends. Thus runs one version—whether true or not—of a joke on an ancient theme, that of the relation between appearance and reality. Nowhere are appearance, reality, and the relationship between the two so diverse as in American schools and colleges. Any difference which may exist between some typical British student and some American student as to either the appearance or the reality of his academic effort is as nothing compared to the differences between American students, themselves, and among American educational institutions. In the amount of effort put forth by teachers and students, in the quality of their product, in the direction of their efforts toward one kind of learning or another, in their conception of their purposes, certainly our educational institutions differ from one another more than they do from those of any country.

Varying Academic Rhythms

Our schools and colleges are also different from one another in more subtle things which might be called rhythm and style of effort. David Daiches has recently written some observations concerning the rhythm of academic effort in Britain and America.[1] In Britain he observes that youngsters put

Reprinted with permission from *College Admissions 5: Planning College Policy for the Critical Decade Ahead,* New York: College Entrance Examination Board, 1958: © 1958 by College Entrance Examination Board.

1. D. Daiches, "Education in Democratic Society," *Commentary,* April 1957, pp. 336–343.

on the great push in secondary school, achieving quite remarkable knowledge of some subjects; in the university, they take it easier, and perhaps do
not make equivalent progress. The American youngster comes to college
not very learned, and often not accustomed to working, but he may enter
into his college work with such verve and lively curiosity that he comes out
the better man in some respects. That is what I mean by rhythm of effort.

At Oxford, I hear, one must preserve the appearance of doing little but
enjoy the intellectual and other amenities of the place during term, while
also giving the impression of doing naught but "swat" between terms. That
is a matter both of rhythm and style, since everyone there knows he really
must work hard to survive. A man who teaches in the most gentlemanly of
our state universities reports, without bitterness, that the students cannot
be made to work except for a mad orgy of burning of the midnight oil for
the last 10 days of term; only out-of-state "characters" start work at the
opening of the term and do all of the assignments.

It may be that these gentlemanly students accomplish more than those of
another, much larger and more folksy state university at which, according
to a former student of mine who taught there, the students are kept so busy
at little daily assigned chores that they have no time to develop or pursue a
program of study (not that most of them had ever thought of doing such a
thing in the first place). In the effort to get some reasonable level of
accomplishment and effort in his own course, each instructor had resorted
to the device of assigning a quota of daily chores. The student gives each
teacher his due, claiming in return the right not to be held responsible
several months from now for debts for which he already has a receipt. The
rhythm is one of small, slight pulsations of effort.

At McGill University, where I began to teach just about the time the
young ladies from the upper-middle and upper slopes of the Westmount
section of Montreal stopped going to finishing schools and started going to
college, these same young ladies seemed to have as their goal a good, solid
Second-Class achieved by competent, unstrained effort. *First-Class* would
have indicated eager competitiveness worthy only of those "pros" who
were working for prizes and graduate scholarships; *Third-Class* would
have betrayed either slackness or lack of ability to take things in one's
stride.

There is an analogy in industry. Groups of skilled workmen will nearly
always set, by informal understandings, the proper level of production. If
they hate the ratebuster, they also despise the man who has to strain to
"make bogey."

How unlike were those young ladies at McGill to the piously
hard-working students in a certain sectarian college who lack goals and
style altogether, having no one to give them a model of either. How unlike

were they also to the moderately bright, frightfully earnest young man who is rewarded with a teaching assistantship by a professor grateful to have at least one promising "major," who stays on for a dreary second-class M.A., and, as an instructor at his home university or one of its satellites, becomes that drone of American education, the premature pundit teaching too many subjects, and driven by his wife, the administration, and the accrediting boards to get a Ph.D. by applying what are known as tests of significance (sic) to what are indeed *data,* since they were handed him by his academic master. The poor fellow may have life made even worse by having to teach at a college where, as reported to me by a man who teaches in one, the students simply say, "Everybody has a right to go to college, even though they don't want to work hard." Or by having to teach at another, a state teachers college which has had its name changed by law to "state university," where the students will not answer any examination question based on a book not on the list of those issued free (as a perquisite for being part of the public school system of the state).

Why multiply these illustrations? Everyone associated with education is familiar with them. The excellent case descriptions of educational institutions given us to read before this meeting suggest how great is the variety of American colleges as to administrative and financial situation, historic concept of function, sensitivity to community forces, actual and potential numbers and kinds of students, and other characteristics. My immediate point is that this variety is matched by one equally great in the amount, styles, and directions of effort and accomplishment expected of students by each other and by the people who teach them.

While we have a good many tests of the levels of accomplishment of students in various schools and colleges, we have less knowledge than we should have of the manner in which various levels of effort are set and maintained. From studies in industry we know that levels of production are set by many factors other than the wishes of management, ability of individuals to perform tasks at a certain rate, and by the formal rewards of wages, promotion, and security. I think it safe to say, as did Max Weber about 50 years ago, that any group of workingmen possessed of any solidarity whatsoever, and with some common image of themselves and their situation, will not easily yield to any authority full control over the amount of work they do or over the strenuousness of the effort they put forth. They will wrestle with management whenever a change is made in the conditions of their work and in the concept of normal effort. We apparently have assumed that students have stronger individual goals than workingmen, and that the main thing required to raise levels of accomplishment is simply to raise standards required of individuals for entrance and graduation.

I am perhaps putting up a straw man when I say this, for I know well how many people have paid sensitive attention to social atmosphere, to the collective images which student bodies form of themselves and of their proper efforts. But it is not altogether a straw man; we have not systematically studied the way in which student bodies, as collectivities, form their own "student cultures," if I may use a term given me by my colleagues, Dr. Howard S. Becker and Dr. Blanche Geer, in a study of the students of a certain medical school. By the term student culture, Dr. Becker and Dr. Geer mean a whole body of definitions of problems and situations and of understandings about proper and justifiable solutions to them arrived at by the students. These are in part passed along from one generation of students to another, in part apparently rediscovered—or at least reinforced—by each succeeding generation as they pass through the same experiences.

The students in a medical school, even though every one of them accepts as his own the goal of becoming a physician, and even though they recognize the knowledge and wisdom of their physician-teachers, do not accept without revision the assignments made them. For one thing, they are assigned more work than they can do, and must decide what part to do, what to neglect. For another, they hear other voices than those of their own teachers talking about what knowledge is most valuable—the voices of physicians out in the community. For still another, they talk together of their problems, and often decide in favor of the short-term goal of surviving as students rather than in favor of the long-term goals of becoming great diagnosticians and therapists (as those goals are ideally defined).

"Student Culture" Important

By and large, the students of a college or university will be less homogeneous than those at medical schools as to goals and problems. That may make for a less distinctive and homogeneous student culture in colleges and universities; in the case of institutions with heterogeneous student bodies it may be more difficult to discover what the student culture is. But it does not mean that there is not a student culture, or that the understanding of it is not essential to the making and carrying out of educational policy.

A certain urban "underdog" college prides itself on providing education for those neglected by other institutions. Since the students work for a living, many classes are held in the evening. The students, in spite of all the difficulties of their individual situations, have an exceedingly active collective life in the corridors and lounges. In their discussions, they—that is, an articulate group of them, at least—have come to the notion that since their education is so hard to come by, it is up to the professors to make it good, and that allowance in outside assignments and in course marking should be made for the fact that they work long hours at some hard or tiresome task to earn their bread. Theirs is not the attitude of passively accepting a handout from the professor, but of aggressively demanding it and of reserving the right to decide whether it is a good handout.

These students work out their particular student culture not so much in relation to a specific common goal (such as medicine), as in relation to a common set of difficulties in their immediate careers as students. And they have definite expectations as to what their professors owe them. When these students turn up in graduate school, as a good many of them do, they are at first resentful of the load of work given them and of what appears to them the indifferent attitude of the teaching staff. Since, however, they are usually bright students and really eager, they often pick up the slack quickly. Their previous experience with life often makes them the good observers we prize in sociology and anthropology.

One solution offered for the problem of undesirable student cultures is to pick the right young people to go to college, or, at any rate, to one's own particular college. This is all very well for those few institutions which can afford, like exclusive specialty shops, to offer a single line of goods to a select clientele. There are some such in the country, and perhaps there will presently be more of them. But it should be pointed out that even in those cases where the college can and does pick its students from a national market, the student society creates itself without subservience to the wishes of the faculty.

Most academic institutions, in any case, appear fated to offer several kinds of goods to several kinds of clients. And in colleges, as in hospitals for chronic ailments (which keep their patients around for a long time), the clients — or patients, as you wish — develop their own notions of what is wrong with them and of what to do with the medicines dispensed to them.

Although we all know it, it is well to remind ourselves of a certain great difference between the institutions called colleges and universities in this country and those of the same designations in Europe. There, colleges and universities provide for the later education of only a few young people in a very few lines of work. The great burden of vocational training is allocated to other institutions. In this country, a great and increasingly greater amount of vocational training is done in colleges and universities.

The postponement of the working age, in our era of automation, combined with the notion that he who does not yet work goes to school and that college comes after high school, has brought about a huge increase in the student enrollment in colleges. It has also brought about a great increase in the number of things taught in American colleges, and in the number of vocational bachelor's degrees. The difference between this country and others is not that we or they do or don't support vocational training but that in this country a greater and greater part of the vocational training is done in the very institutions which also carry the burden of higher education. There is no way out of this situation, even if we wanted to find a way.

Let me hasten to say that I am not in the least opposed to the community supporting, with either public or private funds, any kind of educational or training enterprise whatsoever — even courses like those in "sister diving acts" or in "circus clowning" that are actually offered at one American college. We have more leisure and presumably require more professional entertainers to amuse us. Nor do I believe that we can, in the foreseeable future, substitute for our catch-all institutions a series of specialty-shop colleges and schools, cach providing only one kind of training, or only one level of education for one kind of student. As a matter of fact, even in the specialty-shop schools there was in the past more variety than met the eye.

If the professors of an earlier day at Harvard, for example, had time to be scholarly, it was because they got paid for teaching a good many students who did not work very hard; students who don't work so hard don't bother one too much. I have a friend who stays on in a certain university because he can earn his keep by teaching courses in American government daily until noon to students who won't bother him. In his afternoons he has written a number of masterly books. We forget that teaching used to be the main subsidy of research and the scholarly life. In the going concerns that we call universities there are many hidden subsidies and relationships of this sort. The idea that a man should do but one kind of thing for his academic keep may not be a sound and feasible idea. Whether so or not, most American colleges have and will continue to have a considerable variety of students, and most teachers will teach a variety of students.

Our major means of raising standards, and especially in increasing the number of students who want and get the best, will almost certainly not be a great and massive sorting by which all the best students and all those wanting general education of high quality will get into colleges intended for such students only. The major means will have to lie in experimenting in institutions which do a great variety of things for a great variety of people. We will have to undertake experiments in maintaining still another kind of variety; variety of student cultures within the great colleges and universities in which there are masses of students, many with no great intellectual ability or interest in studying or being exposed to all sorts of things.

Dynamic Sub-Cultures

We are all aware that in many colleges and universities where the general level of aspiration and effort is miserably low, there are small nuclei of students of great intellectual verve. Such groups, in effect, create little sub-cultures all of their own, contrary in many respects to that of the prevailing mass student culture. We need to study such groups in order to learn more of the circumstances in which they arise and disappear, and to learn how they may be planted, cultivated, and emulated. There are many experiments of this kind going on. I suspect that those experiments in quality will succeed best which make most use—possibly through the sound instincts of wise administrators and teachers—of the knowledge of the propensities of groups of students for developing their own conceptions of their abilities, of setting their own group standards and goals.

I don't think that encouragement of individual rate-busting will succeed in more than a few cases (although all of us know of students who have wrung an education from an unwilling college). Nor do I think that a general raising of minimum standards, or a purging of so-called extraneous matter and unworthy material, will create and increase the number of nuclei of students of superior effort and accomplishment. Added to all other efforts, I would lay my bets on efforts to create or encourage groups of special quality within the bosom of the conglomerate institutions which go by the name of university or college.

These institutions, in addition to other differences, are enterprises established for widely varying purposes and with diverse conceptions of their special mission. Some were established as definitely anti-intellectual training schools for the people of a certain sect, although it is notorious that the educational institution may eventually modify the sect. It is one of the fascinating things about this country that anti-scholarly sects nearly always end up by producing their own colleges and their own moderately intellectual elite to teach in them. The intellectual drive may, of course, like the well-known Freudian libido, be contained or directed toward limited goals—with peculiar results. Perhaps even Jehovah's Witnesses will found a school some day, and go professional.

Other colleges, not anti-intellectual by any means, were nevertheless established to educate some religious group in relative isolation from nonbelieving or wrongheaded teachers and fellow students. Some were established to give education, and a chance in the world, to underdogs. The city night colleges, the colleges for Negroes in the South, and some of the schools established for white people of the mountains and backwoods, were designed for particular groups of disadvantaged people. Still others were the product of social movements which required a special educational institution for their full realization. The movement for popular education led to the establishment of normal schools to provide teachers. The movement for application of science to industry and agriculture led to establishment of the agricultural and mechanical colleges.

Some enterprises have had combined functions from the beginning. The typical Catholic university in this country did not grow up around a monastery, but around a group of night classes in vocational subjects in large cities; Catholics were, in large proportion, poor city people who had to study nights if they were to get up in the world. The Catholic university gave them opportunity, but did it under Catholic auspices and with an admixture of Catholic social doctrine and philosophy. It is not uncommon to find a large Catholic university and a large urban university which grew out of protestant (YMCA or other) efforts to provide night college training for Horatio Alger (who came in from the farm) now competing for the growing market for a wide range of general and vocational classes in a large city.

These varied enterprises have tended, in time, to become standardized toward a common model. They give the same degrees for approximately the same kinds and numbers of course; many of them seem, on the surface, to have lost their original function. Generally, however, they retain some vestige of the original enterprise, while taking on new characteristics in the attempt to get a new identity as general universities and to meet changing conditions in the regions in which they operate.

Some of these colleges and universities are atrophied little company-town dictatorships left over from great movements and enterprises. This is so of quite a number of Negro colleges and of many denominational colleges in regions or communities that have remained poor. They can't compete for good students or good teachers; but the power of deans and presidents is great by virtue of the fact that the miserable teachers can't compete for jobs, either, and are held in ineffective servitude.

Other institutions have opportunistically added new functions to the old, as in cases like that of a sectarian college which has become a commuting "bus college" for local students who are not of the sect but are also not of the classes who go away to college, or like that of a teachers college which was made the "state university" for a region and became a "suitcase college" to which students travel by bus or car and return home on weekends. In such cases, we should learn more of the influence of the original function on the newer ones. I have heard some fantastic tales of the carry-over of an elementary schoolroom atmosphere in former normal schools which now purport to be general colleges, a carry-over which develops and encourages pettiness and resistance in the student culture. (For we must remember that student cultures are, in part, reactions to an atmosphere created by faculties and administrations.) One also hears of sectarian colleges which, in order to survive and expand as community or regional colleges, introduce new subjects but insist on teachers of sectarian background to the injury of their academic standards.

Colleges' Formulae for Survival or Expansion

American colleges and universities are enterprises, in a measure quite unknown in other countries; it matters little whether they are private or public, they are still enterprises seeking formulae for survival or expansion in competition with others. A common formula for survival is retention of some measure of monopoly over an original function (such as the training of county agricultural agents, high school teachers of agriculture, schoolteachers, or ministers for a certain denomination; or the providing of night vocational or general education for a given community or for some category of people), while also entering into competition with other institutions for other functions and other kinds of students. Many of our colleges and universities are going concerns which have come to their present state through such processes and are still making adjustments of this kind to survive, consolidate their positions, or to expand. In each, the students—usually several kinds of them—come with certain expectations and, in interaction with one another and with their faculties and with circumstances, work out some culture of their own, including notions of how hard to work and what to work at.

Our problem is to develop the means which will make it possible for experiments in excellence to be carried out in an ever-increasing number of these weird and interesting going concerns; we waste our breath in dreaming up the one ideal kind of institution with the one ideal kind of student. The problem is to develop, in real situations, combinations of functions and of kinds of students in which the number who will try to achieve more will be made greater. This is, in turn and in part, a matter of getting some college students—and their teachers—to create new images of themselves and their possibilities.

FIVE

Quality and Inequality:
American Educational Enterprises·

No country has had, or now has, so great a variety of educational enterprises as we. And in no country is the word "enterprise" so appropriate a designation for educational and, indeed, for many other kinds of institutions.

France, I hear, has decided to establish a number of universities in provincial cities. France will do it. An edict will be issued. The bureaux will move. And lo, there will be new universities very much like the older ones in form and quality. But this is not the way we do it in education, although our big corporations and the armed forces may establish plants and operations in that way. The State of New York is an exception, with its intangible university (with no campus and no teams) which sets down colleges and professional schools here and yon according to present and predicted population and needs. In Illinois our state university and the several teachers' colleges, some of them now crowned with the name University but clinging to their prerogatives as normal schools, compete with each other before the legislature for money—and woe to him who suggests an overall organization and plan. We may see a great deal more of the New York style of planning in the future, but our present American educational system (sic) has grown out of many social and religious movements, experiments and enterprises. I do not use the word "enterprise" in any sentimental way or to refer to private more than to public institutions.

The founders and developers of state universities, such as this, were and are very enterprising people.

In the eastern, and especially in the northeastern states, the early educational enterprises which have since become famous colleges and universities, were nearly all private. They were, of course, the product of collective effort, often of people with strong religious beliefs which the schools were to cherish. Even as far west as my native state of Ohio, a number of private colleges and universities are much older and, in some circles (not athletic), more famous than the Ohio State University. But one must note that Ohio also pointed the way by establishing two state universities, Ohio University (1804) and Miami University (1809) in towns appropriately dubbed Athens and Oxford, very shortly after the state was admitted to the Union.

But as one goes west one encounters state universities established by the pioneers and which are the outstanding ones of the region. Given present trends in the growth and support of public institutions of higher learning, they will undoubtedly maintain their leadership, although they may have to share it somewhat with other state institutions whose enterprising officers want university standing for them and are working to get it. It is also a sign of the times that even in New England there is a great spurt of growth of state institutions. What was long the Massachusetts Agricultural College is now the University of Massachusetts, with an expanded student body and a varied curriculum. It even has joined in a cooperative arrangement with Smith, Mt. Holyoke and Amherst colleges, all private and famous, by which they will pool resources in certain fields where staff and equipment are expensive. The relative position of private and state institutions is changing rapidly throughout the country. Furthermore, the country is becoming so closely knit that no educational institution, private or public, can continue to act as if it were alone with its constituency. All are subject to contingencies which arise from the presence of others, far or near.

The country is full of institutions, many of them private, founded for a great variety of reasons or causes. Oberlin, founded in 1833, was a gathering place of pious, intellectual fanatics. They experimented in coeducation at an early date. They accepted Negroes as students and helped with the Underground Railroad. They thought of having all their students work on a farm, more for their souls' sake than to feed them. One pre-feminist wanted the women to wear the same clothes as men. She was ahead of her time, but the incident gives the mood of the enterprise. Unlike some other religious colleges, it was intellectual from the start.[1]

A rather more common kind of educational enterprise in that period and

1. Fletcher, Robert S. *A History of Oberlin College From its Foundation through the Civil War,* Oberlin, Oberlin College, 1943. 2 Vols.

later was that founded by a denomination or sect which wanted to give its children or its ministers some education, but in such a way as to keep them from the dangers of the world, especially from the dangers of worldly education. Some sects which did this were definitely anti-intellectual. One of these colleges or enterprises which I know from a thesis done by one of my students, is Anderson College, of the Church of God. The Church of God did not believe in a professional clergy; they did believe in inspired preaching accompanied by Gospel singing. They believed that no true sermon could be prepared in advance. Most learning was considered dangerous to the soul. They established in Anderson, Indiana, a Bible-training school where people could learn to lead singing, commit the Bible to memory and hold contests in citing texts from Scripture. The students practiced extemporaneous preaching based on texts which were handed out at the moment. All the teachers were members of the sect; only incidentally were they teachers. The students were accepted on the basis of their sound conversion to this particular form of Christianity. They were more likely to be turning thirty than to come straight from high school. The small amount of money required for running the school came largely from the sale of a magazine called *The Gospel Trumpet,* which did a thriving business with sinners as well as with the saved.

The school was founded in this century. By about 1950, the Bible Training school had become an accredited college. While its administrative posts were still held by members of the Church of God and while *The Gospel Trumpet* was still a valuable property, most of the administrative staff and some of the teachers had gone outside to work for advanced degrees. A good many of their teachers were not of the sect, although they had to qualify as members of fairly conservative denominations and, for the most part, moved about in the orbit of conservative denominational colleges. The students now came directly from high school as a rule to take a four-year course leading to a Bachelor's Degree. The students were of two kinds: Church of God people from anywhere in the country; and young people of other denominations, but from the town where the college is located. The college had even begun to accept some money from unconverted people; they finally accepted some from one of the large motor companies which has a factory in the neighborhood. In return for some support from the local Chamber of Commerce it had undertaken to build up a basketball team for the local fans. Basketball brought a third group who were not of the Church of God: basketball players from various places in the South.

Anderson Bible Training School was started as a sort of permanent camp meeting to serve the Church of God. In the course of becoming

Anderson College it has added other functions.[2] It is but one of perhaps hundreds of Bible training schools and colleges established by individuals, or by groups representing some social movement to serve some particular purpose—political, religious, utopian or utilitarian.

Many of the Catholic colleges of this country, although founded mainly for Catholic students, were city evening schools—colleges for the under-dogs who had to get their education in the hard way. They were practically the Catholic counterparts of the YMCA evening schools. They had about the same curriculum in the beginning and got very much the same kinds of students. The Catholic college in this country is much less cloistered than many a little, rustic, Protestant college. The Catholic college is a city college; it gets a dental school and a law school before it gets a medical school, because there is no such thing as an evening medical school.

The normal schools were established to bring school teachers up to normal in their own education. Their problem was to teach the teachers to read and spell as a part of the great movement of taking education to everybody. A good deal of the teaching was done in summer school, and of course a large proportion of the students were women. The teaching was done by people who identified themselves with the school teaching profession, rather than with college teachers. This is so, to some extent, even today. One of my students recently taught for some years in a normal school which was supposed to be in the process of becoming a college of liberal arts. Each morning the students and staff gathered in a hall to sing "America the Beautiful" to the piano accompaniment of an old-time school and normal-school teacher and to swear allegiance to the flag. The president noticed if a member of the staff was often absent. This does not prove that many of the normal schools are not changing in other ways than in name. The names certainly are changed. The way to tell a teachers' college now is that it has three words in its name. The first is the name of a city or region; the second is State or the name of the state; the third is university. Examples are Kent State University and Southern Illinois University. For institutions, like individuals, try to validate a desired change of status by a change of name: the change of name does not prove, one way or another, whether a real change of character has taken place; it is at least a sign that change in a given direction is contemplated. Many normal schools appear to be in a period of transition, with some inner conflict between those of the staff who are strongly identified with the public schools and state departments of instruction and those who identify themselves mainly with colleges and universities and with their colleagues in their special subjects.

2. Nelson, Leona. "A sociological study of a church-related College," unpublished Ph.D. Dissertation, Department of Sociology, University of Chicago, 1953.

The schools of agriculture and mechanics, founded under the provisions of the Morrill Act, were the culmination of a movement which accused the classical colleges of being dominated by clergymen and lawyers who used Latin and Greek as mysteries to keep good common folk from getting ahead in the world. They also were an expression of the belief that we would fulfill our manifest destiny better by applying science to agriculture and manufacture. Many of them have become aggressive rivals of the other state university in states where the state university and the land-grant college were not united from the beginning. They have strengthened their work in arts and sciences, while maintaining their monopoly on research and teaching in agriculture. Within the past few years many of them have sought and gained the right to become universities in name.

After the Civil War, Northern denominations established schools, academies and colleges for the Negro freedmen and for other poor people of the South. Others have been started for backwoods, mountain or frontier people. There have been experiments in labor and workers' education; they ordinarily have not lasted long. A number of these enterprises have been built on the "earn while you learn" system. Sometimes, the work itself was considered part of the education, as in Hampton and Tuskegee Institutes for Negroes (and in Antioch College today). In 1912, Robert E. Park, sociologist and co-worker of Booker T. Washington, said of Tuskegee:

> One distinguishing feature of Tuskegee, Hampton and other industrial schools of the same character is that, not perhaps with any intention to do so, they have always maintained their early reputation as places where a poor boy or girl who was willing and able to work could learn a trade and get an education. In spite of the difficulties of such a policy, Tuskegee at least has kept its doors open. It has been and still is a place where every black boy or girl no matter how poor, no matter how ignorant, may have a chance.[3]

There are still a few Negro colleges in the South which take a few young people, straight from plantations, barefoot, and hardly able to read and write.

Many of the varied enterprises in education started with people as they found them, asking nothing of them except willingness to work and perhaps adherence to some sect or cause. Very often they provided a means for the students to make a living as they went; few American colleges do not make some such provisions today. Many of the sectarian colleges were also underdog colleges, from the fact of the poverty of their adherents. They also were likely to accept people of any age or previous education, since the call to preach is no respecter of age in new and lively sects. Many of

3. From an unpublished Founder's Day Speech, 1912. Recently circulated by Lewis Jones, Tuskegee Institute, Tuskegee, Alabama.

the experiments and enterprises were intended, at least incidentally, to bring some sort of education or practical training to people who had not had access to it before. There was an intense, practical democracy in these many efforts.

That particular phase of enterprise and experiment is about at an end. A large number of the resulting institutions have become, like Anderson College, the local college but retain some vestiges of their origin. In outward form, the great majority have become standard American colleges. They take young people after four years of high school and after another four years give them a Bachelor's Degree. Their curricula contain about the same names of courses. Standardization is helped by the mass-produced text book. They strive, of course, to get more Ph.D.'s on their faculties in order to get accreditation. They offer about the same undergraduate professional courses. All of them are, in some measure, teachers' colleges; they have departments of education which offer the work required for getting teachers' licenses. Most of them try to be pre-medical, pre-law and pre-graduate schools. They compete for the philanthropic and corporation and foundation dollar while, at the same time, hanging on to any non-competitive sources of funds available to them. In the case of Anderson College the non-competitive source of funds is the *Gospel Trumpet.* In the case of the teachers' colleges it is the fund especially assigned to the Normal Schools; in the case of the Agricultural College, the agricultural experiment station and other funds for vocational agriculture. In the case of the Negro colleges there is a certain amount of money that is given specifically for Negro education. The thing to do to make one of these enterprises boom and strive is to combine a slight monopoly on the old function with a competitive position in some part of the new educational order. Some of the sectarian colleges combine a certain orthodox piety with unbelievable availability to those who just want to come to college, any college.

In the course of all this, the old distinctions between the denominations and between the purposes of these colleges have very largely been lost. New groupings, new names and new classifications have arisen. The old denominational colleges are now called church-related colleges to indicate that they are not quite so devoted to any one denomination as they were. Some of them have become élite colleges. Several of the Ohio colleges, once strongly denominational, have now become Eastern overflow colleges. There aren't enough "Eastern" colleges in the East for the present demand, so students spill over the mountains into Ohio.

This has another effect. The small denominational colleges which used to favor the children of their own graduates now are a little cautious about it because such children don't always meet the new standards. The question is how to keep the loyalty and the money of the alumni without letting their children into the college — a difficult feat of public relations.

These colleges, so long as they remained each the organ of a social movement, could avoid comparison. They were not competitive. They stressed the fact that they had a peculiar mission. They got their students from their denomination and from the children of their alumni. But as choice by denomination declines, the colleges come into competition and must find some other criteria of distinction. Some of them have become, as I have suggested, simply the local college, the one cheapest to go to — for, as the percentage of young people who go to college increases, more and more of them want to go to college near home for financial, family, dating and other reasons. The demand for the local college is certainly increasing.

The many colleges which were established for special purposes, and which have outlived their original purpose in varying degree, have to find some other basis for existence. Some have made themselves very good indeed. Others, as I have suggested, have made themselves available. All have outwardly conformed to the four-year pattern. The result is that, while we have outwardly more colleges than any other country and a much larger proportion of our young people in them, we have also a great and deep built-in inequality of quality in our educational system. We have come closer than any country in history to giving our children equal opportunity to get to college. A working-man's son has a good deal more chance to get to college here than he does in Russia. The class differences in educational opportunities are certainly less here, although in this country the best way to get to college is still to have a father who went; if one can manage to have both father and mother go to college then it is practically a sure thing.

We have, on the other hand, a measure of inequality among our colleges and inside our colleges unmatched in any other country. Some say that the unevenness of quality is the price which we have to pay for the equality of opportunity to get to school and to stay there more years than is common. A few people think that too many people go to high school and college. They may think what they like. But our industry will want youngsters even less in the future than in the past. The child labor laws, for which the generation of my parents fought so hard, are absolutely obsolete. Industry wouldn't have children and young people working for them, no matter what the laws were. As production per man-hour goes up, and more and more machinery is used, the less industry wants of adolescents. Unless we are going to let our young people do nothing at all for a few years, they will go to something called schools even longer in the future than in the past. This trend now is found in other industrial countries.

So the question is not whether young people will go to school: the question is what the institutions will be like which go by the name of school, and to which we send the young people. As one who believes in both equality of opportunity and in quality, I would not, in any case, like the solution of having fewer people going to higher schools. The experimenting of the future will have to be in the direction of greatly expanding the opportunities for young people to get education of high quality. If it is objected that few are moved to get quality education, the answer is, in part, that motivation itself is a social product and one which we must learn to distribute more widely than we do. For motivation is not spontaneously generated; it is sown and cultivated. Just as a child who has never seen a piano cannot want to become a Schnabel, no matter what his native abilities, so a bright youngster who has never seen a person who used his mind with great skill can hardly have the motive, let alone the defined ambition to use his own mind in that way. Motivation is not simply something that people bring to school with them; it is in part the product of the school itself.

James Coleman, now of the Johns Hopkins University, has lately completed a study in which he seeks to relate motivation to the social atmosphere in a number of Midwestern high schools.[4] The youngsters from the "plush" suburban high school, who have successful parents and excellent teachers and school facilities are courted by representatives of leading colleges. They do not merely get to college, but to "right" colleges, although often for the wrong reason that everyone they know goes to them. They do well — school success is built into them — but they do not all do their best. The athlete, even from a small and obscure school, is also courted, although not necessarily by colleges of great academic reputation. One high school basketball player had never thought of going to college until sought out by a coach with an athletic scholarship to offer. His only ambition before that had been to "fight chickens;" that is, to breed fighting cocks and to match them with others. The lost soul, however, is the brilliant student from a small high school which does not have someone on the staff to see that he gets the courage and the information necessary to admission to a college that would give him full opportunity to realize his talents. He may end up (although Coleman does not say so) in a college where there is simply no model of intellectual excellence before him; and there was no one to tell him beforehand how different colleges are from each other, and no one to tell him he could make his way to the best. Coleman did find one small, rather deprived school with one teacher who performed this function and got youngsters of talent off to the better colleges. Motivation is not complete without information and adequate models. We have no real estimate of the number of capable young people

4. Coleman, James. *Social Structures and Social Climates in High Schools,* Glencoe: The Free Press, 1961.

in this country who are not moved to high intellectual attainment simply because such a goal has never been presented to them in any effective way.

I have got ahead of my story. While we have had a great increase in the proportion of young people who go to college or university, we have changed the meaning of the terms college and university. In Europe, the term, university, has a known and universal meaning. One knows what subjects are taught in them, and at what level. The traditional professions of law, medicine and theology are prepared for in the universities. And, of course, the academic profession itself gets its education in the universities. Other vocations are taught in a separate system of schools. A few of them, such as engineering, architecture, forestry and agriculture, are taught in technical high schools, high school being used in the continental sense of an institution of higher learning. (The universities are called high schools there.) A fairly significant change has occurred in Germany, where a very large proportion of the post-war increase in enrollment in universities is accounted for by students of business administration who take what is, in effect, a vocational diploma in the faculties of economics and social science. In England, the only country where the term, college, is used in anything like the sense in which we use it, the universities and the university colleges, generally speaking, are even more strict about admitting vocational subjects, except for a few anomalies such as agriculture and estate management at Oxford. But England has, as do most continental European countries, an elaborate and excellent system of vocational schools. Better scholastic standing is required for entry to many of them than for entry to colleges and universities in this country.

In this country, the vocational schools have grown up inside the colleges and universities. When they have grown up outside, as in the case of normal schools, schools of agriculture, schools of nursing, and many others, they eventually seek to become affiliated with universities, to require four years of study and to award a Bachelor's degree. The degree becomes, in effect, the license to practice the profession, — for in such cases the occupation seeks professional standing.

Colleges and universities in this country thus include the whole galaxy of vocational schools which in most countries of an equivalent measure of industrialization are maintained separately. An industrial urban economy requires a variety of vocational schools. We may expect to see more of them in the future. They are subsidized by the state in the European countries, just as they are here. By our peculiar history, and in keeping with our national culture, these schools, in this country, are incorporated in the institutions known as colleges and universities. In the other countries they are not. And when we say that so-and-so many of our young people go to college and university and we say that they do so more than in any other country, we have to stop and find out what goes by the name of college and university in the countries which we are comparing with ourselves.

It is very easy to say that our problems would be solved if we simply separated the vocational schools from the colleges and universities. So far as I can see there is no particular merit in one system or the other. One might argue that they weren't originally in the University. What of it? We don't have to cut our institutions to fit the name; we cut the institutions to fit circumstances and goals. We are stuck with this system, whether we like it or not; public opinion is behind it, and the result is, of course, that a much smaller per cent of our so-called students are studying arts and sciences than is the case in European countries. The vocational Bachelor's degree is certainly more common in this country than the arts and sciences degree, and even among those which appear to be arts and sciences degrees are hidden many vocational degrees. For some vocational sub-jects—education and commerce are the most common—are offered as majors in a good many colleges of arts and sciences, although their intent and content are essentially professional. There is, to be sure, a certain trend toward requiring two years of arts and sciences in the undergraduate professional schools and this may in time strengthen our arts and sciences. Along with this goes the phenomenon of service-teaching, which has its handicaps but which also has its advantages; that is to say the system in which there is, for example, a special course in English for nurses, home economics people, and special courses in chemistry for particular groups. There is some move, as I say, in some professions which have undergraduate vocational degrees, to require more arts and science work. On the other hand it is doubtful whether the students in undergraduate professional courses would themselves choose to increase the arts and sciences work. Studies of one degree school of nursing show that the students are very proud that they are in a collegiate school, and that they want to have college degrees. On the other hand, when asked whether they would like more liberal arts and sciences in their course, they said "No." They would really like to get into the direct work of the hospital earlier than they do. They want the degree but they do not want the liberal arts.[5] To what extent this is true in other undergraduate and professional schools, I don't know; it would be interesting to find out.

5. Simpson, Ida Harper. "The Development of Professional Self-Images among Student Nurses," unpublished Ph.D. thesis, University of North Carolina, 1956. Simpson found that many of the students did not see the value of courses in the social sciences and the humanities. Joseph Kahl, in an unpublished study of the same school, found that $1/4$ of the freshmen voted for a curriculum that was 90% nursing and 10% general; $1/2$ for a program that was 70% nursing, and that only $1/8$ voted for the equal balance of the two which the present curriculum calls for.

In addition to the great growth of undergraduate professional schools there is a tendency for the Master's degree to become a professional degree. More than half of the sixty-two thousand Master's degrees awarded in this country in 1956 and 1957 were in secondary education; and twelve thousand more of them were in other professional fields. In other words, Master's degrees in the liberal arts and sciences counted for less than one/third of all the Master's degrees.[6] As a matter of fact, only five thousand of the nine thousand doctoral degrees in the same year were in what one might think of as basic science and art subjects. The rest were essentially professional degrees. In quite a number of fields, the Ph.D. is what one does at that point in his career where he believes that he can make it in the big league but needs a new label to do it. School superintendents, librarians and nurses use the Ph.D. degree in this way. The institutions where they work press them to get the degree for accreditation's or prestige's sake. When a school superintendent comes up for his Ph.D., this is what his sponsors say to the other examiners: "This is a very intelligent man. He is a fine superintendent. He really needs this degree. We know that research is not really quite his line, but after all, he did fairly well." There are a lot of Ph.D. degrees, we may as well face it, which are merely steps in a career of administration. The so-called research is an ordeal, never repeated.

Again, let me say that there is nothing wrong with training people for vocations; there is nothing wrong in an occupation insisting on longer schooling and on calling the certificate given for it an M.A., a Ph.D., or by any other name, but there is something wrong in fooling ourselves about it. Part of our problem of quality in education in this country is the matter of getting things sorted out, so that we know what the names mean; so that young people who are working for degrees or certificates know what they are getting for their money and their effort, and really know what league they are playing in. Along with the sorting, we need some set of devices that will enable young people in high schools to learn more of the distinctions underlying the common terms: college, Bachelor's degree, Master's degree, and all the rest of it.

James Coleman's study suggests that the youngsters in most high schools are not given any adequate conception of these distinctions of quality or of kind of education. Enough young people who graduate from high school know about those few colleges which are known as elite or Eastern to make the pressure for places in them terrific. Radcliffe College claims that it turns away five girls as good as the one it accepts. The

6. Rosenhaupt, H., and Chinlund, T. J. *Graduate Students: Experience at Columbia University, 1940-1956.* New York: Columbia University Press, 1958. See pp. 4, 5 et passim.

pressure is overflowing into certain small colleges in the Midwest and even on the Pacific coast.

There may be some snobbery in this, but it is not all snobbery. There is, undoubtedly, an increasing number of parents who want to give their children a much better education than they got themselves. (Incidentally, I am amazed at how much better the education of our daughters is than what I got in college. We must not overlook certain tremendous general improvements in quality of education.) I think the number of people who want education of quality is going to increase. The total demand for college is increasing and will keep on doing so. A great many of the parents and many of the youngsters do not have their sights set very high, but, within that larger demand there is a strong and rising wave of demand for better quality. Now, if it is American to want to give a chance to everyone, it is also very American to want to give one's own children the chance that everyone has, plus a little bit more. This I call the equality-plus principle. I want for my children the same opportunity as everybody else, plus as much more as I can give them. The demand for equality-plus is going to be much greater than could possibly be met by some slight increase in the number of élite colleges. Such colleges will continue to exist and some of them may be in a position to carry on experiments that can serve as models to other institutions. But they cannot do the whole job, nor, in the long run can they do any large part of it.

The main bulk of the job is going to have to be done throughout the country. A large and ever increasing part of it will be done in the large state-supported institutions, which are not usually in a position to achieve quality by simply restricting admission. They have to take people pretty much as they get them, for which, as I mentioned earlier, there is a strong American tradition. And who is to say that some of the people with poorer school backgrounds may not gain a great deal from college? So long as our high schools are as varied in quality and climate as they are, just so long are many people going to come to college without much notion of what a good education can be and how exciting it is to get one. I recently interviewed in Boston a young man who wants to come to our graduate school. Here is his story: He is one of eight children of an illiterate Italian-born laborer. Somehow he got the idea that he could go to college, and entered one of the two cheapest ones in Boston. (There are at least six universities in Boston and Cambridge, not to mention those in the suburbs. Not all of them are considered "Eastern.") He was advised by the Dean to take the business course because he was a poor boy and should take something practical. As he went on, however, he got more interested in theoretical economics, sociology and literature than in marketing and accounting. So he set his sights higher, and having got a Master's degree in business, is now going on to pure graduate study. I may say that he has the slight advantage of belonging to the house-painters' union, and all summer long earns $26 a day. When he got to the top of the little hill he for the first time saw the bigger hill beyond: his perspective expanded as he went. I don't know how often that happens but it may be more often than we know. Such expansion of perspective is a process that we really have not studied. The European system would have made his first choice irrevocable. We will have in this country for a long time the job of making it possible for people to discover higher goals after they get to college, and of facilitating the painful change from lower goals to higher.

There is no one kind of institution that can solve the problem of quality. Certainly, most of our institutions are going to have to accept people of widely varying backgrounds, taste for work and goals. The kinds of experiments which we need most are those which will be designed to create within the existing institutions nuclei of students who stimulate each other to work of high quality, who are given opportunity to set and reach long-term goals and who are given a quality of instruction and stimulation which will make high effort and accomplishment seem the natural thing. This can be done. It *is* being done in varying degrees in a good many institutions. Our institutions are of an infinite internal variety already. Our own University of Kansas almost certainly has some students who could match the best in any university and, unless it is a very unusual institution, it has some who can't read or figure.

May I point out here the great American anomaly: the married undergraduate student. A married student of any kind is something of a rarity anywhere else. These young people who are married and who are allowed unbelievable freedom in everything else, are counted in and out of classes and fed on small hourly doses of prepared formula of technical pabulum and given small daily and weekly chores, as though they were children. I honestly believe that we cannot raise the level of long-run effort of our students very much until we give them the same freedom in academic matters as we do in other affairs and expect from them the responsibility that goes with it. On this point, we need some very bold experimenting; it will include some experimenting in teaching loads. Neither a student nor a teacher can study sitting in a classroom with a lot of other people. The teacher doesn't live who can give a dozen or fifteen good lectures a week. And the student who listens or dozes through that many poor lectures a week is being robbed of the time he might use in studying and thinking on his own. By having so much time in classroom, we reduce the time for the faculty to study and to be of use to the students and we reduce the time which the students have for study.

We have our American schools and colleges outwardly standardized in number of credits, years of study, general curriculum, and we call all the degrees by the same name, no matter what is in them. We have a maximum of external standardization. Our next step is to de-standardize. To sort out things so that we know exactly what variety of substance and quality we have. The next step after that will be to experiment boldly in creating nuclei of high quality all through the country; each institution may do this in its own way, yet I suspect they will find that there isn't an unlimited number of ways. The further step will be to make these experiments in quality widely available. More power to the University of Kansas for its share in any program of this kind! May you prove our educational gadfly, Robert M. Hutchins, wrong in his provocative and, at present, true statement about us:

> History will have trouble with American education in the twentieth century. It will see a people who say they are dedicated to education and who are the richest in the world, indifferent to education and unwilling to pay for it. It will see an educational system that delivers less education per dollar than any I can think of, saying that all it needs is more money.[7]

7. Hutchins, Robert M. *Is Democracy Possible?* (An address on receiving the Sidney Hillman Award, Jan. 21, 1959), The Fund for the Republic, p. 5.

Going Concerns: The Study
of American Institutions

American sociologists have, on the whole, been quite willing to study lowly people and humble aspects of life. Yet when they study institutions — or, rather, when they talk about studying them — they fall into the highbrow fallacy. They forget that, as John Dewey put it, "there is no immaculate conception of meanings or purposes."[1] Everyone agrees that institutions should be the central object of sociological study, then promptly defines them in such a way that the most interesting and significant kinds of human collective enterprises are left out of account. The term *institution*, in short, suffers from an overdose of respectability, if not of hypocrisy; perhaps also from overmuch definition and classification.

The usual classified list varies but slightly from that given by Williams in his *American Society*:[2] kin, family (marriage); economic institutions (property, distribution, work); political and legal (law, the state, etc.); religion (magic); education. Although this also about covers the list one finds in ethnological monographs describing primitive societies, there are additions in some ethnological works that should give us pause. The Melanesian *kula* and the Bantu *lobolo* seem to defy classification.[3] They appear to be

---

The original version read at the American Sociological Association, 1957. The present version read at the Southwestern Sociological Society in 1962.

1. John Dewey, *Human Nature and Conduct,* New York: Holt, 1922, p. 31.

2. Robin M. Williams, *American Society*. New York, Knopf, 1951.

3. B. Malinowski, *Argonauts of the Western Pacific*. New York, E.P. Dutton, 1922, 1961. Pp. 88–104, "The Essentials of the Kula." Concerning *lobolo,* consult any work on the Bantu.

economic, familial, religious, legal, and I am sure they are considered educational as well. We would be inclined not to study them, if they occurred in our society, because they have so many functions—which leads one to ask whether classifications are made to aid investigation, or investigation to serve classification. Since our culture shows a high degree of institutional specialization, so we can indeed find some institutions that really do not suffer much from being put into one of Williams' or others' categories. But others do not fall easily into any category. Even those that do so fall have a complex of functions not suggested by the category into which they seem to fit. Furthermore, the usual definitions make *institution* a great name, one deserved only by those things which embody the highest of human values. The result is that many even of the more enduring forms of collective effort are left out of consideration, as being too lowly to merit the name. New enterprises are studied as social problems or as new trends to be treated as a different series requiring different concepts for study and analysis. The rural Baptist congregation and the store-front church would not qualify for most American lists of social institutions. The social agency and the art museum finally make it in Hertzler's *American Social Institutions*.[4]

Since a common feature of definitions of institutions is that they are clusters of conventions, the obvious things to put into a list are those phenomena that are beyond dispute conventional, the things that have a place in the more established public statements of how we do things (strongly tinged with the notion that these are the right way to do things). But if we close our lists there, we miss the main and more fascinating part of the sociologists' work, which is to understand how social values and collective arrangements are made and unmade: how things arise and how they change. To make progress with our job, we need to give full and comparative attention to the not-yets, the didn't quite-make-its, the not quite respectable, the unremarked and the openly "anti" goings-on in our society.

A part of the argument concerning institutions has to do with their relations to associations and to organizations (I emphasize concreteness by use of the plural). Sumner made an important point on this subject when he said that the constituent elements of an institution are a concept and a structure and that the structure may be as unpretentious as "perhaps only a number of functionaries set to cooperate in prescribed ways at a certain conjuncture," that is, a few people who act when the time comes.[5] His statement puts emphasis on an active nucleus of people and upon social definition (a conjuncture appears to be what Thomas might have called a

4. Hertzler, *American Social Institutions*. Boston: Allyn & Bacon, 1961.
5. William G. Sumner, *The Folkways*. New York: Ginn & Co., 1906, p. 53.

"defined situation") of how and when they are to act. It puts people into the institution but does not close things artificially as the terms *association* or *organization* do with their implication that some known numbers of people are "associated" or "organized." It does not say what people other than the functionaries are involved and in what ways. It leaves us free to discover what people are mobilized, and in what measure, in what terms, capacities, and ways they are mobilized around the smaller, more active nucleus of people—be they functionaries in the ordinary sense of that word or upstarts, entrepreneurs, or prophets. One of our chronic temptations is to assume that the limits of the systems of action that we study are a known instead of being, as they are, one of the unknowns which it is our business in each case to discover. One can imagine (and find cases to match) small, closed groups of fervent people testifying in and out of season (the political or religious sect); in these cases the small central nucleus and the total mobilization of people coincide. One can imagine small active nuclei of constantly active people, with several smaller to larger and even immense mobilizations of other people from time to time, occasion to occasion, crisis to crisis, being drawn into the orbit of action and reaction along lines that, in theory at least, could always be dis-covered—the preacher and a few elder ladies all week, more on Sunday, still more on Easter. The small active nucleus may act with or without a firm mandate. They may be moved by various sentiments or the desire to attain many different kinds of goals, from revolution to money making (which can also be revolutionary if enterprising enough).

It is to the very great number and variety of things that may be sug-gested by these remarks that I give the name *going concern*. They occur in many forms, and may be in any stage of having, getting, or losing moral, social, legal, or simply customer approval. But they are identifiable going concerns—enterprises, institutions, organizations, associations, fami-lies—and have existed at least long enough to be seen. They may have persisted so long, undergone so many turnovers of generations in their various mobilizations (from center to circumference, each usually with its own rate of generational turnover) and have been so changed in other ways that philosophically minded people may ask whether the present entity is indeed the same thing as that of the past, and, if so, in what the identity consists.[6] At any rate, they have a present existence and an historical dimension; discovery of the relations between the two is one of our chief sociological tasks. This requires that we try to make some sort of order out of the various contingencies to which going concerns are subject and the

6. Karl Rothenbücher, *Über das Wesen des Geschichtlichen und die gesellschaftlichen Gebilde*. Tübingen, J.C.B. Mohr, 1926. This remains the best discussion of this matter in sociological terms.

kinds of changes that occur in them as they survive (of course, they often fail to survive) these contingencies (joinings of events and circumstances). We will probably fail if we attempt to make a very tight system for ordering contingencies and changes; however, we will fall far short of our intellectual duty if we simply record events unsystematically on a sea of change.

I should like also to state my belief that the dichotomizing of events and circumstances as functional and dysfunctional for systems is likely to be of limited use in the long run; in part, because it may carry the assumption that someone knows what is functional—that is, good for the system; in part, because these are value terms based upon the assumption that there is one right and known purpose for which the system (going concern) exists, and that actions and circumstances that appear to interfere with achievement of this one purpose are dysfunctional. Argument over purposes, goals, and functions is one of the commonest forms of human discourse and many are the going concerns that thrive upon it, although it is both conceivable and likely that some survive such disputes and actual shifts of purposes better than others. It is quite common to have an annual meeting to decide on the purpose for the year to come. Do we play basketball for the glory of God this year, or destroy communism? I am certainly not suggesting that either purposes or functions be left out of consideration in study of going concerns; on the contrary, I am suggesting that discovery of them and of their relations to going concerns is another of our chief businesses.

And finally these terms may be misused because one may assume the existence of one system where several are involved whose "needs," while interdependent, may not completely agree.

It is time for me to turn from these general and critical remarks to some illustrations and cases. This continent, in its post-Columbian times, has been the scene of the burgeoning of a tremendous lot of enterprises, organizations, and movements. Some have eventuated in lasting going concerns; others, equally intriguing, did not last long. One of the services of earlier sociology in this country was to direct attention to these phenomena and to make some attempts to study them in at least a semi-systematic fashion. Their preoccupation turned upon some, rather than others, of the experiments in doing, changing, and organizing people and things. There have been many new sorts of going concerns since then to which we might in these days pay attention—the foundation, the concentration camp, the kibbutz, gambling syndicates, shopping centers, insurance—to take a few that would be missed in a conventional list.

The pioneers of American sociology—the Columbia group around Giddings, and more especially the Chicago group around Small, Thomas, et al. — showed great interest in the fate of various sectarian and reform movements that arose in America or were transplanted here and in the many experimental communities that were established on our moving frontier, as well as in the many organizations and enterprises established as a result of our ethnic and racial diversity and events connected with it. There emerged from their discourse over these matters Park's and Burgess' classic statement, published in 1921, on the relations between social movements and established institutions. They took the sect as their main example but suggested that it would be profitable to follow other kinds of social movements and to look at the origins and development of other kinds of institutions in the same manner.[7]

A good many people followed the clue of studying the course of sects, finding, of course, that not all follow the same course and not all become the same kind of going concern and that not all who do follow the general course toward becoming tolerated and competing denominations do so at the same rate. In fact, the sect toward denomination cycle seems to occur most generally in nonconformist Protestant movements so placed that both

---

7. "This sketch suggests that the sect, like most other social institutions, originates under conditions that are typical for all institutions of the same species; then it develops in definite and predictable ways, in accordance with a form or entelechy that is predetermined by characteristic internal processes and mechanisms, and that has, in short, a nature and a natural history which can be described and explained in sociological terms. Sects have their origin in social unrest to which they give a direction and expression in forms and practices that are largely determined by historical circumstances; movements which were at first inchoate impulses and aspirations gradually take form; policies are defined, doctrine and dogmas formulated; and eventually an administrative machinery and efficiencies are developed to carry into effect policies and purposes. . . .

A sect in its final form may be described, then as a movement of social reform and regeneration that has become institutionalized. Eventually, when it has succeeded in accommodating itself to the other rival organizations, which it has become tolerant of and is tolerated by, it tends to assume the form of a denomination. Denominations tend and are perhaps destined to unite in the form of religious federations — a thing which is inconceivable of a sect.

What is true of the sect, we may assume, and must assume if social movements are to become subjects for sociological investigation, is true of other social institutions. Existing social institutions represent social movements that survived the conflict of cultures and the struggle for existence.

Sects, and that is what characterizes and distinguishes them from secular institutions, at least, have had their origin in movements that aimed to reform the mores — movements that sought to renovate and renew the inner life of the community. They have wrought upon society from within outwardly. Revolutionary and reform movements. on the contrary, have been directed against the outward fabric and formal structure of society. Revolutionary movements in particular have assumed that if the existing structure could be destroyed, it would then be possible to erect a new moral order upon the ruins of the old structure. . . .

A violent, confused, and disorderly, but enthusiastic and popular movement arises. Finally the movement takes form; develops leadership, organization; formulates doctrines and dogmas. Eventually it is accepted, established, legalized. The movement dies, but the institution remains."

R.E. Park and E.W. Burgess, *Introduction to the Science of Sociology,* Chicago: University of Chicago Press, 1921, pp. 873-874.

the group as a whole and the individual members thereof can concurrently rise in the world. In Catholicism, the counterparts of sectarian movements have, when not nipped in the bud, become new religious orders or new auxiliary organs of the church itself.[8] The sort of going concern which grows out of a successful religious movement is then a function of the kind of larger social system in which it occurs and of the ways in which it makes the changes that allow it to survive. It is this story that Frazier tells so well in his book, *The Negro Church in America.*

There is a rich literature in Europe on the concerns that emerged from the socialist and other labor movements. Karl Kautsky carried out an elaborate comparison of the adjustment of the early Christian movement to the world with that of modern socialism.[9] More in line with what I have in mind are the works that describe the development of the several kinds of concerns that grew directly out of the labor movement: the cooperatives, the unions, the study and recreational centers and clubs, and the press.[10] The developments described parallel in amazing detail those of successful religious movements in America.

Park's suggestion that similar analyses be made of other movements and enterprises has not been very widely followed. One kind that might profitably be followed are the many educational movements and enterprises that have been undertaken for some single purpose. Among them are the agricultural and mechanical colleges, given sustenance by the Land Grant Act nearly a century ago; the mechanics institutes that were to raise workingmen and city life to a new level by spreading knowledge of applied science; the normal schools that were to establish norms of learning and of skill among our then rapidly growing and rag-tag, bobtailed army of public school teachers; the sectarian Bible schools designed to train people to preach the gospel but to keep them at a safe distance from the worldly and overly intellectual established colleges and universities with their faculties addicted to higher criticism; the various movements to teach workers the

8. For comparative studies of sects see: Harold W. Pfautz, "The Sociology of Secularization: Religious Groups." *American Journal of Sociology*, LXI (Sept., 1955), pp 121-128; Thomas F. O'Dea, "Mormonism and the Avoidance of Sectarian Stagnation: A Study of Church, Sect, and Incipient Nationality." *American Journal of Sociology*, LX (November, 1954), pp. 285–293. Religious orders that grew out of movements within Catholicism are The Order of Preachers (Dominicans); Order of Frairs Minor (Franciscans), and the Society of Jesus (Jesuits).

9. *Foundations of Christianity; a Study in Christian Origins.* New York, International Publishers, 1925. Part IV, Chap. 5. "The Evolution of the Organization of the Congregation."

10. Theodor O. Cassau, *Die Gewerkschaftbewegung; ihre Soziologie und ihr Kampf.* Leipzig: C.L. Hirschfeld, 1930, *Die Konsumsvereinsbewegung in Deutschland.* Leipzig: C.L. Hirschfeld, 1924, Kantorowicz, Ludwig. *Die sozialdemokratische Presse Deutschlands, eine soziologische Untersuchung.* Tübingen: J.C.B. Mohr, 1922. These works and many similar ones were written when these going concerns were at the height of their glory in the Weimar republic. New contingencies arose when Hitler came to power.

philosophy of Marx, of the Knights of Labor or the wonders of the Single Tax; the institutes and trade schools established as home mission enterprises for freed slaves, backwoods mountaineers, and Indians; the vocational night classes for underdogs in cities, whose main entrepreneurs were the YMCA and the Catholic Church; the schools and colleges founded by immigrants to preserve the culture of the homeland; and finally, the educational enterprises undertaken by people who just wanted to reform education itself by dissociating it from football, teaching men and women together, adopting new methods or setting new standards (the Antiochs, the Reeds, the Oberlins, the Benningtons). These were enterprises undertaken generally for a single and well defined purpose. However, one might say of them, as Hetherington says of all collective enterprises, that their purposes were single and clear only at the moment of their inception.[11] We have studies of enough of them to construct at least one general line of development (not the only possible one) of those that continue to exist.

A certain sect established a Bible school in the midwest on a campground where members gathered for prolonged "revivals" in large pavilions. Nearby were the houses occupied by the leaders of the movement and used as a combination religious house and editorial headquarters for a gospel periodical that sold far beyond the limits of the sect itself, and brought in a good deal of money. All who had any connection with the Bible school were primarily of the sect, only secondarily or instrumentally of the school. Teaching was merely a special form of preaching, or of training others to bear true testimony. The students came because of some decision to change their way of life; there were no fixed academic standards of entrance. The course was short and did not lead to a degree. Study at the school led only to a new position in the sectarian movement. The money that came in was the money of the sect.

One might say that there was a single, unequivocal point of reference for all people and activities — their religious movement. But, by a series of processes we will not here describe in detail, the school, as a going concern, got more and more outside references. The students came more and more to be youngsters who simply went to college there, rather than

11. H.J.M. Hetherington and J.H. Muirhead, *Social Purpose*. New York, Macmillan, 1918. For material on the course of some of these educational enterprises see Earle D. Ross, *A History of Iowa State College,* Ames, Iowa State College Press, 1942; R.S. Fletcher, *A History of Oberlin College from its Foundation through the Civil War.* 2 vols., Oberlin, Oberlin College, 1943; John Flint, "Kent State From Normal School to University. The Study of an Institution in Process." Unpublished M.A. thesis, University of Chicago, June, 1951; Channing Briggs, "George Williams College, 1925-50. A Study of Institutional Change." Unpublished M.A. thesis, University of Chicago, June, 1952; Leona B. Nelson, "The Secularization of a Church-Related College." Unpublished Ph.D. thesis, University of Chicago, June, 1953. There are many anniversary histories of colleges pertinent to the discussion, and recently some studies of the changes in normal schools.

elsewhere, and at the usual age — not as a function of a belated call to preach. A dual student body grew up; one part comprised of children of members of the church, who might come from anywhere where such people lived; the other of non-members, mostly from within daily bus-riding distance. The teachers came, in ever-increasing number and degree, to act and to think of themselves as teachers among teachers of their particular subjects; some of them began to move about, becoming part of a wandering group of college teachers considered more or less interchangeable parts in an unofficial, small-time league of evangelically religious colleges. The College — eventually so named — sought accreditation. To do so, it had to adopt standards set by the educational world, some of them at odds with the traditions of the church. Eventually even some money came from industries with plants in the community, and there is talk of appointing community and industrial leaders, not of the church to the governing board. The College clings jealously, however, to its near monopoly on training the clergy and lay leaders of the church.

The similar changes in the agricultural colleges and normal schools are on the record. Two of my students have analyzed in detail the development of two normal schools; another has followed the course of a school founded for the training of YMCA secretaries. Let me summarize the kinds of change. The courses of study are at first narrowly instrumental for the founding movement or organization and do not correspond in length to those of other schools and colleges. They approach those of the regular school and college system, in both content and in length.

The students are highly specialized, study at varying periods in their lives, and start from various amounts of previous schooling; in time the student body corresponds more and more in age and sex distribution and periods of attending school to the general school and college population. The staff starts as a group of people who are primarily something else — preachers, school teachers, so-called "scientific farmers," YMCA secretaries. In time it includes people who teach in this particular college as a part of their roving careers as academic people. The administrators and authorities are some sort of selection from among the people in the movement or other concerns involved; they tend to approach in general character and selection the boards of other colleges. The money in most cases seems to come at first from sources devoted especially to the cause the new enterprise serves, not to education as such; in time, the new going concern seeks money, more or less successfully, from those people and organizations accustomed to granting money for colleges and to couch their plea in some slightly varied version of the usual terms and symbols.

One might summarize this by saying that in the beginning these educational enterprises were contained within a movement or other going concern; they were, one might say, a sub-mobilization within such movements. Eventually they became articulated with the larger society, and especially with the whole system of colleges and universities and related things. They became like other colleges; what is more important is that they came into competition with them, and had to take advantage of their own real or potential differences as well as of their likenesses.

Hundreds of colleges in the country are in the throes of deciding in what academic procession they are to march. Some that once had an assured place as the only proper college for families of some religious denomination find that those families no longer choose colleges on denominational grounds. Suppose such a college decides to try for a place among the *ultra-montane* little elite, west of the Appalachian Mountains. These days no doubt it can find the students, for there is a big overflow of applicants rejected by the so-called "Eastern" colleges. But can it get the faculty and can it get the money to make the change? And almost certainly there will be among the existing faculty some who, from devotion to the old denominational role and simply from dislike of change, will oppose the actual changes of faculty and curriculum necessary to the new role. Furthermore, perhaps new money cannot be obtained from foundations, the government, and the new industrial committees to save the colleges, without endangering the old sources of money.

Similar problems face teachers' colleges that aspire to the standing of liberal arts colleges. What will happen to the many schools and colleges that were establised for the people called *freedmen* in the Methodist church reports I used to see in my father's study as a child? Some of these institutions were established by white northern people as an act of home missions. Some were established by Negroes, generally with money from some sort of white people. You know how various they are. There is one whose president used to write me a letter by hand each year asking for money. There are some where the president and perhaps one or two henchmen lord it over a miserable little empire consisting of faculty who can't leave because no one would have them and students who are so lacking in preparation that they couldn't go to a better college and so limited in knowledge of the world that they probably don't know there are better ones. They may also be kept in debt to the college and made to pay it off by cutting the president's grass at a few cents an hour under the guise of being helped to pay their way. They are academic sharecroppers. They are, of course, indistinguishable from many white colleges. It's too bad the Negro and white entrepreneurs who run these colleges draw a color line, for I am sure they could learn a great deal from each other.

There are, need I tell you, institutions of quite different calibre established for Negro students. What will be their fate? In what academic procession can they and will they march? For many years they have had a monopoly, created by segregation, over the better Negro students and the pick of the Negro faculty. They never had a monopoly over much of anybody's money, although some of what they got was money dedicated to the particular end of Negro education rather than simply educational money looking for the best college to give itself. Insofar as present movements are successful, the fact of being Negro will not give these institutions, even the best of them, a monopoly over anything in the future. Things are still such, it appears, that many Negro students prefer to study in these institutions. Courtship is, I hear, one of them. It is, however, increasingly difficult for them to compete for Negro scholars and scientists. As for money, all educational institutions, even the most richly endowed, have to raise new money to meet present costs. What the fate of Negro colleges will be in raising new money, I do not know. But the contingencies have to be met—whether the Negro institutions will survive, and, if so, in what form, with what students, staff and money. I have no idea. I am sure some in this audience are at work on the problem. There are, of course, communities where the Negro university is the one that should survive desegregation.

The case of the Negro colleges is but one of many like it. Many American going concerns—churches, colleges, hospitals, professional practices, insurance societies, cemeteries and undertaking establishments—were established to exploit a near-monopoly market created by ethnic, religious, or racial distinctions. In some cases, the monopoly was based on the tastes of people for goods and services peculiar to their own group. In other cases, it was a monopoly created by exclusion. One of the contingencies of such institutions in this country is the disappearance of their monopoly market through assimilation of tastes and integration of customers, clients, and participants into the main stream of American life. Some institutions survive these processes; others do not. The Negro case will be a crucial one. The Negro hospital, the Negro insurance and burial societies and businesses, perhaps even the hair dressing businesses all have contingencies and may all be caught in dilemmas of various kinds.

Negro hospitals are already caught. In some cities the Negro patients still do not have the same freedom as whites to choose doctors and hospitals (to put it mildly), yet they have enough so that the Negro hospital gets only the poorest patients. This creates a problem in getting Negro medical staff, although the Negro physician still does not have full access to hospitals and so may have to go on the staff of a Negro hospital so mediocre that it hurts his reputation to work there. The money problems thus created are catastrophic for the Negro hospital, although not necessarily so for the quality of medical service available to the population.

All sorts of gaps and faults lie in the way of going concerns. The money may disappear first, or perhaps the staff, or perhaps the customers. In what order the entrepreneur would like to have the changes occur is an interesting question.

Even those institutions that seem least changed by the sea voyage to America are far from being the same here as in the home country. Catholicism is Catholicism everywhere; but a French abbé who visited this country found the pastor's job quite different from that in Europe.

In America, when a new city is built, or even when an existing parish becomes too large, the bishop calls in a young priest and marks out a territory for him. "You are assigned the area between such and such streets; go do your best." There is no question of building or money; he must shift for himself. In a few years everything is created, organized and almost paid for. . . . It is understood that to do his job the priest must be active and must keep on good terms with his parish.[12] The American pastor has to be an entrepreneur; it is a far cry from the "country living" of an English incumbent, where to be enterprising would probably upset everyone. The assured resources that make it possible for a man to be called an "incumbent" of an office are usually lacking in this country; at least, they were in the beginning. All institutions in this country have enterprise in their past; many must show it constantly to survive. And the enterprise that keeps a concern going may change its character, its function, and even its environment.

When we speak of institutions as enterprises, we are indeed emphasizing that they must continue through time in environments to which they must adjust themselves. Many of the current studies of organizational systems ignore the environment. They talk of the internal organization of businesses, hospitals, and schools. They do not pay much attention to the actual environment in which the institution has its being. In some measure an institution chooses its environment. This is one of the functions of the institution as enterprise. Someone inside the institution acts as entrepreneur. He may be acting as entrepreneur for himself and be using the institution as something of an instrument. Whether that is so, at least there is some center of enterprise in most institutions, and one of the things the enterprising element must do is choose within the possible limits the environment to which the institution will react; that is, in many cases, the sources of its funds, the sources of its clientele (whether they be clients who will buy shoes, education, or medicine), and the sources of its personnel of various grades and kinds. This is an ecology of institutions in the original sense of that term.

12. From a book written by Abbé Felix Klein about 1905. A selection is reproduced in Oscar Handlin, *This Was America*. Cambridge, Harvard University Press, 1949, pp. 423–433.

The change in the environment may come about without any special attempt on the part of the entrepreneurs of the institution, or it may be sought out consciously. Generally what happens is a mixture of both. Think of Oberlin College, for instance, which has become in due time—from having been an experimental, exceedingly religious institution, expressing the New England spirit in a midwestern environment—a wealthy college with students from all over the country, selected from a certain class of young people who are the children of certain rather well-defined classes of parents. It has, in effect, become a preprofessional college, of which some of its students complain. They say that the interest in a course is not in its subject matter but in its value as a step to get one accepted in the graduate or professional school of his choice.

In choosing their environments, institutions develop a division of labor among themselves. What, for instance, are the functions of the various educational institutions in the city of Washington, or Boston, or Chicago, or New York? All of these cities have a number of institutions known as universities. For example, in Boston it appears clear that the environment of Northeastern University, the largest in the city, is Boston itself and the immediate region and certain classes of people within that region. It started as a night school. Harvard, of course, has a national or international environment. It draws its students from everywhere and makes this a matter of policy. Its staff also comes from a large environment.

As a matter of fact, an institutional enterprise has several environments. One is its clientele environment, the environment from which it gets the people whom it serves. Another environment is that from which it gets its personnel. A third is that from which it gets its financial support. These may be the same. In the case of a sectarian college they are, in the beginning, the same. As time goes on, they cease to be the same. The students may be drawn from one environment, the staff from another, and the money from still a third. The government being more and more one of the sources of money for all sorts of institutions, one of the most important forms of enterprise in institutions nowadays is to make themselves conform to the requirements of the government, that is to say, to meet the requirements for getting public money. This of course brings up another kind of environment, what one might call the political environment of the institution, or, let us say in one sense, the sentimental environment. Who are the people who believe in it and feel that they have a right to criticize its courses of action? I suppose the job of the ever present public relations man is to discover who these groups are and to define the institution for them, to give it a satisfactory, indeed, more than a satisfactory, image, an image such that these people will not merely approve it but will actively support it in competition or conflict with others.

Another way of saying environment, I suppose, is to call it a market. An institution is in the market for money, students, staff, ministers, whatever kinds of help and personnel it wants. There is a significant description of the environment or market in which any given institution manages to bring these desired things to itself. We need more study of this sort of thing, which will, incidentally, be more historical than sociologists are generally inclined to make their work.

May I bring these rather profuse remarks to an end by saying again that the way to study American institutions is not by defining them closely in advance, but by having a good look at the kinds of collective enterprises that have arisen in this country and to follow them through the many contingencies they have to meet in the course of survival—if they do survive. While I have taken my illustrations mainly from educational enter-prise—in which I am especially interested at present—they could equally be taken from families, businesses, and many another kind of going con-cern.

SEVEN

Disorganization
and Reorganization

The Revolution of Organization

A world-wide revolution of organization, long under way, is now more widespread and profound than ever. In certain countries, called "Western" for some obscure reason, it has been called the industrial and urban revolution. In its earlier phases, as Paul Mantoux says in his *Industrial Revolution in the Eighteenth Century*,[1] it consisted in the invention not merely of new machines, but of new institutions of production and exchange, of new ways of organizing men for work, exchange, and communication. It also consisted, in part, of the rise of new breeds of man, unscrupulous — according to Werner Sombart in *Das Wirtschaftsleben im Zeitalter des Hochkapitalismus*[2] — in the strict sense of not feeling bound by the hampering scruples of the older mercantile families; hence, able to act in new ways and in new combinations. The revolution, in the earlier phase and now as well, consisted of massive internal and international migrations to the growing industrial regions and urban centers; and of a good deal of shift and drift of other populations to fill the vacuum left by those who went to industry and cities. Europe, in course of all this,

Read before the Society for Applied Anthropology, 1962. *Human Organization,* Vol. 21, No. 2, Summer, 1962. Reprinted by permission of *Human Organization* and the Society for Applied Anthropology.

1. Paul Mantoux, *The Industrial Revolution in the Eighteenth Century.* (Rev. ed.; trans. by Marjorie Vernon), London, Jonathan Cape, 1928. Part III, Chap. II, pp. 374-408.

2. Werner Sombart, *Das Wirtschaftsleben im Zeitalter des Hochkapitalismus,* Munich & Leipzig, Duncker and Humbolt, 1927. Chap. 3, esp. pp. 29-31.

underwent such a drastic demographic explosion that it was able to populate America and other parts of the world while becoming itself more
densely populated than ever. Migrations and increase of population almost
of necessity break up kin and other patterns of organization, and lead
eventually to their reorganization in new places and in modified forms.

As the institutions and new men developed, so also did an ideology — social, economic, political — to support them. This ideology persists
vigorously even now, although the institutions it supports may long since
have ceased to correspond to the definition of them contained in the
ideology. The ideology makes much of private enterprise, of voluntary
association (to do business), individual freedom (of the entrepreneur and of
the buyer), and other concepts.

We now have colossal organizations run by huge bureaucracies in business as well as in government, with rationalized division of labor in which
every man's job is, in principle at least, a computer's solution of the
problem of locating humans in relation to machines, not machines in
relation to humans. The reversing of these terms — man and machine — of
the equation was first pointed out sharply, to the best of my knowledge, by
the French sociologist, Georges Friedmann.[3] The first industrial revolution
was that which, by the use of power, made the machine a much more
effective extension of a man's hand. The second industrial revolution,
according to Friedmann, made the man the tender of the machine. Perhaps
it is a third revolution, brought on by true automation and the computer,
that sets the conditions for Kenneth Boulding's post-civilization.

One part of the more recent revolution of organization has been an
intertwining of government and business. One can now speak of public
enterprise and private bureaucracy, not merely of public bureaucracy and
private enterprise. We have been accustomed to believe and say that what
is private is enterprising and what is public is bureaucratic. Many so-called
private enterprises are woefully unenterprising, except on the political
front in defense of themselves. The owners of a corporation (I mean the
stockholders) may be notoriously passive and conservative, while hired
men run the company with great verve and while outside raiders show
great enterprise in trying to take it over and reorganize it. In business, one
is probably right in saying that the most enterprising companies without
exception have elaborate bureaucratic arrangements designed to make every employee an interchangeable part. At the same time, the heads of
governmental agencies and the presidents of state universities are perfect
dynamos of promotion and enterprise, in spite of, or perhaps even because
of, the bureaucratic structure of their organizations. With day to day

3. Georges Friedmann, *Problèmes humains du machinisme industriel,* Paris, Gallimard,
1946. And several more recent works and articles.

matters settled by rule, the head man is free to show enterprise. We live in a day of public entrepreneurs and unenterprising small private businesses.

Professionalization

The phase of massive organization and bureaucracy is also characterized by the professional trend; in industry it might be called the staff trend. Many occupations, old or new, offer esoteric, technical, and organizational advice and services to large organizations, including government. The members of these professions may move from one organization to another, keeping themselves detached in that particular fashion thought appropriate to the relation of professional to client. Each case is, according to the ideology, given full attention and skill, but the professional leaves one client for another without a pang. Indeed, his value to the new client comes from his experience with other clients. But many of the new professional people are employed by one client—a contradiction in terms of the old professional ideology, in which a client could only retain, not hire. They become part of the staff of an organization. They may internalize its interests and values to such an extent that their identification with and loyalty to the free-floating professional colleagueship is in question. The professions of medicine and law, which serve as models for all newer professions, are themselves undergoing the organizational revolution. The practitioners work in complex organizations with colleagues, near-colleagues, and with a line organization of people not of their profession at all. The successful lawyer, with high income and the privilege of working intensively at a special branch of law of interest to him, characteristically works in a large law firm or is house counsel for a corporation or a government agency. The lawyer who practices alone is generally scarcely a lawyer at all; if he had a law problem, he would call a lawyer.[4]

Likewise, the general practitioner of medicine, especially if he works in some isolation from colleagues, becomes a specialist by default. Whatever his medical knowledge may have been at the moment of graduation, it becomes a limited, certainly not random, sample of all medical knowledge. The individual physician develops some favorite diagnoses which turn up as the immutable morbidity and mortality statistics of the territory in which he works. He also develops favorite treatments. The most general thinkers in medicine are probably highly specialized men who see how many things one must know to understand one thing. Such men generally work in some complex medical organization such as a clinic, teaching hospital, medical school, laboratory; more and more often they work for salaries.

4. Jerome E. Carlin, *Lawyers on Their Own,* Rutgers University Press, New Brunswick, New Jersey, 1962.

Thus we observe a double professional trend. On one hand we see the development of many new professional occupations which take as their model the old "privately" practiced professions. On the other, we see the older "model" professions becoming rapidly bureaucratized, thus departing from their own earlier standards. Perhaps it is our penchant for attempting to follow organizational models which no longer exist that makes us over-developed and gives us a certain isolation from the rest of the world.

Now applied anthropology, the very broad application of social and related sciences, is a product or a by-product of these organizational changes. In effect, we give services and advice to these changing organizations and systems.

The Tempo of Change

Of recent years, and I am repeating a cliché here, a revolution, similar in its results if not in its rate and form of development, has occured in Russia and certain associated countries. It is not at the same stage as here, but there is no reason to believe that it will go through the same stages as here. I will return to that point. Let us remember that we have been carrying an organizational revolution to the rest of the world for a very long time indeed. Kenneth Boulding has called this period the phenomenon of civilization, or exploitation. This exploitation was the thing on which our great empires were built. The great Western empires have always from their beginning had some effect on what we speak of as the native peoples, through recruiting them to new kinds of labor and through taking their land or otherwise causing drastic changes in their economy. In this country and in Canada, civilization made the fur trade. The Indian who used furs to clothe himself was a quite different Indian from one who lived by selling furs to traders. We have caused many basic industrial revolutions or economic revolutions throughout the world from the very period in which the industrial revolution occurred in the West and even before. Now the tempo of these changes that we have induced in other parts of the world has become very rapid among the very peoples that anthropologists, rather than sociologists and political scientists and economists, conventionally were supposed to study. The anthropologist has for some time been a one-man division of social science. He went out on an expedition and studied something. That, too, is changing, but perhaps not as rapidly as it should. Perhaps the other social scientists are not integrating themselves as rapidly as they should to understand these outlying societies, but that is a different point. To sum up, we have caused industrial or economic revolutions and demographic revolutions almost throughout the world. There are very few of the simple peoples of the world, as they were called before they became underdeveloped, which were not touched by this and which did not have some fundamental part in the development of industry in the Western countries.

Africans, as you know, were moved to this country in such numbers that they are the biggest single immigrant group next to one or two Western European nationalities. There are fifteen million of them and they are old-stock Americans, although they are African in origin. There have been other migrations of this sort — that of the East Indians to Africa, to the West Indies, and to British Columbia is only one example.

The rate of change in these outlying parts has lately been greatly accelerated. It is happening very rapidly in the places under Russian control. It may happen quickly in the places that are under or will come under Chinese domination. Do not forget that the Chinese have a long history of commercial and industrial activity throughout the world. Wherever Europeans have gone to do big business, they have created a need for little business which the Chinese have eagerly filled and then have sometimes themselves turned into big business.

The Nation-State

One of the by-products of this industrialization of the world has been the nation-state. We think of the nation-state as a European phenomenon, but I should like to point out that the successful and powerful nation-states of Europe, almost without exception, became great nation-states concurrently with their development as great empires. The concept of the nation-state is that of a country with fixed boundaries, the people within these having one language, one culture, and descended from one God-hero, perhaps. Actually, however, the great nation-states have all been developers of empires. Modern nation-state England was also Imperial England. Nor are we a nation-state in the accepted sense. We were an empire until we became a people. We were an imperial power whose territory happened to be all in one piece, like the Russian Empire. We had plantation economies with African and Oriental labor; we had the Southwest with the Spanish-speaking labor of that area. Somehow we have made something of a nation-state of what we first developed as an empire. Note that when Germany became a nation-state, it immediately set out to become an empire as well and got itself some colonies, and tried it twice in this century. Spain and Portugal did it a long time ago, although perhaps too early to make themselves modern industrial nation-states at the same time.

One of the anomalies here is that ideology of the nation-state never corresponded to reality except in a very few places, not even in Switzerland, the oldest one. One cannot point out any European national boundary that is really strictly an ethnic or linguistic boundary. I think it could be shown that the concept was itself a phenomenon of empire and grew up along with empire, perhaps serving the function of making the distinction between us at the center and those people out there that we are civilizing, of making it clear that we had the mission of civilizing those people out there who could not be full citizens of the state. In this country, we did it by racial ideology. We had people inside our nation-state who were not of it.

The interesting and ironical thing is that the ideology of the nation-state was a European luxury which we carried out to the whole world, but did not allow to be realized fully out there. It is backfiring on us now, for the notion that every people has a right to be a nation-state is now flourishing most in just those parts of the world where empire went. People are allowing themselves the luxury of being nation-states. We could afford it because we were developing a large-scale industrial economy and could make use of the outlying colonies in various ways. Whether the new nations in Africa and elsewhere can become effective states without large internal markets and without empires to develop remains an open question. It will be interesting to see whether industrial nation-states can exist without colonies.

This is yet another case of an ideology which was very powerful in the Western world, but never corresponded to reality, being picked up in other parts of the world whose economic history is quite different and who can never go through the same phases of industrial development as the West. In the West, the very instruments of modern industrial production were invented as we went along. These instruments are now going out to other parts of the world, at least we think so, ready-made. It may be that it will require quite different forms of organization to bring off industrial revolutions in the outlying parts of the world.

Overdevelopment and the Specialization of Sociology

I should like now to turn to the subject of overdevelopment. I do not think that democracy in this country is overdeveloped, and I can think of many other things that are not overdeveloped, but I do think I see what people mean when they say that we are overdeveloped. I think that we might almost call it the new isolation. Not the new isolationism, for that is a doctrine, but the new isolation. It may be that we are developed, in our affluence and in our technology and in a great many ways, out of the possibility of effective contact with the rest of the world. It is not merely that we are so rich, at least not that we are rich in a material sense. I think that our very mode of thinking about the world has become very much adapted to understanding ourselves, in part, but not to understanding the other parts of the world.

Here I make reference to the branch of social science that I more or less officially belong to — sociology. The sociologists, although they invented the word ethnocentric, have themselves become methodologically ethnocentric. They have developed methods which are based on the assumption of huge populations which speak a common language, in the sense that given words mean more or less the same thing to most people. Our technology, or methodology as it is called, assumes that the important things to study are minor differences against a massive background of homogeneity. This means that one can select small samples which will stand for the gigantic whole and assume that everyone has the choice between a Ford and two or three other kinds of cars. There is no place in the scheme for people who cannot afford cars at all. That is to say, the whole method is based upon people who have so much that they have many easy choices to make. It is not based on situations where people have no choices, in societies where change is very rapid, or where the population is heterogeneous. It is based on a stable society, where it is almost un-American for people to have tastes that fall out of the middle range that the sociological surveys are designed to describe.

Whether this methodological bias has gone over into other social sciences I do not know. I think, perhaps, that the anthropologists are as a whole ethno-eccentric. They still have a method based upon relatively small societies and have done little about studying rapidly changing societies and societies which are moving from the small to the large very rapidly. There are, no doubt, some anthropologists conducting such studies, but their number must be small. The very specialization of the social sciences, our organization of them into divisions which do not occur in this form in other parts of the world, makes us captive of our own professional academic organization, which in turn reflects the institutional structure of our own society. Our departmental specialization is only one of a number of things that isolate us from other peoples. It isolates us in the sense that it impedes penetration into these other societies, differently organized.

I should like to close with a comment on our great love of the neutral, non-controversial, middle bulge of the curve of social phenomena. Our methods of social science are not gauged to the understanding of radical, wild people, and of the more extreme forms of discontent and conflict. We are so anxious to predict that we avoid the unpredictable. It seems to me that the biggest job that we, as applied anthropologists, and as Americans, interested in our own welfare and that of the rest of the world, have to do is precisely to take a crack at looking at the least predictable parts of the world, which is most of the world. If some of the things that we hope not to see happen do happen in the rest of the world, I would not give much for all our predictions about what will happen to us as part of that world.

EIGHT

Queries Concerning Industry and Society Growing Out of Study of Ethnic Relations in Industry

A number of sociologists about two decades ago focussed their studies of race relations on ethnic divisions of labor found in the colonial regions of the world which capitalistic industry had but recently penetrated.[1] More recently American sociologists have joined in study of race relations in industry in their own country with the aim of learning how we may make fuller use of the American labor force regardless of racial or ethnic distinction. I think it now profitable to draw these two perspectives together; and in so doing, to raise some general questions, not merely about the role of industry in mixing peoples, but concerning the relations between industry and society in various situations. For whenever one scratches a problem of racial and ethnic relations, he uncovers problems concerning society itself; and in this case, concerning industry and society.

Paper read at the annual meeting of the American Sociological Society held in Chicago, December 28-30, 1948. Reprinted by permission of the publisher from the *American Sociological Review*, Vol. 14, April, 1949. Copyright 1949, American Sociological Asssociation.

1. See E.B. Reuter (Editor), *Race and Culture Contacts* (New York: McGraw-Hill Co., 1934), in which papers of the 1933 meeting of the American Sociological Society appear; especially R.D. McKenzie, "Industrial Expansion and the Interrelations of Peoples," and R.E. Park, "Race Relations and Certain Frontiers." See also McKenzie, "Cultural and Racial Differences as Bases for Human Symbiosis," in Kimball Young, *Social Attitudes* (New York: Henry Holt, 1931). For still earlier work on the problem see Sidney Olivier, *White Capital and Coloured Labour* (London, 1906) and *The Anatomy of African Misery* (London, 1927); James Bryce, *The Relations between the Advanced and the Backward Races of Mankind* (London, 1902.)

First, let me make three sweeping statements which are germane to the whole problem of ethnic relations in industrial economics.

The first is that industry is always and everywhere a grand mixer of peoples. War and trade mix them, too, but chiefly as precursors to the deeper revolutions of work and production in which the more fateful mixing occurs. In no considerable industrial region of the world has an indigenous population supplied the whole working force. Some of it comes from such a distance as to be noticeably different from the local people. The resulting ethnic differences within the industrial population may be small, as between the various parts of Great Britain, or as between Yankees and Southerners in this country; or great, as between Poles, eastern Germans and western Germans in the Ruhr and Rhineland, or as between English and French-Canadians in Quebec. They may be extreme, as between South African natives and Europeans, or between North Americans and native Indians of Peru. In short, the differences may range in magnitude from those between regions of the same country, through those between different European nationalities, to those between European and non-European, the latter being most extreme when some of the people are of tribal cultures whose institutions of property and work are entirely different from those known in Europe.

Industrial regions vary also as to the positions of local people relative to those of immigrants. At one pole are those regions in which the working force is built around a nucleus of native controlling and technical personnel and skilled workers, and where successive waves of immigrants enter the working force at the bottom of the skill hierarchy. At the other extreme are those regions in which the controlling and highly skilled nucleus goes out to establish industry in a remote, unindustrialized part of the world; the labor is recruited either from a native population, or—and this is common—is imported from still other ethnic areas. It thus may happen that practically the whole industrial personnel is alien to the region, while the various ranks are alien to each other, as in the mines and plantations of the Malay peninsula.

Finally, the industrial regions vary as to the kinds of industrial and social structures which develop and in the degrees of upward mobility possible for various racial and ethnic elements of the working force. Again, at one pole are the somewhat open structures in which there is a theoretical, although practically limited, possibility for a person of any ethnic kind to fill any position; at the other, rigid systems of stratification in which the people of each ethnic group are limited to a narrow range of jobs or ranks. Each of these kinds of variation has its accompaniments in the industrial community, and eventually in the political and social conflicts, alignments and movements which follow the development of industry.

My second sweeping statement is that modern industry, by virtue of being the great mixer, has inevitably been a colossal agent of racial, ethnic, and religious segregation. For segregation, if it means something more than that isolation in which the peculiarities of race and culture develop, refers to some degree of functional separation of different kinds of people within a common system. Industry brings people together and sorts them out for various kinds of work; the sorting will, where the mixture is new, of necessity follow racial and ethnic lines. For cultures (and when races first meet they are always unlike in culture) differ in nothing more than in the skills, work habits and goals which they instill into the individual. These differences may tend to disappear in the course of industrial experience, although segregation may tend to keep them alive in some modified form for a long time. At any rate, there is not yet—even among the older industrial regions, where ethnic differences have been reduced by common experience and intermarriage—one in which one may not discern some deviation from chance expectation in the distribution of ethnic and religious groups among the various kinds of work and the several ranks of industrial organizations.[2]

The third of the sweeping statements is that industry is almost universally an agent of racial and ethnic discrimination. There is no question about it if we take the word discrimination in its basic sense of the action of making distinctions. For those who hire industrial help must nearly always choose from among people who are not all alike ethnically, and very often from among ethnic groups whose industrial experience and training are far from equal. Furthermore, when industry actively seeks labor from new sources, it generally has to make an ethnic choice.

In sociological language, discrimination has taken another meaning: that those who pick people for jobs consider, intentionally or unwittingly, traits not directly relevant to work. If we accept this meaning, industry is still almost universally an agent of ethnic discrimination. In all industrial regions, again including the oldest, there is current among managers, foremen and industrial workers a body of opinion and lore concerning the work capacities and habits of various ethnic groups. Insofar as such belief and lore do not correspond to verifiable fact, they point to discrimination. Certainly they hinder clear perception of the differences between in-

2. This is so obviously true in North America as to need no proof. For evidence concerning western Germany see: Wilhelm Brepohl, *Der Aufbau des Ruhrvolkes in Zuge der Ost-West-Wanderung,* (Recklinghausen, Bitter & Co., 1948). Everett C. Hughes, "The Industrial Revolution and the Catholic Movement in Germany," *Social Forces,* XIV (Dec., 1935). There are marked differences between the positions of Flemings and Walloons in Belgium; Protestant and Catholic in Holland; Flemings, Italians, etc., and French in France. It is commonly said that such differences of distribution still exist as between Welsh, Scotch, Irish, and English of various regions of the British Isles.

dividuals of a given ethnic or racial group. In some industrial regions, discrimination is openly defended; in a few, enforced by law.

We have defined industrial segregation as deviation from chance in the distribution of people of various ethnic groups among the positions in industry. Discrimination we have defined as consideration of racial, ethnic or religious traits in selection of workers even when the traits are not known to be relevant to work behavior. But segregation is not of itself evidence of discrimination. For there are undoubtedly cases in which even the most objective and sharp selection of workers by known or probable work performance would result in racial and ethnic segregation. On the other hand, we do not know how long it would take, under an aggressively objective policy, for all racial and ethnic disparities in job distribution to disappear. The truth is that no one has worked out a statistical device for establishing the existence or degree of ethnic discrimination. It would be very difficult to do so. For a given organization may have a great variety of jobs and positions, each of which has its own complex of activities and skills, and consequently of required training and experience. The positions have each their own rate of turn-over, so that they vary in their sensitivity to ethnic change in the labor supply. Past discrimination leaves its mark in varying degree and for varying length of time. But the lack of such an index need not worry students of the problem unduly. For discrimination is generally admitted, although it may be called by other names when discrimination becomes a bad word. In fact, the evidence of recent studies indicates that at least an unconscious discrimination tends to permeate industrial organizations even in the rare moments when conscious effort is made to avoid it.

It is an interesting and apparently paradoxical observation that modern capitalistic industry, which has developed a strong, sometimes ruthless ideology of indifference to persons, of choice of the best article for the purpose, and of the best man for the job, and which has shown a great drive, almost a mission, to sweep away beliefs, customs and institutions which stand in the way of industrial development, should also have become not merely—as one might have expected—an aggressive and grandiose mixer of peoples. but also a great and sometimes stubborn agent of racial and ethnic discrimination and a breeder of racial doctrines and stereotypes. This raises the general question whether and under what circumstances modern industry is really guided by the impersonal concepts of the market and efficiency in choosing and assigning its labor force.

Another tenet of the ideology of modern industrial management has been that all barriers to free movement of labor should be removed in the interest of its economic use. This appeared in the movement to remove restrictions against internal migration in the early days of the industrial revolution in Europe, and in the insistence on treating each worker as an individual whose employment could be terminated at will by either party without interference of any third party. With reference to this tenet we may ask: To what extent and under what circumstances *does* industry rely on purely economic means and incentives applied to freely moving individuals to get and keep a labor supply, and under what circumstances does it use or encourage essentially political means, such as restriction of movement, fixed terms of employment, or differential rules governing the movement and activities of certain categories of people? There are other questions like these concerning the behavior of industrial management in various social settings. I believe it one of the major tasks of people interested in a sociological view of industry to seek the answers to these questions, and that the way to do it is to compare the ways of industry in a variety of settings, including a variety of inter-racial and inter-ethnic settings.

A first and evident comparison is that between the mother-countries of modern technology and industrial institutions, including their closer satellites, and the outlying, newer industrial regions which we may call colonial whether they are so in a political sense or not.

In the mother-countries (England, Belgium, Holland, Germany, parts of other western European countries, and North America), those who manage industry and perform its higher technical functions are native, as are also the central core of skilled workers. At least, they are native to this general area and feel themselves at home in it. Even within these areas, however, managers and technicians may be ethnically somewhat strange to the particular smaller regions in which they work. Many of the founders, engineers and skilled workers of the early industries in the German Ruhr came from Britain and Belgium where coal mining and the iron industry had first developed machinery. It was not long, however, before Germany could supply such people in number sufficient for her own industry and for export.

There has been a constant flow of managers, accountants, engineers and skilled workers from these mother countries to the outlying newly industrialized regions of the Western world itself, as well as to the colonial regions. This movement takes them, and the industries they operate, into regions where they are ethnically strange enough for it to be remarked by themselves and by the native population. Examples are the central and eastern countries of Europe, the French parts of Canada and even our Southern states. As the prime movers of industry get out into the less industrially-minded parts of the Western world one begins to hear from them those impatient complaints about the perversity of local institutions and people which they utter more or less openly in colonial regions.

In the older industrial regions of the mother-country the rank and file working force was generally built around a nucleus of people native to the region and of the same ethnic kind as management. But as industry grew, large and long-continued internal migration and immigration from other countries were necessary to keep up and expand the working force. The consequent ethnic differences are of the order of national differences within the European world. Of the mother-countries, only the United States has recruited a sizable part of its labor from outside the European cultures and races. Such people, Negroes, Orientals and Latin American mestizos, were generally brought here as labor, not for manufacturing but for industrial agriculture and construction work, just as in the colonial areas. It has been only after a long experience in the Euro-American culture and economy, and usually after turn-over of generations that people of other than European ancestry have found their way into the labor force of American manufacturing industry. In spite of these facts, the ethnic differences show up in the strata of power, skill and prestige in industrial organizations in all Western countries. To the extent that they do not, it seems to be because the ethnic differences have, in effect, ceased to exist.

Now these mother-countries of modern industry all have open social-class systems and social ladders of a similar kind. Social mobility is part of their philosophy. The Western communities in which industry is established generally have landed, commercial and professional middle-classes who, being accustomed to prestige and power, may be jealous of the new leaders of industry. This jealousy is perhaps more apparent when the new leaders of industry differ ethnically from the local middle class. On the other hand, the latter often encourage the coming of industry, and seek to take advantage of it by speculating in land for industrial sites, and by building new houses or businesses which, they hope, will be patronized by the incoming industrial population. In any case, some combination of cooperation and antagonism of local middle-class people with the leaders of industry develops; this becomes a major theme of politics. To it is added the politics of labor, as the industrial working force takes form and becomes defined in its own eyes and those of management and the local non-industrial middle class. Some of the workers, whether native or immigrant, will try to rise in the industrial structure; their success or failure will almost certainly become symbolically important to the workers at large. If it be failure, the flames of ethnic consciousness will be fanned thereby, and local politics will reflect the fire. There may develop a labor movement which defines its enemy, management, in racial or ethnic terms, and which may, at the same time, endeavor to keep out workers of other ethnic or racial kinds. Since these are areas in which all, or nearly all, classes of people are accustomed to take some part in politics, and therefore may be quickly mobilized against industry, management cannot ignore local politics. The various political alignments which develop in such industrial communities, and the circumstances which change them have been talked of, and have, in a few cases, been described and analyzed.[3] There is need of systematic comparison of them in a variety of situations.

Although it must reckon with unfavorable alignments and opposition, industry can count on finding in the Western world the basic matrix of law, institutions and ideologies in which the special institutions of capitalistic industry grew up. I think it a fair generalization that in the mother-countries, industry prefers as little interference of government as possible, excepting only use of the police power to protect their "property" and "right to operate," and of legislation to protect markets. In such countries, industry is, as a rule, against attempts to restrict the flow of labor into and out of the region. An exception appears in marginal areas which share some of the characteristics of the colonial world; such as in the southern United States, where an industrial agriculture had developed slavery and when that was abolished, other devices for holding people to their jobs — a pattern taken over to some extent by early manufacturing industries in the region.

At the opposite pole from the Western mother-countries of modern industry, stand the colonial areas of the world,[4] whither men of European extraction have gone or sent their agents to gather and fetch to world markets vegetable and mineral products wanted for consumption or manufacture in the industrial mother-countries. The first capitalistic industrial enterprises in such regions are usually plantations or mines, which marshal large numbers of people to labor under what is to them an alien system.

Often not enough native people can be immediately recruited to meet the newcomers' demand; in this case, laborers may be imported under indenture or contract from some other non-industrial, non-European country; generally, the imported labor has come from among the non-tribal peoples of Asia where large masses of landless people accustomed to wage-work are willing to hire themselves out for a period of years without hope of advancement. When their terms of work are up, they often go into small trading or commercial farming. They thus become a middle caste of small entrepreneurs, as have the Chinese in the East Indies and the East Indians in South Africa.

The natives themselves are often not accustomed to individual wage

3. e.g., W.L. Warner, and J.O. Low, *The Social System of the Modern Factory* (New Haven: Yale University Press, 1947).

4. For a general definition of colonial status see Raymond Kennedy, "The Colonial Crisis and the Future," in R. Linton, *The Science of Man in the World Crisis* (New York: Columbia University Press, 1945). He notes that Japan is (or was) the one non-European nation to have developed modern political and economic colonies, and that these colonies showed the essential features of colonies of European countries.

work, at least as a continued and sole means of getting a living. They may have worked only as members of communities, their tasks and their rewards determined by their places in a social system. Hence they are not always willing to work for long periods, if at all, in the new enterprises. In such case the political force of the colonial power is used to recruit and hold workers. A head-tax payable in money of the new system may be used to compel families, tribes, and communities to send out members to work for a time. Penal sanctions may be applied to those who leave jobs. Restrictions on movement in and out of the district and earlier, colonial chattel slavery served the same end.[5] In short, the usual economic incentives do not bring in a labor supply. Industry departs from its mother-country practice of encouraging free movement of labor, and uses the police power instead. The problem of early industry in England was to make the people free to move from parish to parish so that they might be available to industry; one could assume that the poor would use the freedom in a way profitable to industry. In colonial regions, that assumption proves not true, and there is a complete reversal of tactic.

This raises the whole question of the relation of industry to the law, institutions and mores of the communities and regions where it establishes enterprises. In the Western world the representatives of industry claim to believe in as little government as possible, and generally claim to respect the mores, religion, and social beliefs of the communities in which they operate. Indeed, local custom and belief are often plead by industrial management as their reason for racial and ethnic discrimination and segregation. On the other hand, industry has eaten away at many customs and beliefs by its very insistence on continuous operation. But, in the main, the law, sentiments and symbols of the community are essentially those of the leaders of industry themselves. In the purely colonial regions, they are not. Local institutions and law may not allow for the kind of organization that industry regards essential to its operation; and the policing power may be neither strong enough nor properly minded to support industry. The evidence from colonial situations makes it appear that where the local legal and institutional framework stands in the way, industry is prepared to modify it as much as need be. This it does by support of imperial interference with local authority. An additional means is the establishment of separate industrial communities in which industry and its representatives exercise political and police functions over their employees: thus the famil-

5. For material on this subject see: J.H. Boeke, *The Structure of the Netherlands Indian Economy,* New York: Institute of Pacific Relations, 1942. John A. Noon, *Labor Problems of Africa,* Philadelphia: University of Pennsylvania Press, 1944. Sheila van der Horst, *Native Labor in South Africa.* London: Oxford University Press, 1942. Sydney Olivier, *White Capital and Coloured Labour* (London: The Hogarth Press, 1929), and *The Anatomy of African Misery* (London: L. & V. Woolf, 1927).

iar colonial institutions of the labor compound, the plantation, and that institution of areas marginal to the colonial world, the company town. One of our tasks should be the close analysis of the behavior of industrial management toward local law, institutions and beliefs in a whole series of situations, from those in which local society is apparently most favorable to industry to those in which it is least favorable. At the colonial pole we get evidence of a belief in the divine right of industry to modify any society as much as need be to allow it to exploit local markets, resources, and labor; perhaps it is undertaken with the least pang when the local people and culture are of some kind with whom industrial managers feel little human identification. This is one meaning of the "white man's burden."

On the other hand, it may turn out that industry will lose its sense of identification with the law, institutions, and people of an older industrial community if they develop in a way unfavorable to industry beyond some point of tolerance. It is possible that law, institutions and sentiments are most favorable to industry in Western communities with well-developed concepts of the law relating to property, organization of voluntary corporations, free individual contract, and the like, but not yet highly nor long industrialized—communities still virgin, but ripe for willing embrace.

To resume our comparison, as a result of the importation of labor from other regions, the industrial hierarchy in colonial areas often consists of several ethnic groups, each of which performs some rather distinct function.[6] The new recruits of each group come into the structure at a given level and tend to remain there. There is no ladder of promotion by small rungs from the bottom to the top of the structure. Mobility tends to occur mainly by leaving the industrial organization for some new commercial or service function brought into being by the social revolution accompanying the growth of the new economic system. There is almost complete absence of the kind of industrial mobility which is so strong in the ideology of industry in the Western countries.

A related feature of the colonial regions, well described by J. H. Boeke in his works on the Dutch East Indies, is that the native labor is for a long time only halfway in the new system. When not working in it for wages, they are absorbed again and kept by the familial, tribal or village societies to which they still belong. In course of time, the power of the native society and economy to re-absorb the industrial workers declines, through loss of land to the new system of things or through pressure of population. At the same time, some of the natives become so weaned from their mother culture as to have no wish to return to it. Their goals are already

6. R.D. McKenzie, "Cultural and Racial Difference as Bases of Human Symbiosis," Amos H. Hawley (ed.) *Roderick D. McKenzie on Human Ecology.* Chicago: University of Chicago Press, 1968; pp. 170-201.

turned toward the new life. Thus there grows up a group of people who are completely dependent upon the new industrial system, people who—when not working for wages—must now be considered the unemployed of the new system. Such people are inclined to become discontent, to demand a new and higher scale of wages so that they can buy the consumer's goods of the new system, and even to demand that they be allowed to climb higher in the industrial hierarchy.[7]

A similar cycle occurs even in the mother-countries of industry when people of "backward" rural regional or ethnic elements are drawn into the less skilled jobs of industry in times of acute labor shortage. We have seen it in the United States in the case of the rural Southern people, both Negro and white; and in Canada, in the case of "backwoods" people from Quebec and the Maritime provinces. It is a process which contains the problem of hidden social subsidies to industry, and the question whether industry can maintain the level of profit which it has come to expect when all such hidden subsidy has wasted away and the population must be kept from industrial income even when not working for industry.

In the colonial regions, there is either no middle class of natives in the European sense (South Africa), or the middle class (as in India or China) is far removed from any place in industry of control over it. The middle classes may pick up some crumbs of prosperity or power from the presence of the new economic order, or they may be threatened and destroyed by it. In either case, they may be without political power. The masses are at first politically inactive, but may begin showing signs of forming new groups, of a feeling of nationality where once there had been only tribal or village solidarity. A new nationalism may arise, and economic and ethnic unrest may be joined in it. Hence that confusion of racial and class conflict so common in the colonial areas of the world.

Within industry itself, one finds in these colonial areas almost no admission of the native population to the inner and higher positions of prestige and control. The tendency to exclusion of ethnically alien elements is here seen in its extreme; or perhaps it is only more visible because of race and

7. For one of the best analyses of this process see A.W. Lind, *Economic Succession and Racial Invasion in Hawaii,* University of Chicago Libraries, 1936. In this work (p. 404) is the following passage: "The process by which Hawaii imports large numbers of unskilled laborers from various sections of the globe, exploits their labor power for a few years on the sugar and pineapple plantations, and at the same time initiates them into the great American scramble for a place at the top of the economic ladder, is apparently irreversible and is cumulative in its exactions upon the existing economy and culture. Each new generation of plantation workers occasions an addition to the surplus of competitors for the preferred positions within the system, not alone by graduation of the majority of its number to the ranks of non-plantation pursuits, but even more by the creation of a second generation even more thoroughly inoculated with the American success virus." See also his *An Island Community: Ecological Succession in Hawaii,* Chicago: University of Chicago Press, 1938.

the sharp cultural distinctions between the working many and the managing few. Where this line of effective exclusion is drawn depends upon circumstances and upon the nature of the industry. In South African mining, white men came from England to do the skilled work at first; now that a native labor force which could do the work has been developed, the politically active white men use the full power of the state and racial solidarity to preserve their own monopoly. The line is held at the gate to skilled work; industry puts up with it at great cost. In other cases the line is drawn at supervision and authority. In others, the main concern is to keep merely the higher control of policy and money in the hands of representatives of the dominant, European group.

Here we meet that peculiar phenomenon, the straw-boss, and can see his essential function. A native is given supervision over native workers; or a person of some ethnic group alien both to management and the mass of the workers is given this function. The notion is that such a person will know the peculiar ways of the workers, and will deal with them accordingly. He is a liaison man, a go-between. And wherever there are workers of some kind extremely alien to industry and to the managers of industry, someone is given this function. He documents, in effect, the gap between the higher positions and the lower; and symbolizes the fact that there is no easy ladder of mobility from the lower position to the higher. He may be literally bilingual, transmitting the orders given in the European tongue into some vernacular; he is also bilingual in a broader figurative sense. He understands the language—the symbols and meanings—of the industrial world, and translates it into symbols which have meaning to people from another culture, who live in a different set of life-chances. And here we can begin to push harder toward comparison of the mother-countries of industry and the colonial industrial regions. In the latter, the straw-boss symbolizes limited mobility. He is himself mobile, and ambitious. But the nature of his job rests on the lack of mobility of the masses. In the mother countries, the straw-boss turns up, too. He is found wherever some new and strange element is introduced into the labor force in number. The Negro personnel man is one of the latest straw-bosses; he acts as a liaison man between management and Negro help. He cannot himself be considered a candidate for any higher position or for any line position in industry; his is a staff position which exists only so long as Negroes are hired in fairly large numbers, and so long as Negro help is considered sufficiently different from other help to require special liaison. If the race line disappeared, or tended to disappear in industry, there would be no need of the Negro personnel man. There might be personnel men who are Negroes. Thus, the Negro personnel man is performing a racial function; he is not part of the regular line of authority, and does not represent a rung in the ladder of regular advancement to higher positions. Industrial organizations in the colonial regions abound in such liaison positions. Just what such positions are, the features of social and industrial organization which they reflect, and the kinds of persons who fill them are all matters whose further analysis would throw light on the nature and internal functioning of industrial organization. It is but one of the several features which appear in clear form in colonial industry, but which may also exist, although commonly overlooked, in the industry of the mother-countries.

Now these considerations of structure and mobility again raise questions concerning the fundamental ideology of industry. For industry in the Western world promoted an ideology of mobility, that is, of ambition. In the colonial world, ambition is often regarded as unjustified and dangerous. Even in the Western world, managers speak with nostalgia of the unambitious first-generation of Poles, French-Canadians, or peasant-workers of other ethnic groups; people who were content with their jobs, willing to work hard without hope of advancement. Of course, such people often had objectives outside industry to keep them at work and content; notably, the desire to save money for buying property. In spirit, they were not completely industrialized. A second or later generation which insists on advancement within industry is compared unfavorably with their fathers. The hostile reaction of many managers to ambitious Negroes is too well-known to require documenting.

Here is apparently a contradiction: Industry encourages ambition, and complains a good deal about lack of it. On the other hand, it praises some people for not having it, and complains of others who do. This raises another general question: Just how much ambition does an industrial organization want and in how many people and in what kinds of people does it want it? In the colonial world, there is generally a limit on the possibilities of promotion for persons of each ethnic category, although this may change through time. For certain kinds of work, it may actually be to the advantage of industry to hire only people whose ambitions are directed to goals completely outside the industrial system. For others, they may want ambitious people. There may, however, be some balance between the proportion of ambitious and unambitious people which works best even in the oldest of the industrial regions. A clue appears in a phrase current in a large concern in this country. They have a breed known as the "Thank God for" people; the unambitious people who can be counted on to stay where they are, and who keep things running while others are busy climbing the mobility ladder from one job to another. Analysis might show that in the mother-countries of industry some adjustment between symbol and reality has occurred, so that a large proportion of workers may give lip-service to the mobility ideal, but not too many take it seriously.

Just what proportion of ambitious workers industrial organizations of various kinds can tolerate is a question which merits comparative analysis, although it may be difficult to make the necessary observations in a society where people generally claim to believe in ambition and to be ashamed of lack of it. In colonial regions, the talk on the subject is often franker.

I have already noted that ethnic exclusiveness tends to develop at all levels of colonial industrial hierarchies. The dominant managerial and technical functions remain pretty much in the hands of the founding ethnic group. Sometimes a European group of skilled workers, as in South African mines, holds to its level of jobs and succeeds in excluding the natives. In the less skilled jobs, some group of natives may manage to keep out others. Even in American industry, such a tendency shows clearly. A number of forces play upon hiring and selection to reinforce or to break up this tendency. If I were to venture an hypothesis it would be something like this: the tendency to exclusiveness is present in all organizations, and in the segments thereof, but the power to maintain it varies. In industry, the necessity of keeping a full labor force operates against exclusiveness in those categories where large numbers are required; generally, the lower levels of skill. The people at these levels have little or no formal power of hiring. They have, in varying degree, informal power of selection and rejection.

The people in the higher levels of the hierarchy have the power to keep their own ranks ethnically exclusive. In the colonial or semi-colonial industrial regions, management often quite frankly talks of the necessity of keeping management in loyal hands; that is, in the hands of people closely identified with one another by national sentiment as well as by general cultural background. In the mother-countries of industry, one does not hear such talk, but it is possible that the mechanism operates without people being aware of it. It may operate through the mechanism of sponsoring, by which promising young people are picked and encouraged in their mobility efforts by their superiors. In the course of their rise, they are not merely given a technical training, but also are initiated into the ways and sentiments of the managerial group and are judged by their internal acceptance of them. Ethnic, national and class loyalty are undoubtedly factors in the original choice of people to be sponsored and in their later rise. In the Western world individuals ethnically different from those at the top of management may be drawn into the sponsorship circle, but in the course of it effectively lose all symbols of identification with the ethnic group from which they have come and take on those of the receiving group. Where skin color and other racial features are involved, this is not so easy to do. Thus, while modern industry is opposed to nepotism, as contrary to the best choice of people in an open market, as an operating organization it tends to hold power in the hands of a group whose new members are picked from among people thought to be loyal not merely to the particular organization but to the management class and its culture. In the selection and sponsoring process ethnic background plays a large part.

The sponsoring power of lower ranks may be less, but is by no means completely lacking in many situations. Coal miners and railroad workers notoriously have great sponsoring power. And even in the colonial regions the members of an ethnic group or clan, or the inhabitants of a village, may have, in effect, the power to recruit new workers. In a sense, when industry brings in some new ethnic group it has to do it in opposition to the present workers. The actual ethnic composition and changes therein seem then to be a resultant of the operation of demand for new help against the exclusive tendencies of the various segments of the existing working organization. The search of modern industry for new help that can be used with profit has certainly been active and persistent. On the other hand, for a given kind or level of job, the field in which the search is made may be limited by management's own state of knowledge and sentiments. Certainly the evidence is clear that in the colonial regions, and to some extent in the mother-countries, there grows up a body of belief about the special working qualities of various ethnic groups. These stereotypes, which may or may not correspond to the facts, act to limit the vision of those who select help and who inititate sponsorship. In a sense, this is like any marketing situation, in that the bargaining of the marketer is limited by his own knowledge and sentiments. The role of sentiments is, however, made somewhat stronger in the hiring and utilization of human labor than in the buying and selling of inanimate commodities by the fact that the human labor is, so to speak, consumed by industry. Industry is not a labor broker, for it uses the labor to build a continuing organization for work; it must live with its laboring people. And in the course of working together the social and political processes get under way as they do in any organization. Industry thus considers its people not merely as technical help, but as actual or potential participants in a struggle for power within industry and society, and as potential close colleagues (or as unfit to be such). When one takes these points into account, many of the contradictions and paradoxes in the behavior of industrial management and workers begin to move toward possible solution. A complete resolution of them might be approached by systematic comparison of the various situations in which industry has operated. I suspect that in such comparison racial and ethnic differences will act as a sort of litmus paper to bring out characteristics and processes which might otherwise be overlooked.

NINE

Good People and Dirty Work

"... une secte est le *noyau* et le *levain* de toute foule. ... Etudier la foule c'est juger un drame d'après ce qu'on voit sur la scène; étudier la secte c'est le juger d'après ce qu'on voit dans les coulisses."

Sighele, S. *Psychologie des sectes*. Paris, 1898. Pp. 62, 63, 65.[1]

The National Socialist Government of Germany, with the arm of its fanatical inner sect, the S.S., commonly known as the Black Shirts or Elite Guard, perpetrated and boasted of the most colossal and dramatic piece of social dirty work the world has ever known. Perhaps there are other claimants to the title, but they could not match this one's combination of mass, speed and perverse pride in the deed. Nearly all peoples have plenty of cruelty and death to account for. How many Negro Americans have died by the hands of lynching mobs? How many more from unnecessary disease and lack of food or of knowledge of nutrition? How many Russians died to bring about collectivization of land? And who is to blame if there be starving millions in some parts of the world while wheat molds in the fields of other parts?

Reprinted by permission of the publisher from *Social Problems,* Vol. X, Summer, 1962. Copyright 1962, Society for the Study of Social Problems. (Delivered as public lecture at McGill University shortly after a long visit to Western Germany in 1948.)
1. "... a sect is the nucleus and the yeast of every crowd. ... To study a crowd is to judge by what one sees on the stage; to study the sect is to judge by what one sees backstage." These are among the many passages underlined by Robert E. Park in his copy, now in my possession, of Sighele's classic work on political sects. There are a number of references to this work in the Park and Burgess *Introduction to the Science of Sociology,* Chicago, University of Chicago Press, 1921, 1969. In fact, there is more attention paid to fanatical political and religious behavior in Park and Burgess than in any later sociological work in this country. Sighele's discussion relates chiefly to the anarchist movement of his time. There have been fanatical movements since. The Secret Army Organization in Algeria is but the latest.

I do not revive the case of the Nazi *Endlösung* (final solution) of the Jewish problem in order to condemn the Germans, or make them look worse than other peoples, but to recall to our attention dangers which lurk in our midst always. Most of what follows was written after my first postwar visit to Germany in 1948. The impressions were vivid. The facts have not diminished and disappeared with time, as did the stories of alleged German atrocities in Belgium in the first World War. The fuller the record, the worse it gets.[2]

Several millions of people were delivered to the concentration camps, operated under the leadership of Heinrich Himmler with the help of Adolf Eichmann. A few hundred thousand survived in some fashion. Still fewer came out sound of mind and body. A pair of examples, well attested, will show the extreme of perverse cruelty reached by the S.S. guards in charge of the camps. Prisoners were ordered to climb trees; guards whipped them to make them climb faster. Once they were out of reach, other prisoners, also urged by the whip, were put to shaking the trees. When the victims fell, they were kicked to see whether they could rise to their feet. Those too badly injured to get up were shot to death, as useless for work. A not inconsiderable number of prisoners were drowned in pits full of human excrement. These examples are so horrible that your minds will run away from them. You will not, as when you read a slightly salacious novel, imagine the rest. I therefore thrust these examples upon you and insist that the people who thought them up could, and did, improvise others like them, and even worse, from day to day over several years. Many of the victims of the camps gave up the ghost (this Biblical phrase is the most apt) from a combination of humiliation, starvation, fatigue and physical abuse. In due time, a policy of mass liquidation in the gas chamber was added to individual virtuosity in cruelty.

This program—for it was a program—of cruelty and murder was carried out in the name of racial superiority and racial purity. It was directed mainly, although by no means exclusively, against Jews, Slavs and Gypsies. It was thorough. There are few Jews in the territories which were under the control of the Third German Reich—the two Germanies, Holland, Czechoslovakia, Poland, Austria, Hungary. Many Jewish Frenchmen

2. The best source easily available at that time was Eugen Kogon's *Der SS Staat. Das System der Deutschen Konzentrationslager,* Berlin. Verlag der Frankfurter Heft, 1946. Many of my data are from his book. Some years later H. G. Adler, after several years of research, wrote *Theresienstadt, 1941-1945. Das Antlitz einer Zwangsgemeinschaft* (Tübingen, J. C. B. Mohr, 1955), and still later published *Die Verheimlichte Wahrheit, Theresienstädter Dokumente* (Tübingen, J. C. B. Mohr, 1958), a book of documents concerning that camp in which Czech and other Jews were concentrated, demoralized and destroyed. Kogon, a Catholic intellectual, and Adler, a Bohemian Jew, both wrote out of personal experience in the concentration camps. Both considered it their duty to present the phenomenon objectively to the public. None of their statements has ever been challenged.

were destroyed. There were concentration camps even in Tunisia and Algiers under the German occupation.

When, during my 1948 visit to Germany, I became more aware of the reactions of ordinary Germans to the horrors of the concentration camps, I found myself asking not the usual question, "How did racial hatred rise to such a high level?", but this one, "How could such dirty work be done among and, in a sense, *by* the millions of ordinary, civilized German people?" Along with this came related questions. How could these millions of ordinary people live in the midst of such cruelty and murder without a general uprising against it and against the people who did it? How, once freed from the regime that did it, could they be apparently so little concerned about it, so toughly silent about it, not only in talking with outsiders—which is easy to understand—but among themselves? How and where could there be found in a modern civilized country the several hundred thousand men and women capable of such work? How were these people so far released from the inhibitions of civilized life as to be able to imagine, let alone perform, the ferocious, obscene and perverse actions which they did imagine and perform? How could they be kept at such a height of fury through years of having to see daily at close range the human wrecks they made and being often literally spattered with the filth produced and accumulated by their own actions?

You will see that there are here two orders of questions. One set concerns the good people who did not themselves do this work. The other concerns those who did do it. But the two sets are not really separate; for the crucial question concerning the good people is their relation to the people who did the dirty work, with a related one which asks under what circumstances good people let the others get away with such actions.

An easy answer concerning the Germans is that they were not so good after all. We can attribute to them some special inborn or ingrained race consciousness, combined with a penchant for sadistic cruelty and unquestioning acceptance of whatever is done by those who happen to be in authority. Pushed to its extreme, this answer simply makes us, rather than the Germans, the superior race. It is the Nazi tune, put to words of our own.

Now there are deep and stubborn differences between peoples. Their history and culture may make the Germans especially susceptible to the doctrine of their own racial superiority and especially acquiescent to the actions of whoever is in power over them. These are matters deserving of the best study that can be given them. But to say that these things could happen in Germany simply because Germans are different—from us—buttresses their own excuses and lets us off too easily from blame for what happened there and from the question whether it could happen here.

Certainly in their daily practice and expression before the Hitler regime, the Germans showed no more, if as much, hatred of other racial or cultural groups than we did and do. Residential segregation was not marked. Intermarriage was common, and the families of such marriages had an easier social existence than they generally have in America. The racially exclusive club, school and hotel were much less in evidence than here. And I well remember an evening in 1933 when a Montreal business man—a very nice man, too—said in our living room, "Why don't we admit that Hitler is doing to the Jews just what we ought to be doing?" That was not an uncommon sentiment, although it may be said in defense of the people who expressed it, that they probably did not know and would not have believed the full truth about the Nazi program of destroying Jews. The essential underlying sentiments on racial matters in Germany were not different in kind from those prevailing throughout the western, and especially the Anglo-Saxon, countries. But I do not wish to over-emphasize this point. I only want to close one easy way out of serious consideration of the problem of good people and dirty work, by demonstrating that the Germans were and are about as good and about as bad as the rest of us on this matter of racial sentiments and, let us add, their notions of decent human behaviour.

But what was the reaction of ordinary Germans to the persecution of the Jews and to the concentration camp mass torture and murder? A conversation between a German school teacher, a German architect and myself gives the essentials in a vivid form. It was in the studio of the architect, and the occasion was a rather casual visit, in Frankfurt am Main in 1948.

> The architect: "I am ashamed for my people whenever I think of it. But we didn't know about it. We only learned about all that later. You must remember the pressure we were under; we had to join the party. We had to keep our mouths shut and do as we were told. It was a terrible pressure. Still, I am ashamed. But you see, we had lost our colonies, and our national honour was hurt. And these Nazis exploited that feeling. And the Jews, they *were* a problem. They came from the east. You should see them in Poland; the lowest class of people, full of lice, dirty and poor, running about in their Ghettos in filthy caftans. They came here, and got rich by unbelievable methods after the first war. They occupied all the good places. Why, they were in the proportion of ten to one in medicine and law and government posts!"
>
> At this point the architect hesitated and looked confused. He continued: "Where was I? It is the poor food. You see what misery we are in here, Herr Professor. It often happens that I forget what I was talking about. Where was I now? I have completely forgotten."
>
> (His confusion was, I believe, not at all feigned. Many Germans said they suffered losses of memory such as this, and laid it to their lack of food.)

I said firmly: "You were talking about loss of national honour and how the Jews had got hold of everything."

The architect: "Oh, yes! That was it! Well, of course that was no way to settle the Jewish problem. But there *was* a problem and it had to be settled someway."

The school teacher: "Of course, they have Palestine now."

I protested that Palestine would hardly hold them.

The architect: "The professor is right. Palestine can't hold all the Jews. And it was a terrible thing to murder people. But we didn't know it at the time. But I am glad I am alive now. It is an interesting time in men's history. You know, when the Americans came it was like a great release. I really want to see a new ideal in Germany. I like the freedom that lets me talk to you like this. But, unfortunately that is not the general opinion. Most of my friends really hang on to the old ideas. They can't see any hope, so they hang on to the old ideas."

This scrap of talk gives, I believe, the essential elements as well as the flavor of the German reaction. It checks well with formal studies which have been made, and it varies only in detail from other conversations which I myself recorded in 1948.

One of the most obvious points in it is unwillingness to think about the dirty work done. In this case—perhaps by chance, perhaps not—the good man suffered an actual lapse of memory in the middle of this statement. This seems a simple point. But the psychiatrists have shown that it is less simple than it looks. They have done a good deal of work on the complicated mechanisms by which the individual mind keeps unpleasant or intolerable knowledge from consciousness, and have shown how great may, in some cases, be the consequent loss of effectiveness of the personality. But we have taken collective unwillingness to know unpleasant facts more or less for granted. That people can and do keep a silence about things whose open discussion would threaten the group's conception of itself, and hence its solidarity, is common knowledge. It is a mechanism that operates in every family and in every group which has a sense of group reputation. To break such a silence is considered an attack against the group; a sort of treason, if it be a member of the group who breaks the silence. This common silence allows group fictions to grow up; such as, that grandpa was less a scoundrel and more romantic than he really was. And I think it demonstrable that it operates especially against any expression, except in ritual, of collective guilt. The remarkable thing in present-day Germany is not that there is so little reference to something about which people do feel deeply guilty, but that it is talked about at all.

In order to understand this phenomenon we would have to find out who talks about the concentration camp atrocities, in what situations, in what mood, and with what stimulus. On these points I know only my own limited experiences. One of the most moving of these was my first post-war meeting with an elderly professor whom I had known before the Nazi time; he is an heroic soul who did not bow his head during the Nazi time and who keeps it erect now. His first words, spoken with tears in his eyes, were:

"How hard it is to believe that men will be as bad as they say they will. Hitler and his people said: 'Heads will roll,' but how many of us—even of his bitterest opponents—could really believe that they would do it."

This man could and did speak, in 1948, not only to the likes of me, but to his students, his colleagues and to the public which read his articles, in the most natural way about the Nazi atrocities whenever there was occasion to do it in the course of his tireless effort to reorganize and to bring new life into the German universities. He had neither the compulsion to speak, so that he might excuse and defend himself, nor a conscious or unconscious need to keep silent. Such people were rare; how many there were in Germany I do not know.

Occasions of another kind in which the silence was broken were those where, in class, public lecture or in informal meetings with students, I myself had talked frankly of race relations in other parts of the world, including the lynchings which sometimes occur in my own country and the terrible cruelty visited upon natives in South Africa. This took off the lid of defensiveness, so that a few people would talk quite easily of what happened under the Nazi regime. More common were situations like that with the architect, where I threw in some remark about the atrocities in response to Germans' complaint that the world is abusing them. In such cases, there was usually an expression of shame, accompanied by a variety of excuses (including that of having been kept in ignorance), and followed by a quick turning away from the subject.

Somewhere in consideration of this problem of discussion versus silence we must ask what the good (that is, ordinary) people in Germany did know about these things. It is clear that the S.S. kept the more gory details of the concentration camps a close secret. Even high officials of the government, the army and the Nazi party itself were in some measure held in ignorance, although of course they kept the camps supplied with victims. The common people of Germany knew that the camps existed; most knew people who had disappeared into them; some saw the victims, walking skeletons in rags, being transported in trucks or trains or being herded on the road from station to camp or to work in fields or factories near the camps. Many knew people who had been released from concentration camps; such released persons kept their counsel on pain of death. But secrecy was cultivated and supported by fear and terror. In the absence of a determined and heroic will to know and publish the truth, and in the absence of all the instruments of opposition, the degree of knowledge was undoubtedly low, in spite of the fact that all knew that something both stupendous and horrible was going on; and in spite of the fact that Hitler's *Mein Kampf* and the utterances of his aides said that no fate was too horrible for the Jews and other wrong-headed or inferior people. This must make us ask under what conditions the will to know and to discuss is strong, determined and effective; this, like most of the important questions I have raised, I leave unanswered except as answers may be contained in the statement of the case.

But to return to our moderately good man, the architect. He insisted over and over again that he did not know, and we may suppose that he knew as much and as little as most Germans. But he also made it quite clear that he wanted something done to the Jews. I have similar statements from people of whom I knew that they had had close Jewish friends before the Nazi time. This raises the whole problem of the extent to which those pariahs who do the dirty work of society are really acting as agents for the rest of us. To talk of this question one must note that, in building up his case, the architect pushed the Jews firmly into an out-group; they were dirty, lousy and unscrupulous (an odd statement from a resident of Frankfurt, the home of old Jewish merchants and intellectual families long identified with those aspects of culture of which Germans are most proud). Having dissociated himself clearly from these people, and having declared them a problem, he apparently was willing to let someone else do to them the dirty work which he himself would not do, and for which he expressed shame. The case is perhaps analogous to our attitude toward those convicted of crime. From time to time, we get wind of cruelty practiced upon the prisoners in penitentiaries or jails; or, it may be, merely a report that they are ill-fed or that hygienic conditions are not good. Perhaps we do not wish that the prisoners should be cruelly treated or badly fed, but our reaction is probably tempered by a notion that they deserve something, because of some dissociation of them from the in-group of good people. If what they get is worse than what we like to think about, it is a little bit too bad. It is a point on which we are ambivalent. Campaigns for reform of prisons are often followed by counter-campaigns against a too high standard of living for prisoners and against having prisons run by softies. Now the people who run prisons are our agents. Just how far they do or could carry out our wishes is hard to say. The minor prison guard, in boastful justification of some of his more questionable practices, says, in effect: "If those reformers and those big shots upstairs had to live with these birds as I do, they would soon change their fool notions about running a prison." He is suggesting that the good people are either naive or hypocritical. Furthermore, he knows quite well that the wishes of his employers, the public, are by no means unmixed. They are quite as likely to put upon him for being too nice as for being too harsh. And if, as sometimes happens, he is a man disposed to cruelty, there may be some justice in his feeling that he is only doing what others would like to do, if they but dared; and what they would do, if they were in his place.

There are plenty of examples in our own world which I might have picked for comparison with the German attitude toward the concentration camps. For instance, a newspaper in Denver made a great scandal out of the allegation that our Japanese compatriots were too well fed in the camps where they were concentrated during the war. I might have mentioned some feature of the sorry history of the people of Japanese background in Canada. Or it might have been lynching, or some aspect of racial discrimination. But I purposely chose prisoners convicted of crime. For convicts are formally set aside for special handling. They constitute an out-group in all countries. This brings the issue clearly before us, since few people cherish the illusion that the problem of treating criminals can be settled by propaganda designed to prove that there aren't any criminals. Almost everyone agrees that something has to be done about them. The question concerns what is done, who does it, and the nature of the mandate given by the rest of us to those who do it. Perhaps we give them an unconscious mandate to go beyond anything we ourselves would care to do or even to acknowledge. I venture to suggest that the higher and more expert functionaries who act in our behalf represent something of a distillation of what we may consider our public wishes, while some of the others show a sort of concentrate of those impulses of which we are or wish to be less aware.

Now the choice of convicted prisoners brings up another crucial point in inter-group relations. All societies of any great size have in-groups and out-groups; in fact, one of the best ways of describing a society is to consider it a network of smaller and larger in-groups and out-groups. And an in-group is one only because there are out-groups. When I refer to *my* children I obviously imply that they are closer to me than other people's children and that I will make greater efforts to buy oranges and cod-liver oil for them than for others' children. In fact, it may mean that I will give them cod-liver oil if I have to choke them to get it down. We do our own dirty work on those closest to us. The very injunction that I love my neighbor as myself starts with me; if I don't love myself and my nearest, the phrase has a very sour meaning.

Each of us is a center of a network of in- and out-groups. Now the distinctions between *in* and *out* may be drawn in various ways, and nothing is more important for both the student of society and the educator than to discover how these lines are made and how they may be redrawn in more just and sensible ways. But to believe that we can do away with the distinction between *in* and *out, us* and *them* in social life is complete nonsense. On the positive side, we generally feel a greater obligation to in-groups; hence less obligation to out-groups; and in the case of such groups as convicted criminals, the out-group is definitely given over to the hands of our agents for punishment. That is the extreme case. But there are other out-groups toward which we may have aggressive feelings and dis-like, although we give no formal mandate to anyone to deal with them on our behalf, and although we profess to believe that they should not suffer restrictions or disadvantages. The greater their social distance from us, the more we leave in the hands of others a sort of mandate by default to deal with them on our behalf. Whatever effort we put on reconstructing the lines which divide in and out-groups, there remains the eternal problem of our treatment, direct or delegated, of whatever groups are considered somewhat outside. And here it is that the whole matter of our professed and possible deeper unprofessed wishes comes up for consideration; and the related problem of what we know, can know and want to know about it. In Germany, the agents got out of hand and created such terror that it was best not to know. It is also clear that it was and is easier to the conscience of many Germans not to know. It is, finally, not unjust to say that the agents were at least working in the direction of the wishes of many people, although they may have gone beyond the wishes of most. The same questions can be asked about our own society, and with reference not only to prisoners but also to many other groups upon whom there is no legal or moral stigma. Again I have not the answers. I leave you to search for them.

In considering the question of dirty work we have eventually to think about the people who do it. In Germany, these were the members of the S.S. and of that inner group of the S.S. who operated the concentration camps. Many reports have been made on the social backgrounds and the personalities of these cruel fanatics. Those who have studied them say that a large proportion were *gescheiterte Existenzen,* men or women with a history of failure, of poor adaptation to the demands of work and of the classes of society in which they had been bred. Germany between wars had large numbers of such people. Their adherence to a movement which proclaimed a doctrine of hatred was natural enough. The movement offered something more. It created an inner group which was to be superior to all others, even Germans, in their emancipation from the usual bourgeois morality; people above and beyond the ordinary morality. I dwell on this, not as a doctrine, but as an organizational device. For, as Eugen Kogon, author of the most penetrating analysis of the S.S. and their camps, has said, the Nazis came to power by creating a state within a state; a body with its own counter-morality and its own counter-law, its courts and its own execution of sentence upon those who did not live up to its orders and standards. Even as a movement it had inner circles within inner circles; each sworn to secrecy as against the next outer one. The struggle between these inner circles continued after Hitler came to power; Himmler eventually won the day. His S.S. became a state within the Nazi state, just as the Nazi movement had become a state within the Weimar state. One is reminded of the oft quoted but neglected statement of Sighele: "At the center of a crowd look for the sect." He referred, of course, to the political sect; the fanatical inner group of a movement seeking power by revolutionary methods. Once the Nazis were in power, this inner sect, while becoming now the recognized agent of the state and, hence, of the masses of the people, could at the same time dissociate itself more completely from them in action, because of the very fact of having a mandate. It was now beyond all danger of interference and investigation. For it had the instruments of interference and investigation in its own hands. These are also the instruments of secrecy. So the S.S. could and did build up a powerful system in which they had the resources of the state and of the economy of Germany and the conquered countries from which to steal all that was needed to carry out their orgy of cruelty luxuriously as well as with impunity.

Now let us ask, concerning the dirty workers, questions similar to those concerning the good people. Is there a supply of candidates for such work in other societies? It would be easy to say that only Germany could produce such a crop. The question is answered by being put. The problem of people who have run around (*gescheiterte Existenzen*) is one of the most serious in our modern societies. Any psychiatrist will, I believe, testify that we have a sufficient pool or fund of personalties warped toward perverse punishment and cruelty to do any amount of dirty work that the good people may be inclined to countenance. It would not take a very great turn of events to increase the number of such people, and to bring their discontents to the surface. This is not to suggest that every movement based on discontent with the present state of things will be led by such people. That is obviously untrue; and I emphasize the point lest my remarks give comfort to those who would damn all who express militant discontent. But I think study of militant social movements does show that these warped people seek a place in them. Specifically, they are likely to become the plotting, secret police of the group. It is one of the problems of militant social movements to keep such people out. It is of course easier to do this if the spirit of the movement is positive, its conception of humanity high and inclusive, and its aims sound. This was not the case of the Nazi movement. As Kogon puts it: "The SS were but the arch-type of the Nazis in general."[3] But such people are sometimes attracted for want of some-

3. *Ibid.,* p. 316.

thing better, to movements whose aims are contrary to the spirit of cruelty and punishment. I would suggest that all of us look well at the leadership and entourage of movements to which we attach ourselves for signs of a negativistic, punishing attitude. For once such a spirit develops in a movement, punishment of the nearest and easiest victim is likely to become more attractive than striving for the essential goals. And, if the Nazi movement teaches us anything at all, it is that if any shadow of a mandate be given to such people, they will — having compromised us — make it larger and larger. The processes by which they do so are the development of the power and inward discipline of their own group, a progressive dissociation of themselves from the rules of human decency prevalent in their culture, and an every-growing contempt for the welfare of the masses of people.

The power and inward discipline of the S.S. became such that those who once became members could get out only by death; by suicide, murder or mental breakdown. Orders from the central offices of the S.S. were couched in equivocal terms as a hedge against a possible day of judgment. When it became clear that such a day of judgment would come, the hedging and intrigue became greater; the urge to murder also became greater, because every prisoner became a potential witness.

Again we are dealing with a phenomenon common in all societies. Almost every group which has a specialized social function to perform is in some measure a secret society, with a body of rules developed and enforced by the members and with some power to save its members from outside punishment. And here is one of the paradoxes of social order. A society without smaller, rule-making and disciplining powers would be no society at all. There would be nothing but law and police; and this is what the Nazis strove for, at the expense of family, church, professional groups, parties and other such nuclei of spontaneous control. But apparently the only way to do this, for good as well as for evil ends, is to give power into the hands of some fanatical small group which will have a far greater power of self-discipline and a far greater immunity to outside control than the traditional groups. The problem is, then, not of trying to get rid of all the self disciplining, protecting groups within society, but one of keeping them integrated with one another and as sensitive as can be to a public opinion which transcends them all. It is a matter of checks and balances, of what we might call the social and moral constitution of society.

Those who are especially devoted to efforts to eradicate from good people, as individuals, all those sentiments which seem to bring about the great and small dirty work of the world, may think that my remarks are something of an attack on their methods. They are right to this extent; that I am insisting that we give a share of our effort to the social mechanisms involved as well as to the individual and those of his sentiments which concern people of other kinds.

TEN

Bastard Institutions

Institutions distribute goods and services; they are the legitimate satis-fiers of legitimate human wants. In the course of distributing religion, play, art, education, food, and drink, shelter, and other things — they also define in standard ways what it is proper for people to want. The definition of what is to be distributed, although it may be fairly broad and somewhat flexible, seldom if ever completely satisfies all kinds and conditions of men. Institutions also decide, in effect, to serve only a certain range of people, as does a shop that decides not to carry out-sizes and queer styles of shirts. The distribution is never complete and perfect.

Some institutions have resulted from collective protest against either the institutionalized definition of the service, function, or goods in question. One kind of protest is sectarian — protest against the brand of religious doctrine and expression distributed by official clergy. It may be protest against the definition of religious practice, against its distribution, or against alleged connections and identification of the church and its functionaries with the vested interests of certain social classes. Another such protest was that against the established definition of education by the classical colleges. Out of that protest came new educational enterprises such as the Land Grant colleges devoted to pursuit of some single, clearly defined purpose. In time such institutions devolved toward the very patterns against which they revolted and from which they departed. Established institutional pat-terns are hidden traps into which the best of protest enterprises may fall.

But there are other chronic deviations from established institutions, other kinds of escape from the legitimate channels. There are chronic deviations and protests, some lasting through generations and ages. They

Regular class lecture in Social Institutions, University of Chicago, Nov. 26, 1951.

98

may gain a certain stability, although they do not have the support of open legitimacy. They operate without benefit of the law, although often with the connivance of the legal establishment. They may lie outside the realm of respectability.

Let us call them *bastard institutions*. Some are the illegitimate distributors of legitimate goods and services; others satisfy wants not considered legitimate. Among bastard institutions are gambling, prostitution (the second oldest profession), rackets, black markets (whether of babies for adoption, food, or foreign exchange), the fence, professional crime, bootlegging (of alcoholic liquor or of forbidden drugs or literature). All take on organized forms not unlike those of other institutions. Homosexuality takes on certain fairly stable forms: the homosexual menage, clubs, cabarets, and such.

Kangaroo courts in prison and armies and the tong courts of the earlier Chinatowns meted out the justice of a particular group that did not accept or trust established justice. The popular justice of the frontier and the lynchings that continued in several Southern states until the 1920's were bastard institutions, not formally legitimate but highly conventional and supported by popular opinion. The underworld has its hidden courts for offenses against its rules and interests, and when an enemy is abroad in the land, the underground—the maquisards—may try and execute traitors.

Something called quackery lies on the margins of legitimate distribution of medical services. On the outskirts of the educational establishment are the cram schools, to prepare students for admission to universities or to help them pass the examinations for admission to the bar. Beyond the gates of military centers, just outside the limits of middle-class suburbs that allow drinking but not the sale of alcohol, and just off the property of Utopian industrial towns lie the "Bumtowns" where people can satisfy their all-too-human wants. Hell is probably the Bumtown of Heaven.

Some of these bastard institutions are directly against the law, or the declared moral values of society. They are in direct conflict with accepted definitions and institutional mandates. Others offer a less than fully respectable alternative, or allow one to satisfy some hidden weakness or idiosyncratic taste not provided for, and slightly frowned on, by the established distributors. Still others quite simply offer a way to get something not readily available to people of one's kind in the prevailing institutional system. They are corrections of faults in institutional definition and distribution.

Whatever they be, and whatever they have in common, these bastard enterprises should be studied not merely as pathological departures from what is good and right, but as part of the total complex of human activities and enterprises. In addition, they should be looked at as orders of things in which we can see the social processes going on, the same social processes, perhaps, that are to be found in the legitimate institutions. Weber was interested in the way in which the not-legitimate becomes legitimate, but not especially in the manner in which the chronically illegitimate enterprises of men continue to exist and through what course they run in their effort to survive as against the legitimate definitions of behavior. Park was interested in some of these phenomena. In his later years he became especially interested in the underworlds of the great cities of the world. In them, he believed, there were unusual mixtures of people who, to survive, had somehow to establish a social order among themselves with a minimum of recourse to police and law. Because of their doubtful means of living, it was unwise to attract unnecessarily the agents of law. Because of their variety of origins, traditions, and languages, they could not rely on the customary norms of any one element among them as the basis of their rules of conduct.

Institutions may be described as man's self-created modes, or modal points, of behavior in areas in which there might be many ways of behaving other than the modal one. A mode, of course, is a point in a distribution. The institutional tendency is to pile up behavior at a modal point by definition of what is proper, by sanctions applied against deviating behavior, and by offering devices for distributing only the standardized opportunities and services to people. But while institutions cluster behavior, they do not completely destroy the deviations.

Marriage, for example, is the modal way of organizing the relations between male and female as sexual mates and as procreators and rearers of children. But not all males and females enter into marriages, and not all of those who do so confine their mating to their marriage partners. Some of those who do not enter into marriage have sexual partners, nevertheless, or at least some occasional sexual relations. Now marriage is always defined not merely as an enduring relation between a man and a woman, but as between a man of a certain class, religion, ethnic character, age, income, kin relations, and a woman with appropriate, although not always identical traits. There are people, in short, who are appropriate mates for each other. Further, as Margaret Mead says in *Male and Female,*[1] only human primate males feed, clothe, and shelter their mates. The ability to do so is not equally distributed among the male population. These factors, combined with the tendency of men and women to move about at different tempos and to congregate in relative isolation from one another, bring it about that there are many people for whom no appropriate marriage partners are easily available or who are not in a position to undertake the obligations of

1. Margaret Mead, *Male and Female,* New York, William Morrow & Co., 1949 Mentor Book, 1955.

marriage without depriving themselves of other things they value. The upper-class women of Yankee city, whose brothers are slightly less particular about whom they marry, are often without mates. The men of the frontier, the waterfront, the sea, and of armies may be far from the gathering places of the women they might expect to marry. A prolonged military occupation always brings some relief, sometimes resulting in new definitions of what is the acceptable marriage partner—as witness the Japanese wives of the G.I.'s. In present-day England, as Rowntree found in his study of *English Life and Leisure*,[2] many middle-class men, being unable to contract marriage without falling to a lower class level in their style of living and in their associations, merely establish more or less secret liaisons with women of similar circumstances who are quite willing to continue to make their own livings and to enter into such relations rather than to live the life of isolated career women among other career women. A few of the men interviewed said they simply went to prostitutes because the prostitute put no claims on one. A mistress might in time come to have the expectations of a wife, and the man might feel these expectations as obligations. One may, from one point of view, quite properly speak of marriage as a device for distributing men among women, and the available women among the men. The terms of the distribution seem not to fit the facts of present-day English middle-class life so well as they once did.

Now the ancient institution of prostitution is one of the organized ways in which the faulty distribution of mate selection has been compensated for. The most obvious concentrations of houses of prostitution are at those points where men congregate away from home: along the main stems and waterfronts of cities, on the skid roads where loggers and workers on great construction enterprises in the mountains or forests come for relief from the isolation and monotony and complete maleness of their camp life; about hotels, from flop-houses to expensive convention hotels; and about military establishments. In the western world at least, prostitution is always frowned on, yet is invariably to be found, and is found most where the distribution of men and women sharply deviates from equality in number and from appropriateness of social status. (Miner found, incidentally, in his French-Canadian rural parish where it was considered very improper for young people to marry without an assured place or piece of land, that a certain married woman in the village was more-or-less tolerated for many years as a prostitute.)

There is another fault in distribution in sexual relations. Because of the very moral code instilled in children or the vagaries and accidents of temperament, child-rearing, and personal experience, often people who are

2. B. Seebohm Rowntree and G. R. Lavers, *English Life and Leisure*, New York, Longmans, Green & Co., 1951.

otherwise appropriate marriage partners are not mutually satisfactory sexual partners. There have been various ways of adjustment allowed and various illegitimate (as evaluated by society) ones developed and practiced in various times and among various classes of people to compensate for this maladjustment.

Now this leads me to another side of this same problem, which we do not ordinarily consider in connection with such frowned-upon things as prostitution. One has not discussed the problem of the institutional (the legitimate) and the bastard (the illegitimate) in any aspect of life and behavior until he has also drawn into view the deviation from the institutional norm and from the established way of distributing men and women, in the angelic or saintly direction as well as in the devil's direction. Now, on a quite simple level of analysis, the reason prostitution is such a viable device is that it requires so few women for so many men. It is an economic use of a small number of available, in two senses, women. There is no major contrary device by which one man is distributed among a large number of women (although there are women in modern industrial organizations, hospitals, offices, schools, etc.), gathered in large numbers about a man, or a few men, who occupy enhanced positions and who undoubtedly become for these women, in some measure, substitutes for husbands in many aspects of their relationships. From observations of school teachers and civil servants, it seems to be likely that the man who is nominally their superior and performs merely bureaucratic functions does not become the object of womanly protection and affection, but in their eyes is merely that most unsatisfactory of all males, an old woman in trousers. While the organization of business and industry offers a good many women a share in a man in this way (often, perhaps, a better man than they are likely to pick up on the marriage market), it remains true that in our society there are very large numbers of unmarried women who are not by temperament and vocation devoted to the spinster state. (As a dean of a nursing school remarked lately, it doesn't even do any good to get into a university hospital with an exceptionally good lot of interns. The boys come to medical school already taken these days. This is a blow to women who propose to use their professions to meet men.)

The household of several career women living together in which (although all work) there is some domestic division of labor not unlike that between man and wife, is an essentially unstudied — shall I say institution — that has developed as a result of the maldistribution of males and females under our condition of instituted monogamy. It is not a bastard institution in the extreme sense, but it is often suspected of being one. Those who deviate from expectation in the direction of the angels, but through no wish of their own and through no vocation to blessedness;

those who are in the position of having to be better than they would like to be, or better than anyone has a right to expect them to be, are a group seldom studied, although for any full understanding of the operation of moral codes as realized institutional definitions and actual distributions, their case is of special interest. (They are said to be prone to arthritis.) It would be especially important to find out at what points there develops some institutionalizing of adjustments to the position of being better than one wishes. In some countries there is a slight institutionalizing of spinsterhood in the traditions of the Day of St. Catherine. On this day children call at the doors of women recognized as old maids and are given a special candy prepared for the occasion. There must be some inward burning over the decision whether one is to make taffy ahead of time for this occasion, thus recognizing one's estate. Perhaps the children of the neighborhood, egged on by their mothers, enforce the status upon the spinster who clings too long to her youth.

Beyond this, in appearance at least, lies the institutionalizing of celibacy in the name of religion, the spiritual marriage of man or woman to the church accompanied by all the symbols and language of human marriage. There are those who point out that a son dedicated to God by his mother is safe from the clutches of any rival woman. But this is not the order of things that I have in mind to discuss now. It is rather that religious celibacy is the realization in institutional form of deviation from marriage in the direction of the angels—a deviation rationalized in the terms of supposedly supreme values, the higher-than-normal ideals of human conduct. For the individual in such an institution the function may be clear; these institutions allow one to live up to some ideal more nearly than is possible out in the world and in marriage. I emphasize the word *allow*, for the world would merely think a person queer to so live without special declaration, without attachment to an ongoing body devoted to this special deviation from the normal way of life. (In passing, one should not neglect to mention the frequency of stories of famous nuns who had run from the ball where their lovers paid too much attention to someone else to the convent, and there threw themselves into the arms of the mother superior. In the legend they stay on to become themselves mothers superior. There are always stories of girls who enter the convent when their fiancés are lost at sea or in battle.)

Leaving that aside, the institutions of celibacy offer a declared, established, and accepted way of not accepting the modal norm of behavior; perhaps a nobler and more satisfying way of accepting the fate that a fault of distribution in existing institutions condemns one to. They may be considered also as institutional provision for those highest lights of idealism that, although engendered by the established teaching of the virtues, are not provided for in the modal definitions to which institutional machinery is generally geared. Let it be noted, however, more emphatically than I stated it earlier, that society very often accepts such deviation in an organized institutional form, when it would scarcely accept it as isolated individual behavior. In recent decades, the decades of the Great Wars, the western countries have been more and more inclined to regard military service as an obligation of every man and yet to accept somewhat the pacifism of certain historic religious sects. They have, however, been hard on the individual who arrived at pacific philosophy and behavior on his own account or who considered himself individually called to set the Christ-like example of turning the other cheek. The individual deviation may appear as a threat to the whole accepted system; the organized deviation, however, may appear as a special adaptation of the system itself, perhaps as a little special example of what humans are capable of. The institutional angels may have some vicarious role of pleading for us all in heaven. Even so, the public nearly always balks when the saints, not content to be symbolic paragons of virtue, seek to become active leaders.

There is an important analogy to this in the heresies. One student of the heresies of the Middle Ages proposes that one kind of heresy was the doctrine that all men should absolutely live up to some ideal of virtue commonly proclaimed by the church.[3] Thus, suppose someone says that all sexual relations are sinful and draws the conclusion that people are in danger of perdition if they marry. Or suppose that someone turns the virtue of adoration of the sacred Host, enjoined upon all men, into a mandate that all men should spend most of their time in such adoration before the altar, to the neglect of their worldly duties. The church would declare these to be heresies, argues the author in question, because society, hence the church, would be destroyed by so extreme and absolute practice of any one virtue. The church could argue further that true virtues must be commuted with each other if man is to live. Without going further, it is clear that society idealizes, in statements and symbolic representation, degrees of virtue that are not in fact realizable by all people or are not realizable in combination with other virtues and in the circumstances of on-going real life. It appears that society allows some people to approach these levels of one virtue or another in some institutionalized form that will at once provide the spiritual lift and satisfaction of seeing the saintly example before one, without the personal threat that would come from mere individual saintliness offered as something that all of us should seriously emulate and the social threat of a contagious example. The saint's saintliness should be contagious, but only slightly, so that only a few should catch it as badly as he, and the rest of us,

3. Emmanuel Aegerter, *Les Hérésies du Moyen Age*. Paris, Ernest Leroux, 1939.

though we should catch it, should catch it only in its lighter form. In effect, these apparently heroic deviations stand, in a functional sense, in a parasitic relation to the rest of life: they breed in, are the products of, and live upon the larger, less heroic organism.

When I drew up my outline for this discussion, I meant only to mention, but not to discuss at such length, the bastard substitutes for marriage. And I did not propose to explore the deviation from the norm of institutionalized virtue in the better-than-modal direction. In any case, I have not really said much about the many social phenomena to which the term *bastard institution* might be applied, some of which I named at the beginning. The prototype of all bastard institutions is perhaps that kind of thing which has come to be called "the racket." It is likewise, in its true form, a sort of parasite on the shady side of the institutional tree. On second thought, discussion of that problem had better wait. And I am not too unhappy about my departure from the outline planned, for I think we have done something not common in sociological discussion: namely, to take some matter, some aspect of human life, which is highly institutionalized and is the object of much moral sanctioning, and to treat the whole range of behavior with respect to it: the institutionalized norms and the deviations in various directions from the norm. I do not say that we have surveyed all deviations; that was not the aim. But we have seen the norm, the institutionally defined and distributed relations between adult males and females, as a special point in the fuller range of possible and actual behavior, and have at least indicated some possible functional relations between the instituted and the deviation in both the bastard and the angelic directions.

ELEVEN

The Cultural Aspect of Urban Research

The social scientists of this university cut their teeth on the problems of city life in the 1890's. About thirty years later, Albion W. Small, as Leonard White has told some of us, called them together and proposed a joint offensive on the city of Chicago. The city, it seems, is always with us; it appears to be creeping closer. It is, therefore, appropriate that Philip Hauser, in his exhaustive bibliography of publications about cities, should have mentioned a great many written about Chicago and by people who worked or now work here. Many of the works he mentions concern other facets than the ecological. I will not list them again, nor will I try to give an exhaustive bibliography comparable to his. One reference to his paper I cannot refrain from making. If anyone is spoiling for a fight, I will gladly enter it to support the distinction between the moral aspect of society (the moral order) and the survival aspect (the ecological) and to deny that Robert E. Park's work on cities was atheoretical. It only seemed so to people who were used to drinking their theory in straight philosophical draughts, unmixed with the empirical juices of life. But, before the argument starts, let me recommend that you read the last of the three volumes of Park's papers, happily just now published with the title *Society*.

The burst of academic interest in cities and in this one in particular was but the culmination of a movement, both academic and popular, that had been under way for a long time. Chicago was a new city, built on flat ground by men adventurous in speculation and in building. Only a few Indian trails and a sickly river warped the expanding grid of streets. No

Read at an anniversary symposium at the *University of Chicago. The State of the Social Sciences,* Leonard D. White (ed.), Chicago, University of Chicago Press, 1956. Reprinted by permission. © 1956 by the University of Chicago.

high hill, no rugged rock, no mighty sacred oak offered resistance to the surveyors and the builders. Our greatest historic event was a fire, fit symbol of a city where tearing down to make way for the newer and bigger (hence better) was and is as important as building itself. Sometimes the grid gets ahead of the houses, and the tearing down ahead of the building. An upstart university, founded by people *parvenu*—just in—from the East, with money made by other upstarts from the East, as a matter of course undertook an upstart program, with a faculty pirated from the East. Men with state-of-Maine accents studied the upstart city, the city where flat terrain and the absence of sacred precincts allowed city growth and city rot to approximate as closely as one can imagine the form of concentric circles. Ernest Burgess, the youngster of the team, drew the circles on a map. He practiced a bit first on Columbus, Ohio, which is as flat as Chicago, but has a nastier river and did not grow quite fast enough or quite big enough to make the perfect case.

What happened here was a break-through, both of certain tendencies of city growth and of certain movements and interests of the public and of the academic world.

The academic people of Europe and America had been speculating a good deal on the difference between great states and great cities (not always saying which they meant), on the one hand, and the smaller, more conservative, more homogeneous, and more self-contained communities in which most human beings had lived throughout most of the history of the race. Most of those who wrote about the evolution of society (before, along with, and in the wake of biological Darwinism) spoke their pieces on this distinction. One such man was Ferdinand Tönnies; his distinction between society, in which men voluntarily and consciously join forces to gain finite ends, and community, into which men are born and in which they stay because of loyalty and the impossibility of even conceiving that they can leave, is also a distinction between modern, industrial socialism (to which Tönnies would have had us aspire) and a primitive communism of kin, which he and others supposed to have been the early state of man.[1] When, in Tönnies' last years, a movement called national-socialism smote down the Weimar Republic, its leaders shouted as moral pronouncements some of the speculative propositions made by Tönnies and others concerning city and simpler societies: cities destroy racial and moral purity; they elevate reason and trade above sentiment and loyalty. Hitler shouted against the city with the voice of an Amos, but, as he shouted, he led the very urban mob to a feast of bread, circuses, and blood. I join the speculations of Tönnies' kind on the distinction of city society from

1. R. Heberle, "Ferdinand Tönnies' Contributions to the Sociology of Political Parties," *American Journal of Sociology*, LXI (November, 1955), 213–20.

folk-community with the ranting of an urban demagogue who idealized the country, not to suggest any necessary connection between them, but to document interest in the problem, and the tendency to cast not only philosophical speculation about society but also sermons, political talk, and journalistic stereotyping in the terms of the dialectic between city and something conceived as its opposite.

It was not only in the perverted political philosophy of the Nazis that the themes of academic thought concerning city and country joined with political movements. Folklore also became a link between both the emerging social sciences and the humanities, on the one hand, and certain political movements. The same ethnologist who went abroad to study the simpler cultures and the smaller and not yet literate societies could find corners of his own country where old tales were told, old songs sung, old traditions and superstitions preserved. The student of literature, music, and art, seeking the origins of the themes which turn up in works of art produced in and distributed from the cities, got to the back country and talked to the old folks. There he met, at least in spirit, the ethnologist, and they both studied a bit of the "living past." One folklorist and ethnologist, who had published things on Australian myths and legends as well as on the folklore of France, invaded the territory of political science and sociology with a treatise on nationalities;[2] he notes in it that the many peoples who sought national self-determination in Europe before and during the first World War used folklore as proof that they were true historical peoples, entitled to political autonomy. The evidence, as a rule, stressed not the urban but the rural and folkish past. Folklore and vernacular apparently are preserved in the country, in the remote places, and with them the virtues and soul of a people. These things cities, full of strangers and the temptation to betray one's past, apparently tend to destroy. If the city man takes them up again, it is as symbols of a past for which he believes he ought nostalgically to yearn. It is not without relevance to the history of social research in America that our cities, in the early days of empirical social study, were full of people from the very areas in which folklore was being mustered in support of the claim to be politically free of alien domination. It was in American cities as well as in European that Lithuanian, Polish, Czech, Rumanian, and Yiddish legends were gathered, watered, and manured by self-conscious national gardeners. It was this joining of circumstance that may account for the fact that the American sociologist, almost by definition a student of cities, is so much more kin than is the English sociologist to the anthropologist; for the anthropologist has been almost by definition a student of whatever lies at the other end of the scale from the urban. The

2. Arnold van Gennep, *Traité comparatif des nationalités* (Paris, Payot, 1922).

English sociologist has been not only a city man but usually a city planner and social politician.

Into American study of cities there came also the influence of the surveys of the great growing cities of England and of this country; studies which were directed at describing and altering the conditions of life in the great slums, where there was a poverty of a new kind, different from feudal and preindustrial rural and town poverty. These surveys, although they used statistics of a simple sort and gave the matter on which much of the earlier work of statisticians was based, were not polls of opinion (for which the term "survey" is now used) but descriptions of the life, habits, and institutions of the slum, more like an ethnologist's description of a folk community than like a "sample survey."[3] They were a sort of scientific counterpart of the novels of Dickens and Zola, sprinkled with tables on wages, household expenditures, housing, health, drinking, and crime. In the British surveys the pawnbroker's shop, the gambling club, and the gin-shop appear as the villain; in the American ones, the ethnic colony is always in the center of the stage, although not presented as a villain. The villains are the exploiting landlord, the corrupt politician, the saloonkeeper, and, sometimes, the labor agent. In both cases, the eye of the investigator was upon the slum and the poor, not on the city as a whole, And, in the main, he paid only lip service to the grander statements concerning the city-country or city-folk distinction.

But the theme was not forgotten. Maine, Bagehot, Tarde, Le Play, Spencer, and their precursors were introduced into the discourse of American social scientists who talked of and studied cities. Park, a man of philosophical as well as of journalistic bent, was steeped in this literature. In one of his latest papers he wrote:

> Modern society is an urban and secular society. Earlier societies were organized on the pattern of the family and the kinship group. Present society grew up about the market place. The great cities which have reared their towers about these market places have been the melting pots of races and cultures, and the centers of intellectual life. But great cities, where men live together in relations that are symbiotic rather than social, have not yet, it seems, developed a tradition, a body of mores, or a moral solidarity sufficient to insure either the perpetuation of existing social institutions, or the orderly succession of those economic, political and cultural changes which embody the aspirations of this modern world.[4]

The general issue presented in that rather typical paragraph is by no means a dead one. Robert Redfield has devoted his career to study and

3. D. Caradog-Jones, *Social Surveys* (London, Hutchinson's University Library, 1950).
4. R. E. Park, "Modern Society," in *Society* (Glencoe, Ill.: Free Press, 1955), p. 341. This was read at the Fiftieth Anniversary of the University in 1941.

reformulation of it. In *Tepoztlán* (Chicago, 1930) he studied a folk village; in *Chan Kom* (Washington, D.C., 1934), a village in relation to changes coming from the town; in *The Folk Culture of Yucatan* (Chicago, 1941), a series of communities on what he thought of as a folk-urban continuum. The emphasis, in those monographs, was put upon the impact of city and town upon individuals, culture and social organization in its more direct and immediate aspects. In his much more recent *Primitive World and Its Transformations* (Ithaca, N.Y., 1953) and *The Little Community* (Chicago, 1955) he treats of the problem more broadly and in deeper historical perspective and to some extent explicitly as a single historical event on the grand scale rather than as repeated and repeatable proccss. This perspective is explicit in the first paragraph of *The Primitive World*: "After the rise of cities men became something different from what they had been before. . . . History is here conceived of as a single career, that of the human race." In these works one will find a critical review of the classic formulations of the city versus not-city distinction.

Redfield and his co-worker, Milton Singer, are now turning from study of the "little traditions" developed within and carried by little communities to that of the "great traditions" which, under certain circumstances, build upon and integrate the small, giving them great dimensions and longer perspectives, and turning conceptions of what is right and wrong from particular to general and universal abstract principles, transcending the local world.[5]

Redfield's work is, more than any other that I know, a continuation and a further development of the urban versus primitive, folk, or rural distinctions made by so many of the precursors of modern social science. The work on great and little traditions goes beyond previous work in that it is based on modern ethnological, sociological, archeological, and historical research rather than on the contrived stereotypes of at least some of the early work. There are, however, certain difficulties involved in carrying their work (Redfield's and Singer's) further. One of them is methodological. Redfield's *The Little Community* bears the subtitle "Viewpoints for the Study of a Human Whole." It is much easier, in practice, to study a little community as a whole than to study a great civilization, with its immense

5. R. Redfield and M. Singer, "The Cultural Role of Cities," *Publications in Economic Development and Cultural Change* III (Chicago: University of Chicago Press, 1954), 53–73. See also Redfield, "The Social Organization of Tradition," one of a set of lectures entitled "Peasant Society and Culture: An Anthropological Approach to Civilization," delivered at Swarthmore College, 1955, and now in preparation for publication. In it occurs this passage: "The great tradition is cultivated in schools or temples; the little tradition works itself out and keeps itself going in the lives of the unlettered in their village communities. The tradition of the philosopher, theologian, and literary man is a tradition consciously cultivated and handed down; that of the little people is for the most part taken for granted and not submitted to much scrutiny or considered refinement and improvement."

cities and its great systems of technique, thought, institutions, and arts, as a whole. He deals with the problem in a thoughtful chapter on "Wholes and Parts" but resigns himself (or perhaps there is not in his conclusion that regret which would warrant the word "resign") to saying that "the study of human wholes lies today in a borderland between science and art" (p. 163). The prolegomena of Redfield and Singer to the study of the great civilizations and the great traditions seem almost completely to abandon the study of huge communities and societies, as something existing on the ground, and having, as it were, a body in space. This is a fundamental change in method from Redfield's own studies of villages and folk societies. I do not say that the shift may not be necessary if they are to achieve their aim; I only contend that it is a shift. Nor do I suggest that anyone else has any very good set of devices for studying cities as wholes in the same way that anthropologists have done in very small communities and sociologists in somewhat larger ones. The point, however, is important; for it is not precisely the same thing to study some men and some things in cities as it is to study the city as a whole.

A second comment on this very interesting and promising work is that, like most dichotomous schemes, a lot of the boxes in a possible set of contingencies tables are left empty, although there are undoubtedly cases to put into them. There is, in Redfield's work, almost nothing about that very important part of human society—the city man who participates but superficially in the great, or high, tradition and who, in company with the masses of his fellows, makes the vulgar or popular culture. They mention such people, but I have the impression that they do not mean to include them very seriously in their scheme of studies.[6] These are the people and the cultural products to which our colleagues, Riesman, Benny, Denney, Meyersohn, and others are attending in their Center for the Study of Leisure.

I want, however, to make clear the direction of the wind I am stirring up. The Redfield and Singer enterprise is moving in a direction in which we need to go; I only wish to say that to get full benefit of it will require ingenious, brilliant, and, although I hate the thought, massive attacks upon the problems of method which are involved.

6. Mr. Milton Singer has, since I wrote this paper, reported some of his last year's work in India to the Seminar on Comparative Study of Cities. He did, in fact, find that urban popular culture supplied the links between the great tradition contained in the ancient Sanskrit writings and carried by learned Brahmin scholars, on the one hand, and the little traditions. Ritual storytelling in the vernaculars, interspersed with secular and even comic matter, and movie shorts on traditional tales and religious themes are among the forms of popular art in modern Indian cities. One is reminded of the morality plays of the Middle Ages in England, in which Noah and his wife became comic relief and the symbols of henpecked husband and the scolding wife.

I am happy to have been a little wrong as to the present trend of their project as well as to have been a little right in my counsel.

Perhaps I have now earned license to bring up one or two of my own pet problems. One of them has to do with the interaction between the little traditions and the great. Another is that of the image of the ideal man in various religions and cultures. In a seminar on cities which Professors Sylvia Thrupp and Gustave von Grunebaum initiated and in which I have joined them for the fun of it, it has come out that the ideal Moslem is a city man, who moves from bazaar to mosque and back again, from trade to disputation and prayer, whether at home or in a strange city. Yet Islam has become the religion of some very isolated folk—who tend to make Islamic tradition smaller.[7] Julien tells us that rustic Berbers consider the men of the cities less devotedly and fanatically religious than themselves. The city Moslems of North Africa, for their part, regard the rustic Berbers as but crude and impure followers of the finely and curiously worked patterns of thought and practice of the true faith—a faith whose nuances can be expressed truly only in the tongue of the Prophet. The case recalls the relations between rustic fundamentalist sects, say, the snake-handlers of the South, and the learned seminaries of the great universities; or the strain between the rustic thaumaturge or fanatical unlettered ascetic, whom the Roman Church has sometimes canonized, and the very learned masters and aesthetes of the cult who must do the canonizing. In Christianity, during its first centuries an urban movement but scarcely one of intellectual or sophisticated people, the case is not always clear. An Augustine—who was a sophisticated man—writes of the City of God, but many of the sects and orders sought the Kingdom in rural settings and idealized supposedly rural kinds of piety. One may doubt whether any of the great religions has consistently held to either an urban or a rural image of the ideal man or has avoided some conflict between divergent images. In Catholic Christendom, the religious orders appear to act as a connecting tissue; sometimes they bring to the cities, and even to Rome, the naïve enthusiasms and visions of the provinces and the country; again they carry back the idea of the great universal church to nationalistic and regionally minded branches and to particularistic movements, often anti-urban. The problem is not merely that of an opposition of great and little traditions but of the forms of interaction between them and the organs of that interaction or dialectic. One thinks of Chaucer's pilgrims exchanging corrupted Greek tragedies, folk tales, and bawdy yarns of the towns as they ride to Canterbury; of wandering monk and preacher; of merchant and peasant on the way to Mecca. In these cases, however, the great and the little are fruit of the same tree, although the rural-urban differences are, or were, in many respects much greater than, say, in our own part of the world. For among us the rural-urban

7. C. A. Julien, *Afrique du Nord en marche: Nationalismes Musulmans et souveraineté française* (2d ed.; Paris, Julliard, 1952).

differences in most matters of belief, knowledge, attitude, and sentiment appear measurably slight; I do mean *measurably slight,* for they appear to be of such order that it takes a bit of statistical manipulation to determine whether they exist. Samuel Stouffer has recently found some measure of difference in tolerance of certain unpopular political opinions and actions between rural and urban people in a national sample; it was still there after eliminating the influence of region, education, and certain other factors.[8] But it can scarcely be said that rural people in this country tend to produce little traditions which are either integrated with or opposed to the great systems of thought and value of our civilization as a whole or of the urban part of it; city and country are cut of the same cloth. But the parts of the world where the rural-urban contrast is great are still large, and a large proportion of the world's population is still in them. The question is still current. The Far East, most of the Middle East (leaving out, I suppose, Israel), Moslem Africa, and Black Africa certainly are regions where the difference between city and country is so great as to be one apparently of kind rather than merely of slight or moderate statistical measures on scales of common values. Students of cities ought to be and are at work in these parts of the world. A spate of work on African cities is being produced by anthropologists turned sociologists, by economists and colonial officials turned anthropologists, and by historians turned students of the current. (Even economists seldom remain pure in Africa.) The historian turned student of current matters appears somewhat the mode in Moslem Africa. It may be that the reason is that the very recent transformation of centuries-old urban layouts and institutions puts the historian's traditional objects in juxtaposition with the changes which are in the day's news. Thus Le Tourneau, who has written a history of Fez,[9] going back centuries, is in demand for meetings of administrators and scholars who want to know what is up in the cities of Algiers and the Magreb. In this case the transformation of the cities, although undoubtedly set in motion by forces from the outside and especially by European political and economic intervention, is swept on by huge immigration of poverty-stricken, uprooted people from the countryside. These rustics live on the outskirts of the growing and great cities of Africa in oil-can and shanty towns. The links between town and country appear in this case to be precisely these half-rustic, more or less unwilling, city dwellers who have one foot in the country and the other in the back yard of the cities. They are certainly neither carriers of a great tradition nor creators of folk tradition.

8. Samuel Stouffer, *Communism, Conformity and Civil Liberties* (New York: Doubleday & Co., 1955).

9. Roger Le Tourneau, *Fès avant le protectorat* (Casablanca, Société marocaine de librairie, 1949); "Social Change in the Muslim Cities of North Africa," *American Journal of Sociology,* LX (May, 1955), 527–35.

In Black Africa the studies of cities all point to an extreme lack of cultural links between the most urban and the most rural people. The East African studies I have read,[10] and the work of Balandier on French Equatorial Africa, picture aggregations in which the more urban people are so far removed by residential segregation, culture and language, and income and standard of living that the rural people who come to town as well as the people still in the country have no effective contact with them. The models of urban life are not accessible to the people of the country in any great degree. The city is as alien to the country as it is possible to imagine. Singer and Redfield have taken such cases into account in some measure in their memorandum on the culture roles of cities. It is a point that wants a great deal of closer study. One has to ask, then, not merely what the organs are of interaction between great traditions and the little ones where the basic cultural differences between city and country are small or moderate and within the same basic civilization; he has also to ask what happens when people are drawn to the precincts of cities that are alien in origin and style of life and where the cultural and economic gaps are so great that the organs of effective diffusion in one or both directions are lacking. As I read of the cities of East and Central Africa, and even of South Africa, I get the impression that perhaps this is what Rome was like when her outlying precincts were full of barbarians who did not know what the plumbing, the theater, the spoons, and the temples were for. But my heart goes out, I must say, to the barbarians rather than the Romans. The barbarians were, after all, the ancestors of a good many of us. It will be interesting, and a crucial part of the study of cities, to see how the status gap between native rural people and foreign urban people will be filled and what ladders will be built by which people may climb from the disorderly life of the half-rural, half-urban, poverty-stricken shanty towns to a more urban and prosperous way of life.

In the meantime, it is clear that what is happening in some of these places is not the mutual fructifying of the rural and urban but an opposition between the two. A portent of integration, however, may be seen in the nativistic movements which adapt symbols and ideas from the great traditions (Christianity, Islam) to the stirring-up of new half-religious,

10. *East Africa Royal Commission (1953–1955) Report* (London: H.M. Stationery Office, 1955), Part IV: "Conditions for Urban Development."

C. Sofer and R. Sofer, *Jinja*. (Kampala, London, East African Institute of Social Research, 1955), This monograph reports a survey of the rapid'y growing town at the head of the Nile where a great power project has been built.

G. Balandier, *Sociologie des Brazzavilles noires* (Paris, Presses Universitaires de France, 1955); *Sociologie actuelle de l'Afrique noire* (Paris, Presses Universitaires de France, 1955).

Social Implications of Technological Change and Urbanization in Africa South of the Sahara (Prepared under the Auspices of UNESCO by the International African Institute [London, 1955]).

half-political movements on a grander scale than any one tribe or primitive community. These are described in Sundkler's *Bantu Prophets* and in several papers and chapters of George Balandier's work.[11] These so-called native or separatist churches are considered bastard mixtures of Christianity with native beliefs, symbols, and practices; certainly their leaders do not have benefit of the laying-on of hands by European or other authorized clergy. Still, it may be possible that this is part of the way in which the great traditions of the past have spread to new parts of the world and have taken root among hitherto tribal or rural peoples. This is certainly not the first time that missionaries have given weapons into the hands of cultural "children" only to have them twisted and turned upon their teachers and masters.

But let us return briefly to the problem of the city man, as ideal, as stereotype, and as reality in our own world. We have long since passed the stage at which it is easy to tell rural from urban people in our part of the world. The margins are too slight. Yet the image of an urban man who is different from the rural is still with us. Wohl, writing of the middle and later nineteenth century, finds in fiction (the Horatio Alger, Jr., series) and in other writings the myth that it is the virtuous country boy who succeeds in a big way in the city and it is precisely because of certain rural qualities that he does succeed.[12] A certain ambivalence is revealed by the fact that it is in the city that success lives and that the successful boy does not go back to the country. Yet the notion is there that it is the country that breeds virtue. William E. Henry, in his studies of personality, has canvassed the literature on the concept of the normal man, the good man, in a certain sense, and finds in even the scientific literature (of psychology) a sort of built-in notion of simplicity, stability, perhaps even of not being too awfully and disturbingly bright; the whole is somehow associated with a simpler, quieter life than that of the city, or at least than that of the stereotype of the city. Rural life and rural people are simple and good; city people are complex, not so good, and perhaps even a little perverse and immoral. It remains to determine what personality types and what modes of personal conduct actually exist in our society, to what kinds of experience and environment they are related and how; and, finally, what the associations of these things with actual living in the cities are.

This has led us to the threshold of the problem of deviation, of the extent to which and of the manner in which city and other communities breed and/or tolerate behavior not considered close to the proper norms. This is a problem on which I am sure that the talk has generally been bigger than

11. Bengt G. M. Sundkler, *Bantu Prophets in South Africa* (New York, Oxford University Press, 1961); Balandier, *op. cit.,* Part III, chap, ii: "Le Messianisme Ba-kongo."
12. R. Richard Wohl, "The Myth of the Country Boy as an Aspect of American Urban Tradition" (unpublished manuscript).

our knowledge. The late Nicholas Spykman, translator and interpreter of the great urban sociologist and philosopher, Georg Simmel, wrote: "The metropolite is an individualist, a relativist, and a formalist in all aspects of moral life. The city inhabitant is a dweller in a pluralistic social universe. He participates in a great many social circles, and is thus subject to a great many different sets of social standards."[13]

"Deviation" is a term of relativity; it also is a term of evaluation and judgment when applied to human conduct. There are many dimensions in which people may deviate from either statistical modes or moral norms—in belief, in action, in combinations of beliefs and actions, alone or in company, occasionally or habitually. We, in fact, need a fresh start in study of social deviation, which ought to be almost the central problem of social science; by the time we get a real anatomy of conforming and deviating, it is likely that our conception of the conduct of both city men, as individuals and groups, and of rural people, also as individuals and groups, will be much more complicated than pictured in any of the prevailing images of either city or country man. We may well start by taking a lead from W. I. Thomas, who insisted that there cannot, in effect, be any effective description of behavior without definition of situations. We will have to study both city and country as the loci of social situations before we will get far with the complex problem of studying the differences between city men and other men and the whole related problem of deviation.

I fear I have rather abused the title and function given me. I have certainly neglected some of the most important aspects of research concerning cities. A great many historians, for instance, are taking particular cities or groups of cities as their fields of study. France seems especially to abound in such historians. Their papers made up a considerable part of a program of the French Sociological Society devoted to the relation of city and country not long ago.[14] The thing that has impressed me about these historical monographs on cities is that, no matter what the period or the cultural setting, the problems of the historian and those of the sociologist or anthropologist or other students of contemporary social institutions seem to converge. The problems seem not to be those of determining who did what but of determining the whole of which available evidence reports and reveals a part. I find this especially so in the work of Le Tourneau on Fez, in Philippe Wolff 's work on medieval Toulouse, in Asa Briggs's study of Birmingham since 1865, of Bridenbaugh's study of American Colonial cities, of Sylvia Thrupp's various works on medieval cities, and very

13. "A Social Philosophy of the City," in *The Urban Community,* E. W. Burgess (ed.) (Chicago: University of Chicago Press, 1926).

14. G. Friedmann (ed.), *Villes et campagnes: Civilisation urbaine et civilisation rurale en France* (Paris, Armand Colin, 1953).

markedly in the work of the late sociologist-economist-historian Robert K. Lamb.[15] In the recent studies in Kansas City in which some of us have been engaged, the historian of the group has turned out to be one of the most important members, even though we are dealing mainly with things which are happening now. His particular value comes from the fact that he helps us solve the difficult problem of seeing the community as an entity; his memorandums and comments enable us to see that the particular institutions and events in which the individuals in a number of samples participate are parts of a continuing whole whose present is more a function of the past than we may believe. So the proposition I made about the historians who study cities works both ways. They, who cannot go back and check their samples by new observations and interviews, have nevertheless to meet the problem of building out the whole as of a given moment. It is a problem on which students of contemporary going concerns and processes have something to say to the historian; yet, for all our building out our conceptions of a whole, or universe, we are a bit prone to regard the whole thing as static and as held together by some mechanical force, some social glue. The happy circumstance of having a historian who studies with us and digs up the fairly recent, but nevertheless purely documentary, past creates an optimal situation for learning from each other.

If I have not mentioned more often and by name studies made by people who belong to the other social science fraternities—economists, planners, educators, psychologists, political scientists—it is because it would have been a bit forced to do so. I am so accustomed to work with people of the various disciplines that it hardly occurs to me to make note of the fact. Furthermore, we live in an epoch when any social scientist who would avoid studying cities would have to be a very determined and ingenious escapist indeed.

15. Philippe Wolff, *Commerce et marchands de Toulouse (vers 1350–vers 1450)* Paris: Librairie Plon, 1954.

Asa Briggs, *History of Birmingham, Vol II: Borough and City 1865–1938* (London and New York, Oxford University Press, 1952).

Carl Bridenbaugh, *Cities in the Wilderness: The First Century of Urban Life in America, 1625–1742,* New York, The Ronald Press, 1938. *Cities in Revolt: Urban Life in America, 1743–1776,* New York, Knopf, 1955.

Sylvia L. Thrupp, *The Merchant Class of Medieval London* (Chicago, The University of Chicago Press, 1948).

TWELVE

Desires and Needs of Society

The general trends and problems of such a society as ours, which are likely to be found in all of the highly urban and industrial parts of the world, most certainly affect professional education of all kinds, not medical education alone. I have never made a study of public opinion on health or any other matter, nor have I ever tried to assess the needs of the public for health services or for the kinds of education which produce people who deliver such services. I have, with E. Clarke Wescoe and his colleagues of the School of Medicine of the University of Kansas, been party to a study of medical students; I have also studied a number of other professions. Those studies have provided some of the point of view which is presented here.

We live in the professional age. Two great trends characterize our society, and others like it, including that of the Soviet Union. The first of these is a great and continuing increase in the standard of living. That trend has gone furthest in this country, although we still have many very poor people — more in proportion to our population, perhaps, than have England and some other western European countries. Yet our average standard of living has reached heights not known before.

A second trend is a great and accelerating increase in the dependence of society, organizations, and individuals upon professional services. Since great many professional services are required to maintain societies and individuals, there has been a great increase in the number of professions and the proportion of the working force engaged in professional or quasi-professional services.

Read before the Annual Congress on Medical Education, 1963.
Reprinted from *JAMA* 185: 120–122, 1963. Copyright: American Medical Association.

The training for these services consists of higher general education plus special professional training, and the services are such that the consumer or client is not a very good judge of what he gets. He has to take quality on faith.

This is certainly the outstanding characteristic of medicine and that which creates your basic educational problems — you have to train a man to give his best even when the person who receives his services does not know whether that best is very good or not. All of your patients die. It is a question whether they die before or after you.

The individual does not really know whether he has received high-class service or not; this is so of a great many professions.

The increase in the standard of living takes the form of availability and use of such services, among them professional health services. There is a limit to the increase of use of material goods such as food, housing, clothing, and so forth. There seems to be no such limit on the consumption of services. It is an axiom of consumption economics that the proportion of income spent on food goes down as income and standard of living go up. We have reached the point in this country at which a great many people overeat, although some of them, I need not tell you, can overeat and be undernourished at the same time. But there is a limit to the amount of food people can eat.

Housing is another matter. Some people may be overhoused, although I don't know what that means, unless maybe that a family has a larger house than it can keep in order without hired help. But who has hired help? At any rate, we know that many families can reduce the amount of their housing when their children have grown up. They take smaller quarters, with perhaps built-in service.

Our working people are not overhoused, they are underhoused. Housing is economically a very sticky item. Free supply and demand do not seem to make everyone well housed. But it is true that, as the income goes up, the proportion of the income spent on housing goes down.

But when one gets over to services, the situation is different. There appears to be little limit on the amount of professional services an individual can use, and none on the amount of services which society at large can use.

In this country, more than anywhere else, we seem to be touching the point at which the proportion of income spent on housing, food and so on, will go down, and that on services will go up.

Now let me illustrate some of the consequences of this increase in the consumption of services by reference to education. This is perhaps the most spectacular example of increase in the consumption of a service, consumption both by the individual, in that he gets more, and by society, in that it makes more use of higher education.

We send practically all of our children to school and we keep them there longer than any people in history did or does. The time is apparently not far off when half or more of our high school graduates will continue in school for some time at least. We are making a study in the Boston area of people who thought they were through with school and who now, in their thirties, are going back. There are thousands of them. Either their old jobs became obsolete and they had to be retrained or they decided that they didn't have enough education and had better go on. It was room at the bottom that brought us millions of immigrants a couple of generations ago. Whether or not there is room at the top, there is certainly no room at the bottom of our economy any more. Great numbers of Americans are going to school, some by day, some by night, in youth, in middle age, and beyond, in order to move a little distance up from the disappearing bottom. College degrees, not all of them the best in the world, are achieved sooner or later by a very large proportion of our people.

Now it is evident that this increase in the consumption of education depends upon a tremendous increase in the productivity of our economy. Children in most parts of the world cannot be spared from work until they are 17 or 18 years old. In this country, we not only spare them, we don't want them to work. We take a great deal of credit for sending children longer to school than anybody else, but we do it because we don't know what else to do with them. Children attend school from the time they get away from their mothers' skirts (or slacks) until they go to work. And since our economy does not want the young except as consumers, that period increases. So we consume a great deal of schooling for one great reason: our industrial production per man-hour is so very great.

In education, we have an example of the unlimited increase in the consumption of a service when an economy is producing about all the material things that people can handle and sometimes a little more. We are approaching a time at which there is going to be a colossal increase in the consumption of many services. Medicine is one of these services.

There are some things that I think happen whenever a great deal more of some service is produced and consumed than in the past. One is that the method of delivering and distributing the service changes when it is delivered to everybody. At the present time, something approximating the same level of medical service is being delivered to most of the population.

Until the past few generations, a great many people saw doctors very seldom. In Europe, many didn't see them at all. They may have seen a midwife once in a while, but a large proportion of the population did not get medical care directly from the medical profession. They do now in most instances. I suppose practically everyone in this country now sees a doctor at other than the two inevitable times, the signing of the birth certificate and of the death certificate.

I do not know exact figures, but the number of people who receive professional medical services is approaching that of the total population, and the amount of service received by each individual is increasing. The increase of age of the population alone would have these results, but that increase is itself related to the increase in available medical services. The method of distributing a service always changes drastically when the amount consumed is increased and when it is distributed to a very much greater percentage of the population.

As the population gets used to a higher level of service, its expectations rise equally or even more rapidly than does the availability of the service. In other words, the public becomes more demanding.

In this country the public has become very demanding with regard to education. We are in course of becoming very demanding, indeed, about medical education and medical services.

In any population the laymen vary greatly in their knowledge of the value and quality of the professional services available. A great many parents, for instance, who are sending their young people to college, are unable to tell a good college from a poor college. They want their children to have good educations, but they do not know the difference between colleges.

The same thing is true in the field of medicine. There is a tremendous difference in the degree of sophistication about medical education among various segments of the population, such as people of various occupations and income. One of the problems then becomes massive education of the public as to the nature of good service in the fields of higher education, recreation, medicine, dentistry, etc.

When a professional service is widely distributed, its basic organization changes. One of the problems of education in law, medicine, and other professions is that the educators are usually operating on an organizational model that is about half a century old and perhaps never existed. There was never a time in this country when the majority of families had a family physician in any full meaning of that term. Families were too casual, they were too poor, they had no real connection with a family physician. Many of them do not have one in this country now. Some think more people have family physicians now in England than ever before. Families can now stay with a physician for a long time so that he knows them.

We also seem to be operating on the assumption that there is such a thing as a general practitioner. The term "general practitioner" could mean a number of things. It could denote a man who has a statistically random sampling of all medical knowledge, which would not be of much use to anybody, or a good knowledge of the things likely to turn up in a given area and population. The latter is what counts—that a man should know his people well and know the ills to which they are commonly subject.

The amount of medical knowledge available now is so great that the proportion of it which any one man can master is smaller than ever before. When Dr. Caughey spoke on community practice, it is assumed that he was talking of training groups of young men who have some realistic notion how to fulfil all the medical needs of a community, rather than having any one man try to fill all of them by himself.

We are still operating with an old-fashioned idea of education and on the notion that the children who go to college are the children of people who went to college and have a good idea of the conditions of the occupations which they are going to take up. This is no longer the case. In all of our professions, one of the ultimate needs of the public is that the profession be trained to distribute its care in a realistic way under modern conditions.

The one-man-office lawyer finds himself so tied down to the smaller chores of his clients that, when he has a problem that requires fundamental legal advice, he is unable to give it. He becomes a specialist by default. He becomes the captive of the particular problems that are brought to him, and he is so busy with those particular problems that he cannot develop a very general knowledge of law.

The problem in medical education is to teach young men to group themselves so they will not be bypassed by the important problems and will have some kind of organization through which people will channel their medical problems, small and large, i.e., some sort of grouping in which they can meet all problems. It is clear that one man can no longer do this alone.

One might raise the question as to whether a patient doesn't get more personal attention from his physician when there is more elaborate organization than merely one man in an office.

Medical educators are a little concerned with the quality of the young men who come to them, but there are very few professions which have applicants of equal caliber. Certainly if the students of the medical school studied are any sample of the young men in medicine today, they are highly motivated and they work very hard; of course they do not always agree with their teachers as to the nature of important work. They would like it to be more practical than the teachers do.

The basic problems of quality are well in hand, but perhaps what is not in hand is that part of medical education which has to do with making the young men fully and completely aware of the social organization of medicine which is required to give full, complete service to everybody in a society such as ours. I am not, at the moment, talking about the financial end of it, which is another, although related, matter, but about organizing relationships among doctors and the relations of doctors with the other people who work with them.

There are now at least four or five other health people at work in this country for every physician. The medical profession has not learned to understand as fully as it might the professional and personal situations and aspirations of these other four or five people who are so crucial in medical practice. Medicine is not practiced by doctors alone, and one of the things the medical men must look to in the future is the division of labor between the doctors themselves and these other professionals — nurses, technicians, therapists, etc. There is still much to be desired in those relationships. Part of the medical training must be presentation of the student to good experimental and realistic models of the way in which medical practice can be organized.

THIRTEEN

Cycles, Turning Points, and Careers

Every man is born, lives, and dies in historic time. As he runs through the life-cycle characteristic of our species, each phase of it joins with events in the world. In our society, the successive phases of his life tend to be defined in terms of his relations to the world of school and work: pre-school, school, work, and retirement. But some people come to the age of work when there is no work, others when there are wars. A man may learn the trade of, say, furrier, start a small shop in a solid city neighborhood only to have technological and economic changes make him and the shop slightly obsolete and to have his customers desert to the suburbs when he is too old to learn the new techniques and to raise the new capital required for a smart suburban shop, yet too young to retire decently. Such joining of a man's life with events, large and small, are his unique career, and give him many of his personal problems.

But not all of a man's life is his work; and not all of it is unique in the sense of being very different from the courses of other men's lives. There is a certain order in the lives of men in a society. Some of the ordering is open, intentional, and institutionalized; some of it happens without people quite knowing it until it is turned up by investigation. The ordering in our society, as I have mentioned above, is very much a matter of a man's relation to the world of work. It is also true that our institutions of work are highly developed and are, in unusual measure, formally separated from others. There are a time and a place for work; times and places for family life, recreation, religion, and politics. The mood and frame of mind of the

Prepared for the Eighth Annual Conference on Theology in Action, Adelynrood, South Byfield, Massachusetts, September, 1950. (Published by National Council of the Episcopal Church, 1952, New York)

place of work are supposed to be different from those of the rest of life. The study of the more or less orderly and predictable course of a man's work life has become a major concern of several branches of academic endeavor. Some of the essays which follow in this volume have to do with careers in just this sense. This essay, however, treats of the phases and turning points of a man's whole life. It is included in a volume of essays on work just because it does see a man's life as a whole, of which his work is but one facet.

Every culture develops a calendar, some cycle of days, moons, positions of sun and stars, or rain and drought, heat and cold, of plenty and want; of germination, growth, and harvest of plant; of breeding, birth, growth, and migration of the animals upon which they depend. These cycles of nature are interlaced with man's cycle of work and play and with his movements from place to place. Anthropologists have given us a rich body of descriptions of these cycles among the peoples of the world and of the myriad rites, festivals, exorcisms, and the like which mark their turning points. They tell us of cycles of mood as well as of natural occurrence, of periods of black despair followed by gay renewal of life and hope. A tribe may, with its most powerful rites, compel the sun to stop his flight to the south and to turn northward so as to bring summer again. It may combine abstinence, fasting, and repentance of sin with its most impressive ceremonials to make the rains come after seasonal drought or to make them stop ere the earth dissolve in moisture. We are all aware of the way in which the ancient cycle of solstice and equinox has become woven into the Christian calendar. Whether the rites which accompany the turning of the wheel of time among so many of the peoples of the world are of the essence of religion or not, certainly one cannot say much about religions without taking the calendar of rites into account. And certainly no people has for long lived without some established groupways which turn with the sun.

All cultures also recognize and mark in various ways the biological life-cycle of the human individual. Birth is attended by rites which acknowledge the social existence of the infant and make him a member of his kin-group and of his community. At the same time, his parents are ritually made into father and mother and assume responsibility for developing and training their offspring into good members of the community. Further rites often occur at puberty, when membership in one sex or the other becomes a more fateful matter; or when a boy is ready to go to sea, to war, or to the hunt with adult males. Entering upon a trade, marrying, growing old, and dying are also celebrated. These are all cases of passage from one status to another, from one patterned combination of duties and privileges, with its attendant perils and joys, to another. After the phrase of van Gennep, they have come to be called *rites de passage,* rites of transition. Sometimes the transition from one status to another is considered of such import that the candidate is given special instructions in the canons of conduct appropriate to his new estate. He may be sent upon a lonely journey in search of a vision, separated from other people and ordinary activities for a time, subjected to severe ordeals, and bound by solemn vows. He may be made symbolically to die as a child and to be born again as a man. Finally he may appear again in the world transfigured, in a new costume and like St. Paul, bearing a new name.

Not only is the biological life-cycle of the individual thus related to the corresponding social cycle of his standing in society, but account is also taken of occasional cycles of mood and condition, that is, of the things which, while not so fixed in their order as are birth, puberty, aging, and death, are pretty sure to happen to all men, life and human nature being what they are. One may violate a tabu, commit a sin, or do an injury to another. A man may have been ill and in his fever may have seen the spirits of the dead. A woman may be bereft of the man whose bed and board she shared so closely that they were as one life. These things alienate one from other men and women and from the routine and banality of life. Many societies have institutionalized this alienation. In India the widow jumped into the funeral pyre and joined her husband in death. More commonly, there are rites for bringing the person, in due time, back into the world. In French Canada, a young widow mourns her young husband for a time, starting with the severest of black costume and gradually returning to one which suggests that though she be a woman with a sorrow, her youth, attractiveness, and fruitfulness are not to be wasted. There is a period and a depth of mourning appropriate to every age and state of the mourner and the mourned and to every degree of kin. In some societies, mourning is brought to an end after a stated period and in a ceremonial way. The bereaved arises, puts on new garments, and goes among men again.

How well, in each case, does the proper institutional expression suit the felt grief of the bereaved individual? How often is it a hypocritical cover? How often a woefully insufficient expression of deep feeling? How often does the fixed penance for sin really liquidate the sense of guilt? How often is the rite gone through with defiant unrepentance? These are appropriate questions, but one cannot answer them in the mass. I suppose that if the instituted rites no longer correspond fairly well to the cycles and degrees of feeling accompanying the crises they are intended to carry one over, one would have to say that something is out of joint in society; that is, if the psychological reality and the social institution are no longer in some good functioning relation to one another. However that may be, there is one great thing to be said for conventional and instituted rites for carrying people over such crises, and for passing them on from one state of life to another; namely, that so long as the rites are practiced there is no attempt to deny the realities of the human life-cycle and the contingencies and changes of status that occur during it, and there is no pretense that the rhythms of mood, of guilt, of unhappiness and grief do not occur. I am afraid that many of us, in our culture and in our time, do try to deny these things, to exorcise the reality by the negative rite of looking firmly in the opposite direction so as to pretend nothing is happening.

The number of phases of the social life-cycle varies from society to society and may be altered by social changes of many kinds. The passage from one phase to another may be obscured or prolonged. In our society, the ages of entering and leaving school and of going to work and supporting one's self have been undergoing great change. We are far from the simple state of rural Quebec where a boy is a man when, for the first time, he goes to the field and handles a team of horses. On that day, when he comes in to dinner he eats with the men and, before returning to the field, hauls down a pipe from the rack near the kitchen stove and smokes a pipeful of home-grown, home-cured tobacco, even if it nearly kills him. With us, a man's graduation from college or professional school may be attended by his own children. A physician, on the average, does not make ends meet until he is past thirty years of age. It is therefore difficult to say when childhood ceases, when adolescence begins and ends, when one is really adult. The onset and the risks of middle age are altered by technological and social change. The functions of old age are perhaps less clearly defined than ever before, in spite of the fact that there is an increasing tendency to standardize the age of retirement from work and the movement to provide pensions and thus economic security for all people.

As for marriage, the women of our time run a greater risk of having no man at all than have the women of any other civilization; yet they are completely without ritual defences and without clear definitions and rationalizations of their enforced celibacy. It may be the confusion of age lines, the lack of moments of clear-cut change, which makes us a bit unwilling to recognize the turns from one life-phase to another. That we are loathe to recognize many of the crucial turnings is, I think, beyond dispute. And we much dislike to mark one age from another by costume and ornament or by terms of address and etiquette. And, while the psychiatrist is familiar with the private rituals by which people try to reduce their sense of guilt, we are especially loathe to recognize it socially as something requiring periodic public ceremonial liquidation. And as Margaret Mead has pointed out, we even try to do away with death. The modern hospital, in its anxiety to appear to be a place where all patients get well, refuses to allow relatives to gather for a ceremonial parting from a loved one and condemns the dying to sanitary solitude. If there be any triumph in death, our generation will not be there to see it. As for mourning, we are so fearful of wearing sorrow upon our sleeves that we eat our hearts out in a mourning which cannot be brought to a decent end, because it has never had a proper beginning. I have had dear friends who have done it so; and so has anyone who is of that well-meaning generation who believed that all good things could be attained by science and all bad things avoided by emancipation from old formulae and freedom from old distinctions, the people who got it into their heads that anything formal is cold—not sensing that ceremonial may be the cloak that warms the freezing heart, that a formula may be the firm stick upon which the trembling limbs may lean, that it may be a house in which one may decently hide himself until he has the strength and courage to face the world again.

How ghastly can be the smile of a suffering man who is pretending that all is well, how pathetic the stiff but tottering stance of a man who, because he does not know how to share his troubles with others through the historic liturgies, is about to break under them. How pathetic, also, the man who, in his time of trouble, expresses the ultimate of that individualism in which we have all been reared—the insistence that his troubles are so private and so unique that no social salve can soothe them.

The trouble may have been that, since we believed in progress, in things getting better and better, we were—and are—unwilling to face the implication of inevitability that lies in a repeated rite. A rite is something which is set off, so to speak, by a trigger, by something which happens again and again. To observe a rite is a sort of confession that the occasion of it may happen again and again in the future as it has in the past. It is as if the magnitude of progressive changes had blinded us to the limits within which change occurs. The average life expectancy of the child at birth has increased so marvelously that we overlook the fact that the oldest man alive now is probably no older than the oldest man alive in the days of great Caesar, and no older in medically progressive America than in backward India. Our average health is so good that we forget that man is as mortal as ever. And perversely enough, as the belief in life after death has declined, we have become less and less willing to make an occasion of death itself. Those who have the cure of souls in their charge—pastors, psychiatrists—can tell better than I what burdens break and what sicknesses ravage the souls of people who, in the name of self-reliance, emancipation, or progress, try to act as if there were no cycle of youth, maturity, old age, and death; no rhythms of inner peace and conflict, of guilt and freedom from guilt, of grief, and of the healing of its wounds.

I began with some statements concerning the calendar and went from that to the problem of the life cycle of the individual. Let us return to the calendar, for the two are closely related. Revolutionary movements are invariably enemies of the existing calendar for the very good reason that the calendar embodies the social memory. Every day is rich with meaning; the more festive days and seasons blow into flame the cooling embers of sentiment. The calendar is the warp of the fabric of society, running lengthwise through time, and carrying and preserving the woof, which is the structure of relations among men, and the things we call institutions.

The men of the French revolution tried to cut off the warp of memory by changing the names of days and even months; they went further and tried to break the rhythm of life itself by changing the number of days in the weeks and of months in the years. This is a logical thing for men to do when they want to change society completely. Its relation to rites is obvious.

Sectarian movements, bent upon religious revolution, likewise attack the calendar. Insofar as purification of an ancient religion is their aim, they see in the calendar and the rites that are timed by it, the barnacles of corrupt tradition which have gathered upon the strong, clean hull of doctrine and practice. But there is another logic behind the sectarian attack. It is hinted at in Dom Gregory Dix's *Shape of the Liturgy,* in a magnificent chapter entitled, "The Sanctification of Time." The early Christians developed little in the way of a calendar in the centuries before Constantine. Why? Because they were a little band of faithful people holding themselves in constant readiness for the end of the old and the beginning of the new. They did not look back. Since the danger of death and damnation and the hope of Christ's coming were equal in all moments of time (*Ye know not the day nor the hour*), one had to be equally in a state of grace at all times. Hence, one day could be no more dedicated to the service of God than another. As time went on, the Christians made some peace with the world; as generations turned, they began to accumulate memories, to take account of rhythms and cycles, to recognize that some among the saints are more constant than others and that the best of us have our ups and downs. So they developed devices for meeting the recurrent smaller crises of life while waiting for the great final crisis. Thus it is with the recurring revivals and movements for the purification of religion. Some man, himself at white heat, conceives of a church of people all at constant white heat. Only those who are aware of their lost condition and who have consciously repented and believed, only those whose devotion is full and complete, are members of the true church. You will see this ideal described in John Locke's famous *Letters Concerning Toleration.* It was embodied in the Quaker meeting in its early form.

Since it could not be allowed that devotion could or should vary from moment to moment, or from day to day, there could be no holy days, no

cycles, no calendar. Thus Edmund Gosse in *Father and Son* tells how his
father, Philip Henry Gosse, threw into the garbage can the Christmas
pudding which a sympathetic cook had secretly prepared for the small boy.
The father was of the Brethren who did not approve of special Christian
days and especially hated joyous festivity in the name of religion. The
ceremonies of renewal imply that faith and fervor cool and want reheating.
That the true sectarian zealot cannot allow.

Likewise, since entering the Church is purely a matter of reasonable
conviction, it must be a single, catastrophic act of a person of the age called
that of discretion—hence that horror of infant baptism so common among
strict sectarian groups. Edmund Gosse, again, reports his childish wonder-
ing about what terrifying sinful practice lay behind the mysterious epithet,
paedo-baptist—the anxious fear that something less than unwavering white
heat of fervor is inimical to the cycles of growth and changes of state
implied in a series of rites of religious initiation and transition beginning in
infancy or childhood.

Now these features of early Christian and of sectarian mentality generally are of more than historical interest. For the sectarian revolt against
calendars and cycles is something that occurs again and again. And as
often as it occurs, the facts of life slowly or rapidly catch up with the
revolting group. For one thing, even sectarians have children. In theory,
these offspring of the saints may be outside the Church until they are
violently converted at some age called that of discretion. But people are
not really that hard hearted when they become parents. Besides, conversion in course of time tends to come and to be expected to come at a
certain age, usually adolescence. A Baptist student told me how, when he
was fourteen, his parents and the pastor openly expected him to be soundly
converted between Christmas and that time in the spring when the water
would be warm enough for an open-air baptizing in New Brunswick. His
age-mates, who were with him in a special class for the purpose, saw the
light one after another. He alone got no sign from heaven. He got to feeling
so guilty that he finally felt compelled to testify to an experience which he
had not had. The words came easily from the formulae in which he had
heard others tell what they had felt in conversion. Then for weeks, while he
basked in the sunlight of general approval during the day, he lay awake at
night fearing that his lie was the unpardonable sin. James Weldon Johnson
tells a similar story of his Negro Methodist youth in Florida. He, too, lied,
but in verse and made a career of it.

One could go on with examples of the growth of calendars. The early
Methodist camp meeting and revival were outbreakings of the spirit,
whenever and wherever it might please God; but in due time God pleased
more and more often to have the camp meeting right after harvest when a

joyous spirit coincided with a slack in the farm work and to have the revival in the dead of winter when life was dark and dreary. Gradually the revival has merged back into Holy Week. The shoutings of the Negro meeting have settled into rhythms and chants.

The single-minded logic of hard reason, of unwavering devotion, of equal sanctity of the days, gives way to the rhythms and cycles of birth, growth, and decline and death. The fanatical insistence that all men be equally strong and constant gives way to a measure of charity for the young and the weak and to devices to bring both weak and strong back into grace after a fall. It is, I suppose, the dialectic of time and eternity, of the absolute unchanging ideal and of the relative changing reality.

The manner in which any society or epoch handles this dialectic is one of its distinguishing marks, and is one of the things which will, I am convinced, determine the kinds of soul sickness from which its members will suffer.

As for our own times, William Graham Sumner said of us even half a century ago that we no longer like to take vows, that is, to make commitments for ourselves. He might have added that, in the name of emancipation and of respect for the individual, we do not like to make commitments for others, even for our own children. And in all rites of initiation or transition there is commitment either for one's self or for someone else, or for both. I even know a woman who did not want to name her children more than tentatively so as to leave them the freedom to pick their own names to suit whatever notions they might get of themselves. She could not bear being a *paedonomist,* I suppose. When and if it becomes possible to control the sex of unborn children, we will no doubt breed a generation of hermaphrodites for fear of committing our children to an identity and a fate not of their choosing.

I wonder what is back of all this. Perhaps it is that sectarian Protestantism has lost the individual faith and fervor which allowed several magnificant generations of rugged individualists to do without a calendar and without the support, direction, and comfort of liturgy and rites of passage. Without their faith, but with a scruple for the feelings of others, and especially of our own offspring that our immediate predecessors lacked, we are unwilling to commit ourselves and even more unwilling to commit our children to anything, even to a social identity. And in so doing, we rob them of the ultimate inalienable right of every child: a good and sound reason for running away from home. That is the last indignity which the child-centered home heaps upon its miserable victims.

FOURTEEN

Institutional Office and the Person

The conscious fulfilling of formally defined offices distinguishes social institutions from more elementary collective phenomena. This paper will discuss the nature of institutional offices and their relations to the peculiar roles and careers of persons.[1]

Office and Role

Sumner insisted that the mores differentiate, as well as standardize, behavior, for status lies in them.[2] Status assigns individuals to various accepted social categories; each category has its own rights and duties. No individual becomes a moral person until he has a sense of his own station and the ways proper to it. Status, in its active and conscious aspect, is an elementary form of office. An office is a standardized group of duties and privileges devolving upon a person in certain defined situations.

In current writing on the development of personality, a great deal is made of social role. What is generally meant is that the individual gets some consistent conception of himself in relation to other people. This conception, although identified with one's self as a unique being, is a social product; Cooley would have said, a product of primary group life. But role, however individual and unique, does not remain free of status. Indeed,

Reprinted by permission of the publisher from *The American Journal of Sociology*, Vol. XLIII, November, 1937. Copyright 1937, University of Chicago Press.

1. W. G. Sumner, *The Folkways,* New York, Ginn & Co, 1956, pars. 40, 41, 56, 61, 63, 67, *et passim;* C. H. Cooley, *Social Organization,* New York, Scribners, 1929, chaps. iii, xxviii; E. Faris, "The Primary Group: Essence and Accident," *American Journal of Sociology,* XXXVIII (July, 1932), 41–50.

2. *Op. cit.,* par. 73.

Linton says "a role is the dynamic aspect of a status."[3] Role *is* dynamic, but it is also something more than status. Status refers only to that part of one's role which has a standard definition in the mores or in law. A status is never peculiar to the individual; it is historic. The person, in status and in institutional office, is identified with a *historic role*. The peculiar role of a prophet or a political leader may be transformed into the historic role or office of priesthood or kingship. Every office has had a history, in which the informal and unique have become formal and somewhat impersonal. The story of an institution might well be told in terms of the growth of its offices, with which have been identified the personal roles of series of individuals.

Entrance into a status is not always a matter of choice. That does not prevent persons from being aware that they are entering it, from focusing their wills upon it, or from fulfilling the attendant obligations with consciously varying degrees of skill and scruple. Status gives self-consciousness and the conscience something to bite on.[4]

Every social order is, viewed in one way, a round of life. Anthropologists almost invariably describe it so, and show how persons of different status fit their activities into this round. But beyond routine, even in simple and stable societies, occur great ceremonial occasions and crucial enterprises. On such occasions some person or persons become the center of enhanced attention. Collective expression and effort are co-ordinated about them. Status may determine the selection of these persons, but they must perform special offices appropriate to the occasion. They become, within the limits of their offices, especially responsible for the fate of their fellows and for the integrity of their communities.[5]

The person who fills such a great office is judged not as the common run of mankind but with reference to his predecessors in office and to the

3. Ralph Linton, *The Study of Man*, New York, Appleton, 1936, chap. viii, "Status and Role."

4. B. Malinowski, in *Crime and Custom in Savage Society*, London, Routledge, 1926, chap. v *et passim*, attacks the notion, so prominent in evolutionary social theory, that the member of a primitive society adheres to custom unconsciously and automatically. He maintains that among the Trobriand Islanders there is considerable margin between the maximum and minimum fulfilling of obligations and that, within these limits, persons are impelled by motives very like those recognized among us. Some men show an excess of zeal and generosity, banking upon a return in goods and prestige. He points also to a conflict of offices embodied in one person; a man is at once affectionate parent of his own children and guardian of the property and interests of his sister's children. Malinowski suggests that the man is often aware of this conflict.

5. See R. Redfield, *Chan Kom, a Maya Village*, Washington, Carnegie Institution, 1934. Chicago, Univ. of Chicago Press, 1962, pp. 153–59, for description of the *fiesta* and the office of *cargador;* B. Malinowski, *Argonauts of the Western Pacific*, New York: E. P. Dutton, 1922, 1961, for the office of the chieftain in canoe-building and expeditions, and that of the magician in gardening.

popular conception of what the office should be. He is exposed to special demands. He is also protected, in so far as the office sets the limits of his responsibility, from both the bludgeons of critics and the sharp thrusts of his own conscience.

Objective differentiation of duty reaches its ultimate rigidity in ritual office. The subjective aspect of such rigidity is punctiliousness.[6] The responsibilities of ritual office are so clear-cut as to allow the incumbent a feeling of assurance that he is doing his whole duty. The anxiety lest he fall short is but the greater.[7] Anxiety and responsibility are alike focused upon the office, as something transcending the individual. The incumbent tends to be impatient of the criticisms of others. He wards them off by declaring that whoever criticizes him attacks the sacred office.

In the performance of ritual one may realize profoundly that he, even he, is playing a historic role; he may be transfigured in an ecstasy in which his personal attributes are merged with those of the office. Each meticulous gesture bursts with symbolic meaning. E. Boyd Barrett writes thus of his feeling while celebrating his first mass.

> On the snow-white altar cloth before me lay a chalice of wine and on a paten a wafer of unleavened bread. Presently *at my words,* at my repetition of the eternal formula of consecration, the wine would become the blood of Christ, and the bread the body of Christ. My hands, soiled and sinful though they were, would be privileged to raise aloft in adoration the Son of God, the Saviour of the world. . . . . Surely the words "Sanctus! Sanctus! Sanctus!" were none too sacred to pronounce in presence of this mystery of mysteries. . . . . My first mass was an ecstasy of joy. . . . . I gave myself confidently and wholeheartedly to God and I felt that He gave himself to me.[8]

While devotion and sense of office may be at their maximum in such moments, judgment is in abeyance. It is in the nature of ritual that it should be, since each action is part of a sacred whole. Furthermore, rituals are performed under compulsion often backed by a vow. A vow allows no turning back, no changing of the mind, no further exercise of judgment.[9]

6. Sumner, *op. cit.,* par. 67.

7. The psychoanalysts trace ritual to anxieties arising from unconscious guilt. In compulsion neurosis the individual ceaselessly performs rituals of *Buss* and *Nichtgeschehenmachen* (see A. Fenichel, *Hysterien und Zwangsneurosen,* Wien, Internationaler Psychionalytischer Verlag, 1931, chap. iv). J. Piaget, in *The Moral Judgment of the Child,* London, Kegan, Paul, 1932, finds that young children play marbles as ritual before they play it as a game. In this early stage they observe punctiliously such rules as they know, attributing their origin to their fathers, the city alderman, and God. They are quick to accuse and facile at self-excuse, but show little regard for their fellow-players.

8. *Ex-Jesuit,* London, Geoffrey Bles, 1931, p. 124. Many Catholics expect special blessings from a priest's first mass.

9. See W. G. Sumner, *War and Other Essays,* New Haven, Yale University Press, 1911, "Mores of the Present and Future," p. 157, in which he says: "One of the most noteworthy

An office may eventually become so ritualistic that the successive incumbents are but symbols rather than responsible agents. A rigid etiquette is observed in approaching them, and sentiments of reverence become so intense that the office is worshipped. This final point of impersonal institution of an office is reached at the cost of the more active functions of leadership. In ongoing collective life, contingencies arise to require decisions. Even a ritual may not go on without a stage-manager. Furthermore, every ritual is proper to an occasion. The occasion must be recognized and met. An office may become purely symbolic only if the meeting of contingencies is allocated to some other office.[10]

Coming down to earth, the person cannot, apart from ritual, escape judgments. His peculiar social role asserts itself and may come into conflict with the office which he fills. The fusion of personal role and office is perhaps never complete save in ritual.

One of the extreme forms in which one's personal role appears is that of a call or peculiar mission. The person's conception of his mission may carry him beyond the conception which others have of his office. As an office becomes defined, there arise devices by which one's fellows decide whether one is the person fit to fill it. The first leader of a sect may be "called" to his task; his successors, too, are "called," but the validity of the

---

and far-reaching features in modern mores is the unwillingness to recognize a vow or to enforce a vow by any civil or ecclesiastical process . . . In modern mores it is allowed that a man may change his mind as long as he lives." The belief that a man may change his mind is an essentially secular attitude. Catholic doctrine recognizes this, by distinguishing resolutions, promises, and vows. Vows are the most sacred, since they are promises to God. "A subsequent change in one's purpose is a want of respect to God; it is like taking away something that has been dedicated to Him, and committing sacrilege in the widest sense of the word." Resolutions are mere present intentions, without a commitment; promises between man and man or to the saints should be kept, but the breach is not so serious as that of a vow (*The Catholic Encyclopedia*, Vol. XV, "Vows.") It is perhaps the residue of the compulsion of a vow that gives ex-priests the sense of being marked men. See E. Boyd Barrett, *op. cit.* Ordinary life may be something of an anticlimax for these men once dedicated to holy office. Such men are also suspect. A French-Canadian recently dismissed all that a certain psychologist might say by remarking, "C'est un homme qui a porté la soutane."

There are many instances in sociological literature of the profound changes in an institution that accompany the decline of compulsion in its offices. Redfield, *op. cit.*, tells how in towns and cities the *fiesta* becomes something of a secular enterprise. No longer is it a sacred festival, led by a *cargador* who accepted "the holy burden" from his predecessor. The Webbs, in *English Local Government: the Parish and the County*, London, Longmans, 1906, describe a similar decline of the sense of obligation to serve as parish officers in growing industrial towns.

10. Max Weber, in his "Politik als Beruf" (*Gesammelte politische Schriften*, München, Drei Masken Verlag, 1921, pp. 396-450), essays a natural history of various types of political office. He shows how certain offices, as that of sultan, became purely symbolic, while the wielding of political power and the risk of making mistakes were assumed by others. The position of the emperor of Japan is similar; the emperor is divine, but he speaks only through the voices of men. It is not suggested that these two features do not sometimes appear in the same office. They do, as in the papacy. Offices vary in their proportions of symbol and action.

call is decided by other men, as well as by himself.[11] Thus the "call," a subjective assurance and compulsion, is brought under the control of one's fellows. But the sense of mission may be so strong that it makes the person impatient of the discipline exercised by his colleagues.[12]

There are other ways in which personal role and office may conflict. It is sufficient for our present purposes to suggest that the very sense of personal role which leads one into an institutional office may make him chafe under its bonds. The economy of energy and will, devotion and judgment, peculiar to the individual does not completely disappear when he is clothed with an established, even a holy, office. The more secular offices make fewer formal demands upon the individual; they require less suppression of the individuality. They are less symbolic and more subject to the test of effectiveness in action. A free, secular society, from this point of view, is one in which the individual may direct his energies toward new objects; one in which he may even succeed in creating a new office, as well as in changing the nature and functions of existing ones.

Career And Office

In any society there is an appropriate behavior of the child at each age. Normal development of personality involves passing in due time from one status to another. Some stages in this development are of long duration; others are brief. While some are thought of as essentially preparatory, and their length justified by some notion that the preparation for the next stage requires a set time, they are, nevertheless, conventional.

In a relatively stable state of society, the passage from one status to another is smooth and the experience of each generation is very like that of its predecessor. In such a state the expected rate of passage from one status to another and an accompanying scheme of training and selection of those who are to succeed to instituted offices determine the ambitions,

11. See the *Catholic Encyclopedia,* Vol. XV, "Vocation." While the Catholic church admits the possibility that divine light may be shed so abundantly upon a soul as to render deliberation about the validity of a vocation unnecessary in some cases, it does not regard such inner assurance necessary to vocation. The spiritual director is to discover and develop the germ of vocation by forming the character and encouraging "generosity of the will." The church insists that two wills should concur before one can enter the clergy: the will of the individual and the will of the church. The latter is "external vocation," which is "the admission of the candidate in due form by competent authority."

12. The ardor of a person with a peculiar mission may become an insufferable reproach to his colleagues and contain a trace of insubordination to his superiors. The neophyte who is too *exalté* can be borne, but a certain relaxation of ardor is demanded in course of time. In a well-established institution, ardor must be kept within the limits demanded by authority and decorum; it may not necessarily reach the state in which "men, fearing to outdo their duty, leave it half done," as Goldsmith said of the English clergy.

efforts, and accomplishments of the individual. In a society where major changes are taking place, the sequence of generations in an office and that of offices in the life of the person are disturbed. A generation may be lost by disorder lasting only for the few years of passage through one phase.

However one's ambitions and accomplishments turn, they involve some sequence of relations to organized life. In a highly and rigidly structured society, a career consists, objectively, of a series of status and clearly defined offices. In a freer one, the individual has more latitude for creating his own position or choosing from a number of existing ones; he has also less certainty of achieving any given position. There are more adventurers and more failures; but unless complete disorder reigns, there will be typical sequences of position, achievement, responsibility, and even of adventure. The social order will set limits upon the individual's orientation of his life, both as to direction of effort and as to interpretation of its meaning.

Subjectively, a career is the moving perspective in which the person sees his life as a whole and interprets the meaning of his various attributes, actions, and the things which happen to him. This perspective is not absolutely fixed either as to points of view, direction, or destination. In a rigid society the child may, indeed, get a fixed notion of his destined station. Even in our society he may adopt a line of achievement as his own to the point of becoming impervious to conflicting ambitions. Consistent lines of interest and tough conceptions of one's destined role may appear early in life.[13]

Whatever the importance of early signs of budding careers, they rarely remain unchanged by experience. The child's conception of the social order in which adults live and move is perhaps more naïve than are his conceptions of his own abilities and peculiar destiny. Both are revised in keeping with experience. In the interplay of his maturing personality and an enlarging world the individual must keep his orientation.

Careers in our society are thought of very much in terms of jobs, for

13. Psychoanalysts trace to very lowly motives the lines of consistency in the individual's conception of his life and the way in which he disciplines and marshals his efforts. Their more important point is that these phenomena rise out of intimate family relationships. They also use the term "mobility of the libido" (cf. Klein, "The Role of the School in the Libidinal Development of the Child," *International Journal of Psychoanalysis,* V [1924], 312-31) to indicate the child's capacity to transfer his affections and energies to objects in a larger world as he grows and extends his circle of activity. A great deal, however, remains to be done in the way of understanding the bearing of early experiences on the subsequent careers of persons. It is evident that the age, as well as the frequency, of appearance of a sense of career varies greatly from family to family and from class to class. The pressure on children to discipline themselves for careers likewise varies; the psychological by-products of these pressures want studying, for they seem sometimes to thwart the ends they seek.

See H. D. Lasswell, *World Politics and Personal Insecurity,* New York: McGraw-Hill, 1935, pp. 210-12, for a discussion of "career lines."

these are the characteristic and crucial connections of the individual with the institutional structure. Jobs are not only the accepted evidence that one can "put himself over"; they also furnish the means whereby other things that are significant in life may be procured. But the career is by no means exhausted in a series of business and professional achievements. There are other points at which one's life touches the social order, other lines of social accomplishment — influence, responsibility, and recognition.

A woman may have a career in holding together a family or in raising it to a new position. Some people of quite modest occupational achievements have careers in patriotic, religious, and civic organizations. They may, indeed, budget their efforts toward some cherished office of this kind rather than toward advancement in their occupations. It is possible to have a career in an avocation as well as in a vocation.

Places of influence in our greater noncommercial organizations are, however, open mainly to those who have acquired prestige in some other field. The governors of universities are selected partly on the basis of their business successes. A recent analysis of the governing boards of settlement houses in New York City shows that they are made up of people with prestige in business and professional life, as well as some leisure and the ability to contribute something to the budget.[14]

It would be interesting to know just how significant these offices appear to the people who fill them; and further, to whom they regard themselves responsible for the discharge of their functions. Apart from that question, it is of importance that these offices are by-products of achievements of another kind. They are prerogatives and responsibilities acquired incidentally; it might even be said that they are exercised ex officio or *ex statu*.

The interlocking of the directorates of educational, charitable, and other philanthropic agencies is due perhaps not so much to a cabal as to the very fact that they are philanthropic. Philanthropy, as we know it, implies economic success; it comes late in a career. It may come only in the second generation of success. But when it does come, it is quite as much a matter of assuming certain prerogatives and responsibilities in the control of philanthropic institutions as of giving money. These prerogatives and responsibilities form part of the successful man's conception of himself and part of the world's expectation of him.[15]

Another line of career characteristic of our society and its institutional

14. Albert J. Kennedy, Kathryn Farra, and Associates, *Social Settlements in New York,* New York: Columbia University Press, 1935, chap. xiv; T. Veblen, *The Higher Learning in America,* New York: Sagamore, 1918, p. 72 *et passim.*
15. The Junior League frankly undertakes to train young women of leisure for their expected offices in philanthropic agencies.

organization is that which leads to the position of "executive." It is a feature of our society that a great many of its functions are carried out by corporate bodies. These bodies must seek the approval and support of the public, either through advertising or propaganda. Few institutions enjoy such prestige and endowments that they can forego continued reinterpretation of their meaning and value to the community. This brings with it the necessity of having some set of functionaries who will act as promoters and propagandists as well as administrators. Even such a traditional profession as medicine and such an established organization as the Roman Catholic church must have people of this sort. By whatever names they be called, their function is there and may be identified.

Sometimes, as in the case of executive secretaries of medical associations, these people are drawn from the ranks of the profession. In other cases they are drawn from outside. University presidents have often been drawn from the clergy. In the Y.M.C.A. the chief executive officer is quite often not drawn from the ranks of the "secretaries." But whether or not that be the case, the functions of these executive officers are such that they do not remain full colleagues of their professional associates. They are rather liaison officers between the technical staff, governing boards, and the contributing and clientele publics. Their technique is essentially a political one; it is much the same whether they act for a trade association, the Y.M.C.A., a hospital, a social agency, or a university. There is, indeed, a good deal of competition among institutions for men who have this technique, and some movement of them from one institution to another. They are also men of enthusiasm and imagination. The institution becomes to them something in which dreams may be realized.[16]

These enthusiastic men, skilled in a kind of politics necessary in a philanthropic, democratic society, often come to blows with the older hierarchical organization of the institutions with which they are connected. Therein lies their importance to the present theme. They change the balance of power between the various functioning parts of institutions. They change not only their own offices but those of others.

Studies of certain other types of careers would likewise throw light on the nature of our institutions—as, for instance, the road to political office by way of fraternal orders, labor unions, and patriotic societies. Such careers are enterprises and require a kind of mobility, perhaps even a certain opportunism, if the person is to achieve his ambitions. These ambitions themselves seem fluid, rather than fixed upon solid and neatly

16. The reports made by the American Association of University Professors on conflicts between professors and college presidents sometimes reveal in an interesting way the characteristics of both and of the offices they fill. See *Bulletin of the American Association of University Professors,* XXI (March 1935), 224-66, "The University of Pittsburgh;" XIX (November, 1933), 416-38, "Rollins College."

defined objectives. They are the opposites of bureaucratic careers, in which the steps to be taken for advancement are clearly and rigidly defined, as are the prerogatives of each office and its place in the official hierarchy.[17] It may be that there is a tendency for our social structure to become rigid, and thus for the roads to various positions to be more clearly defined. Such a trend would make more fateful each turning-point in a personal career. It might also require individuals to cut their conceptions of themselves to neater, more conventional, and perhaps smaller patterns.

However that may be, a study of careers—of the moving perspective in which persons orient themselves with reference to the social order, and of the typical sequences and concatenations of office—may be expected to reveal the nature and "working constitution" of a society. Institutions are but the forms in which the collective behavior and collective action of people go on. In the course of a career the person finds his place within these forms, carries on his active life with reference to other people, and interprets the meaning of the one life he has to live.

17. Mannheim would limit the term "career" to this type of thing. Career success, he says can be conceived only as *Amtskarriere*. At each step in it one receives a neat package of prestige and power whose size is known in advance. Its keynote is security; the unforeseen is reduced to the vanishing-point ("Über das Wesen und die Bedeutung des wirtschaftlichen Erfolgstrebens," *Archiv für Sozialwissenschaft und Sozialpolitik,* LXIII [1930], 458 ff.).

FIFTEEN

Dilemmas and Contradictions of Status

It is doubtful whether any society ever had so great a variety of statuses or recognized such a large number of status-determining characteristics as does ours. The combinations of the latter are, of course, times over more numerous than the characteristics themselves. In societies where statuses[1] are well defined and are entered chiefly by birth or a few well-established sequences of training or achievement, the particular personal attributes proper to each status are woven into a whole. They are not thought of as separate entities. Even in our society, certain statuses have developed characteristic patterns of expected personal attributes and a way of life. To such, in the German language, is applied the term *Stand*.

Few of the positions in our society, however, have remained fixed long enough for such an elaboration to occur. We put emphasis on change in the system of positions which make up our social organization and upon mobility of the individual by achievement. In the struggle for achievement, individual traits of the person stand out as separate entities. And they occur in peculiar combinations which make for confusion, contradictions, and dilemmas of status.

I shall, in this paper, elaborate the notion of contradictions and dilemmas of status. Illustrations will be taken from professional and other occupational positions. The idea was put into a suggestive phrase by Robert E.

Reprinted by permission of the publisher from *The American Journal of Sociology,* Vol. L, March 1945. Copyright 1945, University of Chicago Press.
1. "Status" is here taken in its strict sense as a defined social position for whose incumbents there are defined rights, limitations of rights, and duties. See the *Oxford Dictionary* and any standard Latin lexicon. Since statuses tend to form a hierarchy, the term itself has — since Roman times — had the additional meaning of rank.

Park when he wrote of the "marginal man." He applied the term to a special kind of case—the racial hybrid—who, as a consequence of the fact that races have become defined as status groups, finds himself in a status dilemma.

Now there may be, for a given status or social position, one or more specifically determining characteristics of the person. Some of them are formal, or even legal. No one, for example, has the status of physician unless he be duly licensed. A foreman is not such until appointed by proper authority. The heavy soprano is not a prima donna in more than temperament until formally cast for the part by the director of the opera. For each of these particular positions there is also an expected technical competence. Neither the formal nor the technical qualifications are, in all cases, so clear. Many statuses, such as membership in a social class, are not determined in a formal way. Other statuses are ill-defined both as to the characteristics which determine identification with them and as to their duties and rights.

There tends to grow up about a status, in addition to its specifically determining traits, a complex of auxiliary characteristics which come to be expected of its incumbents. It seems entirely natural to Roman Catholics that all priests should be men, although piety seems more common among women. In this case the expectation is supported by formal rule. Most doctors, engineers, lawyers, professors, managers, and supervisors in industrial plants are men, although no law requires that they be so. If one takes a series of characteristics, other than medical skill and license to practice it, which individuals in our society may have, and then thinks of physicians possessing them in various combinations, it becomes apparent that some of the combinations seem more natural and are more acceptable than others to the great body of potential patients. Thus a white, male, Protestant physician of old American stock and of a family of at least moderate social standing would be acceptable to patients of almost any social category in this country. To be sure, a Catholic might prefer a physician of his own faith for reasons of spiritual comfort. A few ardent feminists, a few race-conscious Negroes, a few militant sectarians, might follow their principles to the extent of seeking a physician of their own category. On the other hand, patients who identify themselves with the "old stock" may, in an emergency, take the first physician who turns up.[2]

2. A Negro physician, driving through northern Indiana, came upon a crowd standing around a man just badly injured in a road accident. The physician tended the man and followed the ambulance which took him to the hospital. The hospital authorities tried to prevent the physician from entering the hospital for even long enough to report to staff physicians what he had done for the patient. The same physician, in answer to a Sunday phone call asking him to visit a supposedly very sick woman, went to a house. When the person who answered the door saw that the physician was a Negro, she insisted that they had not called for a doctor and that no one in the house was sick. When he insisted on being paid,

If the case is serious, patients may seek a specialist of some strange or disliked social category, letting the reputation for special skill override other traits. The line may be crossed also when some physician acquires such renown that his office becomes something of a shrine, a place of wonderful, last resort cures. Even the color line is not a complete bar to such a reputation. On the contrary, it may add piquancy to the treatment of a particularly enjoyed malady or lend hope to the quest for a cure of an "incurable" ailment. Allowing for such exceptions, it remains probably true that the white, male, Protestant physician of old American stock, although he may easily fail to get a clientele at all, is categorically acceptable to a greater variety of patients than is he who departs, in one or more particulars, from this type.

It is more exact to say that, if one were to imagine patients of the various possible combinations of these same characteristics (race, sex, religion, ethnic background, family standing), such a physician could treat patients of any of the resulting categories without a feeling by the physician, patient, or the surrounding social circle that the situation was unusual or shocking. One has only to make a sixteen-box table showing physicians of the possible combinations of race (white and Negro) and sex with patients of the possible combinations to see that the white male is the only resulting kind of physician to whom patients of all the kinds are completely accessible in our society (see Table 1).

One might apply a similar analysis to situations involving other positions, such as the foreman and the worker. the teacher and the pupil. Each

Table 1*

Patient	Physician			
	White Male	White Female	Negro Male	Negro Female
White male...	....	....	....	....
White female.	....	....	....	....
Negro male..	....	....	....	....
Negro female	....	....	....	....

* I have not used this table in any study of preferences but should be glad if anyone interested were to do so with selected groups of people.

---

the people in the house did so, thereby revealing their lie. In the first instance, an apparently hostile crowd accepted the Negro as a physician because of urgency. In the second, he was refused presumably because the emergency was not great enough.

case may be complicated by adding other categories of persons with whom the person of the given position has to deal. The teacher, in practice, has dealings not only with pupils but with parents, school boards, other public functionaries, and, finally, his own colleagues. Immediately one tries to make this analysis, it becomes clear that a characteristic which might not interfere with some of the situations of a given position may interfere with others.

I do not maintain that any considerable proportion of people do consciously put together in a systematic way their expectations of persons of given positions. I suggest, rather, that people carry in their minds a set of expectations concerning the auxiliary traits properly associated with many of the specific positions available in our society. These expectations appear as advantages or disadvantages to persons who, in keeping with American social belief and practice, aspire to positions new to persons of their kind.

The expected or "natural" combinations of auxiliary characteristics become embodied in the stereotypes of ordinary talk, cartoons, fiction, the radio, and the motion picture. Thus, the American Catholic priest, according to a popular stereotype, is Irish, athletic, and a good sort who with difficulty refrains from profanity in the presence of evil and who may punch someone in the nose if the work of the Lord demands it. Nothing could be farther from the French or French-Canadian stereotype of the good priest. The surgeon, as he appears in advertisements for insurance and pharmaceutical products, is handsome, socially poised, and young of face but gray about the temples. These public, or publicity, stereotypes — while they do not necessarily correspond to the facts or determine peoples expectations — are at least significant in that they rarely let the person in the given position have any strikes against him. Positively, they represent someone's ideal conception; negatively, they take care not to shock, astonish, or put doubts into the mind of a public whose confidence is sought.

If we think especially of occupational status, it is in the colleague-group or fellow-worker group that the expectations concerning appropriate auxiliary characteristics are worked most intricately into sentiment and conduct. They become, in fact, the basis of the colleague-group's definition of its common interests, of its informal code, and of selection of those who become the inner fraternity — three aspects of occupational life so closely related that few people separate them in thought or talk.

The epithets "hen doctor," "boy wonder," "bright young men," and "brain trust" express the hostility of colleagues to persons who deviate from the expected type. The members of a colleague-group have a common interest in the whole configuration of things which control the number of potential candidates for their occupation. Colleagues, be it remembered, are also competitors. A rational demonstration that an individual's chances for continued success are not jeopardized by an extension of the recruiting field for the position he has or hopes to attain, or by some short-cutting of usual lines of promotion, does not, as a rule, liquidate the fear and hostility aroused by such a case. Oswald Hall found that physicians do not like one of their number to become a consultant too soon.[3] Consulting is something for the crowning, easing-off years of a career; something to intervene briefly between high power and high blood-pressure. He who pushes for such practice too early shows an "aggressiveness" which is almost certain to be punished. It is a threat to an order of things which physicians—at least, those of the fraternity of successful men—count upon. Many of the specific rules of the game of an occupation become comprehensible only when viewed as the almost instinctive attempts of a group of people to cushion themselves against the hazards of their careers. The advent of colleague-competitors of some new and peculiar type, or by some new route, is likely to arouse anxieties. For one thing, one cannot be quite sure how "new people"—new in kind—will act in the various contingencies which arise to test the solidarity of the group.[4]

How the expectations of which we are thinking become embodied in codes may be illustrated by the dilemma of a young woman who became a member of that virile profession, engineering. The designer of an airplane is expected to go up on the maiden flight of the first plane built according to the design. He (*sic*) then gives a dinner to the engineers and workmen who worked on the new plane. The dinner is naturally a stag party. The young woman in question designed a plane. Her co-workers urged her not to take the risk—for which, presumably, men only are fit—of the maiden voyage. They were, in effect, asking her to be a lady rather than an engineer. She chose to be an engineer. She then gave the party and paid for it like a man. After food and the first round of toasts, she left like a lady.

Part of the working code of a position is discretion; it allows the colleagues to exchange confidences concerning their relations to other people. Among these confidences one finds expressions of cynicism concerning their mission, their competence, and the foibles of their superiors. themselves, their clients, their subordinates, and the public at large. Such expressions take the burden from one's shoulders and serve as a defense as well. The unspoken mutual confidence necessary to them rests on two assumptions concerning one's fellows. The first is that the colleague will not misunderstand; the second is that he will not repeat to uninitiated ears.

3. Oswald Hall, "The Informal Organization of Medical Practice" (unpublished Ph.D. dissertation, University of Chicago, 1944).

4. It may be that those whose positions are insecure and whose hopes for the higher goals are already fading express more violent hostility to "new people." Even if so, it must be remembered that those who are secure and successful have the power to exclude or check the careers of such people by merely failing to notice them.

To be sure that a new fellow will not misunderstand requires a sparring match of social gestures. The zealot who turns the sparring match into a real battle, who takes a friendly initiation too seriously, is not likely to be trusted with the lighter sort of comment on one's work or with doubts and misgivings; nor can he learn those parts of the working code which are communicated only by hint and gesture. He is not to be trusted, for, though he is not fit for stratagems, he is suspected of being prone to treason. In order that men may communicate freely and confidentially, they must be able to take a good deal of each other's sentiments for granted. They must feel easy about their silences as well as about their utterances. These factors conspire to make colleagues, with a large body of unspoken understandings, uncomfortable in the presence of what they consider odd kinds of fellows. The person who is the first of his kind to attain a certain status is often not drawn into the informal brotherhood in which experiences are exchanged, competence built up, and the formal code elaborated and enforced. He thus remains forever a marginal man.

Now it is a necessary consequence of the high degree of individual mobility in America that there should be large numbers of people of new kinds turning up in various positions. In spite of this and in spite of American heterogeneity, this remains a white, Anglo-Saxon, male, Protestant culture in many respects. These are the expected characteristics for many favored statuses and positions. When we speak of racial, religious, sex, and ethnic prejudices, we generally assume that people with these favored qualities are not the objects thereof. In the stereotyped prejudices concerning others, there is usually contained the assumption that these other people are peculiarly adapted to the particular places which they have held up to the present time; it is a corollary implication that they are not quite fit for new positions to which they may aspire. In general, advance of a new group — women, Negroes, some ethnic groups, etc. — to a new level of positions is not accompanied by complete disappearance of such stereotypes but only by some modification of them. Thus, in Quebec the idea that French-Canadians were good only for unskilled industrial work was followed by the notion that they were especially good at certain kinds of skilled work but were not fit to repair machines or to supervise the work of others. In this series of modifications the structure of qualities expected for the most-favored positions remains intact. But the forces which make for mobility continue to create marginal people on new frontiers.

Technical changes also break up configurations of expected status characteristics by altering the occupations about which they grow up. A new machine or a new managerial device — such as the assembly line — may create new positions or break old ones up into numbers of new ones. The length of training may be changed thereby and, with it, the whole traditional method of forming the person to the social demands of a college-group. Thus, a snip of a girl is trained in a few weeks to be a "machinist" on a practically foolproof lathe; thereby the old foolproof machinist, who was initiated slowly into the skills and attitudes of the trade, is himself made a fool of in his own eyes or—worse—in the eyes of his wife, who hears that a neighbor's daughter is a machinist who makes nearly as much money as he. The new positions created by technical changes may, for a time, lack definition as a status. Both the technical and the auxiliary qualifications may be slow in taking form. The personnel man offers a good example. His title is perhaps twenty years old, but the expectations concerning his qualities and functions are still in flux.[5]

Suppose we leave aside the problems which arise from technical changes, as such, and devote the rest of this discussion to the consequences of the appearance of new kinds of people in established positions. Every such occurrence produces, in some measure, a status contradiction. It may also create a status dilemma for the individual concerned and for other people who have to deal with him.

The most striking illustration in our society is offered by the Negro who qualifies for one of the traditional professions. Membership in the Negro race, as defined in American mores or law, may be called a master status-determining trait. It tends to overpower, in most crucial situations, any other characteristics which might run counter to it. But professional standing is also a powerful characteristic—most so in the specific relationships of professional practice, less so in the general intercourse of people. In the person of the professionally qualified Negro these two powerful characteristics clash. The dilemma, for those whites who meet such a person, is that of having to choose whether to treat him as a Negro or as a member of his profession.

The white person in need of professional services, especially medical, might allow him to act as a doctor in an emergency. Or it may be allowed that a Negro physician is endowed with some uncanny skill. In either case, the white client of ordinary American social views would probably avoid any nonprofessional contacts with the Negro physician.[6] In fact, one way of reducing status conflict is to keep the relationship formal and specific.

5. The personnel man also illustrates another problem which I do not propose to discuss in this paper. It is that of an essential contradiction between the various functions which are united in one position. The personnel man is expected to communicate the mind of the workers to management and then to interpret management to the workers. This is a difficult assignment. The problem is well stated by William F. Whyte, in "Pity the Personnel Man," *Advanced Management,* October-December, 1944, pp. 154–58. The Webbs analyzed the similar dilemma of the official of a successful trade-union in their *History of Trade-Unionism* (rev. ed.; London: Longmans, Green, 1920).

6. The Negro artist can be treated as a celebrity. It is within the code of social tufthunting that one may entertain, with a kind of affected Bohemian intimacy, celebrities who, on all counts other than their artistic accomplishments, would be beyond the pale.

This is best done by walking through a door into a place designed for the specific relationship, a door which can be firmly closed when one leaves. A common scene in fiction depicts a lady of degree seeking, veiled and alone, the address of the fortuneteller or the midwife of doubtful practice in an obscure corner of the city. The anonymity of certain sections of cities allows people to seek specialized services, legitimate but embarrassing as well as illegitimate, from persons with whom they would not want to be seen by members of their own social circle.

Some professional situations lend themselves more than others to such quarantine. The family physician and the pediatrician cannot be so easily isolated as some other specialists. Certain legal services can be sought indirectly by being delegated to some queer and unacceptable person by the family lawyer. At the other extreme is school teaching, which is done in full view of the community and is generally expected to be accompanied by an active role in community activities. The teacher, unlike the lawyer, is expected to be an example to her charges.

For the white colleagues of the Negro professional man the dilemma is even more severe. The colleague-group is ideally a brotherhood; to have within it people who cannot, given one's other attitudes, be accepted as brothers is very uncomfortable. Furthermore, professional men are much more sensitive than they like to admit about the company in which nonprofessionals see them. The dilemma arises from the fact that, while it is bad for the profession to let laymen see rifts in their ranks, it may be bad for the individual to be associated in the eyes of his actual or potential patients with persons, even colleagues, of so despised a group as the Negro. The favored way of avoiding the dilemma is to shun contacts with the Negro professional. The white physician or surgeon of assured reputation may solve the problem by acting as consultant to Negro colleagues in Negro clinics and hospitals.

For the Negro professional man there is also a dilemma. If he accepts the role of Negro to the extent of appearing content with less than full equality and intimacy with his white colleagues, for the sake of such security and advantage as can be so got, he himself and others may accuse him of sacrificing his race. Given the tendency of whites to say that any Negro who rises to a special position is an exception, there is a strong temptation for such a Negro to seek advantage by fostering the idea that he is unlike others of his race. The devil who specializes in this temptation is a very insinuating fellow; he keeps a mailing list of "marginal men" of all kinds and origins. Incidentally, one of the by-products of American mores is the heavy moral burden which this temptation puts upon the host of Americans who have by great effort risen from (*sic*) groups which are the objects of prejudice.

There may be cases in which the appearance in a position of one or a few individuals of a kind not expected there immediately dissolves the auxiliary expectations which make him appear odd. This is not, however, the usual consequence. The expectations usually continue to exist, with modification and with exceptions allowed.

A common solution is some elaboration of social segregation. The woman lawyer may become a lawyer to women clients, or she may specialize in some kind of legal service in keeping with woman's role as guardian of the home and morals. Women physicians may find a place in those specialities of which only women and children have need. A female electrical engineer was urged by the dean of the school from which she had just been graduated to accept a job whose function was to give the "woman's angle" to design of household electrical appliances. The Negro professional man finds his clients among Negroes. The Negro sociologist generally studies race relations and teaches in a Negro college. A new figure on the American scene is the Negro personnel man in industries which have started employing Negro workers. His functions are to adjust difficulties of Negro workers, settle minor clashes between the races, and to interpret management's policies to the Negro as well as to present and explain the Negro's point of view to management. It is a difficult job. Our interest for the moment, however, is in the fact that the Negro, promoted to this position, acts only with reference to Negro employees. Many industries have had women personnel officials to act with reference to women. In one sense, this is an extension of the earlier and still existing practice of hiring from among a new ethnic group in industry a "straw boss" to look after them. The "straw boss" is the liaison officer reduced to lowest terms.

Another solution, which also results in a kind of isolation if not in segregation, is that of putting the new people in the library or laboratory, where they get the prestige of research people but are out of the way of patients and the public. Recently, industries have hired a good many Negro chemists to work in their testing and research laboratories. The chemist has few contacts with the production organization. Promotion within the laboratory will put the Negro in charge of relatively few people, and those few will be of his own profession. Such positions do not ordinarily lead to the positions of corresponding importance in the production organization. They offer a career line apart from the main streams of promotion to power and prestige.

These solutions reduce the force of status contradiction by keeping the new person apart from the most troublesome situations. One of the consequences is that it adds new stories to the superstructure of segregation. The Negro hospital and the medical school are the formal side of this. The Negro personnel man and foreman show it within the structure of existing institutions. There are evidences that physicians of various ethnic groups are being drawn into a separate medical system of hospitals, clinics, and schools, partly because of the interest of the Roman Catholic church in developing separate institutions but also partly because of the factors here discussed. It is doubtful whether women will develop corresponding separate systems to any great extent. In all of these cases, it looks as if the highest point which a member of these odd groups may attain is determined largely by the number of people of his own group who are in a position to seek his services or in a position such that he may be assigned by other authority to act professionally with reference to them. On the other hand, the kind of segregation involved may lead professional people, or others advanced to special positions, to seek—as compensation—monopoly over such functions with reference to their own group.

Many questions are raised by the order of things here discussed. One is that of the place of these common solutions of status conflict in the evolution of the relations between the sexes, the races, and the ethnic groups of our society. In what circumstances can the person who is accepted formally into a new status, and then informally kept within the limits of the kind mentioned, step out of these limits and become simply a lawyer, foreman, or whatever? Under what circumstances, if ever, is the "hen doctor" simply a doctor? And who are the first to accept her as such—her colleagues or her patients? Will the growth of a separate superstructure over each of the segregated bottom groups of our society tend to perpetuate indefinitely the racial and ethnic division already existing, or will these superstructures lose their identity in the general organization of society? These are the larger questions.

The purpose of the paper, however, is not to answer these large questions. It is rather to call attention to this characteristic phenomenon of our heterogeneous and changing society and to suggest that it become part of the frame of reference of those who are observing special parts of the American social structure.

PART II

The Meeting of Races
and Cultures

SIXTEEN

The Study of Ethnic Relations

Since so many people are making a desperate effort (perhaps the last before they meet their Maker) to understand and modify the relations between peoples, ethnic groups and races, it is appropriate to note some of the biases and false assumptions that vitiate well-intentioned study and discussion of these relations. The relations between French and other Canadians are not one of the desperate cases. Quite the contrary. The points I have to make, however, apply to the Canadian case as well as to those that threaten the peace of the world.

I have already used the term *ethnic group,* a colorless catch-all much used by anthropologists and sociologists; it is a term likely to be taken up by a larger public, and consequently likely to take on color that will compel the sociologists to get a new one, for it is one of the risks of our trade that our words lose the scientifically essential virtue of neutrality as they acquire the highly desirable virtue of being commonly used. The anthropologists will probably not have to change, since they study people who cannot read. To return from this digression, which does have a point for the subject in hand, what is an ethnic group? Almost anyone who uses the term would say that it is a group distinguishable from others by one, or some combination of the following: physical characteristics, language, religion, customs, institutions, or "cultural traits." This definition is, however, exactly wrong-end to. Its wrongness has important consequences, not only for study of intergroup relations, but for the relations themselves. An ethnic group is not one because of the degree of measurable or observable difference from other groups; it is an ethnic group, on the contrary, be-

Dalhousie Review, Vol. XXVIII, No. 4, Jan., 1948 Reprinted by permission of the *Dalhousie Review.*

cause the people in it and the people out of it know that it is one; because both the *ins* and the *outs* talk, feel and act as if it were a separate group. This is possible only if there are ways of telling who belongs to the group and who does not, and if a person learns early, deeply, and usually irrevocably to what group he belongs. If it is easy to resign from the group, it is not truly an ethnic group.

These points should be clear and dear to any English-speaking Canadian. By the kind of measures usually used, the English-speaking part of the Canadian people would be considered a colony of Great Britain or a part of the United States. About all the evidence to prove that Canadians are a separate ethnic group is a little extra virtue and the fact that they export their Aimee Semple McPhersons, Tex Guinans, Norma Shearers, Pidgeons, and Masseys—and buy them back at the box-office. Yet Canadians are Canadians just as naturally as Englishmen are Englishmen, and they never yield to the temptation to belong to other nations. Well, hardly ever.

To be sure, the living of a common life and the facing of common problems—conditions that lead to the growth of an ethnic group, nationality and even a race—will almost certainly encourage the development of a peculiar language, at least of peculiar turns of expression and meaning, and of some unique customs and institutions. Some of these peculiar traits will become the dear symbols of the group's distinction from others; their value for group solidarity may exceed their measurable degree of uniqueness. The essential fact remains, however, that the cultural traits are attributes of the group, and not that the group is the synthesis of its traits.

What difference does this error make? It warps study both of groups and also of the relations between them. When I first went from Chicago to McGill University, I took with me the conventional notions of studying the assimilation and acculturation (to use both the sociologists' and the anthropologists' lingo) of European immigrants in North America. I looked up all the studies I could find of what was happening to the French Canadians. In the census I sought figures on the number of French Canadians who speak English. Now the assumption was that French Canadians are being gradually assimilated to the English-Canadian culture and world, and that the trait of language was the index thereof. If a French Canadian spoke English, he was presumably less French. It took me a long time to discover that the French Canadian who speaks English best is generally pretty stoutly French in sentiment and way of living, and that sometimes one who speaks but little English has often suffered severe lesions in the integrity of his French culture and loyalty. Eventually I learned that one of the commonest errors of English Canadians is to take the use of English, a tweed coat, or something else considered an expression of Englishness, as evidence that some French Canadian they meet is about to resign from his group. Later, when they discover that he is more French than they have thought, they decide that he has reverted. In fact, the English Canadians have simply learned more about him. A certain withdrawal of cordiality often results. The misunderstanding arises from the error of considering that individual cultural traits are the measure of a man's belonging to an ethnic group, and of the solidarity of the group itself. This error is usually accompanied by the hidden assumption that the individual traits are, or ought to be, disappearing and that one fine day they will be gone—and the French-Canadian people will no longer exist. This is misjudgment, of course, in line with the common tendency to regard one's own group as immortal and the other as relatively a passing thing. It might, incidentally, be interesting to speculate upon what will have become of English Canadians as an ethnic entity by the time French Canadians have disappeared as one.

An additional consequence or expression (I will not try to be too nice about deciding which) of this point of view is the judging of a group's right to exist on the basis of the quality of its cultural peculiarities, called for this purpose "cultural contributions." An English-Canadian teacher of French in a Canadian university used to maintain—in a stout Ontario twang—that since French Canadians had corrupted the French language into a "patois" and since they had made no worthy contributions to French literature and culture, they had no right to hold out from the English-Canadian language and culture. This argument could cut both ways. Whether in the Canadian case it cuts either way is not at issue. Before deciding the case of any people, one would have to agree upon some canons of linguistic and literary aesthetics and upon some standards by which to determine when a contribution to culture has been made. Need I dwell upon the difficulty of getting such agreement from people of two cultures?

Thus far I have myself contributed to another and graver error, that of implying that one can study the relations between groups by analyzing only one of the groups concerned. It takes more than one ethnic group to make ethnic relations. The relations can be no more understood by studying one or the other of the groups than can a chemical combination by study of one element only, or a boxing bout by observation of only one of the fighters. Yet it is common to study ethnic relations as if one had to know only one party to them. Generally the person who studies such relations is a member of one of the groups involved. One might suppose that he would assume that he knows his own group and would therefore study the other.

That is not quite what happens. Most studies turn out to deal with whichever of the groups is considered the minority. The student who is himself of the minority wants to make his group known and appreciated by the dominant group; one who is of the dominant group is likely to assume that he knows his own and that the problem is, after all, one of how the minority will adjust to the dominant group. In conducting a seminar on race and cultural contacts, I have found that the majority of students propose projects that are simply studies of some minority group, with the word *problem* attached: the Nisei problem, the Flemish problem, the French-Canadian problem. In the resulting reports, the dominant group gets off with a drubbing because of its prejudices, although it may be shown that there is hope of a more "liberal" attitude's arising in some hearts. The wounds and virtues of the minority are exposed to view and their relics to veneration. The *relations,* however, are never studied. Since it is generally true that members of a minority have a more lively experience of the dominant group than members of the latter have of the minority, more can perhaps be learned about the inter-group relations by studying the minority than by studying the dominant group. This might give some justification for starting with the minority, but not for leaving the matter there, as is often done. Even that would not be so bad, if the study were pushed into all realms of life and experience, and not limited to political and economic relations. Much is to be learned about inter-group relations by probing to the depths of personal experience, by discovering through what experiences the individual learns both the realities and the fictions of his position as a member of an ethnic group. To what literature can one turn to study this aspect of French-English relations in Canada?

But whether a student studies one or all the groups in a situation—and he should study all—he must study *relations* if that is what he claims he wants to know. If he puts the emphasis on relations, he will find out fairly easily what kind of things he will have to know about the groups themselves in order to understand the relations. He will learn, for instance, that study of folklore, as such, is not study of inter-group relations; but he will also become sensitive to the hints of group loyalty and aggression in tales and songs. He will sit up and listen to a French-Canadian folksong in which, long ago, the rich old man whom the pretty young maid does not want to marry was turned into a *maudit anglais.* He will turn to the folklorist, who will be able to tell him more of the history of the song and who will correct his impressions—as one of the several excellent French-Canadian folklorists will probably do to my interpretation of the above song. He will also learn, however, to discipline his own passion for curio and antique hunting by keeping his eye firmly on the objective of studying relations. He will find his curiosity about both groups greatly enlivened and his eye sharpened, but he will not try to be a specialist in all matters concerning the group and will turn willingly to others for their specialized knowledge.

Now the way to keep this disciplining objective in mind is to start quite consciously with an assumption; namely, that if the groups in question have enough relations to be a nuisance to each other it is because they form a part of a whole, that they are in some sense and in some measure members of the same body. With this idea firmly in mind, one can set about finding out what the whole is and what is the part of each in the whole. In doing this, one will almost certainly not fall into the errors so far considered, and will avoid another one: that of studying only the conscious surface of the relations between groups — their quarrels, opinions, propaganda and counter-propaganda. Among the respects in which the two groups are parts of a larger whole may be some of which people are not ordinarily aware and of which, if they are aware of them, they do not ordinarily think in ethnic terms at all. This conception will also keep one from thinking that either of the groups has so independent an existence that it could be studied without reference to other groups around it.

Almost anyone will agree that the French-Canadian people has become what it is, not merely by virtue of what its ancestors brought with them from France, but also because of its long contact with Anglo-American life and civilization. I refer not to anglicisms in its speech, its love of baseball, or other English or North American customs which it may have adopted, but to its very peculiarities. French Canada has never had to swallow its own spit. Its balance of population has long been maintained by spilling the excess into a continent until recently thirsty for settlers and industrial labor. Its malcontents and heretics have been able to find companions and a place to exercise their peculiar talents somewhere in North America. How much relief from inner pressure of number and of psychological and social tension French Canada has been afforded by being part of something much larger than herself, no one can say. Nor can I prove, although I think it is so, that the failure of the continent to continue this function of absorption for French Canada is partly responsible for the current brand of more bitter nationalism and nationalist in Quebec.

I stress the functions that the rest of Canada and North America perform for Quebec, not to reinforce any feelings that other Canadians may have about French Canada's debt to the English-speaking world, but to prepare for the kill. There has been some study of the economic, demographic, and political functions of French Canada in the development of Canada as a whole, but not much of her cultural and deeper psychological functions in the development of the rest of the Canadian people. During the war, the two-thirds vote of French-Canadians against conscription served beautifully to obscure the one-third vote of other Canadians against it. In those years, I frequently heard my United States compatriots most unjustly and ignorantly criticize the magnificent Canadian war effort. How often I heard English-Canadians, instead of answering with the eloquent facts, defensively impugn the patriotism of their French-Canadian fellow citizens! The temptation was great. Indeed, the critic often suggested this way out himself, since he usually wanted to think well of the Canadian. Proving oneself a good fellow on the other fellow's terms, however, does not generally increase the other fellow's respect for the group to which one belongs; and in this case it may be doubted whether Canada was well served. The presence of a minority whose sentiments vary from one's own, either in direction or intensity, is a wonderful salve to the conscience. If one wear the salve thickly and conspicuously enough, who shall dare question whether there is really a wound under it? Just what the fact of having always had a minority in its bosom has done to the national conscience and self-consciousness of English Canadians is worth study. I offer this very controversial point, like others in this paper, as bait to those who would explore the full depth and subtlety of the effects upon each other, of two ethnic groups who are parts of a larger whole. Note, too, that in pushing the conception of the relations between two groups so far, we have gone beyond the effort to be merely impartial and just. Impartial judgment implies a standard of justice, legal and moral. This is precisely what two groups are least likely to agree upon, especially in a crisis.

I plead, however, not for less justice of word and action between ethnic groups, races and peoples, but for a more drastically objective, a broader and more penetrating, analysis with which to work.

SEVENTEEN

The Sociological Point of View:
The Challenge of the Deep South
to Research in the Social Sciences

We could review, just as well, not the challenge of the Deep South to research in the social sciences, but rather the challenge of social research to the Deep South. Any society presents a challenge to those who would study it: the challenge to unlock its secrets, and to question its image of itself. The secrets are of two kinds, those which people hide from outsiders, and those which they hide from themselves. Human beings are adept at keeping both, and are equally adept at prying out other people's secrets. The social scientist, insofar as he becomes adept at finding out things about other people, and about societies, plays the uneasy game of the thief catching a thief. His relation with the people he studies is never comfortable. It is a toss-up whether it is easier for an insider, or for an outsider.

Every region, or society, is at any given time a sort of God-given laboratory for study of some particular problem, and in time of crisis, especially so. A situation of great tension and crisis is, however, not necessarily easy to study. This is indeed a time of crisis in the Deep South. The crisis, however, is more than regional. It is national; indeed it is

Read at a symposium at the dedication of the Social Science building at the University of Alabama, 1963.

Reprinted by permission from *The Deep South in Transformation,* edited by Robert B. Highsaw, Copyright © 1964 by The University of Alabama Press.

world-wide. It is here the crisis that comes from the determined and widespread effort of Negroes to take possession of the rights which they consider to belong to all Americans and from the bitter-end fanatical resistance of many other Americans to their exercise of those rights. There has been equally bitter resistance to social changes in other times and places, but usually social scientists have not been there to study it, or have either not had the courage to do it, or were prevented from it by Draconian measures. It is this extreme resistance which offers the two-way challenge of social research to the Deep South, and of the Deep South to social research.

Sociologists in these, the years of their prosperity, have tended to limit themselves to the middle range, not only of theory, but of social behavior itself. In the large survey, a national sample of people are asked at their front door or inside the house a set of standard questions about some matter of general concern. Allowance is made for a variety of answers; there are "probes" to follow out unusual atitudes. Yet the mass survey, whether of political opinion or consumer preferences, loves the small differences in the great clusters at the middle of the curve. In the recent studies based on an interviewing of a national sample of the college graduating class of 1960 about their plans for further study, one finds an analysis of the characteristics of students who plan to study law; but women are excluded from the analysis because they are too small a percentage of the total. In a study of the religious practices of Catholics in a Florida town some years ago, the Spanish speaking majority was left out because they were not "typical." Negroes similarly are omitted from the sample in many market surveys. There was no Negro college included in the sample which Paul Lazarsfeld studies in the book, *The Academic Mind,* on academic freedom. People may be left out because they are few, are not typical, or because their behavior shows some extreme deviation from the expected and the respectable.

The people at the extreme ends of the scale in their opinions and people who differ basically in their social experience from the rest of a population (women from men, Negroes from whites) confuse the findings. One can understand certain practical reasons why exceptional people and exceptional behavior are excluded from large surveys. There are, one suspects, often more subtle reasons, such as conscious or unconscious exclusion of the odd ones from the ranks of those who count socially, morally, politically, or economically. It is fair to say that the methods used by most American sociologists tend to keep them away from peculiar people and from extremes of behavior. Their mood of objectivity is also sometimes taken to mean a certain lack of concern with people of queer beliefs. It is the trend that counts. There are certain assumptions, though, underlying both the mass survey as method and the attitude that it is the mass that counts. One is the assumption of peace, of a continuation of the status quo, or of none but rather small changes from year-to-year. When there are drastic changes, great movements for social change, it usually turns out that social scientists, if they have been predicting catastrophe, have predicted the wrong one.

Since the mass destruction of European cities from the air during the last war, the searing of Hiroshima and Nagasaki, and the subsequent development of the power to destroy to unbelievable heights, certain government agencies have studied how people will behave in extreme disaster. Teams of graduate students were recruited to be ready to go at a moment's notice to scenes of accident, storm, or flood. It was difficult to get them since a disaster, being unpredictable, might occur at examination time or on a holiday. The routine of life and the demands of the academic career militate against doing research which requires that one be ready, as is a fireman, to answer a call day or night. Not the least part of the difficulty was to "pre-test" questions for unpredictable events, although that was, in fact, overcome fairly easily on the assumption that the problems of meeting major community disasters vary less than the causes of the disaster.

Whatever the failings of social scientists themselves—timidity, love of the routine and of the expected—some extremes of behavior are hard to study because the people so behaving do not easily submit themselves to observation. When one of my students wanted to study the people who call themselves Jehovah's Witnesses, he had to pose as a potential convert. The Witnesses admit no neutrality. A postulant must try to convert his own mother by giving her the hard word that she will go to hell if she does not believe. One must be an insider, one of the faithful; or one is an outsider, one of the damned. The only third position is that of postulant, undergoing instruction and passing the hard tests of initation into the church. Objective observer is not an admissible role. The Witnesses, however, are ordinarily without influence or power in their community. They can prevent inquiry only by not letting the observer into their houses and meetings or into their confidence.

A variation on this theme is found in the study of a science-fiction sect, *When Prophecy Fails,* by Leon Festinger. The members of the sect, so few as to meet in a private house, gathered to prepare themselves for the coming of their master in a flying saucer to save the faithful few from a new deluge. The only possible way to observe the group was to join it. Festinger and several associates did so. They joined in the preaching, prophesying, and the visions. At times the observers, feigning full faith, were nearly as numerous as those whom the observers believed sincere members. It was a small, tense group in which the role of objective observer on the sidelines would have been impossible. Although some students of mine took part in the study, I did not like the pretense involved, partly on principle and partly because of the possibility that great harm might be done.

Thus, on the bias, we approach the question of sociological research in the Deep South, asking in what role it can be done on the problem that is the most crucial one. There are many people in the South who allow no free discussion of the relations of people of European descent with the American Negro. Some have resorted to extreme forms of behavior to prevent such discussion and any deviation from practice. Some would defend their beliefs and the current practices to the death, the death certainly of others and probably of themselves. It is a case in which people feel and act upon the notion that he who is not fully with us is against us. Part of the challenge, taken in either direction, then is that of studying last-ditch defense, for people engaged in it are not likely to allow themselves to be studied fully and freely.

One of the problems in such a case is that unanimity of attitudes may not be so great as the unanimity of outward expression. Indeed, studies made by the survey method show marked changes in racial attitudes on the part of many people. Insofar as the survey method uses the private interview, and insofar as the people interviewed trust the interviewer's promise not to reveal identities, the survey may be, contrary to what I suggested, the best way to study situations of tension. But it does not study the aspect of things we are most interested in, namely, the circumstances in which those who may in privacy express a contrary opinion will state that contrary opinion in the political and social discourse of the home town. Indeed, we might ask in what circumstances people will state their contrary opinion with the same force as the extreme defenders of the publicly prevailing extremist opinion. A few people do so in the Deep South, perhaps more do so in South Africa. In either case, if they are white people, they may have a very difficult time. I know a professor whose telephone has been tapped, whose wife and daughters are given obscene scoldings over the phone at all hours of day and night because of exercising a freedom of expression and action that would have been considered normal in universities throughout the world throughout most of the history of the university as an institution. He is not alone. A young man who teaches in a private white college has related that he has moved within a block of the campus because life has become unpleasant for his wife and children. In both cases, the attacks came from outside the academic community, but they came. There is evidence that in a Virginia community, where last-ditch defense took the form of closing the public schools, the traditional leaders of more moderate views gave way, without a struggle, to people of extreme views who in normal times would not aspire to positions of leadership and would not be considered for them. It may be that last-ditch defense of this kind brings about a shifting of leadership away from the moderates. It would be good to know in what circumstances and by what means that shift could be prevented, or its direction reversed.

Some of the mechanisms involved in last-ditch defense seem to be of a universal character; others may be peculiar to American culture. A probably universal one is that of being hoisted on one's own rhetoric. To be elected to office a man declares that he will resist racial change to the death; thus he has made compromise, the essence of politics, impossible. If he retreats, he will be destroyed, politically and perhaps in other ways by the extremists whose cause he has espoused. Fanatical defenders are not unlike the political sects such as the nineteenth century anarchists in Europe in this regard; defectors were sometimes erased. Here is the phenomenon of people having talked themselves beyond the point of no return.

A more American mechanism is one adopted by the vigilantes in early and frontier days, that of not allowing the person of deviating opinion or action to remain in town. It has been used in most parts of the country at one time or another, against revenue agents, labor leaders, people of queer religion, and nowadays against peacemarchers and integrationists. What once was a defense of the vigilantes has now become a device of police, as well as of elements of the populace. Although common in the Deep South, it is by no means confined to any one region of this our country. It makes the way of the social researcher difficult, and certainly limits his ability to probe whatever differences may lie behind the wall of apparent unanimity.

If there is one thing we should have learned about modern complex societies, it is that surface unanimity is always suspect. Hitler managed to get votes of 98 per cent to 99 per cent in his favor in every election when he was in power. The question that he raised was always the same: Are you for me or against me? Unanimity on a great public issue usually is obtained only by what amount to totalitarian methods. Behind the façade of unanimous assent may hide many nuances of feeling and conscience. The presence of fanatics who have power always leads to distortion of public expression and, indeed, of private action if not of thought. One problem for social research is to find out what lies behind the façade of unanimity, and to learn how the hidden contrary opinions might be brought to expression and action.

Perhaps the most extreme of all forms of social behavior is physical violence, either in limited degree to control behavior or gain power, or to destroy other human beings. Once a popular legal form of punishment, it has lost favor in the western world both in the family, in the disciplining of children, and by public authority. In Great Britain it is part of the approved armory for educating small and middle-sized boys. It is also used in some places as punishment of incorrigible prisoners convicted of felonies. In this country the law, in the abstract, tends to disapprove much use of corporal punishment. But unofficial use, sometimes furtive, sometimes open, is probably much greater in this country than official and unofficial combined in British countries. Beating, roughing up, shocking with electrical wands, are practices used to make people move on, get out of town, or disperse. In many places in our country the police shine bright lights in the eyes of people for hours on end, weaken them with fatigue, or make them miserable in other ways either as punishment or as a form of brainwashing. If they do not have official permission to use these forms of behavior, there is at least no effective effort to make them stop. The public gives an implicit mandate to the police to conduct themselves as they do. It is no secret that these extremes are used to control Negroes more often than whites in those parts of the country, South or North, where there are Negroes in any considerable number, to control alleged "vagrants" in certain regions where migrant labor is wanted only in season, and to deal with people accused of crimes, if they are not members of some protecting group.

An opposite extreme form of behavior is non-violence, or passive resistance. In this country, violence is used by the representatives of the law as well as by many who have no mandate to punish or control others. Non-violence, with its partner passive resistance, as a rule is used by those who claim that the representatives of the law are themselves breaking the law. They maintain that legitimate authority is acting beyond or contrary to its true mandate. In India, passive resistance was eventually successful because the British-led police were loathe to use the butts of their guns on inert bodies. It has not been successful in South Africa because the police continue shooting and using their clubs. The limit of what their stomachs can stand has not been reached. The encounter of passive resistance with violence is not one of the more pleasant of human encounters, but it is one which occurs. Since it does occur, it is the business of the social scientist to observe and learn its dynamics. It is an encounter in which the role of neutral bystander (observer) is most difficult to bear as well as one in which that role is not likely to be tolerated.

There is no intent to belittle sociological research done in the South. Some of the best research done in this country has been done in the South, some of it in the Deep South. There come to mind the many studies of regional life and culture initiated by the late Howard Odum at the University of North Carolina and carried on by his successors. Fisk University and the Tuskegee Institute have carried out many important studies on the economy and the social life and problems of the rural South. Robert E. Park and William I. Thomas, fathers of sociological research on racial and ethnic problems, held their first discussions on the dusty roads around Tuskegee just over fifty years ago. Much good work is being done now.

In the main those earlier studies had to do with problems that were real at the time. The South was rural. Its agriculture, at least the agriculture that gave the region its character, was plantation agriculture, more akin to that of the West Indies and Northern Brazil than to that of Illinois and Wisconsin, with the rotation of crops on family farms, or that of the grain-producing prairies and the ranches of the great plains. Good sociological work was done on the plantation as an institution. Those are not the problems of today. The South is becoming urban and industrial; regionalism is not a concept of much use in analyzing industrial and urban societies.

The people who worked on those plantations, where, Negro or white, literacy helped them little, are now going to the cities of the South and of the North. They are making the move not with great hope, but out of necessity. And they are making it at a time in industrial history when the demand for unlettered, unskilled labor has dwindled to naught. The result is still another kind of extreme behavior, the extreme alienation of the new urban masses, mainly from the South. They came too late, mainly because they were detained too long in the doomed plantation agriculture. It is the same whether they are Negro or white. Go into those Chicago neighborhoods invaded by rural white people from the South, and you will hear exactly the same descriptions of their behavior as of the behavior of Negroes of the same social class. They are fewer, and they are not confined behind a wall of caste, but their situation is tragic.

Those white people are, in some sense, symbolic of the present last-ditch resistance to allowing Negroes their full rights as citizens. For those unlettered whites gained nothing more than a purely symbolic victory from their position in the dominant group. They had none of the instruments of domination except their race. Whatever mutual satisfactions there may have been in the system of race relations in some places and times did not reach those people, and, indeed, have not those satisfactions pretty well disappeared throughout the South? They certainly do not exist and probably never did for most of the people who fanatically resist basic changes in the racial system. That may, indeed, lie behind their resistance; they are engaged in what Joseph Gusfield calls a symbolic crusade, when writing of the crusade against drink carried on by the people who profited least and suffered least from the evils of alcohol.

Study of the last-ditch defenders would lead one into basic changes in the social and economic structure of the South. The best of the South's social research was done on a system and social structure which no longer exist. The men who did it were good sociologists, studying what they considered the problems of their day. Even they, however, did not study the extreme behavior of the time. The study of lynching was done in the main by Negro organizations; they used for that purpose for many years, the late Walter White, a white man physiologically, who was a Negro by American definition. He could visit the site of a lynching and find out what had happened with, of course, a certain danger to his person.

One must also say that some sociologists have made it their special mission to study what happens in racial crises in the South. Thomas Pettigrew of Harvard University led a research team in Little Rock, and has continued to be as nearly Johnny-on-the-spot as possible in a number of crises, when the more extreme forms of behavior are in evidence. Others are following his lead.

Perhaps the time will soon come when many more join the effort of observing and analyzing these extreme forms of behavior so characteristic of our country, and, in this epoch, especially of the Deep South. It is the role of the sociologists to find and observe not merely those social situations which tell us new and hitherto unknown things about human behavior, but those which are the key situations which must be described fully in objective terms if we are to understand and solve the problems of our own country in our own time. It is a task which requires great courage and great ingenuity. It is not a task for the social scientists of any one region, but for those of all regions of our country.

The challenge of the Deep South to social research is the challenge to bring in an epoch when any American can move to any part of his country and carry on his normal activities, including social research, provided they are done fairly and courageously. The general message of my words is that we are all in this together — social scientists or not, Negro or white, northerners, southerners, westerners. The Deep South like the rest of the country is going through a technological revolution which has made it urban and industrial, and will make it more so with each passing year. The challenge of the Deep South and to the Deep South is quick adaption of our institutions to this new situation with as little human destruction as possible.

EIGHTEEN

The Nature of Racial Frontiers

Dr. Park used to talk a good deal about the nature of things in general and of the orders of things in which he was especially interested. One way to define the nature of things was to talk of their essence, after the manner of the scholastics. He often indulged in this kind of discourse, but he preferred the question of science, namely "What kinds are there?" and "What are the marginal cases?"

It was in keeping with this bent of mind to be more interested in the relations of things than in the things themselves; it was race relations, rather than race, that he was curious about. And race relations occur on racial frontiers.

He wrote two articles whose titles contain the phrase "racial frontier." The first of them, "Our Racial Frontier on the Pacific," appeared in 1926 in a colorful special issue of the *Survey Graphic,* entitled *East by West.* The second, "Race Relations and Certain Frontiers," was read before the American Sociological Society in 1933, at a meeting devoted entirely to Race and Culture Contacts by plan of the president of that year, E. B. Reuter.[1]

In the first paper he says "The Pacific Coast is our racial frontier. All the problems of the Pacific tend to focus about this racial barrier." The racial frontier is, then, both a meeting place and a barrier. Later he speaks

Reprinted by permission of the publisher from J. Masuoka and P. Valien (eds.), *Race Relations: Problems and Theory.* Copyright 1961, University of North Carolina Press.

Read at the dedication of the R.E. Park Building, Fisk University, March, 1955.

1. "Our Racial Frontier on the Pacific," *Survey Graphic,* LVI (May, 1926), 192-96; "Race Relations and Certain Frontiers," in E.B. Reuter (ed.), *Race and Culture Contacts* (New York: McGraw-Hill, 1934), pp. 57-85. Both articles also appear in Robert E. Park, *Race and Culture* (Glencoe, Ill.: The Free Press, 1950).

of a tendency for race relations in any given case to be at first merely geographic, only to end up by becoming human and social; or it may be at first economic and utilitarian, only to become moral, social, and political. "We have imported labor as if it were a mere commodity, and sometimes we have been disappointed to find, as we invariably do, that the laborers were human like ourselves."

The essential nature of a racial frontier, as suggested by this article, is that it is a meeting place of two or more racially distinguishable peoples, but a meeting place where barriers are set up to slacken the tempo of eventual assimilation — barriers which, Park goes on to say, may "perhaps halt it [assimilation] for a time; but cannot change its direction; cannot at any rate, reverse it." Without commenting on the theory of irreversible cycles, we may throw Park's conception of racial frontiers into high light by asking the question: Where is there not a racial frontier? There are two answers, corresponding to the two points in his implied definition. (1) There is no racial frontier where there is no contact of races, that is, in a society racially homogeneous both within and on its frontiers. (2) There is no racial frontier where people do not take notice of race in any of the crucial concerns of social relations, that is, where race does not matter. The study of the kinds of racial frontiers is, then, the study of the ways in which racially distinguishable people meet and the subsequent course of events, with respect to the things in which race matters or is thought to matter, until such time, if it ever comes, as race no longer matters at all or as there are no longer easily perceptible racial distinctions in the population. The two terminal points may, in fact, be one and the same.

The other paper is built around a distinction that has nothing to do with race, the distinction made by the geographers, Brunhes and Vaillaux, between the active and expansive areas of the world and those areas which — although in some cases they are densely populated — are politically and economically passive. (I feel a certain sentimental interest in this paper since my wife, at that time my fiancée, and I translated the passages for Dr. Park in which this distinction is made.) Modern race relations, he in effect says in this paper, are the accidental result of the meeting of the active with the passive peoples. They are thus a product of economic, political, and ideological empire. The kinds of racial frontiers are than a function of the various forms which this expansion has taken. The emphasis is put upon the "moving frontier," to use a phrase of American origin picked up and developed by W. K. Hancock, in his little book, *Argument of Empire*.[2] Mr. Hancock speaks of the moving frontiers of various ex-

2. W.K. Hancock, *Argument of Empire*, Chapter VII, "Moving Frontiers," (Penguin Special, 1943). See also reports on the Institute of Commonwealth Studies, London, of which he is a director.

panding societies, North American, Australian, and South African especially. He classifies them according to the kinds of people who led the
expansion: settlers, traders, missionaries, and the people who established
the colonial or power frontiers. Hancock, like Park, see racial frontiers as
an accidental by-product of the pursuit of various human designs; but one
would do both of them injustice if he were to take this to mean that contact
with, or exploitation of, people of other races has not been, in many cases,
itself part of the design. The design has often been that of mobilizing
potential labor, and the new laborers were of another race than their
employers. But design, individual and collective, seems to bear directly
upon racial relations in the setting up of those barriers which limit the
intermingling that would let the frontier vanish through the racial blending
that nature does so willingly and often so beautifully. Racial frontiers, once
established, vary in the bounds which are set, in the means resorted to in
order to maintain them, and in the relative power and determination of one
or another of the racial groups to maintain, move, or destroy the barriers.

There is a large literature on these varying aspects of racial frontiers,
although one would by no means be justified in saying that all of the actual
or possible cases have been sufficiently analyzed. The questions for present
and future investigation are perhaps these: How are the racial frontiers of
the present like or different from those which Park and his generation
described? To what extent do his and similar theoretical formulations fit
the present state of the case? And, are these descriptions and theoretical
formulations of use in predicting the course of racial relations?

Park lived at the end of the epoch of European expansion, at least of
imperial expansion. European missionaries, settlers and soldiers are not at
present extending the hegemony of western Europe. Park knew this, and
often spoke of it in his later years; what might happen next is, however, not
talked of much in his work.

As a matter of fact, in the parts of the world not dominated by Russia,
empires are breaking up. New nations or self-governing commonwealths
are constantly in the making. There is certainly no flood of European
settlers going out to take possession of lands. With a few exceptions, the
trend of migration is from frontiers of settlement back into such urban and
industrial centers in the countries which were most recently drawn into the
European empires. One may indeed say that it is the world of the
non-European races that is on the move. There are a few places where
there is talk of getting rid of the white man.

Yet this is not the whole story; the checking of European empire building by many forces, of which native and racial nationalism is but one, came
before the industrial revolution introduced by Europeans had reached
completion. It is evident from the events of the past generation that people

may become politically active, or at least effectively reactive to the imperial powers, before they have become active and independent carriers of
modern industrial organization and technology. We may expect, in one
form or another, expansion of the main features of the European industrial
complex for a long time to come. I think we may also expect that people of
European races will continue to play a great role in the spread of this
complex; what their economic and political role will be is another matter.
The many economic and technical missions being sent out to what we
consider the far corners of the earth are but one aspect, perhaps a small
one, in the continued expansion of the industrial frontiers. To what extent
race will be forgotten, while still existing as an observable and statistically
significant fact on this industrial frontier, is a question of major interest.

While the expansion of European modes of industry goes on in the
so-called free parts of the world, in the part dominated by Russia it appears
to be going on equally actively. The primary difference is that there it is
accompanied by an ideological campaign that is as fervent as, and much
more highly organized than, the Christian missionary campaign which
accompanied the expansion of Europe. The main non-European objectives
of Soviet expansion are peoples of race noticeably different from the
European, poor and non-industrial, as were the countries occupied by
European empires previously. However, they have all previously been in
some measure parts of European empires and have all become aware,
likewise in varying measure, that the Europeans have set up racial barriers
against them. The propaganda job of the Russian imperial and Communist
missionaries is thus made somewhat easier; racial discrimination and capi-
talist economic and political domination can be made into one and the same
sufficient explanation of the poverty and of the landlessness of the masses
of people. Although Walter Kolarz has shown fairly convincingly that the
Soviets depart from their doctrine of racial indifference as drastically as
imperial Christians have done, this evidence may not be more convincing
than is usually the case when a boy tries to get out of trouble by saying of
his accuser, "He's worse than me."[3] We may at least conjecture that
industrial expansion will go on and that it will continue to make the races
meet in situations such that there will be strong differences in their distributions among positions of various kinds. What the role of race itself as
political and social symbols will be is another matter; the role of ideologies
is still another.

It should be clear by this time that I cannot possibly discuss all the
questions I have raised concerning Park's notions and descriptions of racial

3. Walter Kolarz, "Race Relations in the Soviet Union," paper prepared for the Conference
on Race Relations in World Perspective, University of Hawaii, 1954. See also A. W. Lind
(ed.), *Race Relations in World Perspective* (University of Hawaii Press, 1955), Chapter 9.

frontiers. I will make some remarks about the racial frontier that is of closest interest to most of us here, the one in our own country. The racial frontier in America was, of course, a product of the same expansion of Europe that made the other frontiers. We were simply the most successful of all the settlers' frontiers, so successful that we soon became a center of expansion in our own right. The ancestors of some of us wanted and by various means got the ancestors of others of us to come here to work and, in so doing, created a great racial frontier. It was a meeting place, certainly, to such an extent that several new racial subgroups resulted. You all know the history of the barriers which form the other term in the definition of the racial frontier. We Americans have, in the course of time, become that people in which the major racial groups, Negro American and European American, are less divided by cultural differences than is the case in any country which has equal racial diversity. The cultural differences of ethnic quality which do occur between the races come largely from the greater cultural diversity of the so-called white element, as compared with the Negro. (I am ignoring smaller racial groups for the moment.) Americans classified as Negro are of longer ancestry in this country, on the average, than those classified as white. The racial frontier in this country has no ethnic quality. There are significant differences in the statistical distribution of certain cultural characteristics among the people of the two races; the range of the differences is essentially the same for the two groups. The most ignorant white man of old American stock and the most ignorant Negro are of an essentially identical ignorance in what they do and do not know of the American culture. The most learned are alike in the same way. Our racial frontier is perhaps the most purely racial of all the racial frontiers of the world. It is a theoretically crucial case. How long can the barriers of race last without buttressing by an objective or symbolic cultural difference? The white man can lamely and pathetically, even with tears, speak of his mission, but no one believes him; he does not believe himself. The Negro can buy a few African trinkets and some may join pseudo-Islamic sects to give themselves a prouder past, but he remains an American in his culture, in his past, present, and future.

Meantime, there is still expansion of industry into the South and other more rural parts of the country and a continued mobilization of the remaining untouched sources of labor. It is moving white and Negro rural Southerners to town and to the North. We all know this story. Apparently the racial barriers are not strong enough to prevent Negro Americans from moving both spatially and to new positions in the American economy and in American society; they are apparently strong enough to maintain a considerable differential between the spatial, occupational, educational, and income distributions. No one seems to be proposing an economic *apartheid* as in South Africa. We seem rather to be moving with accelerated speed toward a fuller and more varied contact of the races, but one continually blocked somewhat by barriers. The crucial questions in race relations in this country have to do with the rates at which these barriers break down in various regions, aspects of life, occupations and institutions, and with the processes which hasten or retard the breakdown.

It is significant that at just this moment economists should be invading the sacred sociological precincts of race relations. Several young economists at the University of Chicago have been going into racial differentials in the market, that is, into discrimination, using data on occupation and income, land ownership, and other related matters. The one of their studies which is already available, that of Morton Zeman,[4] seems to show that the white American and the Negro American are most nearly alike in income when both have the least education, skill, and experience but that the Negro gets smaller increments of income for each increment of education, skill, and experience. This seems to sum up the nature of the American racial frontier; the odds are not yet even. Donald Dewey of Duke University adds to this impression by pointing out that there are still many Negroes in the bracket of least education and skill and that many of them in the South are not even yet fully in the labor market. Another of the young economists at the University of Chicago, Gary Becker, has pursued his analysis in a refined set of formulae for measuring what he and other economists call the "taste *for* discrimination," a legitimate phrase in their system for what we would call prejudice against the Negro. I mention these studies because it seems to me indicative of the present state of the racial frontier in this country that Negroes and others of us are so nearly interchangeable items in the same labor market that economists, who like their variables reduced somewhat ahead of time, find the problem of discrimination one to their liking. It would be difficult to apply their analysis in South Africa, although I am sure it would be worthwhile to do so. The reason that this kind of analysis is moderately easy appears paradoxical. It may be attributed to the fact that we have gone as far as we have gone from the situation in which race relations were (to repeat Park's phrases) merely geographic, economic, and utilitarian, toward that in which they are moral, social, and political. As the moral, social, and political barriers disappear, so will the Negro and white Americans be able to compete on equal terms in the same markets, on terms in which their racial characteristics are less and less relevant to economic decisions, leaving the bargainer

4. Morton Zeman, "A Quantitative Analysis of White-Nonwhite Income Differentials in the United States" (Ph.D dissertation, University of Chicago, 1955). See also, Gary S. Becker, *The Economics of Discrimination* (University of Chicago Press, 1957).

with only his increasingly expensive "taste for discrimination" as excuse for an irrational choice. The American racial frontier is becoming more and more pervasive. One finds it everywhere, in the school, the hospital, the learned society, the circle of friends. And the more pervasive it becomes, the less it is a racial frontier.

NINETEEN

New Peoples

The Jews are one of the oldest peoples in the world; the Israeli, one of the newest. The Indian people is both old and new in the same senses.

One of the most ancient of living books is a collection of Hebrew folklore, law chronicles, proverbs, poetry and religious exhortation. The Hebrew language and alphabet are old. From time so immemorial that it takes archeologists, aided by physicists with Geiger counters, to reckon it, people of something like Hebrew or Jewish identity have lived in the region where the language and the book grew. Thus are the Jews old.

The Israeli, as a people, are new. Their government is one of the newest in the world. Their constitution, effective law, and their political boundaries are scarcely cooled from the heat in which they were forged. Their population is newly gathered from many parts of the world and is of many cultures and tongues. Even the charter members of the population, the old-time Zionists, are much newer to their country than were the Americans who revolted against England. The country has as strange a mix to blend as had the United States of America in the late nineteenth and early twentieth centuries. What it lacks in size is so much more than made up in the speed and intensity of assimilation that Israeli speak of it as a pressure cooker rather than as a melting pot. While the Hebrew language is old as a symbol and as a medium of religion and lore, it is new in two senses. It is not the native language of most of the adult Israeli, and it is a language consciously revived and in the course of being remodeled to suit modern living and learning. Finally, while there are certain traditional and ceremonial ways of making a Jew of a person or of casting him out of the fold, the tests to determine who is and who is not an Israeli are still being argued over. There are claims and counterclaims concerning who should be loyal

174

to Israel, who should help bear her financial burden, and who should have a voice in her policies.[1]

The Indians are also old; their ancient books are much more numerous than those of the Jews. Their learning is more finely spun and its working out is like a design in fine lace. Their plastic arts—which the Jews eschewed in an over-compulsive reaction to religious art as a symbol of polytheism—are rich; their architecture lives in buildings and cities still existing. Furthermore, they live in their ancient homeland and speak their ancient tongues. They need not be brought back from Diaspora and taught a forgotten language.

Yet, as a political people, the Indians of the Government of India are new. Many Indians scarcely know that they are citizens of a new state. The language of the movement which made an independent people was English; it is not yet clear whether Hindi will be the language of the people. For there are many languages, and already there are movements to redraw the boundaries of some states to correspond to linguistic areas, and to establish some regional tongue as the official language of such states. One such has already been established. The constitution of the new Government of India is British in its essence; but what will be the relation between national law and the rich bodies of religious and local law and custom? If the Indians are a new people, so also are the Pakistanians. Their boundaries, language, and constitution are in an even more uncertain condition.

These examples will suggest what I mean by a new people. A people may be old in culture, literature, language, and art; yet it may be new if age is counted from the time of effective political self-consciousness and unity. The several tribes of the Gold Coast and of Nigeria are old. To the extent that they begin to feel themselves one for the purpose of gaining and maintaining a new political standing at home and in the world, they become a new people. A new people is one only recently or scarcely even yet come to that kind of self-conscious unity in which it is capable of political expression and/or action. I say both *and* and *or* so as not to prejudice the question whether a people capable of political expression is of necessity also ready for political action; or whether, if ready to act to gain new status or even political independence, it is also of necessity capable of administering a political state and an economy. It is at least theoretically possible that a people may have found a common language in which to sing the glories of their past and future without having learned to debate their affairs and go peaceably from debate to effective administration, diplomacy, and defense.

1. I am overlooking neither the ambiguities of the outside world's ascription of the status of Jew to individuals nor the equally great ambivalence which many persons feel about whether they are or want to be Jews.

Now we come to the main question of this paper: What new peoples are arising and will arise in those parts of the world where racial and cultural contacts are most active? It would be almost the same question if put concerning those regions of the earth where colonial governments do now or recently did prevail. Those colonies which have large populations of European origin have already, most of them, become nations with as much political autonomy as they wish. Canadians, Australians, and New Zealanders have become well-established political peoples with relatively minor problems of their relations with indigenous minorities of other races. It is not so with those colonies where the settlers of European race, even though in some places they are numerous and possessed of political power, are greatly outnumbered by indigenous people of other races, as is the case throughout Africa. Where racial and cultural contacts are active, and where the politically subordinate races and ethnic groups are not hopelessly outnumbered, new political peoples are in the making. The coincidence of the processes by which peoples are made with racial and ethnic frontiers is the subject of this discussion.

The main question concerning what new peoples will arise contains and consists of many related questions. What will be the racial, ethnic, religious, and linguistic composition of the effective political peoples of the future in the areas of racial and ethnic contact? Who will unite with whom; and whom will new peoples reject from membership in their bodies social and politic? How homogeneous will the members of new peoples be outwardly, to the eye and to the ear; inwardly, in their sentiments and aspirations? What will be the symbols of their solidarity? What will be their territories and boundaries? How sovereign will they be; with whom and against whom will they ally themselves in the larger struggles of the world? What powers and resources will they have or develop for balancing their sovereignty against that of other peoples and powers?

The most familiar model of a people coming into self-conscious being is that developed in the voluminous literature written during and after the first world war on nationality, European national revivals and movements, and the self-determination of peoples. To be sure, the notion of national revivals had already turned up and been written about before that time, both in connection with the movements for unity of Germany and Italy in the nineteenth century and in connection with the growing self-consciousness and political discontent of the mid-European peoples who were minorities within the three great continental European Empires (German, Austro-Hungarian, Russian) and the Ottoman Empire, with its head in Europe and its body in Asia and Africa. But the great flood of books and articles on the subject of self-determination of peoples came during the war and after.

About the same time came the development of a sense of nationhood in those of the British colonies (new Dominions) which had large populations of permanent settlers of European descent. Two of these, Canada and the Union of South Africa, include large minorities of European background and language other than British. Both of these minorities, the *Canadiens* and the *Afrikaner* — to use their own names for themselves — have long been accustomed to political activity. As responsible self-government took the place of colonial government, both these minorities became especially concerned lest their fellow citizens of British descent and English language infringe upon their rights and cultural self-determination more than the British Colonial Office had done. A distant colonial office may preserve a protecting impartiality against which one's new and close neighbors may chafe. These two minorities became part of the stock of cases discussed by those who were developing a generalized description of the growth of new national peoples. The one of them which I know best, the French-Canadian people, does not appear likely to push for independent sovereignty, although a strain is put upon the unity of Canada in times of war, when the English Canadians are more eager to fight on the side of other British peoples than are the French Canadians (even though France is on the same side), and are inclined to demand a more ardent worship of sacred British symbols than the French can wholeheartedly give. In the Union of South Africa, the relations of the Afrikaner (Boers) and the other white South Africans are hopelessly entangled with the fateful relations of both to the Negro Africans. How far the three elements are from having become a single new people is indicated by the punctiliousness one must observe in referring to them respectively as Afrikaner, South Africans, and Africans. National feeling has also been growing in several regions of Islamic and Arab-speaking North Africa and the Middle East. The movements were directed in some cases and for a time against their Islamic, but not Arab, overlords, the Turks, but eventually turned more and more against the European powers who had rushed in to gather up the fragments of the disintegrating Ottoman Empire. Most of the familiar European literature on nationality movements takes little account of the Islamic peoples of North Africa and the Middle East.[2]

The nationalist movements of the great Eastern peoples, the Chinese and Indian, are well enough covered in the literature, although it is their

2. *L'Afrique du Nord en Marche: Nationalismes Musulmans et souveraineté française,* by C.A. Julien (2nd ed.; Paris: R. Julliard, 1952), covers the developments in Tunisia, Algiers, and Morocco in detail and in historic perspective. The nationalist movement in Iraq has recently been described and analyzed by Hatim Sahib in an unpublished Ph.D. dissertation at the Universtiy of Chicago (1954).

earlier rather than their later phases that have been the more discussed; and the reaction to the race-minded, imperial Europeans has been more studied than the welter of moving racial, linguistic, religious, and national frontiers within Asia itself. It certainly is not yet clear how many Asiatic peoples there will be in the future.

Even a cursory inventory of the cases from which one might get models for comparative analysis of the process of making new peoples must also include the movements for improved status among the many ethnic and racial groups who, voluntarily or involuntarily, have migrated to the New World in the past few centuries and of the indigenous populations of the Americas and the West Indies on whose territory they encroached. The racially mixed Haitian people sought and got independence. Those descendants of the Africans forcibly imported to North America who have not passed into the white race have fought sometimes for symbolic separation—by return to Africa—from other Americans, but have more generally demanded their right, as citizens, to full incorporation into the American people. Central and South America have had many movements, small and large, of native or immigrant groups who have felt deprived and estranged from the prevailing governments, societies, and economies.

Last of all, come the nativistic and other movements among the many smaller peoples who are being "detribalized" at precisely that moment in the world's history when, to quote a phrase from a recent article on Africa, it is also being *de*-colonized. These are the movements which lie closest to the interests of people interested in race relations in world perspective; the strivings of black Africans and of the dark-skinned peoples of the East Indian islands and of Southeast Asia to become new political peoples.

The general model of a national or nationalistic movement has been, as mentioned before, developed upon the basis of European cases. It is to be found in generalized form in a number of works.[3] The features essential to our purpose are the following. Some group of people find themselves under what is to them foreign rule; they may also find themselves separated from

3. See Robert E. Park and Ernest W. Burgess, *Introduction to the Science of Sociology* (Chicago: University of Chicago Press, 1924, 1969) for extensive bibliographies, "Nationalities," p. 659, "Language Revivals and Nationalism," p. 945. Herbert A. Blumer, "Collective Behavior," in A.M. Lee, ed., *Outline of the Principles of Sociology* (New York: Barnes & Noble, 1946). Clarence Glick, "Collective Behavior and Race Relations," *American Sociological Review,* XIII, No.3 (June, 1948), 287-294. Herbert A. Miller, *Races, Nations and Classes* (Philadelphia: J.B. Lippincott, 1924). Arnold van Gennep, *Traité comparatif des Nationalités.* Vol I, *Les éléments exterieurs de la nationalité* (Paris, Payot 1922). I find no record in available libraries of two more volumes which van Gennep listed as in preparation. They were to be called Vol. II, *La formation de la nationalité,* and Vol. III, *La vie des nationalités.* Etienne Fournol, *Les Nations Romantiques* (Paris, Editions des portiques 1931). Erich Voegelin, *Rasse und Staat* (Tübingen, J.C.B. Mohr, 1933). Florian Znaniecki, *Modern Nationalities* (Urbana: University of Illinois Press, 1952). The well-known works of Bryce, Barker, Zimmern, and many others have contributed to the generalized description of nationalities, national peoples, national movements, etc.

others of their own culture and tongue. Through some set of circumstances, some element or elements among these people become discontent with the foreign rule or at least consider that they and their kind suffer disabilities within the body politic, economic, and/or social. The self-consciousness accompanying the discontent may take the form, at the very least, of revival of interest in the history, culture, and language of the group; it may be a revival not merely of interest in these symbols of the separate past, but of their very substance. History may be dug up; half-forgotten literature got back into print and circulation; folk tales and folk songs cultivated and taught to people who had no previous knowledge of them. The discontent may also be expressed in agitation for improvement in the political, social, and/or economic status of the group. The agitation generally has two directions. The one is inward; the discontented seek to get others of their people to share their discontent and to join their movements. The other is outward, an agitation directed at the people and powers who dominate them and who are said to oppress them.

As the movement goes on, its goals are defined and redefined. Leadership may change as the classes of people involved in the movement change and as the general situation is altered. The goal may be at one time defined as recognition within the present body politic. At other times it may be complete political independence or the shifting of political frontiers so as to unite under one sovereignty all or most of the people of a given nationality. The methods also change. In Ireland there was continued harassment of the English authorities; activity of the kind now known as "under-ground" went along with public agitation at home, in England, and abroad (especially in the United States where there was a large population of Irish emigrants). The method might be open armed revolt; guerrilla warfare and raiding (of the Mau Mau kind) may become general, and even formal, warfare. Van Gennep was probably right, however, when he maintained that the minority peoples who got independence in Europe at the end of the first world war got it largely by default. The empires, in which they were encysted and among whom some of the minority peoples had been divided, collapsed just at a time when the winning powers were in a mood to allow self-determination. Although Van Gennep does not mention it, an added favoring circumstance was that these people were largely represented in the population of the United States. A good share of enthusiasm for American participation in the war was based on the desire of immigrant groups to help their people at home to political freedom. They also supplied money for the movements for independence.[4]

4. Helena Znaniecki Lopata, "Polonia: A Study of the Polish American Community" (Ph.D. dissertation, University of Chicago, 1954). Mrs. Lopata found that once Poland had her freedom, the Polish-Americans were much less interested in Poland and in their own organizations. Supporting the Poles in Europe appears to have served the function of making the Poles in America feel they were somebody.

The minorities so freed in Europe, most of them at any rate, had a body of leaders who had taken part in the agitation for national recognition and who could take over as leaders of the newly founded states (although in not all of them was the passage from agitation to the administration of a democratic state either peaceful or outstandingly successful). It is thus apparent that whether the movement of a people to establish a new sovereign state or to otherwise get recognition of what they consider their rights depends on factors other than the strength of the movement and the sense of solidarity of the people concerned. Economic, military, and political factors are involved, and these not merely in the region concerned; the play of such forces in the world at large may influence both the strategy of the movement and its outcome. This is so obviously true of Israel, Egypt, India, Indonesia, and Indo-China, to mention only a few that one need not argue it. The situation in which England found herself in relation to France was not without influence upon the outcome of the American war for independence in the eighteenth century. External circumstances will certainly affect the outcome of the attempts of various new peoples to establish their own governments and to maintain them in our time.

Now I would like to go back to some of the features of the national or nationalistic movements of which we have record, and by putting a certain emphasis on them raise questions concerning the probable developments in Africa, Asia, and the Pacific.

In all of them, as indeed in any case where people have a sense of belonging to a collectivity, there is choice and cultivation of effective symbols of their unity — past, present, and future. The concept of race as a political and national symbol in racial ideologies, rather than as a term used by physical anthropologists, is very much a creation of the national movements of Europe in the nineteenth century. Oddly enough, however, it was developed not by minority peoples but by peoples of great political power. It belongs among the collective symbols used in strengthening national solidarity, and specifically among the great social myths by which people get a conception of themselves as having a common past that sets them off from other people from the beginning of time, gives them peculiar rights now and a special mission for the future. The racial myth, as it occurs in political ideologies, was developed in Europe where observable racial differences are very small as compared with those of the present great racial frontiers. Furthermore, race remains a myth in Europe, in that nowhere there in the past or present — not even in Nazi Germany — were physical characteristics taken as the identifying marks by which an individual was included in or excluded from a people. In Nazi political cartoons and posters, the true German was a tall blond, and the Jew a small dark man. In the concentration camp, the opposite was sometimes true. The physical traits were taken, in the European racial myths, rather as historical symbols associated with certain cultural or spiritual qualities supposedly peculiar to a given people.

Erich Voegelin, in his acute analysis of racial ideology in Europe,[5] quoted Schelling as saying that it takes some sort of psychological crisis to combine people into a group conscious both of its internal unity and of its separation from other people. In such a crisis people may become anxious lest they, as a group, die. In such a case they seize upon some symbol that gives them a sort of eternal life, as a group. Race becomes such a symbol. It seems an entity more eternal than language or dialects, or even religions, which are known to change. Keeping the race pure, in some mystically biological sense, meant ensuring the continued existence of the political, national, and cultural people. But the tests of belonging to the mystical racial body were not biological tests at all. Some might argue that we should limit a discussion of race relations to relations between peoples easily distinguished by physical differences or skin color and other traits of physique or physiognomy. There is something to be said for that view as a way of limiting our field, but I would answer that race as a social myth, as a symbol of unity, must be considered as part of the process with which we are concerned. The myth of race is found far beyond the parts of the world where physical racial characteristics can be and are used as criteria for inclusion in or exclusion from social clubs, voters' lists, and trade unions. One of our questions must be whether and to what extent the new black peoples of Africa, to take the part of the world where race relations in the narrower sense are undoubtedly most acute, will use the myth of racial origin as a symbol of such unity as they may achieve. The Europeans have taken their racial myths to Africa and have developed them further. There, as nowhere else, the racial myths appear supported by the cultural condition of the masses as well as by color. Will the people on either side of the race line drawn in Africa find some new myth that will allow black men, so-called white men, and men who are of both ancestries to belong to new political peoples with some self-conscious sense of a common fate, common rights, and a common mission? If so, what will be these myths that transcend race? Christianity as interpreted and practiced by most colonists of European ancestry will hardly do it, for in both South Africa and the southern states of the United States of America, the dominant Protestant denominations have used Christian dogma as the ideological support of racial separation and of special privilege for white men. And, at least in the southern United States, the Roman Catholic church has until recently gone along with racial segre-

5. *Rasse und Staat, op. cit.* pp. 149 ff.

gation. To be sure, many Christians have used their symbols against racial divisions. Such attacks are numerous and strong in many Christian bodies at present; it remains to be seen how effective they will be. Meanwhile, the Communists work very hard at making their creed transcend all racial and national differences (although they have sometimes capitalized on the aspiration of colonial peoples and national or racial minorities to be independent or to achieve better status).

In the European national movements a great deal was made of language as a proper basis for political unity, and for separation from other peoples. It, like race, was used as a symbol of eternal existence of a people. Fichte claimed for the Germans a special mission in the present and future on the ground that they alone of the Germanic peoples (unlike the French and the English) have kept their original German tongue.[6] They had not kept it free of foreign phrases, however. Many German national leaders from his time until Hitler sought to rid the German tongue of Latin roots and even to banish from the German alphabet the equivocal letter *c*, as the independent consonant where *k* or *z* should be. Such purification of language is a common feature of national movements, or even of periods of enhanced national self-consciousness. The French Canadians are constantly at work to weed out Anglicisms, which are for them the symbol of the ever-present danger of assimilation of their people to the English-speaking world. The Turks, who were trying to make of themselves a Western and secular nation, sought to restore their language to pre-Islamic purity by getting rid of Arabic phrases. The Arabic phrases were reminders that, while the Turks had been political masters of Islam, the inward frame of Islamic civilization was Eastern and Arabic. The Turkish language was somehow evidence that the Turkish people had an existence and a national character prior to conversion to Islam and were therefore entitled to run their affairs without too much influence by Islamic religious leaders.

In these cases, the German, the French Canadian, and the Turkish, the linguistic aspect of the movement had or has nothing whatever to do with finding a medium in which people can communicate with one another. It was purely symbolic.

The few authors whom I have read on the political movements of North Africa do not speak of any movement among the Berbers to substitute their dialects for Arabic as the language of their national aspirations. The Berbers are said to be sensitive on the point of foreign domination, even by Arabs.[7] They are xenophobic and are said generally to regard themselves as more devout Moslems than the more urban Arabs. The Arabs, for their part, have not always disguised their contempt for those more rustic brands

6. *Ibid.*, p. 146.
7. Julien, *op. cit.*, p. 12.

of Berber piety which lack sophisticated faithfulness to the letter of the Prophet's Law. Yet, as I understand the situation, there is, among the great numbers of rural Berbers who are moving into the cities of northwest Africa, no resistance to learning Arabic. This may be because they consider the greater threat to their culture and national identity to come from their European political masters. What prouder symbols could there be of their ancient and honorable past than those of the Arab, Islamic world?

There are some national movements of which it is difficult to say to what extent the emphasis on their own peculiar language serves merely to strengthen their sense of solidarity and to mark off the one people from others, and to what extent there is a problem of finding a common medium of communication. The Zionist movement and the new Israeli people is such a case. Hebrew was certainly not the bread-and-butter language of many of the immigrants to Israel. The movement to make Hebrew the language of the new country is something more than an attempt to find the medium of communication which can be most economically diffused to the polyglot immigrants to the new country.

Another case in which the matter of language is difficult to understand, for outsiders at least, is that of India. Now that the goal of national self-government has been achieved, people of some languages are asking that provincial (or state) boundaries be so altered as to correspond more closely to linguistic frontiers. The Telugu have already got themselves a new state so bounded as to free them from domination by their Tamil-speaking fellow citizens.[8] Since many of the existing provincial or state boundaries were set by the British, it is but natural that there should be movements to make them correspond more closely to ethnic and linguistic realities. On the other hand, language and ethnic boundaries are seldom so near and narrow and the linguistic territories seldom of such shape and geographic composition as to make good administrative and economic units. It may be these movements for linguistic states are no threat to India's basic unity, although they obviously will hamper any movement to make any one or two languages prevail in the new nation. India, of course, has many other symbols of her ancient cultural unity.

Some observers believe that these ancient elements of common culture, and an earnest desire to maintain political unity will outweigh the linguistic divisions. Another view of the matter is that the present generation of political leaders, brought up in the Congress movement, of broad English education, and possessed of a certain world-mindedness, will be succeeded by locally bred and provincially minded politicians who will have less of a vision of all India and its place in the world. The older leaders, some say,

8. This movement is said to have a racial tinge. The Telugu insist that in blood, as in language, they are descended not merely from the Dravidians, but also from the Aryans.

are still marginal men, not close to the masses of India. Their very success in increasing the proportion of Indians who are interested in politics may bring a new kind of man to power, men more concerned about the local vote, and hence more inclined to foster local aspects of the Indian heritage than were Gandhi or Nehru. I do not know to what extent the movements for new linguistic states are prompted by a desire to get better communication in government and other affairs of the states of India, as against the wish of various groups of Indians to acquire a new pride and a new status by emphasizing their historic differences from people of other Indian languages, sub-cultures, and even races.

It may be that we of European tradition overemphasize the importance of a single language as a condition of the feeling of being one people. We know that Canada, Belgium, and South Africa (the South Africans of European ancestry) get along with two linguistic groups which are in some conflict over the roles of their respective languages.[9] Yet we generally suppose that knowledge of a common language by most of the people of a country is necessary to national unity of sentiment as well as to operation of a modern economy. This may turn out not to be true in all parts of the world. On the other hand, great increase in literacy generally reduces the variety of speech. To just what point the reduction will go in the newly literate peoples remains to be seen.

I suppose the problem in Africa beyond the Sahara will be that of choosing the language or languages in which literacy will be spread, although there is not much choice other than the European languages of the colonizing countries. South Africa, it is reported, is attempting to reduce the spread of English and Afrikaans literacy by encouraging schools in native languages. Whatever the motive for this, I think most students will agree that it will have no great long-run success. Nevertheless, one can imagine a good deal of ambivalence over the matter of language in Africa. I have lately had a letter from a native in West Africa, a man of university training in two countries, who asks wistfully whether there is no solution except to take to European language and European clothing in order to have literacy and progress at all.

The problems raised here are the ones which Kenneth Little presents so well in his paper. The dilemma is that of the strength of language as a symbol of tradition, as something that gives one a social identity, as against languages as a means of communication in a new, larger, and technologically complicated world. The languages of tradition, in which senti-

9. In South Africa and Belgium what were once the minority languages (Afrikaans and Flemish) appear to be becoming languages of the majority and may soon be the languages of the politically dominant group. In both cases the language coming to ascendency is a local, rather than a world, language. What effect this will have on South Africans of English speech and descent and on the French-speaking Walloons of Belgium remains to be seen.

ments may be aroused, may not be those in which the newer communication can be carried on. If there are to be large political peoples of native Africans, they will have to face this dilemma of language. In addition, there are problems which arise as in India from the fact that the European powers made no attempt to make the boundaries of their African colonies correspond to those of language and tribe.

One might follow out in much the same manner as I have done for race and language, the whole problem of territory and boundaries. In the European national movements a great deal was and is made of the notion of the historic territory. People, language, and territory are considered to belong together; and claims are made concerning natural and historic boundaries and original possession of territories. These are countered by other claims.

As van Gennep has so well shown in his chapters on territorial frontiers, none of the theories concerning natural boundaries between languages and peoples hold up against the facts of migration, changes of language, and the shifting of political boundaries. Boundaries are where they are because of many past events, including dynastic changes and wars, as well as migrations. Whether nations are content with them apparently depends on a good many things. The boundary between the United States and Canada is a fairly new one; and both sides are now relatively content with it. They were not always so. I imagine a great deal of emotion would be aroused if either nation were now to propose a minor alteration. The boundary has already become a sacred thing. How this is and will be in Africa is a matter for discussion and prediction. The Afrikaner certainly have the notion that they live on ground that is theirs by battle and already ancient right. There are territories outside the Union which they think they should control, not by this same ancient right, but as part of the larger strategy of their policy toward the native peoples. One can imagine this strategy opposed both by people of European ancestry in the other African territories and by natives.

To what extent natives of Nigeria or the Gold Coast consider the present boundaries of their territories good ones, I do not know. They may at least consider that they have some vested interest in them, both politically and economically. But would they defend them, and could those natives who do value the boundaries as they are muster much feeling for them among the masses of the people? We certainly cannot expect that native populations will enthusiastically support boundaries established by European conquest and diplomacy and which are now used as barriers to free movement to the places where their jobs are, even though those places are centers of discrimination and exploitation. People in search of a living are not particular about boundaries set by other breeds of men for their own purposes.

Territory involves also the question of the actual tenure of land for cultivation. Where tenure is involved people may be aroused to wild and desperate action. There is scarcely a part of the world where the moving of cultural and racial aliens onto the land has not stirred people to riots, destruction, and revolt. Kenya is but one of the many in the long history of racial and cultural contacts. It takes less political sophistication to be stirred by alien tenure of farm land than to get concerned about a detail of the placing of an international frontier. As with reference to the other matters I have had the temerity to talk of, on this one of territory I again merely ask for discussion of the problem.

To carry out to the bitter end comparison of European national movements with the things which are happening and may happen in those parts of the world where the new peoples are destined to arise, we must speak of literature and art. In the European movements, and in others also, the restoration of old literature and art has been part of the stirring up of national self-consciousness. Fournol has given the classic statement of this process in his work, *Les Nations Romantiques,* where he describes the role of the German folklore movement in the movement for a united and powerful German state. For folklore is a kind of *proto*-literature. A Germany that had been divided for centuries could and did find a symbolic unity in a common body of lore which antedated all existing political units. The minority peoples of middle Europe followed suit.

To be sure, the folklore movement eventually spread over most of the world. Its political function, however, is greatest among those peoples who are in a crisis of identity and political status. In Canada, it is the French who cultivate folklore the more assiduously, who have chairs of folklore in their universities, and who see to it that the children in school and the common people gathering in the parish hall sing the old songs and hear the old tales.

Generally, the folklore symbolizes an era in which the people, now in danger and in too much contact with others, were alone and showed their traditional culture in a more pure form. The heroes of lore are thought to have possessed the true virtues, the virtues that distinguish this people from others. The true German of folklore was unspoiled by foreign influences, whether Roman or Jewish. He was set up as a model for the new, restored, true German. Something like this is happening in the Zionist movement, too, where a hardy, sometimes belligerent, athletic Jewish youth is set up both as the original and as the true model for the future.

As the people of Africa and other parts of the world take form, what will be the parts of their past which they will attempt to restore? What will be the virtues extolled as the original ones of their own past and the desired ones for their future? The function of the symbolic past is in fact to presage and set the model for the future. This has been obviously so in many small nativistic movements, although in some of them the sacred past is taken as ground for bitter, hopeless resistance to changes brought by strangers. In others, certain features of the past are used to rally the people for change and for triumph through change. A third possibility is that of taking some of the symbols of the invading or dominant peoples and blending them in some way with the symbolic past. This appears to have occurred many times in the half-sectarian, half-nativistic movements of Berber tribes. It has happened among American Indians. It appears also in the quasi-Christian native religious movements described by Balandier and Sundkler.[10] How powerful such blending of Christian symbols of equality with racial symbols will be among recently urbanized and detribalized Africans is another of those questions which I hope will be discussed. At least such movements offer an alternative to revivals of purely tribal lore and heroes; perhaps they can move a greater variety of people to some sense of common fate than could any purely tribal revival. They give people a bigger past, including more people, and also a greater, more expansive symbolic future.

As a people develops its symbolic past, its present strategy, and its claims for the future, there appears in its talk an implicit, and perhaps an explicit, time perspective. As Voegelin shows, Fichte made the symbolic time of the German people like the Logos, which was in the beginning, is now, and ever shall be. The earlier gospels were content to give Jesus a genealogy from David, long but historical and finite. John made his time transcendent and infinite, a timeless time. There appears to be a tendency for people to like the groups with which they identify themselves most deeply to be so enduring as to be eternal; that is, timeless.

But there appears another kind of time perspective[11] in movements for

10. Georges Balandier, "Messianismes et Nationalismes en Afrique Noire," *Cabiers Internationaux de Sociologie,* XIV (1953); Bengt G.M. Sundkler, *Bantu Prophets in South Africa* (London, Oxford University Press, 1948).

11. Pars Ram and Gardner Murphy, "Recent Investigations of Hindu Muslim Relations in India," *Human Organization,* XI, No 2 (Summer, 1952), 13-16:

"Especially significant is what Kurt Lewin used to call 'time perspective.' For the Hindu, events are sketched on an infinite canvas of time; for the Muslim history is dynamic and even explosive. Important things are occurring at this instant. Without a single clear exception to the present time, when a Hindu in Aligarah is asked: 'What is the most recent example of communal trouble?' he embarks upon a broad historical sketch of Hindu-Muslim relationships down to events of a year or so prior to the interview. 'It seems to me,' he says, 'that there was a scuffle in the streets and somebody was killed ten or twelve months ago,' or, 'I think I remember some Muslims leaving at night for Pakistan. That must have been a year ago.' Ask any Muslim the same question—and no exception has yet been found among those interrogated—and he tells you of events of a week or two ago, events still burning deeply within him: 'Why last week three men learned that their shops were to be looted and they left for Pakistan at once,' or, 'This very day my children came home from school crying, saying that Hindu children had taunted them.' In the same way, for the Hindu the future is a vast open change; time as patience or impatience. The radical is the person who wants change now; the conservative, the sensible, reasonable fellow is the one who can wait. Perhaps there is a special time for underdogs and another for top dogs.

In the United States, white men used to say that it took them thousands of years to rise to their present civilized state; it would therefore take Negroes a long time to equal them. *Ergo,* there is no hurry about removing the disabilities of Negroes. The Negro, it was and is said, is not ready. But under the pressure of change, a new apology is given for delay; it has now become the white man who is not ready. He must be allowed time to get used to the idea of having a Negro beside him in school, restaurant, or bus. In a recent conversation with a southern white man who hoped the Supreme Court "would not disrupt progress" in the South by making a decision against segregated schools, he said that in twenty-five or fifty years the South might be ready, but not now. I asked him who weren't ready, the Negroes of the South or the whites of the South. He replied sharply (in an otherwise friendly conversation about his own outstanding role in improving Negro schools) that the whites are the South. He implied, and in good faith, that the sentiments about race are so deep that people will have to get used in advance to the idea that things will not always be as their own sentiments decree.[12]

A similar case of implicit time turns up in conversation with people from

---

space, for the Muslim a sharply structured region wherein that which is closest is most vivid. Ask any Hindu, 'If you had the power what would you do to stop the communal troubles?' and you would get this sort of reply, 'Well, we've had these troubles a long, long time, and it will be a long, long time before we get rid of them.' Ask any Muslim what he would do to stop the difficulties and he replies, 'The police can stop them tomorrow if he wants to.'

"Two hypotheses immediately suggest themselves. The first hypothesis is that this difference in time perspective is due to the unstructured nature of time in Hindu culture compared with the highly structured nature in Islamic culture. If this hypothesis is true, we shall find similar responses among Hindus outside of India, notably among those few who are still living in Pakistan. We shall find these same responses characteristic also of a later period of interrogation when the present crisis is past. Similarly, we should get the same responses from Muslims in Pakistan, or indeed in Iran, Jordan or Egypt. The second hypothesis is that the difference in time perspective is a characteristic difference between majority and minority groups or between secure and insecure people. From this point of view the secure need not remember crisis incidents nor need they be concerned with the immediacy of their removal. The insecure, subject to continuous threat, must take note of all that threatens them, and recent past and immediate future must be sharply defined."

12. A few days after I wrote this, the United States Supreme Court decided that segregation in public education "is a denial of the equal protection of the laws," hence unconstitutional. But it allows a breathing spell. Several questions concerning application of the ruling are to be argued before the Court again. One of the questions to be so argued next year is, "May this court, in exercise of its equity powers, permit an effective gradual adjustment to be brought about from existing segregated systems to a system not based on color distinction?" *(New York Times,* May 18, 1954.) A great deal of the newspaper discussion of the decision turned upon the timetable of enforcement.

the Union of South Africa. It has happened to me several times in recent years that South Africans have talked about the great long-run economic future of their country, of its vast quantities of uranium and other valuable earths and ores. But when one asks them for a prediction of what the racial situation will be in twenty years, they bridle. The future which looks so attractive in one respect may be feared when seen from another side.[13]

So much for the symbolic time of individual and collective psychology; what of time as measured by changes of the various kinds involved in race relations and in social movements? And what of the consciously tactical and strategic time of the people pressing for change or resisting it? Certainly we should by this time be aware that industrialization of a country can be much more precipitate in our age than in the time when England and her neighbors made their own industrial revolution. We should be skeptical of any notions of either the sequence or the rate of social and political changes based upon the slow-moving models of the countries who had to invent and make their machines as they went. I should like to hear the members of the Conference discuss the problem of time and of timing in the social, economic, and political events and changes of the various racial frontiers of the world.

I have left until last what is perhaps the most crucial question of all in the formation of new peoples, that of the classes of people who form them. As Julien describes the nationalist movements of Morocco, Algiers, and Tunisia, one becomes aware that the social structures of these three countries are quite unlike. The bearers of nationalism are not the same kinds of people in all. It sometimes happens that those who feel most anger against foreigners are also alienated from the masses of their own people. I gather that something like this is true in Iraq, where the so-called nationalists are of an economically powerful class and are also of another Islamic sect than the masses of the people. In Algiers, Julien and other observers speak of a class of young men who thought they could become Frenchmen and could lead their people in that direction; when they come home from Paris they find the local French colonists want none of them, and that they know too

---

13. In the discussions at Honolulu, Mr. Olivier of the South African Bureau of Racial Affairs turned this completely about. In effect, he recognized that complete Apartheid is impossible in the near future, but thought that it might be accomplished in twenty-five or fifty years. It would be interesting, indeed, if the Apartheid of the Malan Nationalists were to become a symbolic thing, an ideal for some distant time, a sort of Second Coming, instead of a political program for the immediate future. One ordinarily thinks of this as the fate of great things greatly desired, not of unworthy goals. Perhaps some Afrikaan Nationalists do regard Apartheid as some great thing, to be attained by pure men above wanting the cheap labor of Africans or the custom of the African with a shilling, perhaps even a pound, in his pocket. It does seem an odd moment in world history for anyone to expect racial inequalities to be restored by eschatological catastrophes.

little of their own people and language to be acceptable leaders of the nationalist movement.

There are many changes rung on these themes in parts of the world where racial and cultural contacts are changing the shape of societies. Who can successfully speak for whom? What rivals are there for leadership? What are the relations between the classes of people who traditionally had prestige and power and those possessed of new kinds of learning and of new techniques? What are the kinds and numbers of uprooted people and what are their relations to those still close to traditional ways of living? These questions come to the fore in other papers in this series.

In the United States, it has been remarked that colleagueship is often more important than race, when the two run counter to each other. Entry of a Negro into the nursing staff of a hospital may be strongly resisted by the white nurses; but once she is there, these same white nurses will fight to have her treated as a nurse should be treated. It is possible that colleagueship in learned and technical professions, and even in trades or in common industrial jobs (where such exist) can draw people together in an operating social structure across racial and ethnic lines. To what extent is this happening in Africa and the East? And what influence will it have on the formation of new political peoples?

Whatever the answers to those questions, it appears certain that both the composition and the fate of any people will depend upon the distribution of its members among the various occupations and positions in its economy and its political body. And race has in almost all countries of the world appeared as a factor in their distribution, whether because of differences of training and background or because those with power to determine the distribution favored one race over another. It may, in fact, be that the distribution of literacy, land, and jobs will be more important in determining the growth of new political peoples than any of the things I have discussed. On the other hand, collective unrest, agitation, struggles for status, the efforts to define self, friend, and foe in symbolic terms will go on but the more actively as people attempt to change these distributions of learning, skills, land, and jobs. Our problem is to describe and, if possible, to forecast how the resulting lines that divide people politically and the bonds that hold them together will relate to the lines of race and ethnic origin.[14]

14. After I had written and revised this paper I remembered my debt to Karl Rothenbü-cher's little book, *Uber das Wesen des Geschichtlichens und die gesellschaftliche Gebilde* (Tübingen, J.C.B. Mohr 1926). In it the author makes a distinction between old and new nations very like the one I have made here. The old peoples are old in the sense in which I have said that India is old; but the new peoples are, for Rothenbücher, simply those peoples of the East or those preliterate tribes which are suddenly transformed by European impact. He says nothing of the processes by which they are regrouped or otherwise made into active, self-conscious unities.

TWENTY

A Sociologist's View

The Undiplomatic Relationship

On January 11, 1964, some fifty Canadians are reported to have marched in front of the United States Consulate in Montreal to protest rough treatment of other protesting marchers by the police in the state of Georgia. The picketing of a United States office by Canadians is relatively new, but the lack of diplomacy it expresses is as old as the two countries.

The relations of the people of the Government (formerly Dominion) of Canada and the United States of America have been as notoriously undiplomatic as they have been, in a formal military sense, peaceful. That, indeed, seemed to me one of the chief findings of the study of Canadian-American relations made under the auspices of The Carnegie Endowment for International Peace in the 1930's. As I put it in a review of four volumes resulting from that study, "[The relations] have been exceedingly undiplomatic, for the contact is so close that almost any citizen of either country is ready to venture an opinion upon the affairs of the other;" I see no reason to change the statement now, except to make it stronger and to go into detail. In doing so, I shall state facts known to many Canadians and Americans, but to a larger proportion of Canadians than Americans, for one of the findings of nearly all studies of Canadian-American relations is that a Canadian is more apt to know the States well than an American is to know Canada well. Thus, an American writing to Americans about Canada may appear to Canadians to be writing for ignoramuses; he is also likely to display his own ignorance at some point. No American should ever write

The United States and Canada (ed. John Sloan Dickey). Published for the American Assembly by Prentice-Hall, Inc., Englewood Cliffs, New Jersey, 1964.

about Canada, just as no English Canadian should write about French
Canada; not if he wants to come out with a whole hide. The underdog has
always the sharper tongue; lacking other weapons, he needs it.

HOW DIFFERENT, HOW ALIKE?

At the risk of being both obvious to Canadians, and condescending to
Americans, let me go into some detail on how our countries, and the
relations between them, differ from those of the classical diplomatic type.
We are close to each other; how close? We are alike in language and
culture. How much alike, and what is the significance of both likeness and
differences? We are both new peoples and new states. How new, and to
what extent do the people of each country accept the eternal existence of
the other? Our boundary seems political, not cultural; is it? We are obviously not equal; Canada has the larger territory and heaven knows what
hidden resources under her ice and snow; we have a ten-times larger
population, more capital, bigger military establishments, and consequently
greater international responsibilities.

Suppose we start with closeness. Two of the longest international
boundaries in the world join the United States with the other two large
countries of North America. The Mexico-United States boundary, more
than 2,000 miles long, makes those countries very close indeed to each
other. The penetrations of culture, people, goods, and capital across that
border are, and always have been, massive and fateful. Mexico has boundaries to her south, but taken alone or together, they are as nothing in social,
economic, and political importance compared to her United States boundary. The Canadian-United States boundary is even longer. It is Canada's
only boundary, although polar air navigation is giving her a new border
with the Soviet Union, made more tangible by the Dew-line: for the first
time Canada is physically between the United States and another country.
The effect is not so much to make her close to Russia as to make her
proximity to the United States more acute.

Both these long boundaries, although not among those being actively
questioned at present, are the result of wars, declared and not declared,
and of long conflict between people pushing on beyond "the border"—the
border, that is, in the peculiar North American sense of the edge of
settlement. The settlers of North America paid little attention to frontiers
agreed to by treaty. As Frederick Merk shows in *Manifest Destiny and
Mission in America,* the United States in effect recognized no boundaries
on this continent for a long time; it was all ours to occupy, to civilize and to
prosper in. Having pushed the Mexican border back to its present place
(deep in what had long been Mexico), we lost our taste for "continen-
talism" in that direction, perhaps because we were now sure of our Pacific

front and also perhaps because we had, as Merk says, "a national reluctance to add peoples of mixed blood to a blood that was pure, and an
unwillingness in some parts of the population to have unfree blood added
as well."

The Canadians, being of European origin and, outside Quebec, Protestant, seemed fit candidates for the blessings of our kind of democracy. We
are always a bit astonished that Canadians do not want to be United States
Americans. We did not quickly give up the notion of including the northern
and northwestern portion of the continent within our boundaries.

Border Migrations and Intermingling

But the fixing of the boundary had little to do with actual migration. As
Canadians and Americans moved west, they paid slight attention to boundaries. As students of migration have shown, more people make short
moves than long. The Jenks, Cushings, Haights, and many others pushed
across the uncertain boundary from Vermont and New Hampshire into the
Eastern Townships of Quebec. The Painchauds moved down over the
Quebec boundary back of the Adirondacks; one can follow them today as
the name on the rural mailboxes changes letter by letter, until it becomes
Pinchot in the neighborhood of Tupper Lake, a lumber town of the kind to
which French Canadians gravitate in Maine, New York, upper Michigan,
Oregon, Washington—and British Columbia. The French Canadians have
never been border minded. A Catholic bishop of Burlington, Vermont,
estimated at 500,000 the number of French Canadians in the United States
in 1869. Whether he was right or not, the number of residents of that
extraction was certainly much beyond a million in 1900. Being sensitized
to French-Canadian surnames, I see them in pure or modified form pretty
well wherever I go in the United States. Indeed, I think it likely that there
are more people of French descent in the United States than in Canada.

The emigration of great numbers of rural people was, I believe, the chief
reason why French Canada remained relatively unchanged as long as it
did. Now that the French have swarmed to their own cities, in such
number as to become more urban in residence, though perhaps not in
mentality, than other Canadians, they are clamoring for change in their
educational system, their constitutional arrangements, and, to some extent,
the traditional leadership of their clergy. In Canada they remain an ethnic
minority with a strong home base; in the United States they become
assimilated, as do immigrants.

Meantime Pennsylvania Dutch (Germans), on their way west, got over
into Ontario and founded Berlin, which became Kitchener in World War I.
Assorted Americans, some of them not long from Scandinavia, moved

north into the Prairie Provinces when that part of the country was being settled. Some of my great-uncles and uncles went to the Dakotas; one of them, during his brief career of cow-punching, got over the line. He brought back a pretty, blue-eyed, black-haired bride, an Ontario Irish Protestant girl who had gone west. Her adventures turned into the rearing of a large family of children in rural Ohio. For if people went west, many came back — on one side or another of the border. The night boat of sentimental memory brought Maritime girls to be maids in Boston houses and young men to work in the factories or go to Harvard and become famous professors, doctors, businessmen, or just common men.

Along all that long boundary short-distance movements have confused whatever tendency the border may have had to become an ethnic or linguistic frontier. Even if those who crossed stayed on the other side of the boundary from where they were born, they generally did not consider themselves emigrants and were not considered immigrants by their neighbors. In fact Americans who live in Canada are notorious for acting exactly as if they were at home, for not becoming naturalized, and even for taking it for granted that their children will remain American. Yet Raymond Bréton, a Canadian sociologist, recently found that while immigrants from most countries form societies of their own in Montreal, Americans do not. They simply join the Canadian organizations. Some years ago there were 50,000 people of Canadian birth in Chicago; it was difficult to keep a Canadian Club going. It had to be revived periodically. Neither Canadians nor Americans act like immigrants when they cross the line. Trains, planes, and cars take people across the border in greater number than ever — in the normal course of business or pleasure, to visit relatives and friends, to go to weddings (sometimes their own), to attend universities, or to take new jobs.

Along this border there is intermingling scarcely to be found along any other. It seems a boundary that is stable and will not be moved. Yet during much of the history of the two countries there has been pressure on the boundary from one side or the other. Since Canada became a political entity, the pressure has been from the United States side. To Canadians, who feel pushed, the United States must seem very close indeed. Apart from that feeling, Canadians are indeed closer to Americans than Americans are to Canadians.

A Border People

There are approximately ten Americans for every Canadian: about 190,000,000 to 19,000,000. The proportion has remained about the same for many decades. Drop them all on a flat plane and each Canadian will fall closer to the nearest American than will each American to the nearest Canadian, several times over. But we aren't distributed by chance. When at home, the average Canadian appears to live about 50 miles from the endless border. The average American lives hundreds of miles from it. One-fifth of all Canadians live in Montreal and Toronto, which are almost on the border; add Vancouver, Winnipeg, Windsor and Hamilton—all close to the border—and one has caught over 5,000,000 of the Canadians—between one-third and one-quarter of all of them.

In Canada as in the United States, rural population is an ever smaller part of the total; only about 11 per cent of Canadians live on farms. Growth is in the cities; most of the cities are close to the border. But even the rural population hugs the border. Canada's open frontier is to the north rather than to the west. It is a chronic frontier; preaching and subsidies have failed to shift the rural population much to the north where they would be safe from baneful urban (American) influence.

Industry, especially the exploiting of ores and earths in demand in these nuclear times, takes people and activity northward; but it takes more machinery rather than people, for machinery does the work. All in all, the Canadians are probably moving closer to the border; Americans probably are not. Florida, Texas, and California, the great American population magnets, take people—some of them Canadians—farther than ever in physical distance from that peaceful border.

Canadians are the greatest telephoners on earth, with their more than 600 calls per person per year. Americans are not far behind. The people of both countries have cars, radios, and television sets in similar proportion. I should think them likely to travel about the same distances from home. If all Canadian territory were easy to travel over, a Canadian could travel further and stay in his own country than any other car-owning national. In fact, it is the American who can and does travel farthest in his own country. The same considerations that make the Canadian live close to the border make the lines of travel run close to it. A look at any Canadian map shows that travel routes not merely run close to the border, but are inclined to dip over into the United States. Only in 1962 was the Trans-Canada highway complete. The odds are greatly in favor of the Canadian visiting United States. Since there are ten times as many Americans as Canadians, it is many times more likely that a Canadian will take an American spouse, have American friends and associates. Mass and distance, in the absence of language barriers and with only a mildly troublesome passing of the border, conspire to make the Canadian closer to Americans as measured by contacts.

Another asymmetry of closeness and difference of size may be called the "headquarters" effect. These two countries are highly industrial, and have high standards of living. Both production and distribution are organized into a large-scale system of institutions. Given the tendency to large-scale organization one would expect the dominant centers to be in the larger part of the two-country system. And so they are, not only in the control and financing of industry and advertising, but in fashion, communications, the arts, learning and science, the professions, unions, and probably the rackets.

Learning and Science

The same wave of growth of higher education is sweeping over both countries as the birth cohort of the war and postwar years comes of age and as the technological revolution reduces the demand for people of little education and increases the demand for technical training, and scientific and humane learning. The 129,000 full-time students in Canadian institutions of higher learning in 1961 were 65 per cent more than the enrollment of 1956; the estimate for 1970 is about 312,000. As in so many things, Canada falls somewhere between the United States and Britain in the proportion of her youth who go on to higher studies. The increase in enrollment is accompanied by expansion of existing institutions and by an increase in the number of colleges, universities, and post-high school vocational and technical schools. The greatest increase seems to be in Ontario, the most populous province, where there are already a number of new universities and some new colleges attached to existing universities; a total of nineteen institutions, I am told, in which one may work for a degree. This represents in part a movement of higher education out to the smaller cities and to the northern industrial towns; in part an elevation of technical and teachers' colleges to university status. A similar increase occurring in the Western provinces is so rapid that the new institutions must seek staff in the larger United States market.

Although differences between the educational systems make it hard to compare the French universities and classical colleges with the English, it is clear that there is a great expansion in higher education in French Canada as well, but that the proportion of French young people in universities is far below that of English. The new nationalists call for making French-Canadian institutions the equal of English ones in preparing people for positions of leadership in the new industrial era. A recent article in a French paper estimates that to equal the United States, French-Canadian universities would have to multiply by eight the number of doctorates given per annum.

Canadian institutions of higher learning have had more uniform standards of admission and graduation than American ones; the standards have been good, if sometimes stodgy. Some academic people fear that the great increase of students and institutions will lower standards. I think this unlikely, for the power to grant degrees is much more closely controlled than in the United States.

Although there has been a great expansion of graduate enrollment in Canada (118 per cent from 1956 to 1961), it is still relatively small compared to that in the United States. A large but unknown number of Canadians pursue graduate studies in the United States; surveys indicate that about two thirds of them take employment in Canada. The dependence of Canada on American graduate schools and research establishments is a matter of much concern in Canada. An editorial in *Le Devoir,* a leading Montreal daily, asks whether Canadians are not colonials in the matter of scientific research, since a good part of the medical research done in Canada is supported by the United States National Institutes of Health. The United States spends several times over as much for medical research per capita – and remember there are ten times as many American capita.

The editorial writer goes on to say that French Canada is even poorer in its research establishment. He might have noted the analogy with the South, where – until Texas bloomed with the black roses of oil – there were not many great fortunes and where the colleges ran to religion, letters, and law, rather than to science. Canadians who have made fortunes are great enough givers, and for the same kinds of things – universities, hospitals, churches, charities. But there are not so many Canadian fortunes; and as for great French-Canadian fortunes, is there one? The larger American foundations usually offer their grants and fellowships to Americans and Canadians, treating America north of the Rio Grande as a unit. No Canadian foundation has yet become known as a continental giver of scientific support; as far as I know, only one offers its grants on the southern side of the border.

One should note, however, that in Canada the government has long supported education, science, and the arts in a more forthright way than does the United States government. The National Research Council, the Film Board, the Canadian Broadcasting Company, and the Canada Council are government agencies which support and encourage a broad range of activities. Canadians seem not to have to think up devious reasons for such support as Americans do. Much of the liveliness of musical composition and performance, ballet and theater and the documentary movie in Canada has been due to this continuous support, given without any nonsense about making Canadians fit to fight communism.

The Common Market for Talent

In the upper-middle range, the Canadian is probably on the average better read and more sophisticated in the arts and in international affairs than his

American counterpart. Yet the finer edge of sophistication is to be found in certain centers in the United States. Certainly the headquarters in art, science, learning, is apt to lie on the southern side of the border; and the eye gets fixed on the main stage, the big tent. "We [French-Canadians] see our best men go to the English-Canadian institutions who lose theirs in turn to the Americans." How many times have I read that allegation (which was stated in a paper of January 4, 1964) in newspapers, magazines, and books and heard it in Canadian sermons, lectures, and political speeches, French and English, in the more than thirty years of my contact with Canada! It is often accompanied by complaint that the Americans have more money and buy off the talented Canadians. That is probably not the correct statement of the case. The range of positions and of incomes is probably greater in the United States; the headquarters in many lines is south of the border. The concentrations of activity are larger and absorb more people.

It is a characteristic of the industrial, urban world—perhaps more true of the United States and Canada than of any other countries—that it is a world of professionals: professional managers, engineers, accountants, scholars, scientists, doctors, lawyers, and the others, old and new. The new professionals tend to be itinerant, to get up in the world by moving about from one place of work to another. In industry and business, the tendency is to be moved about within the same large company, which has plants or offices in many places. In the academic world, the system includes many institutions, independent of one another yet in close communication. Professors get ahead by moving about, as well as by going up through the academic ranks. So do scientists, and even physicians in those specialties which are practiced in large clinics, hospitals and laboratories. Every profession or line of work has its orbits; a man may move in a small one or a large one. In the newer sort of profession, involving work in organizations and promotion by moving around, the leading orbits pay little attention to the border between the United States and Canada, except when the United States government gets worried about "security" and stops the American with a secret from leaving or a suspect Canadian from coming in.

At a given point in a man's career, the next step may often be made quicker in the larger continental market than in the smaller Canadian one. It happened to me both ways. When I was ready to take an academic post, McGill University in Canada was clearly one of the better things going for a new Ph.D. in sociology. When Chicago offered me a very modest salary eleven years later, McGill was quite willing to let me go rather than raise the ante. I'm afraid crossing the border was the least of my thoughts in either move; I suspect it is more so, but hardly an over-riding consideration, for Canadians in the same box. A Canadian, however, is more likely to be in that fix than is an American, for the reasons already given. An actor, athlete, scholar, scientist may cross the line simply to keep in a job, or to go to the top. An author may stay at home, but publish in New York.

It is hard to speak of this phenomenon without getting into very hot water, for one appears to be judging quality. It is not that. The headquarters institutions usually have exaggerated opinions about their monopoly of quality. We all know the professor who made his name in some midwestern state university, or a Canadian one, but grew his paunch in New England. We are speaking of systems of institutions, with a common market for personnel of certain kinds. Some are nearer the apex in reputation, money, and power than are others. That apex, in factors involving both countries, is more likely to be in the United States even though average quality may be better in Canada and the lowest of the low may be in the United States. Given the very great similarity of our cultures and institutions, a common market for talent is inevitable. Given the disparities of size and distance, the movement is bound to be more in one direction than in the other. It is also bound to be a matter of greater concern to Canadians; it is one of the things which gives Canadians, in some measure, a sense of being a minority. The poor French Canadians are a minority within a minority (and a very good thing for this great agglomeration of car-driving, telephoning, TV-baseball-football-movie-watching, do-it-yourself English-speaking North Americans to have in their midst).

Whether a Canadian professional man (including the itinerant professional business executive) actually crosses the line for a job or not, he will have connections over the line. He will belong to trade associations, scientific, professional, or learned societies. Very likely if he is, say, a hospital administrator, he will belong to a provincial or country-wide Canadian organization (if there isn't one for hospital administrators in most provinces, a French one, and one for all of Canada, there soon will be). If he moves in a larger orbit, he will also belong to a larger association, probably called American, which has its headquarters in the United States and generally meets in the United States. The American of the same profession will belong to a state, perhaps a regional, and certainly the "American" association. If the Canadian is the publishing kind of man, he will sometimes publish in the Canadian organ of his trade; but sometimes, unless his specialty is distinctly Canadian, he will seek to have his work published in the "American" journal, with a continental circulation. I find that the articles which I have published in Canadian journals are less known to my American colleagues than those which appeared in American periodicals. My Canadian colleagues, who live in the "Provinces," know both their own journals and those of the larger world.

Let me hasten to put the record straight on Canadian science and scholarship. Canadian scholars and scientists have their own problems to work upon and have always worked upon them. As in the United States, private institutions of higher learning were established early in the East; as one goes west, provincial (state) institutions predominate. The chronology of settlement and of establishment of institutions of learning is about the same except that when one gets west of Ontario it is generally later in Canada. Scholars and scientists who work on peculiarly Canadian matter tend to stay in Canada. A considerable portion of those who work on more universal matter start and finish their careers in Canada as well. There is a lively itinerancy in all professions within Canada itself, and there are many scholarly journals of quality. Canadian learned societies meet in the charm and informality of their university campuses, not as in the United States in great hotels. I go to the Canadian Political Science Association meetings not merely to see friends, but also to refresh my memory of what sociological meetings used to be like in the United States (when we were fewer and poorer).

The Myopia of Ethnocentrism

This is the point at which to say something about Canada and the United Sates in general. A feature of ethnocentrism in a large country is that its people find it hard to understand that a much smaller country is just as mature, viable, well-established, and distinct as the larger. Add to this the relatively small overt differences of culture and language, and one gets a situation in which the larger is inclined to assume that the smaller is an accident which will soon fade away. English Canadians seem to assume that French Canada will go away, that it won't always be French. Americans seem to imply, by many words and deeds, that Canada will not always be Canada. Every people likes to believe itself eternal. Neither kind of Canadian, nor the American, can pretend that their people existed, as a distinct group, from the beginning of time. But we can argue about who got here first. The French Canadians can do pretty well on that argument, speaking as a "national" group. The United States can do better than English Canada, and can point to a considerably earlier establishment of an independent state. But some Canadians can get around that by saying their ancestors lived in the American colonies, but were of more aristocratic origins than the Franklins and Adams' and elected to remain true to King George III. Thus there are in both countries people who claim peculiar merit because of their ancestors: the United Empire Loyalists in Canada, whose merit it is to be descended from people who fought the ancestors of the Daughters of the American Revolution. They are incidentally quite indistinguishable from each other, and should by all rights arrange for joint membership, not merely on the grounds of the likeness of their place in and views of the world, but because in many cases their many eighteenth-century ancestors include some of both sides. (Typically, my Canadian wife is eligible by descent for both, not to mention any organization of people of French-Canadian descent. I, typically, have no ancestors who ran off to Canada during the Revolution. They ran off to the mountains instead.)

There is a certain strain between the two countries over the matter of time past and time future — about our age, and about our duration. French Canadians are the oldest group in our triangle; the United States is the older independent political entity and the largest. But the English Canadians, too, opened up country and set up government. Indeed, they say that they are the true carriers and practitioners of Anglo-Saxon responsible government on this continent, while yielding to no one in independence from outside controls. Yet Americans find it hard to feel in their bones that a Canadian is as Canadian as an American is American, and needs take no more thought (although he does) to be so; the English Canadian for his part, finds it hard to believe that a French Canadian is French Canadian simply because he was born so, and not for any contrived reason, although of course, being under pressure, he does contrive a reason.

The Overseas Input

Our two peoples are modern mixes, blended from European overseas migrations which began in the seventeenth century and still continue, and later migrations from other continents. The United States got fewer of the early French migrants, but it is not at all unlikely that there are as many people of some French ancestry in the United States now as in Canada, although they have no strong centers of culture and have largely lost their identity. The United States generally got more British immigrants than did Canada year by year, until very recent times, but they are less in evidence in the larger country.

On the frontier of both countries, as that frontier moved west, religious sects sought to establish their peculiar kingdoms of God in peaceful isolation from the World: Mennonites, Hutterites, Doukhobors, Latter Day Saints. The world always caught up with them, tempting the saints to follow the world and attacking them if they did not. The United States, with larger territories suitable for plantation agriculture, had a larger part in the forced migration of Africans to America — thus making her social structure in the Southern regions resemble that of the West Indies and some parts of Latin America. Westward migration and expansion, with military force, gave the United States a considerable dark-skinned, Spanish-speaking population, which Canada does not have.

Trans-Pacific migration provided Chinese and Japanese laborers for construction and agriculture on the western coast and in the western mountains of both countries, together with communities of active small entrepreneurs in the coastal cities. Recent migration from Europe is probably of about the same composition in both countries but the United States continues to get, in addition, large numbers of Latin-Americans, poor, unskilled, and of little schooling.

The Minorities

Although a large proportion of the two peoples are of about the same mix, the largest minority of each country is quite different from that of the other. Obviously the two great minorities are the French in Canada and the Negroes in the United States. In one respect, the two are alike; both are native. Find that part of any large American city in which 90 per cent of the population is native-born of native-born parents; it is a Negro district. Find it in Canada: it is French. Although much of the talk and thinking about such matters in both countries assumes that minorities are immigrant, unassimilated immigrant minorities are no longer a problem in either country. The immigrants of yesterday are part of the majority which today deals with the large native minority.

The United States literally created its own minority. White Americans brought Africans to serve as plantation labor, bred with them, and so organized the lives of the progeny that they lost the culture of their African ancestors without having full access to Euro-American culture. They were given, in practice and in law, a special status far out of keeping with the principles of equality written into the American Constitution. The members of the resulting minority, similar in number to the total population of Canada, still suffer from the poverty, lack of schooling and skills, physical peril, and personal insult and humiliation visited upon them a century after their nominal emancipation from slavery. They are engaged in a massive struggle to remove the distinction of status, in law and in practice. They ask that the concept *Negro* disappear from American law and custom. But other Americans have not yet allowed the special status of Negro to disappear. Some wouldn't mind, providing the Negroes were at a distance. A few join in the struggle. A large and concentrated group fight the change so bitterly as to change the very course of government.

Canada's great minority, the French, antedates the creation of a Canadian government. It is a classical territorial, linguistic, and cultural minority, a self-conscious, stubborn group of people whose ancestors got there first and sent down deep roots. They seek to maintain an historic special status. Many of them insist that there is not a Canadian people, but two peoples, or nations, bound into one state by an agreement which they do not consider sacred or immortal.

However much may be made of differences in our cultural liturgy which I shall mention later, I doubt whether they are of great importance in the relations between Canadians and Americans. The deeper misunderstandings probably come from strains which, in turn, are caused by the different situations in which we find ourselves and the different internal problems which we have to meet. Of the different internal problems, perhaps the most important is that more than a third of all Canadians are of a cultural and linguistic minority demanding its rights in one way, while twenty million Americans are of a racial minority demanding their rights in quite a different way. The tone, the rhetoric of internal politics, is different because of these two great internal problems. It is the stress and strain of meeting problems that makes our relations what they are, not merely our very similar culture and history.

Contrasting Constitutional Crises

Thus both these countries are involved in fundamental constitutional debate aroused and colored by the struggle over the status of the large minority in each country. The debate brings out some perhaps rather fundamental differences. In the modern nation state one is supposed to believe that his immortal people has now got its just dues, a state which will also be imperishable. The notion that any state can be of tentative constitution, and probably not immortal, is political heresy; especially where there is no sacred, symbolic monarch. Americans are especially absolute in their ideas on this point.

Canadians generally are probably less absolute in their notions about nations and constitutions, within which changes can be made. But English Canadians often seem to regard French Canadians as a group which will, or ought to, disappear into the "Canadian people," which they think of as having a long, if not eternal, future. Many French Canadians think of the present constitution of Canada as a contract, a *mariage de convenance* — probably not so contracted as to come under the Church's protection as a valid marriage — subject to renegotiation when no longer *convenable*. I believe that these differences of view about the nature of the constitution often confuse communication between Americans and Canadians.

During the war I sometimes went out to talk to American audiences about Canada's war effort. On more than one occasion my companion, a

Canadian offical, blamed the French Canadians for the fact that Canada did not send drafted men overseas. The Americans who had raised the question clearly implied something like this: "What kind of country is it that can't draft its people if it wants to? The French are Canadian citizens, aren't they? Canada is in a war, isn't it?" The poor Canadian, who knew very well that large numbers of Canadians, French and English, were serving abroad before the United States was in the war still thought he had to apologize for the lack of a drafted overseas army. This story illustrates what I mean by the absolutism of American political philosophy, and a certain greater flexibility of Canadian. The minute we got into the war, our way was the right way. The Canadians should follow it. The official who accompanied me on these excursions was driven to the common defense of accusing some one else. The Americans, with a divine assurance that they are right, feel quite free to ask the Canadians, "why don't you do as we do?;" that is, as we have been doing since yesterday noon. There is a certain pressure of American criticism on Canada, especially with respect to such matters as Cuba, the Cold War, and China. Forty years ago, it was prohibition. Canadians, I think, feel that they must excuse the fact that they do not follow American policy and actions. Perhaps their ambivalence about the United States and Americans comes partly from the fact that they have, on so many points, similar sentiments and might come to similar decisions, yet being independent and acting separately, they do not come to identical and simultaneous decisions. There is nothing so infuriating as to have the detail and timing of one's actions dictated, or urgently proposed by some one else who has no more commitment to the ideal or cause than oneself. Again the French Canadians are a minority within a minority. The English Canadian sometimes comes stiffly to attention and tells the French their duty. The French like neither coming to attention nor being told their duty. They would rather do their duty in secret than to have it thought they were doing it because they had been told.

It's not that Canadians would not gladly, and do not, tell Americans their faults and their duty. But Americans are so numerous and far off from Canadians; they simply don't listen, and hence bear no malice.

But if some of the features of ethnic composition of the two populations (and the two or three peoples) appear to make both internal relations and the relations between the two countries more difficult, they also make them closer and more harmonious. Most special kinds of Americans—by religion, race, national origin, occupation, or other identifying traits—have their counterparts with similar problems in Canada. Hearty athletic Irish priests have to deal with their Latin counterparts in both countries. Mormons in Alberta are of the same community as those in Utah and have similar neighbors to contend with. Beyond that, however, the people of each country can use some of their fellow-countrymen as scapegoats for their own sins and failures. Thus are we drawn together in uneasy peace, a *pax familias*.

Cultural Liturgies and Attitudes

Thus far I have woven what I have had to say about the relations of the two countries into a web of structure and ecological relations. I have done so because I think the conscious attitudes, such as are uttered in opinion surveys, of the people of the one country toward those of the other cannot be understood without keeping these ecological relations in mind. It is customary to say that Canadians and Americans are annoyed with each other because they are so alike that any deviation of either from their common culture is regarded as sacrilege by the other. That reaction does, indeed, occur. Battles rage over the "or" as against the "our" ending of words, and over small or large differences of pronunciation. This is not to be wondered at in the particular case, although it is one of the more fantastic of human phenomena. Alphabets, spelling, pronunciation, vocabulary are the stuff of which nationalist movements are made; at least, much is made of them in such movements. Poor Canada is caught between England and the United States in this, as in many other matters, such as the handling of knives and forks. On the whole, it is the Canadian who has deep feelings on these matters, probably just because of being in the cross fire between Mother Britain and Uncle Sam.

But we must speak of "attitudes." Canadians have attitudes about almost everything American: Americans are not well enough informed to have so many about Canada. Canadians participate in the World Series of baseball and the American presidential election; at least, the talking and betting at the McGill Faculty Club used to be concentrated on those events at the appropriate season (and not by my initiative or that of other Americans). Canadian papers are full of news from the United States; Canadians talk about the American news of business, of sports, scandal, and whatever else is stirring. Attitudes are expressed, but they are generally not explicitly "attitudes about" Americans and things American.

Of course, there are such attitudes. Some English Canadians are bitter about the United States and about Americans; it is a deep, dark bitterness and dislike, expressed in a waspish way. It does not turn up in the polls of opinion, so far as I have seen them. I have no idea how widespread it is. But it exists, and there is no use pretending it does not. So far as I know, it never caused me, an American, to be kept out of a house or a party; but one never knows that sort of thing. An elderly cousin of my wife's did introduce me thus at a tea a few weeks after my arrival in Canada: "This is my niece's husband. He's an American. But you would never know it!" She was drawing me into the inner circle of kin and friends, not reflecting on Americans. She was of that convent-bred generation of Montreal and Quebec women, French and English, who thought that they lived at the center of the world beyond which lay the outer darkness. Another cousin of the same kind kept asking me for ten years when I would finish my course "up at the college." An American could only be at McGill to take a course! Such provincialism is to be found, I suppose, wherever there is a local in-bred society with strong sense of class and family. Americans, being outside that system, were odd. One could be kind to them, as to other people one had never heard of.

The prevailing stereotype is of another kind. As Professor S. D. Clark, now of the University of Toronto, reported it in a study based on interviews with English-speaking Protestants in Montreal in the 1930's, the American is boastful, excitable, materialistic, inclined to law-breaking and divorce, and very ignorant of Canada. One finds them hospitable and perhaps agreeable, taken individually, but one can't take them in a group. A good many exceptions were made for people one knew well. Canadians who live in cities, and especially those near the border are apt to be influenced by American ways, especially the bad ones. In fact, as I reread Clark's report on *Canada and her Great Neighbor* (1938) I am reminded — as I was at the time — of the way my rural Ohio relatives talk about people from New York and Hollywood, and about how the young people who went bad did it under the baneful influence of those centers of sin.

Since the studies of the 1930's the techniques of surveying opinion have been refined — and more money is available for them. Raymond Bréton, a young Canadian sociologist who has been reviewing the polls, notes as a first significant point that Canadians are never asked about the influence of England, France, or Europe as a whole on Canadian life; they are asked only about the United States. The United States is the constant, inevitable point of comparison.

In a 1961 study of a representative sample of people in the cities of Montreal and Quebec, only 21 per cent were found to agree with the proposition that "the immorality which we observe in Quebec is often due to the evil influence of the Americans;" 62 per cent did not agree. In the province outside the cities only 25 per cent agreed, while 54 per cent did not agree. In a general Canadian poll people have been asked in several years whether they think the Canadian way of life is too much influenced by the United States. They have answered thus:

	1951	1956	1957	1961
Too much...................	36	27	21	38
Not too much..............	48	63	57	49
No opinion.................	16	10	22	13

In the 1961 poll, 23 per cent thought, for example, that "We copy the Americans in our way of life; they are faster living; more materialistic." From the figure it appears that a good solid core of Canadians continue to have about the same opinions that Clark found twenty-five years or more ago. But it is a minority countered by a larger percentage who say they do not hold those views. It also appears that the percentage fluctuates rather widely. It would be interesting to know with what conditions and events the opinions rise and fall, for the actual influence of Americans and their actual character, however volatile, can scarcely vacillate so rapidly. No doubt economic conditions and political events affect these opinions.

Opinion as to whether economic control is a good thing or not also fluctuates. In 1956, nearly 70 per cent of people questioned in all regions of Canada thought it a good thing that "a lot of Canada's development has been financed by United States money." In 1963, the percentage had dropped to about 55 throughout the country. Even the percentage of Canadians who believe Canada is becoming more dependent on the United States fluctuates somewhat, although it is more stable than the other opinions we have noted. One Canadian, whom I do not have the right to quote at present, believes that the instability of Canadian opinion about the United States may come from a certain feeling that their own Canadian actions are without great significance, a feeling which may breed a certain alienation which is expressed in negative attitudes. I repeat his idea because it suggests that the matter is one that is not completely understood and should be probed. As more and more countries become industrialized with capital from the great central industrial countries, similar situations and attitudes may occur in many parts of the world. In the poll figures which I have seen, there are no correlations of attitudes toward American economic control with judgments of American people and morals. One would expect such correlations. In our civilization morality and economics are considered strongly connected in people's judgments.

Aggression by Communications

This is also a world in which people read newspapers and magazines, listen to radio and watch television. Control of these media and the content of their messages is considered very important in determining behavior. Canadians have always been great consumers of "mass communications"—to use the awkward common phrase—from the American side of the line. And it worries them. I sensed this when I first crossed that border. In fact, when I went to Vancouver in 1927 to "speak to father," he gave me quite a talk about how in Canada they were a little more restrained and modest in advertising than in the United States, and about how the press was not so sensational. As he was talking he was showing me through Vancouver, the Canadian Pacific railway yards and docks, the gateway to the Orient. In the yards stood an express car with a great banner on it: "The First Carload of Kotex to Cross Canada." That, of course, though embarrassing, illustrated the point; Kotex and the advertising of it were American inventions.

When I first went to live in Montreal I thought it would be interesting to see what parts of Canada preferred United States popular magazines to Canadian and those from England. It was a naïve notion, but I learned much by trying it out. The city of Victoria on Vancouver Island turned out to have the highest circulation per capita of the Canadian *MacLean's Magazine, The Saturday Evening Post,* and also of a couple of popular English weeklies. The circulations moved up and down together. In some parts of Canada people simply read more magazines of all kinds. The circulation of magazines from England was quite small; *The Saturday Evening Post's* circulations were of the same order of magnitude as in American cities. As for Victoria, when people weren't looking after their roses, they had to have something to do. As another index of American influence I took divorce rates. The rates in the Canadian Provinces were much lower than in the various States, but as one went west the rate went up: the peak was on the west coast in both countries. Magazine circulation also went up as one went west, but Ontario (with much the largest urban English-speaking population) stood high on these measures of "Americanism."

Canada has met the "problem" of American publications in various ways. There have been attempts to control the amount of advertising by United States businesses, to require Canadian advertising and to "clean up" the content of what comes in. The protection of Canadian business from an excess of United States advertising is, of course, one of the strong motives for discouraging circulation of American magazines. *Time* magazine years ago established a Canadian edition to meet the requirements; its Canadian circulation was apparently large enough to warrant it. Other magazines have not done so; as far as I know there has been no decline of the reading of United States magazines. But the Canadian *MacLean's Magazine* has prospered so greatly that it has established a French edition, the only English-Canadian publication to do so.

The penetration of Canada by American communications has been made more massive by radio and television. Not only are a large proportion of all Canadians within easy tuning reach of American stations; the Canadian stations also run many programs of American origin. In the control of radio and television, Canada lies somewhere between Britain and the United States. Commercials are less blatant, long, and frequent than on the United States radio and television. From the early time of radio, the Canadian Broadcasting Company, a government agency, has owned stations and run programs. Until the burgeoning of FM stations, there was nothing in the United States to compare with the CBC programs for quality and for relief from interruption by silly ditties, commercials spoken in various kinds of affected voices, and generally unpleasant noises and talk. A greater measure of control was also exerted over the private stations in Canada than in the United States.

The Canadian Broadcasting Company has recently made a survey of opinions of its listeners. Nearly all the respondents thought nearly all the stated goals of the CBC were important: to encourage Canadian talent, to educate, tell the news and entertain the people, and to help Canadians understand each other. Very few people thought too many performers were hired from the United States; indeed, a larger number thought more should be hired. A fifth of all respondents thought that even their own CBC-run programs for children are harmful to them, and 24 per cent that too many of the plays show the seamy side of life; yet only 12 per cent believe that many CBC programs have a bad influence on people's morals. Those who think things are bad tend to be rural, English, elderly, and Bible Protestants — like Americans of similar opinions about radio and television. No doubt those same people would think independent and United States radio and television programs even worse.

Whatever some Canadians may think of United States programs, a very large number of Canadians hear and view them in a big way. In November 1963 three Buffalo affiliates of United States networks took 43 per cent of the total viewing audience during peak evening hours in Toronto; United States stations, presumably those of Seattle, took 37 per cent of the Vancouver audience in the same period. In addition many popular United States programs are carried on both independent Canadian and CBC stations. It is reported that Canadians absolutely loved the fourth Nixon-Kennedy debate, which was presented on CBC-TV. Apparently Canadian viewers simply take to the programs which they can enjoy, without much thought about their origins. Origin is mentioned by the audience mainly when they are for some reason annoyed.

Yet there are differences between those Canadians who say they prefer CBC stations and those who prefer independent Canadian and United States stations. Among those who prefer the CBC stations are distinctly more people who have been to university, who are in professional occupations, and who are older. Among those who prefer the other stations are distinctly more young people and workers, from skilled to unskilled. It seems clear that there is a substantial group of people whose preference for the CBC is marked. From my own experience, and from listening to comments of Americans who have heard CBC programs, I believe that there is a group in the United States who would like programs such as those of the CBC, and that this group is very like the Canadians who like the CBC. Paul Gardner wrote a piece along these lines in *The New York Times* of January 19, 1964. He spoke mainly of the quality of the drama done on CBC, and of the opportunity for actors to develop professionally on CBC-TV as they cannot on United States television, with its guest appearances and star system. American visitors to Canada find CBC discussion of international affairs much more free of attempts to justify government policy than on the supposedly private stations in the United States. It may be that Canadians are just annoyed enough by United States attempts to keep the media in line to insist on their freedom of discussion. The main effect of having government-supported radio and television in Canada has certainly not been bias in political news or discussions; nor has it been neglect of popular taste. It has been a determined, if moderate, attention to other tastes, so that more time is given to plays, intellectual programs, and good music. To achieve this end in an American city requires a committee of public-minded citizens with money, university people, and people engaged in the arts; they must carry on a campaign in competition with other philanthropies, and generally must avoid programs of political significance.

In radio and television, as in other matters, we are dealing with a continental system in which the Canadian part cannot be understood without the rest. It might be hard to show that the Canadian part has any great influence on the rest. At least one may speculate that the presence of such an independent system (to reverse terms as generally used by suggesting that the government-owned Canadian Broadcasting Company stations are more independent than privately-owned stations in the United States) may check some of the extremes of American communications, and may give an example which can be followed and material which can be used.

The Neglected Study: The Integrity of the System

In conclusion, it is important to keep in mind that these two complicated urban industrial countries are part of a common system, that each is deeply dependent upon the other, and that they are bound by kinship, economy, organization, tastes, standard of living, and many common problems. One cannot describe either country without taking the other greatly into account. It is, however, amazing how little the two countries have been studied as parts of a system. One studies a system not by showing the likenesses and differences between its parts, as in classifying butterflies on pins, but by analyzing the functions of each part for the others and for the whole.

TWENTY-ONE

Principle and Rationalization
in Race Relations

One of the most distressing and dangerous of the symptoms of our sick world is the distortion of people's minds and sentiments, and of our social practices and institutions along the axis of racial and cultural (ethnic) differences. It is right and proper that students of society should direct their attention to these symptoms and to their underlying causes. This social scientists have been and are doing. Much valuable work has been and is being done. More power to the people who are doing it; to those anthropologists who have not merely accelerated their investigations into the nature of racial differences but have also launched programs of popular education to clear up misapprehensions. All credit also to those sociologists, political scientists and other specialists who have turned their scientific effort in this direction; and to those people, of various professions, who have undertaken, by bold experiment, to bring more justice into the relations between people of different racial and ethnic backgrounds. And if scholars and other persons who are themselves members of the disadvantaged groups of our society show a special penchant for studying problems of this order, no less credit is due them. It is not only their right, but also their special duty, to undertake research and action which will benefit society at large none the less for being directed especially at

Presented at the Eighth Annual Convention of the American Catholic Sociological Society, Dec. 28, 1946.

Reprinted by permission of the publisher from the *American Catholic Sociological Review*, Vol. VIII, March 1947, pp. 3–11. Copyright © 1947, The American Catholic Sociological Society.

injustices done to the group to which they themselves belong. The others of us in social science might, however, search our professional consciences to see whether we do not passively conspire to confine Negro social scientists to study of Negro problems, women to study of the problems of women and children, and so on (for this is one of the subtler forms of discrimination—"Go up higher, brother, to the head of your own table").

The main business of this paper is, however, not to praise, but to criticize the way in which we have gone about the business of improving the relations between races and ethnic groups.

Our main fault has been opportunism, and especially an opportunism of logic, a fault common enough in American social science and social action. I do not mean that there is necessarily any opportunism in the turning of our attention to the problems of our own time and country. On that point we should not yield an inch to those who would have us choose our objects of study purely on the basis of something called "the state of knowledge" without reference to what is currently going on in the world. There has undoubtedly been some opportunism in choice of problems for investigation by American social scientists; we may have respected sacred cows and may have run after the problems for whose investigation funds are easy to get. An opportunism of logic is, however, much more serious.

The main evidence of the kind of opportunism to which I refer is that we allow the direction of our research and educational effort to be dictated by the enemy, the defenders of racial and ethnic injustice. It is common for people to defend their sentiments and actions by rationalizations. In some societies a given set of rationalizations may last so long as to become traditional. In our society, we are quick to change them. We actively seek new ones; this is one of the functions of annual conventions—to find more up-to-date reasons for our old policies, interests and sentiments. Being scientifically minded, we Americans dress our new rationalizations in the sheep's clothing of science. The inequality of the position of the races in this country was once defended by scriptural quotation; now it is defended by what are called "facts" of biology and psychology. And those of us who are interested in getting new light on and more just action in the relations between peoples, take up the chase. If someone says Negroes have such poor jobs because they are biologically incapable of learning complicated skills, we set about to prove that Negroes can learn to do anything anyone else can learn to do. If then the "fact" of incapacity to learn is modified to say that Negroes are good with their hands, but not with their heads, we get busy to prove that that isn't so, either. Then someone comes along with the defense that although they can learn as well, or almost as well, as other people, Negroes lack sexual or other controls necessary to the nicer positions in our society; we chase that one. Or perhaps Negroes don't smell nice; so we start counting sweat glands. We store the sweat of people of various races in bottles and have it smelt by noses of several shapes, sizes and colors, just as advertising agencies say they do with cigarettes in their "scientific" blind-fold tests—and note with glee that women have more sweat-glands than men and that while the smellers couldn't tell what race the samples came from, a Chinese man picked as worst of all the sweat of an Anglo-Saxon. Someone will no doubt soon analyze the oil from the skin and hair of some group unfortunately dubbed "greasers." Perhaps some day a broad-minded East Indian will be disturbed by the disgust his fellow-countrymen are said to feel at the sight of lobster-red sunburned English skin. Desirous of eliminating this unwarranted prejudice against Europeans, he will have chemists make tests; if all goes well, they will find no chemical difference between the beautiful bronze skin of Hindu vegetarians and the parboiled hide of a beef-eating Colonel Blimp.

Now I have no basic objection to the making of such tests, and none to the dissemination, to as many people as possible, of whatever findings result from them. Truth is better than error, and should be spread with the more vigor when the error is one that does great damage. What I do object to is giving the terms of the game into the hands of the enemy, who, by inventing a new rationalization every day, leads us a merry and endless chase. We attack the devil's changing disguises instead of the devil himself.

Each of these rationalizations brought up in defense of racial and ethnic injustices is part of a syllogism. The minor premise, stating an alleged fact, is expressed; the major premise, a principle, is left out. Instead of driving our opponents and ourselves back to the major premise, we are content to question and disprove the minor premise, the allegation of fact.

Suppose we take a couple of the common statements: "Jim Crow practices are justified because Negroes smell bad," and "Jews should not be admitted to medical schools because they are aggressive." The first, completed, would read something like this:

There should be separate public facilities for people who smell bad.

Negroes smell bad.

Therefore, Negroes should have separate facilities.

The second would read like this:

People who are aggressive beyond some determined degree should not be admitted to medical schools.

Jews are aggressive beyond this degree.

Therefore, Jews should not be admitted to medical schools.

The orders of fact alleged in these two examples are quite different. But they serve equally well for our purpose. The major premise is ordinarily not stated in either case by the persons who use the statement; nor is it often stated or answered by those who oppose racial and ethnic discrimination of the kinds they refer to.

I suspect — though it might be hard to prove — that the suppression of the major premise in these and similar cases is not a psychological accident. There is said to be a kind of shrewdness in the fevered reasoning of the neurotic, as well as in that of the devil. The shrewdness in these rationalizations lies in the use of implied major premises that people of our culture, those who believe in racial and ethnic equality, as well as those who use these rationalizations, do not care to bring out into the open.

Let us look again at the syllogism about odors. We are a people who can be frightened by advertisements which tell us that we will not be promoted to be superintendents of factories and sales-managers of businesses unless we smell nice; and the American woman can be frightened by the threat that she will not get her man or that she may lose him over a matter of a little unpleasant odor of which her best friend can't bring herself to speak. We are not told at what point in his rise to authority and higher income the man must begin to make himself pleasant. Nor do we learn whether the man who is about to be lost had so sensitive a nose when he got the girl, or whether he picked up this nicety later. But the reference to the great — and legitimate — American dream of getting ahead is obvious enough. And it is perhaps not difficult to understand why we do not question the main premise behind the alleged fact of Negro odor.

Or let us take the defense of restrictive covenants by the statement that the presence of Negroes in a neighborhood destroys property values. The major premise would be something like this: People are justified in preventing property in their neighborhood from being occupied by people whose presence reduces property values. Now it is true that residential property values respond in some degree, under certain circumstances, to a change in the kind of people who live in the area. This may be due to the way of living of the new people, or it may be due to an attitude toward them, or to both. It is also true that Americans in great numbers try to turn an improvement in their economic condition into an improvement in their social standing by moving to a new neighborhood. This is a perfectly natural and generally proper thing for them to do. But the trouble is that there is always some later comer treading on one's heels. So that it is, in a sense, the great American game to break in where one is not wanted. It is a game that is successful just to the extent that one seems not to be playing it: to seem to play it is to be aggressive, and one gets punished for that although he may not necessarily be rewarded for not being aggressive. Herein lies the great American dilemma, although I do not mean to belittle Mr. Myrdal's statement of it. The thought that I may be one of those whose presence in a neighborhood might — through other people's attitudes toward me — reduce its desirability to them is not a pleasant one to face, especially when combined with my own concern lest some group of people from whom I wish to be dissociated may some day threaten the neighbor-hood in which I have achieved a social footing and perhaps a dearly bought family house.

The preceding paragraph contains a clue to the effectiveness of the use of alleged Jewish aggressiveness as justification for limiting their entry to the professions. We Americans do not like to talk about just what degree of aggressiveness is proper; we might find that the amount of this virtue necessary to realize our ambitions is greater than the amount which turns it into a punishable vice. I am tempted to pursue a like analysis of what is hidden in the question, "How would you like your sister to marry a nigger?" I will spare you—and myself—that ordeal. To those of you who are still college students, I recommend it as an exercise for the brain and the spine.

Let me repeat that I do not pretend to prove that the enemies of interracial and interethnic justice exercise conscious slyness in the choice of their defensive rationalizations. Nor can I prove that it is the discomfort of facing major premises about which we are fearfully ambivalent, rather than mere logical carelessness and the love of empiricism at all costs, that prevents us from filling out these syllogisms. But certainly we are ambiva-lent about the principles hidden in these statements. We, like those who defend the racial and ethnic inequalities of our society, are all Americans. They and we share the same aspirations; the hidden fundament of our minds is the same as theirs. I only suggest that that gives them a certain advantage over us, and that we have allowed them full benefit of it.[1]

Whatever causes it, the failure to ferret out major premises has other consequences than merely leading us on to a merry chase for facts. It leads to too much protestation as well. We counter the exaggerated statements of our opponents with exaggerations in another direction. Nearly all of the statements in favor of racial and ethnic discrimination allege faults in the minority groups in question. These faults range from serious moral defect to slight departures from the canons of good taste. In our counter-arguments, the members of the racial or ethnic groups involved appear as paragons of virtue, delightful in their manners—better, in fact, than it is common for human creatures to be.

This brings up the whole problem of the differences between people of different racial and ethnic categories. Those opposed to racial prejudices and inequalities have shown a tendency to slight, or even to deny, the existence of any differences at all. Fishberg's book on the Jews has long served as a text to prove that no one can tell a Jew when he sees him—a very dubious compliment to Jewish parents who have put forth great effort

1. For a penetrating analysis of hidden factors in interethnic sentiment, see Ichheiser, Gustav, "Diagnosis of Anti-Semitism," Sociometry Monographs, No. 8.

so to bring up their children that they will respect and practice conduct which the parents consider rooted in their Jewish faith and culture. All that Fishberg says about the physical characteristics of Jews may be true; and there are occasions when statement of his or other such findings is called for. But to use them to try to prove that there are no discernible or significant differences between one ethnic, or religious, group and another can lead to no good.

In the first place, overuse of such argument implies that the only basis for social, political and economic equality is the lack of differences between the groups concerned. That would put our faith in the rightness of social equality on a very dubious foundation, both because it might some day turn out that there are some differences we don't know about and because it would imply that the price of equality is the elimination of peculiar traits which some group of people may properly cultivate and cherish. Heaven knows that in our prejudiced world members of some groups are given plenty of temptation to deny that they belong to the groups in which they were born and bred, and in so doing to eliminate all identifying marks. That is a matter for their own consciences. We can only have sympathy for such victims of racial, ethnic and religious injustice. Our sympathy should not lead us to engage in counter-propaganda which expressly or implicitly denies or tones down the differences which really exist between groups.

There is, further, the danger—so cogently stated by David Riesman in an article entitled "Equality and Social Structure,"—that common people will consider the whole propaganda for tolerance a fake intended to obfuscate them. For, as Riesman says—speaking of the way into which the democratic world played into the hands of the Nazis:

> That (democratic) world denied that there was any difference between races. . . . [Anthropologists] insisted . . . that only the ignorant and the prejudiced could find any differences between Jews and non-Jews, and sociologists supplemented this with statistics to show that, in all tangible ways, Jews were just like everybody else. . . . One can see now that it would have been better strategy to admit the differences while denying that they justified political and economic stratification in most cases. . . . For the differences *are* there, no less so for being subtle and impalpable, or being mostly culturally conditioned, not biological in origin. . . .
>
> At any rate, in the eyes of the ordinary man, there were differences between races and between the sexes and between men in general. He could not always put his finger on them, but he could feel them, and feel that there was something fishy in the liberal denials.[2]

Riesman's warning applies not only to those differences which merely distinguish, or are supposed to, one group from another; it applies as well

2. *Journal of Legal and Political Sociology,* Vol. I, 1943, pp. 79-80.

to those real or alleged differences which imply faults. For if groups of people maintain somewhat different virtues in their peculiar cultures, is it not likely that they will differ somewhat in their vices also? A record of the problems with which practical theologians have had to deal in different times and places, and of the special questions of conscience which have turned up in the confessional in various periods and countries, and among people of different ethnic background and social position, would—I am sure—give ample evidence of differences in the sins for which people have a predilection. In this matter, it would probably be more effective to gloss over nothing; and especially not to gloss over our own sins. The doctrine of original sin, which rests equally on all, is a sounder starting point than protestation that the groups which are the special objects of prejudice do not have any special vices. For, again speaking of our logical opportunism, the use of the denial of special faults as an argument against racial or ethnic prejudices and injustices implies somehow that we who are not dis-criminated against are in that blessed state because at some time or other we were without special disqualifying faults or vices, and were therefore elevated to our privileged position. It further implies the right of those who consider themselves without special faults or vices to give or withhold full equality from others.

In this kind of argument, incidentally, we again play into the hands of the enemy, for in arguing so hard that groups of people whose rights we have limited are without fault we encourage the idea—implicit in the "fault" justification of prejudice and limited rights—that justice and equality are something to be earned, and that the wage is to be paid by and at the discretion of the more privileged group. This argument turns up in the statement that Negroes are not ready for full political rights and for access to all kinds of jobs, supported by a false use of evolutionary ideas—"the Negroes are only yesterday out of the jungle." "It will take another hundred years," etc.

I do not mean to suggest that the problem of the relation between faults and access to full privileges in a society is an easy one, either in theory or in practice. There are circumstances in which society withdraws full free-dom from an individual because of a weakness betrayed in his actions towards others. But the principle on which this is done is not that the other members of society have the right to do this because they are virtuous. They do it not in the name of and by right of their own virtue, but in the name of the good of the community and through functionaries of the law who—although they should certainly be people of uprightness and as far above reproach as possible—act with an authority delegated by society. The principles involved are far from those implied in any rationalization which justifies one group of people, supposedly free of faults, in limiting the social privileges of another whole category of persons because of the latter's alleged faults. It is some such principle that we give consent to if we answer the "fault" argument for discrimination by protesting that the minority concerned is not different in any way from other groups. It makes us parties to a revolting self-righteousness.

Allow me to mention briefly one more consequence of the denial or glossing over of differences, and especially of faults. It has already led to a feeling, in this country, that no one not a member of a certain group may express any but the most laudatory sentiments or judgments concerning it. Even those who are members of the group are enjoined to say nothing critical in such a way that it may reach ears outside the group. Again, the abuses and misunderstandings have been so flagrant that one can understand the effort to enforce a certain censorship upon criticism of one group by members of another. But that kind of tolerance which prevents statement of honest opinion and conviction is a false tolerance. It is the kind of tolerance which requires us to look about the room, and ask of our neighbor in a whisper, "Is there a Lower Slobbovian present?" before we open our mouths to speak. Granting that a careful tongue is an organ of great virtue, it does not follow that an honest one is less to be valued.

I have made but one point, or sung but one theme, with some variations: that it is worse than of no avail to gather and disseminate the true facts which refute the alleged facts offered in defense of racial and ethnic inequality of social rights, unless at the same time we dig out and bring to our own view, as well as to that of our opponents, the major premises, or principles, which lie hidden beneath the disguise of rationalizations.

TWENTY-TWO

Social Change and Status Protest:
An Essay on the Marginal Man

The phrase "marginal man" and the phenomenon it designates came formally into the study of society with the publication of Robert E. Park's essay, "Human Migration and the Marginal Man" in 1928. I call it an essay, for it has depth, breadth and richness of hypotheses, neither required nor expected in an ordinary scientific paper. Park planted seed enough to keep a generation of scientific cultivators busy.

While the phrase came with this publication, the essential idea is much older. Park refers to many others who had sensed the problem; notably Simmel, in his passages on the "stranger" in his *Soziologie* and Gilbert Murray, in his *Rise of the Greek Epic*. He takes Heinrich Heine as a living example of the thing about which he is talking. What Park did was to put the "marginal man" into a broader setting; to see him as a function of the break-up and mixing of cultures attendant upon migration and the great cultural revolutions. He turned a literary and poetic insight into a cluster of related scientific hypotheses. In doing so, he brought it down from the glamour of antiquity and the grandly historical to the level of the most modest European immigrant as well as the oft despised mulatto, and indeed even to all men in his remark that there are "periods of transition and crisis in the lives of most of us that are comparable with those which the immigrant experiences when he leaves home to seek his fortunes in a strange country."

From *Phylon*, The Atlanta University Review of Race and Culture, Vol. X (1st quarter, 1949), pp. 58–65. Reprinted with permission of *Phylon*.

The first part of Park's paper sketches broadly the relation of migration to cultures and social organization, leading up to its part in the break-up of the smaller traditional societies of which anthropologists have become the most expert students. The latter part focuses attention on the subjective aspects of migration and its effect upon human persons.

The first such effect he notes is "emancipation," the freeing of a man from customary expectations by travel and migration. Sometimes, we gather, the emancipated man is eager for new things; he explores and invents. In other cases, he may be painfully homesick for that which he left behind. Perhaps this homesickness is greatest when, as in the case of the Greek, that warm and sacred world for which he yearns no longer exists.

From the completely emancipated man, Park moves on to the "cultural hybrid;"

> . . . a man living and sharing intimately in the cultural life and traditions of two distinct peoples; never quite willing to break, even if he were permitted to do so, with his past and his traditions, and not quite accepted, because of racial prejudice, in the new society in which he now sought to find a place.

The prototype of the "cultural hybrid" he found in the Jew emerging from the Ghetto. However, the person of mixed blood—to use the most misleading phrase of common talk about the races—is perhaps the most permanently and fatally condemned of all to the condition of marginality. And that fact, in so far as it is one, points to the true nature of the marginal position; for while the racial hybrid is ordinarily also a cultural hybrid, by virtue of the fact that both cultures and races develop their distinguishing marks in relative isolation, we have plenty of evidence in America that the racial hybrid need not be a cultural hybrid at all. The American Negro—whether of mixed blood or not—is not conspicuously a cultural hybrid. But he is a man with a status dilemma, and the more he, as an individual, acquires of those elements of American culture which bring to others the higher rewards of success, the greater is his dilemma.

In addition, the American Negro is a living contradiction of the canons of status in the American culture. The contradiction lies in the fact that a member of a group assigned a very humble and limited status bears other characteristics which ordinarily give or allow the individual to acquire higher status. The contradiction is objective, in that it appears to the eyes of others. The dilemma lies in the fact that he cannot accept the status to which Negroes are ordinarily assigned, but neither can he completely free himself from it. The dilemma, on the other hand, is essentially subjective. The Negro who passes as white no longer presents any contradiction to the eyes of others, but he still has the inner dilemma.

It is from the angle of status that I propose to analyze the phenomenon of marginality. Status is a term of society in that it refers specifically to a system of relations between people. But the definition of the status lies in a culture. In fact, one of the essential features of a person's status may be his identification with a culture.

Imagine a society in which the statuses are very well established. The rights and duties pertaining to each are well understood and generally beyond doubt and discussion. The ways by which an individual is assigned to and enters a given status are likewise well defined: by descent, sex, social learning and accomplishments of various kinds, arriving at a certain age, or by certain rites of passage, such as initiation and marriage. In such a case, one would expect—and the evidence on such societies seems to warrant it—that persons of a given status would exhibit a whole complex of social attributes, all of which seem naturally to pertain to that status. These attributes would be unconsciously woven into a seamless garment. Finally, everyone would know exactly who he is. His status identification would be clear and unquestioned by himself or others.

Imagine now the opposite—a society which is a complete free-for-all. Talents, both the virtuous and the nefarious, have full play. Everybody gets exactly what he has coming to him by virtue of his own efforts. It is a society without a hang-over from its past. If an enterprising lad of twenty were fittest to be head surgeon of a great hospital, he would be it. Make it more drastic; if a Jewish Negro girl of twenty, born in Russia and converted to the Witnesses of Jehovah were fittest to be head surgeon of Massachusetts General Hospital, she would be it. In such a society one could, in effect, say that status did not exist. Competition, of some purer sort than any we know, would determine without time-lag what each person would do and be. No such society ever existed. The ones we know are somewhere between this and the other pole. Relatively, our society is nearer the free-for-all than have been most others we know of.

Free as is competition in our society, and strong as is the strain toward allowing talent and accomplishment free rein, there are many positions about which there is a halo of technically irrelevant, but socially expected characteristics. Thus the physician is still rather expected by most people to be a man. He is expected, further, to be of a certain age, and, often, to have certain ethnic and class characteristics. But in our mobile and changing society new kinds of persons continually acquire the technically and formally demanded skills or qualities of a profession, or other position. Whenever it happens, sociological news is made and a new and unexpected combination of social characteristics appears; thus, the woman senator, the Negro judge, a boy president of a university, a professor in the White House, Cinderella in the Rockefeller mansion. For certain positions there is a long period of training for inculcating the auxiliary characteristics of a status as well as the technical skills. Thus, a medical course is a long *rite de passage*. So is the seminary of the priesthood and the novitiate of a religious order. Essentially, the function of the novitiate is to guarantee that there shall be no *marginal* priests or monks. The marks of the world are washed off, so that the newborn priest shall be fully a priest, acting as such and judged as such by all other priests and by all the faithful.

Now it is not merely that the new people who come into positions lack certain expected characteristics, but that they positively belong to groups which themselves have a status definition which includes a combination of expected characteristics (such combinations are called stereotypes). The woman has certain traditional expected characteristics; she plays certain traditional roles. People are accustomed to act toward women in certain ways. Likewise, the Negro has a traditional role. The traditional roles of neither woman nor Negro include that of the physician. Hence, when either of them becomes a physician the question arises whether to treat her or him as physician or as woman or Negro. Likewise, on their part, there is the problem whether, in a given troublesome situation, to act completely as physician or in the other role. This is their dilemma. It arises from the fact that the culture has not yet provided a series of accepted definitions of behavior for the various situations which arise from the existence of this new kind of person. So long as the dilemma is present in the mind of the person, and so long as the existence of such a person appears a contradiction to others, just so long are the persons concerned in a marginal position.

Their marginality might presumably be reduced in several ways.

1. All such persons could give up the struggle, by retiring completely into the status with which they are most stubbornly identified by society. This people sometimes do. There are records of turning back to one's own people, culture or status which read like those of religious conversions, with conviction of sin, seeking and finding the light, doing penance and retiring into an exclusive world as into a cloistered religious order. Sometimes, however, such people become leaders of a cultural revival, which may be either religious or militant in temper.

People of the statuses threatened by marginal people generally favor this first solution—that of putting them back into their traditional places. Measures of repression and of exclusion are used to this end.

2. One of the statuses could disappear *as a status*. The word "woman" could cease to have social meaning, and become merely a biological designation without any status or role connotations. A few women have set this as the goal of the feminist movement. The word Negro would disappear—as it has tended to do in certain times and countries—in favor of a series of terms which would describe complexion and feature. These terms,

in a continuum from black to white or white to black, would be of use mainly to people who are careful about the color of their dresses and neckties and to the police, whose vocabulary for identifying complexions of wanted persons has always been meagre. In short, there would be no Negro group to which to belong.

3. Persons of marginal position might individually resign from the status which interferes with their other status aims. A woman who became a physician would simply not be a woman any more, although other people might remain identified with the status of women. A Negro would declare himself no longer a Negro. Such resignation is both subjectively and objectively difficult. The interplay of these two aspects of the difficulty constitutes a fascinating and sometimes tragic theme of human drama. The temptation to resign, and even to repudiate, is put heavily upon marginal people, as many a Negro can testify. If a Negro worker is somewhat accepted by white fellow workers in industry, they generally seem inwardly compelled to extract from him an admission that he is an exception among Negroes. If he is like them in the rest, why should he not be like them in their stereotypes also. It is a kind of betrayal to which we are all subject in some degree. When we yield, the cock crows thrice.

4. One or both of the statuses might, without disappearing, be so broadened and redefined as to reduce both the inner dilemma and the outward contradiction.

5. Another possible solution is elaboration of the social system to include a marginal group as an additional category of persons with their own identity and defined position. A number of people of similar marginal position may seek one another's company, and collectively strive to get a place for themselves. The Cape Coloured of South Africa, and the Eurasians of India are groups of this kind. In this country, the colored creoles of Louisiana, certain rural communities of light-colored people in both South and North, and the free Negroes in certain Southern communities in slavery times all attempted with some success to establish themselves as recognized groups, neither Negro nor white. During their time of success, they were exclusive of other persons who sought admittance to their ranks as every new member was a potential threat to their special status. They became, in fact, groups of kin-connected families; hence, something closer to Indian castes than anything else in America has been. But the strain toward keeping the American race system a simple dichotomy has worked against them. In recent times, when nearly everyone must have "papers" for relief, the draft, school, and the like, only the most "backwoodsy" of such groups can escape the fatal dichotomy.

The marginal groups just mentioned consist each of people who are marginal in the same way, and who consciously seek to fortify a common marginal position. Sometimes it happens that marginal people establish and live their lives in a marginal group, hardly knowing that they are doing so. There are whole segments of marginal society, with their marginal cultures among various ethnic and religious groups in this country, some of whom even developed a distinguishing speech. Large numbers of unmarried career women in American cities live in essential isolation from other women and with only formal contacts with men. In addition, there are other marginal groups who are not quite aware of their marginality, by virtue of living together a somewhat insulated life, but who are, furthermore, made up of people of the most diverse backgrounds; people who have in common, to start with, nothing but their marginality. These are to be found in cities and especially among young people. They are the American Bohemians.

All of these solutions appear as themes in the process of social and cultural adjustment and conflict. One can see in social movements — cultural, national, racial, feminist, class — all of these tendencies. The woman's movement has had its advocates of complete eradication of sex as a status determinant, its women who individually resigned from their sex and encouraged others to do so and those who have quietly or fervently gone back to and idealized the old roles. The main trend has been toward redefinition and broadening of the roles consonant with the status of women, and toward seeking also the integration of women into formerly exclusively male roles. One or another solution may be tried and given up. The internal politics of a social movement turns about choice of these solutions. If you will look inside any movement concerned with the status of a group of people and of their culture, you will find these conflicting tendencies. Shall it be a Negro Renaissance with return to Africa, individual passing, a fight for disappearance of Negro as a status identification, or some broadening and easing of the definition of the Negro status. I need not remind you of the many contingencies in such choices. In reality, a given solution is seldom adopted and stuck to to the exclusion of all others. There is a sort of dialectic of them as the pursuit of one changes the situation so as to bring another to the fore.

Up to this point, I have kept women and Negroes before you as illustrations of people with a status dilemma. American Negroes, product of migration and of the mixing of races and cultures that they are, are the kind of case to which the term marginal man has been conventionally applied. I have used the case of women to show that the phenemenon is not, in essence, one of racial and cultural mixing. It is one that may occur wherever there is sufficient social change going on to allow the emergence of people who are in a position of confusion of social identity, with its attendant conflicts of loyalty and frustration of personal and group aspirations. Migration and resulting cultural contact simply create the grand fields on which the battle of status is fought out among humans; a confusing and bloodier battle because its essence is that so many people are in doubt about which side they want to be on or may be allowed to be on.

In our own society the contact of cultures, races and religions, combines with social mobility, to produce an extraordinary number of people who are marginal in some degree, who have some conflict of identity in their own minds, who find some parts of the social world which they would like to enter closed to them, or open only at the expense of some treason to things and people they hold dear. American fiction has been full of such people, as it must be if it is to tell the story of America. Even English fiction of the nineteenth century abounds in such characters. Anthony Trollope's heroes and heroines are generally people who have more breeding than money, or more money than breeding. There are young men who can go into politics and stay in high society if they remain single or marry pots of money; but can be true to a half-promise to some poorer, dearer girl only by giving it all up and going to work for a living. Trollope's own story, told in his autobiography, is that of a boy who went to Harrow School so shabby and penniless that he was the butt of cruel jokes from masters and fellow pupils for the twelve years he was there.

In Trollope's England, marginal social position was almost entirely a matter of class mobility. There was little of ethnic difference in it. In America, marginality is thought of as resulting solely from the mixtures of cultures, races and religions. There may be more of the problem of class mobility in it, however, than Americans have been accustomed to admit.

In mentioning what you may think the trivial case of Trollope's young man who must choose between his career (class position) and his sweetheart, I incidentally introduced a crucial problem of marginality to which there is little allusion in the formal discussion of the subject, that of life or career contingencies in relation to status marginality.

I suppose a person is furthest from a marginal position if he is so placed that he can go clear through his life without status dilemma. Each of us lives part of his life in retrospect, part in the fleeting present, part in prospect. We see ourselves in a running perspective of the human life cycle. Each phase of our lives offers its own status definitions, rewards and punishments; each phase also has meaning as the preparation for the next. In Jules Romains' *Men of Good Will* there is a conscientious little boy who promises himself the indulgence of leisure after completion of self-appointed tasks of study repeated so and so many times. The tasks get greater and greater and the indulgence gets put off further and further as he grows up. In the end he becomes very like a case reported by the psychoanalyst, Abraham; that of an artist who promises himself a vacation as soon as he shall have produced a really worthy painting. He ends up, a sleepless wreck, in the hands of a psychiatrist. This is, in varying measure, the theme of life of all people who set high goals for themselves. It is the theme of balancing present and future.

Looking at this same problem from the standpoint of social organization, there are phases of life in which society is more open and more tolerant of diversity than others. Student life is traditionally such a phase. People of various races, ethnic groups, class backgrounds, and of the two sexes mix in an adventuresome spirit of Bohemianism. The essence of Bohemianism is disregard of convention. Convention, in its turn, is in large part a set of definitions of status, hence of proper behavior. Student Bohemianism is a conventional relaxation of convention.

Now university life is two things, a *rite de passage* and a preparation for careers. In England, the two things are crystallized in two kinds of degrees. The Pass Degree is a *rite de passage* for sons of aristocrats and plutocrats; the Honors degree, which requires work, is for people who have to make their way in the world, as most American students must do. But university life is here also a *rite of passage,* not merely from the status of adolescent to that of adult, but from one way of life to another and in many cases, from one culture or sub-culture to another.

The freedom of student life has always been tolerated by older adults on the assumption that it would, for each given individual, soon come to an end. We must then ask, both as social scientists and as persons with a life to lead, what are the hazards of passing from so free a phase of life into those which follow: of the transition from school to work, from irresponsible singleness to more or less responsible marriage, from young childless marriage to parenthood. Each of these has its hazards. Each of them generally brings one face to face with a stiffer set of status definitions, with greater mutual exclusiveness of social roles and consequently, with the greater possibility of status dilemma. This aspect of the problem of marginality has been very little studied. It is one of the crucial areas of study if we are really to advance our knowledge of modern society.

Before stopping, let us ask, with regard to social mobility and social change, the same question as we did earlier concerning the relation of migration to marginality. Are mobility and change necessary conditions of marginality, or are they, too, merely the favoring gale? Might there not be, in the most settled society, persons who are in protest against the roles assigned them; persons, even, who want to play some role for which there is no precedent or defined place in their culture? Need one have a woman's movement in order to have the individual woman who feels the masculine protest? Are all the inglorious village Miltons of unpoetic cultures so mute as those in Gray's churchyard? I have often thought that the

French-Canadian culture is so stable, not because of its isolation, but because there has been a whole continent for its free-thinkers and other rebels to escape into. I do not think we know the answer to these questions. But we have some clues. They suggest that the human individual does not always passively accept society's answer to the question, "Who am I?" with all its implications of present and future conduct. I suppose we might distinguish between that kind of protest which is merely a squirming within the harness, and that which is a questioning of the very terms and dimensions of the prevailing status definitions. At any rate, there is still much work to be done on the genesis of status protest; or, to put it the other way, on the processes by which the human biological individual is integrated—always in the presence and by the agency of other humans—into a status system.

TWENTY-THREE

Anomalies and Projections

The papers of this volume present vividly and in detail most of the orders of fact one would want programmed into a computer set up to predict the future of American society with respect to race. Some of the interacting variables considered are the development of our population, economy, ecology, and institutions; the distribution of our population among whatever occupations and whatever "nonoccupations" there are and will be; the distribution of goods and services among the population; the importance attached to race by various elements of our population as individuals and as incumbents of various roles and offices in our institutional systems; and the part of social doctrines, movements, and law in maintaining or changing the place of Negroes in our American society and economy. Gunnar Myrdal[1] spoke of the place of the Negro in American society as presenting a dilemma. The present volume presents it not as a dilemma, but as a complex of anomalies and paradoxes. My contribution is comment *en marge* on some of those anomalies and paradoxes.

In some respects Negro Americans have got out of the place in which it used to be said they were all right, only to find that, in some respects, the new place is worse or, at least, less comfortable. Their original place was that of cheap illiterate labor on plantations which produced crops for world markets in which they—the laborers—could not buy much. The illiteracy was "functional" for the system as long as it wanted labor more than

Written for a special issue on The Negro American. Reprinted by permission from DAEDALUS, Journal of the American Academy of Arts and Sciences, Boston, Massachusetts, Vol. 94, No. 4, 1965.

1. Gunnar Myrdal, *An American Dilemma: The Negro Problem and Modern Democracy* (New York, Harper & Bros., 1944).

customers. That "place" is rapidly disappearing by force of economic and technological change. The plantation workers have moved from the cabin and shanty rural slums of the South to the crowded Black Ghettos of converted mansions and luxury apartments in the "central cities of the Standard Metropolitan Areas," which are larger and more numerous in the North. Negroes have become more urban than their nearest racial and religious kin, the more-or-less Anglo-Saxon white protestants who are numerous in Appalachia and other rural slums, who still own and operate a large proportion of the more prosperous family farms of the country, and many of whom—after success in urban business and professions—have become the ex-urbanites. But in course of becoming more urban, the *under*employed, illiterate, ill-fed, underpaid share-cropper or gang-laborer has become the latterday, unskilled, illiterate, *un*employed of an urban, industrial, and partially post-industrial economy. He has come to the foot of the ladder only to find the bottom rungs gone.

As the unemployed poor man of the city he is not so ill-fed and clothed as in his old place; he is enough healthier to produce more surviving offspring, so that the proportion of Negroes in the population is increasing slightly. He has plenty of leisure, but without the work that gives it meaning, or the money to make much of it. The whole country is richer, and so is even the poor Negro, but he is becoming relatively poorer in comparison to white people. And, as Esther Peterson of the Department of Labor has so convincingly shown in a recent report, it costs money to be poor. It also costs money to be a Negro.

In fact, Philip Hauser shows us that "the cost of being a Negro increases as his education increases." Education, as everyone knows, is the American means of climbing out of poverty; it takes more of it than ever for anyone. It takes still more for the Negro to get the same benefit in income; the income, in turn, will buy him less housing, services, and goods than it would a white American. Yet a large number of Negro Americans have risen above their traditional place by way of education. By tradition and doctrine, every Negro was supposed to be inferior to the lowest white man in education, income, and standard of living.[2] There was never a time when all Negroes were so low as that, but there were and still are—as Thomas Pettigrew shows—places and situations where any Negro who wants to live should act as if it were so. The late E. Franklin Frazier had hair-raising stories to tell of the dangers of talking a more grammatical English than the Georgia cracker from whom he had to buy gasoline for his old Buick car. There are more Negroes of education in this country than in any other. In

2. Robert E. Park, *Race and Culture* (Glencoe, Ill.: Free Press, 1950), p. 242 ". . . the traditional social order . . . assigns every Negro to a position inferior to that of every white man." (First published in *The Annals*, 1928).

spite of the strictest race line outside South Africa, we have the greatest population of people classified as Negro who are effectively literate, work in a modern economy, and want and buy the goods other Western industrial people produce and buy. Since their wants and ambitions are those of other Americans of similar education and income, it is they who notice that it does indeed cost a great deal — in money and dignity — to be a Negro in the United States. It was the younger among them who first "sat-in" for the right to consume goods and services, including education, as other Americans do. Participation and consumption are much the same thing in our world. Those young middle-class Negroes have since been joined by people of all ages, of other ranks and races, in their "nonviolent" but aggressive battle to destroy their traditional "place." The violent opposition has generally been led by white Americans inferior to "nonviolent" Negroes in education and all status-giving characteristics except race itself.

About one in ten of us United States Americans is known to himself and others, and was probably counted in the census, as a Negro. This fact affects the manner in which that one earns his living and "chooses" his place to live. It will be paramount in determining many of his associations: religious, professional, and social; the more intimate the association, the more paramount is race. But little is said of the nature of the race line itself and of those most intimate and inescapable of all relationships, kinship and marriage. We Americans may have poor relations, if we are rich; rich ones, if we are poor. For people who get ahead in the world do not usually immediately or completely renounce the kin they have left behind; and those who do not get ahead are not inclined to lay embarrassing claims on those who have done so. Compared with the kin systems of most societies, ours is flexible. People are relatively free to set the boundaries of their own complex of kinfolk. If we cannot get rid of relatives in any other way, we can move a thousand miles away from them.

We are also unusually free to choose our spouses. Kinship is reckoned on both sides of the house and kin names are the same on both. As a result our children may have relatives of two or more religions, ethnic groups, and social classes. If the relatives on both sides are very much alike and there are no active feuds, they may comfortably meet on social and festive occasions. The family get-together, small and large, is a great American institution and at greater distances than ever. But for various reasons the two sides may not be comfortable together, except perhaps at those most universal of festivals, funerals. If a marriage be ethnically, religiously, or otherwise mixed, one side or other — or both — may absent itself from the wedding. A naming (I was about to say christening) calls for a lining up of the forces on the side of the one true faith for the once-and-for-all identification of the child with one side or another. If there be, as often in

Quebec, marriage of French with English, the kinship may be bilateral, but not symmetrical. Family gatherings are apt to be lopsided—either heavily French or heavily English. And when the time comes to send children to school, a choice of language must be made.

North American kinship is bilateral and marriage selection is relatively free. People may prefer one set of relatives to another. They may draw the line within which they give mutual aid more or less as they wish. They may and do pick from among their ancestors those who will reinforce the conception of themselves which they wish to hold and have their neighbors accept.

But on one point of difference this grandly flexible system is hard and unyielding. The essence of the race line in North America is that no person identified as Negro will be admitted as effectively social kin of any person classified as white. In those states which have laws against intermarriage of the races, there can be no legitimate offspring of a mixed mating.[3] In all states, the offspring of such a mating are popularly considered Negro whether legitimate or not. What would happen to a white woman who had an illegitimate child of a Negro father today, we can only guess. The treatment might vary according to region, community, class, and family. The result, if not the means, would probably be the same as in the case of the Southern white grandmother of Horace Cayton:[4] complete separation of mother and child. Neither the white mother-to-be of a Negro man's child nor the Negro mother-to-be of a white man's child can invoke the American woman's right to a shot-gun wedding. The Negro mother can at least keep her child. Here is a great American anomaly—a case in which the general rules and duties of kinship are not merely not invoked, but are completely denied. More than denied, they are taboo, even at the graveside. Those who would violate the taboo are cast out from the socially "superior" and more powerful race. They might be killed, in the name of virtue. For with respect to those classified as Negroes, virtue becomes vice and vice, virtue.

This may be illustrated by the phrase, "Would you want your sister to marry a Negro." Its meaning is that if she were to marry a Negro she would no longer be your sister, that her Negro husband would be no kin of yours, and that any children of the marriage, being Negroes, would likewise not be kin of yours. But the shame brought upon you, because of

3. Charles S. Mangum, Jr., *The Legal Status of the Negro* (Chapel Hill, University of North Carolina Press, N. C., 1940), Chap. I, "Who is a Negro," p. 18. "Every court which has considered the question has held that writing that a white man is a Negro is libelous per se. In the case of spoken words, however, the courts have disagreed."

4. Horace R. Cayton, *Long Old Road: an Autobiography,* New York, Trident Press, 1965. Also Seattle, University of Washington Press, 1969.

the former kinship, would justify not merely the withholding of the usual aid to kin, but violence, even killing. Thus there is a great moral fault—in the geological sense, and let us not quibble about the other sense—in American society when it comes to obligations to Negroes who would be kin if they were not Negro.

It is a fault that is crucial to any projection of the future of what Talcott Parsons calls "full citizenship" of Negroes or any other Americans of less than full standing. For citizenship as he conceives it, and as Americans generally do, is more than a legal status; a citizen is a member of a moral community. The definition of the white and Negro serves the function of limiting moral obligations of whites to Negroes; it makes the relationship not reciprocal, but one-sided. The function of the American definition of race has been to justify that one-sidedness; and the essence of the justification is exclusion of Negroes from full membership in the "human race." To make sure, all doubtful cases must be cast into the less-than-human group.

The American definition of racial categories—as that of most social categories—seems very odd indeed if considered from any other point of view than that of setting the limits of social obligation. Yet there is a consistency in the definition, a consistency worked out in social history, not in a laboratory or by a scientific taxonomist.

The historical situation in which the categories were worked out has been one in which it was greatly to one's advantage to be classed white, and in which the people already called white had and have power to determine the criteria and to settle disputed cases of identity. If we talk of the future of Negro Americans we of necessity talk of the manner in which Americans are and will be categorized, of the importance which they will attach to the various categories, of the relative power of groups to control the definitions of these classifications and to assign people to them, and of the advantages of belonging to one group rather than another.

If the criteria for classifying us by race remain the same, continue to be applied to all Americans except a few exotics—American Indians and those Asiatics who comprise the majority of the human species but are not at the moment numerous in America—and continue to be important, projection of the relative numbers of Americans of the two major racial categories will be a matter of predicting rates of marriage, including intermarriage, rates of reproduction properly corrected in the many ways required in such a society as ours, and rates and directions of migration. In view of the genocide practiced by the German National-Socialists and occasionally advocated here, one would have to consider the possibility of political and military action—with methods not yet known—of one race against another and would have to predict the winner.

The significance of race in North America and our definition of it have given us sharp and suspicious eyes. Most Americans will immediately place another with but few Negroid characteristics as a Negro. People in other parts of the world may have sharp eyes or ears for people of the categories crucial in their societies, but not necessarily for ours. Once we have placed a person in the Negro category, it takes strong proof to the contrary to alter the assignment. We may even place them without any biological signs. Twice in my career a blond blue-eyed student has drawn my office door shut after her in a way that told me—from experience as a college teacher—that she was about to reveal her troubling secret, and before she could speak I knew—from being an American—what the secret was to be. One, a young woman, had come from the West to Chicago to escape from her Swedish mother and become a Negro—when it suited her. Her father was a Negro jazz musician whom she found fascinating, though he had abandoned his family. The other, a middle-aged woman, had moved North to become white so that her daughter could do likewise. A middle-class woman, she required letters of recommendation; all of hers betrayed that her previous employers had been Negro institutions. I do not go around looking for Negroes behind pale faces and blue eyes, but I carry the experience of America in me. I am quick to classify by race; I do not mean to be, but I am.

Our definition of races is then both complicated and simple. There is no American who could not be a Negro, so far as physique is concerned. In that sense it is complicated. It is simple, however, in that anyone is a Negro if it is obvious that some of his ancestors were Negroid, and in that anyone is considered a Negro if it is known or strongly rumored that one or more of his ancestors were Negroid. The American white race is a residual category whose members have developed an uncanny and suspicious eye for any who do not belong. Such sharpness and suspiciousness of eye can be developed only about something which people regard as of paramount importance. Negroes of course equal, indeed probably excel, whites in their eye for race; they have even greater reason to recognize race. It can mean the difference between friend and enemy, one's own to be trusted or outsider to be feared, between life and death.

The sharpness of eye is developed not merely with respect to physical characteristics. There are findings which show that race is more easily detected, or sought, by the white eye in some circumstances than others. If the Negro does not wear one of the many uniforms of deference or of poverty or play some role in which we expect Negroes to appear, the Negro-ness might not be noticed. On the other hand, there might be situations in which it would be doubly noticed. Imagine a handsomely purple-black Negro woman in a decolleté white gown at the ball celebrating her husband's inauguration as President of the United States. The future of the perception of race is an important part of the future of this country. Television, the founding of new nations, and the United Nations have shown to the world people of every tint and physiognomy in nearly all social roles. This raises again the question of the power of costume, role, and office to determine what we see and accept. The priest, the pope, the king, the supreme court justice—in our image of them does the office outshine race or does race dim the luster of the office? Or might it be that a situation would arise in which race and office would enhance each other? As Negroes appear in a greater variety of prestigeful positions, perhaps whites will allow the Negro-ness to blend into the shadow of the office or role—after, of course, we have given ourselves (the whites) credit for allowing the Negro to occupy the position and after we have given him some condescending credit for his sterling character and hard struggle.

We do not in this country, as in South Africa, have card-carrying Negroes. But the assignment to the Negro race is probably just as fateful, except for the possibility for white Negroes to resign from the race by going where they are not known and denying the bonds of kinship. But we are all card-carriers: social security, insurance, military registration, Blue Cross, Union, credit, driver's license, blood-group, allergies. All of us have our pockets full of them. There are dossiers especially on people of the middle class to which an increasing proportion of us of all races belong. The internal revenue and the FBI know all about us. The Educational Testing Service and the College Entrance Examination Boards have the word on an ever increasing proportion. The colleges of the country and the mail-order houses have the most amazing mailing-lists. By a trick of history racial classification is being left off cards and dossiers just when everyone in the country is getting cards and dossiers. There are few of us who could not be unerringly classified as white or Negro by the IBM machines or computers, because of combinations of characteristics on tapes or cards. The isolated communities where certain groups of peculiar mixtures of ancestry once maintained a special racial status are disappearing. We are all classified. There is no hiding place from our past; the question of the future then is whether those agencies which inquire so relentlessly into our pasts will bother to pay attention to race.

So far as I know there has been no movement in this country for a long time to change the criteria by which persons are assigned to the social category, Negro. There have always been criteria, including color, of distinction within the Negro world. But no one appears to be proposing any elaboration of the racial classification or any new set of devices to determine whether any given individual is indeed Negro or not. As a frontier the racial line is quiet, except for the drive to keep race off documents and even to forbid tell-tale photographs. If the Black Muslims were to gain the day, they would have to set up tribunals to decide who is truly of their morally superior race rather than of the bestial white race. But the general movement is to make race line unimportant, to have Negro-ness forgotten. Suppose there were no longer any distinct social advantage in not being Negro; suppose, as Edwin C. Berry of the Chicago Urban League puts it, it were really and fully all right to be colored. Suppose the time came when a court would no longer hold it libelous to put it in writing that a white man is a Negro.[5] There might still be a period in which it would be newsworthy to be the first Negro to be named, say, a justice of the Supreme Court or president of the Dupont Company (and the latter might be the more newsworthy!). One's identification as Negro might be used to push a special claim to some position because of previous disadvantage. Those would be passing phases. But would Negroes really want their past as Negroes forgotten in an essentially race-less world? It might be a world in which traditional American claims on social prestige would hold.

For here is a paradox of identity and prestige. Except for being black, American Negroes have most of the symbols necessary for being considered rather more American than average. They were a larger proportion of the population in 1790 than now. Not long ago, the way to find the Negro sections of Northern cities from the census was to look up those tracts with very high proportions of the population native-born of native parents. Negroes are "old Americans," a characteristic that earns one prestige. They are almost WASP's. If only they were not black, some of them would be eligible for the Daughters of the American Revolution; maybe that is why the organization is so adamant on race. Too many of the "wrong" people are eligible. One of my eight great-great grandmothers was held up to a window to see the British soldiers marching in the streets of Philadelphia in the War of 1812. She was the granddaughter of a German bondwoman who had married a veteran of the American Revolution. The bondwoman part can be forgotten or even used as proof of early immigration, but color cannot be forgotten. Yet in this world of prestige by date of immigration of the earliest known American ancestor, the Negroes have one of the valued symbols. Some Negroes have shown themselves all too ready to make the claim, by way of African princes taken into slavery or by emphasizing unacknowledged kinship with white families of renown. It will of course be interesting to see whether Negroes, by the time that there is no advantage in not being one, will want to claim any kinship with the people who so stubbornly denied them the human rights they so loudly preached—for whites only—from pulpit and platform. Perhaps they will ask the Jewish question: If I were not a Jew, what would I want to be? A descendant of the Mayor of Selma, Alabama? Or of any whites, for that

5. Charles S. Mangum, Jr., *op. cit.,* Chap. II, "Libel and Slander."

matter? One possibility, pleasant to contemplate, is that all of our descendants will have found better canons of social prestige when our eye for race has grown dim. If any emphasis is, in that day, to be put upon descent from those who cleared the land, contributed to America's arts, and struggled up patiently—until they got impatient and got results—from humble origins, the Negroes will have a foremost claim.

Here, earlier, as also in South Africa, some people of Negro descent sought to differentiate themselves from others, thus increasing the number of racial categories and modifying the criteria of racial ascription. That day is past, partly by fiat of the white world supported by bureaucratic identification of everyone, partly by the very definite improvement of the position of Negroes with the promise that integration—tendency toward disappearance of the race line—will continue, perhaps at an accelerated rate. It certainly will not disappear for a long time, but it seems likely that there will be no new movement to multiply the categories or change the criteria. Nor is there any movement to have Negroes rather than whites decide who is a Negro. Perhaps the system has gone on so long, and the web of association and kinship within the American Negro race is so great, that there is essential consensus on who belongs to each race.

If we assume that the races will continue to be defined as they are, what of number? That is a problem on which demographers are working. As one extreme model, one might take a situation in which every marriageable Negro would be married to a white and in which those marriages would be as fruitful as marriages between whites. Approximately one white in nine would get a Negro mate and—as now defined—Negro children. In a few generations about half the children born would be Negro by definition, but it would be very hard to tell which were Negro and which not unless a strict record were kept. It would require card-carrying!

Perhaps we should have a geneticist on this problem. If, as some say, the ten per cent of Negroes in our population already carry a gene pool of which approximately one quarter comes from Europe, and if intermarriage were complete, Negroid genes would probably not leave much trace in our population. I set this up as a sort of absurdity. Only a completely totalitarian government could bring about such high intermarriage; genocide has been more to totalitarian liking thus far. The case does indicate, however, how greatly in favor of an essentially white race the proportions in our population work even with our racial definition which eliminates all doubtful cases from the white race.

Suppose even the milder—but equally improbable—case of mathematically random intermarriage between two groups which are in proportions of nine to one. The larger one would exist practically forever as a "pure" group of some size, even if all the mixed specimens were taken from it, while the smaller, even with the addition of all the known mixed cases, would become so diluted that apparently "pure" specimens would become very few and the mixtures who might "pass" would become a great majority of the total population. I apologize for even mentioning this subject. If the demographers and geneticists wish to slay me, let them first set up the various models, probable and improbable, of future breeding and interbreeding of these peculiar categories of people who are, by Americans, classified as of one race or another. The Negroes ought to disappear, but probably will not. Nuclei of people persist even when intermarriage is not strictly forbidden. I am trying only to imagine the genetic situation which would be least favorable to the survival of a large number of Americans discernibly of Negroid descent, perceptibly different, that is, from another large number of Americans.

Suppose we take the much more likely, but still not very likely, case of an America which had become completely indifferent to racial characteristics but which retained its other ways of rating people: education, income, manners, speech, occupation, and family connections. There are societies in South America which are relatively indifferent to racial characteristics, but are exceedingly sensitive to the signs of social class, including "good family" or connection with prestigeful kin-webs. Those societies are economically such that it is much more difficult to get ahead in the world than it is in the United States. A few women, in nearly all societies, have been able by beauty or other talents to rise from the slums to palaces—as in Hollywood. Let us not go into the question of the fascination of the exotic or of the universality of the canons of female beauty. Negro women have not succeeded as young stars in Hollywood; there have been many who would have done so had uncensored male admiration been the only requirement. Perhaps even now a Josephine Baker would not have to emigrate to Paris, but in her earlier years talent cum beauty was not enough. Leaving aside fame by bedazzlement, a very common thing in America, if we became relatively indifferent to race, but kept our other criteria of status and prestige, and rewarded people for about the same activities as now, what would be the future of Negro Americans?

American Negro women have always had more security and less risk of physical and social attack, other than rape, than the men. Already there is a large group of middle-class Negro families in the country. The labor force includes an increasing proportion of people of white-collar occupations and an even larger one of a somewhat lower-middle-class style of life. The Negro family has been stable, but not so Negro marriage. One would expect that with more nearly equal opportunity for jobs at all levels, Negroes might approach white families in their characteristics, become more stable in those matters where they are less stable than white families, and less so where they are more stable than white families of similar class. A real break-through is likely to come only when an inter-racial marriage could be based on a sound mutual bet that, together, the mates could get on at some appropriate class level in some American community other than The Village, Chicago's Hyde Park, Cambridge, or their likes and could dare to have children there. A wise and strong Negro woman and a white man who is sensitive and intelligent—and knows some of his own weaknesses—might make a winning combination given half a chance or better. Let us not be over-skeptical of such radical changes. One-fourth of the Jewish men in Germany were marrying Christian women when Hitler came to power; rather, Christian women were winning one-fourth of the marrying Jewish men in a tight market. Those women, given the small proportion of Jews in the population, were—lucky or not—a few.

Even if we were to have a breakthrough of that magnitude in Negro-white intermarriage, we Americans would still probably consist of a number of endogamous lumps plus certain interstitial, more or less open groups resulting from previous mixtures. My favorite minority people, the French Canadians, have absorbed great numbers of Irish, Scotch, and English, and probably some Negro Americans. Their English-speaking descendants in the United States are probably as numerous as the apparently homogeneous French people of Quebec. Many ethnic and sectarian communities lose large numbers of their children to the "world," yet remain identifiable, endogamous nuclei. Perhaps it will be so with Negroes and whites if, and long after, there is a great deal of intermarriage and interbreeding. As for interbreeding without intermarriage, it will surely dwindle to nothing when the differences between income, power, and social class sharply decline.

The most drastic imaginable change in American race relations would be the full extension of the American bilateral kinship system to include mixed couples and their in-laws on both sides. A mixed marriage—as to race, nation, politics—is often one which ends up not mixed, that is, one in which kin connections are kept on one side only, the other being more or less excluded. Many American marriages are, de facto, like that. The poor, or otherwise embarrassing, relations are suddenly or gradually dropped. The people who make odd marriages of the same kind may in a short time create new homogeneous nuclei of congenial people who hold what are scarcely distinguishable from family reunions. They may hive off and form a new social grouping.

It may well be that, while we will not see new racial categories defined, an increase of intermarriage will be part of that forming of new nuclei of families with common style. Perhaps the common experience of sit-ins, marches, and demonstrations will, as some Southern and other whites predict, create new groups whose common élan and whose common experience of cattle prods and the evil-eye of hatred will lead to continuing associations, including marriages.

Perhaps there will come to be cases where mixed couples and their children will be able to lead normal lives, with real uncles and aunts and cousins on both sides, or at least with those *ersatz* relatives so many Americans have—especially those who have left home and found a breathing place in a moral and intellectual atmosphere other than the one they were brought up in. While we may be a card-carrying people, we appear also to be a people of myriad informal nuclei of common style, fêtes, cuisine, play, and moral causes.

Even if many whites and Negroes were drawn into such common social nuclei, there would remain the problem of the great hang-over from centuries of discrimination. And even if all discriminatory practices based on race alone were to disappear, their accumulated effects would remain. How long would it be before Negroes would have, in the same proportion as other Americans, the characteristics which would allow them to move freely in our society and economy; how long before they would be distributed in the same proportions as others among occupations, and would be like them in income, consumption habits, education, and in all respects but race itself? It would certainly take a long, long time. Many other social events and currents could change the direction and rates of change in the Negroes' condition—and that of others—in the interim.

In the first paragraph of this essay I spoke of the Negroes' place in American society and of the ways in which they have been kept in it. People have searched Scripture and come up with proof that God made the races one day and means them to stay apart—in a peculiar kind of apartness, to be sure, since He equipped them to be strongly tempted and able to get together in the way most fatal to apartness. People have developed elaborate ideologies to justify excluding Negroes from full membership in the human race. Having excluded them from the human race for nobler purposes, we have thought ourselves justified in adapting our legal institutions in whatever ways turn out to be necessary to keep a lower breed in subjection. Thus the sheriff's posse was changed from an occasional device by which citizens might protect themselves from the outlaw into a permanent institution with membership and leadership going from generation to generation—an "almost institution" always ready to mobilize people to keep the Negro in his place and destroy any local whites and to get rid of outside whites who take the Negro's side. A chronically sloppy police in not quite open collaboration with eternally vigilant posses with good horses and guns, back street gangs with old cars and whatever weapons come to hand, and occasional fanatics who are good shots at a distance confront our society with a combination of legitimate and bastard institutions which is very difficult to combat. We have seen some successes of law and vigorous police work against this combination. We must ask whether continued progress against this system of keeping Negroes in their place will result in general improvement of our policing institutions, by which they would approach the quality of policing in England and the countries of western Europe. We must also ask whether increasing application of our constitutional principles to Negroes will be accompanied by a return to the more obvious interpretation of the great documents of the Christian tradition, which are broadly humane. Once there is not even any apparent gain in reading the Gospel backwards will there continue to be great numbers of apparently sincere people who find themselves driven to make that backwards interpretation?

I remember Robert E. Park once saying that even the most benighted Southern Baptist usually gets right on the race question after service as a missionary in Africa. In our own time we have Billy Graham preaching the "Bible" gospel, so cherished as a symbol by many Southern whites, only to integrated congregations. Will increasing integration bring release from those constrictions of mind and sentiment which have certainly had some part in the perversion of doctrines, principles, and institutions themselves? Noble principles have been perverted in defense of vested interests other than those of whites in exploiting the Negro; and noble principles have — with the aid of courageous men — been cleaned, sharpened, and well-used for their true purposes. We have also, in our American institutions, many that have degenerated to very low level without any connection with keeping Negroes in their place. Yet we must ask, at this time of actual and impending great change in the relations of Negro with other Americans, what is likely to be the general effect on our institutions and conduct of this one great change — occurring as I suppose it was bound to do — along with other great changes in our institutions and way of living. Perhaps all that it is wise to say on this subject is that we ought to keep a sharp eye out for the clues to directions of change, take hold of those clues and follow them out quickly and imaginatively, make the most of them in directing social policy and practice, with a sober reminder that we cannot do very well at home unless we do equally well abroad on these matters of humane conduct.

TWENTY-FOUR

French and English in the Economic Structure of Montreal

We propose to examine herein the position of the French and the English in the hierarchy of the economic structure.[1] Not occupation as such, but positions of control are the centre of interest. Something of what we have in mind is indicated in the following quotation: "[Since] economic activity is quite as much organized through systems of administrative or canalizing controls as it is by the market, it is impossible to outline the structure of American economy without covering the structure of such controls . . . In the conduct of economic activity the controls exercised by individuals or groups arise from three main sources: possession of one or more of the factors of production, possession of liquid assets, and position in relation to a functioning organization."[2]

It is common knowledge among the residents of Quebec that the English exercise a greater share of financial control than their proportion of the population would warrant. The English and French are quite conscious of this difference and each have their accepted *clichés* for describing or

The Canadian Journal of Economics and Political Science, Vol. 7, No. 4, November, 1941, pp 493-505.

1. This study proceeds from the conviction that discussions of the relations between the French and English in Quebec have been confined too much to the problems of acculturation. In general the relations between ethnic groups have been studied in terms of the taking over of culture traits, matters of spatial succession, and occupational specialization. Less attention has been paid to place or position in the institutional relations within the economic structure.

2. National Resources Committee, *The Structure of the American Economy*, part I, *Basic Characteristics* (Washington, D.C.: Government Printing Office 1939), pp. 153,155.

explaining it. As yet no detailed analysis has been made of the measure of this financial control or of the ways in which it has been exercised. Nor has any previous study shown just how important the ethnic factor is in the structure of financial control. In this study our analysis is confined to Montreal.[3]

We shall be concerned with three phases of the relations between the English and the French within the economic structure: first, the differences in terms of role or position within a given industry or occupation; second, the general division of labour in terms of occupational specialization; third, differences in terms of ownership or control of enterprise with regard to size and kind of interest held. These differences are manifest in the concentration of one group above or below certain limits in the given structure.[4]

The first two points have already been established in the unpublished theses of Messrs. William J. Roy[5] and Stuart M. Jamieson.[6] In both of these studies we find an emphasis on the concept of *division of labour* between the two cultural groups. They show that the French majority furnish the large and relatively undifferentiated labour supply and that the English are in positions of control and in those which demand a greater mastery of modern technical knowledge.

Mr. Roy dealt with the role and position of the ethnic[7] groups in manufacturing industries. In making his study he obtained data on the

3. In Montreal the French constitute 60.8 per cent of the population, as compared with 79.0 per cent in the province, and 28.2 per cent in the Dominion. Montreal is the great meeting place for the French and English in business affairs. Here, if anywhere, we would see the extent to which the French have entered into the control of nation-wide corporations. As the largest city in Canada, Montreal transacts a great deal of business for its million consumers; it is also the headquarters city of the region and shares with Toronto the headquarters of most large corporations.

4. While it is not the purpose of this article to deal with more than contemporary statistics of certain phases of the relationship between the French and English in Montreal, and while certain obvious conclusions can be derived from the data presented, we should keep in mind the history of the colonial pattern of military conquest, and of the commercial, industrial, and financial development of the country, and the roles played by the French and English. The French were the "native" population in Quebec; the English the "invaders," taking full advantage of their conquest by developing the as yet unexploited labour power and resources of the region. Cf. D. G. Creighton, *The Commercial Empire of the St. Lawrence* (Toronto, The Ryerson Press 1937); E. C. Hughes, "Industry and the Rural System in Quebec" (*Canadian Journal of Economics and Political Science,* vol. IV, Aug. 1938, p. 341-9); E. C. Hughes, "Position and Status in a Quebec Industrial Town" (*American Sociological Review,* vol. III, Oct., 1938, pp. 709-17).

5. William J. Roy, "The French-English Division of Labor in Quebec" (M.A. Thesis, McGill University, 1935).

6. Stuart M. Jamieson, "French and English in the Institutional Structure of Montreal: A Study of Division of Labour" (M.A. Thesis, McGill University, 1938).

7. In Quebec the population is predominantly French-Catholic or English-Protestant. There are, of course, marginal groups but this "ethnic" distinction is the major one involving both language and religion.

nationality and position of 15,283[8] employees in the following types of Montreal concerns: iron and steel, textile, boot and shoe, wood-using, mattress and springs, furniture, chemicals and allied products, printing and allied graphic arts. This selection—in no sense a sample of all manufacturing industries in the city—represented a range from "big" English concerns relatively new to the province to small concerns, owned and operated by the French over a considerable period of time.

Of the 15,283 employees, 30.8 per cent were English, 62.6 per cent French, and 6.6 per cent "Other."[9] Assuming that the ethnic factor is of no consequence in determining position in industry, we would expect to find an approximation to each of these proportions in each of the rank groups. The data, however, showed that 73.8 per cent of the managerial group were English and 22.6 per cent were French. In the sales force 62.4 per cent were English and 34.3 per cent French. In the clerical, foremen, and assistant foremen groups we also find, though in a decreasing degree, over-representation of the English and the reverse for the French. When we come to the skilled workers only 25.3 per cent were English and 69.4 per cent were French and in the semi-skilled group only 19.4 per cent were English and 74.6 per cent were French.[10]

Thus we find that as one goes up the scale of important positions in industry there is an increasing proportion of English in each rank group, and conversely that as one goes down the scale the proportion of French increases until it becomes overwhelmingly great at the bottom. Roy also points out that such French as are in top managerial positions are in smaller industries.

The ethnic difference in iron and steel, and primary textiles, is typical of the big business in Montreal. These are owned by the English and have a high proportion of French in all categories below the rank of foreman. Iron and steel have a higher proportion of English because of the skilled nature of much of their work. Textiles are low-skilled and low paid and have the highest proportion of French. Highly speculative enterprise, such as the garment industry, is usually owned by Jewish entrepreneurs. The French are likely to own concerns in which there is relatively little elaborate machinery or involved financial relations. Most of these, such as boot and shoe, wood-using, and printing, are native to the province, have always been owned by the French, and employ a large number of French workers.[11]

8. This number constitutes one-sixth of the total gainfully employed in manufacturing industries in Montreal.

9. In the total population of the city these nationalities are found in the proportions 26:61:13, respectively.

10. Roy, *op. cit.*, p. 137 and Appendix, Table 41-C, p. 31.

11. *Ibid.*, p. 92 and chap. VIII.

When a French firm becomes a serious competitor of the large English companies, it is likely to be bought and become a part of the big business owned by the English.[12] In the case of the larger boot and shoe concerns which are still operated by the French, the machinery used is rented and serviced by a large American company. The English are also taking over some of the sash and door factories.[13]

In an analysis of occupational data from the 1931 *Census of Canada,* Mr. Jamieson shows that the English are employed in more than proportionate numbers in industries which require a high ratio of skilled or technical to unskilled labour. Participation of this language group is highest in those industries which are new to the province, having little or no trained labour force among the French Canadians. This is especially marked in specialized industries such as air-transportation, ship-building, telegraph and telephone, communications, non-ferrous metals, lithographing, and engraving. Other comparatively newly developed industries requiring a trained labour force, such as chemicals, pulp and paper, and most lines of iron products have a similar predominance of English gainfully employed in them. Mr. Jamieson notes that with the exception of lithographing and engraving, all of the above industries are dominated by English controlled corporations.[14]

Industries organized on a basis of mass production and standardization are dominated for the most part by English capital. The participation of English gainfully employed is far more than proportional in sugar-refining, and declines through flour-milling and rubber goods. In liquor and non-metallic minerals there is no marked specialization. Animal foods, primary textiles, and tobacco products have an over-representation of French.[15]

The English-speaking group, owners and directors as well as employees, predominate in highly specialized and corporate-controlled industries requiring heavy investments of capital and a wide market. The nationality of employees appears to have little direct relation to that of the owners. It is, rather, a matter of industrially useful skills which members of a group can apply regardless of their cultural backgrounds. The characteristic large business unit is preoccupied more with the search for profit than with the ethnic[16] character of its labour force.

12. In view of the trend towards centralization in modern industry, it is to be expected that the small firm will be bought out by the large one. Small units with local control are combined with larger units with more distant control. This process is affecting both French and English firms. As the majority of large firms are English, the process of centralization would seem to indicate the passing of French control.

13. Roy, *op. cit.*

14. Jamieson, *op. cit.,* p. 69.

15. *Ibid.,* p. 72.

16. *Ibid.,* p. 74 ff.

The predominance of French-Canadian employees in French-Canadian owned industries is to be expected. The latter manufacture perishable goods, such as bread, biscuits, and canned goods for a local market. They also predominate in industries which are perhaps most native to the province such as leather goods, wood products (especially furniture), and to a lesser extent tobacco. Mr. Jamieson also notes, as did Mr. Roy, the American control, through ownership of machinery, in the boot and shoe industry and mentions that the same type of relationship is to be found to some extent in canning and preserving.[17]

In brief the points established in these studies concern the relative position of the French and English within industry, and the general pattern of occupational specialization. They also indicate certain broad differences with regard to the size and type of control exerted through ownership.

In order to carry this point still further, we made a more detailed analysis of the differences in size and kind of enterprise carried on in Montreal. We were able to make a complete tabulation of all merchandising firms[18] listed in the Dun and Bradstreet Directory (March, 1940) for the city of Montreal, showing the relationship between type of business,[19] estimated pecuniary strength of firms,[20] and nationality.[21]

17. *Ibid.*

18. The Dun and Bradstreet Directory lists nearly all merchandising firms by city or town. This list includes firms engaged in the production, processing, wholesale, and retail distribution of goods, and the servicing of merchandise.

19. We divided the merchandising firms into four main groups: (1) production, processing, etc.; (2) wholesale, commodity, brokers, manufacturer's agents, etc.; (3) retail trade; (4) miscellaneous services. The latter includes a wide range of services from large construction companies, to various sized printing, trucking, garages, and laundry establishments.

20. Estimated pecuniary strength is the index given (in dollars) along with the credit rating in the Dun and Bradstreet Directory. There were twenty-one ratings of financial strength which we reduced to five. The original groups ranged from under $500 to over $1,000,000.

21. "Nationality" is used here as a convenient term to describe apparent ethnic affiliation. In designating the nationality of the firm, we do not mean to discount the possibility of another nationality having some control over it, either through a directorship, owning part of the means of production or some other way. It has been noted that certain large French firms have one or more English directors, and that certain English firms have French directors. We have already noted that an American company produces and rents machinery for making boots and shoes. It may be objected that we use the term "ownership" loosely, in view of the fact that the stock of corporations may be widely distributed. In answer, we remind the reader that it has been amply shown in various studies, that the group who own a very small proportion of the total stock of a company may effectively act *as if* they owned the company. In making our tabulation nationality was assumed in the following manner: (a) from the name of the firm — that is, a firm with a French name would be considered French by the general population. For the individual familiar with the French and English names in the province, this is not too difficult. (b) In addition to name, the address of the firm is usually written in French or English according to the nationality of the owner. The term English includes British, English-Canadian, American, and Jewish. It might have been profitable to separate the Jewish from the other firms in this group, but the task of tabulating over 16,000 made it impossible, as time did not permit checking such a list against other sources of information. French means French Canadian, but might include a few from France. "Others" includes

In our analysis of these merchandising firms we considered nationality as one dimension and size of firm as the other. Of the 16,401 firms tabulated, 7,943 or 48.4 per cent were English, 7,378 or 45.0 per cent were French, and 1,080 or 6.6 per cent "Other." It should be noted that 5,707 or slightly more than one-third of the firms, were listed but not rated. The proportion of unrated firms varies in each nationality group—the English having the highest proportion, namely 41.1 per cent, the French 28.7 per cent, and "Others" 30.6 per cent. The higher proportion of unrated English firms can in part be accounted for by the fact that only the headquarters of a large corporation is rated. Subsidiary branches listed in other cities are referred to the main company. In our tabulation we noted several such concerns of considerable size. These would probably fall into the first or second size groups. If it were possible to include these, the overloading of the English at the top would be even more marked. The large French firm is very unlikely to have its headquarters in a place outside of Montreal and there is little likelihood that an unrated French firm would fall into Groups I or II. In the remainder of our analysis we shall deal only with the rated firms.

Chart I gives in summary form the percentage distribution of the French and English in the various estimated pecuniary strength groups. As one would expect, there are few very large size firms and a great number of

Chart I. Percentage Distribution of English and French Merchandising Firms by Their Estimated Pecuniary Strength*

Estimated Pecuniary Strength Groupings	English	French
I = $750,000 and over		
II = $125,000 to $750,000		
III = $20,000 to $125,000		
IV = $2,000 to $20,000		
V = Less than $2,000		

```
20   15   10   5   0   5   10   15   20   25   30
                   PER CENT
```

*From tabulation of all firms listed and rated in Dun and Bradstreet Directory, March, 1940. Of the firms classified as "Other" (7 per cent of the total) two-thirds belong in Group V.

names that were Greek, Chinese, etc., and certain doubtful cases. As the "Other" category makes up but 7 per cent of the total number listed, and as two-thirds of this 7 per cent were in the lowest size grouping, possible errors are not too significant.

small ones. The English have a majority of firms in the first three categories
and the French a majority in the last two. By estimating the total financial
strength of the firms in each category we get a much better picture of the
relative financial strength of the English and French. A rough estimate of
financial strength is shown in Chart II. This estimate was derived by
multiplying the number of firms in each group by the lower value of the
estimated pecuniary strength.[22] This estimate is *most* conservative for
several reasons. First, we used the lower limit of the estimated pecuniary
strength group. Secondly, the two original groups included in what we have
designated as I were open end groups (Aa =*over* $1,000,000 and
A+ = *over* $750,000). Third, included in II are a large number of firms
which had "one-legged" ratings. Instead of having both an estimated
pecuniary strength and a credit rating, they were given the rating of—!
which meant that they fell within the range of $125,000 and over
$1,000,000 and that their credit ratings fell within the range of those with

---

Chart II. Approximate Percentage Distribution of Estimated Pecuniary Strength by Nationality and E.S.P. Group

Estimated Pecuniary Strength Groupings	English	French
I = $750,000 and over		
II = $125,000 to $750,000		
III = $20,000 to $125,000		
IV = $2,000 to $20,000		
V = Less than $2,000		

```
                                 45  40  35  30  25  20  15  10   5   0   5  10
                                               PER CENT
```

---

the above-mentioned estimated pecuniary strength groups. These firms we
multiplied by $562,500, or the midpoint between the above-mentioned
limits but a good number of them probably could be rated Aa.

However, from this conservative estimate we find that 86.6 per cent of
the estimated pecuniary strength is English and only 12.0 per cent French.
It should also be noted that at least 45 per cent of all estimated pecuniary

22. In order to make our estimate more precise we used the twenty-one original E.P.S.
groups in our computation. We then regrouped the twenty-one products so that the E.P.S.
groups would correspond to the five used in this paper.

strength—probably nearer 55-60 per cent on the basis of the above-mentioned limitations—is held by the 208 largest English corporations.[23]

In discussing the financial strength of the large English corporations we have confined our statements to our data giving estimated pecuniary strength. It is important, however, to keep in mind other factors which are bases of control such as the various kinds of interrelations found between corporation managements—either through interlocking directorates, intercorporate minority stock-holding, interrelationships resulting from the servicing of large corporations or the control over investment funds, and corporation interest groupings.[24] Consideration of such factors is beyond the limits of this paper but if accounted for would reinforce the pattern of English control to an even greater extent.[25]

Of all firms rated there were 15.7 per cent engaged in production, 8.3 per cent in wholesale trade, 59.2 per cent in retail trade, and 16.8 per cent in services. Table I gives the distribution of each nationality within these categories. The English constitute a large majority of the production group, a lesser majority in the wholesale group. The French are in the majority in

23. The term estimated pecuniary strength seems to correspond to liquid assets. It has been pointed out in the *Structure of American Economy* that "possessor of liquid assets is in a position to buy action from others" and sometimes the mere possession without actual expenditure can influence the action of others, "though for the most part the controls derived from liquid assets depend on the expenditure of liquid assets in the market" (p. 155).

24. *Structure of American Economy*, p. 158.

25. Mr. Jamieson in Appendix A of his thesis gives us some indication of the number of directorates held by English and French in certain types of business or industry. From this table we have compiled the one below showing the nationality of the directors in firms of a given type.

Industry or business	Number of firms	Directors	
		English	French
Banks.....................................	10	140	26
Transportation and communication......	7	73	6
Iron and steel.............................	10	87	7
Non-ferrous metals.......................	8	76	5
Milling....................................	6	49	6
Pulp and paper............................	11	102	10
Electric power............................	8	68	7
Chemicals.................................	5	48	1
Non-metallic minerals....................	13	98	18
Liquor and beverages.....................	5	27	7
Total directorates........................	83	768*	93*

*This total does not eliminate duplication arising through interlocking directorates.

*Table I. Percentage Distribution of Each Nationality
Within the Merchandising Categories*

Type of firm	Total number of firms	Per cent English	Per cent French	Per cent Other	Per cent total
Production.................	1,674	81.2	15.7	3.1	100.0
Wholesale...................	888	67.0	27.5	5.5	100.0
Retail.......................	6,334	29.8	62.0	8.2	100.0
Service.....................	1,798	46.8	46.2	7.0	100.0
Total......................	10,694	43.8	49.2	7.0	100.0

the retail trade and the two nationalities have about equal proportions in the services. Again we should note that the service group covers a large range of firms from big construction companies and privately owned utilities to a multitude of medium and small size service shops, such as laundries, trucking companies, and print shops.

In Table II we show the median estimated pecuniary strength of firms of a given nationality and type. As we would expect, the 1,674 industrial firms are the largest having a median estimated pecuniary strength of $19,520. The 6,334 retail firms have a median of $937; the 1,798 service firms have a median of $1,293. Service and retail trade are the important fields of small enterprise and have as a rule the highest mortality. The 888 wholesale firms, though one-seventh the number of retail firms, have a median estimated pecuniary strength of $12,750, which is 13.5 times larger. This would seem to indicate the corporation orientation of this group.

When comparing the differences in the size of French and English firms we find that *for all firms* the median estimated pecuniary strength of English firms is approximately 2.9 times greater than the median estimated pecuniary strength of French firms. This difference varies in each of the merchandising categories, the English being 5.5 times larger in production, 2.4 times larger in wholesale, 2.1 times larger in service, and 1.2 times larger in retail.

In comparing the average estimated pecuniary strength (Table III) we find that the English are 3.9 times larger than the French in production, 1.8 times larger in wholesale, 2.6 times larger in retail, and 3.4 times larger in service. For all firms the English are nearly 8.2 times larger.

The domination of the English is most obvious in the fields of production

26. Large manufacturing corporations produce a larger proportion of the total value added by the manufacturing than their proportion of the total man power employed. This reflects to some extent the large volume of capital per unit of man power which they employ as compared with smaller companies (*Structure of American Economy*, p. 102).

Table II. Median Estimated Pecuniary Strength of Firms of Given Nationality and Type*

	English	French	Other	All firms
Production.................	$27,200	$4,926	$6,250	$19,520
Wholesale.................	18,310	7,500	6,430	12,750
Retail......................	1,128	913	777	937
Service....................	1,987	958	693	1,293
All firms...................	$ 2,861	$1,000	$ 884	$ 1,871

*In deriving the median estimated pecuniary strength of firms we used our original twenty-one estimated pecuniary strength groups.

Table III. Average Estimated Pecuniary Strength of Firms of a Given Nationality and Type

	English	French
Production.......................	$206,543	$52,713
Wholesale.......................	85,161	46,191
Retail...........................	13,496	5,093
Service..........................	37,096	10,956
All firms.........................	$ 82,944	$10,284

and wholesale trade. In production the English predominate in every size group, having 98.3 per cent in estimated pecuniary strength Group I[26] and decreasing to 67.0 per cent in estimated pecuniary strength Group V. The French increase from, 1.7 per cent in Group I to 25.9 per cent in Group V. Correspondingly in the wholesale group the English decrease from 80.0 per cent in Group I to 57.2 per cent in Group V. The French increase from 13.3 per cent in Group I to 35.9 per cent in Group V.

Among the retail firms we find the greatest differences. The English decrease from 85.7 per cent in Group I to 28.2 per cent in Group V. The French increase from 14.3 per cent in Group I to 62.5 per cent in Group V. As we have stated before, the French constitute the majority in retail trade, having 62.0 per cent compared with 29.8 per cent English. We have also noted that the median size English firm was only 1.2 times greater than the median size French firm, or 2.6 times greater than the average. This, however, tells only part of the story. Our data so far would seem to confirm the belief that the French always have had and have retained their place in small-scale enterprise. There are several important points which are not brought out in our statistical analysis.

Along with large-scale production units there have grown up large-scale distributing units—the department store, mail-order house, and the chain store. These units are frequently parts of vertical corporations which produce, distribute, and/or service their products. In Montreal nearly all these large-scale distributing units are English. In estimating the relative financial strength of the English and French retail firms we run into difficulties on two accounts: first, because the home companies of certain chain stores are located in another city, and secondly because in the case of vertical corporations the concern was probably tabulated as being in some other category (e.g., certain candy, clothes, and other manufacturers have their own stores for selling their products). These difficulties are greater obstacles in the retail category than any other because they affect a greater proportion of the large size firms—at least half of them. We can, however, state on the basis of our data that the English retail firms, approximately 30 per cent of all retail firms, control at least 55 per cent of the estimated pecuniary strength—if not a great deal more—and the French, 62 per cent of all retail firms, less than 45 per cent.

From these indications it would seem profitable to make a more detailed analysis of the retail firms in the city. Significant factors which would throw more light on the relations between the French and English in retail trade would be: (*a*) more accurate data on size and ownership; (*b*) analysis of directors; (*c*) the trend in the growth of large-scale distributing units; (*d*) mortality of small concerns; (*e*) volume of trade; (*f*) amount of merchandise handled that was produced by an English or French concern; (*g*) analysis of vertical combinations.

Much of what we have said about retail firms is equally applicable to the service ones. Here we would also need a more refined classification of types of service rendered. From the data we have we find that the English vary from 93.3 per cent in estimated pecuniary strength Group I to 41.5 per cent in estimated pecuniary strength Group V. Correspondingly, the French increase from 6.9 per cent of estimated pecuniary strength Group I to 49.3 per cent of estimated pecuniary strength Group V.

In conclusion we may say that the pattern of ethnic differences within the economic structure is not a simple clear-cut division of labour; it is, rather, one that involves a complex set of controls. These controls may be derived through being a corporation director, a factory manager, or a superintendent within the authority hierarchy. Or, on the one hand, the owner of a small enterprise may within certain limits determine the use made of certain resources without himself owning a significant volume of assets. But the large corporation, because of its position in corporate organization, shares in the controls arising from the assets of the corporation and the institutional relationships which develop out of its operation as a going concern. Large corporations have come to play an increasing role in relation to all corporations and in relation to the national economy.[27]

The pattern of ethnic relations must be seen within the structure of these controls. The distribution of all French and English firms within the various estimated pecuniary strength groups is as shown in Chart III. The controls derived through the possession of "estimated pecuniary strength" are effective both within size groups and between these groups. From the diagram it may be seen that the proportion of English in estimated pecuniary strength Group I is very large. This group though small in numbers controls such a large proportion of all estimated pecuniary strength (see Chart II) that it is in a position to influence the very small proportion of French firms of the same size. They may also determine policy which affects the smaller English and French firms. If we assume that what is generally said about the role of large corporations[28] holds true in Montreal, then the English are in a position to exercise a control over economic policy of tremendously greater magnitude than the French. We neither assume nor suggest that the English consciously use this power

---

Chart III. Place of French and English in the System of Economic Controls

Estimated Pecuniary Strength Groupings	English
I = $750,000 and over	
II = $125,000 to $750,000	
III = $20,000 to $125,000	
IV = $2,000 to $20,000	
V = Less than $2,000	

This is in effect an area chart. The area left and above the light diagonal line is English; that to the right and below is French. The proportions shown approximate the actual percentage distribution of English and French within each E.P.S. Group.

A — Heavy arrows show the directions of controls.

27. *Ibid.,* chap. IX, "The Structure of Controls."
28. Cf. *ibid;* L. G. Reynolds, *The Control of Competition in Canada* (Cambridge, Harvard Univ. Press 1940).

against the French. Yet, however much the few English who have economic power think and act in purely business terms, the French cannot but
think, act, and feel in ethnic terms. The French-Canadian small business
man suffers from the feeling of oppression and frustration so common
among small business men throughout the western world in our epoch. His
restless eye, casting about for a villain, catches the English names of the
corporations and persons of great economic power. If it rests there, it does
not mean that the French Canadian's vision is less penetrating than that of
other humans who feel the frustrations of a large and impersonal order of
things.

TWENTY-FIVE

The Industrial Revolution and the Catholic Movement in Germany

Modern industrial civilization is essentially a single historical phenomenon. It spreads from centres, and as it does so, brings tremendous changes in the lives of the individuals and groups which it reaches. Its enemies say that it destroys culture. In the search for markets, materials, and labor, the boundaries of cultural and political provinces are violated. New industrial regions grow up within which people of various traditions have to live and work together.

In the parts of the world inhabited by the colored races, the industrial revolution has been initiated by outsiders of European race and culture. The masses of the native population are usually drawn into the new economic structure in menial capacities. Those natives who had a measure of prosperity and prestige in the indigenous economy may find position and fortunes undermined. New goods threaten the markets of the native industries; new opportunities divert their supply of labor. Other natives, less bound by traditional interests and scruples, may assume leadership in the new types of exploitation. Such become the newly rich, hated as usurpers by the traditional aristocracy, and feared as competitors by the Europeans from whom they learned their lessons.

In such situations nationalistic movements may arise. Some native leaders attack the new system as such, and seek a revival of the old economy, or of some symbolic part of it. Others accept the new economy, but protest

Reprinted by permission of the publisher from *Social Forces,* Vol. 14. No. 2. December 1935. Copyright 1935, University of North Carolina Press.

against the inferior position of the natives within it. The traditional distinctions of sect, caste, class, and vested interest become hopelessly confused with newer ones based upon the varying extent and nature of native participation in the new economic life. The period of economic change is also one of enhanced cultural self-consciousness.

It is not so apparent that in more thoroughly industrialized countries, with a large measure of common culture and even a common language, various elements of the population are drawn into the newer industrial life at different rates and in distinct capacities. Nor is it so clear that apparently minor cultural differences, buttressed and accentuated by economic distinctions, may play an important rôle in the political life of a country. It is perhaps here that one should search for the solution of an apparent anomaly in many social and political movements and organizations. A Catholic trade union, for instance, appears to bear a contradiction in its very name; and when we hear of National-socialism, most of us assume that only a very calculating scoundrel could have thought of such a combination.

The anomaly in question is that of taking cultural differences as symbols of economic differences, so that political and even economic battles are fought in the name of language, religion, and tradition. The fact that these cultural factors, apparently so irrelevant to the issues of political and economic life, become the basis of political movements, would indicate that the industrial revolution does not rob people of their cultural peculiarities so completely as is often thought. It may indeed lead to self-conscious defense of traditional culture; a defense in which differences of opinion and discussion arise as to the implication of ideas previously taken comfortably for granted. If, as is often the case, an industrial revolution is ushered in by one element of the population, another element may regard the change as an attack on it and its traditions. One element may even conceive that it is being oppressed because of culture and tradition, when—in economic terms—it is simply being exploited by people who have little or no interest in its culture. This is but one of the by-products of social change.

The Catholics and Protestants of Germany furnish an excellent example of such difference in participation in the newer industrial life. At the beginning of the nineteenth century Catholics and Protestants were distributed on an essentially territorial basis. One's religion was part of his local cultural heritage; it was an attribute of the community, of saint and sinner alike. The political union of Germany brought Catholics and Protestants somewhat closer together, sometimes in bitter political struggle. It was, however, the transformation of German economic life in the latter half of the century that effectively broke down the denominational boundaries. To their horror, the good Protestants of old Prussia found a Catholic *diaspora* in their midst. The Catholic small tradesman of the Rhineland was forced to compete with aggressive Protestants, and the Catholic peasant was drawn from the land to work in industries established nearby by Protestant capitalists. Some parts of Catholic Germany, such as Upper Bavaria, remained relatively untouched by this revolution; others, especially the Rhineland and Westphalia, were transformed, both economically and politically.

The difference between the participation of Catholics and that of Protestants in the new industrial life may be clearly seen in the accompanying tables, compiled by the author from the German occupational census of 1907.[1] There is every reason to believe that the contrast was more marked at earlier dates.

As one proceeds down Table I from the so-called primary industries, through "industry" in the narrower sense, to commerce, transportation, and the free professions, the ratio of Catholics to non-Catholics steadily decreases. Seen in another dimension, of all Catholics engaged in occupations of Groups A, B, and C, 46 per cent were in A, 43 in B, and II in C; while the corresponding distribution of non-Catholics was: A, 36.5; B, 47.5; and C, 16 per cent.

Table I. The Number of Non-Catholics for Each 100 Catholics in Major Groups of Occupations

Total gainfully employed population, except domestic servants	167
A. Farming, gardening, animal husbandry, forestry and fishing	126
B. Industry, including mining and building	177
C. Commerce and transportation, including the hotel, restaurant and retail liquor trades	233
D. Military, civil service, the church and the free professions	212
E. Same as D, but excluding military and church; i.e., including the civil service and free professions alone	230*

*The ratio in the free professions is somewhat obscured by the fact that teaching, nursing, and similar services are performed by the clergy and by members of religious orders among the Catholics. The Catholics are disproportionately represented in ecclesiastical professions, and have less than the expected proportion in the secular professions. The military, then compulsory, is of no great interest to us.

This sequence from farming toward the free professions is also one from less mobile toward more mobile, as appears in Table II. The Catholics are relatively more numerous in the less mobile occupations. It is fair to assume that they tend to work closer to their birth-places than do non-Catholics.

1. The data were taken from *Statistik des Deutschen Reiches,* Vols. 203, 204, 206, 207, 211. This census was chosen because it shows the situation shortly before the disturbances of the Great War, and yet after the major development of German industry. The Jews, comparatively few in number, appear as "non-Catholics" in the compilations.

Table II. Mobility of Persons Engaged in Various Groups of Occupations

Occupational Groups	Percentages Living		
	In Gemeinde* where born	Outside Gemeinde but in Gebiet* where born	Outside Gebiet where born
A. Farming, etc..................................	53.2	38.2	8.5
B. Industry, etc..................................	39.3	34.6	26.1
C. Commerce, etc...............................	28.9	38.8	32.1
E. Professions...................................	13.1	45.2	41.7

*A *Gemeinde* is a municipality or rural district, roughly corresponding to our township. The *Gebiet* or district is sometimes the state, principality or province, but is often not so large as these units.

In those industries in which large corporate organization is the rule, the non-Catholics hold the majority of the dominating positions (Table III). In these industries, as in any organized into large units, the number of people in the higher positions is very small in relation to that in the lower. Neither Catholic nor Protestant has any great chance of becoming an employer. That does not, however, obscure the fact that these industries have been organized on their present basis and are largely controlled by non-Catholics. The Catholic in these industries is likely to have a non-Catholic employer and foreman. The technical and administrative staffs, the "white-collar" people, are also largely non-Catholic. Catholics are proportionately more numerous in the positions with less prestige.

The industries in question are those in which the modern type of large corporate enterprise prevails. In the case of spinning and weaving, the newer type of enterprise was imposed by outside entrepreneurs on an existing household and small shop system, which—in Catholic regions—had been in the hands of Catholic masters.

Ore and coal mining and the related industries are largely found in Catholic provinces because the raw materials are there. Again non-Catholic entrepreneurs brought in the new era; they got a large part of their labor force from among the Catholic peasants nearby. So far as the

Table III. People Engaged in Certain Industries, According to Religion and Position

Industry and Position*	Non-Catholic	Catholic	Non-Catholics Per 100 Catholics
Mining and preparation of ores:			
a. Managers, etc..............................	649	226	288
b. Salaried help...............................	3,343	1,790	186
c. Wage workers..............................	37,955	37,717	101
Total.......................................	41,947	39,733	106
Smelting and foundry and related industries:			
a..	1,020	328	312
b..	10,937	9,506	115
c..	79,335	142,344	56
Total.......................................	91,392	152,178	60
Coal mining, making of coke and briquettes:			
a..	1,068	312	343
b..	15,508	11,821	131
c..	218,101	355,504	61
Total.......................................	234,677	367,637	64
Spinning and weaving:			
a..	12,930	3,851	314
afr..	29,925	11,858	252
b..	37,017	16,756	221
c..	337,943	261,733	129
Total.......................................	417,815	294,198	142

*The category "a" includes independent entrepreneurs, leading officials and other managers of industries, including owners, partners, lessees, master workmen (in the old sense), directors and administrative officers.

"b" refers to non-managing (nichtleitende) officials, especially the scientifically, technically and commercially trained personnel, as well as inspectors and the accounting and office personnel. This category is covered roughly by our term "white collar" employees.

"c" includes other help and apprentices; factory, wage and day workers, including members of the family engaged in the industry. (The latter refers especially to household industries.)

"afr" is a special category for a few industries in which small units still persist. It includes small jobbers, doing contract work at home or in small shops, but hardly to be classed as independent entrepreneurs.

Catholic regions are concerned, the industrial revolution was not a spontaneous local affair, but an invasion led by non-Catholics.

Apart from the highly industrialized and almost purely Protestant Kingdom of Saxony, and the metropolitan centres, Berlin, Bremen, and Hamburg, the heavy industry of Germany was then, and is now, largely concentrated in the three strongly Catholic provinces of Westphalia, the Rhineland, and Silesia. Ninety-one per cent of the coal miners in Prussia, and 83
per cent of all in Germany were in these provinces. In the period from
1895 to 1907 there was an increase of 6,133,296 in the population supported by industry; over 2,000,000 of this increase were in Westphalia and
the Rhineland alone.

The industrial invasion of Catholic Germany has put the Catholic not
only into a new economy and under Protestant masters, but also alongside
non-Catholic workers. Table IV shows the extent to which the workers
of the two religious groups work in the same industries within the same
census areas. The 41 census areas are small states and the provinces of the
larger states.[2] In spite of their inequality in size and population, one may
assume that if large numbers of Catholics and non-Catholics work in the
same census unit and industries, they will have considerable contact with
each other. This assumption is especially justified in case of the industries
concerned, for they have large plants rather than small shops.

Instead of being completely isolated from each other, and instead of
being evenly distributed so that the ratio of Catholic to non-Catholic
workers in each census area would be the same as for the whole of
Germany, there is a wide variation in the ratios in the various census areas.
In all industries taken together, well over half the Catholic workers are in
the mixed areas. This is also true of the individual industries shown except
the textile industries in which just under half are in such areas. In none of
these industries are nearly one-half the Catholic workers in areas in which
they constitute 70 per cent or more of all the workers.

On the other hand, in all of the industries concerned, except mining, far
more than half the non-Catholic workers are in predominantly
non-Catholic areas. Even in mining, more than half the workers of each
group are in the mixed areas. The Catholic workers tend to be concentrated in areas in which there are large numbers of non-Catholic workers,
while the majority of the non-Catholic workers are in areas where there are
but few Catholic workers.

We may now summarize: (1) The growth of modern industry in the
Catholic regions of Germany was in fact a sort of non-Catholic invasion.
(2) The Catholics have, as a group, an inferior position in industry. (3) The
Catholic regions have not experienced the industrial invasion equally. It

---

2. A better unit would have been the municipality or the industrial plant, but such data were
not available.

Table IV. Percentage Distribution of Workers among (1)
Predominantly Catholic, (2) Mixed, and (3) Predominantly
Non-Catholic Census Areas*

Areas	All Industries		Mining and Smelting		Metal Industries		Textile Industries		Making of Machinery	
	Catholic workers	Non-Catholic workers	Catholic workers	Non-Catholic workers	Catholic workers	Non-Catholic workers	Catholic workers	Non-Catholic workers	Catholic workers	Non-Catholic workers
Catholic............	22.0	2.5	36.9	7.8	13.8	1.3	33.0	3.2	13.5	1.6
Mixed...............	61.7	28.1	59.3	57.1	69.4	36.1	49.9	20.5	68.2	29.0
Non-Catholic......	16.3	69.4	3.8	35.1	16.8	62.6	17.1	76.3	18.3	69.4
Total...............	100.0	100.0	100.0	100.0	100.0	100.0	100.0	100.0	100.0	100.0

*For the purpose of this table Catholic areas are those in which 70 per cent or more of the workers in the industry or industries concerned are Catholic; mixed, 30 per cent but under 70; Non-Catholic, less than 30 per cent Catholic. An area may thus be classed as Catholic with reference to one industry, and as mixed or Non-Catholic with reference to another industry.

has been most felt in those regions which had raw materials necessary to heavy industry. (4) The Catholic industrial workers were so distributed that they were usually mixed with a strong proportion of non-Catholic workers.

It was precisely in those regions and in those industries in which workers of the different religious affiliations were mixed that the "Christian trade unions" took root and flourished. These unions, nominally inter-denominational but actually almost entirely Catholic in leadership and membership, became enough like the "free" or socialistic unions in spirit and tactics to be troublesome both to employers and to the more conservative of the Catholic clergy. They remained Catholic enough to be thorns in the flesh of the Marxist free unions. Life has been hard for them, as for any organization with a chip on each shoulder; one on the right for the exploiting employer and the too conservative priest to knock off at their own risk; one on the left as a warning to Pope-baiting Protestants and godless socialists.

The earliest and one of the most vigorous of these unions was that of the miners. Although Silesia had 186,199 workers in mining and smelting, and Alsace-Lorraine, 41,058, of whom 86.5 per cent and 91.2 per cent, respectively, were Catholic, it was not in these provinces that the Christian union of miners was founded and had its best growth. It was founded in the Ruhr, and spread from there throughout the Rhineland and Westphalia. In the Rhineland there were 255,887 workers in mining and smelting, of whom 69.8 were Catholic; in Westphalia, 276,784, of whom 52.8 were Catholic. In other industries, too, the Christian unions had their early vigorous growth in the mixed, rather than in the more purely Catholic areas.

In the mixed areas, the Catholic worker seems to have received from his non-Catholic comrades enough working-class philosophy and fighting spirit to make him a trade-unionist. Every one of the important Christian unions was founded in the face of an active socialist or independent union. Indeed, most of the earlier leaders of the Christian unions had at one time been members of independent unions. Many Catholic workers apparently remained true enough to their faith to resent attacks on the church and the clergy. The independent unions gave ample cause for such resentment, as did also many of the employers. The latter showed lack of respect for Catholic holidays and customs, and were often outspoken about the superiority of the Protestant. In such a situation the sense of being a minority — in effect, if not in number — gave Catholic workers an *esprit de corps* on which they could build an organization. The trade union had given them a pattern of action.

Catholic labor clubs of a sort grew up more slowly in the more strongly Catholic and less industrial regions, but they were less spontaneous and less vigorous. They did not follow the usual pattern of trade-unions closely enough to worry either clergy or employers.

It was also in the industrial and religiously mixed Rhineland that the Catholic Centre Party took its democratic and somewhat progressive form. There has been continual and bitter conflict within Catholic ranks over the policy of this party. The bishops of safely Catholic dioceses have fought the more compromising attitude of those who, faced by class-consciousness and socialism among their flocks, fear that they may lose them. The Catholic nobility, as all landed gentry, hate modern industry; they also hate those leaders of the Centre Party who have come up through the ranks of Christian labor unions and are imbued with a moderate, but stubborn, labor point of view.

Bavaria, while very Catholic, is the least industrial of the larger German states. It was not fruitful soil for the Centre Party. It retained its Bavarian People's Party, which was provincially, rather than religiously, sensitive. Catholicism is taken for granted in Bavaria; in the industrial Rhineland and Westphalia it must be fought for, and that with weapons adapted to the presence of big industry and resulting class-consciousness. In the east, the admixture of Slavs hindered the free growth of the German Catholic movement.

A third branch of the modern German Catholic movement, "Der Volksverein für das katholische Deutschland," was also born and did its most effective work in the Rhineland and Westphalia. This organization was conceived as a sort of mothering body for the lesser Catholic organizations. Its function was to adapt the propaganda of the church to the conditions of modern life. It encouraged lay discussion of social problems, and attempted to develop a lay leadership for Catholic organizations, including the trade unions and the Centre Party.

In Germany, as elsewhere, small business and industrial enterprises have suffered from the rise of "big business." In the Catholic parts of the country, this takes the form of a threat to the existence of the small Catholic tradesman, the "Kleinbürger." Since this threat comes from non-Catholic sources, it is not surprising that this lower middle class should confuse its hatred of "capitalism" with suspicion of the Protestant world. This class also hates the socialistic movements of the Proletariat into which they may fall at any moment. To them, Catholicism means their traditional world of comfortable small business. One wing of the Catholic party is made up of these small, harassed people, fighting a big world. They sharply criticize their more liberal Catholic brethren of the Christian trade unions and of the Volksverein for having made peace with big industry and the socialists.

Such people seek salvation in the "Catholic morality" and Catholic "natural law." Even the more realistic Catholic trade unionist mixes with his coöperative insurance and labor tactics a measure of distrust of the whole modern capitalistic system. He sees the way out, not in simon-pure socialism, but in a Golden Mean, maintained by the steadying influence of the Catholic faith. Thus would he avoid the chaos of Protestant Capitalism as well as the communism which he regards as its sequel.

In this confusion, it is at least clear that the industrial revolution has made Catholics self-conscious. It has provoked discussion and even conflict within the Catholic ranks, as well as between Catholics and non-Catholics. The social and political implications of Catholic doctrine have been disputed, and have become the concern, not of the clergy alone, but of every Catholic. The struggle to remain safely within the fold and yet to meet the problems of a new economy has given rise to movements which push forward into the new world with one step, and withdraw for shelter in the old at the next.

A similar situation, involving nationality and language, arose in pre-war Austria. The Czech social-democrats and trade unionists, whose employers were mostly German, saw a nationality problem even in the labor problem. In spite of Marxian class philosophy and internationalism, these Czechs eventually split off from their German-Austrian comrades.[3] In Canada, the entry of the Catholic French Canadian into industry has resulted in the splitting of the labor movement on lines of language and religion.[4]

These are but a few of the many instances in which industrial invasions and revolutions have brought peoples with a degree of cultural difference into contact in such fashion that cultural and economic problems have become confused. The social movements which arise in such a situation present a Gordian knot at which doctrinaire socialists, Manchester liberals, and the economic man — in the persons of captains of finance and industry — argue and rave, but which they do not quite loosen. The battles of a new, secular civilization may be fought in the name of an older and more sacred culture.

3. Ludo Hartman, "Die Nation als politischer Faktor," *Verhandlungen des Zweiten Deutschen Soziologentages,* Tübingen, J.C.B. Mohr (1912), pp. 80-97.
4. Allen Latham, *The French Catholic Labor Unions of Canada.* Toronto: The Macmillan Co. of Canada, 1930.

TWENTY-SIX

The Knitting of
Racial Groups in Industry

Elton Mayo has recently given the name "rabble hypothesis"[1] to the assumptions which, he claims, still guide not merely many managements in dealing with workers, but also many of those who investigate industrial behavior. He refers to the belief that an industrial organization is an aggregation of individuals each seeking his own gain without reference to other persons, and consequently each capable of being induced to greater effort by devices focused upon this desire for advantage. To this assumption Mayo opposes the view that a working force normally consists of social groups, whose members are highly responsive to each other's social gestures and identify their fates with those of their fellows; social groups which, further, are related to others in the larger system of social relations in and about industry. Mayo argues that a state of good cooperation is dependent upon the existence of such groups, even though one of their functions may be some restriction of individual production. He believes, finally, that the "solitary," the person who does not feel himself part of any such group, is actually somewhat disorganized, and not likely to function well in the long run.

The theme of my remarks is that a fruitful way of analyzing race relations in industry is to look at them against whatever grid of informal

Paper read before American Sociological Society at 40th Annual Meeting, 1946. *American Sociological Review*, Vol. XI (Oct., 1946). Reprinted by permission.

1. Elton Mayo, *The Social Problems of an Industrial Civilization*. Boston Graduate School of Business Administration, Harvard University 1945. Chapter II et passim.

social groupings and of relations within and between such groups exists in the industries, departments and jobs in which Negroes or other new kinds of employees are put to work. Recent experience suggests that this grid of relationships, and the manner in which Negroes are introduced into it, are more significant in the success of a policy of hiring Negroes than are the generalized racial attitudes of the white workers concerned.

Polling of white workers to find whether they favor the hiring of Negroes as their equal and close fellow-workers would almost anywhere result in an emphatic "No." Workers generally prefer not to have any new kinds of workers introduced among and equal to themselves. But Negroes have been successfully employed among white workers; and many other new kinds of workers have been introduced among older kinds of workers who were not enthusiastic about them. Polling of attitudes, on this simple basis, gives little clue to the probable behavior of the old workers to the new. The simple "No" of the workers to many proposals of management is not to be taken at face value; for industry has not been run by majority vote of the workers, and a "No" is often no more than a demonstration of protest. In fact, workers more or less expect each other to object to changes proposed by management.

It does not follow that racial preferences and dislikes have no bearing on the question whether the races will work well together. Racial attitudes themselves take on new dimensions when looked at in the framework of the human relations prevailing in industry. It is characteristic of industry that groups of workers who have knit themselves into some kind of organization in and about their work develop some set of expectations, considered little short of rights, that their jobs and their work-fellowship should be limited to persons of some certain kind—as to age, sex, race, ethnic qualities, education and social class. Mr. Orvis Collins, in a recent paper,[2] shows how the management of a New England factory got itself into an impasse by violating the expectation that certain kinds of jobs should belong to Irishmen. We could do with a good deal more investigation of what workers in various jobs and industries consider the proper kind of fellow-worker, what they think are their own rights in the matter, and of the devices which they use to expel newcomers not of the kind they want and of those which management and unions have used to get the new-comers accepted. Such expectations are not likely to be stated formally; they may not even be admitted informally. Defense of the breach of them is likely, as in the case reported by Mr. Collins, to be hidden by indirection of various kinds. It is also probable that some of the so-called non-economic behavior attributed to people new to industry—erratic

2. Orvis Collins, "Ethnic Behavior in Industry." *American Journal of Sociology.* LI (January, 1946), 293-298.

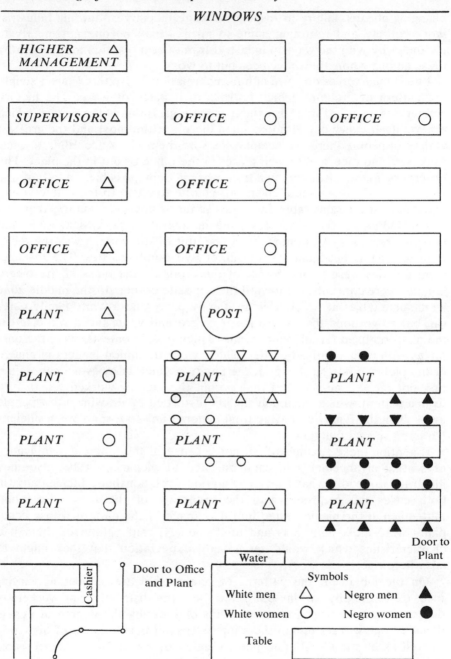

Figure 1. Seating by Rank, Sex and Race in a Factory Cafeteria.

changing of jobs, failure to respond to wage incentives, quitting industrial work entirely and returning home to farms—may be due not merely to unfamiliarity with the ways of industry. It may be a reaction to rejection by those among whom they have been put to work.

I used the expression "grid of informal relations." By this I mean simply the pattern of grouping which prevails in a place of work. The factory cafeteria, shown in Figure I, exhibits such a grid; this is the pattern which renews itself every day at noon, when there are the most and the greatest variety of people there. The employees sort themselves according to their rank, sex, and race, and to their places in the office or out in the plant. The observers found also, that while it was seldom possible for all of the workers who belonged to a given close circle to come to the cafeteria and find places at the same table, they did—so far as possible—eat together.

The individual thus finds his table in a grid of rank, sex, race, and personal relations. At a union picnic the unit of the pattern was the table, each serving as headquarters for one or two family parties. The management families were in one corner of the grounds; the mass of the Negro families were concentrated toward the opposite corner. In the middle zone were some tables at which a Negro family party and a white family party sat, but so grouped that Negro faced Negro and white faced white. Near the platform used for announcements, dancing and contests, were the only tables with racially mixed parties. These were the union leaders in charge of the picnic. Thus, in this grid, the family—which is by American definition not racially mixed—and rank within the factory worked together to form a pattern, which the union slightly disturbed by drawing a few people away from the family and away from factory rank to form a small nucleus based on special function.

I mention these examples first, not because of the inherent significance of seating arrangements in cafeterias and at picnics, but because they illustrate so vividly what I mean by a grid of relationships. Incidentally, in both cases the Negroes—with the exception of the few union committeemen at the picnic—fitted into that space in the pattern whose occupants were most numerous and of the lowest rank. None of them had characteristics which would set up any expectation that they might fit anywhere else.

On the job itself, the patterns of relationship are subject in varying measure to the physical lay-out of the shop, the distribution of workers of different races among the various kinds of jobs, by the degree of dependence of one worker upon others for successful performance of his work, as well as by the social atmosphere created by management, supervision, the union and the workers themselves. Furthermore, the informal relations among workers are not always so immediately visible as in the cafeteria and at the picnic. But generally such relations are there, although not all workers are part of any network of groups of people who cooperate in some special way to control what goes on with reference to work or other matters.

The Fixing Room

A department called the Fixing Room in a certain plant illustrates one kind of grid or grouping at work and its consequences for race relations. The work is done by teams of three men. The members of a team meet and exchange tools and materials without a word and without even a direct look at each other. In fact, there is something of a cult of silence among them. The bonus, which is a large part of their income, is based upon the product of a team. The skills are learned on the job from the other members of the team to which one is assigned. The men are nearly all Poles, past middle age, bound together by kinship and neighborhood. The teams and the whole group together are notoriously and successfully impervious to management's attempts to control their relations, and even the choice of new employees. They pick their own fellows. The labor shortage of the war dried up the sources of new men of their kind and management tried to get new help—Negroes. Several Negro men were hired, but all left after a few days. Interviews with these Negro men revealed that they were subjected to a not very subtle, but very effective torture by the other members of the teams to which they were assigned. Later, the management tried the device of hiring a whole Negro team, which complicated the matter of learning the job; they stayed for some time, achieved a very creditable rate of production, and recently quit in a group. We have not yet found out what happened, but I venture to say that it was fundamentally a case of rejection by the older workers. In this shop there is no place for the solitary individual. One must be integrated into a team-clique to work at all. The homogeneity and traditional solidarity and autonomy of the whole department conspired to make the men unwilling to accept new kinds of

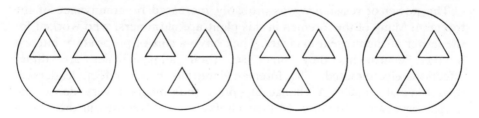

Figure 2. Fixing Room. (Each circle is a closed work team of three men.)

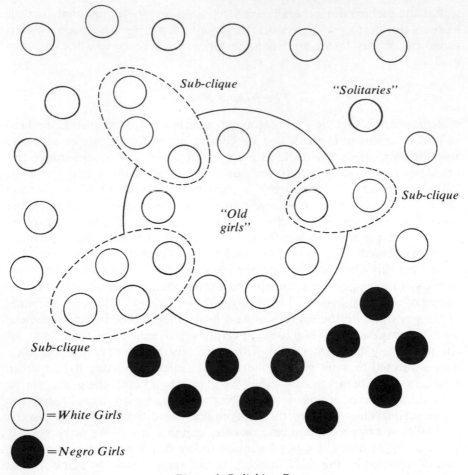

Figure 3. *Polishing Room.*

workers and make management impotent to bring about change against their will.

The power of resistance was probably increased by connivance of the foremen. Many of the foremen in this plant are old-timers, who worked for the father of the present manager. They have a sort of proprietary interest in the departments they supervise; their idiosyncrasies are rather affectionately tolerated. The foremen can thus be, in effect, leaders of departmental cliques. A change of policy thus meets a very dense and intricate resisting structure. In their efforts to hire Negroes in the Fixing Room, management did not succeed in penetrating it.

The Polishing Room

The Polishing Room in another plant shows another type of both formal and informal organization operating in relation to race. In this room, each girl works independently on a machine like all the others. At intervals, all workers are moved along to the next machine. No one has a vested interest in a machine. By dint of good production and long service workers hope to get on the day shift. Many of the white girls of longer service have gravitated to this shift; it is about two-thirds white, in fact. The swing shift has a larger proportion of Negroes; the night shift, a strong majority of them. The few white girls on the night shift appear to prefer it because of some family reason. A girl cannot by especially high production increase her income; seniority alone brings small fixed increases of hourly wage; long service also brings certain benefits and an annual bonus. Something is made of the principle that only those who have good production records will be kept on when and if lay-offs become necessary. There is thus very little in the situation and in the policies of management to induce either a strong individualism or a close grouping of the employees. One would expect it to be a situation into which Negro help could be fairly easily introduced, and so it has been. But there is, nevertheless, an informal organization of workers. To quote from the report of the observers:

> An analysis of clique formation and membership provides some clearer insights into such acceptance as the Negro has achieved and into the attitudes and expectation of Negro workers in the plant. There are several recognizable cliques in the Polishing Room; their functions are well defined by their members. The clique is concerned with production and procedure, and with the status and behavior of the individual workers.
>
> The cliques in this room are not mutually exclusive and sharply defined. There is a central group, the 'Old Girls,' made up of young women of from twenty-two to thirty-three years of age and of an average length of service of about five years. The 'Old Girls' eat in the cafeteria; each usually manages to eat with at least one or two of her clique fellows. Another group, also of long service, bring their lunches and eat in the lounge. But there is little association between them and the 'Old Girls' clique. There are a number of smaller satellite cliques, each attached by at least one common member to the 'Old Girls.' It appears likely that a new girl may be sponsored into the organization through the satellite cliques. We observed one girl who was, when first interviewed, unfriendly toward other workers, a 'lone wolf.' Two months later she had been accepted, had ceased to be a rate-busting 'horse' and had even become much more tolerant to the Negro girls.

The clique organization of the Polishing Room may be shown as in Figure 3.

The girls in the central clique, and those oriented towards them seem to be of such skill that they are without anxiety about being able to keep up to or even to surpass the usual rate; they maintain good levels of production, but make statements which make it clear that one of the functions of the group is control of the average rate of production.

White workers have defined a "good day's work" as falling within the limits of one hundred and one hundred and six. Many say that it would be easy to produce more. The girls who say this claim to be fast workers; they explain their failure to produce more by a well-developed rationale: to do more would be to ruin the job for the diligent, but slower workers. But "ratebreaking" is condoned for a day or so for a worker who has fallen behind and wants to bring her average up to par. Apparently a girl who is socially well established in the group can consistently break the rate a little with only mild teasing as punishment. But outsiders who break the rate are severely punished by ridicule and scorn; if they persist, they remain outsiders and, if associations are important to them, they may be forced off the job. Here is an apparent paradox: Admittance to the group may be secured only by adherence to the established definitions of the group, while unquestioned membership carries the privilege of some deviant behavior.

This is, of course, not a paradox at all; for it is characteristic of social groups to demand of the newcomer a strict conformity which will show that he accepts the authority of the group; then, as the individual approaches the center of the group and becomes an established member, they allow him a little more leeway.

Outside the organization are some white women and all the Negro women. The white women outsiders are a varied lot. Some are older women who must, or think they must, struggle to produce enough to keep their jobs. Some of them say that they are no longer young enough to be able to play. Others show in one way or another that some outside concern is so important as to make them defy or ignore the opinions of their fellow-workers. Some are probably not acceptable for one reason or another—perhaps dress, personal hygiene, or general queerness.

But no Negro girl, no matter what her length of service, her production rate, or her personality, has found a place in the system of cliques of the white girls. The observers report that among the girls in the cliques,

"It is generally understood that Negro workers are to be accorded tolerance and a measure of friendliness. There is ample evidence that there was opposition at first to the hiring of Negroes. In the two years that have elapsed a studied, but tentative acceptance has occurred. Negro and white workers meet each other with good will and friendliness on the job. They carry on conversations at their machines. But this friendliness does not extend beyond the work situation, and it varies in degree within the lesser cliques. White and Negro workers do not eat together except occasionally by accident. Not in any case is a Negro a member of a clique of white girls, and apparently conversation between the races seldom touches problems that are mutually important."

This means, in effect, that the Negro girls do not take part in the conversation of social gestures by which the rules and sentiments of the group are communicated to the newcomer, and by which she is offered membership in the clique as a reward for accepting its discipline. Insofar as white girls complain of the conduct of their Negro fellow workers, it is in precisely the terms they use about white girls who are not in the cliques. The Negro girls, they say, "are all for themselves; they don't try to help each other." One white girl summed up the matter thus:

> Some colored girls . . . don't care what the next person does. They're that way about everything. If one of them makes a hundred and ten (a very high production), the rest of them don't care. Now when a white girl makes that much, we make her slow down because we know how hard it is for some of 'em to make the average.
>
> *Interviewer:* Why do you think the Negro girls don't try to pull their rates down?
>
> Well, they're just like that about everything. They don't even try to help each other.
>
> *Interviewer:* What do you mean?
>
> They don't get into a group. They just mingle with everybody. I don't think the colored girls have any little groups like we have. . . .
>
> *Interviewer:* How do you account for that?
>
> It's 'cause they're all for themselves. Now you take the white girls; the younger ones will mix with the older girls and they find out what they are supposed to do.

The same worker said of a new white girl "She won't keep no high average. She's mingling more with the other girls, now." Thus she implicitly recognized mingling with other girls and sensitivity to their opinions as a desirable, steadying experience. She apparently did not see that the very reason for the Negro girl's undesirable production habits is probably that she is excluded from the rewards of group membership. In effect, she is complaining that the Negro girls do not form their own cliques.

That the Negro girls have not developed an organization in this case is borne out by the observers. We do not know why this is so. But certain considerations concerning the probable reasons bear directly on the points thus far made and on the final one which I have to make.

Some of the white girls are, to use Mayo's expression, "solitaries." Most of the Negro girls are so. The records of production seem to indicate this, as well as their other actions and talk. A few Negro girls have very high

rates, and indulge in racing with other workers. Some are erratic in production. Others anxiously struggle to get their rates up to the point where they
can feel secure against being the first to be laid off. There is evidence that
they think that they are on trial. This is highly individualistic behavior; it is
also typically anxious behavior.

We may ask, although we cannot answer with much assurance, why the
Negro girls in this room are so unorganized. First, they are not in the white
clique organization because they are not given the chance to be in it. Then,
why do they not form an organization of their own? Perhaps because they
are new, relatively speaking. Perhaps because on the day shift, where the
main white clique developed, they—the Negro girls—are in the minority
and would hesitate to form what would be considered a rival group.
Perhaps it is that there are no Negro girls who feel secure enough in their
positions to form a disciplining group which would, as part of its discipline,
control production. In this particular plant the management has undoubtedly made a strong attempt to reduce discrimination. Now the way they
have done it is to emphasize that the Negro girl will be hired, kept and
promoted strictly according to her individual merits.

This is a point on which we may make some tentative generalizations.
This very emphasis on treating the individual on his merits can become a
source of over-individualistic anxiety. For the statement "You will be
judged on your own merits," repeated too often becomes a dinning into
one's ears of the thought, "You are on trial. I doubt whether you can make
it, but if you do I will give you credit. Most people of your kind can't make
it. I shall be astonished if you do. If you do, you will certainly be an
exception. You've got to show me." This bit of imagined talk is, in fact, not
far from what foremen do say to Negro workers in many plants. It contains
an invitation, almost a threatening command, to the Negro worker to be a
"solitary."

Now this might not work with Negroes of the least ambitious class or
those working at traditional Negro jobs. But in the Polishing Room the
Negro girls show potential or actual middle-class behavior and sentiments,
as do also most of the white girls; nor are they employed at "Negro jobs."
And this brings us to our general point. The individualistic or "rabble"
hypothesis of industrial management—that each worker is an individual
who may be induced, and who ought to be able to be induced to work for
his own ends without regard to his fellows—is almost unconsciously applied with redoubled force to the Negro worker. The behavior it encourages is, in its essence, the behavior of the ambitious person. The ambitious
white worker may dissociate himself from his fellows to some extent, and
in spite of being somewhat disliked he may get promotions for it. The
Negro worker apparently feels and is made to feel in some situations that

he has to dissociate himself from others and be a "solitary" in order merely to keep his job. I do not think the Polishing Room is a situation in which this is unusually so. But the combination of individually separate work, with the particular pattern of white informal organization from which Negroes are excluded, and a management policy which gives the Negro girls definite hope that they can gain security by individual effort—and in no other way—might be expected to keep them a somewhat anxious series of solitaries rather than a stable organized group.

The Fixing Room illustrates the problem which arises in a shop where the informal organization consists of a series of closely related tight teams into which the individual worker—white or Negro—must fit in order to work at all. The Polishing Room has an open formal structure, easy for the individual to enter; and a moderately open, but nevertheless, powerful, informal structure of cliques. But it is not quite open to Negroes, and the results are as have been reported.

These two cases are, however, alike in that no attempt has been made to modify the informal organization so as to relate Negroes to it. In the Fixing Room, after a first attempt to put Negroes into existing teams failed, management attempted to set up Negro teams, but without trying to define their relations to existing teams. In the Polishing Room, management tried to create general tolerance. In other cases, a union or management has made a more definite effort in this regard. It seems fairly common for a vigorous union administration successfully to encourage bi-racial groups of shop leaders. We have observed a few cases in which foremen who are the centers of informal groups of their own workers, have developed something of an inter-racial organization. More often the opposite occurs where the foreman occupies such a position. I cite these additional cases, without the description necessary for you to judge of them, to indicate the variety of situations which may occur, and also to introduce a final point; namely that the situation may often be changed by some active force, either union or management, which takes the pattern of informal relations into account.

TWENTY-SEVEN

Leadership and
Inter-group Cooperation

In an article published in the first issue of this journal, William Foote Whyte[1] notes that the people who run settlement houses, probably because of class bias, select for special grooming for such positions of leadership as the settlement is willing to trust to local hands, young men who are already somewhat out of the main stream of neighborhood life. He further shows that the settlement staff then, wittingly or unwittingly, demand as the price of their sponsorship that the chosen young man should further alienate himself from his neighborhood. Scudder Mekeel[2] recently published some Comparative Notes to the effect that the Indian Service does much the same thing in the selection of Indians for collaboration and in what it does to these chosen Indians later.

May I point out similar facts in the attempts of English Canadians to get the collaboration of French Canadians in various movements and organizations. The situation differs in several regards from that of settlement workers of middle-class origin seeking the collaboration of Italian Americans of a slum district, and obviously it differs from the relation between the white Indian Service functionary and his protégé, the Indian. For the

Applied Anthropology, Winter, 1945. By permission of *Human Organization* and The Society for Applied Anthropology.

1. "The Social Role of the Settlement House," *Applied Anthropology*, Vol. I (Oct.-Dec., 1941), pp. 14-19.
2. "Comparative Notes on the 'Social Role of the Settlement House' as Contrasted with that of the United States Indian Service," *Applied Anthropology*, Vol. III, No. 1 (December, 1943), pp. 5-8.

French Canadians number millions, and have a social structure of all the social and economic classes common in western societies. They are a self-conscious people, with full political rights. They are under no guardianship. But they are a minority people.

In the two cases previously reported, the members of a dominant group fail to accept as reality the actual social organization of the group with whom they wish to deal. The leadership which arises within the minority group is either overlooked or purposely passed over. The same is true in the case I am to report. It is, in fact, one of the commoner forms of ethno-centric action. The people of the dominant group who want to do something for the minority or subordinate group may recognize certain picturesque values in the latter. Thus the settlement house may try to revive the folk-dancing or peasant art of a group of slum-dwelling immigrants. And the Indian Service (I do not speak with much knowledge in this case) may encourage the cult of Indian arts. But to recognize the social organization of the group, and especially its leaders, is quite another thing.

I have observed, over some years, the relations between the French and the English Canadians. It frequently happens that English people interested in social movements of various kinds (adult education, cooperatives, progressive political movements, social welfare programs, or merely in inter-group good will) set about to get cooperation from the French. The very terms in which it is put contain an ethno-centric bias. Such movements want a committee, and, as usual, want "big names" for the letterhead and lesser persons who are wanted for the work they can do rather than for their names. I have frequently been asked by English people to supply the names of French-Canadian leaders, or to say whether certain French Canadians would be "cooperative."

Note, first of all, the assumption that the French Canadians who are to "cooperate" and who are to "represent the French" are to be picked by English Canadians. This is, of course, a common thing. Men choose the woman to represent women on a committee concerned with a civic matter. White men pick the Negro to represent other Negroes in questions involving race relations. What usually happens in the French-Canadian case is that the persons picked are much more cooperative than representative. The very fact that French Canadians know very well by whom and why the individual is picked lessens his power to represent. The idea of asking a number of French Canadians known to be interested in the matter in hand to select their own representatives apparently seldom occurs to the English-speaking leaders. In any case, the English promoters usually get fine cooperation, on the verbal level at least, from their hand-picked French Canadians. But the latter seldom mobilize any support for the movement or cause, whatever it may be. The English then proceed either to make statements about how the French can't be counted upon really to do anything or bemoan the fact that, while their picked man is all right – hardly distinguishable from an English person, in fact – reactionary or nationalistic forces block his efforts.

Two factors seem to be involved in the failure of English people to pick – which still, you see, assumes that it is the English who will be doing the picking – French Canadians who would really be representative of their group in the dynamic *rather than the sampling* sense. One is failure to see inside the French-Canadian society sufficiently well to recognize the forces at work and to know who the leaders are. A French Canadian is apt to be known to English people in one of two opposed capacities. If he be a notorious "nationalist trouble-maker," he will be known as public-enemies are known when they rise high enough in their chosen line of endeavor. If he be a conspicuous exponent of the *bonne entente* between the two ethnic groups, he will likewise be known. That there is a much larger number of leaders in the various institutions and movements of the French-Canadian world who merit neither of these kinds of notoriety is always a bit of a surprise to the few English people who learn it. The communication between the English and the French world is not such as to bring these people to English public attention.

The second factor is that the leaders of English movements, and especially of the kind of movement most concerned about inter-racial cooperation, may be actually a little afraid of French-Canadian leadership. It is not by cooperation with English people that a French Canadian becomes a leader. On the contrary, every French-Canadian leader must be in some measure known as a defender of his people as against the English. And he is so by sentiment, quite apart from the requirements of getting a public reputation. Of course, it is equally true that English people do not become leaders in their group by and because of cooperation with the French. The leadership mechanism of the two groups are, in most areas of life, completely separate. But the English who wish to muster French for cooperation cannot quite face this fact, at least not to the extent of trying to cooperate with French Canadians who are primarily leaders and only incidentally, if at all, *bonne ententistes*. The result is that, while they can easily get verbal cooperation from some hand-picked individual, effective cooperation seldom occurs in social movements. Of course, a great deal of effective cooperation occurs in business, politics, trade unions and other such concerns where there is a more realistic approach to leadership, and where the rituals of cooperation are not so much valued as is action.

These cases raise problems of importance for those who would promote cooperation between groups different as to race, culture, class or what have you. They suggest a research problem of practical importance, that of the devices of getting leadership for cooperation between such groups.

BOOK II

Work, Self,
and the Study of Society

PART III

Work and Self

TWENTY-EIGHT

The Study of Occupations

Any occupation in which people make a living may be studied sociologically. Many have been so studied in recent years, especially those which are undergoing changes in techniques and social organization and in their social and economic standing. Sometimes the study is instigated by those in the occupation; sometimes by people not in it but affected by it. The motive may be immediate practical advantage; it may be greater understanding and general social advantage. Sociology has much to gain from such studies, provided that those who undertake them make and keep a sociological bargain with those who support them and those who allow themselves to be studied. The maximal gain can be reached, however, only when the sociologist keeps clearly in mind his ulterior goal of learning more about social processes in general.

In the following pages, we are frankly preoccupied with this ulterior goal of learning about the nature of society itself from the study of occupations.

The Labor Force

Modern industrial and urban societies and economies, no matter what the political systems under which they operate, are characterized by a wholesale mobilization of people away from traditional and familial activities into more formally organized work activities. These activities are named and categorized in payrolls, organization charts, and union-management contracts, and in income-tax, licensing, and social-security legislation.

Chapter 20 of *Sociology Today*, edited by Robert K. Merton, Leonard Broom, and Leonard S. Cottrell, Jr., © 1959 by Basic Books, Inc. Publishers, New York. Reprinted by permission.

In the sense that they work at some times in their lives in this system of things, more people are engaged in occupations than in other kinds of societies and at a greater variety of occupations. In industrial countries, the census more and more serves the end of informing government and business about the actual and potential labor force and about the actuarial problems of providing for people who are not at work, whether because of age, physical condition, lack of the skills needed in a changing technology or simply because they live in the wrong place. Race, sex, marital status, and other characteristics formerly determined civil estate quite directly; now it is work that counts (although it has always been a great determiner of status), and the other characteristics take their importance by virtue of their influence on one's place in the labor force.[1]

It also seems that everyone who is not too young, too old, too sick, or too burdened with household duties is rather expected to have an occupation in the sense indicated. In Soviet Russia, this expectation has become compulsion; a man may not stay away from his work without a doctor's certificate, and the physician who gives such certificates too freely is called on the carpet.[2] In this country, those who look to our national resources have lately added womanpower to the list, not because women did not work in the past and are now expected to do so, but because they have become mobilized away from the household and into the labor force in greater proportion and for longer periods of their lives than previously.[3]

I leave to others the task of counting the occupations in industrial economies and the changing numbers of people engaged in each of them, and the tiresome business of fitting the many occupations into a small enough number of categories to permit crowding them into tables. I can think of no set of categories that has been given such heavy sociological work to do, both theoretical and practical, as those of occupations in census tables. Measures of social stratification and of mobility, both territorial and social, are based upon them, as are international comparisons. They are used as independent variables against which to weigh differences of political opinion, taste, religion, and many other things. One is tempted to ask whether they are equal to the burden; it is a question on which many people are very competently breaking their heads.

Work and Leisure

Oddly enough, at a time when nearly everyone is being drawn into the

1. See Evelyn M. Kitagawa, *The Family as a Unit in the Work Force: A Review of the Literature*, Population Research and Training Center, University of Chicago, 1956.
2. Mark G. Field, "Structured Strain in the Role of the Soviet Physician," *Amer. J. Sociol.*, 53:5 (1953), 493-502.
3. National Manpower Council, *Womanpower*, Columbia University Press, 1957.

labor force, the proportion of a man's daily, weekly, annual, and life time that he is expected to devote to work is falling so drastically that the days of leisure in each seven may become nearly equal to the days of work. Already the waking hours spent away from work are, for many people, more than those spent at work, even on working days. At the same time, a new concept has been introduced, that of underemployment. It refers not to hours, weeks, and months of idleness so much as to the supposed underuse of human effort; the standard of efficient use applied is that of an economy which, like ours, provides great amounts of capital per worker and thus allows great per-man-hour production. The underemployed man may put forth great effort, but his product is small. It is as if the famed Protestant ethic had been transferred from the individual to the system; it is the machinery which is supposed to put in seven days a week and almost, if not quite, 52 weeks a year. The machine-tenders can take it easier at work, although they are expected to keep their eyes and ears piously glued to the "media" so that they may keep their consumption up to expectation. For, as G. Tarde said in his *Psychologie économique,*[4] a return to the early evangel, with its belief in the vanity of human desires, would be the death of modern industry.

Although the great masses of people who are occupied are taking it easier, a minority appears to be bound to the tireless wheels of the machines. Those who manage the machines and the organization required to keep them and their products moving appear to require an extra dose of a certain brand of the Protestant ethic, a brand which does not leave time for prayer or other solitary and idiosyncratic activities. The new distribution of work and leisure in the life of the individual, and as between people in various positions in our society and economy; the new concepts, values, and expectations with respect to them, and to the levels and kinds of effort expected or required of people in the various positions; these are fundamental problems of society and of occupations. The change of balance between work and leisure has given new emphasis and a new turn to studies of leisure. The demand for men of unlimited ambition and drive to fill certain of the positions in our economy of abundance has, in its turn, given a new impulse to studies of social mobility into the higher ranks of management.

The Division of Labor

Division of labor, one of the most fundamental of all social processes, finds one of its most explicit expressions in occupations. The phrase,

---

4. Paris, 1902, Vol I, p. 186. Tarde's chapters on the economic role of desires and beliefs are good reading for those who are working on a theory of consumption and leisure.

however, is but a poor term for differentiation of function in a social whole. It is poor because it emphasizes the division and neglects the integration, the relations among the functions so divided or differentiated. All organization of behavior consists of differentiation of function. Economic division of labor is but a special case, or a special aspect of it.

An occupation, in essence, is not some particular set of activities; it is the part of an individual in any ongoing system of activities. The system may be large or small, simple or complex. The ties between the persons in different positions may be close or so distant as not to be social; they may be formal or informal, frequent or rare. The essential is that the occupation is the place ordinarily filled by one person in an organization or complex of efforts and activities. Sociologically speaking, the division of labor is only incidentally technical. It consists, not of ultimate components of skill or of mechanical or mental operations, but of the actual allocation of functions to persons. Individual components of motion or action are combined in ways that sometimes appear fearful and wonderful to a mechanically oriented or rational and detached mind. The logic of the division and combination of activities and functions into occupations and of their allocation to various kinds of people in any system is not to be assumed as given, but is in any case something to be discovered. Likewise, the outward limits of a system of division of labor are not to be assumed but are to be sought out. Analysis of systems whose limits have not been determined can be very deceiving.

Homans[5] has recently emphasized exchange as a basic social process the analysis of which might bring us closer to a sound general theory of social behavior. Although this is not an entirely novel idea, it is an important one and especially pertinent to the analysis of division of labor. Where there is differentiation of function, there is exchange — and exchange not merely of money, goods, or tangible and easily described services. Durkheim's book, let us remember, is entitled *De la division du travail social* — on the division of social labor. And although it may be true that more and more kinds of exchange tend to have an expression in money, it is also true that it is very difficult to keep money exchanges free of other kinds.

One of the problems of the purest markets is to limit exchanges to the purely economic. Glick has recently found this to be so in the market in egg futures.[6] The rules and signals for buying and selling are made explicit so that the dealers will not be able to give private information or to

5. George C. Homans, "Social Behavior as Exchange," *Amer. J. Sociol.*, 53 (1958) 597–606.
6. Ira O. Glick, "Futures Trading: A Sociological Analysis," unpublished Ph.D. dissertation, University of Chicago, 1957. See also Max Weber, "Die Börse" (1894), in *Gesammelte Aufsätze zur Soziologie und Sozialpolitik*, Tübingen, J.C.B. Mohr, 1924, pp. 256–322.

exchange favors on the floor. I mention this case only to emphasize that the division of labor involves many kinds of exchange, many of them not at all apparent, and that several kinds may go on at once. This is true of occupations as well as of those differentiations of functions found in families and other systems of relationship. In many occupations, the exchanges occur on at least two levels. There is exchange between a person and the various others with whom he interacts in his occupational role. It is of this exchange that Henderson wrote in "Physician and Patient as a Social System."[7] It is also described in studies of industrial relations, and especially of the informal relations among people in the same work situation. One must remember, however, that much interaction occurs in formally defined relationships and that much involves persons not in personal contact with one another. The other level is that of exchanges between the occupation and the society in which it occurs; they underlie those characteristic features of certain occupations, license and mandate.

License and Mandate

An occupation consists in part in the implied or explicit *license* that some people claim and are given to carry out certain activities rather different from those of other people and to do so in exchange for money, goods, or services. Generally, if the people in the occupation have any sense of identity and solidarity, they will also claim a *mandate* to define—not merely for themselves, but for others as well—proper conduct with respect to the matters concerned in their work. They also will seek to define and possibly succeed in defining, not merely proper conduct but even modes of thinking and belief for everyone individually and for the body social and politic with respect to some broad area of life which they believe to be in their occupational domain. The license may be merely technical; it may, however, extend to broad areas of behavior and thought. It may include a whole style of life, or it may be confined to carrying out certain technical activities which others may not carry out—at least not officially or for a reward. The mandate may be small and narrow, or the contrary.

License, as an attribute of an occupation, is usually thought of as specific legal permission to pursue the occupation. I am thinking of something broader. Society, by its nature, consists in part of both allowing and expecting some people to do things which other people are not allowed or expected to do. Most occupations—especially those considered professions and those of the underworld—include as part of their being a license to

7. L. J. Henderson, "Physician and Patient as a Social System," *N.E.J. Med.,* 212 (1935), 819-23.

deviate in some measure from some common modes of behavior. Professions, perhaps more than other kinds of occupation, also claim a broad legal, moral, and intellectual mandate. Not only do the practitioners, by virtue of gaining admission to the charmed circle of the profession, individually exercise a license to do things others do not do, but collectively they presume to tell society what is good and right for it in a broad and crucial aspect of life. Indeed, they set the very terms of thinking about it. When such a presumption is granted as legitimate, a profession in the full sense has come into being. The nature and extent of both license and mandate, their relations to each other, and the circumstances and conflicts in which they expand or contract are crucial areas of study, not merely for occupations, but for society itself. Such licenses and mandates are the prime manifestation of the *moral* division of labor — that is, of the processes by which differing moral functions are distributed among the members of society, as individuals and as categories of individuals. These moral functions differ from one another in both kind and measure. Some people seek and get special responsibility for defining values and for establishing and enforcing sanctions over a certain aspect of life; the differentiation of moral and social functions involves both the area of social behavior in question and the degree of responsibility and power.

Since this is the aspect of occupations to which I give most emphasis in this paper, I will illustrate it in a manner which I hope will stimulate discussion and research.

Many occupations cannot be carried out without guilty knowledge. The priest cannot mete out penance without becoming an expert in sin; else how may he know the mortal from the venial? To carry out his mandate to tell people what books they may or may not read and what thoughts and beliefs they must espouse or avoid, he must become a connoisseur of the forbidden. Only a master theologian can think up really subtle heresies; hence Satan is of necessity a fallen angel. A layman would be but an amateur with a blunderbuss where a sharpshooter is wanted. The poor priest, as part of the exchange involved in his license to hear confessions and to absolve and his mandate to tell us what's what, has to convince the lay world that he does not yield to the temptations of his privileged position; he puts on a uniform and lives a celibate existence. These are compensating or counter-deviations from the common way of dressing and living; they would not be admired, or perhaps even tolerated, in people who have no special function to justify them. The priest, in short, has both intellectual and moral leeway, and perhaps must have them if he is to carry out the rest of his license. He carries a burden of guilty knowledge.

The lawyer, the policeman, the physician, the reporter, the scientist, the scholar, the diplomat, the private secretary, all of them must have license to get — and, in some degree, to keep secret — some order of guilty knowledge. It may be guilty in that it is knowledge that a layman would be obliged to reveal, or in that the withholding of it from the public or from authorities compromises the integrity of the man who so withholds it, as in the case of the policeman who keeps connections with the underworld or the diplomat who has useful friends abroad. Most occupations rest upon some bargain about receiving, guarding, and giving out communications. The license to keep this bargain is of the essence of many occupations.

The prototype of all guilty knowledge is, however, a different, potentially shocking, way of looking at things. Every occupation must look relatively at some order of events, objects, or ideas. These things must be classified, seen in comparative light; their behavior must be analyzed and, if possible, predicted. A suitable technical language must be developed in which one may talk to his colleagues about them. This technical, therefore relative, attitude must be adopted toward the very people whom one serves; no profession can operate without license to talk in shocking terms behind the backs of its clients. Sometimes an occupation must adopt this objective, comparative attitude toward things which are very dear to other people or which are the object of absolutely held values and sentiments. I suppose that this ultimate license is the greatest when the people who exercise it, being guardians of precious things, are in a position to do great damage. (No one is in so good a position to steal as the banker.)

Related to the license to think relatively about dear things and absolute values is the license to do dangerous things. I refer not to the danger run by the steeplejack and the men who navigate submarines, for that is danger to themselves. (Even so, there is a certain disposition to pay them off with a license to run slightly amok when the one comes down and the other up to solid ground.) I speak, rather, of the license of the doctor to cut and dose, of the priest to play with men's salvation, of the scientist to split atoms; or simply of the danger that advice given a person may be wrong, or that work done may be unsuccessful or cause damage.

License of all these kinds may lie at the root of that modicum of aggressive suspicion which most laymen feel toward professionals, and of that raging and fanatical anger which burns chronically in some people and which at times becomes popular reaction. Many antivivisectionists, according to Hughes,[8] do not love beasts more but love doctors less, suspecting them of loving some parts of their work too much. It is a chronic protest. Of course there are people who believe that they have suffered injury from incompetent or careless work or that they have been exploited by being acted upon more for the professional's increase of knowledge or income than for their own well-being.

Herein lies the whole question of what the bargain is between those who

8. Helen Hughes, "The Compleat Anti-vivisectionist," *Sci. Mon.,* N.Y., 65:6 (1947), 503–07.

receive a service and those who give it, and of the circumstances in which it is protested by either party. Of equal or greater sociological significance is the problem of a general questioning of license or mandate. Social unrest often shows itself precisely in such questioning of the prerogatives of the leading professions. In time of crisis, there may arise a general demand for more conformity to lay modes of thought and discourse.

One of the major professional deviations of mind, a form of guilty knowledge, is the objective and relative attitude mentioned above. One order of relativity has to do with time; the professional may see the present in longer perspective. The present may be, for him, more crucial in that it is seen as a link in a causative chain of events; the consequences of present action may be seen as more inevitable, rippling down through time. The emergency, in this sense, may appear greater to the professional than to the layman. In another sense, it appears less crucial, since the professional sees the present situation in comparison with others; it is not unique, and hence the emergency is not so great as laymen see it.

Something like this seems to lie in the attack upon the Supreme Court following its decisions on civil rights and upon professors who insist on freedom to discuss all things in this time of Cold War. They are thought to be playing legal and academic tunes while the Communists plaster us with firebombs. In time of crisis, detachment appears the most perilous deviation of all, hence the one least to be tolerated. Their deviation, in these cases, consists in a drastic reversal of what many laymen consider the urgent as against the less urgent aspects of our situation. And it arises from their license to think in different terms.

Militant religious sects give us an instructive illustration. They ordinarily, in Christianity at least, consist of people convinced that they are all in imminent danger of damnation. So long as they remain militants sects, they are in chronic crisis. It is perhaps not without sociological significance that they do not tolerate a clergy, or much differentiation of function at all. It is as if they sense that professionalizing inevitably brings some detachment, some relative and comparative attitude. In a large society the clergy are generally more ardent than the laity; a sect might almost be defined as a religious group in which the opposite is true. Inquisitions to the contrary, it is probable that the professional clergy tend to be more tolerant than ardent laymen. Although it may seem paradoxical to suggest it, one may seriously ask under what circumstances religious people tolerate a professional clergy.

The typical reform movement is an attempt of laymen to redefine values and to change action about some matter over which some occupation (or group of occupations or faction within an occupation) holds a mandate. The movement may simply push for faster or more drastic action where the profession moves slowly or not at all; it may be a direct attack upon the dominant philosophy of the profession, as in attempts to change the manner of distributing medical care. The power of an occupation to protect its license and to maintain its mandate and the circumstances in which licenses and mandates are attacked, lost, or changed are matters for investigation. (And one must not overlook movements within a profession.) Such work is study of politics in the fundamental sense — that is, in the sense of studying constitutions. For constitutions are the relations between the effective estates which *constitute* the body politic. In our society, some occupations are among the groups which most closely resemble what were once known as estates. While there has been a good deal of study of the political activities of occupational groups, the subject has been somewhat misunderstood as a result of the strong fiction of political neutrality of professions in our society. Of course, a certain license to be politically neutral has been allowed some occupations, but the circumstances and limits of such neutrality are again a matter for study. Special attention should be given to the exchanges implied and to the circumstances, some of which we have mentioned, in which the license is denied, and the ways in which it is violated and subverted, from within or without.

One can think of many variations of license and mandate, and of the relations between them. School teachers in our society have little license to think thoughts that others do not think; they are not even allowed to think the nastier thoughts that others *do* think. Their mandate seems limited to minor matters of pedagogy; it does not include definition of the fundamental issues of what children shall be taught. Educational policy is given into their hands very grudgingly, although they have a good deal of power by default. Mandate by default is itself a matter for study. The underworld, to take another example, has a considerable license to deviate; in fact, members get paid to help respectable people escape the norms of everyday life. But the license is not openly admitted. The manner in which the people of the underworld find spokesmen and the nature of the exchanges involved have often been discussed as a pathology of politics. The full circle of exchanges is seldom analyzed with an eye to learning something significant about the very nature of social exchanges. Study of the license of artists and entertainers could also yield much knowledge concerning the degrees of conformity possible in a society and the consequences of trying to reduce deviation to something like zero. For these occupations seem to require, if they are to produce the very things for which society will give them a living of sorts (or, in some cases, unheard-of opulence), at least some people who deviate widely from the norms more or less adhered to and firmly espoused by other people. Their license is, however, periodically in a parlous state, and there seems no guarantee that it will not, at any moment, be attacked. There has recently been a case which turns upon whether poetic license includes speaking for an enemy country in time of war.

Occupations and Social Matrices

If an occupation is a more-or-less standardized one-man's part in some operating system, it follows that it cannot be described apart from the whole. A study of occupations, then, becomes in part a study of the allocation of functions and the consequent composition of any given occupation.[9]

Although an occupation may conceivably consist of but one activity in a narrow and mechanical sense, it takes an extremely rationalized organization to keep it so. Most occupations consist of a number, a bundle, of activities. Some may be bundled together because they require similar skills; others, simply because they can conveniently be done at one place, or because taken alone they do not occupy a man's full time; still others, because they are, or seem to be, natural parts of a certain role, office, or function. The physician's repertoire, for example, includes technically unrelated activities, bound together by the demands of his basic function. Only in those specialties which can be practiced without personal contact with patients can physicians group their activities on strictly technical lines. One might, indeed, try to scale occupations according to the dominance of technical as against role factors in determining combinations of activities.

The extreme of technically rational division and grouping of activities, under conditions of constant and aggressive invention of new machines and forms of organization, would lead to continual destruction and reforming of occupations.[10] The problems of adjusting self-conceptions and social roles in such a case have been much studied lately. The opposite of this would be a system of strongly traditional and entrenched occupations whose activities, whether bound together by technical considerations or not, are considered to belong rightfully and naturally together.

This leads us to the distinction between historic and less historic occupa-

9. Throughout this paper, but especially in what follows, it would be hard for me to distinguish what is, at least in some small sense my own combining of ideas and what I owe to my colleagues in recent studies, Howard S. Becker, Blanche Geer, and Anselm Strauss. I am sure that many of my former students and other colleagues will have reason to think that I am borrowing liberally from their work.

10. Georges Friedmann has been the leading student of this problem. See his *Où Va le Travail Humain?*, Paris, Gallimard, 1950; *Problemes Humains du Machinisme Industriel*, Paris, Gallimard, 1946. He has also written a fundamental criticism called "La thèse de Durkheim et les formes contemporaines de la division du travail," *Cahiers Internationaux de Sociologie*, 19 (1955) 45–48.

tions. An historic occupation is historic, not because its chief activity is an old one but because it has long had a name, a license, and a mandate, a recognized place in the scheme of things. In the extreme case, an historic occupation has a strong sense of identity and continuity; a galaxy of historic founders, innovators, and other heroes, the saints or gods of the trade; and a wealth of remembered historic or legendary events, which justify its present claims. The aspirant to such a trade is expected to acquire a strong sense of belonging to an historic estate, somewhat set off from other men. New occupations, like new families, seek an heroic genealogy to strengthen their claims to license and mandate. Occupations vary greatly in the degree to which they become the master determinants of the social identity, self-conception, and social status of the people in them.

In an occupation which is strongly historic, one would expect the combination of activities also to have a certain historic quality, reinforced by a traditional logic. Historic or not, occupations vary greatly in their autonomy in determining what activities are their duty and prerogatives. One would, however, expect occupations of long standing to resist attempts, especially of outsiders, to determine the content of their work or the rules governing it.

The various activities which make up an occupation are, of course, given varying values both by the people inside and by others. Sometimes the name of the occupation expresses an emphasis upon one rather than other activities; note the use of "preacher," "priest," and "pastor" in referring to clergy of various denominations, and the insistence of some gynecologists upon being called gynecological surgeons. Some one activity may be symbolically valued beyond its importance in the present complex of activities. Changes in technology, economics, and organization may change the balance between the named symbolic activity and others; in extreme cases, the symbolic activity may be lost or dropped from the repertory of the occupation while the name persists.

Nursing is a striking example of such a series of shifts. The word has a certain connotation in the lay mind; it refers to a role and an attitude, but also to certain comforting activities considered consonant with the role. The elaboration of the organization of hospitals, clinics, and public-health agencies, combined with great technological change in medicine and an immense increase in the demand for medical services, has led to a great reshuffling of functions in the whole medical system. Doctors need much more technical help than before; the system also requires much more administrative activity. A host of new occupations has arisen. The physician has passed along many activities to the nurse; the nurse has in turn passed along many of hers to other occupations. The result has been upward mobility of the nurse, since a good number of the new occupations stand below her in the hierarchy and since there are some posts of high prestige, income, and authority to which nurses alone may aspire. But there has been a certain dissociation of the occupation called nursing from the activities traditionally associated with it in the lay mind. The case is not peculiar, but it is so clear cut as to allow sensitive observation.

Every occupation has some history which may in part be described in terms of changes in the bundle of activities, in the values given them, and in the total system of which the occupation is a part. Changes may occur in ownership and control over access to appropriate tools (pulpits, operating rooms, law libraries, stages and properties, Univacs and laboratories), methods of payment and exchange, the formal authority and status systems in which work is done, the terms of entry to the occupation, and competition among individuals, occupations, and whole complexes of goods and services for the patronage of consumers. Of course, these same matters are crucial to study of an occupation at present; but sociologists have to be reminded of the pertinence of history rather more than of present doings.

I hope I have not put so many things into the last few paragraphs that the main points will be overlooked: namely, that the items of activity and social function which make up any occupation are historical products. The composition of an occupation can be understood only in the frame of the pertinent social and institutional complex (which must in turn be discovered, not merely assumed). The allocating and grouping of activities is itself a fundamental social process.

The Work Situation

I should at this point mention work situations as systems of interaction, as the setting of the role-drama of work, in which people of various occupational and lay capacities, involved in differing complexes of *Lebenschancen,* interact in sets of relationships that are social as well as technical. Some of the best work in contemporary sociology[11] is being done in such settings and is giving us new knowledge of reciprocal expectation of role performance, definition of roles, group solidarity, and development and definition of reference groups. We are by this time alerted to the value of work situations as posts for observing the formation of groups and the generation of social rules and sanctions. I am not sure that we are using the findings of such observation vigorously enough in building our theories of social control and of the larger legal and political processes.

Let me conclude with some remarks on the individual and his occupa-

11. See Erving Goffman, *Presentation of Self in Society,* University of Chicago Press, 1956.

tion and his career. Career, in the most generic sense, refers to the fate of a man running his life-cycle in a particular society at a particular time. The limitations put upon his choice of occupation by his own peculiarities (sex, race, abilities, class, wealth, access to and motivation for education, and access to knowledge of the system itself) in interaction with the "times" have been the object of many studies. Not all the problems of logic and method involved in such studies have been adequately attacked or solved.

Occupations vary in their strength as named reference-groups, as the basis for full and lasting self-identification and firm status. They vary also in their demand for full and lasting commitment and in the age and life-phase at which one must decide to enter training for them. Some occupations are more visible to young people than are others, and effective visibility varies also by class and other social circumstances. The inner workings of the best known cannot be seen by outsiders. Add to this the fact of changes in even the most historic occupations, and it is evident that young people must choose their occupations, as they do their wives, largely on faith (if, indeed, they choose at all). The career includes not only the processes and sequences of learning the techniques of the occupation but also the progressive perception of the whole system and of possible places in it and the accompanying changes in conceptions of the work and of one's self in relation to it. A good deal of work is being done on these matters; the phrase *adult socialization* is being applied to some of the processes involved.[12]

The processes are complicated by the fact that some occupations, strong as their symbols of common identity (their license and mandate) may be, are inwardly very heterogeneous. Within medicine, there is wide choice of specialties; each of them is not merely a unit of technical work but a position in the huge and complex system of health institutions. They offer alternative career lines, some of them mutually exclusive from an early stage. These career lines are variously ranked within the profession itself as well as outside; the people in each of them have their own ethos and sometimes their own variant system of relative values concerning many things in medicine. They differ, for example, in their notions of what knowledge and skills should be taught in medical schools. How these factors act upon and are reacted to by students who are in the process of choosing their specialties is discussed in a current paper.[13] A part of the

12. Howard S. Becker and Anselm Strauss, "Careers, Personality, and Adult Socialization," *Amer J. Sociol.,* 72 (1956), 253-63. See also Robert K. Merton, George Reader, and Patricia Kendall (eds.), *The Student Physician: Introductory Studies in the Sociology of Medical Education,* Harvard University Press, 1957.

13. Kurt W. Back and Bernard S. Philips, "Public Health as a Career of Medicine: Specialization within a Profession," paper read at the annual meetings of the American Sociological Society, 1957.

individual's career may be the making of the finer decisions concerning his hoped-for place within an occupational system, the projecting of his self-image in the direction of one rather than others of the available models of mature members of his occupation.

Career involves, at each stage, choices of some rather than other activities in one's economy of effort. A career consists, in one sense, of moving — in time and hence with age — within the institutional system in which the occupation exists. Ordinarily, career is interpreted as progress upward in the system, but a man can make progress in a number of ways. He may become more skillful at the basic activities of the occupation; the increase of skill may be rewarded by increase of income, security, and prestige among his fellows. If his occupation is practiced directly with customers or clients, he may get more of them and better ones. However, progress and advancement also consist in part of change in the proportions of time and effort devoted to various activities, and even in rather complete change of organizational function or role.

Sometimes the greater success is paid for by a complete abandonment of the activities symbolically most closely associated with the occupation, a consequent loss of skill in those activities, and passage from identification with the basic colleagueship to some other. This is a career contingency of much importance to the individual's self-conception. It often creates severe guilt. We might expect the severity of such crises to vary with the sense of commitment and the strength of the colleague-group as a significant other for its members. Some occupations appear intense, others weak and indifferent, in commitment. In some there is a casual attitude toward particular activities and perhaps a full acceptance of the right of employers to determine just what work one shall do. In others, there is a rich culture and a strong sense among the members of being different from other people. There are songs and lore about logging, railroading, and going to sea. In these occupations there are strong feelings about who really shares in the dangers and fate of the group, and who consequently has a right to the name. Jazz musicians, who live life wrong-end to — for their night is day, and other people's pleasure is their work — have a similarly strong sense of who is and who is not one of them. Some of the professions also have a sense of identity and a tendency to be self-conscious about who is a true member of the group.

Today, there are great numbers of people in occupations which are, in fact, products of modern industrial and business technology and organization and in which there appears to be little sense of belonging to a closed circle of people with a peculiar fate. The sense of identification of such people with their work, or with classes and categories of people at work, is a matter for study. Many of them are said to be alienated both from their work fellows and from society. Not the least problem of such people is the balance between work and leisure—not merely as proportions of their lifetimes, years, weeks, and days, but in terms of their importance and meaning. This is also, in the broad sense, a problem of career, of a man and his work seen in the perspective of his ongoing life and life chances. We may then think of man and his work, of careers, as an immense area of problems, embracing a great many of the problems of formation of social personality and of adjustment of individuals to their social surroundings. Careers in various occupations are patterned in varying degree. In the narrowest sense, career—as Mannheim wrote—is a predictable course through a bureaucracy.[14] But the patterns, the possible positions and sequences in work systems, themselves change. And each human career is worked out in some particular historical phase. Ours is a rapidly changing phase, which means that careers and career contingencies are changing, too. This gives the study of careers, and of other facets of occupations and work, a certain timeliness and excitement that adds to their basic relevance for study of social and social-psychological processes.

14. Karl Mannheim, "Über das Wesen und die Bedeutung des wirtschaftlichen Erfolgsstrebens," *Archiv für Sozialwissenschaft und Sozialpolitik,* 63:3 (1930), 449–512.

TWENTY-NINE

The Sociological Study of Work:
An Editorial Foreword

All of this issue of the *Journal* treats of people at work; not all of it has to do with industry, even as currently defined. People nowadays do indeed speak of the "restaurant industry," the "advertising industry," and even of the "amusement industry," although I am not sure they would include boxing in it. No one has yet, so far as I know, talked of the medical, educational, and labor-union industries, but I suppose someone will.

The extension of the term "industry" to include so much more than manufacturing is itself an interesting datum. I take it to mean that in the minds of many people the ideal organization for getting work done is the manufacturing industry operated by a limited liability company. Just as certain occupations look to the professions as models, so others look to industry. One raises the prestige of his line of business if he thinks of it and persuades others to speak of it as an industry (the junk-dealers are busy renaming their business the salvage or recovery industry). It is not surprising that sociologists who study people at work should go along with the trend and call themselves "industrial sociologists."

Some huge proportion of our working force is hired by the large manufacturing concerns which people generally have in mind when they speak of industry or of big industry. The managements of such industries are, for various reasons, interested in having social scientists analyze at least certain aspects and certain levels of their organizations; what is more, they have money which can be easily turned to the purpose. Trade-unions, professional and educational institutions, small trades and businesses, have not the money and often not the wish to have their organizations so looked at. Accordingly, it is industrial rather than professional or business or labor-union sociology which has flourished. Some say it has become a fad. So it has. It does not follow that research done under the name is sound or unsound in a proportion or degree different from other sociology. For while there may be connections between the motives for undertaking a piece of work and the validity of the method with which it is done and the honesty with which it is reported, such connections are not necessary. A piece of work is not made false by insinuating or even by proving that it was undertaken on behalf of the enemy or from a frivolous motive. Industrial sociology needs no apology if it be good sociology.

Social science appears to have a double burden laid upon it. The one is to analyze the processes of human behavior, and especially of persistence and change thereof, in terms relatively free of time and place. the other is to tell the news in such form and perspective — quantitatively and comparatively — as to give clues for the taking of those chances of which action consists. The balance between these two functions or burdens varies from man to man, from time and place to time and place. Social science thrives on the strain between the two. Industrial sociology is pursued in the main by people who lean to the news-telling side. Since the big story about work lies in problems of huge organizations and nearly automatic machines, we may expect most students of human work to try to make sense out of it. This is what C. Wright Mills does in *White Collar* and Georges Friedmann in *Où va le travail humain?*

Why, then, give a large part of an issue of this *Journal* over to such whimseys as the special culture of the few professional boxers who fly up like moths from the morass of the slums and drop back again in a little while and as the disappearing breed of small custom-furriers; to such oddities as janitors and schoolteachers? In the first place, not even a majority of people work in the big organizations and on the new machines. There are still many ways of working besides those which fill the most space in census tables. Some of these other kinds of work are refuges for those who do not want to work in the big system or are rejected by it. Other occupations may be related in various ways to the larger show and to the major trends. The meanings and functions of work are many, not all of them included in the usual questionnaires and classifications. Part of the duty of even the news-telling social scientist is to be the ethnologist of his own time and place, illuminating the less obvious aspects of his own culture.

A deeper reason for the apparent whimsey is that for an understanding of human work one must look at a wide variety of kinds of work and of their social matrices. Only so will we get that relative freedom from time, place, and particular circumstance that is required of those who would analyze processes. Even that part of social science which is a telling of the news for action's (prediction's) sake depends for its efficacy upon putting of the particular into some larger perspective of other cases described in generalized terms.

The sample of cases for analyzing processes is one thing; that for telling and predicting the news is another. A small error of quantities in the news sample can send one "Galluping" off at a slightly wrong angle that will land him miles from his desired destination. In getting the process sample, one cares less about quantities of each kind so long as he gets that full variety and contrast which will allow him to tell the particular from the general and will, hence, enable him to give his categories just that balance between universality and particularity of reference needed for effective comparison. This issue of the *Journal* does not, of course, draw into view any great variety of the kinds of work current in our society, let alone those of other societies and times. It does go outside the usual boundaries of industry and the professions which have so limited sociological students of work. And it does so in quest of a broader, more useful frame of reference for studying work.

Comparison of widely divergent cases may also help break the bonds of conventional naming. If the big show in the world of work is large-scale industry, the prestige show is still, in some degree, in the professions. Many occupations have lately tried to pattern themselves after their notion of what a profession is and fight to be so named. Part of the process is to prove to the lay world that the work done is of such nature that the client is no judge either of what he needs or of what he gets; hence, it is work to which the principle of *caveat emptor* cannot safely be let apply. But if one studies plumbers and janitors, who do not yet claim to be of professional rank, one finds the same basic contention that laymen are not competent to judge much of the service which they ask and/or get. Furthermore, both the humble janitor and the proud physician have to protect themselves against the overanxious and importunate client (tenant or patient); both must keep their distance in order not to let any one client interfere with one's duties to others or with one's own ongoing program of work and leisure. Now the conventional and evaluative term "profession" carries as connotation the contention that there is no conflict of interest or per-spective between professional and client — or at least that there is none between the good professional and the good client. Consequently, doctors, professors, schoolteachers, and their like conceal in various degree from laymen generally, from naïve investigators in particular, and from themselves their feelings of antagonism and resistance toward their dear but troublesome patients, students, and pupils' parents. The janitor and the jazz musician are troubled by no such problem of public relations or anxious guilt. Basing one's study upon a conventional term, such as "profession," may lead one to group together and observe only those occupations which, since they cherish and publish a common stereotype of themselves, engage in a common concealment. The social scientist may become the dupe of this common concealment; the more so, since he, too, fancies himself a professional. The study and comparison of occupations without regard for conventional categories may sharpen our sensitivity to certain problems which we might otherwise overlook. Almost any occupation is a good laboratory animal for some aspect of work control, organization, or culture. It may disclose easily some aspect which is hidden in other cases, or it may show in developed form something which is incipient in others.

I think it a good rule to assume that a feature of work behavior found in one occupation, even a minor or an odd one, will be found in others. The fact that it is denied at first by the people in some occupation, or that it has not been revealed by previous research, should not be considered sufficient evidence that it is not there. A generation that knows its Freud should know that the difference between what people do about certain matters is often less than the difference in what they reveal to themselves and others.

Restriction of production is a good case in point. As it is generally defined, it means the wilful refusal by workers in industry to do as much work as their employer believes they can and ought to do. The latter, having hired a man's time, expects some large power over its disposition. It is assumed by the employer that his will—enlightened, informed, and reasonable—should determine how hard a man should work. If the worker consciously does less, the employer may use the words "theft" and "bad faith." It has long been recognized that a withholding of paid-for effort—the British ca'canny—is a powerful means of industrial conflict. Employers blame it on trade-unions. But Max Weber maintained that putting on the brakes could occur without unions, and without conscious agreement, as part of the workingman's unending struggle with his employer over the price of his labor—a struggle which he feels in his very body.[1] It can happen in concert either by conscious intent or as an almost instinctive common defensive definition of the situation by workers faced with changes of piece rates, machinery, or other practices.

1. Max Weber, "Zur Psychophysik der industriellen Arbeit (1908-9)," in *Gesammelte Aufsätze zur Soziologie und Sozialpolitik* (Tübingen, J.C.B. Mohr 1924), pp. 61–255. " 'Putting on the brakes' will occur in the absence of union organization wherever the working force or even some considerable fraction of it feels some measure of solidarity" (p. 156).

Mr. Roy gives us a unique record and penetrating analysis of restriction in an industrial shop and of the group interaction by which it is defined and maintained. But why should we not expect some restriction of production to be found in all occupations? In the social drama of most kinds of work, people interact in several established roles. The people of each category have their own conceptions of their interests, rights, and duties toward one another and toward people in the other categories. An object of these conceptions will nearly always be the measure of effort and of product of work, both of which will also vary from person to person, from day to day, and even from hour to hour. Even in organizations where everyone is devoted and hard-working, there is often someone whose effort and product are regarded as heroic in scale, and perhaps even more often persons whose punctilious attention to duty is looked upon as queer. Certainly it is hard to think of occupations in which there is no group preoccupation with definition of proper levels of effort and product and of those levels which, since they may encourage others in the work drama to expect too much, are potentially dangerous for all who share the fate of living by the given trade or calling. Students, even graduate students, learn from their fellows how many of the too many assigned books to read; they may not, as in a certain normal school, write "D.A.R." (Damned Average Raiser) on the door of an eager student whose examination results tend to skew the grade distribution upward to the disadvantage of most. At any rate, I think it good to start one's investigation of any line of work with the assumption that there is some struggle of wills or of consciences or both over the level of effort and of product. But, to use the assumption, one must state it so as to fit his case. If there be no employer, it cannot be stated as the question why workers do not do as much as the employer wants them to or in any other way which uses the employers' will as a criterion. It is better stated, in a general way, as discovering the processes, social and psychological, by which levels of effort and product are determined in various kinds of work and in various kinds of organization for work. When the problem is so defined, better questions can be asked concerning the industrial case itself.

It is of importance for the understanding of human work – in the industrial and in other settings – that we develop a set of problems and processes applicable to the whole range of cases. The terms for describing these problems and processes can be got by comparison of the work drama in various occupations. Each paper in this series was chosen because it deals interestingly with one or more aspects of this drama in one line of work. In so studying work, we are not merely applying sociology to work. We are studying work by sociological methods. We do not learn our method in some pure or generalized society or part of society and then apply it and the findings to industry, crime, or religion. Rather, we study group life and process where they occur, learning our method and developing our knowledge of society as we go. We may learn about society by studying industry and human work generally. In our particular society, work organization looms so large as a separate and specialized system of things, and work experience is so fateful a part of every man's life, that we cannot make much headway as students of society and of social psychology without using work as one of our main laboratories.

THIRTY

Social Role and the Division of Labor

All of the many ways in which the work of human beings is studied lead back at some point to the obvious, yet infinitely subtle, fact of the division of labor. What is a job description if not a statement of what one worker, rather than another, does or is supposed to do? Similar reference to division of labor lies implicitly in study of the number and migrations of the labor force, of motive and effort, of basic capacities and the learning of skills, and in analysis of the price of labor, services and goods.

The division of labor, in its turn, implies interaction; for it consists not in the sheer difference of one man's kind of work from that of another, but in the fact that the different tasks and accomplishments are parts of a whole whose product all, in some degree, contribute to. And wholes, in the human social realm as in the rest of the biological and in the physical realm, have their essence in interaction. Work as social interaction is the central theme of sociological and social psychological study of work.

Social role, the other term in my title, is useful only to the extent that it facilitates analysis of the parts played by individuals in the interaction which makes up some sort of social whole. I am not sure that I would put up much of an argument against the objection that it is not a very useful term, provided the objector has a better one to refer to the same complex of phenomena. I would argue vociferously, however, if the objector implies either that social interaction is not an ever-present and crucial feature of human work, or that the social-psychological description of a division of labor implied by the term social role is of less importance than a descrip-

Reprinted by permission of the publisher from the *Midwest Sociologist,* Vol. XVII, Spring, 1956. Copyright 1956, Midwest Sociological Society.

tion in terms of techniques. I would mention to the objector that even those who work in solitude are often interacting with a built-in father or with God himself, who is known to be worse than any flesh-and-blood slavedriver; and that those who toil upward in the night while their companions sleep may quite simply be seeking access to an as yet unknown, but more admired set of companions or colleagues.

I will not define or further belabor these terms, social role and the division of labor, but rather illustrate some of their dimensions from those kinds of work which consist in doing something for, or to, people. I say *for* or *to* people intentionally, but not cynically. Any child in any school will sometimes believe that something is being done to him rather than for him; the boy in a reform school nearly always thinks so. The patient in a mental hospital is often convinced that things are being done *to* him *for* someone else; although it may be in the nature of his illness so to believe, he may nevertheless often be right. Even the person suffering from tuberculosis, although he knows he is ill and willingly undergoes treatment, considers that many of the rules of society and of the hospital, and even some parts of the treatment are done *to* him, rather than *for* his benefit. Even in short-term illnesses, the patient may view as indignities some of the things allegedly done for his recovery. At the least, he may think they are done for the convenience of those who work in the hospital rather than for his comfort. These are but some of the simpler ambiguities in those kinds of work called personal or professional services. Perhaps it is well to recall that the opposite of service is disservice, and that the line between them is thin, obscure and shifting.

In many of the things which people do for one another, the *for* can be changed to *to* by a slight over-doing or by a shift of mood. The discipline necessary to that degree of order and quiet which will allow study in a class-room can easily turn into something perceived by the children as perverse and cruel; their perceptions may be truer than the teacher's own self-perception. Wherever a modicum of power to discipline by tongue or force is essential to one's assigned task, the temptation to over-use it and even to get pleasure from it may be present, no matter whether one be a teacher, an attendant in a mental hospital, or a prison guard. The danger of major distortion of relationship and function within the framework of a formal office lurks wherever people go or are sent for help or correction: the school-room, the clinic, the operating room, the confessional booth, the undertaking parlor all share this characteristic. Whatever terms we eventually may use to describe social interaction at work must be such that they will allow these subtle distortions of role or function to be brought to light and related to whatever are their significant correlates in personalities or situations.

Another feature of the kinds of work in question lies in the peculiar ambiguities with respect to what is seen as honorable, respectable, clean and prestige-giving as against what is less honorable or respectable, and what is mean or dirty. The term *profession* in its earlier and more restricted usage referred to a very few occupations of high learning and prestige, whose practitioners did things for others. Law and medicine are the prototypes. Yet both of them have always required some sort of alliance, or, at least, some sort of terms with the lowliest and most despised of human occupations. It is not merely in Dickens' novels that lawyers have truck with process-servers, informants, spies and thugs. What the learned lawyers argue before an Appellate Court (and I hear that the cases for textbooks used in law schools are almost all from Appellate Courts) is but a purified distillate of some human mess. A lawyer may be asked whether he and his client come into court with clean hands; when he answers, "yes," it may mean that someone else's hands are of necessity a bit grubby. For not only are some quarrels more respectable, more clean, than others; but also some of the kinds of work involved in the whole system (gathering evidence, getting clients, bringing people to court, enforcing judgments, making the compromises that keep cases out of court) are more respected and more removed from temptation and suspicion than others. In fact, the division of labor among lawyers is as much one of respectability (hence of self concept and role) as of specialized knowledge and skills. One might even call it a moral division of labor, if one keeps in mind that the term means not simply that some lawyers, or people in the various branches of law work, are more moral than others; but that the very demand for highly scrupulous and respectable lawyers depends in various ways upon the availability of less scrupulous people to attend to the less respectable legal problems of even the best people. I do not mean that the good lawyers all consciously delegate their dirty work to others (although many do). It is rather a game of live and let live; a game, mind you, hence interaction, even though it be a game of keeping greater than chance distances.

As the system of which the lawyer's work is part reaches down into the nether regions of the unrespectable and outward to the limbo of guile and force, which people may think necessary but do not admire, so the physician's work touches the world of the morally and ritually, but more especially of the physically unclean. Where his work leaves off, that of the undertaker begins; in some cultures and epochs they have shared the monopoly of certain functions and certain occult arts. The physician has always had also to have some connection (even though it be again the connection of competition or of studied avoidance) with the abortionist, with the "quacks" who deal with obscure and "social" diseases, as well as with the lesser occupations which also treat physical and mental troubles:

the midwife, who has in certain places and times been suspected of being willing to do her work a bit prematurely; the blood-letter, who has at times been also the lowly barber; the bonesetter, who in mediaeval Italy was also the smith; and the masseur and keeper of baths, who is often suspected of enjoying his work too much. If the physician has high prestige—and he has had it at various times in history, although perhaps never more so than now—it is not so much *sui generis,* as by virtue of his place in the particular pattern of the medical division of labor at the time. Two features of that division of labor at present are (1) that the level of public confidence in the technical competence and good faith of the medical system is very high and (2) that nearly all of the medical functions have been drawn into a great system of interlocking institutions over which physicians have an enormous measure of control. (Only abortion remains outside, and even that can be said only with some qualification.)

It is also a division of labor notorious for its rigid hierarchy. The ranking has something to do with the relative clean-ness of functions performed. The nurses, as they successfully rise to professional standing, are delegating the more lowly of their traditional tasks to aides and maids. No one is so lowly in the hospital as those who handle soiled linen; none so low in the mental hospital as the attendant, whose work combines some tasks that are not clean with potential use of force. But if there is no system in which the theme of uncleanliness is so strong, likewise there is none in which it is so strongly compensated for. Physical cleanliness of the human organism depends upon balances easily upset; the physicians and his co-workers operate at the margins where these balances are, in fact, often upset. To bring back health (which is cleanliness) is the great miracle. Those who work the miracle are more than absolved from the potential uncleanliness of their tasks; but those who perform the lowly tasks without being recognized as among the miracle-workers fare badly in the prestige rating. And this gives us a good case for rubbing in the point that the division of labor is more than a technical phenomenon; that there are infinite social-psychological nuances in it.

Actually, in the medical world there are two contrary trends operating simultaneously. As medical technology develops and changes, particular tasks are constantly down-graded; that is, they are delegated by the physician to the nurse. The nurse in turn passes them on to the maid. But occupations and people are being up-graded, within certain limits. The nurse moves up nearer the doctor in techniques and devotes more of her time to supervision of other workers. The practical nurse is getting more training, and is beginning to insist on the prerogatives which she believes should go with the tasks she performs. New workers come in at the bottom of the hierarchy to take over the tasks abandoned by those occupations

which are ascending the mobility ladder. Others come in outside the hierarchy as new kinds of technology (photography, electronics, physics) find a
place in the medical effort. Satisfactory definitions of role for these new
people are notoriously lacking, and that in a system in which rigidly defined
roles and ranks are the rule. Here we have indeed a good case for illustrating the point that a role definition of a division of labor is necessary to
complement any technical description of it. And the question arises of the
effect of changes in technical division upon the roles involved. Sometimes a
desired change of role is validated by a change in technical tasks (the
nurses are an excellent example). Sometimes a change in technical division
creates a role problem, or a series of them. I think we may go further and
say that when changes of either kind get under way the repercussions will
be felt beyond the positions immediately affected, and may indeed touch
every position in the system. Some roles in a division of labor may be more
sensitive to changes in technique than are others. It seems probable, for
instance, that some aspects of the basic relationships of nurse, physician
and patient will not be greatly altered by the shifting of technical tasks from
one to the other and from both of them to other people in the medical
system. (I purposely included the patient, for he has a part in the medical
division of labor, too.)

There will probably always be in this system, as in others, some one
whose role it is to make ultimate decisions, with all the risks that go with
them and with all the protections necessary. This is the role of the physician. He has and jealously guards more authority than he can, in many
cases, actually assume. There will probably always be in the system,
complementary to this position, another of the right-hand man order; a
position which defers to the first but which, informally, often must exceed
its authority in order to protect the interests of all concerned. The nurse
occupies this position. When the doctor isn't there, she may do some
necessary thing which requires his approval — and get the approval when he
comes back. She is the right-hand man of the physician, even and perhaps
especially when he isn't there. The nurse also sometimes fires furnaces and
mends the plumbing, i.e., she does tasks of people below her or outside the
role hierarchy of medicine. It hurts her, but she does it. Her place in the
division of labor is essentially that of doing in a responsible way whatever
necessary things are in danger of not being done at all. The nurse would
not like this definition, but she ordinarily in practice rises to it. I believe
that, if we were to take a number of systems of work in which things are
done for people we could dig out a series of roles or positions which could
be described in some such way, and could see the consequences for the
roles of changes in technique and in other roles in the system. And I would
defend the term *role* as a fair starting term in such an enterprise; for it

suggests a part in a whole act involving other people playing, well or badly, their expected parts.

I have been saying, in various rather indirect ways, that no line of work can be fully understood outside the social matrix in which it occurs or the social system of which it is part. The system includes, in most and perhaps in all cases, not merely the recognized institutional complex but reaches out and down into human life and society. As in the case of law and even in medicine, there are usually some connections which we cannot easily or do not willingly follow out. There are also ambiguities and apparent contradictions in the combinations of duties of any one occupation or position in an occupational system.

One of the commoner failures in study of work is to overlook part of the interactional system. We speak of the physician and patient as a social system (as did the late Dr. L. J. Henderson in an article by that name), or at most include the nurse; or we speak of teacher and pupil, lawyer and client, and the like. Certainly in some occupations there is some basic relation such as these; a relation which is partly reality, partly stereotype, partly ideal nostalgically attributed to a better past or sought after in a better future. Perhaps the commonest complaint of people in the professions which perform a service for others, is that they are somehow prevented from doing their work as it should be done. Someone interferes with this basic relation. The teachers could teach better were it not for parents who fail in their duty or school boards who interfere. Psychiatrists would do better if it were not for families, stupid public officials, and ill-trained attendants. Nurses would do more nursing if it were not for administrative duties, and the carelessness of aides and maintenance people. Part of the complained-of interference is merely institutional. The institutional matrix in which things are done for people is certainly becoming more complex in most professional fields; there are more and more kinds of workers in a division of labor ever changing in its boundaries between one person's work and another's. But it is not so much the numbers of people who intervene that seems to bother the professional most; it is rather the differing conceptions of what the work really is or should be, of what mandate has been given by the public, of what it is possible to accomplish and by what means; as well as of the particular part to be played by those in each position, their proper responsibilities and rewards. Compared to the restrictions, resistances and distortions of purpose, assignments, and efforts in a school, a mental hospital, a social agency or a prison, the much studied restriction of production in a factory is simplicity itself. In the factory, there is at least fair consensus about what the object produced shall be. There is often no such consensus in institutions where things are done for or to people.

Every one, or nearly every one of the many important services given people by professionals in our times is given in a complex institutional setting. The professional must work with a host of non-professionals (and the professionals ordinarily are short-sighted enough to use that pejorative term ad nauseam). These other workers bring into the institutional complex their own conceptions of what the problem is, their own conceptions of their rights and privileges, and of their careers and life-fate. The philosophy—of illness, crime, reform, mental health, or whatever—which they bring in is often that of another class or element of the population than that to which the professional belongs or aspires. Like most humans, they do not completely accept the role-definitions handed down from above, but in communication among their own kind and in interaction with the people served, treated, or handled, work out their own definition. They build up an ethos, and a system of rationalizations for the behavior they consider proper given the hazards and contingencies of their own positions. The proper study of the division of labor will include a look at any system of work from the points of view of all the kinds of people involved in it, whether their position be high or low, whether they are at the center or near the periphery of the system. And those who seek to raise standards of practice (and their own status) in the occupations and institutions which do things for people would do well to study, in every case, what changes in the other positions or roles in the system will be wrought by changes in their own, and what problems will be created for other people by every new solution of one of their own problems.

THIRTY-ONE

Studying the Nurse's Work

People have long nursed the sick, helped the poor and the unhappy, taught the young, and looked after collections of books. But the professions of nursing, social work, school teaching, and librarianship are all new. They are among the many ancient arts that are now being turned into professions.

There are certain symptoms to be seen wherever this happens. The people in the occupation get somewhat self-conscious about many things concerning their work; jealous of their name and badge (the nurse's uniform being her badge); dreadfully afraid that some of their number will not observe company manners and so will hurt the reputation of all; not quite sure what their jobs are or ought to be and consequently not certain what their training should be. The American nurse is in this fix right now. But it is not in such a bad fix, and she is in good company in her misery, for even the older professions are going through changes which make them almost as troubled and self-conscious as the newer ones. They just don't admit it.

One of the things people do when their occupation is changing from an art to a complex profession is to study themselves, their work, and the organization in which they do it. They may have been studied before, but by others rather than by themselves. It takes courage to study one's own work, just as it does to take a good hard look at anything which is dear to one and of which one is proud. It is a little like looking hard in the glass to see if one has wrinkles. The nurses of America (who, of course, haven't a wrinkle) are to be congratulated for undertaking to study themselves. All an outsider can do is to give pointers which come from having watched

American Journal of Nursing, Vol. 51, May, 1951. Copyrighted May 1951, The American Journal of Nursing Company, Reprinted by permission.

other occupations go through it. The basic information concerning nursing has, in the end, to come from the only people who have that information deep in their systems from experience — the nurses themselves.

The particular thing which the nursing profession has decided to study first is the nurse's job. Now a job is not an easy thing to describe. But there are some quite simple points which will help. I shall mention some of them.

The first is that a job — that is, the work done by an individual of some named kind of classification, such as a nurse — is always a position in an organization. No organization, no job. No other people, no work for me. From this it follows that it is impossible to describe the job of one kind of person without saying something about the work of others. Since most nurses do their work in hospitals, it is well to start a study of the nurse's work by thinking of all the things which have to be done to make a hospital go. Seen in one way, the nurse's job consists of all the things which have to be done in the hospital and which are not done by other kinds of people. Of each of these many tasks one must ask, "Why is this done by the nurse rather than by someone else?" About the things done by other people, one should ask, "Why is this done by someone else rather than by the nurse?" This kind of question sets one's eyes on the frontiers between nurse's work and the work of all the other kinds of people in a hospital. There are as many of these frontiers as there are other kinds of people in the organization.

Since the number of tasks to be done in the modern hospital increases from day to day, there are more frontiers between jobs than ever. Every one of them is an area of necessary co-operation, hence also of possible conflict. This applies not merely to the relations between nurses and nurse's aides, practical nurses, and various kinds of maintenance and technical people, but also to the frontier between nurses' work and doctors' work. With every change in medical technology, there comes the question whether the new items of work will be done by the physician or by the nurse in each of the many circumstances which may arise. Never has the frontier between doctor and nurse been more active and mobile than now. A study of the nurse's job will be of little use unless the developments on this frontier are reported and discussed with more than customary frankness.

Finally, let us not forget the frontier of work between the nurse and the patient. What shall the patient do for himself and what shall be done for him? This is an old question, because there is no final answer to it. But the nurse's job will not have been well described without considering the relation of patient and nurse in all the usual situations which arise.

Some may think that nurses are a bit presumptuous in daring to describe everybody else's work in order to learn what is their own. But that is the only way to do it well.

As I have already suggested, an occupation or a job consists of a bundle of several tasks. The thing that holds them together is that they are all done by one person and under a single name. A person, a name, and a bundle of tasks. That the person has a value is something I won't discuss here, although we forget it sometimes with respect to people of other kinds than our own. But the name has a value, too. People are proud to say they are nurses. They jealously try to prevent unauthorized persons from claiming the name or wearing the uniform. But then comes this question: Why are the tasks in this bundle all done by the person who is called a nurse? For not all the tasks in the bundle require the same degree or kinds of skill. Reading in a loud clear voice is one of the tasks required of a professor of mathematics, but it has nothing especially in common with knowing how to work problems.

There are similar cases in the nursing profession, I am sure. One of the aims of a study of the nurse's work is to find out not merely what is in her bundle of tasks in various kinds of hospitals and in various branches of nursing, but also to learn, so far as we can, what holds the bundle of miscellaneous tasks together.

Not all of the tasks in a bundle are equally pleasant to do; nor do they all have the same prestige. Some tasks are unpleasant. Some are considered menial, and beneath one's dignity as a nurse. We may therefore think of each task as having a place in a prestige scale, thus:

Prestige	Old Situation	New Situation
High		A
		B
	C	C
Moderate	D	D
	E	E
Low		F
		G

Now let us suppose that the nurses' work bundle consisted in the past of tasks C, D, and E. C, let us say, is something that everyone would proudly agree is nursing. Let E be something generally considered drudgery, that requires no skill. It has to be done, but is a.low-prestige item in the bundle. It is part of the "dirty work" of nursing. (All occupations have dirty work to do.)

Now suppose that medical technology and hospital organization so change that there are some new tasks in the nurse's bundle. Some of the new things (perhaps new tests, new technics requiring scientific knowledge or high skill; new levels of supervision, planning, coordinating, teaching, et

314 Work and Self

certera) have more prestige than the best of the old tasks. A and B on the chart lift the ceiling of the profession, and hence offer new career lines. Perhaps there are also new tasks considered still lower than any of the old ones (F and G). The result is that there are now not only more tasks in the bundle but that there is also a greater difference in the prestige and desirability of the topmost and the bottom tasks. In this situation it is not surprising that people would like the whole bundle opened up and resorted.

Very likely some will favor having the tasks tied into two or three separate bundles, those with higher prestige (nearly always, in America, the ones for which most schooling is thought necessary) being put together. The occupational name—if it is a proud one, like nursing—will then be reserved for the bundle with high prestige (perhaps A, B, and C). The other tasks, those of less prestige, would then be put together into one or two jobs or positions for which names will have to be found. The process of turning an art and an occupation into a profession often includes the attempt to drop certain tasks to some other kind of worker. And this is exactly what is happening to the nursing profession. One of the aims of the study of the nurse's job is to discover ways in which various tasks, old and new, have been regrouped and with what resulting difficulties and successes.

In studying the resorting, one should remember that an occupation is not merely a bundle of tasks, but a social role, a part one plays in a drama. What part does the nurse play? Sometimes it is that of comforter of the patient. "Physical and spiritual comfort" is the phrase one hears from nurses. Sometimes she is the shock absorber between doctor and patient; or between various technical departments of the hospital which all want the poor patient at the same time. I have a notion that a task that is "dirty work" can be more easily endured when it is part of a good role, a role that is full of rewards to one's self. A nurse might do some things with better grace than a person who is not allowed to call herself a nurse, but is dubbed "subprofessional" or "nonprofessional." At any rate, when the tasks get resorted (as they are almost certain to be in a time of great change and expansion), there arises also the question of how the social roles and names are sorted.

In time, every name tends to stand for an idea which people have of the role played by the occupation. If nurse means comforter and shock absorber, who will be called "nurse" when the nurse's tasks are reshuffled? Will it be the teacher and supervisor? The bedside comforter? Or will it be those who give more humble services?

This suggests that a study of the nurse's job has also to be a study of social roles: that is, of the parts people think they are expected to play or are allowed to play in the social drama of the modern hospital. It may be of some interest to nurses that business and industry, which so long emphasized the purely technical organization of work, are coming back rather quickly in their personnel studies and programs to the consideration of social roles and of the social drama of work. *The nurses can be ahead of them by never making the error in the first place of trying to study technics apart from persons.*

In the drama of treatment of the ill and the injured, the nurse is in the center of the action in every scene. Never the prima donna, she is the stalwart character who must always be ready to pick up a missed cue. She keeps the action moving. Hence she knows the play better than anyone else. In these days of crises and of so much change in the organization of health institutions and services, she can make a greater contribution to the understanding of this great drama than can any of the other characters or any of the spectators. The research program which the American Nurses' Association is undertaking is meant simply to facilitate the nurse's efforts to make this contribution to understanding.

THIRTY-TWO

Mistakes at Work

The comparative student of man's work learns about doctors by studying plumbers; and about prostitutes by studying psychiatrists. This is not to suggest any degree of similarity greater than chance expectation between the members of these pairs, but simply to indicate that the student starts with the assumption that all kinds of work belong in the same series, regardless of their places in prestige or ethical ratings. In order to learn, however, one must find a frame of reference applicable to all cases without regard to such ratings. To this end, we seek for the common themes in human work. One such theme is that of routine and emergency. By this I mean that one man's routine of work is made up of the emergencies of other people. In this respect, the pairs of occupations named above do perhaps have some rather close similarities. Both the physician and the plumber do practice esoteric techniques for the benefit of people in distress. The psychiatrist and the prostitute must both take care not to become too personally involved with clients who come to them with rather intimate problems. I believe that in the study of work, as in that of other human activities and institutions, progress is apt to be commensurate with our ability to draw a wide range of pertinent cases into view. The wider the range, the more we need a fundamental frame of reference.

Another theme in human work is the problem of mistakes and failures. It, too, is found in all occupations. The more times per day a man does a given operation, the greater his chance of doing it wrong sometimes. True, his skill may become so great that his percentage of errors is nearly zero. It

From the *Canadian Journal of Economics and Political Science,* Vol. XVII, August, 1951, pp. 320-327.

is common talk in the medical profession that certain surgical operations really ought not to be done at all, except *in extremis,* by men who do not have the opportunity to do them literally by the hundreds every year. In a large and favorably known hospital, the interns and residents—who are there to learn by practice—complain that the leading members of the surgical staff take all the interesting cases, not merely out of charity, but to keep their level of skill up to the point of least risk for the few patients who can pay a really high fee. This reduces the opportunities of the interns and residents to acquire skill. One may speak of a calculus of the probability of making mistakes, in which the variables are skill and frequency of perform- ance. It is obvious that there are many possibilities. One who never performs a given action will never do it wrong. But one who has never tried it could not do it right if he were on some occasion compelled to try. This is the position of the layman with reference to many skills. Some skills require more repetition than others for the original learning and for mainte- nance. In some, even the most proficient make many failures, while in others the top level of skill is close to perfection. Occupations, considered as bundles of skills, are subject to the contingencies contained in all combinations of these factors of learning and of maintaining skill, and, correlatively, subject to variations in the probability that one will some- times make mistakes. These are matters in which experimental and voca- tional psychologists are much interested and on which they are doing significant work.

But there are other factors in this problem of mistakes and failures. Some mistakes are more fateful than others, either for the person who makes them, for his colleagues, or for the persons upon whom the mistakes are made. Those who train students for research which requires receiving the confidences of living people and getting and keeping entrée to groups and institutions of various sorts are aware of this problem. (We are at present working on a project to discover how to train students to a high level of skill in social observation with the least risk of damage to all concerned.) In occupations in which mistakes are fateful and in which repetition on living or valuable material is necessary to learn the skills, it is obvious that there is a special set of problems of apprenticeship and of access to the situations in which the learning may be done. Later on, when the neophyte is at his work, there arises the problem of his seeming always to have known how, since the very appearance of being a learner is frightening. At any rate, there are psychological, physical, social, and economic risks in learning and doing one's work. And since the theoretical probability of making an error some day is increased by the very frequency of the operations by which one makes one's living, it becomes natural to build up some rationale to carry one through. It is also to be expected that those who are subject to the same work risks will compose a collective rationale which they whistle to one another to keep up their courage, and that they will build up collective defenses against the lay world. These rationales and defenses contain a logic that is somewhat like that of insurance, in that they tend to spread the risk psychologically (by saying that it might happen to anyone), morally, and financially. A study of these risk-spreading devices is an essential part of comparative study of occupations. They have a counterpart in the devices which the individual finds for shifting some of the sense of guilt from his own shoulders to those of the larger company of his colleagues. Perhaps this is the basis of the strong identification with colleagues in work in which mistakes are fateful, and in which even long training and a sense of high calling do not prevent errors.

Now let us approach the subject from the side of the person who, since he receives the services, will suffer from the mistakes when they are made. In a certain sense, we actually hire people to make our mistakes for us. The division of labor in society is not merely, as is often suggested, technical. It is also psychological and moral. We delegate certain things to other people, not merely because we cannot do them, but because we do not wish to run the risk of error. The guilt of failure would be too great. Perhaps one reason why physicians do work gratis for each other's families is to keep completely free from the economic necessity of treating people with whom they are so closely involved that mistakes would be too hard to face.

Sometimes a person requires an assurance that can be had only by being in a strictly lay frame of mind. Belief in the charism of skill is a lay, rather than a professional, attitude. The professional attitude is essentially statistical; it deals in probabilities. But there are matters about which we prefer to think in absolutes. In dealing with such matters we delegate the relative way of thinking to another, who becomes our agent. He runs our risks for us. We like to believe him endowed with charism. Ray Gold, who studied some of the building trades, found that the housewife likes to believe that the plumber she calls in is perfect, not merely *relatively* good. He keeps the mysterious entrails of her precious house in order. How much more does one want to believe absolutely in one's dentist, lawyer, physician, and priest. (There are of course other non-technical factors involved in delegation of tasks. Some work is *infra dignitate*. Some is necessary, but shady, or forbidden by one's particular taboos and aversions.)

Now this does not mean that the person who delegates work, and hence, risk, will calmly accept the mistakes which are made upon him, his family, or his property. He is quick to accuse; and if people are in this respect as psychiatrists say they are in others, the more determined they are to escape responsibility, the quicker they may be to accuse others for real or supposed mistakes.

In fact, I suppose that we all suspect just a little the objectivity of those to whom we delegate the more fateful of our problems. We suspect them for that very experimental spirit which we know is, in some degree, necessary to hardy and progressive skill in meeting our crises. Thus there is probably always some ambivalence in our feelings towards the people whom we hire to make our mistakes, or at least to run the risk of making them. The whole problem or set of problems involved in delegating work — and risks — to others is one on which there is not much to be found in the anthropological, sociological, or psychological literature. For each occupation that one studies one should, I believe, seek to determine just what it is that is delegated to the persons in the occupation and what are the attitudes and feelings involved on both sides.

We now have before us the problem and the characters. The characters are the people who, because they do something often and for others, run the risk of making mistakes and of causing injury; and those other people who, for technical, economic, psychological, moral, or status reasons, delegate some of their tasks and problems to others and who therefore may have mistakes made upon them and at their expense. These are not really two kinds of people, but are the same people in different roles. The relation of these two roles is part of the personal adjustment of everyone who works. The problem is the reduction and absorption of the risk of failure on both sides, and of the kinds of conflicts within and between persons, which arise from the risk of error, mistakes, and failures.

As soon as we go into these problems we are faced with another: that of defining what a failure or mistake is in any given line of work or in a given work operation. This leads to still another which turns out to be the significant one for the social drama of work: Who has the right to say what a mistake or a failure is? The findings on this point are fairly clear; a colleague-group (the people who consider themselves subject to the same work risks) will stubbornly defend its own right to define mistakes, and to say in the given case whether one has been made.[1] Howard S. Becker has found that professional jazz musicians will do considerable injury to themselves rather than let any layman, even the one who is paying their wages, say that a musician is playing badly or even that he has struck the wrong note. An orchestra leader who would even relay a layman's complaint to a member of his band would be thought already on the road to becoming a "square," one of those outsiders who do not understand jazz music. Now you may say that jazz music is so lacking in any canons of correctness that

---

1. The colleague-group does not in all cases succeed in getting and keeping this right. Perhaps they do not always want the full responsibility of convicting one another of error and of applying sanctions. It would be more correct to say that a kind of jurisprudence of mistakes is an essential part of the study of any occupation. Professor Norman Ward has suggested that a study of the official *error* in baseball would throw light on the processes involved.

there is no such thing as a single false note within the larger noise. It is all a matter of individual opinion. There is no clear and objective standard by which a judgment can be made.

But how clear is it in other lines of work? When one starts comparing occupations in this regard one finds that in most of them it is very difficult to establish criteria of success or failure, and of mistakes as against proper execution of work. The cases where all parties to the work drama would agree are few indeed. In factories which make precision parts the criteria are finely measured tolerances, but usually there is an informally agreed upon set of tolerances which are slightly looser than those in the book. Workmen and inspectors are continually at odds over the difference, even when the workmen want the parts they make to be workable. This is a case of the clearest kind of criterion. In medicine the criteria of success and failure are often far from clear. Dr. Bruno Bettelheim recently stated that psychotherapists do not discuss together their successes and failures because there are no standards to go by; that is why, he said, they spend so much time discussing whether their historical reconstructions of the troubles of their patients are correct or not. Health is, after all, a relative matter. Most people are interested in making the old body do as long as possible; this makes medicine quite a different matter from the automobile industry (where the garage man makes his work easier by persuading you the old car isn't worth mending).

Even where the standards may be a little clearer than in medicine and education, the people who work and those who receive the product as goods or services will have quite different degrees and kinds of knowledge of the probabilities and contingencies involved. The colleague-group will consider that it alone fully understands the technical contingencies, and that it should therefore be given the sole right to say when a mistake has been made. The layman, they may contend, cannot even at best fully understand the contingencies. This attitude may be extended to complete silence concerning mistakes of a member of the colleague-group, because the very discussion before a larger audience may imply the right of the layman to make a judgment; and it is the *right* to make the judgment that is most jealously guarded.

In some occupations it is assumed that anyone on the inside will know by subtle gestures when his colleagues believe a mistake has been made. Full membership in the colleague-group is not attained until these gestures and their meaning are known. When they are known, there need not be conscious and overt discussion of certain errors even within the colleague-group. And when some incident makes an alleged failure or mistake a matter of public discussion, it is perhaps the feeling that outsiders will never understand the full context of risk and contingency that makes colleagues so tight-lipped. And if matters have gone to such a point that mistakes and failures are not freely discussed even within the trusted in-group, public discussion may be doubly feared; for in addition to questioning the prerogative of in-group judgment, the outside inquisitor lifts the veil from the group's own hidden anxieties, the things colleagues do not talk about even among themselves. This may be the source of the rather nervous behavior of school teachers when my colleagues and I report to them—at their own request—some of the things we are finding out about them.

One of the differences between lay and professional thinking concerning mistakes is that to the layman the technique of the occupation should be pure instrument, pure means to an end, while to the people who practice it, every occupation tends to become an art. David Riesman,[2] who was once a clerk to Justice Brandeis, and an assistant in the office of the District Attorney of New York, tells of the wonderful briefs which young lawyers draw up for presentation to lower court judges who can scarcely read them, much less judge the law that is in them. The ritual of looking up all the past cases, and the art of arguing out all possibilities are gone through, even when the lawyer knows that the decision will be made upon a much simpler—perhaps also a much sounder—basis. What is more, the ritual and the art are respected, and the men who perform them with brilliance and finesse are admired. The simple client may be dazzled, but at some point he is also likely to think that he is being done by the whole guild of lawyers, including his own, the opposing counsel, and the court. In a sense, the art and cult of the law are being maintained at his expense. The legal profession believes, in some measure, in the cult of the law. The individual case is thought of not merely as something to be decided, but as part of the stream of observance of the cult of the law.

And here we come to the deeper point of Dr. Bettelheim's remark concerning his own colleagues, the psychotherapists. A part of their art is the reconstruction of the history of the patient's illness. This may have some instrumental value, but the value put upon it by the practitioners is of another order. The psychotherapists, perhaps just because the standards of cure are so uncertain, apparently find reassurance in being adept at their art of reconstruction (no doubt accompanied by faith that skill in the art will bring good to patients in the long run).

Another example of these ways of thinking is to be found in social work. This profession is said to make a distinction between successful and professional handling of a case. The layman thinks of success as getting the

2. "Toward an Anthropological Science of Law and the Legal Profession," *The American Journal of Sociology,* LVII (September, 1951), pp. 121-35.

person back on his feet, or out of his trouble. The social worker has to think of correct procedure, of law, of precedent, of the case as something which leaves a record. She also appreciates skillful interviewing, and perhaps can chuckle over some case which was handled with subtlety and finish, although the person never got "well" (whatever that would be in social work).

In teaching, where ends are very ill-defined — and consequently mistakes are equally so — where the lay world is quick to criticize and blame, correct handling becomes ritual as much as or even more than an art. If a teacher can prove that he has followed the ritual, the blame is shifted from himself to the miserable child or student; the failure can be and is put upon them.

Ritual is also strongly developed in occupations where there are great unavoidable risks, as in medicine. In such occupations the ritual may, however, be stronger in the second and third ranks of the institutions in which the work is done. Thus, in medicine, the physician, who stands at the top of the hierarchy, takes the great and final risks of decision and action. These risks are delegated to him, and he is given moral and legal protection in taking them. But the pharmacist, who measures out the prescribed doses, and the nurse, who carries out the ordered treatment, are the great observers of ritual in medicine. Pharmacists are said often to become ritualistic wipers and polishers, flecking infinitely small grains of dust from scales on which they are only going to weigh out two pounds of Paris green. The ritualistic punctiliousness of nurses and pharmacists is a kind of built-in shock-absorber against the possible mistakes of the physician. Indeed, in dramatizing their work, these second-rank professions explicitly emphasize their role as saviors of both patient and physician from the errors of the latter. And here again we get a hint of what may be the deeper function of the art, cult, and ritual of various occupations. They may provide a set of emotional and even organizational checks and balances against both the subjective and the objective risks of the trade.

I suspect that it is a rare occupation whose practitioners develop no criteria of good work, and no concept of mistake or failure other than simply defined successful conclusion of the given case or task. Usually the professional judgment will contain explicit or implicit references to an art, a cult, and a ritual. The function of the art, cult, and ritual is not so much to bring the individual case to an early successful conclusion as to relate it to the on-going occupation itself, and to the social system in which the work is done. In most occupations, a man can be judged as quite wrong by his colleagues for an action which the lay client might consider very successful indeed. The quack, defined functionally and not in evaluative terms, is the man who continues through time to please his customers but not his colleagues. On the contrary, a man may be considered by his colleagues to have done a piece of work properly and without error, even when the client may accuse him of error, mistake, or failure.

In these remarks I have mentioned two concepts of great importance for study of the universal work drama. One is the concept of role; the other, that of social system. A person, asked what his work is, can answer in two ways. He can say *what* he does: I make beds, I plumb teeth. Or he can say *who* he is: I am the person who does so and so. In the latter case he is naming his role. A large part of the business of protecting one's self from the risks of one's own work mistakes lies in definition of role; and in some occupations, one of the rewards is definition of one's role in such a way as to show that one helps protect people from the mistakes of others. Now, roles imply a system of social arrangements. Most work is done in such systems. Part of the function of these systems is to delegate, to spread, or, in some cases, to concentrate, the risk and the guilt of mistakes; and also to spread and to allocate the losses which result from them. The details of these matters are better left until they have been worked out more fully.

This one example of sociological analysis prompts some remarks concerning the academic division of labor with reference to human work. In the historical and conventional division of academic labor, work has belonged to the economists, as do voters and kings to the political scientist, and fun and vice to the sociologist. The historian handled anything which had been written down on paper or other material long enough ago for the author, his characters, and all the relatives of both to be so long dead that no one would bring a libel suit. Indeed, it was better if they were in danger of being forgotten, for the historian's fame depended on rediscovering them. But his mandate allowed him to tell all about his characters — their work, their politics, and their gambols. The anthropologist went about the earth on one-man expeditions discovering people who didn't write and hadn't been written about. Since he was alone in the field and since his reputation depended upon his being the first there, he looked at everything from hair texture and the shape of shin bones to religion, art, kinship, crime, and even the technique and organization of work, and the distribution of the products of labor.

Now the division of academic labor, like other human arrangements, is as much the result of social movements as of logic. Some persons in, or on the periphery of, academic life are seized, from time to time, with a new preoccupation. They pursue it and their successors nourish it. The third generation will have refined out of it some pure essence which will be called a social science; but they will not ordinarily have yielded to anyone else the original liquor from which their essence was distilled. Thus, the pure essence of economic reasoning was abstracted from preoccupation with all sorts of things having to do with the material and moral welfare of man, as may be seen in Adam Smith's *The Wealth of Nations*. Since the quantities which would appear in place of the letters in economic equations—if some economist were to be so impure as to make such a substitution—would include the price of the labor used in manufacturing and distributing those goods which are produced in sufficient quantities to fit the formulae, it is quite natural that work should have been one of the preoccupations of the economist. Indeed, it was natural that economists should extend their interest to whatever might affect the price and supply of labor: migration, the birth-rate, religion and philosophy, laws, trade unions, politics, and even mental and physical capacities, although the latter have become the psychologists' claim to entry into the factory. Economists have been interested in those distractions from labor which have more lately been the concern of the sociologist, but which Daniel Defoe, who never heard of sociology, commented upon in *The True-Born Englishman:*

> The lab'ring poor, in spight of double pay
> Are sawcy, mutinous and beggarly
> So lavish of their money and their time
> That want of forecast is the nation's crime
> Good drunken company is their delight
> And what they get by day, they spend by night.

If the occupation of the economist be economic reasoning, in ever more sophisticated formulae, human work continues to be one of his *pre-occupations*. And this illustrates the fate of each branch of social science; that while it refines and purifies its theoretical core, its logic, it can never free itself from the human mess. Wallowing there, each purist will find himself in the company of others who, although they seek to create a different pure product of logic, must extract it from this same mess. It might be of some use, in these days of the cult of collaboration between the social disciplines, for us to understand the social movements out of which the various social sciences have come, and the consequent development in each not merely of a central and distinguishing logic, but of a large periphery or halo of preoccupation with institutions and events. It is, I believe, treading upon a pre-empted area of events and institutions that brings accusation of academic trespass, rather than borrowing its fundamental logic. Thus a sociologist should stay out of factories because the economist was there first. The economist should stay out of the family. Neither of them should be caught in an insane asylum, which is the domain of psychiatrists.

But, to the extent that there is some logic in the academic division of labor, representatives of each discipline will be found studying not merely some one institution but any events which yield to effective analysis by their particular logic. Economics will cease to be merely—if it ever was—the science of markets; anthropology, of primitive peoples; education, of what happens in schools; sociology, of families, churches, play-grounds, settlement houses, and prisons.

Human work, including the institutions in which people work for a living, has become one of the lively frontiers on which social scientists meet. Without belaboring the point, I refer you to V.W. Bladen for an acute analysis of what is happening among economists, anthropologists, and sociologists on this frontier.[3] Work, I submit, is in all human societies an object of moral rule, of social control in the broadest sense, and it is precisely all the processes involved in the definition and enforcement of moral rule that form the core problems of sociology.

3. "Economics and Human Relations," *The Canadian Journal of Economics and Political Science,* Vol.14 (August, 1948), pp. 301-11.

THIRTY-THREE

Personality Types and the Division of Labor

Introduction

Literature and common sense, and in these latter days, the press, have given us stereotyped pictures of persons engaged in various occupations: the old-maid school teacher, the parson, the village blacksmith, the farmer, the professor, the politician, the financier. All these and many other types so created are expected to react to the situations of life in characteristic manner. To many the cartoonist adds a face and costume. Social scientists and philosophers have taken the cue and have sometimes related types of men to their tasks, as Adam Smith in his classic paragraph on the nature of the differences between the philosopher and the man with a wheelbarrow. In common-sense discussion the question is not asked as to the manner in which the differences arise: it only talks of them as facts or fiction.

In our branch of social science much attention has lately been turned to the classification of persons into types, according to their behavior. Some of the older classifications, as good and bad, criminal and law-abiding, rich and poor, have been called into question—not because the classes indicated do not exist, but because they do not give sufficient clues to the behavior of people. Dr. Burgess has undertaken to study the delinquent as a person, taking into account sequences of behavior, the rôles assumed by the person in his group, the rôle accorded him by his group; and with the

Reprinted by permission of the publisher from the American Journal of Sociology, Vol. XXXIII, No. 5, March 1928, University of Chicago Press.

further provision that one take into account the group in which the person wishes to have status. That is to say, the group in which he "lives." The delinquency, or the breaking of the law, thus becomes a mere item in a pattern of behavior, and emphasis is put on the fact that this one item is not always the same, even when the overt act involved comes under a given legal category. In this is a recognition that behavior types do not necessarily coincide with the common-sense or legal definitions.

In this paper we appear to be reverting from the position already gained; looking for a set of personality types in a classification of people according to the work they do. A number of questions at once arise. To what extent do persons of a given occupation "live together" and develop a culture which has its subjective aspect in the personality? Do persons find an area for the satisfaction of their wishes in the associations which they have with their colleagues, competitors, and fellow-servants? To whose opinions is one sensitive? What part does one's occupation play in giving him his "life-organization"?[1]

A prerequisite for the answering of these questions is study of persons engaged in various occupations, to determine the nature of occupational selection, and what happens to a person once he does find a place in the division of labor. A number of such studies have been undertaken. Some are statistical studies; others are what one might call case studies of occupations, as Mrs. Donovan's work on the waitress.[2] We can go no farther in this paper than to put the problem into a frame of reference, and illustrate from one occupational group.

Human Ecology and the Division of Labor

We are indebted to Durkheim for a distinction between two types of social units, the *social segment* and the *social organ*. The *social segment* is that sort of minute community which exists in independence of all others; its members grow up under conditions so uniform that their consciences are concrete, uniform, and strong. It is also characterized by the presence of as many generations as the longevity of the group allows. It is different in a number of ways from all other communities. The individual cannot imagine any other set of social attitudes than the one common to the people of his own group. The *social organ,* on the other hand, is dependent for life upon other communities; it represents only a unit in the division of labor, and must engage in exchange with other communities. This exchange requires at least a minimum of understanding between the groups of communities

1. See W. I. Thomas, *The Polish Peasant in Europe and America* (New York: Knopf, 1927).
2. Frances R. Donovan, *The Woman Who Waits* (Boston: R. G. Badger, 1920).

involved. The division of labor represents a set of exchanges between communities whereby these communities become involved as functioning parts of a larger community. This larger community, however, has no common conscience, or only a very tenuous, vague, abstract one. As the division of labor proceeds, the life of each social organ is more conditioned by the others; the forces which hold it in place come to include neighbors as well as the soil beneath one's feet. It is this pattern of social organs, treated spatially, with which human ecology concerns itself.

Sacred Division of Labor

In the type of community which Durkheim calls a "social segment" the division of labor is either very simple or very rigid. It may be mere incident of the social organization of the community, consisting in sets of sacred prerogatives, as in the caste system, where a person is born to his trade and station. We may call this sort of division of labor a sacred one. The prerogatives of a given caste may or may not constitute a unit of technique.

In a study of the division of labor among preliterates, done under the tutelage of Dr. Faris at the University of Chicago, the writer isolated a set of occupations which he called "preliterate professions," including healers, performers of rituals, charmers, medicine men, etc. In them he found associated with a certain amount of practical technique a great amount of secret ritual and prerogative whose connections with each other were traditional and arbitrary and fortified by taboos. In a society where the division of labor is of this character, its relation to personality is fairly obvious, especially if it includes the "caste" feature of evaluation and a complete set of social relationships involved with it. This type of division of labor is essentially a phenomenon of an unchanging, immobile society. There may be a tendency for it to develop in a changing society, or at least to persist. For instance, one can think of no principle of technique which naturally associates the activities of the clergyman: he directs the business affairs of his parish, marries, baptizes, comforts the sad, prays for the recovery of the sick, and acts as interpreter of morals and theology. The functions are set in a traditional and somewhat arbitrary complex; they are prerogatives.[3]

3. Cecil C. North, *Social Differentiation*, (Chapel Hill: University of North Carolina, 1926), p. 255. "A group in which status, occupation, and culture have become hereditary is known as a caste. As a matter of fact, however, the distinction between a society based upon caste and one in which open classes prevail is simply one of degree. There are present in all societies forces which tend to crystallize the form of social institutions and social organization. And it is merely a question of how freely these forces have made themselves or worked themselves out to a logical conclusion."

The Secularization of the Division of Labor

In contrast to this type we may characterize the division of labor in our world as secularized. New occupations are created every day, and the concatenations of functions of old ones are subject to change. The industrial revolutions of every day mean to the individual that he is not sure of his job; or, at least, that one is not sure of one's son's job. This is true of whole regions, as well as of individuals; changes in transportation, methods of production, extension of the frontiers of commerce do violence to the most deeply rooted and sacred prerogatives.[4]

Occupational selection becomes a major process, to which social organization is incidental. This selection becomes a fierce process which begins anew each day, atomizing families and tearing them loose from their soil.

We may call the division of labor "secularized" both in that new occupations or units of function are developed, which are not hampered by tradition, and in that the persons who enter the occupation come without very definite, traditional notions about the way of carrying on the occupation.[5] We shall pursue this point further in consideration of what the occupational selection process is and what it does to the person.

Occupational Selection

In his recent work, *Wirtschaftsleben im Zeitalter des Hochkapitalismus*,[6] Sombart has made his major theme the selection of the leaders of industry, as well as that of the proletariat. The chief point in regard to the former is that the life-histories of a very large percentage of them show small beginnings. The corporation and the credit system have made this possible. This fact of democratization does not mean an increase in the chances of the person of low degree to rise in the economic and social scale so much as an acceleration of change, the disappearance of old occupations, and the rise of new ones. Sombart makes this clear in his consideration of the sources

---

4. *Ibid.* "The discovery of new territory or natural resources, the appearance of new inventions or new fields of industry, the coming of war — all tend to upset the old arrangement and make for an exchange of places on the social ladder. A high state of intelligence and communication will make it possible for individuals to pass up or down in the scale according to their abilities and character."

5. Werner Sombart, *Das Wirtschaftsleben im Zeitalter des Hochkapitalismus*, Munich & Leipzig, Duncker and Humblot, 1927, p. 30.

6. Sombart, *op. cit.*, "The Extraction of the Entrepreneur," p. 19. "Finally the economic leaders in the age of *Hochkapitalismus* are new according to their extraction. If we consider first of all the field of recruiting the entrepreneurs with a given body of people, also their social extraction, we shall find as the most important characteristic of our epoch a far-reaching democratization of leadership: the leading men of economic life climb up from ever broader and ever deeper layers of the population."

of the proletariat. The proletariat comes from the ranks of those, says he, who have been dislodged from their traditional places on the soil, and from those whose birth and family do not presume for them any place in the economic system except a place which the individual himself may find. Selection of occupations of the proletarian sort depends largely on time and place availability, both of the job and the person who fills it. Dr. North concludes[7] that "the determination of the precise task that most individuals perform within the larger class of occupations lies in chiefly local, temporary, and fortuitous circumstances." The sum total of conclusions from most of contemporary discussion is that one can predict neither the occupational fate of the individual nor the origin of the person who will next fill a given job. It amounts to a recognition of the essentially complicated nature of the processes involved.

In certain types of occupations the process can be analyzed within certain limits; as, for instance, in the clergy of evangelical churches where one needs a more definite "call" to the profession. This call comes more frequently to rural youths than to urban. The country furnishes the ministers for the city. Also the more evangelical churches furnish the ministers for the less evangelical. The Unitarian denomination furnishes practically no ministers, but must recruit its prophets from emancipated ones of more orthodox denominations. The occupation of the parent undoubtedly has certain tendencies to affect that of the children. The minister's son, for example, has a flair for more emancipated occupations, but still retains some of the father's tendency to appraise rather than participate in the life of the community. Sociology is full of ministers' sons. These processes of selection may well be studied both by case studies of occupations and of families.

The Division of Labor and the Mobility of the Person

The secularized division of labor is a most powerful mobilizer of persons. Durkheim stated this fact as one of the first order of importance among the effects of an increased division of labor upon social life.[8]

The persons who become commodities or functionaries in the division of labor are persons most of whom have been reared in families. In the family the person has acquired a set of social objects and attitudes more or less

---

7. North, *op. cit.*, p. 235.

8. Émile Durkheim, *De la division du travail social,* Paris: Félix Alcan, 1902, 2d ed., p. xx. "For to live by a métier one must have clients, and he must sally forth from his house to find them; he must sally forth also to enter into relations with his competitors, to struggle against them, and to converse with them. Moreover, métiers suppose more or less directly, cities, and cities are always formed and recruited principally by means of immigrants who have quitted their *milieu natal.*"

common to the community. To get into the occupational world, one must be mobilized. This mobilization, according to its degree, implies a removal from the base of one's morals. The study of *The Polish Peasant in Europe and America* (Thomas and Znaniecki) shows nothing more clearly than that this removal ends in radical personality changes. Miss Remmelin, in her study of *The Itinerants,* suggested that the itinerant is, by his very itineracy, cut off from the more settled world over which he moves. These two examples represent, respectively, an extreme of initial movement and an extreme in degree of mobility in a given type of occupation. The essential fact of the mobilizing of the person for participation in economic life is only less, not different in character in other and more common cases. The process of finding a place in competition with others is one involving a great deal of spatial movement in a world where urbanization is proceeding at a rapid rate. Professor Sorokin gives us statistics to show that in 1920 one-third of the people of the United States lived outside the states in which they were born. He assumed that the number living outside the communities in which they were born would be much higher.[9]

The general circulation of population over the face of the earth is continually putting individuals in countries whose language they do not know, and in whose social scheme they have no place. The effect of this mobilization on existing social groups is called, by students of family disorganization, atomizing of the family.

The Catholic clergy probably represents the most complete removal of the person from his *milieu natal* for professional life. In a West Side community in Chicago the writer became acquainted with a number of Irish families who had sons in a seminary. In each case the attitude of the family was one of conflict between pride at the sons's achievement and heartbreak because of losing him. To quote from one father: "The wife is proud of the boy. But he breaks her heart. He ain't our boy any more. He doesn't talk to us the same way. He never stays home long, and when he does he seems like a stranger. We are going to keep the youngest home. We gave two to the church already."

The very process of making a priest is to envelop the candidate in the ecclesiastical world, definitely to limit even the number of letters he can write to his family, to give him a new formalized language; in short, to make a new person of him, with new definitions of his wishes. This does by discipline what sects attempt to do by conversion; namely, to erase the person's past so that he may be completely mobilized for carrying out his mission.

This cutting off of the person from his home base simultaneously with

9. Pitirim Sorokin, *Social Mobility* (New York: Harper & Row, 1927), p. 383.

his entrance into an occupation, with his change from one occupation to another, or even from one job to another, is that characteristic phenomenon of the modern division of labor which carries with it personality change. The change is ordinarily more casual than the change from layman to priest, or from Pole to American. It may begin with a move from a rural to an urban community. Even if it be only the entrance into new groups in one's home community, it may lessen the contacts with the family, and the part of the family in determining one's social attitudes.

Classification of Units in the Division of Labor

We may make a rough classification of the types of places in the division of labor according to (1) the manner in which persons enter, (2) the attitude of the person to his occupation, and (3) the implied standing of the occupation in the eyes of the community. One may be born to his place. There are still hereditary titles and prerogatives. Some are born to a life of leisure, but without the assumption that their parents were so born, or that the person may be assured by society of this position.

1. Those occupations to which a person is called or converted we may call *missions*. The more violent the call or conversion, the less are the ethics within the occupational group. One may become convinced that he is a servant with a special mission. The evangelist, for instance, proselytizes from the congregations of regular denominations; for these regular denominations have departed from the true faith. The missionary easily becomes a fanatic, inspired of God, having no earthly colleagues, and recognizing no one's salvation except his own. A remnant of this attitude may survive in old and well-established institutions. The Protestant minister vaguely hopes to convert the Catholics, and the priest rejoices over one Protestant soul brought into the fold. The missionary belongs to a cult, whether it be a healing, soul-saving, utopian social order cult, or a sacred branch of learning. Editors of organs of opinion acquire this sense of a mission. In such occupations a peculiar language and metaphysics are developed, which one may understand only when he has partaken of the emotional experience common to the group.

2. The *professions* and *near-professions*. The professions are entered by long training, ordinarily in a manner prescribed by the profession itself and sanctioned by the state. The training is assumed to be necessary to learning the science and technique essential to practice of the function of the profession. The training, however, carries with it as a by-product assimilation of the candidate to a set of professional attitudes and controls, a professional conscience and solidarity. The profession claims and aims to become a moral unit. It is a phenomenon of the modern city that an

increasing number of occupations are attempting to gain for themselves the characteristics and status of professions.

3. The *enterprise* deals with a commodity. Sombart makes the point that the entrepreneur finds his function changing almost daily in the modern world. If he enters his business with the sense of a mission or of preserving some value to the world, he is in danger of being superseded by someone less hampered by traditional ideas. To carry on an enterprise it may be necessary for one to have long training of the so-called "practical" sort. If this training makes the person unfit to engage in other enterprises, he becomes something of a professional.

4. The *arts* are presumably entered by a combination of a special talent or ability plus a training in a technique.

5. The *trades* are very close to the arts; so close that some of the arts are associating themselves with the trades for mutual protection. The trade is entered presumably by the acquisition of a certain skill.

6. Beyond these types are the occupations which are called *jobs*. The method of acquiring a job of the more casual sort is simply to present one's self at the proper time and place when manpower of a certain age, sex, and perhaps a certain grade of intelligence, is wanted. The hobo himself, for all of his reputed aversion to work, has an occupation. There are certain jobs for which he is fitted and for which he is wanted.

All of these classes of occupations may demand a degree of mobility. Certain specialists within these classes are especially mobile, as casual laborers, actors, ministers, etc. Others have a technique or skill which is presumably capable of being practiced anywhere, as medicine; but medicine as actually practiced depends on local and personal acquaintance. Others are limited to places where an appreciative client exists, as the artist, the minister, etc. Another important variable in occupations is the nature of the contact of its practitioners with each other, and the nature of competition.

Social Attitudes and the Division of Labor

Within some occupations there may be persons who represent any one of the foregoing types of units in the division of labor. Especially is this true in the world of business. These different degrees of devotion to the business or to one's function, different degrees of casuality, status, different degrees of sensitivity to one's colleagues, represent different types. In the individual these are facts of his life-organization and of his personality.

In those who come to assume the professional attitude the occupation is represented both as a culture and a technique. The technique is developed with reference to certain objects or activities. The technique of the physician is in relation to the human body. It must be for him a different sort of object from what it is for the layman. To the layman it is a sacred thing, and an object of sentiment. To the real estate man, real estate law and the land itself are objects of technique. If he opposes change in real estate law, it is not from sentiment, but as a matter of policy. In relation to its technique and the interests of those who use that technique, the occupational group tends to build up a set of collective representations, more or less peculiar to the occupation and more or less incomprehensible to the community. The interests, which the occupational group couches in a language more or less its own, are the basis of the code and policy of the occupational group. The code is the occupation's prescribed conduct of the individuals within toward each other; the policy represents its relation to the community in which they operate. There is always a limit to the degree in which the code and policy of an occupation can deviate from the general culture of the community. Its members are products of a lay society. The practice of the occupation demands some degree of social sanction by the outside world.

This culture and technique, the etiquette and skill of the profession, appear in the individual as personal traits. The objects become to the individual a constellation of sacred and secular objects and attitudes. In general, we may say that the longer and more rigorous the period of initiation into an occupation, the more culture and technique are associated with it, and the more deeply impressed are its attitudes upon the person.

Some occupations are entered into and left so casually that no collective representations develop. But the casual worker himself, because of the very casual nature of his work, may develop certain characteristic traits. Although distinctly casual, waitresses seem to live together so much that they have developed a language and a set of social attitudes peculiar to themselves, individualistic though they be.[10]

Personality Types on the Frontier

The essential phenomenon of the frontier is a change in the division of labor. By extension of the frontier in China or India, we mean that those countries are being swept into a larger division of labor and that the hitherto local and self-sufficient division of labor is being destroyed or altered. In India, according to Messrs. Joshi and Wadia *(Money and the Money Market in India),* the nexus between the local world of India and

10. Donovan, *op. cit.,* p. 128. "The waitress is markedly individualistic in her attitude toward life, and the status of her occupation as it exists today tends toward the individualistic. She does only what she has to do to earn her wages, and her only real interest is in the tip. In her work she does not often consider the house, the manager, nor her fellow-workers, but herself only, and she seldom hesitates to advance her own interests at the expense of others."

the outside world is made by certain half-caste bankers or money-lenders, the *mahajan* and the *shroff*, who freely swindle the Indian peasant and who translate his crops into European bank credit. A Chinese student says there is a similar type of money-lender in China who literally sells his own people into the hands of the outside commercial world. In Western Canada Chinese are said to engage in the business of hiring men of their own nationality for Canadian employers of labor. These are personality types developed in the changing division of labor on a frontier. Such persons are without ethical or moral precedent. They are unscrupulous in that they operate to undermine the social and economic order of their peoples.

The Person in the New Occupation

In his paper on ecology last year Dr. McKenzie introduced "the center of dominance." Among other things the center of dominance is the place of a very great division of labor. It is, likewise, a frontier in which new occupational types develop. Among these new types is the man of finance, for the center of dominance is a center of credit and finance. Sombart gives us a picture of this new type. The new type must upset the existing order.[11]

When this new type, the financier, was just being developed, he was unscrupulous not only in his dealings with the outside world, but toward his competitors and colleagues as well. The biography of Daniel Drew,[12] one of the first operators on Wall Street, tells stories of boards of directors of corporations who betrayed the very companies they were supposed to represent. The life of Gary by Ida Tarbell tells something of the same story, and tells of the etiquette which in course of time this new element in economic life developed for their protection.[13] As the occupation grows

11. Sombart, *op. cit.*, p. 29. "The new men are as such free from the reference to the tradition of the family, of the business, of mercantile *Sitten*. Earlier large business lay mostly in the hands of aristocratic families with seigneurial tendencies, who shied anxiously before unsound changes or makeshifts, who held the view that it is more honorable to preserve than to win, who therefore were 'neophobes,' filled with a predilection for tradition. That the *Sitten* and usages which regulated the individual merchant in his behavior were very strict stands in close relationship with the essentially traditionally minded entrepreneurship. From all these bonds and barriers the upstart is free; he transforms the world freely according to his purpose . . . The old families live in the continuity of business . . . The new men are unscrupulous."

12. Bouck White, *The Book of Daniel Drew* (Garden City: Doubleday, 1911).

13. Ida M. Tarbell, *The Life of Elbert H. Gary* (New York: Appleton-Century-Crofts), p. v. "Judge Gary belongs to a group of powerful men who in the last fifty years have led in the creation in the United States of what we call Big Business. The most conspicuous of these leaders have been the elder Rockefeller in oil, the elder Morgan in banking, E H. Harriman in railroads, and in the earlier half of the period, Andrew Carnegie in steel. The men of undoubted financial and commercial genius typified certain attitudes of mind toward business and were the sponsors of practices and an etiquette essential to understand if we are to have a realizing and helpful sense of the actual development and meaning and potentiality of Big Business."

older it becomes a social climber, bidding for a fixed or improved status in the community. The individuals in the occupation bear the marks of this social climbing. Once this status is gained, the individuals in it become "regulars," and the persons who attempt to break in with new techniques are in turn unscrupulous upstarts.

Types in the Real Estate Business

The real estate business is a comparatively new one. In its rather brief history it has gone through part of the cycle from an upstart, unscrupulous business to a settled, somewhat respectable one. We may illustrate the types of personality in a unit of the division of labor from the real estate men of Chicago.

The realtor. — The "realtor," or regular real estate man, represents the type who has been in the business longest. He thinks, moves, and has his being in the world of real estate. He is fairly well assimilated to a code of real estate ethics or practice, supports the policies which the leaders of the business conceive to be for the ultimate welfare of the trade. The real estate board is his club, and generally his only downtown club. It is among his fellows there that he has his professional or business status. He sponsors action to make it more difficult for others to get into the business and into the board. A few older members of the Chicago Real Estate Board have made almost a mission of their business, and in so doing have well-nigh lost their business. They are occupationally conscious and jealous. Their name is intended as an advertisement of their place in the real-estate world.

The real estator. — The member of the Cook County Real Estate Board is poorer than the "realtor." He is perhaps less successful, and espouses the cause of democracy in real estate. He accuses the realtor of being a monopolist and a representative of "big interests." When he becomes more successful he usually becomes a "realtor."

The foreign-language agent. — He has a more casual connection with the real estate business. He gets his business with people of his own nationality, and lives in part by accelerating foreign invasions of native communities. The collective representations of the organized real estate world mean nothing to him. He lives in his own language group and capitalizes his acquaintance with this group. His neighbors are his clients.

The salesman. — The salesman is the casual of the real estate business. His services are enlisted by ads which assure the prospect that no experience is necessary. According to the realtor, the salesman is the lowest order of the real estate man. He came into the business because he could not get a job elsewhere. He stays only long enough to get an advance draft on commissions, and will not govern his occupational conduct in the interests of his employer or the real estate business in general. Every salesman complains of mistreatment from his former employer and of "dirty deals" given him by his fellow-salesmen. He is the Ishmael of the business; like the waitress, he accuses his fellows of having stolen his tips, and proceeds to steal theirs. He considers the formulated codes of business as checks upon his enterprise.

The promoter or boomer. — The real estate business in Chicago started in a land boom; the heads of now respectable and conservative firms were once boomers, as wild in their own day as the more recent boomers of Florida and Muscle Shoals. The boomer of today, however, is to them an upstart. He takes money from the sacred local market. The boomer, in turn, calls the conservative local real estate man a selfish, short-sighted pig. This boomer or promoter is the functionary of the land mania. In manner, he is a salesman of the most high-pressure sort; what he happens to be selling at the moment is merely incidental. His optimism turns itself with facility from one thing to another. His ethics are immediate expediency, and he is mobile, changing both the subjects and objects of his activity frequently. To him, likewise, restrictions of any sort put upon the business by law or the trade itself are a handicap.

The center of the real estate business is occupied by a group of men whose fortunes, clientele, and standing in the business are more or less secure. They are no longer upstarts. Their competitors are their bosom friends. To them, their real estate board has become almost a religious organization; it is certainly a fraternity. To be president of that board is an objective to which they look forward when they are well on in their lives and careers. One could name a group of men in the Chicago Real Estate Board who considered it a religious duty to attend meetings of the Board, to serve on its committees, etc. They clearly sought status nowhere so much as in their business group.

Especially when an occupation develops its own institution for control of the occupation, and protection of its prerogatives, is it likely to develop what we may call a culture, an etiquette, and a group within which one may attain the satisfaction of his wishes. This etiquette may be more or less incomprehensible to the outside, or lay, world. The hobo or casual, on the other hand, develops a set of attitudes and wishes such that his wishes are satisfied, not at work, but away from it. He is none the less sensitive to the opinions of people of his own occupational sort, and he undoubtedly constitutes a personality type.

THIRTY-FOUR

Work and Self

There are societies in which custom or sanctioned rule determine what work a man of a given status may do. In our society, at least one strong strain of ideology has it that a man may do any work which he is competent to do; or even that he has a right to the schooling and experience necessary to gain competence in any kind of work which he sets as the goal of his ambition. Equality of opportunity is, among us, stated very much in terms of the right to enter upon any occupation whatsoever. Although we do not practice this belief to the full, we are a people who cultivate ambition. A great deal of our ambition takes the form of getting training for kinds of work which carry more prestige than that which our fathers did. Thus a man's work is one of the things by which he is judged, and certainly one of the more significant things by which he judges himself.

Many people in our society work in named occupations. The names are tags, a combination of price tag and calling card. One has only to hear casual conversation to sense how important these tags are. Hear a sales-man, who has just been asked what he does, reply, "I am in sales work," or "I am in promotional work," not "I sell skillets." School teachers some-times turn schoolteaching into educational work, and the disciplining of youngsters and chaperoning of parties into personnel work. Teaching Sun-day School becomes religious education, and the Y.M.C.A. Secretary is "in group work." Social scientists emphasize the science end of their name. These hedging statements in which people pick the most favorable of several possible names for their work imply an audience. And one of the

Reprinted by permission of the publisher from J. H. Rohrer, and Muzafer Sherif, eds, *Social Psychology at the Crossroads,* Copyright 1951, Harper & Row, Publishers, Inc.

most important things about any man is his audience, or his choice of the several available audiences to which he may address his claims to be someone of worth.

These remarks should be sufficient to call it to your attention that a man's work is one of the more important parts of his social identity, of his self, indeed, of his fate, in the one life he has to live, for there is something almost as irrevocable about choice of occupation as there is about choice of a mate. And since the language about work is so loaded with value and prestige judgments, and with defensive choice of symbols, we should not be astonished that the concepts of social scientists who study work should carry a similar load, for the relation of social-science concepts to popular speech remains close in spite of our efforts to separate them. The difference is that while the value-weighting in popular speech is natural and proper, for concealment and ego-protection are of the essence of social intercourse. But in scientific discourse the value-loaded concept may be a blinder. And part of the problem of method in the study of work behavior is that the people who have the most knowledge about a given occupation (let us say medicine), and from whom therefore the data for analysis must come, are the people in the occupation. They may combine in themselves a very sophisticated manipulative knowledge of the appropriate social relations, with a very strongly motivated suppression, and even repression, of the deeper truths about these relationships, and, in occupations of higher status, with great verbal skill in keeping these relationships from coming up for thought and discussion by other people. This is done in part by the use of and insistence upon loaded value words where their work is discussed.

May I, to illustrate the point that concepts may be blinders, tell you briefly of my own experience in the study of occupations. Maybe one reason we social scientists fall into their trap so easily is that many such occupations have higher status than our own.

My first essay into the field was a study of the real estate agents in Chicago. These highly competitive men were just at that point in their journey toward respectability at which they wished to emphasize their conversion from business-minded suspicion of one another to the professional attitude, with confidence in each other and with a demand for confidence from the public. I started the study with the idea of finding out an answer to this familiar question, "Are these men professionals?" It was a false question, for the concept "profession" in our society is not so much a descriptive term as one of value and prestige. It happens over and over that the people who practice an occupation attempt to revise the conceptions which their various publics have of the occupation and of the people in it. In so doing, they also attempt to revise their own conception of themselves and of their work. The model which these occupations set before themselves is that of the "profession;" thus the term profession is a symbol for a desired conception of one's work and, hence, of one's self. The movement to "professionalize" an occupation is thus collective mobility of some among the people in an occupation. One aim of the movement is to rid the occupation of people who are not mobile enough to go along with the changes. There are two possible kinds of occupational mobility. One is individual. The individual makes the several choices, and achieves the skills which allow him to move to a certain position in the occupational, and thus—he hopes—in the social and economic hierarchy. His choice is limited by several conditions, among which is the social knowledge available to him at the time of crucial decision, a time which varies for the several kinds of work.

The other kind of occupational mobility is that of a group of people in an occupation, i.e., of the occupation itself. This has been important in our society with its great changes of technology, with its attendant proliferation of new occupations and of change in technique and social relation of old ones. Now it sometimes happens that by the time a person has the full social knowledge necessary to the smartest possible choice of occupations, he is already stuck with one and in one. How strongly this may affect the drive for professionalization of occupations, I don't know. I suspect that it is a motive. At any rate, it is common in our society for occupational groups to step their occupation up in the hierarchy by turning it into a profession. I will not here describe this process. Let me only indicate that in my own studies I passed from the false question "Is this occupation a profession?" to the more fundamental one, "What are the circumstances in which the people in an occupation attempt to turn it into a profession, and themselves into professional people?" and "What are the steps by which they attempt to bring about identification with their valued model?"

Even with this new orientation the term *profession* acted as a blinder. For as I began to give courses and seminars on occupations, I used a whole set of concepts and headings which were prejudicial to full understanding of what work behavior and relations are. One of them was that of the "code of ethics," which still tended to sort people into the good and the bad. It was not until I had occasion to undertake study of race relations in industry that I finally, I trust, got rid of this bias in the concepts which I used. Negro industrial workers, the chief objects of our study, performed the kinds of work which have least prestige and which make least pretension; yet, it turned out that even in the lowest occupations people do develop collective pretensions to give their work, and consequently themselves, value in the eyes of each other and of outsiders.

It was from these people that we learned that the common dignifying rationalization of people in all positions of a work hierarchy except the very top one is, "We in this position save the people in the next higher position above from their own mistakes." The notion that one saves a person of more acknowledged skill, and certainly of more acknowledged prestige and power, than one's self from his mistakes appears to be peculiarly satisfying. Now there grow up in work organizations rules of mutual protection among the persons in a given category and rank, and across ranks and categories. If one uses the term "code of ethics" he is likely not to see the true nature of these rules. These rules have of necessity to do with mistakes, for it is in the nature of work that people make mistakes. The question of how mistakes are handled is a much more penetrating one than any question which contains the concept "professional ethics" as ordinarily conceived. For in finding out how mistakes are handled, one must get at the fundamental psychological and social devices by which people are able to carry on through time, to live with others and with themselves, knowing that what is daily routine for them in their occupational roles may be fateful for others, knowing that one's routine mistakes, even the mistakes by which one learns better, may touch other lives at crucial points. It is in part the problem of dealing routinely with what are the crises of others. The people in lower ranks are thus using a powerful psychological weapon when they rationalize their worth and indispensability as lying in their protection of people in higher ranks from their mistakes. I suppose it is almost a truism that the people who take the larger responsibilities must be people who can face making mistakes, while punctiliousness must remain in second place. But this is a matter which has not been very seriously taken into account, as far as I know, in studies of the social drama of work.

Of course, the rules which people make to govern their behavior at work cover other problems than that of mistakes. Essentially the rules classify people, for to define situations and the proper behavior in situations one has to assign roles to the people involved. Thus among the most important subject matter of rules is setting up of criteria for recognizing a true fellow-worker, for determining who it is safe and may even be necessary to initiate into the in-group of close equals, and who must be kept at some distance. This problem is apt to be obscured by the term "colleague-ship," which, although its etymology is perfect for the matter in hand, carries a certain notion of higher status, of respectability. (In pre-Hitler Germany the Social-Democratic workers called one another "Comrade." The Christian trade-unions insisted on the term "Colleague.")

Allow me to mention one other value-laden term which may act as a blinder in study of the social psychology of work, to wit, "restriction of production." This term contains a value assumption of another kind — namely, that there is someone who knows and has a right to determine the right amount of work for other people to do. If one does less, he is restricting production. Mayo and others have done a good deal to analyze the phenomenon in question, but it was Max Weber who—forty years ago—pointed to "putting on the brakes," as an inevitable result of the wrestling match between a man and his employer over the price he must pay with his body for his wage. In short, he suggested that no man easily yields to another full control over the effort, and especially over the amount of physical effort he must daily exert. On the other hand, there is no more characteristically human phenomenon than determined and even heroic effort to do a task which one has somehow taken as his own. I do not mean to make the absurd implication that there could be a situation in which every man would be his own and only taskmaster. But I think we might understand the social interaction which determines the measure of effort if we are to keep ourselves free of terms which suggest that it is abnormal to do less than one is asked by some reasonable authority.

You will have doubtless got the impression that I am making the usual plea for a value-free science, that is, for neutrality. Such is not my intention. Our aim is to *penetrate more deeply* into the personal and social drama of work, to understand the social and social-psychological arrangements and devices by which men make their work tolerable, or even make it glorious to themselves and others. I believe that much of our terminology and hence, of our problem setting, has limited our field of perception by a certain pretentiousness and a certain value-loading. Specifically we need to rid ourselves of any concepts which keep us from seeing that the essential problems of men at work are the same whether they do their work in the laboratories of some famous institution or in the messiest vat room of a pickle factory. Until we can find a point of view and concepts which will enable us to make comparisons between the junk peddler and the professor without intent to debunk the one and patronize the other, we cannot do our best work in this field.

Perhaps there is as much to be learned about the high-prestige occupations by applying to them the concepts which naturally come to mind for study of people in the most lowly kinds of work as there is to be learned by applying to other occupations the conceptions developed in connection with the highly valued professions. Furthermore, I have come to the conclusion that it is a fruitful thing to start study of any social phenomenon at the point of least prestige. For, since prestige is so much a matter of symbols, and even of pretensions—however well merited—there goes with prestige a tendency to preserve a front which hides the inside of things; a front of names, of indirection, of secrecy (much of it necessary secrecy). On the other hand, in things of less prestige, the core may be more easy of access.

In recent years a number of my students have studied some more or less lowly occupations: apartment-house janitors, junk men, boxers, jazz musicians, osteopaths, pharmacists, etc. They have done so mainly because of their own connections with the occupations in question, and perhaps because of some problem of their own. At first, I thought of these studies as merely interesting and informative for what they would tell about people who do these humbler jobs, i.e., as American ethnology. I have now come to the belief that although the problems of people in these lines of work are as interesting and important as any other, their deeper value lies in the insights they yield about work behavior in any and all occupations. It is not that it puts one into the position to debunk the others, but simply that processes which are hidden in other occupations come more readily to view in these lowly ones. We may be here dealing with a fundamental matter of method in social science, the matter of finding the best possible laboratory animal for study of a given series of mechanisms.

Let me illustrate. The apartment-house janitor is a fellow who, in making his living, has to do a lot of other people's dirty work. This is patent. He could not hide it if he would. Now every occupation is not one but several activities; some of them are the "dirty work" of that trade. It may be dirty in one of several ways. It may be simply physically disgusting. It may be a symbol of degradation, something that wounds one's dignity.

Finally, it may be dirty work in that it in some way goes counter to the more heroic of our moral conceptions. Dirty work of some kind is found in all occupations. It is hard to imagine an occupation in which one does not appear, in certain repeated contingencies, to be practically compelled to play a role of which he thinks he ought to be a little ashamed morally. Insofar as an occupation carries with it a self-conception, a notion of personal dignity, it is likely that at some point one will feel that he is having to do something that is *infra dignitate*. Janitors turned out to be bitterly frank about their physically dirty work. When asked, "What is the toughest part of your job," they answered almost to a man in the spirit of this quotation: "Garbage. Often the stuff is sloppy and smelly. You know some fellows can't look at garbage if it's sloppy. I'm getting used to it now, but it almost killed me when I started." Or as another put it, "The toughest part? It's the messing up in front of the garbage incinerator. That's the most miserable thing there is on this job. The tenants don't co-operate—them bastards. You tell them today, and tomorrow there is the same mess over again by the incinerator."

In the second quotation it becomes evident that the physical disgust of the janitor is not merely a thing between him and the garbage, but involves also the tenant. Now the tenant is the person who impinges most on the daily work activity of the janitor. It is the tenant who interferes most with his own dignified ordering of his life and work. If it were not for a tenant who had broken a window, he could have got his regular Saturday cleaning done on time; it it were not for a tenant who had clogged a trap, he would not have been ignominiously called away from the head of his family table just when he was expansively offering his wife's critical relatives a second helping of porkchops, talking the while about the importance of his job. It is the tenant who causes the janitor's status pain. The physically disgusting part of the janitor's work is directly involved in his relations with other actors in his work drama.

By a *contre coup,* it is by the garbage that the janitor judges, and, as it were, gets power over the tenants who high-hat him. Janitors know about hidden love-affairs by bits of torn-up letter paper; of impending financial disaster or of financial four-flushing by the presence of many unopened letters in the waste. Or they may stall off demands for immediate service by an unreasonable woman of whom they know from the garbage that she, as the janitors put it, "has the rag on." The garbage gives the janitor the makings of a kind of magical power over that pretentious villain, the tenant. I say a kind of magical power, for there appears to be no thought of betraying any individual and thus turning this knowledge into overt power. He protects the tenant, but, at least among Chicago janitors, it is certainly not a loving protection.

Let your mind dwell on what one might hear from people in certain other occupations if they were to answer as frankly and bitterly as did the janitors. I do not say nor do I think that it would be a good thing for persons in all occupations to speak so freely on physical disgust as did these men. To do so, except in the most tightly closed circles, would create impossible situations. But we are likely to overlook the matter altogether in studying occupations where concealment is practiced, and this gives a quite false notion of the problems which have to be faced in such occupations, and of the possible psychological and social by-products of the solutions which are developed for the problem of disgust.

Now the delegation of dirty work to someone else is common among humans. Many cleanliness taboos, and perhaps even many moral scruples, depend for their practice upon success in delegating the tabooed activity to someone else. Delegation of dirty work is also a part of the process of occupational mobility. Yet there are kinds of work, some of them of very high prestige, in which such delegation is possible only to a limited extent. The dirty work may be an intimate part of the very activity which gives the occupation its charisma, as is the case with the handling of the human body by the physician. In this case, I suppose the dirty work is somehow integrated into the whole, and into the prestigious role of the person who does the work. What role it plays in the drama of work relations in such a case is something to find out. The janitor, however, does not integrate his dirty work into any deeply satisfying definition of his role that might liquidate his antagonism to the people whose dirt he handles. Incidentally, we have found reason to believe that one of the deeper sources of antagonisms in hospitals arises from the belief of the people in the humblest jobs that the physicians in charge call upon them to do their dirty work in the name of the role of "healing the sick," although none of the prestige and little of the money reward of that role reaches the people at the bottom. Thus we might conceive of a classification of occupations involving dirty work into those in which it is knit into some satisfying and prestige-giving definition of role and those in which it is not. I suppose we might think of another classification into those in which the dirty work seems somehow wilfully put upon one and those in which it is quite unconnected with any person involved in the work drama.

There is a feeling among prison guards and mental-hospital attendants that society at large and their superiors hypocritically put upon them dirty work which they, society, and the superiors in prison and hospital know is necessary but which they pretend is not necessary. Here it takes the form, in the minds of people in these two lowly occupations, of leaving them to cope for twenty hours, day in and day out, with inmates whom the public never has to see and whom the people at the head of the organization see only episodically. There is a whole series of problems here which cannot be solved by some miracle of changing the social selection of those who enter the job (which is the usual unrealistic solution for such cases).

And this brings us to the brief consideration of what one may call the social drama of work. Most kinds of work bring people together in definable roles; thus the janitor and the tenant, the doctor and the patient, the teacher and the pupil, the worker and his foreman, the prison guard and the prison, the musician and his listener. In many occupations there is some category of persons with whom the people at work regularly come into crucial contact. In some occupations the most crucial relations are those with one's fellow-workers. It is they who can do most to make life sweet or sour. Often, however, it is the people in some other position. And in many there is a category of persons who are, so to speak, the consumers of one's work or services. It is probable that the people in the occupation will have their chronic fight for status, for personal dignity with this group of consumers of their services. Part of the social psychological problem of the occupation is the maintenance of a certain freedom and social distance from these people most crucially and intimately concerned with one's work.

In a good deal of our talk about occupations we imply that the tension between the producer and consumer of services is somehow a matter of ill-will or misunderstandings which easily might be removed. It may be that it lies a good deal deeper than that. Often there is a certain ambivalence on the side of the producer, which may be illustrated by the case of the professional jazz-musicians. The musician wants jobs and an income. He also wants his music to be appreciated, but to have his living depend upon the appreciation does not entirely please him. For he likes to think himself and other musicians the best judges of his playing. To play what pleases the audience – the paying customers, who are not, in his opinion, good judges – is a source of annoyance. It is not merely that the listeners, having poor taste, demand that he play music which he does not think is the best he can do; even when they admire him for playing in his own sweet way, he doesn't like it, for then they are getting too close – they are impinging on his private world too much. The musicians accordingly use all sorts of little devices to keep a line drawn between themselves and the audience; such as turning the musicians' chairs, in a dance hall without platform, in such a way as to make something of a barrier. It is characteristic of many occupations that the people in them, although convinced that they themselves are the best judges, not merely of their own competence but also of what is best for the people for whom they perform services, are required in some measures to yield judgement of what is wanted to these amateurs who receive the services. This is a problem not only among musicians, but in teaching, medicine, dentistry, the arts, and many other fields. It is a chronic source of ego-wound and possibly of antagonism.

Related to this is the problem of routine and emergency. In many occupations, the workers or practitioners (to use both a lower and a higher status term) deal routinely with what are emergencies to the people who receive the services. This is a source of chronic tension between the two. For the person with the crisis feels that the other is trying to belittle his trouble; he does not take it seriously enough. His very competence comes from having dealt with a thousand cases of what I like to consider my unique trouble. The worker thinks he knows from long experience that people exaggerate their troubles. He therefore builds up devices to protect himself to stall people off. This is the function of the janitor's wife when a tenant phones an appeal or a demand for immediate attention to a leaky tap; it is also the function of the doctor's wife and even sometimes of the professor's wife. The physician plays one emergency off against the other; the reason he can't run right up to see Johnny who may have the measles is that he is, unfortunately, right at that moment treating a case of the black plague. Involved in this is something of the struggle mentioned above in various connections, the struggle to maintain some control over one's decisions of what work to do, and over the disposition of one's time and of one's routine of life. It would be interesting to know what the parish priest thinks to himself when he is called for the tenth time to give extreme unction to the sainted Mrs. O'Flaherty who hasn't committed a sin in years except that of, in her anxiety over dying in a state of sin, being a nuisance to the priest. On Mrs. O'Flaherty's side there is the danger that she might die unshriven, and she has some occasion to fear that the people who shrive may not take her physical danger seriously and hence may not come quickly enough when at last her hour has come. There may indeed be in the minds of the receivers of emergency services a resentment that something so crucial to them can be a matter for a cooler and more objective attitude, even though they know perfectly well that such an attitude is necessary to competence, and though they could not stand it if the expert to whom they take their troubles were to show any signs of excitement. I have not worked out in any full or systematic way all of the problems of this routine vs. emergency drama. Nor, for that matter, have I worked out systematically any of the problems mentioned in this discussion. My aim has been to call attention to certain problems which lie, it seems to me, on the margin between sociology and psychology, problems on which people of these two disciplines should be working jointly.

THIRTY-FIVE

What Other?

A playwright, novelist, or politician insensitive to the gestures and attitudes of others, and of some others more than other others, is hard to imagine. Indeed, what more common theme is there in literature—and in politics—than this? But systematic attention to the problem of degrees and directions of sensitivity to others turned up rather late among those who study human society in a would-be scientific way.

Adam Smith was a John the Baptist in the field, when, in his *Theory of the Moral Sentiments,* he makes emulation account for so much of human behavior and suggests that the choice of models for emulation is fateful for any man. He is warning, however, not against choosing evil companions but against taking models—of consumption at least—beyond one's effective reach.

This theme is almost the central one of that whole school of American sociologists and philosophers which included J. Mark Baldwin, Charles Cooley, George Mead, William Thomas, Robert Park, Ellsworth Faris, and their students. Perhaps one should mention Josiah Royce, William James, and John Dewey also, for these men and their variety of pragmatism were part of the same movement, each in his own time and fashion.

I need not remind anyone of the place of the theme of "others" in the work of Mead. Fewer people may be familiar with Thomas' classification of men into Philistine, Bohemian and Creative. One of the themes in that classification is the degree of one's sensitivity to others; another is selection of the others.

Reprinted by permission of the publisher from Arnold M. Rose, ed., *Human Behavior and Social Processes: An Interactionist Approach,* Copyright 1962, Houghton Mifflin Company.

348

When I was a graduate student at the Universtiy of Chicago—Thomas' shadow was still there, Mead was still about, and my teachers were Park and Faris—practically all the courses were imbued with the problem of "others." In one of Park's classes a student disputed his statement that most social behavior stems from the fact that we keep an eye on others and their actual and probable reaction to what we do. Park retorted with a question, "Why did you wear pants to school on a pleasant May morning such as this? Think how nice it would feel to have the wind blowing around your legs." Park made a distinction between status and position, sometimes adding adjectives thus: *personal* status and *ecological* or *symbiotic* position. One of his students, Clarence Glick, wrote a dissertation on the Chinese of Hawaii showing that a man might achieve a considerable position in Hawaii while his personal status existed only in relation to the world he had physically left behind. Park spoke of symbiotic or survival relations without social interaction—that is, of relationships without any mutual sensitivity or interpenetration of attitudes and sentiments. This terminology, which was useful, has fallen by the way. Someone may do himself and social science a service by bringing together and systematizing what Park and his students did with the whole problem of sensitivity to others. Nor should Faris be overlooked. It was in a course of his that I first heard developed the notion that the whole fate of sectarian and other Utopian experiments turned upon keeping succeeding generations as impervious to the opinions of the godless as the founding fathers had been. It is an obvious notion, but one which—when enriched by comparative observation—leads to some of the most significant social studies. Indeed, it has lain behind much recent social research, such as that on the spread of influence in politics and consumption, and is the theme of all that is written about reference groups. In what follows I simply add some thoughts on the subject, thoughts which I believe especially appropriate to our times and to the ever increasing breed of people who think of themselves as professional.

Pearl Buck's father, a *Fighting Angel,* knew no "other" but God; sometimes he seems to have thought that even God needed to be told his own mind. Certainly no human "other" could tell where God meant the Fighting Angel to preach the gospel. He violated all cartel arrangements of the denominational mission boards about what territories each could save souls in. He was so consumed by his calling that he could leave his wife alone to look after her sick children in a plague-ridden Chinese town while he went off to give some more souls their chance to hear the gospel and take it and be saved or leave it and be damned. God—and God as the Fighting Angel alone saw him—was his only colleague and his only kin.

Hitler confounding the smart Berlin lawyers when on trial for his Munich Beer Hall Putsch; Edmond Gosse's father (*Father and Son*) persisting in his belief in the creation of the world in one week in 4,004 B.C. in the face of the contrary evidence of geologists and their other scientific colleagues, including Darwin; many of the saints, the heretics and villains, have fanatically rejected the opinions of all "others"—wife, children, kin, friends, class, brothers in the faith, and professional colleagues.

They appear magnificently (if saints) or diabolically (if heretics or villains) indifferent to the opinions of any and all "others." Rather, they would appear indifferent were it not that their own testimony and the analyses of psychiatrists so often reveal that the certainty of their call covers and compensates for some ravaging uncertainty about who and what they are in the eyes of the very "others" they so fiercely defy. Or perhaps they suffer from some deep rejection by the "others" or from unwillingness to accept their humiliating verdict. The possibilities are many, but it is doubtful whether the apparent freedom of "true believers" from the influence of "others" is ever indifference; it is high-strung, not slack. It is not of the same order as that self-contained indifference to the opinions of "others" which one sometimes observes, perhaps more often in women and cats than in men and dogs; not callousness nor want of perceptiveness, but detachment, amused and even bemused.

If absence of direction toward and by "others" is of various kinds as well as degrees, the same is true of such direction itself. What is more pathetic and demoralizing than the fawning attempt to find favor with others not worthy of the suppliant—as one sees it sometimes in homosexuals of intellectual quality whose perversity consists in part of seeking the favor of lesser men than themselves. One thinks of the self-destruction depicted in André Gide's *La Porte etroite,* and *Si le grain ne meurt.* But in that kind of attention to "other," is it not some self-satisfaction that is sought? The "other" is, after all, but an instrument. How different is the thoughtful, sometimes tortured, attempt to understand and respond to the thoughts, feelings, and judgments of others in order that one may do them justice or that one may pursue more effectively some end to which one is devoted. This, too, requires a measure of detachment—as does all true understanding, even of those closest to us. The degrees and qualities of other-directedness—to use the happy phrase with which David Riesman has enlivened our discourse—are, however, but one aspect of the problem.

Another is that contained in the question "What other?" Indeed, degrees and qualities can scarcely be understood without reference to that question. One of the complications of civilized life is that one is confronted with a variety of "others," some of whose directions are not compatible with those of some others. None is completely compatible with all others. Once that oneness of the "others," attributed—correctly or not—to primitive societies, is gone, there is no finding it again except by conversion to a religious, political, artistic, or intellectual sect, disappearance into a monastery, or flight to some totalitarian state, where thought and action are alike controlled by some central authority. In the latter case, some people seem always to seek underground some company of kindred souls, some "other" to give them courage in their struggle to remain spiritually independent of the massive *Big Brother* "other." One need not go to a totalitarian state to find this search for a supporting semi-secret "other;" it may be found wherever and whenever the pressure for conformity becomes oppressive—in a college town, in a closed profession, in a period of McCarthyism or even of Ike-ism—because weakness and blundering in high places are thought to require a more desperate and unquestioning support than strength combined with intelligence (for the weak and blundering man has little to fall back upon except the claim to loyal support that is, he believes, due him).

Certainly we are in a time when part of the very struggle to be a man is the search for one's "others." It takes intelligence to find the "others" that will bring out the best in one's self, and it takes courage to follow—no, not follow, but to walk abreast with that collective "other," ready made or created by mutual effort—when one has found it. Any one of us has certain ready-made "others" by virtue of his birth and the accidents of his schooling and career. Some of them are there from infancy, others gather about him later. Some creep upon him; others he chooses of his own will and seeks that admission to them which will reveal to him the direction in which he must travel if he is to be accepted as one of them.

Some people find, in this welter of "others," some complex balance or compromise among several. Others let one or another tyrannize them. The nature of the combinations and balances is part of the organization of society itself. Judging the relative influence of various "others" upon individuals is indeed one of the problems with which social surveys are most concerned.

Some people manage to remain responsive to only one "other" even in the midst of a complex society. This was the essence of the system of honor among Prussian army officers. Only another of his class could really offend, or give satisfaction for an offense. To be sensitive to the opinions of civilians or of the lower ranks was to be less than an officer and a gentleman. We are no longer a society of closed estates, some of them honorable in that strict sense. We disapprove alike of the dueling sword, used to keep one's face before his honorable peers, and of the horsewhip, used to keep lesser breeds respectful. But we have some very demanding "others" and a certain tendency to become so attached and sensitive to one of them that we lose other attachments and sensitivities.

One order of "others" in which this tendency is strong is the professions, those old and established as well as those new and on the make. Professionalism, in its valued sense, indicates a strong solidarity of those in an occupation combined with a high sense of duty to their clients and a well-developed code of conduct. In its pejorative sense, it refers to a sort of exclusiveness, a group-centrism that makes individual members impervious to the opinions, indeed, to the very terms of thought and feeling, of those outside their professional circle. The professions are not only "functional" in the peculiar sense in which that term has come to be used, they are hyper-functional to a pathological degree in some cases. For professionalism, however worthy the motives for pursuing it, has often led to a hasty crystallizing of the techniques, the apologia, and hence the substance of the training and qualifications required of those who would enter the occupation. This has been clearly true of social work, where the state of the art at a given period was hardened into a curriculum from which the schools of social work are recovering only now. It is also true of education, where certainly there was and is need for tremendous improvement of professional standards and the preparation for practice. The whole business has bogged down in a professionalism that is dogmatic, sometimes bigoted, and generally touchy and impatient of criticism from other "others" — parents, the public, or educated people not of the "educationist" ranks.

A new profession, one on the make, often takes as the common "other" toward which its members direct their conduct some other profession of longer history and firmer place. For social work, the outside looked-up-to "other" has been the psychiatric profession; for nurses, their troublesome superiors, the physicians; for psychologists, both physicians and biological scientists. For sociologists, the emulated outside groups are no doubt several. But the role of older brother is assumed by psychology and sociologists are inclined to allow it. Thus there is a sort of chain reaction: the psychologist must be either a therapist, following the model of the physician, or a scientist, following the model of physiologists or physicists. The sociologists must be scientists, following the psychologists both from wanting to emulate them and from fearing that they may steal their prerogatives. In our world of upwardly mobile occupations, as well as mobile individuals, there thus occurs a sort of collective other-directedness. When an occupational group is actively climbing, and has taken a model, it is likely to be especially severe in its demand for conformity to that model by those in its own ranks — just as a mobile individual puts pressure on his family not to disgrace him before sought-after company. It is to be suspected that some of the rather ritualistic following by sociologists of what are thought to be the only sound techniques of research is due to just such a desire to impress their elder scientific brethren, those who have won recognition as scientists. Somewhere in this complex of things one finds what one might call "bureaucratic other-directedness," an overweening following of the rituals which one believes will get him, by a sort of right, promotion to the next rank in the system in which he works and lives.

Every profession does its work in some social matrix in interaction with whatever kinds of people it defines as its clients, with colleagues in the profession itself and with people in related occupations, with people related to their clients in various ways and eventually with elements of the public. The very word "profession" implies a certain social and moral solidarity, a strong dependence of one colleague upon the opinions and judgments of others. In fact, one depends more upon the opinions of some colleagues than of others; and some professions are more guided by group opinion than are others. In our society it is inevitable that the professions should be among the more significant "others" toward which and by which conduct is directed, for we have more professions than ever and a larger proportion of the working force is in them. That makes it the more important that the relations between profession-directedness and sensitivity to the others involved in the drama of work should be kept flexible, complex, and in balance. A man who stakes all upon his reputation with his clients—patients, students, "cases"—is in great danger of being considered a quack. In fact, the essence of being a quack lies not in the quality of one's work, but in the "other" to which he directs his behavior. A professional who is completely client-directed, without regard to his professional colleagues' judgments, is likely to be declared a quack. He may, in fact, be either a charlatan or a brilliant innovator. The optimum balance between sensitivity to one's professional "other" and one's responsiveness to the people outside—fellow workers of other specialties or professions, one's own and other people's clients, the various parts of the public—will vary from one profession to another and from one situation to another. But in all cases there is some distribution of "directedness" among the various "others" who are involved in one's work. A man's great problem is to see to it that the balance is of his own making and that he finds it intelligently and with perception of the several "others."

One of the great glories of an urban civilization is the complex man, finely tuned to many of the "others" in his life-orbit, consciously selecting the impulses to which he will respond and not being deterred from responding because one of his "others"—and the offender is often the colleague "other"—claims his whole allegiance and demands that he accept and defend its current doctrines and techniques *in toto*. I take it that it is such a man whom William I. Thomas would have called "creative" and David Riesman would call "autonomous." He would be not an automaton, a guided missile, not a Fighting Angel, not a pachyderm impervious to pricks, not a reed blown about by the wind, but a man of many sensitivities who would attain and maintain, by his intelligent and courageous choice of the messages to which he would respond, by the choice of his "others," freedom of a high but tough and resilient quality.

In the academic and professional worlds, such a freedom will show itself in the choice of close colleagues, regardless of department or specialty. The more such freedom is stoutly and sensitively exercised, the more strength we will have to fight off attacks on academic and professional freedom. We will have more freedom to lose, but better weapons with which to defend it. We will also make much greater progress in our common enterprise of understanding man and society.

THIRTY-SIX

Prestige

The occupations most characteristic of industrial-urban civilizations appear to be ranked in about the same order of prestige in all countries of that kind of civilization. Such was the finding of two sociologists in a survey of the pertinent available data.[1] The professions and industrial occupations were ranked most nearly in the same way in the several countries studied. The physician appears to be the world champion of this popularity contest. College professors, scientific workers, and those who manage industries are not far behind. The teacher in public schools does not rate very highly in these countries. He (or she) comes at about the middle of the rating. Urban Africans in Northern Rhodesia rank occupations open to them in a way which suggests that, with more urbanization and industrialization combined with less racial discrimination, they will approach the older industrial countries in their attitudes concerning occupations. Administrators of schools and teachers of secondary schools are rated at or near the top. The medical orderly, who is perhaps as high as an African is likely to get in the medical system there at present, is not far down.[2]

Annals of the American Academy of Political Sciences. Vol. 325, Sept., 1959, pp. 45-49.

1. Alex Inkeles and Peter H. Rossi, "National Comparisons of Occupational Prestige," *The American Journal of Sociology,* Vol. 61 (January 1956), pp. 329-39. They compared studies made in the USA, USSR, Great Britain, New Zealand and Western Germany. Inkeles has continued to make such comparisons and has included other countries. In a recent lecture at the University of Chicago he argued strongly that his evidence shows that, quite regardless of form and doctrine of government, industrial civilizations do produce a common prestige ranking of the most crucial occupations.

2. J. Clyde Mitchell and A. L. Epstein, "Occupational Prestige and Social Status Among Urban Africans in Northern Rhodesia," *Africa,* Vol. 29 (January 1959), pp. 22-40. Police inspectors and ministers of religion are, in fact, higher on the list than the medical orderly. The study rates only those occupations available to Africans. The higher positions in government and industry are not open to them. These authors, anthropologists, are pioneers in study of the urbanization of African peoples.

Prestige Ranking and Occupational Goals

If we could accept the ranking of occupations according to prestige by the public at large as some sort of evidence of the direction of flow of young people of talent, we should have little need to worry about our place in a world where science and its applications count for so much. But the very rankings themselves carry their own damnation. It is common knowledge that the medical schools are not beseiged by great numbers of applicants who cannot get in: the deans of captive state schools — captive in that they must ge most, if not all, of their students from the state in which they are located — speak of scraping the bottom of the barrel. College professors are rated highly, yet they themselves think they are not highly regarded by people whose opinions count heavily in academic and public matters (although many of those in Lazarsfeld's sample allow that perhaps a trustee of their own institution would rate a professor ahead of lawyers, advertising account executives, or branch bank managers).[3] Governors of states, county judges, and heads of departments in state governments stand high in the American ranking used by Inkeles and Rossi. Yet we know that people constantly complain of the low caliber of those who seek public office. As a matter of fact, these prestige rankings are not a sure index of the goals of American parents for their children or of the young people themselves.

Occupational Images

For one thing, most of the ratings simply sample the public in gathering their data. In giving everyone an equal chance to speak, they give no one a chance to speak out with his own voice. For another, the questionnaires do not generally ask people what they mean, let us say, by a lawyer, a physician, or a professor. Do they mean the lawyer who, although he approaches the ideal of individual independent practitioner, is really a chore-boy of small business and politics, captive of a clientele whose drab problems he dare not refuse — since he has long since forgotten how to work at the law?[4] Or do some of them mean the lawyer who, although he may have worked on salary all of his career, can devote his time to the law, or some branch of it, and can do the work he likes? And what kind of physician do they mean? A true general practitioner; a quasi-general prac-

3. Paul F. Lazarsfeld and Wagner Thielens, Jr., *The Academic Mind* (New York: Free Press, 1958), p. 12, Figure 1–5. The college teachers in the large sample used in this study were asked how they thought a typical businessman, congressman, and trustee of his own college would rate a manager of a branch bank, an account executive of an advertising agency, and a lawyer in relation to a professor.

4. Jerome E. Carlin, *Lawyers on Their Own: A Study of Individual Practitioners in Chicago* (New Brunswick: Rutgers, 1962).

titioner who is a specialist by default because fate, pressure, and indolence have progressively narrowed the range of cases he gets and of the names of ailments which he enters on death certificates; a true practicing specialist, respected by his colleagues; an academic research man, with or without patients, in the clinic or in the laboratory? And what professor are they thinking of? For there are wide, even dramatic differences, in the style of work and of life of people called professors. At its best, we professors have a wonderful and stimulating life with access to wider ranges of friends and associates than people in perhaps any other profession—and with a good chance of marrying women of great intelligence and charm and of great powers of sympathy and support. Let us draw the veil over the worst and the circumstances which produce it.

As a matter of fact, many of our leading named occupations are inwardly so varied that to call them by one name is close to misleading. Ratings based on the name alone tell us little or nothing about the actual images which people have of the occupation. They also tell us nothing of how the images held by people of one kind (class, age, ethnic group, religion, region) vary from those held by some other kind. For the kinds of doctor, teacher, businessman, lawyer, or soldier visible to one kind of people may be quite different from those visible to others. And, as Hollingshead and Redlich have shown,[5] the people in a profession do not necessarily show the same kind of face to clients of all classes. The customer may be always right, but in most professions there are some who are righter than others; at least, some are preferred to others, although it does not necessarily follow that the least preferred will be given inferior service.

The Setting of Goals and Standards

The truth is that we do not have a fully worked out anatomy of occupational prestige, including all of the contacts and interactions out of which the images of the various occupations develop. Nor do we know a great deal about what kinds of experiences lead young people to take certain styles of work and life as goals; reality goals, that is, towards which they will effectively strive. Certainly, sociologists and psychologists have learned a great deal about the influence of cliques of peers and about the probability that children of people of certain backgrounds will enter certain schools, colleges, and occupations. Much is being learned at present about the informal social organization of college and university campuses; about the creative "beatniks" who, far from being beat, are often the most hard-working and creative of all students (although they have low opinion

5. August B. Hollingshead and Fredrick C. Redlich, *Social Class and Mental Illness: A Community Study* (New York: Wiley, 1958).

of professors and parents, as of all respectable older folk); about home-town cliques, social cliques, and intellectual cliques of students on different kinds of campuses. But all of this, and much more, needs filling out and drawing together into a general, yet refined, body of theory and knowledge about effective choices of ways of studying, working, and living.

One thing that is quite clear is that students are quick to detect the contradictions in the behavior of those who try to set models before them. "You are not in high school now. You are in college. Be a man. You are on your own," say we professors. Then we deal out assignments in small daily rations and follow with a quiz next day to see if the ration has been properly assimilated, an intellectual toilet-training which is about as creative as any toilet-training. (And note the assumption that high schools are childish.) We claim that we believe in general education; then each of us, as a representative of a "professionalized" department of the university — if not of learning — joins with his departmental fellows in turning colleges into pregraduate schools in which each course is a link in a chain of pre-requisites necessary to graduate work in a given field. The net effect is to force young people to follow another road than the one we proudly point to; they must choose a major field of study with a strict eye to the chance of getting into professional or graduate schools and getting higher degrees without the loss of time which the system brings upon anyone who changes his mind after the middle of college. Many students — I do not know how many — are aware of the discrepancy between preachment and pressure, follow the pressure, and give their slightly younger fellow students the low-down. They work on the daily dose — a principle which experience, in the form of peer-group culture, has convinced them that that is what the faculty really wants; so likewise do they choose between what is in-teresting and a bit out of line and that which is dully more of the same, but prerequisite by decree.

Balance Between the Ideal and the Real

Students, like other people going through the prolonged initiation into adult status, are proud of discovering the true road to success and of learning the prescription for mixing ideal and reality in just the right way. They have to learn to live and survive as students before they can live and survive as members of professions or other occupations. It may be that they receive very confused and contradictory messages concerning the most valued goals and about the ways toward them. What messages are, in fact, being passed along to students by their teachers, those whom they know out in the working world, and by their fellow-students of more experience and sophistication? Part of the study of the anatomy of prestige must be a frank and penetrating study, not of official pronouncements about the roads to glory and about what pursuits are interesting and valuable, but of the messages actually received and perceived by young people.

This is all perhaps merely another way of saying that the prestige-value given to various pursuits is never a matter merely of propaganda and pronouncements but is something worked out by each generation in an atmosphere largely but not completely created by the preceding generation. The problem of prestige is then not a matter of a bit of advertising or of "plugging" in the media, but of learning what we can about various atmospheres and their effects upon young people. If we are to change the canons of prestige we will have to put ourselves through a painful process of analyzing the part of parents, counselors, teachers, future professional and business colleagues in determining them. And I do not so much mean our individual behavior directly toward young people—although that is certainly implied—but our behavior in setting up and playing our roles in educational organizations, in creating the environments in which young people must live and work from day to day.

If young people, regardless of the race, class, or region in which they are born, are to find the best and most satisfying ways of using their abilities, it will be because we manage to make effective living models of such use—and its burdens and rewards—visible to them and in such circumstances that there is a fair chance of them not being diverted by inferior teaching, by confusion of messages which leads them to settle for less than their best, or starts them up intellectual blind alleys (by early "professionalism" and the encouraging of "interested choices" by their teachers). I strongly suspect that close study of what goes on in schools and colleges, a sort of audit of the realities, might start a movement to self-improvement that would be of more effect than any amount of glamour showered on those occupations which we consider a matter of life or death. A good many people are, in fact, engaged in just this self-examination of American educational (sic) environments. One of the things we will certainly learn from it is that no modern civilization can rely for very subtle deployment of its human resources upon a series of childhood and adolescent judgments. Many of the finer judgments concerning a man's special calling are bound to be made later, when he knows some part of the world of work much better than any adolescent or student can know it. The problem of prestige—in so far as prestige is that which leads people to make choices of their pursuits—is then that of creating chains of opportunity to learn more and more about the possibilities within the main parts of the world of work, and to adapt one's self to new demands and to keep setting one's sights further off as he goes. Woe be to him who, through self-interest, doctrine, or laziness, blocks vision and learning at any point on the road.

THIRTY-SEVEN

Psychology: Science and/or Profession

Let me set before you three occupational models: a science, a business, and a profession. Each of these, in the purest case, shows a system of social interaction different from the others in crucial respects. There are other models, but these appear the most useful ones to those who are discussing the institutional aspect of the occupation of psychology.

Scientists, in the purest case, do not have clients. They discover, systematize, and communicate knowledge about some order of phenomena. They may be guided by faith that society at large and in the long run will benefit from continued increase of knowledge about nature; but the various actions of the scientist, *qua* scientist, are undertaken because they add to knowledge, not because of any immediate benefit to any individual or group which may be considered his client. The test of the scientists' work lies in convincing communication of it to colleagues, communication so full and so precise that any of them can undertake to test the validity of claimed findings by following the same procedures. Scientists chafe under secrecy. If laymen do not receive full report of work done, it is simply because they are not sophisticated enough to understand the report. The great point in the scientist's code is full and honest reporting to his colleagues, and, with it, willingness to submit to full criticism. Since this is so, and since no client is involved, scientists ordinarily do not seek the protection of state license. Informal controls are sufficient.

The second model is that of a business. In purest form, business goes on

"Psychology: Science and/or Profession." *The American Psychologist*, Vol. 7, 1952, pp. 441–43. Copyright 1953 by the American Psychological Association and reproduced by permission. (Written at the request of a committee of the APA appointed to consider developing a code of professional ethics.)

among traders. Since the customer is also a trader, he is presumed to be as sophisticated about the object traded in as is the seller. The trading is a game. The principle of *caveat emptor* can apply without injury to anyone. As in all games, however, there are rules designed to allow the game to continue. There is no sense letting anyone in who has not the resources to make good his deals, nor the skill to keep the game going. Hence, stock exchanges have limited memberships. But the state and the public are not especially considered in making the rules of entrance to the game and the rules of play.

Not all business is of this pure form, for goods are eventually sold to an amateur, a consumer. The consumer may know what he likes, but he is not expected to be as good a judge of what he buys as is the man who sold it to him. He expects some little protection from unscrupulous sellers who would impose upon his ignorance. *Caveat emptor* tends to be limited, but not completely — witness the tongue-in-cheek "pitch" of advertising. The customer often, in moments of annoyance, initiates action to license sellers or to otherwise protect the customers from them. I introduce this model merely to high-light the third, that of a profession.

The people in a profession make their living by giving an esoteric service. Nowadays it is commonly said that the service is based upon a science or, as in the case of engineering and medicine, a number of sciences. The essence of the matter appears, however, to be that the client is not in a position to judge for himself the quality of the service he receives. He comes to the professional because he has met a problem which he cannot himself handle. It may be a matter of life or death for himself or a loved one; of gaining or losing a family farm, or one's freedom and reputation; of having one's dream of a house turn into wonderful reality or a white elephant. He has some idea of the result he wants; little, of the means or even of the possibility of attaining it. Indeed, he may want an impossible result, and be bitterly resentful of the professional man's judgment that it is impossible. But the time comes when the physician cannot prolong a life. All patients are lost in the long run. Half of all cases contested at law are lost; there is a losing side. All professions fail in some measure to achieve what their clients want, or think they want, of them. Furthermore, members — even the best — of all professions make mistakes of judgment and of technique. The result of all this is that those in the profession do not want the principle of *caveat emptor* to apply. They do not want the client to make an individual judgment about the competence of practitioners or about the quality of work done for him. The interaction between professional and client is such that the professionals strive to keep all serious judgments of competence within the circle of recognized colleagues. A licensing system adds the support of the state to some mechanism established by the profession itself for this purpose. It is as if competence became an attribute of the profession as a whole, rather than of individuals as such. Thus the public is to be protected from its own incompetence and from its own impossible demands, in that "quacks"—who might exploit them—will not be allowed to practice. And the professional, for his part, is protected from his own mistakes and from the allegation that he may have made one, by the fiction that all licensed professionals are competent and ethical until found otherwise by their peers. The profession sets up institutions which make clients' judgments of secondary importance and colleagues' judgments paramount. These institutions will of necessity require some arrangements for secret discussion. For it is shocking and painful to clients to hear their problems discussed as objectively as must be in deciding whether a professional did, in fact, show competence and whether he acted in accordance with the professional code. In such discussion the question of competence is discussed in complete separation from the outcome for the client. In protecting the reputation of the profession and the professional from unjust criticism, and in protecting the client from incompetent members of the profession, secrecy can scarcely be avoided. Secrecy and institutional sanctions thus arise in the profession as they do not in the pure science.

I have dwelt upon the professional conception because it is so highly valued in the western world, and especially in North America. The people, or some people, in many occupations have sought to have their work conform to the professional model and to be known by the professional name. Social workers, librarians, and many business occupations have tried it. The steps taken are much the same in the various instances. Courses of study are established, and, if possible, professional schools are founded and attached to universities. Prerequisites are required so that a person entering the occupation must decide to so do earlier. Eventually some body is set up to accredit schools and specify the curriculum. Devices are adopted to define more sharply who is and who is not properly in the occupation. Canons of proper practice, proper relations to clients (or employers), proper relations between colleagues, etc., are set up. Although the steps are essentially the same, the results vary greatly. The public may not accept the professional definitions and may continue to take their troubles to people not admitted to the professional group. Employers may simply hire people without consulting the professional group as to their membership or competence. Shrines and various kinds of irregular practitioners continue through the ages to treat the cases which doctors declare either incurable or imaginary. Sometimes the curriculum of the professional schools may be hardened before the techniques have really been tested in practice or in a laboratory. This happened in social work and in library schools. I do not know whether these things have happened or will do so in psychology. I only point out that they are things which do happen in the course of professionalizing occupations.

It is fairly evident that psychologists are torn between the professional and the scientific conceptions of their work. Only their enemies charge them with pursuit of the business conception. Now medicine has been plagued by this conflict through many years. The marriage between clinic and laboratory is still an uneasy one. The wonder-working surgeon (they do work wonders) is still not quite at ease with the sceptical pathologist down in the laboratory. The practicing physician, meeting as best he can the emergencies of patients who refuse to get made-to-order troubles, feels inferior before his patient and learned brethren of the great research schools and foundations; he also resents their detached, leisurely criticism of his hasty blunders.

The medical solution, at least the one prevailing at present, is to instruct physicians in science but not to train them to be scientific investigators. Any physician who learns to do research in a science related to medicine, does so either in prolonged residencies in research hospitals or by taking advanced work in one or more sciences in a graduate school. There are people who believe that a great deal of the time spent in medical school is wasted, unless it be admitted that sheer initiation into the fraternity is a good way to have young men spend time. However that may be, the medical profession has succeeded in enforcing a highly standardized curriculum upon all who would be called doctors of medicine, no matter what skills and knowledge an individual may use in his particular branch of work. Training in scientific research comes later, for the few who want it. I do not know whether psychology could institutionalize its conflict in such a way. But my point is not so much the particular solution as the fact itself that there is a continuing, deep conflict between the model of science and that of professional practice of medicine. In many individuals, it is an ambivalence.

I suspect that psychology's problem is of this order. I also think it likely that whatever solutions are arrived at will be compromises. They will be better compromises if no one has any illusions about settling the problem once and for all; if it is kept in mind that the conflict lies deep in many occupations, and that all solutions to it are tentative, based on limited time predictions about the effects of various actions.

THIRTY-EIGHT

The Professions in Society

"The Recent History of Professionalism in Relation to Social Structure and Social Policy" by T. H. Marshall was published by this JOURNAL twenty years ago.[1] It has since become a classic; and may be fittingly celebrated in this anniversary issue. Its classic quality lies in the skill with which Marshall worked enduring themes with current trends and problems into a common web. He defines professions as, in effect and with some other characteristics, those occupations in which *caveat emptor* cannot be allowed to prevail and which, while they are not pursued for gain, must bring their practitioners income of such a level that they will be respected and such a manner of living that they may pursue the life of the mind. There are certain problems which surround such occupations in all times.

The current changes noted by Marshall are the ever greater dependence of modern society upon professional services, an increase in the variety of such services and in the number of the professions, and the tendency for many practitioners of the older professions and for most or all of some newer professions to work in organizations with an employer, rather than to set up a shop to which clients come, one by one, are served, and pay for the service. He also noted that while the community at large is in all times and places concerned with the manner in which professional services are performed, this is especially so in our times; indeed, the community at large is the client of some new professions and, in increasing measure, of older ones.

Marshall was, of course, not the first among those called sociologists to

From *The Canadian Journal of Economics and Political Science,* Vol. 26, No. 1, February, 1960, pp. 54-61.
1. *Canadian Journal of Economics and Political Science,* V, no. 3, Aug., 1939, 325-40.

have considered the professions as a central feature of society, a key to the understanding of social structure. Auguste Comte had had his say on the subject when he noted (in a passage which I have not lately been able to find) that the same engineer had kept the waterworks of Paris going before, during, and after the Revolution. Some professions, it seems, not merely survive revolutions, but keep the rivers of blood flowing.

Herbert Spencer considered the elaboration of professions the essential feature of a civilized society. Other institutions arose to defend, sustain, and regulate life. "What further general function is there? There is the augmentation of life; and this function it is which the professions in general subserve."[2] There follows an eloquent passage in which he tells us that the medical man increases the amount of life; the artist elevates the emotions and pleasurable feelings; the historian and the man of letters raise men's mental states; the scientist and the teacher increase mental illumination, all in their own way increasing life. His conception of the professions is catholic; dancers are allowed a place among those who increase life.

Emile Durkheim, having devoted his chief treatise on human society to the division of social labour, could not well avoid discussing the place of professions. When he did so specifically in the Preface to the second edition,[3] he referred not to professions in the English sense, as did Spencer, but to all occupations. What concerned him was the propensity of professional groups to generate social rules and sanctions and to become impermeable to attempts of outsiders to control them. He saw professional groups as organs of society, partly autonomous systems of relations which cannot, however, exist except in contact with the other organs of society. As social advocate, he favoured the kind of society in which occupational groups would be the chief organs of control represented as such in government. He did not, so far as I know, deal with the main trends touched upon by Marshall. Nor had any other sociologists done so explicitly.

Tönnies, Park, Max Weber, and Simmel had all written of the multiplication of occupations based on the application of science and reason as a mark of urban society. But none of them had paid special attention to the other trends noted by Marshall. It was Marshall who heralded the up-surge of the new style of professional practice. ·He did not agree with his colleague Harold Laski, who advocated doing away with all private practice

2. Herbert Spencer, *The Principles of Sociology* (New York, Appleton-Century-Crofts, 1896), XI, chap. I. Spencer, Comte, Bagehot, and others of the period, wrote in two moods: in one they presented pretentious theories of social evolution; in the other, they commented sharply and sometimes passionately on the affairs of their day. The work of such men is often completely misunderstood because the notebooks used by graduate students contain the pretentious theories, and those only in brief caricature, but not the more timely discussions and the ideas and theories implicit in them.

3. Emile Durkheim, *De la division du travail social,* Préface à la deuxième édition (Paris, Félix Alcan, 1902), "Quelques Remarques sur les groupements professionels."

of professions.[4] Nor would he join the tirade of Messrs. Lewis and Maude[5] against use of the term "professions" for any but the few occupations which had been so designated in the past, and against any but the style of private practice which they assumed to have been universal in that blessed era.

The merit of Marshall's article is that it did so clearly indicate trends which were to become marked in all of the industrial countries, no matter what political banner floated over them. All have indeed shown a multiplication of professions, as the term is understood in English; and all have shown the same tendency for them to be practised inside complicated organizations—complicated in the sense that the relation of the professional with the client is part of some larger complex of relations. In none, not even in the Soviet Union, has private professional practice completely disappeared.

In the years since 1939 professional services have become a matter of increasing public concern in all of these countries, arising in part from the growing belief that everyone has a right to education, health, and to those other kinds of increase of life which Spencer had said it was the function of professions to provide. One might say that a characteristic feature of our time has been a great increase in the expected standard of living in those very aspects of life of which Spencer had spoken. It has also become apparent that the distribution of such services in the expected measure to all was not likely to be achieved by selling them over the counter by the parcel to paying customers, nor by the simple method of allowing the professional person to charge on a sliding scale, taking much from those who have much and little or nothing from those who have little or nothing. More and more philanthropic and public agencies have become involved in the distribution of professional services; more and more of the cost is paid by various risk- and cost-spreading agencies other than the professional practitioner himself. And one must note, as Marshall did, that many services had never been distributed by that simple method.

The public interest in professions and the services they provide has been reflected in the work of social scientists. In Great Britain, Carr-Saunders and Wilson[6] published a book in 1933 in which they described in general terms the process by which occupations took on the characteristics of professions, and gave the history of a number of cases.

In the United States and Canada, work has lately run rather to the place of professions in prestige-scales derived from surveys of opinion; to the manner in which occupations attempt and sometimes succeed in being

4. Laski had lately argued this point in *Harper's Magazine,* as Marshall observes.
5. Roy Lewis and Angus Maude, *Professional People* (London, Phoenix House, 1952).
6. A. M. Carr-Saunders and P. A. Wilson, *The Professions* (London, Oxford, 1933).

accorded professional standing; to the processes by which young laymen choose to enter professions and to their education and initiation into them; and to that progress of professional people through the maze of the appropriate organizations, formal and informal, which is a man's career.

As has been said by W. Lloyd Warner, North America is not class-conscious, but class self-conscious. Work on the professions, as on other matters, reflects this; it is in part a study of social advancement (mobility). The advancement is of two kinds. The first is the rise of the individual by getting into an occupation of high prestige, or by achieving special success in his occupation. The second is the collective effort of an organized occupation to improve its place and increase its power, in relation to others. That effort, in middle-class occupations, characteristically is directed to achieving professional status. For whatever else the word "profession" may mean, it is in modern English a symbol of high ranking among occupations.

We North Americans are especially sensitive to all that affects the chances of individuals of various backgrounds and qualities to enter various kinds of occupations and to achieve success in them. The achievement of success within an occupation includes, in some professional occupations, choice of one of its several specialties and one of several styles of career. These secondary choices are often as fateful as choice of the occupation itself. We have thus an ever increasing number of occupations which aspire to the title, prestige, and privileges of professions and a great number of people attempting to improve their lot by gaining the education and other qualifications for entry to professions – and all this is happening in a time when no one can be quite sure that any occupation will maintain its present position for as many years as a man's normal career; or that the sciences and arts which one learns will not have become obsolete before one is ready to be retired, even before one has achieved a well-paid, honoured, and secure position.

These changes are all complicated further by the ethnic and racial variety of the two nations of North America, for entry into professions has been a special road to advancement for ethnic groups who first offered themselves for the humbler positions in the labour markets of these two countries; once they have entered professions, their difficulties in following certain specialties or styles of careers become the issues in the battle of discrimination.[7] This is the key to the present phase of racial and ethnic conflict in the United States. As one might expect, this phase is com-

---

7. Oswald Hall did one of the pioneer studies in this field, "The Organization of Medical Practice in an Eastern City," unpublished Ph.D. dissertation, University of Chicago, 1944. David N. Solomon pursued certain aspects of the same problems in his Ph.D. dissertation, "Career Contingencies of Chicago Physicians," University of Chicago, 1952.

plicated by the fact that, just as certain ethnic and religious minorities are entering the professions in large number, the change from private practice to work in more complicated organizations for salary and under authority has also accelerated; so the problem for, say, a Negro is not merely whether he can gain admission to a medical school, and to medical practice, but whether he can find a place in hospitals and clinics or in informal referral systems; for in such systems not even a Negro client can determine whether he will be attended by a Negro physician. Other authorities enter into the choice; so the question of discrimination is not merely whether a given kind of patient will accept a given kind of doctor but whether colleagues and those with the power to place physicians are either prejudiced against Negro physicians or afraid to act without prejudice for reasons of policy.[8] I suspect that the relations between French and English in Canada may be affected by the change from private practice, with clients' choices prevailing, to more highly organized and bureaucratic forms.

And while one is speaking of minorities, it seems not too far-fetched to say that the present demands of the neo-feminists concern a shifting of the place of what have traditionally been women's professions in the whole complex of professional services, and of that minority of minorities, the married women, in the labour force in general, but especially in the professions, for working women of some education are concentrated in professional occupations much more than men. Some would say that the occupations in which they are concentrated are quasi-professional — nursing, teaching, social work, librarianship. That but emphasizes collective mobility; for such occupations are prominent among those which are attempting to gain for themselves a more secure standing as *professions*. This they do by the usual means of attempting to require more schooling of aspirants to their occupations, by insisting that they themselves, and not some outside authority, shall judge what is their proper work, by putting their more routine duties on the shoulders of subordinate workers, and by claiming a mandate to define the public interest in matters relating to their work.

Not the least important of the symbolic steps in raising an occupation to more fully professional standing is to go in for research. The object of research may be the occupation itself, or it may be study of the phenomena with which the occupation is concerned — health, education, human personality. In time these may be redefined so as to bring the research closer to that of older and more general branches of human knowledge. In so far as the people inside the occupation do this research, those who do it tend to become an élite somewhat removed from practice, and to move into pro-

8. See Dietrich Reitzes, *Negroes and Medicine* (Cambridge, Harvard, 1958.)

fessional schools connected with universities or into special agencies, private or public. They tend to have careers quite distinct from those of people primarily in practice. This may indeed be a sign that the occupation has professional status, for this very distinction between careers of practice and careers of research, education, and administration is becoming marked in all of the older professions. Perhaps what distinguishes the new professions from the old is that, in the new, prestige clearly goes to those in the careers removed from practice, whereas in the older ones this is by no means so clearly the case.

I do not mean to suggest that an occupation on the make undertakes research merely to raise its standing, although that may be the result and although those who would elevate an occupation may be quite aware that it will be. A good many of the new occupations are the result of social and technological changes which are not fully understood and whose consequences may affect not merely the way in which some one occupation does its work, and, consequently, the selection and education of the people who are to do it; they may also change the division of labour as among professions and as between them and other occupations in a given field. Thus the division of labour among the specialties of medicine itself is constantly changing; at the same time, the technical division of labour between physicians, nurses, technicians, other therapists, scientists, social workers, and various administrative specialties is changing very drastically (although perhaps the fundamental role of the physician has been less affected by it all than he fears). This is the feature of professional change that has led to the calling in of social scientists. Sociologists, social psychologists, anthropologists, and economists in great number have been invited into the sacred precincts to study changes in the relations of occupations to each other in the great complexes of institutions which have grown up about the major professional services; it is a continuation of the social scientist's role as student of the division of social and economic labour (which political scientists call "constitutions"). One danger is that the social scientists will become pundits when dealing with newer professions of less prestige than their own, and that they will over-identify themselves with professions of greater prestige than theirs when such deign to ask them in.

Whatever the dangers, the gain can be great. For social scientists now have access to crucial data about our culture not previously available and to organizations which do not fit the rather simple models which students of business, of political bodies, and of the family had developed in the time when each branch of social science had its favourite institution. For the organizations in which professions work show patterns of authority and interaction which, according to earlier theories of organization, could not possibly work. They are, in general, organizations with more staff than line; their special importance for the study of social organization is that they give us new models to work on just when business organizations, which students have been inclined to take as the prototype of rational organization, are themselves becoming so cluttered by staff advisors (of various old and new professions) that the line is scarcely distinguishable, and this is very frustrating. The newer generation of business men, instead of proposing that universities, hospitals, and government agencies (in which the efforts of professional people are somewhat co-ordinated) be run in a business-like fashion, may turn to these mad-houses for ideas on how to organize their own enterprises; for the staff people, in so far as they are really professional, have another loyalty than that to their employers; they belong to professions which have some sense of solidarity and autonomy.

The professional trend is doing something to organizations and enterprises. But work in organizations and enterprises is also doing something to professions, both as concept and as reality. It is here that German work becomes of importance. The concept *freier Beruf* (free or liberal profession) once stood for something like a complete philosophy. A man in such a profession was self-employed, learned, devoted to his work, full of the sense of honour of an historic estate (*Stand*), courageously indifferent to pressures from outside, politically neutral (yet, on the whole, *Kaisertreu*). But at the same time there was developed in Germany a model and philosophy of the *öffentlichen Beamten* (civil servant). While all civil servants were to do their work competently and loyally, the higher officials were to be—and were—men of learning, of high professional conscience, and of great prestige. But they were, even more than the men in the liberal professions, to be at once politically neutral and loyal to authority. It was a loyalty which sometimes showed itself in a sort of condescension to those ephemeral and erratic creatures who headed governments and made childishly unwise and impractical policies. There were thus, in German culture, two images of the professional man, one *frei* (self-employed) and one *beamtet* (secure in a bureaucratic position).

One of these conceptions has been rudely shaken by the bureaucratizing of the free professions; the other by the pressures on the civil servants accompanying the violent changes of political régime from Empire to Weimar Republic, to totalitarian national-socialism, and from that to equally totalitarian communism in the East and the return to democracy in the West.

The fate of the older conception of the free profession is dealt with in detail by J. F. Volrad Deneke in *Die freien Berufe*.[9] Herbert Von Borch

9. J.F. Volrad Deneke, *Die Freien Berufe* (Stuttgart, Friedrich Vanwerk Verlag, 1956). *Arbeit und Beruf*, by Theodor Scharmann (Tübingen, J.C.B. Mohr, 1956) is perhaps the best recent German general book on this whole matter.

deals with the second problem, that of the official and his loyalty, in *Obrigkeit und Widerstand: Zur politischen Soziologie des Beamtentums (Authority and Resistance: An Essay on the Sociology of the Civil Servant).*[10] These two books thus deal with one of the problems high-lighted in Marshall's article, that of professional work performed inside agencies rather than independently. Deneke shows, for a number of professions, just how far the reality is from independent practice. In medicine 42.4 per cent were in dependent positions (not in private practice) in Western Germany in 1950, the figure ranging from nearly all under thirty years of age to 14.7 per cent of those between sixty and sixty-five.[11] In the main, Deneke devotes himself not to the figures, but to the problem of maintaining professional autonomy, solidarity, and standards of work under the prevailing condition of working inside organizations and for salary. There is nothing especially striking in his analysis of the problem; the contribution of his book is essentially a statement of the problem and presentation of the current state of things.

Von Borch, in his study of the conflict of loyalties of the civil servant, is dealing with a problem which has not risen in so extreme a degree in the English-speaking countries in recent times as in those countries which have undergone totalitarian revolutions. The conflict of professional and human conscience with the demand of a totalitarian régime that its civil servants not merely carry out all of its orders but that they also become apostles of its doctrines is the problem of the employed professional in its ultimate degree. But the ultimate degree of any problem is very instructive; it brings out the essential features. It does not serve any analytical purpose, however, if used merely as a horrible example. The problem of all professional codes has always been this: Whose agent is the professional? Turned around it is: Who is the client? The extreme ideology of the private practice of professions gives a simple answer. There is but one client, the person who applies for services and accepts them on the conditions dictated by the profession. This obviously cannot be the case when the application does not come in that way. But between that situation and the complete submission of the civil servant in a totalitarian régime there are many degrees. In Russia, the physician must—as agent of the People's Republic which wants everyone at work—take care not to certify too many

10. Herbert von Borch, *Obrigkeit und Widerstand: Zur Politischen Soziologie des Beamtentums* (Tübingen, J.C.B. Mohr, 1954).

11. Deneke, *op. cit.,* p. 124. Deneke compiled a series of tables from the 1950 census of occupations in Western Germany. As one would expect, certain specialties in medicine, law, and other occupations are practised independently more often than others. The newer technical professions are predominantly not independent. The age differences in medicine and law may be due to a secular trend which takes effect first on the young, or it may be due in part to the fact that in some professions a young man must work for older men or in agencies for a long time before he is able to get a private practice.

people as ill enough to stay at home.[12] But the physician and nurse who work for an industry in our part of the world have in some measure the same problem of determining whether the company or the worker-patient is the client. The problem of acquiescence in the demands or pressures from employing agencies is universal, and has always been so. I will not here go into the many means of defence which professional, or other occupational groups, have developed against such pressures. It certainly is demonstrably true that types of organization are being worked out which do allow the maintenance of professional freedom in balance with the controls necessary in large organizations which involve many kinds of positions and many occupations.

As a matter of fact, there are some indications in recent studies of a great paradox. Part of the cherished freedom of a professional worker is not merely to do his work according to his own best judgment and conscience, but also to choose his own style of work and economy of effort. Lawyers who practise alone — at least in a sample of them taken in Chicago[13] — are utter captives and chore-boys of their clients. They have no freedom to choose a branch of law and make themselves expert or learned in it. Most of them, in time, do find their practice narrowed to a special line of chores: they have become specialists by default. Likewise there is growing evidence that something like this is true of physicians who practise alone in certain districts of large cities, and perhaps elsewhere. Joe L. Spaeth found a large number of physicians in Chicago, whose practice has gradually narrowed to a rather low form of industrial medicine, repairing small wounds caused by accidents, examining and treating people who get sick at work, and making due reports for insurance and liability purposes.[14] They, too, have become specialists by default. They could not be called *general practitioners,* for the cases they get are not a random selection of what goes wrong with people, and their knowledge is not any sort of general selection of available medical knowledge.

And here we are at a paradox of modern professional freedom. The effective freedom to choose one's special line of work, to have access to the appropriate clients and equipment, to engage in that converse with

12. See Mark G. Field, *The Soviet Physician* (Cambridge, Harvard, 1958). Also his "Structured Strain in the Role of the Soviet Physician," *American Journal of Sociology,* LVIII, March, 1953, 493-502.

13. Jerome E. Carlin, *Lawyers on Their Own: A Study of Individual Practitioners in Chicago* (New Brunswick, Rutgers, 1962). Carlin compared a sample of lawyers in one-man offices with others.

14. "Industrial Medicine: A Low-Status Branch of a Profession," unpublished Master's thesis, University of Chicago, 1958.

eager and competent colleagues which will sharpen one's knowledge and skill, to organize one's time and effort so as to gain that end, and even freedom from pressure to conform to the clients' individual or collective customs and opinions seem, in many lines of work, to be much greater for those professionals who have employers and work inside complicated and even bureaucratic organizations than for those who, according to the traditional concept, are in independent practice. Penetrating analysis of this paradox and of the problems related to it is a major task of social science. It will centre largely around study of professions, old and new.

THIRTY-NINE

Professions

Professions are more numerous than ever before. Professional people are a larger proportion of the labor force. The professional attitude, or mood, is likewise more widespread; professional status, more sought after. These are components of the professional trend, a phenomenon of all the highly industrial and urban societies; a trend that apparently accompanies industrialization and urbanization irrespective of political ideologies and systems. The professional trend is closely associated with the bureaucratic, although the queen of the professions, medicine, is the avowed enemy of bureaucracy, at least of bureaucracy in medicine when others than physicians have a hand in it.

A profession delivers esoteric services—advice or action or both—to individuals, organizations or government; to whole classes or groups of people or to the public at large. The action may be manual; the surgeon and the bishop lay on their hands, although in the one case manual skill is of the essence, while in the other it need not be great because the action is symbolic. (Yet some priests and religious healers become very effective in their manner of laying hands on the heads of people who seek confirmation or comfort). Even when manual, the action—it is assumed or claimed—is determined by esoteric knowledge systematically formulated and applied to problems of a client. The services include advice. The person for or upon whom the esoteric service is performed, or the one who is thought to have the right or duty to act for him, is advised that the professional's action is necessary. Indeed, the professional in some cases refuses to act unless the client—individual or corporate—agrees to follow the advice given.

Reprinted by permission from Daedalus, Journal of the American Academy of Arts and Sciences, Boston, Mass., Vol. 92, No. 4, 1965.

The nature of the knowledge, substantive or theoretical, on which advice and action are based is not always clear; it is often a mixture of several kinds of practical and theoretical knowledge. But it is part of the professional complex, and of the professional claim, that the practice should rest upon some branch of knowledge to which the professionals are privy by virtue of long study and by initiation and apprenticeship under masters already members of the profession.

The Oxford Shorter Dictionary tells us that the earliest meaning of the adjective "professed" was this: "That has taken the vows of a religious order." By 1675, the word had been secularized thus: "That professes to be duly qualified; professional." "Profession" originally meant the act or fact of professing. It has come to mean: "The occupation which one professes to be skilled in and to follow.... A vocation in which professed knowledge of some branch of learning is used in its application to the affairs of others, or in the practice of an art based upon it. Applied specifically to the three learned professions of divinity, law and medicine; also the military profession." From this follows later the adjective "professional," with the meanings now familiar.

Professionals *profess.* They profess to know better than others the nature of certain matters, and to know better than their clients what ails them or their affairs. This is the essence of the professional idea and the professional claim. From it flow many consequences. The professionals claim the exclusive right to practice, as a vocation, the arts which they profess to know, and to give the kind of advice derived from their special lines of knowledge. This is the basis of the license, both in the narrow sense of legal permission and in the broader sense that the public allows those in a profession a certain leeway in their practice and perhaps in their very way of living and thinking. The professional is expected to think objectively and inquiringly about matters which may be, for laymen, subject to orthodoxy and sentiment which limit intellectual exploration. Further, a person, in his professional capacity, may be expected and required to think objectively about matters which he himself would find it painful to approach in that way when they affected him personally. This is why it is unfair to ask the physician to heal himself, the priest to shrive himself, or the teacher to be a perfect parent. A professional has a license to deviate from lay conduct in action and in very mode of thought with respect to the matter which he professes; it is an institutionalized deviation, in which there is a certain strain toward clear definition of situations and roles.

Since the professional does profess, he asks that he be trusted. The client is not a true judge of the value of the service he receives; furthermore, the problems and affairs of men are such that the best of professional advice and action will not always solve them. A central feature, then, of all professions, is the motto—not used in this form, so far as I know—*credat emptor*. Thus is the professional relation distinguished from that of those markets in which the rule is *caveat emptor,* although the latter is far from a universal rule even in the exchange of goods. The client is to trust the professional; he must tell him all secrets which bear upon the affairs in hand. He must trust his judgment and skill. In return, the professional asks protection from any unfortunate consequences of his professional actions; he and his fellows make it very difficult for anyone outside—even civil courts—to pass judgment upon one of their number. Only the professional can say when his colleague makes a mistake.

The mandate also flows from the claim to esoteric knowledge and high skill. Lawyers not only give advice to clients and plead their cases for them; they also develop a philosophy of law—of its nature and its functions, and of the proper way in which to administer justice. Physicians consider it their prerogative to define the nature of disease and of health, and to determine how medical services ought to be distributed and paid for. Social workers are not content to develop a technique of case work; they concern themselves with social legislation. Every profession considers itself the proper body to set the terms in which some aspect of society, life or nature is to be thought of, and to define the general lines, or even the details, of public policy concerning it. The mandate to do so is granted more fully to some professions than to others; in time of crisis it may be questioned even with regard to the most respected and powerful professions.

These characteristics and collective claims of a profession are dependent upon a close solidarity, upon its members constituting in some measure a group apart with an ethos of its own. This in turn implies deep and lifelong commitment. A man who leaves a profession, once he is fully trained, licensed and initiated, is something of a renegade in the eyes of his fellows; in the case of the priest, even in the eyes of laymen. It takes a rite of passage to get him in; another to read him out. If he takes French leave, he seems to belittle the profession and his former colleagues. To be sure, not all occupations called professions show these characteristics in full measure. But they constitute the highly valued professional syndrome as we know it. Professions come near the top of the prestige-ratings of occupations.

Many occupations, some new, some old, are endeavoring so to change their manner of work, their relations to clients and public, and the image which they have of themselves and others have of them, that they will merit and be granted professional standing. The new ones may arise from the development of some scientific or technological discovery which may be applied to the affairs of others. The people who "process" data for analysis by computers are a recent example. Some of the specialties within medicine are due largely to the invention of some diagnostic instrument, or to an extension of biological or chemical knowledge. After the virus came the virologist, who works alongside the bacteriologist and the person who knows about fungi—together they are the microbiologists, who work with microscopes, and lately with the electronic one. Other new professions or specialties (and specialties follow much the same course of development as professions themselves) may arise from some change in society itself. As impersonal insurance replaced the older, more personal ways of spreading the risk of death, injury, illness, unemployment and loss of property, actuarial knowledge was of necessity developed, and a new profession arose. The professional social worker is a product of social changes. In an epoch of great technological and organizational change, new techniques and new social demands work in some sort of interaction to produce new esoteric occupations.

Perhaps the way to understand what professions mean in our society is to note the ways in which occupations try to change themselves or their image, or both, in the course of a movement to become "professionalized" (a term here used to mean what happens to an occupation, but lately used to refer also to what happens to an individual in the course of training for his occupation). Courses and seminars entitled Professions, Occupations, or Sociology of Work—which I have been holding for more than twenty-five years—invariably attract many people from outside sociology. As often as not, they want to write a paper to prove that some occupation—their own—has become or is on the verge of becoming a true profession. The course gives them a set of criteria for their demonstration. Librarians, insurance salesmen, nurses, public relations people, YMCA secretaries, probation officers, personnel men, vocational guidance directors, city managers, hospital administrators, and even public health physicians have been among them.

These people are serious, often quite idealistic. The changes they want to bring about or to document are directed to the same *terminus ad quem,* but the starting points lie in different directions. The insurance salesmen try to free themselves of the business label; they are not selling, they are giving people expert and objective diagnosis of their risks and advising them as to the best manner of protecting themselves. They are distressed that the heads of families do not confide in them more fully. The librarians seek to make themselves experts on the effects of reading, on bibliography and reference, rather than merely custodians and distributors of books; in schools and colleges, librarians want status as members of the teaching staff. They insist that they are, or must become, jointly with social psychologists, investigators of communications. That is their science, or one of their sciences. People in business management work at developing a science of management which could presumably be applied to any organization, no matter what its purpose. The social workers earlier were at pains to prove that their work could not be done by amateurs, people who brought to their efforts naught but good will; it required, they said, training in casework, a technique based on accumulated knowledge and experience of human nature and its operation in various circumstances and crises. Their first goal was to establish the position of the professional and to separate it from the amateur friendly visitor or reformer. The nurse, whose occupation is old, seeks to upgrade her place in the medical system. Her work, she says, requires much more general education than formerly, and more special knowledge; as medicine advances, the physicians delegate more and more technical functions to the nurse, who delegates some of her simpler functions to practical nurses, aides and maids. The nurse wants a measure of independence, prestige and money in keeping with her enlarged functions, as she sees them. The YMCA secretary wants his occupation recognized not merely as that of offering young men from the country a pleasant road to Protestant righteousness in the city, but as a more universal one of dealing with groups of young people. All that is learned of adolescence, of behavior in small groups, of the nature and organization of community life is considered the intellectual base of his work. The vocational guidance people have trouble in bringing the teaching profession to recognize that theirs is a separate complex of skills, presumed to rest on psychology. The public health men have a double problem. They must convince other physicians that their work—which is generally not the diagnosing and treating of patients—is really medicine. They must also combat the belief of physicians that they should do for fees some of what the public health people do for a fixed salary.

In these examples appear the main themes of professionalization. Detachment is one of them; and that in the sense of having in a particular case no personal interest such as would influence one's action or advice, while being deeply interested in all cases of the kind. The deep interest in all cases is of the sort that leads one to pursue and systematize the pertinent knowledge. It leads to finding an intellectual base for the problems one handles, which, in turn, takes those problems out of their particular setting and makes them part of some more universal order. One aspect of a profession is a certain equilibrium between the universal and the particular. The priest who would fix his attention entirely on the universal aspects of religious behavior might find himself indifferent as to which religion he would attach himself to; and thus, a renegade and a heretic. Churches do not encourage such circulation of the elite. Great corporations, too, although they may seek men who know the science of management, want an executive's curiosity about and love of the universal aspects of human organization tempered with a certain loyalty and commitment to his employer. I suppose there may be a professional man so free-sweeping in his interests that he does not mind what client he serves and what aspects of the client's affairs he deals with. He would be a rarity—a rich outcast or a poor idealist.

The balance of the universal and the particular in a profession varies, but there is always some measure of both, with an appropriate equilibrium between detachment and interest. The balance between universal and particular is related to that between the theoretical and the practical. Branches of learning are not always very directly related to the ordinary business of life. If some occupations become professions by developing an intellectual interest, others do it by becoming more practical. A large number of chemists are now employed by industries. Psychologists are seeking and obtaining legislation giving them monopoly over the name and making it an offense for anyone to "practice" psychology without it. Some sociologists, especially those who do research by the "project" for "clients," would do likewise. Perhaps one should distinguish between professions in essence, such as medicine or engineering, which pursue knowledge to improve practice; and professions by accident, such as, say, archaeology, where the practices are merely the means to increasing knowledge. In both cases, the people engaged may make their living by their activities. There appears to be a trend in certain fields of knowledge for this distinction to disappear and for the learned societies to become professional guilds concerned with problems of practice, employment, licensing and distribution of their services. Many learned societies show strain between the intellectuals and the professionalizers.

This strain, incidentally, is found in some degree in all professions. A physician may be too devoted to research; a lawyer too concerned with comparative law; a social worker overcurious about the roots of human behavior. In fact, inside most professions there develops a tacit division of labor between the more theoretical and the more practical; once in a while conflict breaks out over issues related to it. The professional schools may be accused of being too "academic;" the academics accuse other practitioners of failure to be sufficiently intellectual.

Another set of themes in professionalizing movements has to do with a change of status of the occupation in relation to its own past, and to the other people—clients, public, other occupations—involved in its work drama. Changes sought are more independence, more recognition, a higher place, a cleaner distinction between those in the profession and those outside, and a larger measure of autonomy in choosing colleagues and successors. One necessary validation of such changes of status in our society is introduction of study for the profession in question into the universities. It may be as an undergraduate program, leading to a Bachelor's degree with a major in the theory and practice of the occupation. A large proportion of the university undergraduates in this country are in such professional courses. Other professions seek to have a Master's degree made the standard professional qualification; so it is in social work, hospital administration, business administration, laboratory technology, librarianship and many others. The Master's degree is also used as qualification for a professional or administrative elite in occupations for which the basic preparation is a Bachelor's degree. The Ph.D or some substitute, such as the Doctor of Education, is also used as qualification for higher administrative and teaching positions in professional agencies and schools.

The older professions, law and medicine, have long been established in the universities; at present in this country, they can keep their aspirants in college for four years and in professional school for three or four years after that. Indeed, so sure are they of their place that they tend to encourage undergraduates to pursue what lines of study they will, so long as their achievements are high. One way in which an occupation—or a college—can document its high status is by being able to take its pick of the young people about to enter the labor market, and then to keep them in school a long time before admitting them into the charmed circle.

Some combination of scholastic aptitude, ambition and financial means is required to accomplish this educational aim. The ambition must have been fostered in some social setting, generally in the middle-class family, although occasionally in a working-class family with the aid of a sponsoring schoolteacher who sets sights high. The financial means may come from the aspirant's family, a discounting in advance of the income to be made in the profession, or from an investment in talent by government, industry or the foundations. The latter is of increasing importance in allowing people to continue in higher professional training, especially for work thought to be of use to defense or related industrial development. It is probably effective only when reinforced by the expectation of good income and high prestige.

Not all occupations which aspire to professional standing can promise enough of either of these ingredients to get the most talented and then to keep them in school as long as do medicine, law and the sciences. Characteristically they seek to improve their position in both recruitment and the education system; in the earlier phases of their move toward professionalism, the people in an occupation may have to earn their way slowly and painfully to higher education, and the professional school may have difficulty in getting itself accepted in universities. It may take an operation bootstrap to get a corps of people in the occupation academically qualified to teach succeeding generations and grant them professional degrees.

This competition for status is accompanied by a trend toward prolonging the professional training at both ends: at the beginning by multiplying prerequisites for entry to professional school, at the finish by prolonging the course and the various apprentice or internship programs. This is held in check by the fact that many of the would-be professions cannot offer enough future income and prestige to get people early and keep them long in school. Parents of less income and education also press their children to seek security in known middle-level occupations. This pressure may also work against the movement to lift professional requirements.

Old and new alike, the professions cherish their recruits once they get them. Having picked their candidates with great care, medical schools, for instance, gnash their teeth and tear their hair over a sheep lost from the fold. They wonder what they have done wrong to make the lamb stray. They make it clear to the professional recruit that he owes it to himself, the profession and the school to stick with his choice. Has it not been discovered by all the tests that this is the one right outlet for his talents? Is it not his duty to use his talents for his country in the best possible way? Have not the profession and the professional school made a great investment in him? Has he the right not to give full return on it? The day has passed when the youngsters entering professional school are told to look well at their neighbors in the classroom, for few of them will be there next year. The theme is mutual commitment, reinforced by students' auxiliaries sponsored by the professional associations, and by the use of such terms as "student-physician," which stress that the student is already in the professional family. One owes allegiance for life to a family.

Thus we have a high degree of competition among the professions for talent, combined with a great feeling of possessiveness over the recruits as soon as they have crossed the threshold. The professional student is, to some extent, already an organization man.

But that is not the only respect in which the modern professional is an organization man. Professions are more and more practiced in organizations. The *Freie Berufe* in Germany were considered free not merely because they were worthy of free men, but because those who followed them had no employer. Even the *freier Gelehrte,* or independent scholar, once he had acquired the right to teach, received his income in fees from his clients, the students. The university merely gave him his validation and his forum, as the court gives lawyers a playing field and a referee for their contest. The true professional, according to the traditional ideology of professions, is never hired. He is retained, engaged, consulted, etc., by some one who has need of his services. He, the professional, has or should have almost complete control over what he does for the client.

Especially in medicine, the protest against working in organizations and for salary is very strong. Yet in this country, more than in England, where there is a national plan of medical practice, physicians work in organizations. A decade ago it was reported that for every physician in the United States, there were between four and five people in the related or paramedical professions. There are more now; many people in the medical systems are in nonmedical work such as accounting, housekeeping, engineering and maintenance, and actuarial work for medical insurance schemes. An increasing proportion of physicians are in specialties; the specialist characteristically must work with other physicians. Some specialties never get the first call from an ailing patient; they are reached only after one or more referrals. Some specialties are, like pathology and anaesthesiology, practiced only in hospitals or clinics. All physicians now work at least a year for salary as interns; many work for a salary for several years as residents. In some specialties — those far from the first call of ailing people — work for an organization, possibly for salary, is the rule. An increasing number of lawyers work in large firms where duties and cases are assigned, not completely chosen by the individual practitioner himself. The firm operates as a referral system and allows the individual lawyer enough cases of one kind to permit him to specialize. Many lawyers have but one client, a company; and when there is but one client, it becomes in fact an employer.

Law and medicine — the models which other professions try to approximate — in spite of nourishing free practice of the individual for a number of clients with a minimum of institutional apparatus, are in fact far along the road to practice in complicated organizations which intervene in many ways between them and their clients. Engineers, applied scientists and people in most of the newer professions nearly all work in organizations with others of their own profession, and with many people of related occupations. Indeed, it becomes hard to say who is the client in many cases; in the case of medicine, is it the insurance company or the patient? In the school, is it the child, the parent, the community at large or some class of people within it? In social work, is it the agency — which pays — or the so-called client, who is worked upon not always of his own free will? It is characteristic of modern professions that they do work in such institutional settings, often with capital goods which they do not own and with a great variety of people. Professional ideology prefers a two-party arrangement: the professional and his client. It prefers the client who can speak for himself and pay for himself. This is not the prevailing arrangement, nor is it likely to be.

Thus arise a great number of problems for professions. The problem of finding a clientele becomes that of finding a place in a system of organizations. The problem of colleague relationships becomes that of determining who, in a complex organization of many professions, are indeed one's colleagues, and in what degree. The problem of freedom becomes one of distinguishing between one's obligations to the person, if it be such a case, on which one performs some action or to whom one gives some advice, and to one's employer or organization. For example, does the college physician report the secrets of his student-patient to the dean and, if so, in what situations? There is also a problem of authority; what orders does one accept from an employer, especially one who is not a member of one's own profession and whose interests may not always be those of the professional and his clients?

The other side of this coin is that the employer, even in business, finds himself dealing with an increasing number of professional (staff) people, who will not be ordered about as freely as line people. Indeed, Robert Maynard Hutchins once said:

> ... business may eventually be organized like a university, with the staff claiming a kind of academic freedom, participating in the formation of policy, and enjoying permanent tenure. When that happens the university administrators of America will derive a certain grim satisfaction from the struggles of those captains of industry who have had the habit of complaining about the mismanagement of universities.[1]

As the professions become more organized, business organizations become more professionalized. The result is the development of new patterns of organization. If the professional man giving staff services to business or industry sets a certain pattern of freedom not common among the employees of business, he has also lost a certain kind of freedom which inhered in the private practice of professions for clients of whom enough were solvent to assure him a good income and a fitting style of life.

But it may be possible that under present conditions the private practitioner of a profession does not have so much freedom, or at least not the same kinds of freedom as his colleague working in some sort of larger organization. In theory, the private practitioner is free to move at will; in fact, it is very chancy for a man established in practice in a given community to move. Reputations among the common run of clients are local and may depend upon conformity with local customs and beliefs concerning nonprofessional matters. The man who works in an organization may develop a wider reputation, even a national one; he may improve his lot by moving from time to time. He may be freer of social pressures. The man who practices privately may, in fact, be the choreboy of his clients, doing only those things which they want in a hurry and which do not warrant the

1. "The Administrator," in R. B. Heywood (ed.), *The Works of the Mind* (Chicago: University of Chicago Press, 1947), pp. 135–156.

seeking out of a better known or more specialized practitioner, firm or other organization. He may thus have little or no choice of what kinds of work he will do. The man in the larger organization may apply himself to some line of work and become so proficient in it that he need not accept any work not to his taste. Perhaps the man in the organization may not pick his client, but he can often pick his problems. It may perhaps be that a few men at the very top of a profession can practice privately and as they wish, because of a great reputation throughout the profession and among sophisticated and affluent clients; while the bulk of people in private and "solo" practice will be choreboys without much reputation among clients and without any among their more specialized colleagues.

In between these two extremes there may be — and I believe there are — a large and increasing number of competent people who work in organized settings. They will, in order to be successful, develop reputations among their colleagues and will be, in case the profession is such as to demand it, known as effective with clients. They will work out new systems of relationships, which may be much the same in business, government agencies, universities, hospitals and clinics, and other kinds of organizations; among the relationships to be worked out are those of the balance between obligations to one's professional colleagues, both in and out of one's present organization, and the organizations in which one works. New formulae of freedom and control will be worked out. The people in organizations will be — although in some sense bureaucrats — the innovators, the people who push back the frontiers of theoretical and practical knowledge related to their professions, who will invent new ways of bringing professional services to everyone, not merely to the solvent or sophisticated few. Indeed, I think it likely that the professional conscience, the superego, of many professions will be lodged in that segment of professionals who work in complicated settings, for they must, in order to survive, be sensitive to more problems and to a greater variety of points of view.

On the other hand, the professionals will become more sensitive to outside opinion; and, like other organized groups, they will hire public relations people to perform for them the esoteric service of creating a satisfactory public image in the press, on television and in the schools, where young people learn about the careers open to them. It is all a rather confusing prospect. The professions will, in any case, be a large and influential element in our future, and in that of all societies which go the road of industrialization and urbanization; the organizational structures in which they will work will very likely resemble one another, no matter what the prevailing political ideologies in various countries of the same degree of industrialization.

In the meantime, there are large parts of the world which are not far along this road. In some of them there is an oversupply of professional people and an undersupply, or some lack of balance in the supply, of related professions. A recent paper reports that whereas in this country there are several nurses for each physician, in India there are seven physicians for one nurse. Oversupply means, of course, only more than can be supported by an economy. Lack of demand may be due to lack of money or to lack of acceptance of the very definition of wants to which a profession caters. It is generally both money and sophistication which are lacking. What will be the course of the rise of demand for medicine, education, legal protection and social services in the now poor and nonindustrial countries? It will not be the same course as in the older industrial countries, for the latter had no models to go by; people of the now developing countries know, or soon will know, that such personal services exist and are widely available in the older industrial economies. They will hardly pass through the same stages of professional practice, organization and distribution of services as we did.

Many of the institutions of a modern society depend upon an adequate supply of professionals who perform services for corporate bodies: people to plan and build water systems, communications, roads, industrial plants; people to train others in various trades and techniques and to organize public services. Professionals who do these things have, in the past, come to a new country from abroad as employees or representatives of colonial powers, business concerns or missionary agencies. They have not always sought native recruits or successors; nor have they always given full recognition to local colleagues where there have been some. We are evidently in a new situation with respect to the deploying of professional people over the world. It is not clear who will sponsor such a deployment, what sort of reception professionals from abroad will get in new nations, or how professionals from the highly urban and industrial countries will fit work abroad into their careers.

Again we face the problem of the relation of the particular, the culture-bound, aspect of professions to the universal aspect. The professional may learn some things that are universal in the physical, biological or social world. But around this core of universal knowledge there is likely to be a large body of practical knowledge which relates only to his own culture. The physician may recognize the rhythm of the beat of an East Indian woman's heart, yet lack the slightest knowledge of how to get her to accept his diagnosis of what ails her and his advice about how to live with it. Furthermore, the physician — or other professional — may have become so accustomed to his own society's particular way of practicing, of payment, of dividing labor with others that he will not and cannot adapt himself to these particularities of another society, especially a preindustrial and not highly literate one. An interlude in another part of the world might interrupt the accumulation of reputation, seniority and money so essential to his career at home; whatever he might learn in practice of his profession abroad might or might not be applicable to his future work at home. While professions are, in some of their respects, universal, in others they are closely ethnocentric. In many professions, careers are contained within a single economy and society. One of the interesting developments of the future will be new patterns of international exchange of professional knowledge and professional institutions.

FORTY

Education for a Profession

All cultures in the industrial and urban world name and classify occupations. The naming and the classification are not entirely separate, for the names evaluate as well as describe. They carry praise or blame. They imply high or low rating. They connote social class and economic position. The etymology of the names of classes of occupations, although interesting and useful, is not definitive because overtones drown out the original dominant meaning. Furthermore, the various languages of Europe derive various special meanings and nuances of meaning from the same roots. Profession is one of these class names. A profession in its original meaning is simply an avowal of faith; in German the only profession that is really "professed" is the academic profession. A man professes his subject in a university. In French a *profession* is any occupation at all. *Profession liberale* has a more honorable and special reference. In German all occupations are *Berufe,* that is, callings. Of course, calling and vocation are the same, but in English vocation is supposed to be low and calling high. This reverses the usual distinction because the Latin word ordinarily is applied to the object of higher standing. The French "pork" is on the table and the German "swine" is in the field. But one's calling in German, one's *Beruf,* can be anything from prostitute to priest. In English, we are inclined to use vocation for almost anything; except that the Catholic church speaks of vocation to the religious life. We do say a man is "called to the bar," although nobody called him; he took all the initiative himself; and a man may be called by God, by himself, by the army, or by his future colleagues. Both in German and in French there is a concept of the *liberal* or *free*

From *The Library Quarterly,* Vol. XXXI, October, 1961. Copyright 1961 by the University of Chicago Press.

professions. I believe that our use of the term "profession" goes back to that and to the phrase *liberal profession,* which once meant any profession worthy of a free man — that is, of a gentleman as in distinction from those things which belong to the meaner orders.

In the English-speaking world, the term profession is now used for certain occupations which enjoy a good deal of prestige and which give some esoteric service, often based on science. But let me remind you that some professions are much older than the sciences; science as we know it is modern while the professions are quite ancient. Why should any of the great human arts try to reduce itself to a single discipline of science when it should make use of all the human learning there is, both the scientific and humanistic kinds?

Occupations which are called professions in our society do apply some rather esoteric skill to the giving of a service. Their motto, unlike that of business, is not *caveat emptor* but *credat emptor,* "let the taker believe in us." The essential point is that people in the occupation pretend, not vainly, that they have skill and that they can be trusted to carry out their activities for the good of the individuals or groups served and of society at large.

The Nineteenth–Century Model of the Profession

When people say "profession" nowadays, they often have in their heads a very fleeting model, the model of what the law and medicine are supposed to have been in the liberal nineteenth century — that is, a profession is conceived as an esoteric art practiced by a closed group of people, each by himself, each having relations to a number of separate clients, and each collecting his own fees. This model is not true in medicine in most countries now; only about 35 per cent of the physicians even in this country work in that sort of situation. I think if one were to do a content analysis of professional claims in this country he would find that when people say "profession" they are talking about medicine and about this particular concept of medicine as they think it was at a certain time. Yet the professions old and new are in increasing measure practiced in complex organizations.

There are two important complications: the professional works with several other kinds of people, and it is not at all clear who the client is. For instance, in the library, who is the client? The Daughters of the American Revolution and the American Legion, that is to say, the self-called high priestesses and priests of Americanism? Are they the true client, are the parents of the children the client, is the board the client, are the children themselves the client? In Hersey's *The Child Buyer,* the librarian really wanted to bring along a youngster and help him read whatever he wanted.

It turned out that there were some other clients involved. In the case of medicine, it is again not clear who the client is. It never was completely clear, because if one is in bad need of a physician, if he is very sick, the client becomes whoever is responsible for one and not the patient himself.

Professions are no longer, if they ever were, practiced in that kind of social vacuum which is supposed to surround the physician shut in his surgery or his office with his patient. The rest of the world is there, a very complicated world. I do not know how many kinds of people there are in libraries. The number of people involved in a quite simple case in a hospital is perfectly tremendous. In the health occupations, there are now five people for every physician. The physician is only one among six people who are technically qualified and who have something of a professional interest in handling that case. The bills are often paid by insurance companies, and is not the person who pays the bill the client? Whatever the case may have been in the past, most of the professional services in our society are not delivered on a "fee for individual service" basis. Religious services never were distributed that way. Legal services were distributed that way only for a small part of the population. When medicine was really distributed that way, only a very small percentage of the population ever got professional medical service. Some of the new professions, now very numerous, are based on the application of technology. Professor Goode has told this story very well. Others are organizational in their very nature; whether, however, they are technological in their origin and in their essence, they are all organizational in fact. All professions have to do with the distribution of a service, not merely with producing it. All professions guard rather jealously control over the distribution of their services. I suppose there is quite a lot of new technology involved in the work of the librarian, but when we say "librarian" we say "library." The word "librarians"makes no sense without the fact of the library. There may be a few independent people who do bibliographical consulting, but I hope most of them have a nice secure job in a library.

I have emphasized the point that professions nearly all are practiced in complicated organizations and that a number of other people are involved. The other people are not all at the same level of status; they perhaps do not all require the same kind of education, but they all work together. If any one group enhances its own status without some care for the status of the others, it may find itself in some trouble.

Professional Education: Grading Up and Watering Down

Let us now talk about professional education. There are a few occupations which have been able to restrict recruiting to candidates who have completed a full general college course of liberal arts and sciences. They then have them study, in medicine, four years plus, and in law, three years as a rule, in divinity, three years. A law student and a medical student are apt to enter professional school directly from college, the divinity school student usually or very often not. The notion that people should finish a four-year liberal arts college before their professional training is quite strong, but most occupations have not been able to bring it off. In medicine they bring it off for doctors, but an increasing amount of the medical work is done by people who are not doctors.

Incidentally when one compares physicians per thousand of population, it means little unless one knows how many other people are engaged in health and medical services. We compare the number of physicians per capita in the United States with that of Germany or the Scandinavian countries or Russia and find out that we have fewer, but we have many more people working at health than they do and have a much more specialized and elaborated kind of organization.

Some of the new professions have also taken the model of college plus professional training, but they have done some rather peculiar things with it. They have usually taken the Master's degree as the basic professional degree — so much so that only a minority of the Master's degrees in this country are now non-professional. The Ph.D. is following; 20 per cent of all Ph.D.'s given in the country in recent years were in education alone, without counting the Doctors of Education. It is very likely that within ten years over half of the doctorates in this country will be given in education alone, not to count the other professional Doctor's degrees.

In the movement of an occupation to become more professional, it sets up professional schools. It then establishes a body to accredit the schools. In part, the accreditation is based on the number of teachers with Doctor's degrees; a lot of "doctors" must be created in a hurry, so that the schools can be accredited. In nursing there has been a most terrific drive to increase the number of doctorates. Some have been good doctorates and some have not. There is no use in pretending that the M.A. has not become, for most people who take it, a professional degree. It is the basic professional degree in a number of occupations and the Doctor's degree is becoming in an increasing proportion also a professional degree. In education, for example, the Doctor's degree is taken at a certain point in an administrative career; having taken it, the person does no more research but goes back to a somewhat higher echelon of administration. The Doctor's degree is very often a validation for a step upward in an administrative career. It is also validation for a step in academic position as it is in the non-professional subjects.

Not all professional or would-be professional occupations enjoy such incomes that they can require everybody to finish college and go on to a higher degree. The incomes of physicians in this country are so satisfactory that any medical student can walk into his home town bank and borrow money on practically no security at all except the statement of the dean of the school of medicine that he is proceeding satisfactorily and is in good health. He is a good bet. But all occupations do not have that kind of assured income; the candidates do not have the money to stick through so many years of study. Hence comes a great pressure for vocational Bachelor's degrees. It is doubtful whether any of the increase in the number who take Bachelor's degrees of recent decades has been increase in general liberal arts; it is mainly the vocational Bachelor's degree that has burgeoned. Some of the occupations which have established postgraduate basic professional schools have to contend with teachers' colleges which offer an undergraduate major in the same subject.

At bottom this is partly the result of organized education's strength; it may also be a reflection of the fact that the system demands quite a number of people who have no more training than that and who see no reason for getting the longer more difficult and expensive training. The strain to get the B.A. is very strong. Most elementary-school teachers have the B.A. as a distinctly professional degree; a considerable proportion even of high-school teachers, if they have M.A.'s, got them in education, based on B.A.'s in education. The nurses are going in for the collegiate school, which is a Bachelor's program. Now they are insisting on more M.A.'s and Ph.D.'s and Ed.D.'s to teach in the collegiate schools of nursing in order that they may be accredited. There is now coming up a large generation of nurses with Bachelor's degrees in nursing and no major in any academic subject, who are now, in turn, seeking Master's and Doctor's degrees on the basis of two years of liberal arts work, that is, on the basis of a series of elementary college courses. Many are survey courses cut to the background and supposed needs of the people who are taking them; that is to say, they are a little less rigorous than the regular courses.

This leads to some watering down, but it leads also to a more serious thing, the methodological ritual. A person learns "chi square" and a couple of devices of that kind and goes around stamping work with them to make them kosher. The methodological ritual based on a couple of isolated courses having nothing especially to do with the subject matter concerned is getting to be one of our curses. Research method cannot be so divorced as that from the problems and matters which people are investigating.

The Social Strains on Educational Systems

The trend that I am talking of I think is going to continue. We believe in having people go to school a long time, longer than any other country. This is probably because our economy is more automated than any other. Since industry and the world of work have no use for children, they must go to school. In this country a person is either in school, working, or retired. If one is not yet of an age to go to work, we believe the community should keep him in custody of an institution. We call the institution a school. This is a problem we have to meet seriously because if children are not going to work they must be somewhere with some kind of activity that engages their interest. We have not invented the institutions that will really do this. Failure to do so is having an adverse effect on the more demanding kinds of education. The solution is not snobbery. Anyone who thinks we can solve the problem by sending fewer people to school and not sending them so long is talking through his hat.

But there is a demand in our society for lots of people of moderate literacy who do moderately routine jobs and who have a right to have life made interesting for them, but not without some work on their part. As more people go to school longer, we will have more and more people in colleges because after one has been to school twelve years what he goes to is college. It's going to be called a college and will give a Bachelor's degree. I cannot see any force arising that will counteract it. If we take that, together with the demands of our various systems — medical, educational, and industrial — for large numbers of people with a middle-level education, one gets some sense of the setting in which decisions about professional education for the more demanding professions have to be made.

Let me go back to the fact that nearly every profession is practiced in an elaborate social system. No occupation any longer decides completely by itself what its work is and then goes about doing that work without consideration of the other kinds of tasks which have to be done in the same system. The librarians can go off in a corner and decide that the true librarian would never do anything except, again let us say, bibliographical consultation to practical experts. The decision would not stick.

There is not a profession that I know of whose boundaries are not changing. One might think that medicine is a profession where the people inside can say exactly what their work is and what the boundaries are. They have more power over it, perhaps, than anyone else, but they do not have complete power and the boundary of the medical profession as determined by the allocation of specific tasks is certainly shifting. When the clinical thermometer was first invented, no nurse was allowed to put her hands on this sacred instrument, and when the blood pressure affair came along only physicians could do this. It is against the law for nurses to give intravenous feeding, but it has got so common that it is a nuisance to the physicians. We shall see what happens. There is a constant shifting of technical tasks from the medical profession to other people in the system.

Very often the other people become more skilled in an activity than the physicians themselves. In all these systems, incidentally, there is learning and teaching up the line as well as down it. The more complicated the system the more delegation of work there is, the more shifting of boundaries of actual tasks, the more upward learning there has to be, because the whole thing begins to depend very much more on effective communication among the various kinds of people who are carrying out this work. Division of labor requires communication.

The boundaries of the professions are only apparently measured by tasks that people do. Actually the physician is quite willing to give up any number of tasks so long as he does not weaken his essential role in the system. He passes anything along that does not threaten his role. One may, therefore, look at a division of labor in two ways; as a series of specific tasks or as a set of roles played in a drama. Part of the problem of any modern profession is to preserve its role while at the same time letting its boundaries so shift as to make the organization work well. One thing that professional education has to deal with nowadays is the constantly shifting frontiers of all occupations within the larger system of which they are a part.

The Past and the Future–Pressures on Professional Education

It is very common for an occupation to require some symbolic prerequisites. Professional education is not merely the learning of skills. It is also initiation into a lodge, a semisecret society of people who have cryptic signs and peculiar problems, who have to deal with the ordinary, sometimes stupid and childlike, laymen who just do not understand their own problems. There's a lovely passage in one of Trollope's novels, *The Eustace Diamonds*, in which an old lawyer tells how he regards the whole world from the noble and the royal down as children whose interests must be looked after by wise solicitors. Every profession has this attitude; I would not give much for one that did not. One simply cannot think of educating people for any profession in purely technical terms. It must be in part initiation into a role with its mood, into the understanding of its basic ethic — I do not mean its specific rules but a basic moving spirit that controls what people do. That is one side of it. As time goes on certain courses are thought of as being symbolic, the first degree of initiation into a secret order. Gross anatomy in medicine is like that. All physicians must go through it. Anatomy symbolized a great victory for the medical profession. There is a tendency in all professions to develop certain courses that are thought to have special value. They come perhaps to be a little too religiously guarded. Whether there are such sacred cows in library schools

I do not know. I only say most professions do. I would suggest that, if professional library education is to meet the demands of the modern library and the modern world, someone should look to see whether some courses are not a little too much of this character. I do not believe in doing away with the ritual, but I do like it nicely sung and to have some artistic quality. I do not believe in letting it get out of hand and get in the way of other kinds of teaching.

Another thing one has to do in professional education is to make some sort of prediction about what the work of the profession is really going to be in the future. This is always a guess. One can be almost certain that it will not be what it is now. One can take one of two attitudes. One can just keep it as it was, because the system has worked pretty well—like the British claiming that the best training anyone ever thought of for the British civil service was the classics course. This is one of the great known *non sequitur's* of history. The truth is that at a particular point in time the best young minds in Britain were taking that course and they probably could have been taking anything else and would have done about as well. But I do not think most professions are going to be content with simply doing what they have done on the assumption that it will work forever.

The prediction about what people will really do is difficult. One has to think in several perspectives. The medical students whom we have been studying have a quite different perspective from that of the faculty. The faculty almost always has a longer perspective than the students. In law, medicine, and nursing, the students invariably want the teaching done in a shorter perspective than the teachers. They want to know something specific and immediately practical. If one were to leave it to the vote of the people entering an occupation, they would vote for less general education and more vocational training. At least all the studies I have seen show they believe in starting earlier and having it more practical. One of the functions of people engaged in professional education is to be a long way ahead of the students. No one can be taught how to run a library in a particular town; every library has probably got its own system. What kinds of general knowledge—human knowledge, scientific knowledge—and wisdom are essential for the profession I simply do not know. But I would say that if library educators are not in a continual state of strain with their students over this point they are probably not doing their job very well.

Of course, professional schools vary in this regard. There are two or three medical schools in this country from which half the graduates go into teaching and research, while some medical schools have almost no graduates who go into teaching and research. I would be astonished if there is not some such division of labor among library schools. Again librarianship would be unlike the other professions if its schools did not vary in the particular functions they perform. Some are rather more practical while others, in some sense, look to the future, developing the more abstract knowledge, and training the people who will be leaders on the intellectual and innovating side in the profession.

Let me mention one final problem of education. An occupation going up in the world is very much tempted to do so by casting off its more menial tasks. As it goes up, it drops off signs of lower status. It tries to delegate some tasks downward. There is no more difficult problem for any profession than to decide what it can delegate and at what cost. For instance, the nurses have delegated the bathing of the patients and the brushing of their hair. Have they, in so doing, lost the affection of the patient? There is some evidence that they have. Yet the new thing they are doing, medication and other things the doctor does not want to do or cannot do, are very worthwhile, One thing, I suppose, the profession has to try to decide, but not alone, is what things it will cast off and then at what point to cut off training for the cast-off tasks. Do library schools teach the things that librarians used to do, but in the future are not going to do? Are they going to teach only some central core — legal thinking in a law school, diagnosis in a medical school — or are they going to mix that with other things which do not carry quite so much prestige but which are necessary activities? If a profession isolates its candidates from the other people in the system too much, it may set up strains which lead to reaction. The profession may lose the sympathy of the other people in the system by drawing a strict line and getting high and mighty.

A good many studies show, and it seems common sense, that nobody does the same thing all day year in and year out except people on assembly lines. That is to say, great lawyers do talk to clients sometimes; they do not just sit all day writing briefs. Each of us in his profession has to work out a realistic economy of time and effort as among the various tasks which make up his work. When one grows older, some of these tasks tend to drown out the others, just as the incoming mail becomes so great that soon it pushes the books off one's desk, and diverts one from his main tasks. One problem of a profession is to find out the dangers and threats to its economy of time and effort. Perhaps there will be a few people in a profession who can do only one thing, such as sit and diagnose blood diseases by looking through a microscope. But there are not many of these people and most of them are not at the center of professions. They are only, I would say, marginally professional. They tend to become technicians. Actually all of us do a number of things; part of the problem of a professional school is not merely to educate its people for a place in a complicated system where they will have to deal with a lot of other kinds of people, but also to train them to learn to cope with the problem of economy of time and effort, so that they will not, in the course of five years, become purely administrators or purely this or purely that. The problem is to combine some degree of specialization with some effective understanding of the whole system one operates in.

FORTY-ONE

The Making of a Physician—
General Statement of
Ideas and Problems

Social scientists are being called upon more and more to study training for the various professions and to consult with those who make policy with reference to it. The following pages suggest a general frame of reference for such study. They were written for several people, both medical educators and social scientists, who were thinking of embarking on a modest study tracing the course of students through the maze of a particular medical school. There resulted a daylong discussion which was of great value in planning the study. It was more like a prolonged group interview than a formal discussion. While the ideas refer specifically to medicine, they implicitly refer to other professions as well.

The Medical Culture

Each of the great historic professions is concerned with not just a set of techniques for doing some useful work, but with some aspect of life and/or society, itself. And when, as often happens, an occupation—either an old one transformed by technical or social changes, or a new one—claims for itself the status of profession, it is saying to the world that—like the professions—the work it does has somehow become a matter of broad public concern.

Medicine is the prototype of the professions in this regard. As Sigerist so

Human Organization, Vol. 14, No. 4, 1956. By permission of *Human Organization* and The Society for Applied Anthropology, © 1956.

The period of initiation into the role appears to be one wherein the two cultures, lay and professional, interact within the individual. Such interaction undoubtedly goes on all through life, but it seems to be more lively — more exciting and uncomfortable, more self-conscious and yet perhaps more deeply unconscious — in the period of learning and initiation. To take one example, the layman has to learn to live with the uncertainty if not of ignorance, at least of lack of technical knowledge of his own illnesses; the physician has to live with and act in spite of the more closely calculated uncertainty that comes with knowing the limits of medical knowledge and his own skill.

In the process of change from one role to another there are occasions when other people expect one to play the new role before one feels completely identified with it or competent to carry it out; there are others in which one over-identifies oneself with the role, but is not accepted in it by others. These and other possible positions between roles make of an individual what is called a marginal man; either he or other people or both do not quite know to what role (identity, reference group) to refer him. We need studies which will discover the course of passage from the laymen's estate to that of the professional, with attention to the crises and the dilemmas of role which arise.

STEREOTYPE AND REALITY

We assume that anyone embarking upon the road to medicine has some set of ideas about what the work (skills and tasks) of the physician is, about what the role is, what the various medical careers are, and about himself as a person who may learn the skills, play the role, and follow one of the possible career-lines. We assume also that except in cases of extraordinary early contact with the profession, the medical aspirant's conceptions of all these things are somewhat simpler than the reality, that they may be somewhat distorted and stereotyped among lay people. Medical education becomes, then, the learning of the more complicated reality on all these fronts. It may turn out that it makes a good deal of difference whether the steps toward a more penetrating and sophisticated reality on one of these points come early or late, and whether the reality is learned from supporting teachers and colleagues or rubbed in by punishing cynics or stubborn and uncomprehending patients. It may be that the more complicated reality is in some circumstances traumatic, in others, exciting and even inspiring. Perhaps some aspects of reality can be learned in an early phase of technical training and experience, while others can be effectively learned only at some later point. There has always been considerable talk in educational institutions about what kinds of things are prerequisites for others; only in a few cases does it appear really to be known what should come first, what later—there are those who say that geometry should come before algebra, not after. Some question the time-honored custom of having students learn anatomy from cadavers rather than from demonstrations with living persons. In the study of professional education, we have suggested a distinction between various kinds of prerequisites: conventional and symbolic, technical and role-learning. Learning the realities of medical skills, roles and careers may move *pari passu;* or it may be that some of the roles can be really learned only when a certain level of skill has been attained and certain career corners turned. The realities about career problems might at some points put a damper on the student's eagerness to learn skills and roles; at another point, a new knowledge of career realities might be a stimulus to work on the other fronts.

In professional, as in other lines of work, there grows up both inside and outside some conception of what the essential work of the occupation is or should be. In any occupation, people perform a variety of tasks, some of them approaching more closely the ideal or symbolic work of the profession than others. Some tasks are considered nuisances and impositions, or even dirty work—physically, socially or morally beneath the dignity of the profession. Part of what goes on with respect to a major aspect of life at whose center is a profession, such as the medical, is a constant sorting and resorting of the tasks involved among many kinds of people—inside the profession, in related professions, and clear outside professional ranks. The preparation of drugs, the taking of blood pressures, the giving of anaesthetics, the keeping of medical records, the collection of bills, the cleaning up of operating rooms, the administration of hospitals—these are but a few of the tasks which have been allocated and reallocated within the medical division of labor in fairly recent years. There is constant discussion of what is whose work in medicine and what part of it all is the physician's work, privilege and duty. We assume that the medical student is inducted into the discussion of these problems, and that it has some effect upon his motivation and his sense of mission. We may suppose that the essential, symbolically-valued part of the physician's work is diagnosis and treatment of the ailments of people, and that the other activities are—in theory at least—tolerated only as they appear necessary to it. What, then, are considered essential auxiliary or peripheral activities, and what attitudes do physicians hold toward them and the people who perform them. Hospitals must be administered, and there are some who believe that physicians alone should do it. Yet, physicians do not ordinarily gain great prestige by becoming administrators—indeed, some who are say they are scarcely considered medical colleagues any longer. On the other hand, there is some tendency for auxiliary activities to become valued ends in themselves, sometimes even getting in the way of the presumed basic activity (as discipline becomes an end in itself in schools and, some say, in nursing).

The increasing variety of the central and, symbolically, most valued of medical activities themselves is reflected in the number of medical specialities. Some of the specialities are rated above others both by laymen and the profession, although these ratings are not necessarily the same. We may assume that as the students learns various skills and sees at closer hand the actual tasks of his future trade, he will undergo changes of attitude toward them as components of medical work.

Just as certain tasks and skills of medical work are rated above others, so also are the men who perform them. But we must remember that the various medical tasks differ from each other not merely in the knowledge and technical skill required, but in the social relations and social roles involved. The model member of the profession is a man of certain skills and knowledge, one who keeps proper balance between the more and the less valued activities of the profession, and who plays his role well in relation to himself, his colleagues, other personnel in medical work, and toward his patients and the public. As in other professions, we may find that some models are—like the saints—considered a little too good for ordinary men to be expected to imitate in daily practice, although they are admired as embodiments of the highest values of the profession. A study of medical education should discover not merely the saintly models, but also those the student regards as more practically (even a bit cynically) attainable by himself, the mold being as it is, and he being who he is. The shift in choice of models by the student, his definite steps or his drifting into the path that leads to one model rather than others, is a significant part of his medical education. This is, of course, not merely choice of specialty, but of various ways of practicing medicine: practice, teaching, research; practice in one social environment rather than another: rural or urban, well-off or poor, where the health standard of living is high or is low, among his own or among other kinds of people; alone or in association with others; for salary or for fees; where competition is keen or where there is more security, etc. These matters may all enter as components into models to be admired or followed, which is to say that, as suggested above, a model in effect embodies the whole professional ideology of those who choose it.

The models of the medical world are, of course, not free of influence from the ideologies of other aspects of modern life. We should investigate the extent to which the image of the model businessman has colored that of the model physician. Although the world of business uses the term *private entrepreneur* there is plenty of evidence that the model businessman is seen as a team worker rather than a person who goes it alone. It is possible that in some respects the medical model is a hangover from the outmoded one of the business world. Given current trends in medical organization, it seems obviously important to discover not merely the extent to which the go-it-alone model prevails as against the team-work model, but also to find out what influences continue to reinforce it.

The conception of the model physician contains, by implication, clues to the nature of the model patient. There may be a good deal of ambivalence on this point, since few students are so unrealistic as to believe they can get a practice consisting of only one kind of patient (as to troubles, personal, social, or economic characteristics), or so divinely endowed and blissfully ambitious that they can in fact get such a clientele. It is recognized, too, that all people must be served in some fashion. Yet there are conceptions of the ideal patient: about what is wrong with him, about his social and economic characteristics, about his acceptance of the physician's authority and prescriptions, his understanding, his cooperation and his gratitude. There are apparently at least three important components in these conceptions: the nature of the illness and its amenability to treatment; the nature of the interaction between the patient in his role with the physician in his; and, finally, the effect of the patient on the physician's career (income, reputation, development of further skill, fulfillment of his self-concept as a physician).

We have said little directly about the nature of social roles, and will make only a few remarks on the subject since, by implication, the problem of role is found throughout. In one sense, role is what a man expects of himself and what others expect of him in certain situations. People sometimes expect miracles of physicians; the physician has to learn how to handle this expectation in such a way as to give his patients both the best chance of getting well and the least chance of disillusionment. This is the eternal problem of helping people to face uncertainty, or unwelcome certainty (as the case may be), the problem of maintaining balance in the relations between the more skilled partner (the physician) and the less skilled, but more crucially-affected partner (the patient). Man of understanding, man of patience, confidante, advisor, pillar of strength—and their opposites—these are terms having to do with roles, rather than with techniques as such.

They all involve other people, or oneself considered in one's relations to other people. Everyone has to work out the weights he will give to the various parties to the work drama in which he has a role. Will he play it for the patients alone, dramatizing himself as their champion against the profession itself? Taken to the extreme, this is quackery in a strict sociological sense, whether or not the man be competent in his methods of diagnosis and practice. There are people who play their roles before their colleagues alone, or before some of their colleagues rather than others; still others may be moved by peculiar conceptions of their own rights and duties, impervious alike to colleague and patient. These may be the true missionaries, the sectarians who have no judge except God himself. Every man finds his "significant others," with whom he identifies himself so that he listens to their voices rather than to others. This is what is meant by the recently adopted term, "reference group." Since there are a number of crucial reference groups in modern medicine, it becomes part of the problem of the student to find some balance between his sensitivity to them, his own configuration of significant others. Different configurations may be associated with selection of the specialties and the ways of practicing mentioned above.

It is also likely that as he goes through the medical education, the aspirant will veer from one toward another of his significant others; at one time feeling the aches and pains of the patient more acutely than the patients themselves; at another sharing the angry cynicism of those colleagues who say, in their hour of disillusion with ungrateful humanity, that the only thing to do is get yours while you can; at another, feeling the exhilaration of wonder-working, and yielding a bit to the blandishments of admiring nurses, students, and grateful patients; and at still another, suffering the pangs of uncertainty of his trade and feeling sorry for himself.

This leads to the problem of self-conception and discovery of self. One person's conception of himself is itself something of a stereotype, to which parents, teachers, siblings, peers, and his own dreams have contributed. Some people project themselves far into the future, others operate more or less in the present. But in either case, there come moments of necessary revision and adjustment of one's notions about what he can do and wants to do. One may say, then, that a young man thinking about himself as a physician is thinking about a young man as yet somewhat unknown to himself, doing work and playing roles not yet known, in situations he has never yet been in. This is not to underestimate the anticipatory playing of roles; but no matter how sensitive the individual's anticipation of himself in a future role, there is some gap between anticipation and realization. Certainly, there are more young men in premedical school who think of themselves as potential surgeons than can ever be surgeons, given the qualities necessary and the proportion of the medical profession who make their living as such. There are also fewer who expect to end up in public health than actually will. As he proceeds through medical training and into practice, the young man may be expected to get not merely a better notion of the skills required, of the tasks to be performed, of the roles to be played, and of the positions to be attained in the medical world and the roads which lead toward them, but also to adjust his conception of his own mental, physical and personal aptitudes, his tastes and distastes, and of the chances that a person of his particular social and economic qualities and family circumstances may acquire the skills, the roles and the positions available.

This is an economics of self-conception. The importance of this to the distribution of physicians among specialties and ways of practicing is obvious. Again we have to deal with the problems of fateful or crucial choice. A person may make a discovery about himself only after he has passed the point of crucial decision to do the kind of work he would now like to have been able to do. In the concrete, this means that one cannot enter medicine at all unless one has had certain schooling by a certain age; that some specialties have to be adopted far earlier than others; that some require a longer period of doing without income; that a wife who is a handicap in one kind of practice might be a great asset in another; that, while one can master the skills of a certain specialty, one has no taste or aptness for the social roles required. A study of the progressive self-discovery of students passing through the maze of medical school and training might be used by those who plan the experiences which have a bearing on the choice of effective models, of specialties, and of the ways and places of practice by medical students.

Career

One of the problems in the study of a profession is to discover the career-lines of people who follow it. This in turn requires identification of the significant phases of careers, and the sequences in which they occur. Sequences occur in all the matters we have discussed thus far. Some of them are institutionalized—as the sequence from pre-medical phase, to medical student, to intern, resident, practicing physician, diplomate of a specialty body, etc. Others are not so formally institutionalized and named, but are well known. Still others are more or less unnoticed or not admitted (but nevertheless often anticipated or feared) regularities of change from one ill-defined phase to another. One changes from a young man with teachers and mentors to whom he may turn, into an older man who has become a teacher and a sponsor, even a 'father-figure to younger men. Or one finds that one has less time for the clinic and the laboratory because of the increase of administrative demands upon one's time. One aspect of career is just these shifts from one weighting or combination of activities to another. It is well known that these shifts are accompanied by anxieties, such as shown in the dream of a young woman who had just been made a supervisor of nursing in a large hospital. She dreamed that she suddenly had to get a patient into a respirator at night, and that she had either forgotten how, or else a new model had been brought in—and she fumbled while the patient gasped. The shift from one kind of activity to another entails the danger of losing a skill; it is also a shift from one kind of responsibility to another, from one role to another.

There are, in any kind of career line, points of negative and positive crucial decision. For example, if I have not received my specialty residence in a certain kind of hospital by a certain age, certain further steps are closed. There is also always before a young man the question whether, when, and how often to move from one place of work to another. Some lines of work, and some specialties within medicine, show different patterns of relation between moving and success. One would expect that the career of a man going into private practice might be more affected by his first choice of a place to practice than is the career of a man who goes in for pathology, teaching, or any of the specialties in which work for salary is the rule. There is, in institutions or systems, a certain balance between home-guard success and itinerant success. The home-guard are the people who make their careers with little or no itineracy; the itinerants progress by moving from one place or institution to another. Those who get ahead by moving—from say, smaller to larger schools or hospitals—have to decide whether to move in a small orbit (state or region) or in a large, perhaps national or international, orbit. The decision, or the fact—whether it be by conscious decision or by default—of operating in a small or in a large orbit involves the choice of significant others (reference groups), the people on whose good opinion one stakes one's reputation; those whom one can afford to pay less attention to; and those, perhaps, from whom one must dissociate oneself. It involves, in short, the choice of his closer colleagues, the people who will refer cases to him, the people who will think of him when they want a teammate, the people who see his potentialities and help him to realize them.

Career is, in fact, a sort of running adjustment between a man and the various facts of life and of his professional world. It involves the running of risks, for his career is his ultimate enterprise, his laying of his bets on his one and only life. It contains a set of projections of himself into the future, and a set of predictions about the course of events in the medical world itself. Much is to be learned about career lines, how they are conceived by the students of medicine and how their personal and social backgrounds, school and other training experiences, predispose to turn them in one or another of the many directions in which a medical man may go. It is the sum total of these dispositions and turnings that gives us the kind of distribution of physicians we have among the various ways of practicing and the various places and settings within which medicine is practiced, whether that distribution be good or poor.

We are in a time of great change in the institutions of medicine. Not only is their inner structure changing so that the available positions and careers and the demands made upon those who fill them are in flux both in number and kind, but there are more and more ancillary institutions, more and more connections of medicine with the other concerns and institutions of the world. The younger physician's projection of himself into the future is consequently a projection with more unknowns in it than ever before. The whole trend of the system itself is something of an unknown. So that the problem becomes in part that of adjusting to running, never-completed adjustment. Some will doubtless accept the implications of such open-endedness more than others; some may indeed make it part of their identity to be men who do not seek a fixed identity, men whose constant is that they are open to change, or even men who seek the spots where change is the major assignment. Others may seek, successfully or not, the spots which appear most fixed, the bastions that appear safe from storming. We may find a home-guard of time, as well as of space.

We need studies which will run these various lines of inquiry concurrently, starting in the premedical phase and following the aspirant through into his early years of practice. That is, studies which take him from the time when he is most nearly like a layman in his medical culture, through the full cycle of whatever happens to him in school, to that time in the early years of practice when he is fully a member of the profession, both in his own mind and in that of most people who know him.

FORTY-TWO

Is Education a Discipline?[1]

Is education a discipline? What are the relations between other fields of study and the study of education?

These two questions have been put to us. My first impulse was to dispose of the first with a flat "No" followed by a sentence or two of argument, before proceeding to consideration of the relations of certain kinds of social study to the study of education. I did not follow that impulse; the question becomes more and more important as one gives it thought.

The argument would have been—indeed, it is—that education is one of the major human arts, or complex of arts, but not a discipline. In part, education is custodial care of the young. This is an activity that is increasingly delegated to people other than parents and for a longer period of the child's life than ever before. The school-leaving age is continually being raised, so that nearly all teen-agers are in the custody of public institutions for a good many hours a day. American colleges and universities accept, all too willingly and aggressively, personal custody of young people in their twenties, decreeing the hours of their comings and goings, the objects for which they may organize, and the thoughts which they may think (or at least, express). A young person may escape a good deal of this custody by marrying while he is still going to school or college; the dean of men will

In John Walton and James L. Kuethe, eds., *The Discipline of Education* (Madison: The University of Wisconsin Press; © 1963 by the Regents of the University of Wisconsin), pp. 147–161.

1. I have worked so closely with Howard S. Becker and Blanche Geer that I cannot with certainty say whether an idea came from one or the other of them, or whether it just grew out of our common talk.

then lose interest in the hours he keeps, but they will still count him in and out of the classroom, and his teachers will assign him little daily chores of reading and chide him for not doing them. Such close supervision of college and university students appears amazing to visitors from abroad, as amazing as the freedom which we allow our young children.

The other great art in this complex is the imparting of knowledge, skills, and sentiments. Perhaps there are better ways to word it – the creation of opportunities for learning might be one. This activity is also expanding. There is much more knowledge of certain kinds to be imparted, and we are trying to impart it to a greater proportion of the population than ever before. Because of the rate of technological change, subjects do not stay learned. An increasing number of people are busy learning new things even about the work which they once knew well; they are running the race against obsolescence. Not fewest among these late-learners, or re-learners, are the great numbers of women who, after a spell of child-bearing and rearing, return to work, older and wiser and very industrious, but without seniority and obsolete by a decade. At any rate, the number of people engaged in professional teaching is greatly expanded, as are the subjects they teach and the kinds of people to whom they teach them. Along with this increase, has come a great self-consciousness about methods of teaching and a great deal of experimenting with new techniques, including the use of electronic communication and teaching machines.

The struggle to control the sentiments of the rising generation is likewise engaged in perhaps more self-consciously and on a greater scale than ever before. There are people who make great claims of success in this activity, and who devote a good deal of money to research on it.

Education is, indeed, a major complex of arts. Like the other great arts, it is not a discipline in the sense of offering a single order of phenomena which, when observed and/or manipulated in a systematic way, yield a body of consistent theory. In this respect, education is like the other great practical arts – looking after the sick, keeping order, and distributing justice. All of them, however, give rise to a variety of disciplines and, in turn, use many of their results. These arts are the very springs of human curiosity; they are also great consumers of man's best intellectual and scientific efforts. None of these arts, moreover, is ever completely under the control of the human will, the will of one man or of some small group of men, or even of society at large through its instruments. Yet control over these arts is sought in all societies. The manner of practicing them is the very stuff of the clash of wills and interests; thus, the stuff of politics. Any of these arts is bigger and more perennial than any of the special disciplines.

For disciplines, while they may be established as going concerns within universities, and while each may seek to prove that it was in the beginning, is now, and ever shall be, are passing things. New ones sprout; old ones merge into one another. It is common talk in the physical and biological sciences that the interesting work is being done on the raw edges between the traditional (although still young) disciplines. This is not interdisciplinary work, but work on new frontiers by men who associate with each other because of their interest in the problems at hand; "interdisciplinary work" implies that each party to it means to respect the other's boundaries, while seeing to it that his own discipline gets its share of money, attention, and space in publications. Interdisciplinary work generally means that the parties are determined not to merge their disciplines. If disciplines do not merge, it means either that no intellectual progress is being made, or that there is resistance to reorganization of the university and of research bodies in a way to correspond to the present and emerging state of the frontiers of knowledge. I mean to suggest that organization of the university by disciplines should itself be a matter of study, something on which we keep an open mind. It can choke progress of both the disciplines and the great arts.

Who knows what the disciplines of social science of the future will be? Or the divisions of the sciences of life or of the physical world? Who even knows whether life, society, and the physical world will always be studied so separately as now? Yet we can be quite certain that humans, if there are any, will gather into societies which will have need of the great fundamental arts of which one is education. In any kind of society likely to exist in the future, there will be self-conscious concern over the processes by which people learn and over the ways of organizing the institutions of custody and learning. Education is more enduring than any discipline. To try to cram education into the shell of any discipline is to put the grander into the lesser, the eternal into the temporary.

One might be astonished that the people who are concerned with education should want to bring themselves down in the world by asking that their work be recognized as among the disciplines. Yet it is not surprising, for we are in a period in which professions stand high and in which many occupations, old and new, seek professional standing. As an occupation strives for professional standing, it generally seeks, and may get, a place in the institutions called universities. It will usually claim that the work of the profession rests upon a discipline, perhaps upon a science. Indeed, the rising new professions have brought many aspects of social life under scientific scrutiny; without the pressure of new professions for recognition among the academic disciplines, our universities might be very much more narrow than they are and very much less alive to the possibilities of exploring human behavior. Teachers, the people who administer teaching, and the people who teach teachers and who study schools, have joined the merry chase to be recognized professionally and academically, the latter through declaring education a discipline. Not that many people in education do consider it a single discipline; they are more inclined, I think, to insist upon their *professional* standing. In that, they are like the people in various disciplines, notably psychology, who are now emphasizing, not their character as disciplines, but their proper place as professions. The relation of the academic disciplines to the professions is one of the fundamental problems of our time; it can be stated also as the relation of science to practice, or as the relation of basic to applied research. And this is, in part, the second question to which this paper is directed.

To that second question, I now turn, although it is not really a turning, but a continuing of the same line.

The people engaged in education, in the special sense of teaching teachers and of studying what goes on in schools, are very numerous. They have been so successful in their striving for the admission of their work into the universities that 17 per cent of all Ph.D.'s granted in this country from 1951 to 1958 were given in education; they were half of all Ph.D.'s given in professional fields. Further, 34 per cent of all Ph.D.'s given in these years were given in professional fields, as against 9 per cent in the years from 1911 to 1920.[2] The M.A. has already become overwhelmingly a professional degree; the Ph.D. is following hard, with education leading all other subjects. In the next decade, Ph.D.'s in Education will almost certainly be granted to more people than in all of the physical sciences; they are already about equal in number to those in all of the social sciences. Education is a major—almost overwhelming—part of the American higher academic establishment. Indeed, at a conference called by the New England Board of Higher Education last year, a dean of education openly threatened the critics of education with use of the power which was rapidly passing from the hands of the rest of the university into those of education. Most of the Ph.D.'s, he said, would soon be in education and the rest of the academic profession would have to listen to them. I do not suppose this sentiment is widely shared, but the trend to which it calls attention is not to be ignored.

Education, as an academic subject, is primarily the study of schools; the preparation of schoolteachers and administrators has been the aim of departments of education. To belong to the profession of education, one must have something to do with schools. Just as in the business world, a man is asked whether he has ever had to meet a payroll, so in the world of

2. B. Berelson, *Graduate Education in the United States* (New York: McGraw-Hill, 1960), p. 37.

education he is asked whether he has ever actually taught school. People who have not done so are outsiders; they have not been set upon by parents, school boards, and inquisitorial senators. They have not been assailed by classroom air, thick and sweet with the smell of young America and dusty with chalk. They have not been the butt of academic jokes about departments of education. The people who have worked in schools and who have borne the brunt of the attacks which are made upon school-teachers in this country and have had to cope with the unsolicited advice which everyone has to give about how and what to teach have had plenty of reason to be suspicious of outsiders. They may be pardoned for the belief that they have a sort of monopoly over the study of schools and the teaching and learning which takes place in them.

It is a part of professional ideology to insist that those who practice a profession are the only true and legitimate students of the branches of knowledge applied in it. Educationists do not believe it more than other professionals. Physicians have often been loath to accept biological research except on their own terms. Nurses, who are nowadays much concerned with research, are highly critical of research in which nurses are not the leading spirits. But the fact that education shares with other professions this jealousy does not make it a more sound or justifiable attitude.

The people most concerned, year in and year out, with an institution will of course have more to contribute to a study of it than any other group of people. They will have intimate knowledge of its inner working. They will sense its problems in their bones. But their very closeness to it makes many facts concerning it fall into their blind spot; and close identification is accompanied by vested interest, no matter how high the purposes of those involved.

There are problems which can be studied only by outsiders. Let us take an example. The changing of the name "teachers college" to simply "college," or "state college," prefixed by the name of a town or region of the state, has swept the country like a prairie fire. It is associated, of course, with a change to a more general curriculum leading to a bachelor's degree in subjects other than education (although I have yet to hear of a case in which the program in elementary education did not remain the central feature). One would expect that such a change of name and aim would be accompanied by internal conflicts of greater or less intensity between those who have long been attached to the institution and who have moved in the orbit of school systems and those newer people who come in primarily as college teachers and who have moved about or may move about in an orbit of liberal arts colleges. There is plenty of evidence that there is such conflict. Why should there not be? Changes in the aims, self-image, and public image of institutions are seldom achieved without conflict. It is in the interest of American education that attempts to change existing institutions to fit new needs and standards should be thoroughly understood. This can be done only by objective, comparative study with no holds barred. Yet I sat in a group composed largely of school people who claimed to be (and were) devoted to educational research and who condemned, out of hand, a proposal to study this change in a certain institution. Why? Because, they said, the change in name had already been made almost throughout the country until there are no teachers colleges left. Anthropologists speak of "name magic"! I should have thought that the generality of the change of name would have been a reason for studying its course and consequences. I could only conclude, since they were intelligent men, that they were protecting a vested interest, or perhaps they were merely trying to keep the peace. The people most involved in an institution often prefer not to have its most basic issues brought into the open. The protective device most often used is to deny the existence of the problem.

This is but one example. We, in this country, have an amazing variety of educational enterprises, initiated by various groups for a great variety of purposes. As time goes on, these institutions change in order to survive or in order to achieve new purposes. At the present time we are engaged in a great effort to make these institutions serve our aim, to achieve the national goals of equality of opportunity and high quality of achievement. In some respects our varied educational enterprises are becoming more alike as we pursue these goals; in others, they are becoming more diverse. Certain new enterprises are being initiated to provide education for special kinds of students; others, to provide certain kinds of education and training. Within many larger institutions there are special experimental programs. Incidentally, I have heard the proposal to study such an experiment called unscientific and of little use, because the experiment is unique and not statistically representative of American colleges. An odd conception of science! Many institutions once established for certain kinds of students and for certain kinds of education are being greatly changed to meet new demands. The internal functioning of these many institutions requires penetrating comparative study with particular attention to the problems of change and resistance to change. Their relations to each other require the same penetrating study, with special attention to the actual, as well as declared, division of labor among them. Study of these matters will require the best that we have in skill of observation and in theory and analysis of organizations.

As in all good comparative study of institutions, the concepts and methods of study will have to be drawn not merely from the particular kind of organization under study, but from organizations of many kinds and purposes. While the purposes for which an organization is established may have some effect on its form and functioning, they do not make an organization so peculiar that it can be fruitfully compared only with others devoted to the same purpose and studied only by people devoted to that purpose. Quite the contrary. One cannot gauge the effect of purposes unless one compares organizations of quite diverse purposes.

I say this so emphatically for two reasons. One is that, in this day of necessarily great specialization in the social sciences, there are people who devote their whole careers to study of one variety of institution—medical, business, governmental, educational. This specialization will fail of its goals if it is not countered and enriched by comparisons of organizations of various kinds.

The second reason is that professional specialization often leads to the *specialists' veto* in planning research and in granting the funds for it. By pointing to some small flaw or supposed naïveté in a research plan, those who are specialists on the kind of organization concerned can often prevent the research from being done, thus protecting their own monopoly and perhaps preventing some important issue from being brought into the open. "How can these people, who obviously are naive about our organization since they call our superintendent a manager, and don't know that we have five grades of help instead of four, possibly learn anything of value?"—so runs the reasoning. The ignorance and insight of the outsider do not coincide with those of the insider.

By combining what those inside can see and what they know, with what a comparative, objective student from outside can see, powerfully penetrating and useful studies of American educational institutions can be made. We must make them if we are to meet the educational problems of the country and of the great variety of individuals who compose it.

Although it is not my mandate to talk of fields other than education, I think it important to say that the relation of the inside professional and the outside researcher is essentially the same in all the many fields in our society in which there is a profession, or several professions, especially concerned with an institutional complex. We have many such institutional complexes, and the trend toward professionalism is strong in them. Objective, comparative study of them, with full access to their delicate and sometimes secret inner workings, is itself a delicate thing. It requires frankness between the parties concerned and some sort of responsible understanding in each case.

I have said, perhaps indirectly, that one of the things social scientists can offer to the field of education is study of the whole complement or system of educational institutions, study in which each is seen as a going concern with its own internal working constitution (relations and distribution of functions and power among the categories of people involved, including the pupils and students) and in which each, further, is seen in its relationship with other such institutions and with forces and institutions of other kinds.

One may speak of a basic ecology of education, of a complex of symbiotic relations among institutions. A teacher in a certain state university writes thus: "At —————— we have been particularly hard hit by the general improvement of standards in certain adjacent states. Our out-of-state enrollment runs about 25%, more than half from one state. Their turn-down rate swells their junior colleges—and we get lots of them."

The problem of selection of students in any institution is a function of the selection in other institutions. I do not say that this is a bad thing; only that we need studies of such relationships in metropolitan areas, states, and regions on which to base planning of our educational enterprises. Along with an ecology of selection of students by colleges and of colleges by students, we require one of college and university teachers in which we would learn more about the academic market, of the orbits in which academic people move. This would include also study of alternative careers in various lines of academic work.

But study of the ecology of education should go beyond the conventional schools and colleges, indeed beyond all kinds of schools and colleges. For, in spite of our colossal and growing rate of attendance at colleges, most of our young people do not get and probably do not want to get to college at all. Still, they learn things; they have skills, ideas, and knowledge. What skills, ideas, and knowledge? We do not know. Nor do we know how they learn what they do learn. Schools and colleges represent only part of the total teaching and learning which go on in society. Even in the schools, young people learn a great deal not taught by the teachers—some of it is, indeed, contrary to what the teachers teach, or believe they teach.

Sociologists, anthropologists, and social psychologists should actively study education in the broadest sense and in its total setting, not merely in the institutions ordinarily thought of as the educational system. Those institutions themselves we should study not merely in relation to one another, as suggested, but in relation to family, community, workshop, city streets, prisons, taverns, and the means of mass communication. And all this not merely in order that we may learn to bend these other institutions and groups to the will and aims of educational institutions; that might be one result. Feedback in the contrary direction might be an equally valuable result. This broader study should be done with a sense of history and with an eye to the natural history of institutions and of our society as a whole.

I have said little of the other topic—the inner constitution and workings of educational institutions. A large number of people are working on that problem and in a great variety of institutions. The social climates of high

schools, the culture and perspectives of students in various kinds of undergraduate and professional schools, the levels and directions of student
effort — these things are being studied. The literature is known to all who
are likely to read these pages. Experiments are also being made in methods
of teaching. We talk of the merits of lecturing as against discussion, of large
and small classes, of teaching machines, of spoon-feeding as against putting
students on their own. Yet we have almost no systematic observations of
classroom behavior, of the interaction of teacher with pupils and students.
Obviously, no teacher delivers ten or twelve or fifteen prepared and organized lectures a week, or even five. Teachers are not supermen. But probably most American college teachers do something in their classrooms for
twelve or more hours a week. What is it they do? Do they mumble in their
beards? Do they engage in chitchat? Do they really discuss subject matter
and ideas with their students? In what combinations do they do these or
other things? And how, for their part, do the students take part in what
goes on? What skills have they developed for controlling what goes on in
the classroom? And how is all of this affected by the teacher's conception
of his job, and by what he considers to be the contingencies of his survival
and advancement?

I am convinced that many American college teachers have learned how
to restrict production, their own and that of their students, as a means of
survival, or at least as a means of leading a moderately peaceful existence.
Most of our studies are based on the assumption that the teachers — and the
administrators of the institutions in which they work — have as their goal an
ever higher level of effort on the part of the students. If we were to study
the interaction among administrators, teachers, pupils, and students, we
might very well discover whole systems of checks upon the efforts of all
concerned, a knot of fetters made tighter by the movements of all.

The study of this most basic of all educational activities, the goings-on in
classrooms, combined with study of the other nuclei of interaction — of
student with student, of teacher with teacher, administrator with administrator, and of each with the others and with various lay publics — is something which social scientists can do and which must eventually be done if
we are to understand educational processes.

With it, I leave the matter, knowing that I have not given a catalog of the
kinds of research which ordinarily go by the name of sociology of education.

FORTY-THREE

The Humble and the Proud:

The Comparative Study of Occupations

This paper takes as its point of departure two earlier statements of mine concerning *Sociology of Work*. Almost two decades ago I wrote:

> We need to rid ourselves of any concepts which keep us from seeing that the essential problems of men at work are the same whether they do their work in the laboratories of some famous institution or in the messiest vat room of a pickle factory (Rohrer and Sherif, 1951:318).

and more recently, in a personal communication concerning studies of medical and college students:[1]

> The ideas grew out of study of lowly factories and humble occupations—which is the right place to start, for everything happens in them and people don't try to cover up the seamy side so much as in more mobile pursuits.

Both these sentences refer to method. Both, as do most statements concerning sociological method, express a social rhetoric. For such statements are written at a given moment in the history of the world, in a given

---

Reprinted by permission of the publisher from *The Sociological Quarterly,* Vol. XI, No. 2, 1970. Copyright 1970, Midwest Sociological Society.

1. When Becker, Geer, Strauss, and I had completed the study of a medical school, reported in *Boys in White* (1961), we were asked to study the undergraduate life of the same university and the result was *Making the Grade: The Academic Side of Student Life* (1968). The bulk of the field work on both studies was done by Howard S. Becker and Blanche Geer. Anselm Strauss had a hand in the study of the medical school, doing the "dirty work" of staying up all night with interns and residents. Marsh Ray was a member of the field team in the study of undergraduates. I was the entrepreneur of both studies, a role which very soon passed to my co-workers, Geer and Becker. They also did the bulk of the writing.

place, at a certain point in the development of the science of sociology, and by a given person. That person sees things from a certain perspective; he speaks in the hope that others will accept his perspective and use it in their work. A critic complained that the title *Boys in White* (1961) downgraded medical students; we should have called them men. We called them boys because it seemed to us that, after having been treated like men in the last years of college, they were treated like boys in medical school. *Making the Grade* (1968), even without an "S" on grade, suggests that students misdirect their academic efforts; the book tries to tell why they direct them as they do. Titles, statements of method, and choice of problems for study are all a kind of social rhetoric; one hopes his rhetoric will call attention to neglected aspects of reality, correct biases, and so change methods of study that better findings and theories will result.

Why did we give such titles to those two books? Behind that lies the deeper question: why did we make the kind of study which would naturally be reported under these titles? Why did I make those two statements which I quoted earlier? Would I make the same statement now to students and colleagues going out to study people at their work?

Empirical Beginnings in the Sociology of Work

In the late 1930's, throughout the 1940's, and into the 1950's, several of us at the University of Chicago were engaged in studies of industry.[2] In 1939, I began to teach a course on professions. People from various departments of the university and from many occupations came into the course; many of them wanted to write about the efforts of their own occupation to have itself recognized as a profession. It is said that our image of the devil—the Christian devil, that is—is based on the testimony in ecclesiastical courts of people possessed. From the claims and hopes of people in the many occupations seeking professional status, we learned what the concept means to people. I soon changed the name of the course to "The Sociology of Work," both to overcome to some extent the constant preoccupation with upward mobility of occupations and also to include studies of a

2. W. Lloyd Warner, Robert J. Havighurst, Burleigh Gardner, Frederick Harbison, William F. Whyte, and I were members of a Committee on Human Relations in industry. Many graduate students worked with us, as well as other members of the staff. Among the students of sociology who had a hand in the various projects in industry or in study of occupations were: Robert Dubin, Harold Wilensky, Harvey L. Smith, Melville Dalton, Edward Gross, Robert W. Habenstein, Edith Lentz, Donald Roy, the late Mozell Hill, William Hale, David Solomon, Orvis Collins, Lee Rainwater, and David Moore. There were others at the peak of the enterprise, and also some later. The peak in the study of occupations came later than that of industrial studies. Some members of the committee continued to work together, but on somewhat different projects.

greater variety of occupations and problems. A good many students wrote papers on the occupations of their fathers, their kin, and even on their own. Some of the papers were developed into more systematic studies and were presented as theses. The occupations considered included — I write them down as they come to me — janitors, junk dealers (and how they come to engage in the recovery industry), furriers, funeral directors, taxi drivers, rabbis, school teachers, jazz musicians, mental hospital attendants, osteopaths, city managers, pharmacists, and YMCA secretaries. Others studied lawyers, physicians, and the clergy, as well as the newer professions or the newer specialities in these older professions. We studied workers, union leaders, and management in a variety of industries. As the war wore on, industry wanted more workers and some of them were willing to consider hiring Negroes, women, and even the Japanese (our enemy). That gave occasion to learn something about acceptance and rejection of new kinds of colleagues by workers in industry, as well as by management and the professions. We also got clues about how levels and directions of effort and production are determined in both lowly and proud kinds of work. Those who perform services, it turned out, prefer some customers, clients, patients, or even sinners, to others. Some tasks in any occupation are preferred over others; some are jealously guarded, while others are gladly delegated to those they consider lesser breeds, such as women or Negroes, either inside or outside the occupation (profession). The contingencies which face people as they run their life-cycle, their career at work, turned out to be a constant theme. The great variety of students and of occupations and work situations studied stimulated the search for and the finding of common themes. Some of these common themes I put into an *Outline for Sociological Study of an Occupation* which was used by a whole generation of students.

The historic circumstance was that large numbers of graduate students were coming to Chicago to study sociology. They had come from a variety of ethnic backgrounds, and wrote about them, being at once proud and a little ashamed, most certainly self-conscious! They strove to be both emancipated from and loyal to their backgrounds. In Robert E. Park's time and later in the courses of Louis Wirth and Herbert Blumer they recognized in themselves "the marginal man." The new courses on work and industry perhaps made them more aware of the occupations that lay in their family (and ethnic) backgrounds; occupations to which they had become marginal. Social mobility generally takes the form of abandoning one's father's occupation. If these students started their sociological analysis on the humbler occupations, it was by accident. They started where they were — or had been. They should have been struck into pillars of salt. Those students were not alienated from their milieux; emancipated, yes, but not alienated. Sociology written by the emancipated is different from sociology written — or acted — by the alienated. Emancipation is a very delicate balance between detachment and involvement.

An Emerging Comparative Frame of Reference

If those students — who studied janitors, factory workers, furriers and the like — compared the lowly with the proud, it was not a degrading of the noble, but an ennobling of what some might have considered less than noble. As these studies went on, many of these students, as well as myself, became convinced that if a certain problem turned up in one occupation, it was nearly certain to turn up in all. We were skeptical when someone said, for instance, that in their favorite occupation there was no "restriction of production," no exclusion of some people from the intimacy and protection of colleagueship, no favoring of some clients or customers over others, no codes of behavior with supporting informal sanctions, no secrecy, no sense of rank. The thing was to discover in what form the problem turned up, how serious it was, and how it was handled. Our aim was to discover patterns of interaction and mechanisms of control, the things over which people in a line of work seek to gain control, the sanctions which they have or would like to have at their disposal, and the bargains which were made — consciously or less consciously — among a group of workers and between them and the other kinds of people in the drama of their work. There is no absolute virtue in studying one kind of work rather than another, if the inward frame of one's mind is comparative. The essence of the comparative frame is that one seeks differences in terms of dimensions common to all the cases. If one becomes over-enamored of a particular occupation, he is likely to describe it in terms which suggest that it is not comparable to others. If he seeks common dimensions, the differences between occupations become clearer, and more impressive.

Even at the time of which I am speaking, there were many institutions and many people of various disciplines studying the problems of industrial and professional work. Any student of such matters would be aware of the early work of Werner Sombart on the source of the modern industrial labor force (1927); of Henri de Man on the loss of joy in work (1929); of Max Weber's long — and untranslated — monograph on the sources and adaptation of the labor force of modern industry (1908), and his other one on the psychophysics of industrial work (1908-09);[3] and of Carr-Saunders' book on *The Professions* (1933) — to mention just a few of the classics in

3. Weber's works on science as a profession and on politics as a profession are much better known as are his many references to functionaries and professionals in the body of his *Economy and Society* which is now available in full and in English (1968).

the field. The industrial and post-industrial world has become self-conscious about its labor force, about education for work, and about recruitment in various kinds of work, as well as about the unemployables of city and rural slums. There are endless new problems demanding attention. The economists appear to have lost interest in problems of the organization of work, the motivation of workers, and, to some extent, in the distribution of goods and services. People called sociologists and social psychologists have picked up these problems.

The Encompassing System of Work Organization

It is not my purpose to talk of the state of such studies, but instead I will turn to an aspect of the study of professional work which was not fully developed in the earlier studies. We were inclined to look at the occupation as an entity, thus neglecting somewhat, but not completely, the general system of which it is part. Professions are, in a measure greater than ever, parts within larger wholes. Each profession seeks a monopoly; it does so in part by limiting its activities and the area of its responsibilities and tasks, meantime delegating purposely or by default many related tasks and responsibilities to other occupations. Within the profession itself, specialization marks out limited fields and creates a division of labor internal to the profession.

No profession fulfills all the wants in its general field; nor does it serve the wants of all its potential clients equally. The most complete professional — but not economic — monopoly I can think of in our society is that of the undertaker. No one escapes him; but even he is engaged in a special activity in the great field of birth, health and disease, and death. The core of his activity is the urgent and necessary disposal of human remains. His domain is slightly confused by the new transplanting surgery. It is expanded by his exploitation of some of the deepest of human sentiments and of some of the tragi-comic aspects of the culture of the survivors. Around an almost irreducible core the undertaker creates — in interaction with his clients — a body of wants and then seeks to satisfy them. I take the undertaker simply as an example to suggest that the activities of a profession must be seen in the larger setting and in terms of its place among other occupations and activities. If some occupations are more proud and others more humble, there are differences of prestige within any given occupation as well. It may be that the prouder or more prestigeful the occupation, as measured by its position on the scales used by students of that phenomenon, the greater the differences within it. I suspect that the very fact of a profession being high in prestige gives some of those within it the power to make the most of the symbolic value of their name and to monopolize — or oligarchize — the facilities necessary to practice as they wish and the positions of power and prestige in their work system. As this elite develops, by contre-coup (back-lash) there may develop within the profession a sort of lower-middle class which, in professional matters, will oppose the will of the elite, although they will not completely oppose them; what prestige this lower middle has within the profession depends upon their recognizing in some measure the standards of qualification set up by the elite. They might be called the fundamentalists of the trade, upholding to the letter some conception of their work which they believe was laid down by some founding father- or mother-hero — human, demigod, or divine. Still lower in the scale there may be people who, though legitimate in qualification, so far fail that they are hardly in the colleagueship of the profession at all, and they work in their own way outside it. There are in medicine, law, in the academic profession and the clergy, a number of levels — not merely points on a scale but clusters of practising members.

The Naming Function of Professionals

To understand them one must understand the system, including the clients and their wants. Persons and organizations have problems; they want things done for them — for their bodies and souls, for their social and financial relations, for their cars, houses, bridges, sewage systems; and they want things done to the people they consider their competitors or their enemies. What they want done no doubt has some existence apart from the system of services within which the professions operate. But we scarcely know what their problems would be; that is, in what circumstances they would think they had problems, how they would define the problems, to whom they would turn for help, what they would offer in return for it, what they would consider good service, and what recourse they would have if the service were not satisfactory. For it is in the course of interaction with one another and with the professionals that the problems of people are given definition. Pains and complaints are the lot of the human (and other) species. But, diseases are inventions; they are definitions of conditions and situations. The humans who suffer may or may not accept the professionals' definition of what ails them and their recommendations of what to do. Shame and guilt may be generated without benefit of professionals, but sin and absolution from it have become professional in definition; clients accept or reject in varying degree the professional definition and the professional cure. If belief is general, and supported by political power, the professionals have strong sanctions in their hands. If a given system of religious beliefs is generally accepted and is supported by political power, religion and law become one system. The professionals of religion can make lack of belief not merely heresy, but a crime; the priest is supported by the instruments of the law—by courts and police. Political beliefs may be equally mandatory, as in certain countries; political piety, political guilt and sin take on the quality of the corresponding religious phenomena in a society of one mandatory religion; in both cases the bodies of the guilty may be burnt just in case the fires of hell are not really as hot as they are said to be (an odd bit of unbelief on the part of the professionals of religion; there is always a bit of skepticism in professional belief).

The lawyer, by his efforts on behalf of his client against his client's opponents, has a hand in defining the law. He may defend those who live by setting up a counter-law and a counter-system of protection—as do the leaders of organized crime. But the lawyer's monopoly over his function is practically complete, and the completeness consists in the power of the state to enforce what the courts—the lawyers' institution—decide are proper grievances and proper remedies.

As for education, the power of the academic to say who is learned has been great. He dispenses a powerful instrument—a set of prerogatives, of access to positions and goods. But without a strong prevailing professional definition of learning, what boy ever would have sought to learn to write doggerel verse in school Greek with vowels pronounced in the English way?[4] Certainly it was not by direct application of this bizarre skill that the man earned his place in the world. The ability and the willingness to acquire it made him a member of a select group who were given access to careers demanding high ability, no doubt, but little direct use of that particular kind of learning. The society of learned men had to prove themselves in various activities, and many of them got great pleasure from their classical studies. But the whole system was an artifact. It had a beginning and has come to an end, or nearly so. Other kinds of learning have become legitimate and new professionals foster them. Some of them are of immediate utility, such as in keeping books, in making engines run, in going to the moon and back; the line from academic learning to its application is often long and complicated, and highly institutionalized.

As society changes, the problems of people and institutions change. The changes in professional recognition, definition, and management of the wants which arise from those changes are by no means direct and immediate. What are the relations between changing problems, the definition of personal and collective wants arising from them, and the inward structure of professions, including the place of their elites in leading the way to new

---

4. Ong (1969:627-630) states this point in that portion of his Daedalus article entitled "The Atrophy of Puberty Rites." I had not seen his article when I wrote this paper. I recommend it to social scientists, not to make them smile knowingly at the plight of the poor teachers of Greek, but to make them take thought about their own puberty rites.

definitions and new ways of distributing their services? These are questions to be studied in a great variety of cases. In a rather rambling way, I have been saying that *professionals do not merely serve; they define the very wants which they serve.* Thus, the old dictum that the professions fulfill the basic wants or desires of people and society is much too simple. We must start from the assumption that even with respect to biological wants, the serving professions are in constant interaction with the people they serve, but in contact with and responsive to some kinds of people more than others, and with society at large, in varying degree, initiating changes and responding to them. Often the response is resistance, sometimes active innovation. We know far too little about these processes.

The professions—occupations of high prestige—work only on those wants which are defined as legitimate. In medicine, some diseases or troubles are more respectable than others; some (e.g., venereal diseases) are not respectable at all. The desire to be cured of them is considered legitimate, and in our time it has become permissible to talk about them and to undertake programs of prevention; it is still not common, however, for people to gain great prestige from having cured prestigeful patients of them.

To want to bring a pregnancy to premature end—abortion—has not been considered legitimate, but many women have felt this want most urgently. I believe I would be right in stating that there has never been a society in which there were not some people willing to satisfy this want. One might rank pregnancies from those ardently wanted to those most desperately not wanted, from blessing through neutrality to nuisance to catastrophe. We have seen in our time a tremendous change of attitude toward the legitimacy of abortion. In England changes in the law appear to have created a great international demand. Some physicians have in the past few weeks been struck from the rolls in London for having allegedly drummed up abortion clients from abroad. Thus has an illegitimate want become at least formally legitimate; but that does not mean that those who satisfy the want will gain positions of prestige in the medical system. But to the extent that abortion does become an accepted part of medical practice, one may suppose that the illegitimate abortionist will disappear. The latter have been of many kinds. Some have been apostles of freedom, courageously running the risk of prison and loss of standing in the name of delivering women from their chains. Others have practiced abortion somewhat cautiously on patients referred to them in various ways either by respectable physicians or by respectable women who knew somebody who knew somebody who went to Dr. So-and-So. Women without medical license (the midwife and the granny) have also filled this want, for patients with little or no access to the middle-class referral circle, but also sometimes for the lady in distress. And always there has been, and no doubt will be, the decision as to who is a legitimate case—who has a right to ask for abortion. Class, age, marital status, the pains which threaten if a child is born of the pregnancy—these and other variables will no doubt determine whether a physician will accept a patient for abortion, even if the law allows. The legitimacy of the want—and of the service to fulfill it—thus seems to lie partly in the nature of the difficulty, but also partly in the person, in his status, and the source of his troubles, and partly in the state of society. The boundaries of legitimate want, and of legitimate professional services are not fixed, but tend to vary with time, person, and circumstance. Within the limits of the legitimate, some activities, some services, and services to some clients are more respectable and lend more prestige to the professional than do others.

At the margins of the legitimate and beyond it some professionals operate, as well as persons in other occupations, without professional standing, some even outside the law. Also within the limits of the legitimate and the respectable, the procedures become so numerous and complicated that the profession at the center of the system must delegate a great deal of its work to people in other occupations. This is certainly and noticeably so in matters of health and medicine, where the so-called paramedical professions and occupations have multiplied with resulting problems of authority, the making of decisions, and the allocating of functions to the many members of the medical and health system. Also the specialties of the medical profession themselves tend each to have their own philosophy of medical practice, their own research emphases, and their own notions of the best way to distribute their therapeutic and preventive services. Finally, as the system becomes more complicated, as more kinds of people are involved in it; it becomes crucial to find out how innovations are made and how they become legitimate, if they do.

We may also ask whether there is any field of human wants in which the professional definition is fully accepted by everyone. Perhaps there is always a raw edge where professional definition and practice do not utterly match wants and active demands. There will perhaps always be doomed people who will not accept the professional judgment of their ailment; people who will be curious about things the educational establishment thinks there is no need to be curious about. On these raw edges there may occur what one might call amateur experimenting, experimenting without license or mandate. The mandate of the professional establishment may thus be questioned.

Something of this kind is occurring in the field of education—that of teaching and learning. It is the field in which the professionals are divided into probably the greatest number of discontinuous ranks, each with its own license and mandate. It is the field in which there is probably the greatest range in the measure of authority used in course of performing the service; there is everything from complete dictatorship of the teacher (give me the answer I want or be damned), to equalitarian relations between teacher and learning (both being eager learners), to dictatorship of the pupil. There is always involved in it the relation between generations, as well as relationships between social statuses. The system has depended upon the young — the to-be-taught — internalizing the teaching generations' image of the society into which the young were to be initiated and their concept of the knowledge, skills, and personal traits which would be useful and should be satisfying. Apparently a large number of the younger generation does not see the future through the same glasses as their teachers, and those whom they believe the teachers represent. Perhaps for the first time in history, the young take a gloomier view of the future than do their elders. Certainly their concept of social time and distance — of the relation of learning to action in social matters — is different from that on which modern education has been built.

I believe that the lesson of that earlier advice about the humble and the proud has been pretty well learned. Furthermore, many young people now seek emancipation from their parents' pride, not from their humility. The rhetoric of our time should emphasize study of the whole settings in which particular occupations (professional and non-professional) occur, with attention to the shifting boundaries between them and the kind of cooperation required for any one of them to perform effectively; to the shifting boundaries between the professional systems and the clienteles they serve; and finally, to the development of new definitions of wants growing out of constant social interaction and change. In the course of doing such study, we might learn more about the fate of professional mandates — and pride including our own.

References

Becker, Howard S., Blanche Geer, and Everett C. Hughes
    1968 *Making the Grade: The Academic Side of Student Life*. New York: John Wiley and Sons.
Becker, Howard S., Blanche Geer, Everett C. Hughes, and Anseim Strauss
    1961 *Boys in White*. Chicago: University of Chicago Press.
Carr-Saunders, A.M. and P.A. Wilson
    1933 *The Professions*. London: Macmillan.

de Man, Henri
  1929 *Joy in Work*. Cedar Paul (trans.). London: George Allen & Unwin, Ltd.
Hughes, Everett C.
  1951 "Work and the self." Pp. 313–323 in John Rohrer and Muzafer Sherif (eds.), *Social Work at the Crossroads*. New York: Harper & Brothers.
Ong, W.
  1969 "Crisis and Understanding in the humanities." *Daedalus* 98 (Summer): 617–640.
Sombart, Werner
  1937 "Capitalism." Pp. 195-208 in *Encyclopaedia of the Social Sciences,* Vol. 11. New York: Macmillan.
  1927 "Die Anpassung der Bevölkerung an die Bedürfnisse des Kapitalismus." Pp. 363–469 in Werner Sombart. *Das Wirtschaftsleben im Zeitalter des Hochkapitalismus,* München: Duncker & Humblot.
Weber, Max
  1968 *Economy and Society: An Outline of Interpretive Sociology* (Complete translation of *Wirtschaft und Gesellschaft*). Guenther Roth (trans.). Towata, New Jersey: Bedminster Press, Inc.
  1924 "Auslese und Anpassung (Berufswahl und Berufschicksal) der Arbeiterschaft der Geschlossenen Grossindustrie (1908)," pp. 1–60; also, "Zur Psychophysik der Industriellen Arbeit (1908–09)," pp. 61–225 in Max Weber, *Gesammelte Aufsätze zur Soziologie und Sozialpolitik,* Tübingen: Mohr, 1924.

PART IV

The Study of Society

FORTY-FOUR

The Improper Study of Man

The proper study of mankind is man. But what men shall we study to learn most about mankind, or simply about people? Those long dead, those now living, those unborn? The learned or the unlettered? The lowly, or those of high degree? Those nearby and of color and deportment like the student's own, or men of strange mien and demeanour? The men of the kraal, or those of the city? Faithful or infidel, the virtuous or the vicious? Are all equally human, or are some a little more so than others, so that what one learns about them is of wider application? Where should one start? At the earliest possible beginning, working toward the present by way of the peoples who were in some sense more directly our ancestors? Shall we produce the future from the lines of the past? Or should we, exploiting our experience of living men, apply to both past and future the lessons of the present?

And by what means shall we learn of those whom we choose to study? Suppose we elect to study living people. Shall we put our trust in studying great numbers, or at least such numbers as, properly selected, will represent all sorts and conditions of men in true proportion? Or shall we pick a few whose doings we observe as under a microscope and whose minds we probe for thoughts, desires, and memories, even for such as they themselves know not of? By what ideas, schemes, and formulae shall we reduce what we find to order? And, not least, how much of what we learn shall we tell those whom we have studied, the larger public, or our colleagues? What principles shall guide us in the discovery of men's secrets; what, in the telling of them?

Shall we wait for those crucial things to happen which offer most increase to our knowledge of this or that aspect of human life, and travel fast
and far to catch events on the wing? Or shall we set up experiments,
bringing people together under circumstances so controlled as to get precisely the answers we want next? Shall we study people in small groups
and communities, and hope to find ways of expanding our findings without
distortion to the big world? Shall we look at people where nothing happens
save the turn of seasons and generations, and where men are of one breed
and of one mind, taking that as man's normal state? Or shall we study men
in the seething flux of cities, migrations, crusades, and wars, wherever
breeds mingle and minds clash?

To what of people's doings shall we more closely attend: their politics,
their religion, their work, their play, their poems, their philosophies, their
sciences, their crafts? What, finally, should be the form of our questions:
"What were people like and what did they do?" "What are they doing?"
"What will they do?" or "What would they do if—?"

The academic departments which study people are distinguished from
each other by their choices from among these and similar possibilities.
Some species of academic man insist on a single answer, explicitly stated.
Most of us combine explicit answers with less conscious predilection for
some kinds of human material rather than others. Some like to think of
themselves as scientists; others as artists, critics, or moral judges. Some
love the adventure of digging up manuscripts long buried in dust. Some like
to crack a script, or to put together the fragments of ancient pots or
temples. Others like to express behavior in mathematical formulae. Still
others like to study living men, to discover new things about their own kind
still warm, or to detect commonplace motives under the apparently strange
ways of exotic people. But preference for one kind of study does not
prevent scholars from having a try at other kinds and methods of study
now and again. Again and again some academic people, or even rank
outsiders, discontent with the set ways of academic study, go off on some
new path of discovery, or simply take as their major preoccupation what
others have considered a side issue.

So it was, in the century of evolution, that a number of naturalists,
philosophers, historians, and students of the law assembled, classified, and
sought to put into "evolutionary" order the varied customs reported as
practiced throughout the world, and especially by those peoples most
removed from nineteenth-century Europe in time, distance, civilization,
and race. Some of these men called their work *sociology*. Toward the end
of the century English and American philanthropists and reformers visited
the slums of the great and growing cities, described the ways of the people
who lived there, counted and tabulated the things that appeared the best

indicators of their misery. Their surveys were called *sociology*. Some French legal scholars sought explanations for the alleged penchant of modern people to follow the crowd rather than their ancestors in both virtues and vices. A sharp-tongued Yale professor, Sumner, and, a decade later, an Italian engineer and economist, Pareto, got concerned about those aspects of human social behavior—usages and sentiments—which did not yield good price curves. They wrote treatises on *sociology*.

In addition to a name, these varied pursuits had in common a concern with the classifying of human doings, with the relations of events rather than with the events themselves. They also cut across that organization of the academic studies of man by which the state, the church, economic life, literature, and the like, as well as the various periods of history and the various regions and countries of the world, were each the special domain of some organized group of scholars, and of one department of a university. As historians of human learning have been quick to say, others had gone off on these tangents before. What was new was that these *sociologists,* and people influenced by them, gained a footing in the universities, especially so in the newer American ones. The older scholarly guilds cried, "Trespass," and those of classical bent slew the sociologists with the true but irrelevant accusation that their name, although of noble lineage, was a bastard, being half Latin, half Greek. As do the members of any budding profession or academic specialty seeking access to the sacred precincts, the sociologists sought and found ancient and honored ancestors, founded a society and journals, and have since been arguing about what academic ways to get set in. In the debate and in their deeds they are moving toward a certain combination of answers to the questions raised about the proper study of mankind.

By predilection rather than by logic, most sociologists work on the here and now. Although vast apparatuses have been set up to catch and spread knowledge of current doings, not all is recorded; and of what is recorded, not all is spread abroad. There is an economy of observing, recording, and disseminating the news. There is also a politics of it, a balance between revealing and concealing, in which all people and all organized institutions are in some measure involved. It has become part of the mission of sociologists to catch the goings-on of people and institutions at the time; or at least to catch those parts of them which tend to be overlooked by students of politics and economics, and by those who report on and criticize what are considered the serious works of art and of the mind. The lives of the families across the tracks; the reactions of housewives to the morning soap opera; how the men down in the garage unconsciously weave their own inarticulate anxieties and yearnings into their talk of what happened to L'il Abner this morning; the slow moving changes in the level of

schooling of those Americans who are called Negro. These things don't
make the news, but they make the story comprehensible when it breaks
into the headlines. One might say that part of the calling of sociologists is
to push back the frontiers of the news so as to get at the news back of, or
below the news, not in the sense of getting at the lowdown, but in that of
giving the reported events another dimension, that of the perspective of
culture and of social processes.

One part of this job is undertaken by the surveyors of opinion. They
have invented all sorts of devices for getting at what people think and do
about a great variety of matters, large and small. No one of the particular
opinions or actions they report would make the news columns, as does the
fiftieth home run of a big league player or the visit of a monarch to a
country fair. Neither the actors nor the actions, taken singly, are thought
worthy of note. Put together, they are the ground swell on which prominent
figures and great projects rise and fall, run their courses or founder. Mr.
Unnamed Millions is, as many have noted lately, more and more a gentleman of leisure, a grand consumer of goods and of the popular arts and of
the innumerable "services" of our civilization. His choices make or break
the great institutions and enterprises. Keeping abreast of him is a job
which, like woman's work, is never done. Predicting what he will do, even
in the short run, has some of the features of predicting the weather. Many
sociologists specialize in these very jobs; they are the quantitative historians of their own times. One of the risks of their trade is that their errors
of prediction are more quickly discovered than those of people in some
other lines of human study.

Working on this frontier is not a matter merely of setting up machinery
to watch people and to inquire of them what they do and think. For one
immediately strikes that other frontier, that of conscious and unconscious
secrecy. Even a willing informant seldom can or will tell all that he thinks,
knows, or does about a matter; nor is he able to show or explain the many
connections between his different thoughts and actions. He will tell more
about some things than about others; more in some situations than in
others; more to some people than to others. It is common knowledge that a
human group—a family, school, business concern, a clique—keeps together
and keeps going only by maintaining a delicate balance between discretion
and frankness. Students of group behavior have achieved great skill in
inserting themselves as participant observers into the interstices of groups
so as to observe things which can be perceived only by an insider, but
whose significance can be conceived only by an outsider free enough of
emotional involvement to observe and report accurately and armed with
concepts with which to relate what he sees to other groups. Learning the
role of participant observer, including the subtle practice of its ethic, is a

basic part of training people for social discovery. Each observer, himself a member of society, marked by sex, age, race, and the other characteristics by which people place one another in various roles or relations, must find out not merely what the significant kinds of people are in the groups and situations he wants to study; he must also learn to perceive quickly and surely what role he has been cast in by the people he is studying. He must then decide whether he can effectively and on honest terms get them to see him in such light that they will trust him.

The role of participant observer can be difficult and trying. A young sociologist spent a considerable time as observer in a public mental hospital. The patients would not believe he was not a physician; they pestered him to help them get out. The other doctors were somehow, they insisted, in a plot with relatives to keep them wrongly locked up. The attendants, accustomed to being spied upon, thought him another and more ingenious kind of detective sent to catch them breaking regulations or stealing public property. The physicians, although used to the idea of research and although briefed about his project, were a bit inclined to consider him a spy, too. Only by skillful and strict adherence to his role of seeing much and to his bargain of telling nothing that would harmfully identify any person, did he succeed in staying and in finding out the inward structure of the social groups which even the mentally ill and their keepers and therapists form.

The author of a well-known book on corner gangs "hung on the corner" with a group of young men in a New England city for three years, always torn between whether to get as involved as they wished, which would have bound him to secrecy; or whether to stay just on the edge, where there was a bit of a question whether they could trust him. Except for one essay into helping them get a man elected to public office by voting several times, he stayed on the edge. As it turned out, that was the way the gang wanted it. He wrote the book and is still friends with several members of the group.

It is conceivable that there are social groups so closed and so suspicious that they cannot be studied by participant observers. They may be so tight that they have no place for people of neutral role. Fanatical religious or political sects, criminal gangs, groups planning some secret strategy for either good or ill, bodies charged with knowledge which must be kept close for the common good, people living in great and vulnerable intimacy with each other, these do not welcome even the most trusted outside observers. However, a great deal can be learnt by projecting on these groups what is known of others which approximate them in some degree, and by setting up experiments which simulate them. A group of social scientists has indeed set up an organization to assemble, evaluate, and draw conclusions from the small amounts of information which can be got about people in the Iron Curtain regions. Some of them have written an intriguing book on how to study cultures from a distance. The problems are in part those of the historian, who is limited to the documents left around, since he cannot ask the dead to write documents to his order; but they are also in part the problems of evaluating the testimony of renegades and converts, people who have left some secret group and from various motives tell, or purport to tell, about what they have left. All of these are the problems of the social rhetoric common to all human intercourse.

The fears which lead people to make it difficult for investigators are often enough well-founded; more than that, they lie in the nature of social life. A family has secrets, or it is no family. It is not the public's business, ordinarily, what goes on in the bosom of a family; but it is a matter of basic human and scientific interest to know what kinds of families there are, what makes some hold together and others break up, and what happens to children brought up in one kind of family rather than another. The sociological investigator cracks the secrecy, but buries the secrets, one by one, in a tomb of silence — as do all the professions which deal with the problems of people. This means, of course, that the student of human groups must remain willingly and firmly a *marginal* man in relation to those he studies; one who will keep, cost what it will, the delicate balance between loyalty to those who have admitted him to the role of confidant and to his colleagues who expect him to contribute freely to the accumulating knowledge about human society and methods of studying it.

While some prefer to study people *in situ,* others take them aside and learn from them in long interviews, reassuring their subjects, showing sympathy for the problems of each, and refraining the while from even the gesture of censorship. One of the most powerful of modern social inventions is the psychoanalytic interview, in which the patient is led painfully through a maze of hindrances of conscience, shame, and fear to a fuller expression, hence to fuller knowledge, of his own mind. It is based on the assumption that the injunction to know one's self is one that few of us can follow without help. The prolonged sympathetic interview of the social investigator is less dramatic, but is an effective instrument of social discovery. But every device must be valued by its results. Some students have found that there are situations in which contradiction, calling the subject's bluff, facing him with his own contradictions, and even questioning his sincerity bring out depths and ambivalences which might otherwise remain hidden. Some have undertaken experiments to discover how differences of tactical rhetoric on the part of the interviewer affect the rhetoric of the subjects.

Some investigators prefer to go even further than experimenting with methods of interviewing and observing; they set up their own situations and create their own groups. The social research of the University of

Frankfort on the Main used such a method in study of political attitudes in 1951. They got up a letter in which an American soldier who had spent some years in Germany tells the people back home in the United States what he thinks are the German attitudes towards the Nazis, Jews, Americans, and democracy. Germans of various backgrounds were called together in small groups to discuss social and political issues; the letter was read to them from a tape made by a speaker with an English accent. In the conversation following the reading, attitudes such as have not been caught by any political questionnaire in postwar Germany came to light.

Similar methods have been used in study of various matters in the U.S.A. A team of social scientists engaged to find out how juries arrive at their unanimous decisions, has had the record of a damage suit read on to tape, using different voices for the various persons in the court: the record is played to groups of twelve who are then left alone to decide the case as if they were a jury. A silent observer with a recorder sits unobtrusively in a corner. The subjects play the role of jurymen with great seriousness. The doings of real juries are properly kept a secret; the experimental device provides an approximation with much better observation than one would in any case be likely to get by asking people what had happened in juries on which they had sat. For the observer keeps a record of those who talk the most, those who change their minds, and what alliances are made in the course of the wearing on of the argument. Combined with surveys of the ways in which people of various incomes, education, and other traits say they would judge various cases submitted to juries, these experiments are teaching us a great deal about the operation of one of our cherished institutions.

Some investigators would eventually replace all study of "natural groups" by experimental devices. Only so, they contend, can the many variable factors in social behavior be kept to such number that one can keep track of them and measure their influence. Some would go further than the Frankfort institute or the jury team. For in these projects, the experimenters were interested in the substance of their findings – the political attitudes of the Germans, and the operation of juries in the United States, respectively. The pure experimenters make the substance suit the experiment. They assemble a group of people, and give them a problem to solve to which the experimenter and the subjects are alike utterly indifferent. It is the interaction between people, the influence they have on each other, the way and the mood in which they communicate with one another that is the object of the study. For instance, what difference does it make in the interplay among a number of people whether one of them is so placed that the others can talk to each other only through him, or whether they can all talk to each other at once? One may study the forms of social interaction — social choreography — as a student of poetry may study meters and periods without attending to thought, or as the philologist may analyze grammatical forms and phonetic modulations free of concern for meaning and mood. It is but a narrow step from such study of form in human conduct to the study of form and style in art; one is on the fluttering edge between the abstractions of science and those of art. It is perhaps no accident that Simmel, the German philosopher who first proposed the study of pure interaction, attention to form rather than to content, as the basic concept of sociology, should also have written about money and about art in the same spirit. The more abstract one's way of conceiving things, the more likely one is to make generic discoveries which apply to many concrete fields of natural and human phenomena. As the experimenters penetrate further into the mathematical symmetries of human converse, they may well add to knowledge of other systems of things as well.

If men were gods, big gods with solar systems at beck and call, they might set up control planets, plant people on them, and reproduce millions of years of history, intervening now and then to see what would happen. But students of human society are mortal; our subjects live as long as we do, and usually have as much power over us as we over them. One experimenter has seriously played god by pretending that, in his laboratory as in heaven, a minute is as a hundred years. His naïveté only highlights the problem of translating the findings of small, limited experiments to larger organizations and to the time-scale of history; it does not prove that the transfer cannot, with care and in limited degree, be made.

Social experimenting has also raised the problem, both ethical and practical, of manipulating other people. There has been quite a hue and cry about this lately. A psychologist "running rats" is playing a game; the rats play for keeps without even knowing that it is a game. I believe it is suspected that now and again a sly one makes a game of the experiments and laughs up his metaphoric sleeve at the serious psychologist. No one has objected to playing with the rat, but many believe that to manipulate people is an improper way of studying man. But, of course, all politics and much of social life consist of the more or less successful attempts of people to influence one another. Every profession that deals with people is suspected of looking with an experimental and manipulative eye at its clients; indeed, no one would think of going to a lawyer, physician, or even a clergyman who did not look upon his case as one among many from which they had learned their trades. The real problem of manipulating (hence of experimenting upon) humans is not that of manipulation or no manipulation, but that of the proper conditions, limits, means, and ends thereof.

Some sociologists combine the mood of the experimenter with the roving eye of the reporter. They frequent the places where events of the kinds they are interested in are bound to happen, or they get a wide knowledge of some order of human occurrences or problems, and chase down the crucial cases which will give them the combinations of circumstances of which a more general and abstract, yet more refined and useful, knowledge can be built.

Not long ago some social psychologists were studying what happens to a group of people when a great promised event does not occur as predicted by their leaders. When they were in the midst of their project, a small sect gathered about a man who was predicting an early end of the world. Now this has happened many times before, and there are some records of the cases. For instance, when the world didn't come to end on the due date in 1843, the Millerites decided their arithmetic was wrong. A century later their successors, the Seventh Day Adventists (some of them at least) are beginning to say that while Jesus is indeed coming again in the flesh to establish his Kingdom on earth, it is sinfully presumptuous of men to think they can calculate the day and the hour. For did he not say, "Ye know not the day nor the hour?" But the team of psychologists mentioned above quite properly were eager to see a group of living people go through the experience of waiting for the world to end, and they did. Seldom do scholars have such luck.

We are in a time when we have more than common reason to want to know how people will react when disaster strikes. Flying squadrons have been sent in the wake of floods, tornadoes, explosions, and fires to find out tactfully, before memories are clouded and distorted, how people meet such adversity; who rises to the occasion to help others, and who must, on the contrary, be helped. Immediately after a great fire that destroyed half their town, the citizens told a field worker what a hero a certain obscure sister superior of a small convent-hospital had been. The nun, they said, had simply taken over and run the rescue services and the whole town. Sometime later the proper order of things had been restored; people appeared to believe that the mayor and an ecclesiastical dignitary had saved the day. In another disaster, the minister of one rather popular church went completely to pieces while the representative of a minority church and a school teacher saw the town through its tragedy. The minority minister's hair came out in handfuls some days later when reaction set in; it was the price of his courage. In many cases of such "firehouse" social research, two reports are issued. One is a newsy and perhaps immediately useful report, the other more general, and so phrased as to be useful to others who study human behavior.

If one frees his curiosity of the pecularities of some one time and place by developing a good set of abstract ideas for comparing one case or situation with another, he will see many situations in various parts of the world comparable to those that originally aroused his interest. He will fall into the delicious conflict between wanting to learn more and more detail about the one dear case and the desire to go elsewhere to add both breadth and nuance to his knowledge. A number of students of American race relations have gone off to Africa, the most tumultuous and massive Negro-white frontier of these days. The relative numbers and the historical situations of people of Negro, European, and other ancestries on the racial frontiers of Africa are varied, and are everywhere quite different from the North American racial frontier. Race relations are still vivid in the United States, for we still consider a man's race an important thing about him. Furthermore, these relations are at a crucial point in which much of both practical and theoretical interest is to be learned. Adventure lies at our own door. But there is also much to be learned by going afield. Race relations have occurred in many historical epochs, in great variety of circumstances, accompanied by various degrees of cultural differences; their course has been influenced by intervening events. Sometimes peoples meet who are alike in race, but different in almost all else. The irreducible core of race relations, as distinguished from the relations of peoples different from each other in other regards, might be found by comparing various communities.

To be sure, one's ability and will to learn languages, his health, the adaptability and sense of adventure of his wife, his knack for playing roles such that he can live among various peoples, not to mention the human life-span, limit the number of cultural situations one can study. On the whole, social science has suffered from too little rather than too much getting about (except to conventions). Anthropologists are great people to get around, but only lately have they begun to study the larger and more confused settings where races meet and where new nations are being made. The racially mixed locations and cities of Africa are places where the former subjects of the anthropologists are facing the favorite problems of the sociologist. In fact, sociologists and anthropologists are meeting there, too. In those cities, native prophets and evangelists preach half-Christian, half-tribal gospels and predict great events in which God's black people will come into their own while the white malefactors will be destroyed or driven back to their own land. Such prophets enjoin their people to make themselves pure and ready for their glorious future by a return to some idealized form of the ways of the past. One thinks of the Pharisees tithing mint and rue as part of their program of getting rid of Greek and Roman.

In the *Times* of New York or London, one can follow from day to day the crises of a dozen interracial or intercultural conflicts; in most of them Europeans are reluctantly and bit by bit giving up political, economic, and social power over others. The underdog group is in most cases undergoing revolutionary changes in its culture and social structure and is awakening to a new group-consciousness on larger scale than in the past; it is usually rewriting its history, not because of Carbon 14 or new archaeological finds but because people with a new sense of unity and a new vision of the future seem always to need a new past different both from their traditional ones and from that given them by their foreign masters. Every rewriting of history—especially our own—is grist for the sociologist's mill. Racial and cultural frontiers are but one problem which can be understood only by wide-ranging about the world of the present, either in the flesh or in the mind's eye, and about the past, through the eyes of historians and through the works of art and literature in which men have expressed their hopes, hates, and aspirations.

A basic assumption of the study of mankind—hence of individual branches of study such as that called sociology—is that it is important and fascinating to find out what things do and what things do not repeat themselves in human history. Sociologists work rather more on those which are repeated. They assume that although the people of any race, culture, time, or place inherently merit study as much as those of any others, still each historic social time and place may show some special feature which may make it an especially fit laboratory for study of some problem or process of human society. Part of the adventure of the study of human society is the seeking out of the most intriguing living laboratory, prepared by the fortunes of history, for study of the problems we are especially interested in, for use of our particular skills, and for catering to our particular tastes, curiosities, and preoccupations. Our choices may spring from a sense of political and moral urgency, from a desire to advance knowledge for man's good, from some ill-defined identification with all that is human, or from some aesthetic sense.

Some of the students of man's doings should be creatures ready to invade the territory of others, both figuratively and literally, and to compare anything with anything else without shock or apology. It is a friction-generating and improper pursuit. Any social situation is in some measure dear to those in it. To compare it with others is to seem to dull the poignancy of the wrongs of the underdogs, and to detract from the merits of those who have the better place in it. Comparison may violate the canons of status and prestige, as when one compares the code of secrecy of the gentleman's gentleman with that of the lord chamberlain. Comparison of religion with religion appears to reduce the claim of each to a monopoly of truth. Such invasion is also dangerous and improper on the academic front, for any series of human events, any social time and place, and most of man's institutions are each thought to be the game preserve of one of the learned professions. Shoving over scholarly line-fences is even more dangerous than shifting boundary stones in Vermont.

Most perilous and improper of all is it to compare the academic disciplines with one another by pointing out that each is an historical entity which had a beginning and which will probably be superseded by others in the future. If we study man and his institutions with broad-sweeping curiosity, with the sharpest tools of observation and analysis which we can devise, if we are deterred from no comparison by the fallacy which assumes that some people and peoples are more human than others, if we do not allow loyalty to truth to take second place to department or academic guild, we will all be proper students of man. And when we become too respectable, too much bound to past methods, whenever our means show signs of becoming ends, may we all — even the sociologists — be succeeded by people to whom *nihil humanum alienum est*.

FORTY-FIVE

The Dual Mandate of Social Science:
Remarks on the Academic
Division of Labor

When Carl A. Dawson, a Canadian of American sociological training, went to McGill University in 1922, he went as a pioneer. He succeeded to the directorship of a school of social work, but the sociological point of view he brought was novel in Canada. Robert M. MacIver had taught at Toronto in the twenties. After he left to continue his work with great distinction in the Graduate Faculty of Political Science at Columbia University, the late Professor E. J. Urwick carried on in somewhat the same mood. It was the mood of the British scholarly liberals in which interest in welfare politics joined with social philosophy. Courses called sociology had certainly been offered in other Canadian universities, usually as a sort of sideline.

I do not believe that there had been any formal courses in sociology in the French universities of Canada, but Léon Gérin, Edouard Montpetit, and other French-Canadian scholars had long since studied, and in some measure emulated, the work of Frédéric LePlay, that same LePlay whose name lived on more among British sociologists than among those of his own France. I have no doubt Montpetit was familiar with Durkheim, whose work had so great an influence first on American sociologists and, later, on British and American social anthropologists. One should add that

From the *Canadian Journal of Economics and Political Science*, Vol. XXV, November, 1959, pp. 401–410. Copyright 1959, University of Toronto Press.

during all of this time Marius Barbeau, an anthropologist of British training, was rummaging around for evidence of the nearly lost arts of early French Canada. He had no fixed place in a university. Edward Sapir, also an anthropologist and one who had a great influence on American sociologists and social psychologists, had spent some time in Canada under the same auspices as other Canadian ethnologists—the Bureau of Mines. The sociological mood was not completely wanting in Canada, but sociologists were, to put it mildly, not a group with strong vested interests. In fact, the students of that time were inclined to complain that sociologists assigned them far too many books and articles concerning the States. Professor Dawson warned me, when I joined him in 1927, that my predecessor, also an American, had been given quite a runaround on this point. When it came up in one of my classes, I countered by assigning large doses from English social and housing surveys. When the students complained of that, too, I suggested that we might all get together and create our own research on Canada.

Professor Dawson was already vigorously doing exactly that. He and a number of economists, historians, and others were busy studying pioneer belts; this work was part of a large project initiated by the geographer Isaiah Bowman of Johns Hopkins University. Bowman believed that a study of the settlement of pioneer regions in all parts of the world would yield knowledge of value for social and economic policy-makers of the future. That Canadian sociologists should have joined at the very beginning with other social scientists in a project of national and, indeed, of world importance, was fortunate. It started us off, not in isolation, but in the larger academic family of those interested in Canada's past, present, and future.

A few years later, McGill University got a grant, substantial for those days, to be used in developing social research. A committee, appointed by the late Sir Arthur Currie, decided to devote the fund to the study of what was certainly Canada's greatest problem of that time: unemployment. Mr. Leonard Marsh, fresh from the second survey of *London Life and Labour,* was brought out to co-ordinate the studies that might be made. Many of you are familiar with the publications which came out of that effort. Professor Dawson and I insisted that to understand unemployment in Canada, one must also know the basic pattern of employment. That pattern, we said, was in part ethnic. I need not tell you—economists, historians, political scientists—that when matters of settling the land or recruiting a labour force come up in Canada, the debate very often turns on the ethnic, national, religious, or even racial, composition of Canada's population, not only in the country as a whole but region by region.

Now Professor Dawson not only studied the pioneer belts of Canada; he

exploited them as well. For from Saskatchewan, Alberta, and British Columbia he recruited (not much money was needed to recruit graduate
students in those days) sons and daughters of the pioneers to study employment and unemployment among various ethnic groups, not only in the
west, but also in the more urban and industrial east. He even found me a
couple to work on employment among French Canadians.

Not long after that, the Carnegie Fund for International Peace, goaded
by a former Canadian, Professor James T. Shotwell of Columbia University, allocated money for the study of Canadian-American relations. We
recruited a few more students, among them S. D. Clark, with that money.
Thus, the sociologists, at least the McGill contingent of the 1930's, got
ahead by attaching themselves firmly to larger projects having to do with
Canada's great problem of that moment—unemployment—and some of her
built-in problems—her ethnic diversity and her two frontiers, her empty
one on the north and her overflowing one to the south. (Paradoxically, the
overflowing frontier seemed to draw off more Canadians than the empty
one, and Canadians were, as always, worried about it. Canada's problem
seems always to be that her immigrants will not stay where they are put.)

While I had some small part in the study of Canadian-American relations, I devoted more time and effort to getting acquainted with the history,
literature, and present life of the French Canadians. Eventually, I mounted
a small attack on what I regarded as the most interesting feature of the part
of Canada I was living in—the changes in the structure of French-Canadian society and in the relations between French and English institutions
and people attendant upon the very great increase in industry of modern
style and in urbanization. Although it has been suggested by Philippe
Garigue that this was a poor lead, I believe the evidence shows that
French Canadians, stalwart in their cultural faith as they indeed are, are no
more immune to the effects of social change than are other peoples. I regret
only that I could not remain at McGill to carry out the full programme of
studies which I had planned. Others are, of course, carrying on studies on
the same set of problems; there is still, however, no penetrating study of
the deeper personal problems of those French Canadians who are in some
measure caught between the older culture and the new.

You know the course of sociology and of other social science research in
Canada since then much better than I. There were many things going on
before that; what I have recounted is just one stream, the one I floated on.
Many more things are being done now, and in many places. The enterprises of which I was part might perhaps have turned their energies to
problems other than those mentioned; but the projects in which we did
have a part were important for Canada—immigration and settlement, employment and unemployment, the growth of cities and industries, the rela-

tions among Canada's ethnic groups, and her relations with the United States. As themes of social event and social change, they are still important although in new forms, with new territorial distributions, and with new problems of growth and balance.

Now what has all this to do with the topic of this paper? It has at least this to do with it: I have been talking about what a few people actually did. Presumably they did what they did because they thought it important; they claimed thereby a sort of mandate to tell the Canadian academic and lay world what it needed to know. They also tacitly claimed a licence to practice a certain way of observing (aptly called "intrusive observation" by an English colleague[1]), and analysing social data. They were also elaborating the academic division of labour in the fearful and wonderful way in which it is always done — by barging in where the archangels of the academic world would have shuddered to think of treading; by working in ways that violated old scruples and required a new research bargain with the objects of study.

Every occupation, even social science, consists, in part, of a licence and a mandate. The *licence* is not merely the privilege, somewhat monopolistic, of doing something which other men do not do or perhaps are not allowed to do. It is also the privilege of learning how to do this thing well; to learn and to do the thing well may require a whole mode of thought alien to the accepted beliefs, moral conceptions, and habits of thought of the surrounding society. One cannot do medicine in the modern way without elbow-room in which to handle the human organism and to analyse its nature with radical objectivity. The academic student of man and society, whatever his line, must likewise have elbow-room — a licence to pursue thoughts and events into forbidden territory on certain terms. He has a bargain, implicit or explicit, with the world he lives in and the society he studies.

The *mandate* has two facets. One is the claim of the people in a line of work to the right to define some important matter not merely for themselves, but for society at large. At the very least, they will claim that their way of thinking — for example, objectivity in the study of national heroes, insistence on facts even though they seem to threaten doctrines or vested interests — is good for society. Physicians are not content with a licence to practise; they would like all of us to accept their philosophy of health and disease and their notions about how medical services are to be distributed. It is characteristic of occupations with professional aspirations to attempt to broaden their mandates. In return, and this is the other facet, society expects certain things of the professions. The lay public or publics may, however, be very ambivalent about what they really want of a professional

1. A. T. M. Wilson, "The Social Sanctions of Research," *Sociological Review*, III (N.S.), July, 1955, 109–16.

group. This is nowhere so apparent as in the case of the social sciences, and especially of sociology. Many people would rather not have any sociologists around at all. Some like to hire them to study other people, anyone but themselves. Many expect social scientists, and again especially sociologists, to give answers to all social problems, both great and small: What do you think of fall-out? What is the solution to Little Rock? If a sociologist yields to this flattering demand, he may find his answer sharply rejected on the particular point and perhaps his mandate to speak on it at all questioned. There are no doubt very good reasons why social scientists and the lay public are both ambivalent about the limits of their licence and their mandate. I merely note the point to get the concept of mandate before us.

In some respects an occupation will want a larger mandate than the public is ready to grant it; in others, it may shy away from responsibilities which others put upon it. Discourse concerning its mandate is an important part of the work of any profession of an intellectual character. For it concerns that perhaps most fundamental of all the problems of society — the division of labour. And if Adam Smith may be said to have laid the foundation of economics by calling special attention to the technical division of labour, and its other side, the exchange of goods and services, Emile Durkheim laid an important stone of the foundation of sociology and social anthropology in writing a treatise on *The Division of Social Labor*. But the concept of division of social labour has not been fully worked out. It is the essence of human society. For, in all except the most fanatical sects, and in them usually only in their earlier phases, there is some recognized division of moral labour; at least in the sense that some people are more responsible than others for seeing that certain things get done. The division of moral labour takes in effect two forms. One is the allocation of various functions to different members of society; the other is the placing of common responsibilities more on some shoulders than on others. In the older religions, and most certainly in the Roman branch of Christianity, saints are recognized; they are people who practise the ordinary virtues in heroic (often in an unpleasant and unacceptable) degree.

Now occupations are not simply phenomena of the technical division of labour; they are also (and especially those which claim a professional mandate) positions or clusters of responsibility in a moral division of labour. Each is a sort of node, or focal point, in the division of intellectual labour. The social sciences are one of the more weird clusters of technique, moral responsibility, and intellectual specialty. And if the whole is weird, the division of labour within the general cluster known as the social sciences is positively mad. I do not in the least object to this madness, but I think it well for us to try to understand it. (A sociologist, C. Wright Mills, has lately taken a look at it in a book entitled *The Sociological Imagination.*[2])

One way of making some sense of it is perhaps that of dividing the subjects which are, some of them willingly, others over protest, called social sciences into those which are preoccupied with time and those which try to be timeless. (Oddly enough, the ones which try to be timeless usually end up by being strictly contemporary.) Indeed, the social sciences (and I mean nothing more than those branches of study which work at the business of learning about human societies) may be thought of as a sort of dialectic between the tendency to see everything in historical perspective and the opposite one of trying to conceive things so abstractly that one can ignore time, or at least historical time. The one tendency may be called the St. Matthew tendency; it finds an ancestor and traces a genealogy. The other may be called the St. John tendency; for his gospel starts with an abstract concept, "In the beginning was the Word." One group of economists is very busy trying to make formulations of the game of trading in such terms as to be universally valid, supposing only that there are people who want to play that way and who know how about equally well. Some sociologists are also engaged in making models of all the possible arrangements of human interaction and mutual control. A few (not many as yet) political scientists are doing similar things; one of them, Herbert Simon, has lately been experimenting with simulating human behavior in such a way that electronic computers can carry out sequences of interaction of two individuals who have certain known aims and each of whom has certain items of information useful to the other.

In the extreme case, people who work on this line — one of the possible timeless branches — are quite indifferent to the substance of the behaviour they study. They want to see behaviour in the most abstract way possible; one might suppose that they are people who are indifferent to substance, to the causes and problems which arouse human passions. But in my experience this is not so. The people of this kind whom I know are themselves men of strong social sentiments, much engaged in the problems of their time. Some claim immediate practical usefulness for the findings which they hope to arrive at. All of them, I think, have a sense of the aesthetics of what they are doing; they speak of elegant formulations, elegant experiments, elegant designs of research, parsimonious explanations, and so on.

But in so far as they carry on empirical observations, they are bound to the study of living men and so are strictly contemporary. They could not be historical if they wanted to. But if they are bound to the present, they are

2. C. Wright Mills, *The Sociological Imagination,* New York: Oxford Univ. Press, 1959.

not bound to the study of one institution or another; and in the past the division of labour in the social sciences has been largely a matter of specializing in institutions, regions, and periods of time. The "timeless people" are inclined to find common tools of observation and analysis useful for the study of human interaction no matter what the institutional setting in which it occurs. The result is a new kind of interdisciplinary work, based not on the older belief that it is nice to study a problem from all angles, as in the study of pioneer belts, but on the recognition that the same phenomena are being studied and that common concepts, ways of observing, and tools of analysis are needed for doing so.

People who go at their work in this way may hold to the view that each step in learning of human behaviour is dependent on some previous prerequisite step. To the extent that this is so, social scientists would never pay attention to the news, but would simply pursue knowledge, step by step, impervious to what goes on in the world. The history of curiosity would simply be the order in which new unknowns were formulated on the basis of successive advances of knowledge. Actually, as I need not tell you, even natural scientists do not proceed in quite this way. History and scientific knowledge interact, even, and indeed rather obviously so, in the field of physics. For there is always a choice of things to be curious about, and energies can be concentrated on some problem rather than others for quite mundane, timely reasons.

But before developing the links between those ways of thinking and working which are, or would like to be thought, independent of the times, and other ways of thinking and studying human goings-on, let us look at the other extreme. There are those who would bind all study of human affairs to time and place and, consequently, to substance and institution, which are the more obvious historical aspects of human conduct. They justify this limitation in various ways. Some say that there is so much to learn about any society, or about some part of a society in some period of time or in one place, that the most a man can do in a lifetime is to master what is known and, if he is industrious and lucky, to add a bit to it. They may not believe in comparisons, saying that no one can know enough about two epochs, societies, regions, and so on, to make sound comparisons. They accuse the generalizers of knowing too little about the facts to justify the expressed and implicit comparisons in which abstraction must consist. The classical linguist accuses the archaeologist of being such an ignoramus about languages that one cannot trust what he says about the ruins and artefacts he digs up; the archaeologist says the linguist trusts what people wrote down far too much, since he cannot evaluate the historical sequence of styles of design, and of strata of fragments of various objects which tell how men must have lived. Both, however, have a strong predilection for studying places and periods and are wary of generalizations and comparisons as attempts to cover too much ground.

Other people, including some who call themselves sociologists and anthropologists, share this penchant for time and place. A sociologist of this kind may say that sociology is simply the "here and now" branch of social study; he may go so far in this direction as to merit a term of opprobrium invented by one of his ancestors, William G. Sumner of *The Folkways*;[3] he may become *ethnocentric*, and that in several senses. He may simply lack interest in other social worlds than that of his own country and time. He may eschew all attempts to arrive at general propositions concerning human societies. When he does come into touch with other cultures or countries, he measures them uncritically by his own and finds them wanting to the extent that they deviate from it. The anthropologist of similar bent differs from the sociologist of this kind in that the part of the world he chooses as his standard is at a distance, is generally small, misunderstood by everyone except himself and a chosen few, and must be protected from the baleful influences of economic, political, and religious colonialism, or what is now called "development." He is *ethno-eccentric*.

In these last few paragraphs I have purposely (but the purpose is serious) fallen into a common habit of social scientists—that of stereotyping those who work in fields or in ways other than their own. Each of us tends to exaggerate somewhat the tendencies and preoccupations of others, attributing to them more extreme positions than they actually take. The reason may be the propensity which we academic people have for pedagogical exaggeration as a way of making our points; and partly an anxiety lest laymen (including the students for whose future professional allegiance we contend with each other) underestimate the difference between one of our professional specialties and another. (Each man's specialty, like each man's neurosis, is peculiar; no one else can understand it.)

In fact, neither the time-bound nor the would-be timeless method of work often occurs in pure form. Even those who take extreme positions in argument are generally less extreme in practice. Most of the specialties in social science are in fact some sort of combination of working on timeless, recurring, general problems of man and society with time-bound, historical events, or, if the problems are contemporary, with news. I have recently heard a social anthropologist give a most interesting lecture on that mysterious phenomenon, cross-cousin marriage, relating it to other circumstances of life and asserting that, if one make proper abstractions from the concrete complexes of custom, one finds that it is invariably associated with certain circumstances. He was combining the use of the substantive,

3. William G. Sumner, *The Folkways,* Boston: Ginn & Co. 1906.

bound in time and place, with general propositions concerning the problems which all human societies both create and try to solve. Some historians (my favourite among them is Marc Bloch, and my favourite among
his books is, for the moment at least, the little one entitled *The Historian's
Craft*[4]), handle the historian's view of time in such a generalizing way that
I claim them as sociologists (hoping that my espousal will not cause them
to be excommunicated from the Order of Committed Historians). Another
historian I like is the late Dom Gregory Dix who, in his large history of
Christian liturgy, has written of "The Sanctification of Time."[5] He tells
how Christianity, which started out with naught but a future, acquired a
past; but the terms in which he recites these time-bound facts are such as
to expose the reader to the sociological temptation—the temptation to
make them timeless by seeing the same thing happen to other social
movements which started without a past and, as they succeeded, got one
and sanctified it in a calendar.

Actually, the various social sciences are the institutionalized products of
social movements. Each has its history, of which it bears the marks. Some
are the intellectual aspects or results of movements that were not especially or directly intellectual. Anthropology, for instance, is, as we know,
an intellectual by-product of empire; as European empires grew, some very
un-imperially minded individuals went out and brought back accounts of
strange peoples and customs. To associate these accounts with the intellectual issues raised by Darwin was but a step. There are other threads
in what one might call the anthropological movement. The sociological
movement had several strands: the growth of new urban poverty in industrial England; the conflict between contemporary fashion and traditional
custom in France; Marx and the belated breakdown of the feudal system in
Germany; the simultaneous appearance of city slums and masses of European immigrants in North America just when the Protestant movements
were turning from personal evangelism to a reforming "social gospel;" and
all of that also mixed up with Darwin and the evolutionary and comparative "higher criticism" of the biblical scholars. Few if any of the
branches of social science grew up out of some ineluctable progression of
human knowledge and curiosity and without reference to the movements
and problems of some particular time and place. Few, if any of them,
completely stay away from the search for general and timeless knowledge.
But the combinations are many and peculiar. And each tends to become
the special domain and vested interest of a professional group with a name,
a prescribed course of training, and established careers, and with its own

4. Marc Bloch, *The Historian's Craft* (New York: Knopf, 1962).
5. Dom Gregory Dix, *The Shape of the Liturgy* (Westminster, The Dacre Press, 1945).

claimed and, in various degrees, accepted mandate and licence. Some are, like some of the specialties in medicine, outgrowths of a new gadget—a new instrument of observation, a new mode of analysis. While each of the branches, in some degree, can presumably justify itself as some sort of logical or natural unit in the intellectual division of labour, not one of them can do so completely. For most of them, along with their chosen logical mode of analysing their favourite kinds of data, are preoccupied also with some kind of history or news. Few economists are so preoccupied with the theory of games that they do not follow prices on the great markets. And although in theory there is as much an economics of the wages of church organists as of steelworkers, and although presumably some interesting theoretical models could be built and solved by considering the case of church organists, it is steelworkers whose wages economists are more likely to study.

And this illustrates the dual mandate of social science. Those in any branch are, on the one hand, engaged in a kind of intellectual dialectic between concern over the development of general, abstract (in a sense, neutral) knowledge and the methods of pursuing such knowledge, and, on the other hand, are concerned with what is going on, with the times and news, whether in some particular phase of their own times or of some past time. And, as the intellectual division of labour is formed and reformed, those who give us licence to work and who, in some measure, accept our claim to a mandate, build up expectations in both perspectives—the timely and the timeless; they will perhaps generally incline rather more to the timely, which is also the institutional, the substantive, and the practical, even when the time in question is the past. The balance between the two aspects—between the more general and the more specific and timely—is quite delicate, and perhaps unstable. There are many such balances. Each branch of social science may be described, not merely in terms of substance, but in terms of its balance, in terms of its particular working out of the dialectic.

Each of our branches may also, like other professions, be distinguished by the kinds of data we like to handle; some of us are messier than others. Some of us like data in writing; others of us prefer to get them from living lips; some hate words but like actions. Each breed of us gets his "kick" in a special way. Oliver LeFarge has lately told us what it is for the archaeologist:

> The strongest of archeology's lures [is] the undying wonder about what the next operation may uncover, the answer that may be hidden under the next spoonful of dirt, behind a wall, in the fragments, to be painfully assembled, of a jar, of a carved stone, a multi-millennial flint-tool, or a plaster surface. The wonder is

there from minute to minute and from year to year, and the fact that the answers found are few and usually both minor and abstruse, makes no difference.[6]

Political scientists like to find a hidden document, one someone tried to conceal, that will explain some event. Historians love a document on which no human eye has gazed these many years or centuries. Each branch also has its favourite allies in the academic world, although these alliances change from time to time. These predilections are probably as important in determining the relations of social scientists to each other and to the world as are the purely logical systems of thought which they develop. One may think of the division of labour as a sort of running, never-ending interaction of the timely, or time-bound and substantive, on the one hand, and the more purely logical, general, and timeless, on the other. Since the logical division will be changed by the progress of knowledge, and since timeliness by definition changes in course of time, both of these are principles of change. But even social scientists, in so far as they are human, are ambivalent about change, sometimes inclined to stick to what is, sometimes inclined to change things drastically. I would hate to be able to predict just what the divisions of social science will be in twenty-five or fifty years, for if I could predict, it would mean that there would not have been much change. And that could be only if we made little progress in the pursuit of general knowledge and/or if we were most extraordinarily stubborn and successful in defending our vested professional interests. On the other hand, I would hate not to be able to predict at all, for that would mean that all our traditions of workmanship, of the aesthetic of our work, all our unreasonable interest in this or that part of the human drama would have given way to the exigencies of change, and I would not like that either.

But what about the solution to the problems of a dual mandate for Canadian sociologists? Shall they focus their attention on advancing abstract knowledge of the human social processes, regardless of time, place, substance, and the immediate problems of Canada? I have a theory about the timely and the abstract. It comes in part from Robert E. Park. He was a great enemy of the high-brow fallacy in his insistence that in principle as much is to be learned from one human being, one human situation, one human institution, or one culture, as from another. The series which we have to study is all men, all societies, all events in all times and everywhere. Of course, some parts of this universe are more accessible than others. Some parts require different tools from others. The study of each part entails peculiar temptations and dangers. Each also entails its own kind of research bargain concerning the terms on which the particular kind

6. "The Senior Assistant," *New Yorker,* XXXIV, no. 47, Jan. 10, 1959.

of knowledge required is given, accepted, and communicated. The bargain with the living is different from the bargain with the dead. One need make no bargain at all with rats, and it is said that that is why some psychologists prefer them. It follows from what I am saying that what happens in Canada is no less, and no more, important to the advance of knowledge about human society than what goes on or went on anywhere.

But to this I would add what I call the "more-so" principle. For, while any society at any time is of interest, any one at a given time may show some features of special interest. It may be, because of a combination of circumstances, the ideal laboratory in which to observe certain processes which will give us new knowledge of general interest. If I qualified, at present, as a Canadian sociologist, and were working at my trade, I think I would ask myself this question: In addition to the things which could be done anywhere to add to the knowledge of human societies, what are the features of Canadian life to which the "more-so" principle might apply — those things which are high-lighted somewhat in Canadian life, and from which one might learn something more about some aspect of human society than one would elsewhere? These would turn out, I believe, to be the very things that would be exciting to anyone possessed of what C. Wright Mills calls "the sociological imagination" and what I, who do not attack things so violently, like to speak of as the sociological mood. They would also turn out to be, I am sure, things of great current national interest to Canada, things that are in the news, or, if you can get a bit ahead of the game, things that ought to be and will be in the news. It might be the new Canadian wild east — east, that is, of the Saguenay on the North Shore — or the new north, which is a frontier of a new kind developed in a new way. It might be the New Canadian, a phrase which itself connotes a new way of looking at immigrants. It might be surburbia, or something about the popular arts. Who is to say what it would be?

If you do try thus to unite the timely with the timeless, event with generalization, news with theory, you will find yourself in licence and mandate trouble of a most interesting kind. You will find your licence to gather facts on touchy matters often questioned, but you will find people so intrigued as to be more than willing to give you the information, provided a decent bargain is made and kept. And you will find a similar ambivalence about your mandate to speak a new kind of truth about certain matters. People will question the substance and the mood of your answers, but they will insist on having them. And that should be a most delightful and titillating state of things.

FORTY-SIX

Sociologists and the Public

The sessions of the American Sociological Association which will have preceded the World Congress are to be devoted to discussion of *The Uses of Sociology*. President Lazarsfeld has invited American sociologists to tell the use of sociology in government, business, medicine, and many other institutions. The emphasis is on how sociology is or may be used by policy-makers and professional people, rather than on the relation of the sociologists to the public. Professor Sauvy, in his introductory note to participants in the present session, indicates that when he speaks of policy-makers he refers primarily to members of government. Professor Lazarsfeld has included policy-makers of other kinds as well. I mention this only because many who will attend this session will have read or heard the papers presented at the American meetings. That fact will no doubt influence our discussions. Those papers are not, however, available to me or to others at the time of writing. In any case, the American program will deal primarily with American experience. Our session should deal with experience and problems in a variety of countries. My discussion, as distinguished from that of Professor Sauvy, will deal with the public at large, with the unorganized as well as with the organized publics who may be the objects of sociological study, and who may be also the consumers of sociological analysis, the people to whom sociology is presented in one way or another and who may be affected by it directly or indirectly.

Sociologists are but one of the many kinds of specialists who study some aspect of nature, including human life, for the love of it, for the common good, in order to facilitate effective action on the part of others, or so that they themselves may act with reference to the matter in question on their own account, or for the benefit of clients who seek their services. If the specialists in question pursue their study only in order that they may act, they are professionals in the usual English sense of that term. The learning is a means to the end of effective action. A profession is *practised;* that is, the professional's main business is to provide a service for some body of clients. The clients may be individuals who come of their own accord or who are referred to the professional. They may be institutions or public bodies. The individuals who make up the public are, in varying degree, potential clients of the professional; all of us have been or will be patients of the medical profession. Not all of us will call upon the service of chartered accountants, patent lawyers, or electronic engineers. But we may all be affected by the way in which the members of those professions perform and distribute their services. In any case, the public is considered to be properly concerned about the manner in which professional services are performed; the concern expresses itself in laws which limit the practice of the profession to people licensed by the state, although generally in fact chosen by the members of the profession itself.

Other specialists, although they may be moved by concern over practical matters, follow learning whither it leads without much thought for its immediate usefulness.

Note that I say immediate usefulness. I suppose nearly all who pursue studies of society believe it is better to know than not to know. But some want their knowledge to be applied soon, and are likely to choose their fields of observation accordingly even though they leave application itself to others. Some pursue knowledge in a longer perspective, making their choices of field and problems on grounds other than social urgency. Other sociologists, however, believe that they should be professional in the sense of giving advice or other services to clients who pay for it. I am not among them, but I am not against their following their bent. Others are of the other extreme, divorcing their work completely from all influence by thought of application. Neither am I among them, nor against this. Many of us are ambivalent on this point; perhaps the majority of sociologists refrain from professional application of their knowledge for benefit of clients, but are inclined to choose their problems for study somewhat on the basis of what they consider the problems of the contemporary world, the world we live in and which is here to be seen and observed. Were we to confine our attention to societies distant in time, we might save ourselves most of the problems of our relations to the public; we might pay for it by a competence which would depend upon that built-in ignorance with which the modern historian, E. H. Carr, twits his brethren who study ancient history.[1]

Our problems are those of any group of people devoted to gaining and disseminating knowledge of any aspect of the natural or human world, compounded and made acute by the fact that we generally study our own societies. One of the problems of any such group is that of the relation of its specialists' or professional culture to one or more lay cultures (or sub-cultures). For whenever an aspect of reality becomes an object of study or action by specialists, the latter develop and maintain a specialists' culture with respect to it.

The specialists' culture will consist, in part, of a view of the nature of the phenomena which the specialists study, and of their place among other orders of reality. It will include ideas concerning the nature of evidence, its own line of reasoning and analysis, its concepts, in short, its universe of discourse. Those of us who were initiated into sociology by Professor Robert E. Park, Ellsworth Faris, et al., were made to dwell long and thoughtfully upon Durkheim's discussion of *collective representations,* and especially of those *concepts* which both form our ways of perceiving and conceiving and enable us to communicate more fully with those with whom we have a great body of shared experience. As Park and Burgess put it:

> The significance of the fact that 'every group has its own language' is being recognized in its bearings upon research. Studies of dialects of isolated groups, of the argot of social classes, of the technical terms of isolated groups, of the precise terminology of scientific groups suggest the wide range of concrete materials. The expression 'different universes of discourse' indicates how communication separates as well as unites persons and groups.[2]

The interaction of sociologists with the public, or more exactly, with the several publics of a given society, is the interaction of universes of discourse, of whole systems of concepts which express, respectively, the sociologists' culture, and various lay cultures.

Any specialists' or professional culture — that of the physicist, the pathologist, the biologist, the sociologist — may be so different from the corresponding lay culture as to allow of no understanding between professional and layman. On the other hand, they may be very much alike in basic

1. E.H. Carr, *What is History?,* New York, Macmillan, 1961, p. 9. He refers to the fact that the historian of ancient Greece has no way of correcting the bias of the Athenian sources, the only ones available.
2. R.E. Park and E.W. Burgess, *Introduction to the Science of Sociology,* Chicago, Univ. of Chicago Press, 1921, p. 423. Cf. also pp. 195-198, where they reproduce a selection from Émile Durkheim's *Elementary Forms of Religious Life,* New York, Free Press, entitled "Collective representations and intellectual life."

concepts. In many countries nowadays physician and patient share the same basic notions of the nature of disease. A physician can, with some of his patients, tell the truth in the same terms he would use with colleagues. But the specialist's culture and the lay culture can never be exactly the same; for although specialist and layman may share the same general concepts and body of knowledge, their situation with regard to the aspect of the world in question cannot be quite the same.[3] A theory of the causes of divorce can give but little comfort to those unfortunate people who are sorely in need of one. The snake that has bitten me is something other than a beautiful specimen of a certain order of reptiles. Whether different or similar to each other, the specialists' and the lay cultures will interact in some degree. That interaction, as it concerns sociology, is our problem.

That interaction begins in the very definition of whatever problem is to be studied by the sociologist. For the public will have its own definition, or definitions, of any problem of social life, definitions couched in moral, political, religious, economic or other terms. It is hard to conceive of anything more shocking than to have one's favorite troubles defined in objective, comparative terms. In our society, at any rate, not many people mind it if a physicist redefines some problem, say that of what holds a piece of metal together, in terms other than those used by a mechanic or a foundryman. In general, scientific and professional redefinition of diseases is accepted although with some reservation. But as one moves toward political, economic and social matters, the lay publics are less willing to accept the specialists' definitions of situations. For one thing, most people think they know what ails the state, the economy and society. At least in democratic countries, everyone is expected to be informed on these matters and, indeed, to participate in action regarding them. For another, everyone has vested interests in these matters; they are life itself to him. And, finally, people have deep sentiments concerning these matters. Sentiments do not merely define problems, but contain also the proper answers to them. It is characteristic of the sociological as of any other scientific definition of a problem that it assumes that there can be a variety of answers. It seeks relatively better, but always tentative and limited answers. Sentiments do not seek answers; they *are* the answer.

One may illustrate some of these points by referring to the matter of race in my country. Many people of the race called white define the race problem as biological, insisting that the traditional position of the races in relation to each other is simply a natural consequence of biological differences. Some people define the matter in religious terms. To define the

3. For a classic statement of the problem of communication of professional with client see L.J. Henderson, "Physician and Patient as a Social System," *The New England Journal of Medicine,* Vol. 212, Nov. 1937, pp. 404-413.

problem in historical and sociological terms, to see it as another case of economic, political and social relations among peoples, to compare it with other such cases is not suitable to those who have defined the problem in pseudo-biological or in religious terms.[4]

Even to consider a question open is often considered sacrilege. For where there is question, there lies the implication that the answer is not yet known; that there may be another answer than that generally accepted. One has only to think of going about the United States asking people, "Which system, ours or that of the Soviet Union, will bring greater benefits to mankind?" — or going about the Soviet Union asking it in reverse. One might also speculate on the fate of someone who would go from house to house in white districts of South Africa asking, "Who has the right to rule here? Whites, Natives, Coloured or Indians?" Or, to be even more provoking, consider asking white people, "Who should rule here: Africans, Asiatics or Europeans?"[5]

Involved in this is, of course, the problem of neutrality. In his capacity as a student of reality, the sociologist is presumed to be neutral. In any society there are areas with respect to which intellectual neutrality is accepted; with respect to others, it is not permitted even to play at being the devil's advocate. Within a society, people vary as to the matters on which they will put up with the neutrality implied in philosophical speculation or scientific discourse and inquiry. Even on such an issue as that of free trade as against protective tariffs, a matter of fiscal policy, one may have difficulty concerning neutrality, as Lewis A. Dexter has shown. Some of his respondents took his very putting of questions on the subject as evidence that he was an enemy of the truth.[6]

The areas concerning which sentiments are such as to make objective inquiry difficult will vary from society to society, from country to country, religion to religion, political party to political party. The sociologist, if he is indeed one, will be aware of such sensitive areas in any society he undertakes to study. It is part of the sociological task to be students of this matter, and to be able to interpret our own work and that of others in the light of it.

It is one of our weakness that we do not always make ourselves fully aware of the blind spots of inquiry in our own societies (we are quick to

4. Of course, it is scientifically legitimate to ask questions concerning the biological aspects of race. Those, however, who have attributed the system of race relations to biological difference, are not scientists seeking answers. They are laymen expressing sentiments by dogmatic assertions.

5. The categories used in the second putting of the question are those used by the people whom the whites call Native, Bantu, Kaffirs, etc., but who call themselves African.

6. Lewis A. Dexter, "Role Relationships and Conceptions of Neutrality in Interviewing," *American Journal of Sociology,* LXII, Sept. 1956, pp. 153-157.

smell them out in other societies). The case is fairly simple when some aspect of society is completely closed off from inquiry. More insidious is an apparently detached and objective inquiry which stops short of being completely so. One common manifestation of such a case is the asking of questions about only one end of a full range of possibilities. If I may again speak of race in my own country, I have known of inquiries as to whether Negroes should have rights equal in all respects to those of whites; I have never known any sociologist to ask whether Negroes ought not to be given superior rights for a while to make up for their past disadvantages. Once the parents of the school my children attended were called together to consider the admission of Negro children. One parent moved that we send a ballot to all parents asking whether they favored it or not, and whether they would withdraw their children if Negroes where admitted. Another parent then moved that another question be asked: Will you withdraw your children if Negroes are not admitted? The whole matter was dropped. We consider, very often, but one half of a possible scale, or one quadrant of the possible relations between two variables. This may be quite sensible in some cases. But my point is that sociology, at its best, raises the full range of questions. It is a radical thing to do with respect to matters of sentiment, as most sociological matters are.

Sometimes the very constitution of the state is based on a sociological theory. Indeed, I suppose all legal and political systems rest on theories concerning the nature of society. If those theories are very explicit, the sociologist may at least know where he stands. If they are implicit, he may have more difficulty in discovering the limits of toleration of the inquiring attitude. Of course, there may be in the same society and country competing definitions of any social matter or problem; they are espoused by people of varying wealth, power and sophistication. A recurring problem and a common accusation flow from this fact. The sociologists may be tempted to define a problem in a way that fits more closely one of the competing definitions than another. They may be accused of being the servants of some vested interest. In a recent book[7] American industrial sociologists are accused of accepting management's definition of the problem of industrial morale and production. The case is pertinent, although the author has oversimplified the case. It is true that many sociologists and psychologists have studied, "restriction of production." Max Weber did so fifty years ago in his *Zur Psychophysik der industriellen Arbeit*,[8] and came to the conclusion that "putting on the brakes" is part of the eternal struggle

---

7. Loren Baritz, *The Servants of Power. A History of the Social Sciences in American Industry*. Middletown, Conn., Wesleyan University Press, 1960.

8. Cf. *Gesammelte Aufsätze zur Soziologie und Sozialpolitik*, pp. 61-255. The essay was first published in 1908-1909.

of the worker with his employer over the price of his labor. But both phrases, although useful enough, contain a certain bias. To restrict production is to do less than the employer wants, or less than is physically possible. The phrase assumes that there is a proper standard of production set by someone other than the worker. It asks only half a question. The true question is this: How are levels of productive effort determined in working organizations of any and all kinds—industry, hospitals, universities, government bureaux, etc.,—and among all kinds of workers in those organizations—management itself, professionals, students and apprentices, white-collar workers, skilled and unskilled manual workers? This is a truly open question, relating to a problem to be found in all societies no matter what the form of ownership and control of industries and other institutions. It does not cut its inquiry to those aspects acceptable to any segment of the public.

Sociologists take as their object of study the very public to which their findings may eventually be communicated. The members of the public thus studied become subjects, who collaborate, knowingly or not, in study of themselves. From this relationship flow questions of the extent of the sociologists' access to facts concerning people's behavior and thoughts, of the ethic governing the gathering of their data, and of the terms on which data are gathered and communicated. And one may ask, of course, why people allow themselves to be studied at all and on what terms.

In addition to the point already made, that the sociologist treats in an objective and detached manner the beliefs and institutions which are precious to members of the society studied, there is the additional question whether the sociologist can be trusted with information about one's behavior, that of his family, colleagues, friends and neighbors. For eventually the data of the sociologist come from people; generally, the facts that are of most use are those that are given willingly. True, the sociologist will often have to seek out hidden facts, and will sometimes consider himself justified in revealing them without the consent of persons deeply involved. Most information concerning social life is, however, given willingly. Every human being is the repository of much secret knowledge. Without access to secret knowledge there could be no systematic and penetrating study of human society. The psychoanalysts' greatest invention was probably the interview, in which the subject revealed not merely to the analyst, but also to himself, facts that, in other contexts, would appear shameful and would occasion deep guilt and fear. Sociologists, when they study certain orders of human relationships, must have facts that could cause shame and harm to the person who reveals them. In order to do his work well, he must have the confidence of his subjects (informants, respondents, people observed). They must believe that he will not use his privileged information to do them harm.

In order to have that confidence, the sociologist must deserve it. All of us who have been given access to delicate situations know how difficult it is to get the confidence of people, how great are the pressure and temptations to reveal confidential matter in such a way that sanctions might be visited upon the subject, or his peers. All successful investigation of existing social relationships depends upon some sort of explicit or implicit bargain with the people concerned. That bargain has to do with the terms under which the findings will be made public or otherwise used.

Societies undoubtedly differ greatly in the willingness of people to let themselves be observed for scientific purposes. If internal tension and anxiety are great, we may expect that while many might wish to give information, most people will fear to do it. Where freedom is limited, suspicion of the investigator will be great. In any society we may expect that people of various classes will have their own patterns of consent or resistance to inquiry, based on their experience, or what they have heard of the experience of others. Part of the skill of the sociologist in relation to his public, is to understand their suspicions and the grounds on which they rest, and to know how to reduce that suspicion by correct conduct on his own part. Part of that correct conduct, indeed the heart of it, is a strict ethic of responsibility toward those who give him the data with which he works.

If people are sometimes reluctant to give information or to allow themselves to be observed, they are also as often quite eager to have a part in social investigation involving themselves. With us, in North America, people are generally willing to believe that a study will, in some distant future, be used for the common good; they are quite patient about it. It is believed that the people of some countries, of some classes or occupations, can not be observed or interviewed. That may be so. Nevertheless, it is amazing how successful social research has been in all countries where it has been undertaken. We need to learn more about the differences of access to various people and various segments of society. One of the aims of our session should be to compare notes on this matter, and especially to become aware of the biasses that may creep into comparisons of one society with another through differences in the responsiveness of people to investigation.

The sociologist must, in order to study societies, become familiar with the language of the people whom he studies; not merely the words and what they mean in the dictionary, but the language as expression of society and the culture. He must, of course, also have a second language, that in which he communicates with his colleagues. This second language is, in part, quite technical. It may include statistical or other systems of symbols which are necessary to economic and accurate statement among specialists. But there is eventually a third language which we must learn, that of the public to which the sociologist wants to communicate his findings. Some sociologists consider that they have done their duty when they have reported some findings to a client — the government, a business, or some private or public agency. Not many are content with that alone. They will want to add something to general sociological knowledge and to theories of society; they want to communicate to their colleagues. Many will also want to contribute knowledge and ideas to the public mind. This requires an art at which many of us are not adept. Some, indeed, think we should not try to speak to the public at large. At least one colleague who read my initial statement thought we should not try to communicate with the public lest we yield to the temptation to pontificate. Since we deal with important problems, people expect us to say important things. We sometimes pretend to know more than we do; the temptation is great. Yet, in most countries, it will be expected that something of common interest and value will eventually come out of the great amount of effort spent on social science, including sociology. One of our problems is to become skilful in putting our findings and theories into wider circulation. As a matter of fact, the young colleague who counselled against speaking to the public writes with clarity and wit in language that any one of moderate learning can understand.

It may well be objected that what I have had to say is addressed almost entirely to sociologists who engage in empirical research. I mean by empirical research not mere scurrying about to gather facts, real or presumed, but well considered attempts to join hypothesis and theory with actual observation of human behavior. Those observations may have been made and recorded centuries ago; they may be made now. There are sociologists with great knowledge of historical currents, of various societies of the past and present, but who do not themselves go into the field to gather new social data. They use records made by others. Some of the problems of the relation of the sociologist to the public will apply less to them than to those who do actively study current societies. But the basic problems apply to them as well, for all sociologists analyze the customs, beliefs, and institutions of societies in a systematic and detached way. This analytical view is bound at times to conflict with the view of the lay public (indeed, with our own views in our capacity of members of society). The resulting dilemmas are solved in many ways. They are the matter for our discussions.

FORTY-SEVEN

Professional and Career Problems
of Sociology

Sociology, being itself a social phenomenon, may be studied as one. One might try to find out, for instance, what the circumstances are under which people want to study human society in the way called sociological, those under which they are allowed to do so, and those under which they may publish and otherwise use their findings. Our discussion of the training and professional activities assumes some freedom in these matters. We have before us questions of narrower range, but nonetheless of great practical importance; questions about the organisation of sociological activity. For my remarks on some of these problems I take as my cue the term *profession*.[1]

Reprinted by permission of the publisher from the *Transactions of the Second World Congress of Sociology,* Vol. I, 1954. Copyright by the International Sociological Association.

1. The literature in English on professions in modern society is growing rapidly. The following are a few items especially pertinent to this discussion:

Carr-Saunders, A. M., and Wilson, P. A., *The Professions,* London: Oxford, 1933; "The Professions," *Encyclopaedia of the Social Sciences* (New York: Macmillan, 1932).

Marshall, T. H., "The Recent History of Professionalism in Relation to Social Structure and Social Policy," *Canadian Journal of Economics and Political Science,* Vol. V (1929).

Parsons, T. H., "The Professions and Social Structure," *Social Forces,* Vol. 17 (May, 1939).

Hughes, Everett C., "Work and the Self," in Rohrer, John, and Sherif, M. (editors), *Social Psychology at the Crossroads,* New York: Harper & Row, 1951.

_____. "Discussion of the Bryan Report," in Asheim, L. (editor), *A Forum on the Public Library Inquiry,* New York, Columbia University Press, 1950.

T. H. Parsons and his associates at Harvard University, R. K. Merton and associates at Columbia University, and Oswald Hall at McGill University (Canada) have all been working

Profession has in English a rather more special meaning than has the same word in French and its counterpart, *Beruf,* in German. A profession is an occupation which has attained a special standing among occupations. In the Western world, and more so in the English-speaking part of it, many occupations have sought this status in recent decades. At the same time a great many new subdivisions of learning and scientific investigation have arisen. The people who have founded and/or pursue these new branches have also sought for their subjects and for themselves a place in the academic and scientific world like that of other, older branches, but separate from them. So numerous are these new occupations and branches of learning that one may compare the steps they take to achieve their end of attaining professional status, and thus arrive at a general description of the process of professionalising an occupation. Against such a background one may see with more detachment and perhaps with more penetrating vision the situation and problems of organised sociology.

The first people to practise a new line of work come into it from other occupations. Youngsters do not ordinarily establish new occupations; it is done by more mature people who see a new need or a new opportunity. Sometimes they slip over into a new activity without thinking of it as an occupation, and are only later aware of the significance of the change. In other cases they are apostles, full of enthusiasm and charism, spreading the light of new knowledge and a new cause.

At some point these irregulars, having become aware of themselves as a new group with a social identity, set about setting the terms of entry of their successors, the second generation. Almost invariably they seek to straighten the career line. They set up devices to require their successors to choose the occupation earlier, to make them follow a set course of study and training, to enter into the work as a sole and continued way of making a living, and to do the work under institutional arrangements defined and enforced by the members of the occupation. On the social psychological side they insist that the individual accept identification with the occupation as part of his definition of himself, as a significant and persistent answer to

---

on sociological analysis of professions. In the 13 years in which I have had a seminar on professions at the University of Chicago my students and those of my colleagues have produced upwards of 40 theses on the problems of various occupations and professions.

Several of the American Foundations have become interested in promoting study of professions. The Rockefeller Foundation early encouraged study of the medical profession; the Carnegie Corporation of teachers and librarians; the Russell Sage Foundation, of social workers and lately of several others. Dr. Esther L. Brown has long been retained by the Russell Sage Foundation for studies of the social functioning of professions. The Commonwealth Fund has supported study of the medical professions. More recently the Ford Foundation has taken an interest in the training and functioning of the teaching professions.

There are, of course, other people, universities and private or public bodies engaged in such research, both in the English speaking world and outside of it.

the self-put question, "Who am I?" and the question put by others, "Who are you?" The true members of the aspiring profession will be thought to be those who enter it early, get the conventional training, work at the trade, identify themselves with its collective activities, and leave it only when they leave off working altogether. A person who, once in the charmed circle, leaves it, thereby slights the profession as a whole. He makes light of dedication to it and calls down upon himself that anger which reaches its extreme in the attitude toward a priest who gives up the cloth. The professional group seeks to become an enduring thing in two senses; first, in that membership in it should be enduring and, second, in that the group itself lasts as a known and accepted organ of society.

In this latter aspect, the professional group will claim the mandate to select, train, initiate and discipline its own members and to define the nature of the services which they will perform and the terms on which they will perform them. If possible, they will extend this mandate to the point of monopoly, excluding others from performing their kind of work, and seeking the exclusive prerogative of defining the proper relations (ethic) between the professionals and all other people concerned in their work. In its full form, the mandate will include the function of developing a philosophy for society at large concerning the whole area of thought, value and action involved directly or even remotely in their work. How far these mandates will be realised depends upon many circumstances, including competition and conflicts with other occupations and interests.

The course of a new branch of learning is rather like that of a new occupation which, indeed, it tends to become. Part of its course will depend upon how much it becomes involved in the giving of services to individual clients, or to institutions or the public as collective clients. If it is closely related to a service it will seek to follow the model of a profession, as just outlined. If it gives no immediate service it may follow the model of older so-called pure sciences. In this case the group may not strive so hard to close its ranks or to seek a monopoly from society. In America the psychologists are in a conflict as to whether psychology will be primarily a science or primarily a profession. I do not suggest that they have a choice. The logic of circumstances will almost certainly require them as a group to be both, although some individuals may be purely scientific experimenters while others are therapists. I suspect it is the fate of sociology to suffer a similar chronic conflict. It may not be so acute, as sociology is not likely to be used as an instrument of individual therapy to such an extent as psychology. But if our problem of defining professional relations with individual clients is less acute, our relations with institutions, the state and society are likely to be more trying. Although many sociologists would like to consider their work politically neutral, it is not considered so by those who make revolutions of right or left, or by those who have special interests in the things we study. However strongly we may emulate the model of pure science, claims for applying our knowledge and the fact that what we learn is never a matter of social indifference will continue to put us into the position of people who give a service (or do a disservice) to our client, society. We cannot decide once and for all to be completely a profession or completely a science. The problem is chronic, as are all the basic problems with which professional groups have to deal. The basic parts of any professional code concerns such problems, those which cannot be settled once and for all, but for which—within the limits of lasting principles—different solutions have to be found according to the circumstances of time and place. We should, as an international society, be very chary of trying to determine in any detail solutions to apply to all of the many countries and situations in which sociologists have to work.

In America, at least, we have already gone far upon the road of professionalising our occupation in one respect. We are pushing the point of crucial decision to enter upon sociological study back to an ever earlier point in the schooling, hence in the life, of the individual. This is justified by the contention that, as our methods develop, the prerequisite knowledge and skills become greater. With more to be learnt, if the age of completing training remains the same, the starting point must be earlier. This argument is hard to answer. One must, however, take care to distinguish between conventional and strictly necessary prerequisite training. It is very easy to let prerequisites degenerate into a device to enforce early choice and to ensure proper indoctrination of potential members of an occupation or academic branch. Great is the temptation to raise the status of our subject by proving that it takes as long to become a sociologist as to become a physicist or physician. The best proof is simple; one makes it a rule. I doubt very much whether we know the best possible prerequisite training for sociologists. And since we are still a new and exploring subject we probably should not harden our programme of training too much lest we thereby also harden our subject and methods.

Furthermore, we do not know what effect early choice of sociology as a field of professional study will have upon the kinds of persons who will elect the field. It may be early choice would draw in people of some one bent, with a tendency toward selecting for study only those problems and toward using only those methods which fit the concept of sociology crystallised in the conventional prerequisites. Students entering medical schools show a tendency to pick those specialities which are well known and which are vaunted by their teachers as embodying the true model of medical practice. Choice of others, such as psychiatry, psycho-somatic medicine, epidemiology and public health, often comes quite late and after some ripening experience in which the young man, in effect, unlearns some things and sets out upon a new and less well-charted course of new learning. If we set the point of crucial decision to enter sociology too early, we may prevent that later change of interest which has given us so many of the best sociologists. For sociology is analogous, in this regard, not to a profession, but to a speciality within the larger profession of studying human affairs. If we apply rigid rules of entry to training, we may limit too much the circulation of people, hence of minds, from one branch of social science to another. Since ours is still one of the less known branches, we stand to gain from second and third choices. Furthermore, it may well be that interest in scientific analysis of societies in sociological terms is a mature one, a by-product of other training and experience. Our problem is to develop devices for training people to a high level of theoretical and technical competence without too much restriction of circulation from one branch of social science and experience to another, and without forcing the choice to a too early age.

There is a problem of circulation of sociologists later in their careers as well as during their training. An occupation in course of becoming a profession (and a new branch of learning in course of finding its place) will strive to solve the related problems of circulation and careers in two dimensions at the same time. On the one hand they will seek to set up strong and clear boundaries between their occupation and all others, and to develop career opportunities for those within. On the other hand, they will complement this clear bounding with an attempt to make the profession more universal, so that the professional may carry on his work in a greater variety of situations; so that his skill may meet the needs of any client whatsoever or so that his methods of investigation (in the case of a science) may be applied anywhere and at any time with equal validity. In the purest case the professional would do work which he alone can do, and the work would be of a kind wanted everywhere by all men; a maximum of specific bounding would be matched by a maximum of universality. Armed with his special qualifications, the ideal professional could go from job to job, client to client, place to place, and from country to country; so could the pure scientist. I suppose the best living model of this is the profession of medicine. Physicians have come as close as one can easily imagine to excluding all others from practise of their profession. They also perform a service that may be conceived as universal in character and as universally wanted. Actually, even in this case the reality does not completely corre- spond to the model. The boundaries between physical illness and spiritual illness are not clear and the definitions of illness and health vary from society to society. Sick people may want a doctor of their own kind, and not willingly accept strangers. Other people than physicians also share the treatment of people's troubles. Furthermore, the doctor's knowledge and skills are not completely universal. Some of them refer to the illnesses endemic in his own country. Finally, doctors in one country or place will not willingly allow strangers to come among them and compete for clients. So that, even this most specific and universal of professions does not achieve full monopoly as against other occupations and does not allow completely free circulation of professionals from place to place and situation to situation. The case of medicine shows that even in the extreme case the solutions are relative, not absolute. How sharply should and can sociologists in fact be set off as a peculiar group with specific careers reserved to them alone? How universal can their knowledge and skills of investigation be made? Consequently, in how large an area may they move around freely in course of their careers? I will discuss the last question first, and then return to the other one.

Of recent years there has been a healthy moving around of sociologists. We have met one another, held such meetings as this, worked in one another's universities and institutes. In some countries we have profited from the forced migration of sociologists from other countries. Perhaps we are closer to developing a universal conception of sociological study than ever before. On the other hand it is likely that most sociological careers will be confined to one country. Some sociologists will circulate in two or three closely related countries. A very few will move about in a really wide space. More will visit other countries for varying lengths of time. While the theoretical systems and the basic techniques for studying society should be universal, most sociologists get familiar with the historic conditions of one or two countries, with certain specific problems or institutions and with certain social changes in the setting of their own country or region. The methods may be universal; the data to which they are applied are historical.

In one sense a sociologist—as Robert E. Park used to say—tells the news, although in a more exact way and also in a more general and abstract way than do newspapers. It is not likely that we will ever be free of the demand that we show special interest in and knowledge of the conditions and changes in the world around us. For one thing observation of the human data on which we base our theoretical analysis depends generally on fairly intimate contact with persons and institutions. While playing the rôle of the timeless and disinterested outsider is an important item in the repertoire of the social scientist, it is not the whole of it. Our rôle requires also intense curiosity and personal concern about the people and problems studied. I predict that for these reasons, and for the more embarrassing one that even sociologists may be slightly ethnocentric and perhaps even concerned about foreign competition, most sociological careers will be played out within national boundaries.

Then comes the question of the possibility of having careers within countries, or regions of two or more countries which make up effective circulating areas. The possibilities obviously depend both upon the institutional organisation of academic and scientific activities within a given country and upon the size of the area. America, north of the Mexican border, forms a vast area with essentially the same institutional forms and with a great demand for people who go by the name of sociologist. The career possibilities are great. A young man may be fairly sure that he may choose from among a number of open places when he finishes his training, and that he may from there on move about from position to position to suit his talents and his special interests. If he does not succeed in getting a position where he may do specialised research, or if he does not wish to do so he can become one of the army of college teachers. College teaching absorbs many who are called, but not quite chosen. The number of positions in better known universities, in research organisations and in agencies which want people who can apply sociological knowledge are themselves numerous enough so that no competently trained and talented sociologist need want for a choice of jobs. In these circumstances there is ample opportunity for circulating careers within a fairly closely defined profession of sociologists (although it is still questionable how closely the professional group should be defined).

Many of our ideas concerning the professionalising of an academic subject rest upon the assumption of such a large market. But the academic market for all subjects is small in many countries and especially so for a new subject such as sociology. Generally speaking, there is no great absorbing institution for sociologists in other countries as in the United States and Canada. The sociologist cannot be absorbed by the European Gymnasium or Lycée as easily as by the American college. One of the problems of a new and fairly specialised subject in a small country is precisely the possibility of absorbing those who study the subject, but who do not immediately — if ever — enter upon the main career line in which the training would be used. In French Canada, for instance, there are three universities. Sociology is new in them. Once the few positions are filled there will not be places for an annual crop of talented young men trained as specialists in sociology. But without an annual crop of talented young people the subject itself languishes. Without a position in which he can use his knowledge and skill the young man languishes; or he finds another kind of place, and his skill languishes. The problem might be solved by increasing the area in which the individual may circulate in course of his career. We have already raised that question. It might also be solved by combining sociology with other activities, which means some departure from the ideal of complete professional specialisation. For the model of complete specialisation implies a large market. Even in the large market, it is not completely realised in many occupations. Nor is it all certain that it is the most efficient model for all kinds of activities. Research has never been fully separated from teaching in most academic subjects; in spite of all that has been said there is not the slightest evidence that it would be wise to do so. Few professions have ever achieved such specialisation that the practitioner carries on only one activity. The lawyer writes a brief, but he also pleads and arbitrates. Priests preach, hear confessions and administer the affairs of the Church. Physicians diagnose, treat, and investigate. The historic connection of teaching and research may be weakened in some fields, and certainly the best balance between them is not the same in all. But even where research stands alone as a professional activity, new people must be taught to carry it on. The connection is inescapable, although the weighting of the two activities in a given man's career may vary. There can also be other connections; as for instance, combinations of sociological research with practical activities of various kinds. We who are in the larger countries should be cautious in promoting concepts of professional specialisation which do not suit conditions in other countries. (I think I can assume that we are all more interested in the advancement of sociological knowledge than in the advancement of a profession of sociology.)

Specialisation and the closed profession should be instruments, not ends in themselves. It may well be that sociology will have to be combined with other activities in many countries if there is to be that amount of circulation which will keep new recruits coming into it, and which will make for a large enough group of collaborators to stimulate one another and to get the work of sociological analysis of the life of the country done.

The combination of sociology with other things that comes most easily to mind is that with other branches of social science and with the various kinds of social practise. And here we are back again with our problem of setting the boundaries of sociology, or rather, of the group of people called sociologists. The questions for solution are still both theoretical and practical. We may ask what combinations of sociology with other social or other sciences are best for the advancement of knowledge about man and society. This includes the basic question about what the effective divisions of social science will be in the future; we all know that the divisions of physical and biological science are not what they once were. The practical question—itself not free of theoretical aspects—is that of the best institutional organisation, including that of the best degree of separation of the sociological career from others. All will probably agree that a subject will not advance well unless there are nuclei of people in a position to give their undivided attention to it, nor will it flourish without that morale which comes of being a member of a group with a strong sense of colleagueship and a clear sense of common task. The developing and strengthening of such nuclei is certainly a major problem for sociologists in many countries. Their efforts to create more chairs of sociology, and to get more general recognition of the subject and more money for teaching and research will certainly be supported with enthusiasm by all of us. But I think it likely that these nuclei will function more effectively if the boundaries between us and related social sciences are not drawn too closely. Of course it is sometimes true that those closest to us are our bitterest opponents; nor am I unaware of the fact that economists and historians have sometimes effectively hindered the development of sociology by teaching a little of it themselves and pretending that no more is necessary (just as in the U. S. a university will hire one Negro professor to prove that it doesn't discriminate against Negroes). These dangers, like others, are chronic. I still believe that the best formula for sociology is to develop strong working nuclei of people, without drawing the boundaries too tightly between ourselves and our colleagues in other branches of social science and social practice. Circulation from one branch to another should be easy, so far as institutional and professional barriers are concerned; difficult in the sense that we set high standards of competence for ourselves, our collaborators and our apprentices. Sociology began as the maverick of the social sciences. Bastard child of philosophy, her fatherhood sometimes claimed, sometimes rejected by history, sibling or cousin of economics, political science, anthropology and psychology let her stand on the privilege of her unique parentage by not following too closely the model of an exclusive profession.

FORTY-EIGHT

Ethnocentric Sociology

William Graham Sumner, conservative though he was in many matters, was not afraid to make up words: the folkways, the mores, and ethnocentrism, his innovations, are in the vocabulary, not of sociologists alone, but of many other people. *Mores* was, of course, not a new word. Havoc had been cried for centuries with the phrase, "O tempora! O mores!"; generations of students had sung a heavily facetious and interminable song about Moses and Pharaoh's daughter, ending each chorus with "O tempora! O mores!" The phrase was undoubtedly familiar to the young gentlemen of Yale College, but Sumner's particular application was novel. *Folkways,* likewise, was made of old elements; again the application was new. It enabled people to speak with detachment of matters which, in ethics, they would have argued about with heat. It is always a problem of sociology to find terms conducive to discussion and analysis rather than heat. (God help us when we become content with study of things not worthy of heated argument!)

Ethnocentrism, although it, too, is composed of elements which were familiar to any educated person of that day, was indeed a new word. Sumner had much better luck with his new words than did some other sociologists. Suggestive as they are, Tarde's "gloriometer"—an index of popularity—and his "machinofacture"—to replace manufacture as machine work replaced handwork—did not take on.[1] Popularity ratings and

A paper read at the 24th Annual Meeting, Southern Sociological Society. Reprinted from *Social Forces,* Vol. 40, No. 1, October, 1961, University of North Carolina Press, Chapel Hill.

1. These terms are proposed in G. Tarde, *Psychologie Economique,* 2 Vols. (Paris, Félix Alcan, 1902).

the study of automation did not capture sociological attention until several decades later. Sumner's folkways, mores, and ethnocentrism did catch on and have remained with us into a generation which seems to think that *mores* is the plural of something spelt "m-o-r-e-."

There is more than one way of being ethnocentric. One can think so exclusively in the terms of his own social world that he simply has no set of concepts for comparing one social world with another. He can believe so deeply in the ways and the ideas of his own world that he has no point of reference for discussing those of other peoples, times, and places. Or, he can be so engrossed in his own world that he lacks curiosity about any other; others simply do not concern him. I will not try to complete the list.

The sociologists who preceded Sumner and those who were his contemporaries could hardly be accused of ethnocentrism in any of these senses. Some of them had developed grandiose schemes of comparative and evolutionary sociology. They used data, not all of it valid, from many tribes and nations living and dead. Need I remind you that Sumner uses many more illustrations from other peoples than from our own; and that Émile Durkheim based his *Elementary Forms of Religious Life* not on the study of revivals, sects, millenary movements, glossalalia, and ectasy in the western world—as some later people have done—but on what we are pleased to call "ethnological data"—data about other people than ourselves. None of those earlier sociologists made any move toward going out to the remote parts of the world to collect queer customs and social forms; they left that to others. Indeed, they did not take a great deal of trouble about collecting facts about their own world. They were content with what was in the books and what they could see about them.

As a matter of fact, those early comparative sociologists are hardly the ancestors of modern empirical students of society. Tarde, very much a progenitor of empirical sociologists, did not write about the primitive and exotic world. He stuck to Europe and America—to the industrial and urban world. Charles Booth,[2] who put a team into the streets, households, clubs, pubs, and churches of London in the 1890's, did not think of himself as a sociologist or as an ethnologist (although his people described the customs of working-class London with a detail and detachment worthy of the best of that discipline). The people who started to observe, describe, and count the details of social life in our own cities were mainly of another breed, so far as intellectual bent was concerned—more practically minded, and less concerned with theories of social evolution and change. The people who went forth to do likewise among the primitive peoples of the world were still another breed; they were eventually called anthropologists.

2. Charles Booth, *Life and Labour of the People of London,* 17 vols. (London: Macmillan, 1903).

There were a few conecting links. W. I. Thomas put together a once-famous book of readings on primitive and exotic societies with a name which reveals his way of thinking about them, *A Source Book of Social Origins;* he also wrote *The Polish Peasant in Europe and America* based in part on a major program of empirical observation in Chicago and Poland. R. E. Park, thought of primarily as a student of American cities, sent his students throughout the world to study both race relations and cities. In the main, however, as sociology grew, it became more and more the study of the nearer environment of the sociologist, less the study of other peoples, and less a comparison—for theoretical or practical purposes—of societies and cultures. At the same time, anthropology became the branch of social science which studied primitive peoples, along with prehistory and the evolution of the human species; while the anthropologists went out to observe and gather information on the spot, their eyes were turned rather toward the past than the present. They sought informants who could tell them how things used to be before the anthropologists and other disturbing elements had come. Thus, we came to have in our American academic world one department of people who studied the here and now and another which studied the there and then, provided the "there and then" did not include great cities, political movements, and economic change. This can hardly be said to have given us complete coverage of human societies.

Of course, we sociologists were saved a bit from our stay-at-homeism by the fact that our country is one of great ethnic, racial, religious, and regional diversity. For we are not so much a country as an empire cut of one piece. Britain had her alien breeds—except for the Irish and the Jews—farflung around the world; only now are they turning up in Notting Hill. We have had ours in our home territory,—which we conveniently expanded from time to time to take in some French, Spanish, and Indian peoples. As our industry and commercial industry grew, we imported labor, voluntarily or otherwise, from Europe, Africa, and Asia. By the time sociology got going, we were a very diverse people indeed. We could—and did—study the relations of the races, Italian kinship, communistic sects such as the Hutterites, acculturation and assimilation, the movement of people into cities (we studied without leaving home). We had cultural and racial diversity under our very eyes. In some respects we made the most of our sociological resources. We became very good at studying things in process. It was perhaps all slightly tinged with the notion that the natural and proper outcome of all social change was for people to become like unto us, that is, the American middle class. Even Booker T. Washington appears to have had this idea; perhaps even W. E. B. DuBois had it in his emphasis on the talented tenth.

Certainly in the course of studying his own people, the American sociologist became the most skillful of all sociologists in the gathering and analysis of data on current social behavior. Sociology became very current indeed — a little over-current. Great ingenuity and money have been put into developing methods and organizations for study of this year's voting and buying. In addition to being a very diverse people, we are also probably still that nation which has the largest number of people who can understand and answer questions — by word or in writing — in something approaching the same language. We have the largest number of people with the means to choose from among the various brands of goods offered by a highly standardized industry. We combine, in short, a high degree of likeness in language, taste, exposure to popular arts and news, with a wide, but not unlimited diversity. It is heaven for the sample-surveyor. But heaven can get to be a dull place. As we have become the world's best sample-surveyors (using survey in its present sense rather than that of the earlier survey movement) we have perhaps become a little inclined to believe that only societies amenable to study by this particular method are worth studying at all. Even in studying our own country we are inclined to leave off the ends of the curve. The eccentric are not our concern. Just as Sears, Roebuck will not stock shirts of sizes which are not sold by the hundreds of millions (or some such fantastic number), we sociologists will not count opinions or habits unless they are mass-produced. One finds that most sample surveys simply leave Negroes out of account; they are too few and too queer although they make their presence felt a bit now and again. Perhaps they will restore us to a livelier kind of sociology, interested in the portents of fundamental change and in those more extreme forms of collective behavior in which society is made plastic and ready for a new order.

In the meantime, that great expansion of Europe out of which came new great empires which divided up the new world a few centuries ago and got around to carving up Africa fairly recently is entering a new phase — a phase in which social and nationalistic movements do not smolder along for centuries before breaking into flame as in Europe, but in which they flare up over night. In Europe it took centuries to make a British, German, or French people of one language, culture, and loyalty. In Africa national movements arise where there is no single historical tongue or folklore and no common set of gods or other symbols to unite people. Africans have only their unifying counter-symbol, the white man who taught them nationalism and democracy and then denied access to them. In Africa and in Asia, millions are neither so primitive and rural as to be proper objects of study for the anthropologist; nor so literate, so possessed of a common language, so well-off as to choose goods from a list of advertised brands, and so to be fair game for the sociologist — if by sociologists we mean people who work in a particular way. In short, Africa is full of people who fit neither the specifications of the anthropologists nor those which sociologists, by implication, insist upon for people whom they will study. We have become methodologically ethnocentric; the anthropologists, eccentric. Perhaps we will have to invent some new branch of social science for the study of odd birds, of people who are neither modern nor ancient, urban nor rural, advanced nor retarded—the people who lie between the poles indicated by whatever is the current pair of adjectives used to sum up the world and all that is in it.

I shall be most disappointed if sociology becomes merely the study of the American, the mass, the distribution of moderate range, of the middle of the curve, of the well-established, of the parts of the world where only minor changes occur, where everyone speaks English, and everyone—including the women—wears pants. We have before us a world in which changes are happening on a scale and at a rate unknown in history, yet we remain geared to the slow-moving world of the nineteenth and early twentieth century (for it was slow-moving compared to our decades). And what do we do? We assume that if our present methods of sampling, interviewing, and surveying cannot be applied in a given country, the time has not yet come for a sociologist to go there. If they were proper, decent people, there would be more of them and they would be willing to answer questionnaires with a low rate of "nonresponse." And we pretend that everything worth writing gets translated into English *pronto*. We even have people who become authorities on Durkheim, Weber, and Simmel without having read a word in the original; and, consequently, they do not know whether what they have read is either properly translated or, to speak statistically, is a fair sample of what the men wrote. I am all for the sociological adventure; it will require travel, the eating of strange food, the speaking of strange languages, the tolerance of queer ideas, and the adventure of finding the means and methods suited to the problem.

Tarde, in "La Criminalité Professionelle,"[3] notes that every profession has its own temptations, the crimes to which it is especially subject and that each trade tends to commit murder with its own tools. The blacksmith murders with his hammer; the journalist assassinates with his pen. We sociologists? We invented ethnocentrism. Now we have fallen into it. We invented sampling and precoding, most excellent devices. But let us not eliminate from the human race, the object of our study, all people who are not precodable; nor those who, embittered by the withholding of freedom and human dignity, refuse to answer our coolly put questions about the future but act with unseemly haste and violence to seize freedom, dignity, food, and land.

3. G. Tarde, *Etudes de Psychologie Sociale* (Paris, V. Giard & E. Brière, 1898), pp. 162–194. Originally published in 1896.

FORTY-NINE

Race Relations and the
Sociological Imagination

What is there new to say about race relations? A colleague with great knowledge and deep experience of American race relations—he is a Negro—asked me that. I could have answered that new things are happening in race relations here and all over the world; things from which we can still learn.

A younger colleague who builds models and tries them out in the laboratory wanted to know to what general theoretical problem I would direct this discussion. I could have answered that race relations are so much a feature of most societies, and that they are in such flux that one could find in them a living laboratory for almost any problem of social interaction, social identity and social structure which one could imagine.

While these points are indeed part of my discussion, a deeper question concerning sociology and social life lurks in the background: Why did social scientists—and sociologists in particular—not foresee the explosion of collective action of Negro Americans toward immediate full integration into American society? It is but a special instance of the more general question concerning sociological foresight of and involvement in drastic and massive social changes and extreme forms of social action.

Robert E. Park defined race relations thus:

Presidential address read at the annual meeting of the American Sociological Association, Los Angeles, August, 1963. Reprinted from *American Sociological Review,* Vol. 28, No. 6, December, 1963.

... the term ... includes all the relations which exist between members of different ethnic and genetic groups which are capable of provoking race conflict and race consciousness, or of determining the relative status of the racial groups of which a community is composed. . . .[1]

Park's definition makes study of race relations a part of the study of society itself, not a peculiar problem requiring special concepts for its analysis.

In the same paper Park—it was in 1939—spoke of a great movement among "national minorities to control and direct their own destinies;" a movement "which began in Europe in the early part of the last century, and has now spread, as if it were contagious, to every part of the world; every part of the world at any rate, which has felt or still feels itself oppressed in its provincial, autonomous life, or for any other reason, inferior in its international status."[2]

We of this country ushered in that great movement for national independence a little earlier than the beginning of the 19th century. Never ethnically homogeneous, we became less so by swallowing the remnants of Spanish and French empires, by importing black labor from Africa, and by encouraging immigration from Europe and, for a time, from Asia. The

1. Robert E. Park, "The Nature of Race Relations," pp. 3–45 in E. T. Thompson (ed.), *Race Relations and the Race Problem*. Durham, N. C.: Duke University Press, 1939. Reproduced in Park, *Race and Culture*, New York: Free Press, 1950, pp. 81–116. See p. 82. He continues thus (p. 114): "What then, finally, is the precise nature of race relations that distinguishes them, all the variety of conditions in which they arise, from other fundamental forms of human relations? It is the essence of race relations that they are the relations of strangers; of peoples who are associated primarily for secular and practical purposes; for the exchange of goods and services. They are otherwise the relations of people of diverse races and cultures who have been thrown together by the fortunes of war, and who, for any reason, have not been sufficiently knit together by intermarriage and interbreeding to constitute a single ethnic community with all that it implies."

2. *Loc. cit.* The following longer quotation may be useful to the reader:

"In these cities [of the twentieth century] a new civilization, new peoples, the modern world, with new local varieties of culture, is visibly coming into existence.

"One of the evidences of this is the sudden and wide-spread interest in nationalism and in local nationalities. The struggle of minor racial and language groups for some sort of independent and individual expression of their traditional and national lives, which began in Europe in the early part of the last century, has now spread, as if it were contagious, to every part of the world; every part of the world at any rate, which has felt or still feels itself oppressed in its local, autonomous life, or for any other reason, inferior in its international status.

"It is interesting that this ambition of national minorities, if I may so describe them, to control and direct their own destinies, in accordance with their own tradition and sense of values, has not in the least diminished their interest in, or determination to possess and use, in their own interest, all the technical knowledge and all the technical devices upon which the dominance of Europe in the modern world seems to have been based.

"The present nationalist movement, associated as it is by the practical cessation of migration and the so-called "devolution" of missions, is evidence that we are at the end of one epoch in human and racial relations and at the beginning of another."

movement continued in Central and South America; those new states were also, all of them, racially mixed. The Spanish- or Portuguese-speaking cities were surrounded by latifundia with indigenous, African or mixed labor force, beyond which generally there lay a back country whose inhabitants were not part of any body politic. As in North America, immigration from Europe and even from Asia continued. To our North, Canada gradually took on national status, by a confederation of provinces, the oldest of which was French-speaking Quebec.[3]

In Europe the continental Empires began to break up; Belgium, Greece, Italy, Norway, Finland and the Balkan states became nation-states. At the end of the First World War, the process went on until a belt of independent states was formed between Russia and the west. Established in the name of the self-determination of peoples—of people of common language and culture governing themselves on their historic territory—not one of those nation-states corresponded to the ideal. Every one contained some minority of another people than the one in whose name independence had been claimed. Nor, indeed, was any one of the dominant states from which these peoples had got independence, made into a country of one language and people by this cleansing. Germany tried to reverse the trend under Hitler, but ended up smaller than ever, as two states each racially purer—in our broad sense—than any in Europe. In that sense, Hitler won.

The victors of the First World War were proponents of the self-determination of European peoples, but all had overseas empires to which they did not apply that principle—as Max Weber pointed out in a speech at the time.[4] Their turn came after World War II. Their Asiatic, Oceanic and African possessions then sought and got political independence. None of these former colonies is racially homogeneous. India, Indonesia, the Philippines all contain a variety of languages, historic religions, cultures and tribes. Mass migrations, some voluntary, some forced, have, if anything, made people more aware of those divisions. In the little artificial states of the old French Asiatic colonies, probably few people know what state they do live in. In the Near East and Northern Africa, a series of states, supposedly Muslim in religion and Arab in culture, are in fact a mosaic of languages, sects, tribes, races, classes and "communities." Israel, enclaved among them, is itself an ethnic pressure-cooker; linguistic and patriotic conformity are insisted upon.

In the oldest state south of the Sahara, South Africa, the European

3. New Zealand, Australia and the Union of South Africa became, like Canada, self-governing states with minorities, either indigenous or European, or both.

4. Max Weber. "Deutschland unter den europäischen Weltmächten (October, 1916)," pp. 73–93 in *Gesammelte Politische Schriften*. Munich: Drei Masken Verlag, 1921. See pp. 89–90.

population is divided into majority and minority, which are numerically but a fraction of the total population of the country. The black Africans, once tribal, are being welded into something like an entity by the effort of the Europeans to keep them from it. Among the Europeans themselves, the former minority of Afrikaners has become the dominant group in politics, although English South Africans still dominate the economy. The other countries and the few remaining colonies in sub-Saharan Africa are all diverse in language, culture, tribal loyalties and degree of integration into modern urban economy and life. So diverse are they that the language of the battle for independence is generally that of the oppressor from whom they seek emancipation; language, that is, in both senses, of letters and words and of political and social philosophy. A bit of African chant and rhythm make the rhetoric seem more indigenous than it is. Portugal has thus far saved her empire by not teaching the language of independence, in either sense, to her African subjects.

All of these African countries are observation posts for those interested in the process of nation-making on which Bagehot wrote a classic essay a century ago. The development of a feeling of national, rather than local or tribal, identity proceeds but painfully in some of them.[5] Lucy Mair thinks its growth depends not upon a state of mind induced by propaganda, but upon social structure. Cities, communications, education and experience of industrial employment will create people who identify themselves with a nation. "The structure of an industrial society," she says, "is such that no section of it can pursue its interests by trying to cut itself off from the rest."[6] Whether or not she is right on that point, certainly the new African states are not yet nations. It may be that the state makes the nation, and not the reverse

This tremendous burgeoning of so-called nation-states took place in a time of colossal migrations, voluntary or forced, of people seeking land or wanted as labor for industrial agriculture, the extractive or more advanced industries. Migration makes diversified populations. Even Japan, of all nations perhaps the one with the strongest myth of national homogeneity, got a large population of strange people as she became industrial and an empire—Koreans, Okinawans, her traditional Eta and her tribal Ainu have given the Japanese something on which to exercise their racial exclusiveness. As a final twist, some of the centers of erstwhile empires are now getting a reverse migration from their former colonies. West Indian

---

5. Walter Bagehot, *Physics and Politics*. (New York: Appleton-Century-Crofts, 1873), Chapters III and IV, "Nation-Making."
6. Lucy Mair, "Divide and Rule in the New Countries?" *New Society*, No. 37 (June 13, 1963), p. 18.

Negroes are entering the British labor force at the bottom, as are Algerians in France and Puerto Ricans in New York.

The very era in which the concept of nation-state has been so powerful has been one of empire-building and empire-breaking; an era in which the idea has spread, as Park said, like a contagion; a queer contagion, since the European countries which spread it did their best to prevent others—those in their own empires, at any rate—from catching it. The nation-state, far from eliminating race relations, intensifies them; its ideology of the correspondence of cultural and racial with political boundaries makes internal problems of what were external or international problems in the days of empire or in the more primitive times of tribal rule. It has made great numbers of human individuals aware of race as a fateful personal characteristic, determining the terms of their struggle for a place. It has made whole groups of people conscious of themselves as having a status, not merely in their own region, but in the world. Race, in our broad sense, has been made a part of the political, economic and social processes of much of the world. The United Nations has become an organ of world opinion which makes every domestic racial problem again a diplomatic and international one as well.

The relations among races are now even more disturbed than when Park wrote. They offer a richer and more varied living laboratory than ever for any of us sociologists who would consider going abroad other than to attend conferences. But it is not precisely a laboratory which they offer, for we have but one chance to observe, to understand and to act.

Of course, we need not go abroad. Racial turmoil is here at home. In North America, two elderly nation-states—as those things go—contain two of the oldest established minorities of the world, Negro Americans and French Canadians. When I call them old, I refer to the duration of their position in the nation-states of which they are a part. Negro Americans, aided by some others, are engaged in their most massive, determined, urgent and detailed struggle for equality. French Canadians are vigorously demanding an overhaul of the century-old bargain sealed by the Confederation of the provinces into a single dominion.

Although there have always been agitators in both minorities, there have been long periods of quiet in which there was an entente between the leading classes of each minority and the dominant groups and implicit acceptance of it by the masses of the people. During these periods the dominant group apparently thought that an equilibrium had been established for an indefinite period, with changes going on so slowly as not to upset it. One might have said of both American and Canadian society what Park says of all:

Every society represents an organization of elements more or less antagonistic to each other but united for the moment, at least, by an arrangement which defines the reciprocal relations and respective sphere of action of each. This accommodation, this *modus vivendi,* may be relatively permanent as in a society constituted by castes, or quite transitory as in societies made up of open classes. In either case, the accommodation, while it is maintained, secures for the individual or for the group a recognized status. . . .

In the accommodation, then, antagonism of the hostile elements is, for the time being, regulated, and conflict disappears as overt action, although it remains latent as a potential force. With a change in the situation, the adjustments that had hitherto held in control the antagonistic forces fail. There is confusion and unrest which may result in open conflict. Conflict . . . invariably issues in a new accommodation or social order, which in general involves a changed status in the relations among the participants.[7]

Park's view of society is that status arrangements are always tentative and likely to be questioned. In our two minorities, many of the younger people are questioning the bargain — the status arrangement — made by their forebears and consented to by their elders (for failure to act is considered consent). But what is the time perspective of parties to a bargain? The group with the greatest interest in the status quo may be expected to think of the arrangement as permanent, and to justify it by various devices — such as the doctrine of racial superiority and inferiority. The group disadvantaged in status may use some principle of permanency, which has been violated by the status-bargain forced upon them. Thus a national minority, such as the French-Canadians, will prove that it was there first; that it is an older nation than the oppressor. The function of folklore is to establish antiquity and the rights based upon it. Colonial tribal minorities can achieve a sort of apocalyptic eternity, as Nadine Gordimer says so well of Africans:

You can assure yourself of glory in the future, in a heaven, but if that seems too nebulous for you — and the Africans are sick of waiting for things — you can assure yourself of glory in the past. It will have exactly the same sort of effect on you, in the present. You'll feel yourself, in spite of everything, worthy of either your future or your past.[8]

In both minorities, the Negro-American and the French-Canadian, the time perspectives of past bargains are being called into question; in both cases, the dominant group asks either that the bargain be permanent or that it be changed but slowly.

7. R. E. Park and E. W. Burgess, *Introduction to the Science of Sociology,* Chicago: University of Chicago Press, 1921, p. 665.
8. Nadine Gordimer, *Occasion for Loving,* New York: Viking, 1960, pp. 9-10.

Why the great outbreak of unrest and demand for change in these two minorities at just this moment? Certainly there have been great changes in the situation of both. At the last census, French Canadians had become more urban than other Canadians; Negroes, more urban than other Americans. With the precipitous drop in the agricultural labor force of both countries, these minorities have undergone changes of occupational structure probably greater than those of the rest of the population. Both minorities, in the industrial and urban order in which their fate now lies, are concentrated at lower points of the socio-economic scale than are the dominant groups.

These similarities may appear strained. They cover great differences. French Canadians do not, and never have, suffered civil or personal disabilities; they have not had to give deference to others. No social rank inheres in being French Canadian; the only aristocracy Canada ever had was French. French institutions in Canada are more venerable than English. French Canadians have headed the national government and always control the governments of their province and of most cities within it.

The two minorities are alike in that they have gone from a rural condition to an urban and see themselves as thereby put into a position of increased disadvantage; and at precisely that time in history when such disadvantage is no longer a purely domestic matter. But they seek opposite remedies. The Negro Americans want to disappear as a defined group; they want to become invisible as a group, while each of them becomes fully visible as a human being. Only so will they, in the myriad relations of American life, be judged by the characteristics pertinent to each. They want to be seen, neither as Negroes nor as if they were not; but as if it did not matter. The French Canadians, on the other hand, struggle not for survival as individuals — in which their problems are those of other Canadians — but for survival as a group with full social, economic and political standing.

These two apparently opposite goals represent one of the dialectics of human beings and the groups with which they identify themselves and are identified. How like others, how different from them shall I, shall we, can I, can we, be? And in what respects? Jews in the western world are generally thought to find these questions difficult, and the solutions unstable. Such a group as Negro Americans is at one pole — where all is to be gained from reduction of the social perception of differences. Their end will have been gained when Negroid characteristics and African descent matter no more and no less than other physical traits and quirks of ancestry. At that point, there would be no racial bargain. Whether all persons known as Negroes — and their descendants of that future day — would be content to wipe out their collective past and all features of Negro-American culture is another matter.

Some Negro Americans have given up hope that white Americans will ever live up to the bargain of the American ideology of equal rights for all. They reject everything American — the country, the Christian religion, their Anglo-Saxon names; as so-called Black Muslims they claim complete and eternal difference from white Americans and seek to develop such solidarity among Negroes as will enable them to fight and bargain for a separate realm. To support their claim, they have imagined themselves a glorious past as the Muslims who were the scourge of Europe and Christianity throughout the centuries. They project themselves into an apocalyptic future when, in cargo-cult fashion, their ship will come in and the evil white race will be destroyed.[9] This, mind you, is not in the South Seas, in Black Africa or among dispossessed American Indians, but among urban Americans. The question one must ask is this: at what point do people so far lose confidence in the "others" with whom they are destined to live as to reject all the collective symbols of their common society, and to erase from their talk all phrases which imply common humanity. Such symbolic Apartheid has not been the prevailing mind of Negro Americans, but it lurks ready to be called into the open with every alienating rebuff. The balance is still with the movement for complete integration.

Indeed it is so much so that some Negroes are claiming special treatment in order to make the integration more rapid, on the ground that past discrimination has loaded them with a competitive disadvantage which it will take a long time to overcome. Thus, for the moment, they appear to be asking that their Negro-ness be not forgotten, in order that, in the long run, it may be. It is the vigor and urgency of the Negro demand that is new, not its direction or the supporting ideas. It was that vigor and urgency that sociologists, and other people, did not foresee, even though they knew that Negroes would not be content forever with their situation, and should have sensed that the contradiction between "speed" and "deliberate" would become the object of both wit and anger.

In Canada, the tension between French and English has always existed, and had always turned upon the question of the survival and status of the French as a linguistic, cultural and political entity. French Canadians believe that a large proportion of English Canadians assume that French Canada will and ought to cease to exist, just as English Canadians believe that many Americans assume that Canada itself will and ought to cease to exist. From time to time, the tension becomes great and various French nationalist movements arise. In time of war, English Canadians accuse

9. M. Eliade, " 'Cargo-Cults' and Cosmic Regeneration," pp. 139–143 in S. L. Trupp (ed.), *Millennial Dreams in Action. Comparative Studies in Society and History,* Supplement II, The Hague, Mouton, 1962. See other articles in this volume. The members of such cults are enjoined to prepare for the great day, not by political action, but by strict abstinence from all contact with the enemy and his works.

French Canadians of less than full devotion to the cause, while French Canadians resent the attempt of the others to tell them their duty. In the great depression there was tension over jobs and the burden of unemployment centering about the fact that management and ownership of industry were English, while labor was French.

The present movement is the first major one in time of peace and prosperity, when critics can say, and do, "They never had it so good. What do they want anyway?" To be sure it is a *drôle de paix* in which some other Canadians wish the French might join more heartily in the campaign against Castro—as they ought, it is said, being Catholics and therefore presumably leaders in the battle against Communism. Not only are the circumstances different from the times of earlier national upsurgings, but the very rhetoric is contrary, and some of the most ardent of earlier leaders are dubbed compromisers, or even traitors.

Most earlier French nationalist leaders called upon their fellow Canadians to respect the bargain of Confederation everywhere in Canada; bilingualism and public support of Catholic schools should prevail, or at least be tolerated, everywhere, not only in Quebec. The French were to have parity, their just proportion of all positions in government, and eventually in business and industry. But to merit their survival French Canadians should retain their rural virtues, including a high birth rate which would win for them, in due time, a victory of the cradle. To retain those virtues, their unemployed and the extra sons of farmers should go north to clear and settle new lands. Only so would they save themselves from the vices of the city, which were alleged to be English, American—and Jewish. To document their charter-membership of Canada, they cultivated folklore and song; their novelists wrote of the clearing of the land, of the drive of logs down the rivers after the spring thaw, of the land passing from father to son. They emphasized their place as the true Canadians—*Canadiens* without qualifying adjective—while English Canadians were *Anglais,* or perhaps *Canadiens anglais.*

Thus equal rights with English in a common country was the theme of most of the earlier leaders, and was the sentiment of most French Canadians, whether active in any movement or not. But the new movement talks of separation of the State, not Province, of Quebec from Canada; if not separation, then a new constitution giving Quebec a special status. It calls the French people of Quebec by the name *Québecois.* English Canadians are called Canadians, with English spelling, and the French word Canadien is avoided. The government in Ottawa is spoken of as an alien power maintaining unjust colonial rule; the *Québecois* are chid for allowing themselves to remain the only white colonized people in the world and, indeed, one of the few colonized peoples, white or colored. Instead of seeking bilingualism everywhere in Canada, the more extreme wing—and even some quite conservative groups—ask for a Quebec with one language, French, and complete fiscal independence from Canada. The movement takes the doctrine of the nation-state in its extreme form as defining the goal to be attained.

Instead of praising rural life, they speak of an urban and industrial Quebec, which will solve its problems by becoming master in its own house. They dismiss return to the land and the victory of the cradle as dreams that divert French Canadians from attaining realistic goals. Those goals of well-being for an urban and industrial people are to be gained by socialistic means, and by breaking the power of Yankee capitalism.

Some talk of Freud, Marx and alienation. In literary criticism, they talk of emancipation from obsession with the past, the frontiers, the land and France; not of denying the past and French identity, but of taking them for granted while they deal with their problems as North American city dwellers, as a people who need no justification except that they exist and have the same problems to write about as do others.

The new rhetoric may not be used in extreme form by many, but it has permeated a great deal of French-Canadian writing and political talk. It has spread much more rapidly than any one expected. There are indeed some extreme groups who have turned to the bombing of symbols of British hegemony—a statue of Queen Victoria, an army recruiting station, and mailboxes in what is considered a well-to-do English quarter. The members of this small terrorist sect are not the leaders of the separatist movement, but their existence and temper indicate the intensity of the general feeling of malaise. Those arrested and accused of the bombings are alienated young men of the city, not intellectuals, but part of the white-collar Lumpenproletariat, semi-employed. It has been said that the whole separatist movement is one of the little bureaucrats of business and government. In its more moderate form, the movement has certainly been joined by many people of various classes, whose rhetoric also turns in the direction of a special status for the State of Quebec, of a renegotiation of the terms of Confederation.

To return to this country, the new things about the Negro movement are not its ultimate goals and its rhetoric, but its immediate goals, its mass and its structure. It got under way and took on mass as a struggle for the equal right to consume goods and services—food, transportation, education, housing and entertainment. This is a goal of people with at least some money to spend and with the aspiration to spend as others do. The Negro Americans who led those first sit-ins were indeed so American that they seem more humiliated by not being able to spend the dollar than they would be at not having a dollar to spend. "My money is as good as the other fellow's," is probably the ultimate expression of American democracy. Here we meet the great paradox in American social structure. While our race line is, next to South Africa's, the world's tightest, we have the times-over largest Negro middle class in the world, and the largest group of Negroes approaching middle-class western tastes and with the money to satisfy them in some measure. This may be due to the fact that we are that country in which industry first depended upon its own workers to be its best customers, and in which movement has gone farthest in that direction.[10] Handicapped though Negro Americans are in employment and income, they are well-enough off to resent the barriers which prevent them from keeping up with the white Joneses. This reflects a great change in the Negro social structure itself; goal and social structure are doubtless functions of each other. In the struggle for consumption it appears generally to have been true that the Negro participants were of higher social class than the whites who have set upon them, or perhaps it is that racial struggles bring out the low-class side of white people.

Now that the movement for equality of the right to consume has moved into high gear—and especially in the South—the movement for equality in employment has taken on new momentum in the North. When, during the war, a number of us worked to get Negroes employed in industry in Chicago, our first objective was to get them moved into semi-skilled production jobs, and out of maintenance and unskilled work. The effort now is aimed higher—at the kinds of work controlled by craft unions, and especially those in construction. For in the precariously seasonal construction trades apprenticeships and jobs are notoriously held tightly in ethnic and family cliques. The battle for equality of right to consume may be essentially won long before access to all kinds of training and jobs is open. There are many inaccessible crevices in the American labor market. I have seen no good account of who the people are who are demonstrating at construction sites, but apparently many have been drawn in who never took part in demonstrations before. We may expect, I believe, that each new immediate objective, whether for the right to consume or to work, will draw in new kinds of participants.

One of the most striking cases of this is the apparent mobilization of the National [Negro] Medical Association. It was reported in the press that members of the National Medical Association were to picket the con-

10. F. P. Spooner shows that in South Africa the high standard of living of Whites rests upon the poverty of the Blacks; seven-eighths of the labor in mining, the industry that brings money to the country, is Black. The consumption industries import raw materials with the foreign exchange earned by mining, and produce at prices which only Whites can afford. *South African Predicament. The Economics of Apartheid,* New York: Praeger, 1960, pp. 181 *et seq.*

vention of the American Medical Association in Atlantic City and their headquarters in Chicago. The permanent executive secretary of the Negro association declared himself against the picketing as it would embarrass his good friends in the American Medical Association; but the young president was reported to have said he would himself lead the picketing. Negro physicians have been notoriously conservative in their attack on racial discrimination — even against themselves. Safely ensconced in general practice with patients whom white physicians did not want, they enjoyed a certain security provided they were content to practice in their own offices or in segregated hospitals, letting such Negro patients as could get into other hospitals go to white physicians. But that security is in danger. Negro physicians no longer have a near monopoly on Negro patients, for the patients may be part of insurance schemes which give them access to clinics or hospitals and which will pay their bills. The few segregated Negro hospitals are in generally sad and declining condition. Young Negro physicians do not want to tie their professional fate to them. Back of all this, however, lies a general change in the structure of medical organization. The capital goods of medicine are concentrated more and more in hospitals and clinics; patient and physican meet where the tools and machines and auxiliary personnel are found. If the Negro patient has more access to them than the Negro physician, the latter is in a poor position. Thus a general change in the social structure of medical institutions strikes hard at the position of one of the Negro-American elites. If the younger Negro physicians are to survive, they must get into the main institutions of modern medicine; that means specialization, access to clinics, hospitals and laboratories, membership of various colleague groups and ability to move freely. The American Medical Association is the bastion of the older organization of medicine, for the power to accept members lies completely in the hands of county medical associations, dominated by local physicians out of sympathy with the modern trends in medicine as well as likely to be opposed to recognizing Negroes as full colleagues.

Perhaps it took this combination of changes in the structure of medical institutions, plus the momentum of a great social movement to stir the relatively well-off and well-entrenched to such undignified action as picketing. The change in medical institutions gives the younger Negro physician a motive for rejecting the bargains of the older ones; the new movement gives them the will and the courage.

The older Negro middle class — in the clergy, teaching, law, medicine, insurance and undertaking — had its being in segregated institutions. They got support from white people and organizations with an implicit bargain that there was to be no Negro middle class except what could be supported by giving services to Negro clients and customers; as Park said, the accommodation gave certain Negroes a defined place and field of activity. Now that these institutions are undergoing changes much like those in medicine, the very basis of the older Negro elite would be shaky even without changes in the race line itself.[11]

But that line is changing. With every increase of access of Negroes to consumption and service institutions, the security of the older Negro middle class, which depended upon segregated delivery of services takes another blow; and another front is opened in the battle for equality in the production and distribution of goods and services. Like so many battles in time of great change, it is in part a battle of the generations. In the larger, more itinerant and cosmopolitan system of distributing professional services in which younger men must make their careers, sponsorship of specialized colleagues and the good opinion of their peers about the country counts more than favor with a local clientele or local white leader. While the standards of judgment among professional peers are in some respects objective and universal, yet the specialized colleagueships of the academic, scientific and professional world are small and relations are quite personal. People are loath to hire a stranger. This is the front on which Negro scholars and professional men have to move forward.[12]

Another new feature of the present movement is that some white people have joined not merely in financial support but in direct action itself. A few white Protestant, Catholic and Jewish religious dignitaries have lent not merely their voices, but also their bodies to the demonstrations. Larger numbers of young white persons, mainly students, have joined, perhaps at somewhat greater risk, in marches, demonstrations and sit-ins in both South and North. This is another matter on which Park commented, in 1923, just 40 years ago:

> What has happened to other peoples in this modern world, has happened, is happening, to the Negro. Freedom has not given him the opportunity for participation in the common life of America and of the world that he hoped for. Negroes are restless and seeking. We are all restless, as a matter of fact.
>
> In some respects, however, it seems to me the Negro, like all the other

11. E. Franklin Frazier, *The Black Bourgeoisie*, New York: Free Press, 1957. That was the middle class of which Frazier wrote so mordantly.

12. I have not commented on the role in this movement of the older organizations established to improve the condition of Negroes, to win their rights, or to consolidate their position. The Urban Leagues originally had the form of social agencies, with boards of leading citizens and support by community chests as well as by gifts. The National Association for the Advancement of Colored People was originally both a fighting and an elite organization without the features of a philanthropic agency; it became the organ of legal action. The new direct action has been led by new people. A division of labor seems to be emerging among them, with the whole enlivened by the popular direct action. This is a common enough feature of social movements; as some organizations settle down to one style of negotiation or action, new styles of action spring up around new, unofficial, charismatic leaders.

disinherited peoples, is more fortunate than the dominant races. He is restless, but he knows what he wants. The issues in his case, at least, are clearly defined. More than that, in this racial struggle, he is daily gaining not merely new faith in himself, but new faith in the world. Since he wants nothing except what he is willing to give to every other man on the same terms, he feels that the great forces that shape the destinies of peoples are on his side. It is always a source of great power to any people when they feel that their interests, so far from being antagonistic, are actually identified with the interests of the antagonists. We of the dominant, comfortable classes, on the other hand, are steadily driven to something like an obstinate and irrational resistance to the Negro's claims, or we are put in the position of sympathetic spectators, sharing vicariously in his struggles but never really able to make his cause whole-heartedly our own.[13]

The obstinate and irrational resistance of which Park spoke is certainly in evidence, and apparently more on the consumption front than on the job front. Perhaps the American ego is more centered on symbolic consumption of housing among the right neighbors than on having the right job and colleagues. But what about those white people who join in the lively action on behalf of Negro equality? Are they really nothing more than sympathetic spectators? This raises questions concerning the part of people without status disadvantage in the struggles of those who have a disadvantage. The clergy and many white people are, for the first time, going into overt action on behalf of an eternal principle which they presumably believed and preached all the time. In this case, conscience seems to have been aroused only after the movement, initiated and led by the injured party, got momentum and showed some signs of success. This somewhat cynical suggestion is no answer to this problem: What circumstances so re-define a social situation that some espoused eternal moral principle is considered not merely to apply to it, but to require immediate drastic action of kinds the keepers of the principle ordinarily would not consider proper? Some years ago Samuel Stouffer discovered that the leaders of American communities are more liberal on many issues than are people of less influence. What his study did not throw light on is this: When do those tolerant leaders initiate action to implement their views? The answer on many issues, is that they do not initiate action. In some Southern cities those leaders of the business community who would answer to Stouffer's description, enter to support the Negroes when the movement is under way and when stubborn opposition from another kind of community leader endangers prosperity and peace.[14]

13. Robert E. Park, "Negro Race Consciousness as Reflected in Race Literature," *American Review*, I (Sept.-Oct., 1923), 505-516, reproduced in R. E. Park, *Race and Culture*, New York: Free Press, 1950, pp. 284-300.
14. Charles Levy, in his study of Front Royal, Virginia, in an integration crisis, showed that the more liberal leaders simply abdicated and were replaced by more fanatical people who

Whether white people will remain sympathetic is one question; whether they will remain spectators is another. The alternative to being a spectator is entering the action. The more insistent Negroes become on equality now, the more other people will be forced to act one way or another. To the extent that they must act, the question is whether they will act for or against the Negroes' cause, and with what intensity and persistence. The mood of Negro Americans is, at the moment, one of sticking to the fight until it is won. White people, including the moral and religious function- aries, may persist only so long as they—as Park suggests—are restless and need a cause. Perhaps some other cause will win them away. Or perhaps they will lose their taste for causes.

I should not like to predict what equilibrium, what compromises, sup- ported by what bargains, will be reached in American race relations. But it looks as if no long-term bargain short of fully equal status is likely to be accepted by Negroes. Compromises in some groups and structures will last longer than in others, depending in part upon how rapidly participants turn over. Customers can turn over quickly; where kinship, seniority and long tenure prevail, as in some occupations and organizations, new kinds of people can come in only very slowly. Institutional time is not the time of social movements. Whether Negroes will be content to let old bargains stand where turn-over is slow, and whether they will be able to break slow-moving institutional processes are both questions which cannot be answered now. We must ask: What will be the rate of breakdown of the race line in various segments of society?

Even if we cannot answer these questions about the future state of things, we might at least speculate on them and even on that state in which it could be said that there is no longer a race problem. We might imagine a state of things in which Negroes and whites, as both are defined in our society, would be distributed in their chance proportions among all the occupational, income, educational, residential, or other cells in a great table of the population. That unlikely ultimate state could not be the immediate result of any bargain; it could come about only after a very, very long time in which Negroes could have penetrated, like some slow-moving dye, into the many small capillaries of our complex social system. Indeed, by the time it occured. Negro and white, as discernible racial types, might long since have disappeared. That would take a long time, even if race as a barrier to inter-marriage were to disappear.

Last year I asked some students this question: "Suppose that tomorrow

---

were not, in ordinary times, in positions of leadership. This is, again, a structural problem; in what circumstances does one type of leadership win over another in these crises? See his unpublished Master's thesis, "School Desegregation in Warren County, Virginia during 1958-1960: A Study in the Mobilization of Restraints," Department of Sociology, University of Chicago, 1961.

morning Americans were to wake up blind to all the distinguishing marks of race; what would be the long- and the short-term results?" One student, a mathematician, figured how many people of white, Negro and mixed ancestry there would be in the country after certain numbers of generations. There were, in her formula, certain assumptions which do not correspond to the present reality, but we must allow that license to mathematicians. Another student thought that we are so in need of someone to subordinate, that we would immediately visit upon the Jews or some other minority all we now visit upon Negroes; that might be called the "sick" answer. Others based their answers to this science-fiction question on other assumptions and worked out other possibilities. One student, of his own initiative, imagined that all the inhabitants of Samoa, whom we affect to love and admire, landed one morning, miraculously multiplied but penniless, in Los Angeles — to stay. Whether things would have worked out as he described them, I do not know. The only sociologist of note who ever did anything of the sort in print, was Gabriel Tarde. He imagined a society in which men were all assured of plenty of food and other comforts with but a few minutes of labor each day; the economic friction was taken out of human interaction. He then gave his notions of what would happen to sex, music, the mind, and many other things. He even gave a gently satirical account, by members of that society, of a group called sociologists who had existed in some ancient time — Tarde's own time.

I do not claim that either Tarde or those students to whom I gave that absurd assignment produced probable predictions. At least, they exercised their sociological imaginations in ways that are unaccustomed. Some of them may, in the future, attack problems not by making predictions based on projecting slow trends of opinion a few years into the future, but by imagining a wide range of possibilities, and following out the fantastic and improbable ones as well as those which seem most likely and immediate.

Herbert Hyman has lately complained that "applied social research seems oriented to the immediate issue rather than to be problem oriented. The latent aspects of an issue are neglected and trend designs for surveys have lost prestige."[15] I agree with him if his notion of trends includes a great many lines of change, some of which have no obvious relation to the problem in hand, all going on at the same time and at various rates. The concept of trend, as it is ordinarily used, appears to me too limited to stimulate the sociological imagination to its fullest and most fruitful level of activity. Some have asked why we did not foresee the great mass movement of Negroes; it may be that our conception of social science is so empirical, so limited to little bundles of fact applied to little hypotheses,

15. H. H. Hyman, "England and America, 1962," in Daniel Bell (ed.), *The Radical Right*, New York: Doubleday and Co., 1963, p. 238.

that we are incapable of entertaining a broad range of possibilities, of following out the madly unlikely combinations of social circumstances.

It is sometimes said that sociology deals with only those processes of social behavior which are repeated again and again. That statement, useful in its way, may have been taken too seriously. A process may be repeatable, but it may occur in some set of circumstances which has never happened before or yet. Whenever before was there a race-caste of 20,000,000 people, literate, with the aspirations and basic skills of a modern industrial society, with money to spend and the tastes which make them want to spend it on the same things as do other people of highly industrial societies, yet limited by others in their full realization of all these things; living in a society which has preached that all men are created free and equal, and has practiced it not fully, but enough so that with every increase of education, standard of living and of middle-class achievement of the race-caste, the discrepancy between partial and full practice of equality becomes a deeper, more soul-searing wound. Why should we have thought, apart from the comfort of it, that the relations of the future could be predicted in terms of moderate trends, rather than by the model of the slow burn reaching the heat of massive explosion?

Another possible impediment to claiming our full license to consider every possible human arrangement is that we internalize limits on our sociological imagination. Most of us apparently go about tacitly accepting the cliché that whites and Negroes don't want to marry each other, and that white women are never attracted sexually by Negro men, without considering the circumstances in which it would no longer be true (if it is indeed true now).[16] One of the accomplishments of Freud was to break the bonds of repression so that a person could make his memory match his outrageous impulses. One function of the sociologist is to be that sort of analyst *cum* model-building mathematician for human society, who will break the bonds of ordinary thought and moral inhibition so as to conceive a great variety of human situations, even the most outrageous. Perhaps we failed to foresee present racial movements because our whole inward frame is adapted to study of the middle range of behavior, with occasional conducted tours toward, but not dangerously near, the extremes.

The kind of freeing of the imagination that I am speaking of requires a great and deep detachment, a pursuit of sociological thought and research

16. Certain novelists have dealt with this theme, not merely frankly, but with penetration and some sense of the aesthetics of it. Among them are Alan Paton, *Too Late the Phalarope*, New York: Scribners, 1952; Nadine Gordimer, *The Lying Years*, New York: Simon and Schuster, 1953, and *Occasion for Loving*, New York: Viking, 1960; and James Baldwin, *Another Country*, New York: Dial Press, 1960. Novelists of an earlier day dealt less with the physical attractions of such affairs, and more with the fate of children of such matings *e.g.*, Olive Schreiner and Gertrude Millin in South Africa; Lyle Saxon, William Faulkner and others in this country.

in a playful mood. But it is a detachment of deep concern and intense curiosity that turns away from no human activity. Such curiosity is not likely to develop in minds which are not deeply involved in human affairs, and not concerned with our impossible human race. Detachment and indifference are not the same. I believe those sociologists who will contribute most to the fundamental, comparative and theoretical understanding of human society and of any of its problems are those so deeply concerned with it as to need a desperate, almost fanatical detachment from which to see it in full perspective.

Our problem is not that we are too deeply involved in human goings-on but that our involvement is so episodic and so bound to the wheel of particular projects with limited goals; in short, that we are too professional. While professionalizing an activity may raise the competence of some who pursue it by standardizing methods and giving license only to those who meet the standard, it also may limit creative activity, by denying license to some who let their imagination and their observations run far afield, and by putting candidates for the license (Ph.D.) so long in a straitjacket that they never move freely again. Our problem, as sociologists, in the next few years will be to resist the drive for professionalizing, and to maintain broad tolerance for all who would study societies, no matter what their methods.

I would like to imagine a state of things in which there would be a grand and flexible division of labor among us. Some of us bend our efforts toward making sociology immediately useful to people who carry on action or have problems to solve; I would hope that breed would serve the impecunious and deviant as well as the well-heeled and legitimate, those who seek radical solutions to problems of society as well as those who want merely to maintain stability. Others of us make models of societies, large and small, without much thought as to whether societies corresponding to the models exist at present. Let them be even more free in their imaginations than they are. Let those who perform experiments go ahead, making sure only that they do no harm to the people they work on and that they do not pollute a whole generation with their own particular kind of fall-out (which they might very well do, if everyone goes to college and if all freshmen have to be experimented upon to pass Psychology and Sociology One). Finally there are among us some who look about the world for laboratory cases in which to study the problems of human society; and those who, deeply and passionately involved in some problem of real life, describe reality both with the intimacy and detail which comes from close participation and observation and with that utopian imagination which can conceive of all sorts of alternatives to the way things are now. If we encourage each other, and our students, to work in a variety of ways, and if we all make our projections into the future, the greater the chance that once in a while some of us will hit upon a prediction that will be right.

FIFTY

The Place of Field Work in Social Science

Field work refers, in this volume, to observation of people *in situ;* finding them where they are, staying with them in some role which, while acceptable to them, will allow both intimate observation of certain parts of their behavior, and reporting it in ways useful to social science but not harmful to those observed. It is not easy to find a suitable formula in the best case; it may be impossible in some cases: say, a secret society devoted to crime or revolution or simply espousing "dangerous" ideas. But most people can be studied and most can do more field work than they believe. It is a strenuous, but exciting and satisfying business to expand one's own social perceptions and social knowledge in this way, and to contribute thereby to general social knowledge. Learning to do it—both parts of it, observing and reporting—can have some of the quality of a mild psychoanalysis. But, as in other kinds of self-discovery, one cannot learn more about one's self unless he is honestly willing to see others in a new light, and to learn about them, too.

But perhaps I should say something of the history of the project out of which this volume came. Dr. Junker, a man of much and varied field experience—in Yankee City, in a prison, in southern and midwestern communities, in various professions and institutions, among various racial and ethnic groups, in the United States Army both at home and in Europe—has thought about this subject for a good many years. He has done

Reprinted from Junker, Buford H., *Field Work: An Introduction to the Social Sciences,* Chicago, University of Chicago Press, 1960. © 1960 by the University of Chicago.

field work on field work. In 1951 he joined me in a project whose aim was to do just that.[1]

How did I come to initiate such a project? Certainly not because I ever found field observation easy to undertake. Once I start, I am, I believe, not bad at it. But it has always been a torture. Documents are so much easier to approach; one simply blows the dust off them, opens them up, and may have the pleasure of seeing words and thoughts on which no eye has been set these many years. Yet, in every project I have undertaken, studying real estate men, the Catholic labor movement in the Rhineland, and newly industrialized towns in Quebec, the time came when I had to desert statistical reports and documents and fare forth to see for myself. It was then that the real learning began, although the knowledge gained in advance was very useful; in fact, it often made possible the conversations which opened the field. One who has some information and asks for more is perhaps less likely to be refused than one who has no advance information; perhaps the best formula is to have advance knowledge, but to let it show only in the kind of questions one asks. But if I have usually been hesitant in entering the field myself and have perhaps walked around the block getting up my courage to knock at doors more often than almost any of my students (I have been doing it longer), I have sent a great many students into the field. Listening to them has given me sympathy with their problems; it has also convinced me that most students can learn to do field observation and will profit from it.

When I came to the University of Chicago in 1938, my colleagues assigned me an introductory course in sociology. It was a course taken mainly by young people who had two or more years of social science in the College of the University of Chicago. They were probably better read in the social sciences than their peers in any other college on this continent. But many of them had not yet come to that point in education where one sees the connection between small things and great. They liked everything to be great—events as well as ideas. They were inclined to be impatient with the small observations which, accumulated, are the evidence on which theories of culture and society are built. To quite a number of them real life seemed banal, trivial, and often misguided.

I used various devices to get some of the students to collect social data themselves, in the hope that the experience would give them a livelier sense of the problems of gathering social data and turning them, by analysis, into social facts. Eventually I took a bolder step. Since there was no danger that these students would miss adequate exposure to social

1. The project was supported from a grant made by the Ford Foundation to the Division of the Social Sciences of the University of Chicago. The late professors W. Lloyd Warner and Robert Redfield served as advisers.

theories, I, with the approval of my colleagues, replaced the general course with a full term of introduction to field work.

While we never set the form of the course in any inflexible way, there was a general pattern which did not change greatly. Each student, alone or with another, made a series of observations in a Census Tract or other small area of Chicago outside his everyday experience and reported on these observations almost week by week. We discussed the problems the students met in the field. They were asked to notice especially whom they were taken for by people in the areas where they studied and to find an explanation for the peculiar roles attributed to them. When they had done the several assigned kinds of observation, they were asked to draw up a proposal for a study which might be done in such an area, by a person of small resources.

After some years in which nearly all students of sociology, many students of anthropology, and some others went through this experience, I asked for and received a small grant to be used in putting together what we had learned from these several hundred students about the learning and doing of field work and to learn how people of greater experience and sophistication had gone about field observation.

Dr. Junker took charge of the project. Dr. Ray Gold interviewed the current crop of students about their field experiences. Together we held a seminar in which people who had done field observation on a great variety of problems and in many different situations reported on their experiences. A record was kept of their reports. Miss Dorothy Kittel, a bibliographer, helped us in finding documents which reported experiences of people in the field. We put some of the resulting material into a privately circulated document, "Cases on Field Work." What Dr. Junker has put into the present book is in part a more succinct and readable distillate of that volume. But it is more than that. This book has evolved through eight more years of his thought and work.

Those of us who had a part in this project have been strengthened in our conviction that field work is not merely one among several methods of social study but is paramount. It is, more than other methods of study, itself a practice, consciously undertaken, in sociology itself—in the perceiving and predicting of social roles, both one's own and those of others. It consists of exchanges of tentative social gestures, to use the terms of George Herbert Mead. That theme is developed by Dr. Junker. I shall confine myself to some general remarks on the place of field work in the social sciences.

Field work, when mentioned as an activity of social scientists, calls to mind first of all the ethnologist or anthropologist far afield observing and recording the ways, language, artifacts, and physical characteristics of exotic or primitive people. He is presumably there because the people he is interested in have never written down anything about themselves or because, if they do write, they have not had the habit of recording the things the ethnologist wants to know. The early manuals issued to aid ethnologists told the prospective observer what to look for, not how to look for it. Later anthropologists – Malinowski, Margaret Mead, and others – have told of their field experiences in a penetrating way.

Until a generation ago the phrase field work might also have brought to mind what was then called the "social survey." At the turn of the century the social surveyors were going to the slums of the great cities of Britain and North America to observe the "conditions" in which the new urban industrial poor lived. They then reported them in simple statistical tables on consumption of food and clothing, on wages, housing, illness and crime. But they also described what they found, "fully, freely, and bitterly," as Robert E. Park used to say, in the hope that an aroused public would change things. Their work had its journalistic and literary counterpart in "muck-raking." The seventeen volumes of Charles Booth's *The Life and Labour of the People of London* report several years of observation of the kind known then and for several decades afterwards as "social survey." Among Booth's collaborators were school "visitors," who went from door to door to see conditions and to talk to people. They also visited churches, clubs, public houses, parks, and pawnshops. They got acquainted with the factories, docks, and other places of work of the poor of East London. The work continued for several years; when at last they did the field work for a series of volumes entitled *Religious Influences,* they described not merely the feeble religious institutions of East London, but also the recreational institutions – including public houses – which seemed to have supplanted the church in the lives of working people. They had become rather more sympathetic reporters than muck-rakers. They had also established a tradition of social observation with two facets: (1) the kinds of data which were thought important to description of the social life of the poor, and (2) a way of gathering them. In North America, the tradition was carried on and developed; the Pittsburgh Survey (Kellogg, 1909-14), reporting the conditions of life and work of immigrant steelworkers, was the most voluminous and notorious of such projects in this country. LePlay, in France, had gone about getting data from families concerning their incomes and expenditures. In all of these enterprises, investigators went among the industrial and urban poor to gather information which was not, at that time, to be found in the censuses taken by public authorities. In many of them, the surveyors were betrayed by their humanity and curiosity into noting other kinds of information, into becoming, in effect, the ethnologists of social classes and other social groups than their own.

For the older social surveys discovered and described customs and institutions as well as opinions. Bosanquet, in the course of surveying the standards of living in London, learned the peculiar functions of the pawnshop among the poor of London.[2] Booth described the institutions of East London and came to the conclusion that no recreational or religious institution could survive there without a subsidy: it might be from gambling or the sale of beer, or it might be subsidy from the middle classes in other parts of town. He also described in detail the habits of drinking, by age and sex, among working people, and came to the conclusion that the sending of children to fetch a bucket of beer for their father's tea did not have the horrible consequences the middle class attributed to it.[3]

Although the surveys were not, in Europe, associated with the name of sociology, in England and America the survey movement became part of the peculiar sociological mix. Social workers, important in the earlier surveys, turned more and more to individual case work and seemed to lose interest in communities, groups, and styles of life. "Professionalized" social work abandoned the social survey for psychiatry, which uses a quite different research role and collects information of a different kind.

The unique thing about the early department of sociology at the University of Chicago was that it brought together Albion W. Small, who was both a devotee of German theoretical sociology and of the American social gospel of reform, and a number of people who were even more closely identified with social surveys, social problems, and social reform. W. I. Thomas, who inspired and carried out the great study of *The Polish Peasant in Europe and America* with the collaboration of Florian Znaniecki, was following the tradition of the social survey, but he was also leading it in a new direction, that of a more self-conscious and acute theoretical analysis. Robert E. Park, who eventually joined the department, combined even more than the others, the two facets of American sociology. For he had a Heidelberg degree in philosophy, got by writing a theoretical treatise on collective behavior in the crowd and the public.[4] His interest in the behavior of crowds and publics was, however, developed during twelve years of work as a newspaper reporter and city editor. He did more perhaps than any other person to produce the new American sociology in which people went out and did field observations designed to

2. Helen D. Bosanquet, *The Standard of Life and Other Studies* (London: Macmillan & Co., 1895).

3. For an account of the further development of the social survey in Great Britain see D. Caradog Jones, *Social Surveys* (London: Hutchinson's University Library, 1949); also his article, "Evolution of the Social Survey in England since Booth," *American Journal of Sociology*, XLVI, 818–25.

4. *Masse und Publikum, eine methodologische und soziologische Untersuchung* (Bern, Back, and Grunau, 1904).

advance theoretical, as well as practical, knowledge of modern, urban society.

Under his influence, and that of his colleagues, hundreds of students of sociology at the University of Chicago went to the field in various areas of Chicago. Their work was co-ordinated, for some years, by Dr. Vivien Palmer, who then published a book on how to do such observation.[5] With the development of better quantitative methods of handling social data, the practice of field work declined. It became known, with a certain condescension, as the "anthropological" method. Eventually the very term "survey" took on a new meaning. "Survey research" now means the study of political or other opinions, including consumers' preferences, by interviewing, with set questions, individuals so chosen as statistically to represent large populations about which the information is wanted. Going to the field means getting out to interview the sample. Some place is given to less formal field observation, but it is called "pilot study" or "exploratory study," and is considered preparatory to the main business of getting a questionnaire on the road. Its aim is to learn how to standardize the questions one wants to ask, not generally to learn what questions to ask. Great ingenuity is sometimes shown in such exploration and pretesting, but it is usually done with a certain impatience, since it delays the real work of "administering" the questionnaire. Once the questionnaire is settled upon, any doubts about the questions must be explained away, as it is too expensive and too disturbing to change anything at that point. The survey research of today, valuable as it is, conceives of field observation in quite a different way from that presented in this book.

For one thing, the sample survey still must work on the assumption that some very large population speaks so nearly the same language, both in letter and figure of speech, that the differences in answers will not be due in significant degree to differences in the meaning of words in the questions. This is a condition hard to meet even in Western literate countries; in many parts of the world, it cannot be met at all. The survey method, in this new sense of the term, must work with small variation in the midst of great bodies of common social definition. The preparatory field work is used to determine the limits of common meaning within which one can conduct the survey. Very often, groups of people not in the common social world have to be left out of consideration. In this country many surveys omit Negroes and other "deviant" groups. It is part of the merit of field work of the kind we are discussing in this book that it does not have to limit itself to minor variations of behavior within large homogeneous populations. But even

5. *Field Studies in Sociology* (Chicago: University of Chicago Press, 1928).
The Webbs wrote a classic in this field under the title, *Methods of Social Study* (London: Longmans, Green & Co., 1932).

within such populations, field observation is more than a preparatory step
for large statistical surveys. It is an ongoing part of social science. Most
surveys, again in the new sense, would be much more useful if they were
followed by even more intensive field work than that which precedes them.
There is a tendency for the statistical concentrations and relationships
found in a questionnaire survey to be explained in a text which merely
presents alternative speculations. It is at that point that good field work,
instead of getting "soft" data, would give firmer stuff. In fact, this is what
was done in a recent study of anxiety among college professors.[6] A field
team followed the interviewers. The social science of today requires, in
fact, a great many arts of observation and analysis. Field observation is one
of them.

There were some important differences between the field work of the
ethnologists and that of the sociologists who followed the tradition of the
social survey. The ethnologist was always an exotic to the people he
studied; clearly a stranger in every way except his humanity, and perhaps
he had to establish even that. The sociologist observed and reported upon a
segment of his own world, albeit a poverty-stricken and socially powerless
one. He was usually a class stranger to the people he studied; often, in
some measure, an ethnic, religious, or racial stranger. Still, he was among
people of kinds whom he might see any day in public places and who might
read the same newspaper as himself. In due time, some of the sociologists
themselves came from the segments of society which had been, or still
were, objects of study and began to report on the very minorities — racial,
sectarian, ethnic — of which they were members. The sociologist came to be
less and less a stranger studying strangers and reporting to still other
strangers. Student, object of study, and member of audience for the study
tended to overlap and merge more and more. The sociologist was now
reporting observations made, not as a complete stranger, but in some
measure as a member of an in-group, although, of course, the member
becomes something of a stranger in the very act of objectifying and reporting his experiences.

The unending dialectic between the role of member (participant) and
stranger (observer and reporter) is essential to the very concept of field
work. It is hard to be both at the same time. One solution is to separate
them in time. One reports, years later and when one is at a distance in mind
and spirit, what he remembers of social experiences in which he was a full
participant.

It is doubtful whether one can become a good social reporter unless he
has been able to look, in a reporting mood, at the social world in which he

6. Paul F. Lazarsfeld and Wagner Thielens, Jr., *The Academic Mind: Social Scientists in a
Time of Crisis* (New York: Free Press, 1958), with a field report by David Riesman.

was reared. On the other hand, a person cannot make a career out of the reporting of reminiscenses unless he is so far alienated from his own background as to be able to expose and exploit it before some new world with which he now identifies himself. One has to learn to get new data and to get them in a great variety of settings as demanded by new problems he wants to solve. Other ways of solving this dialectic include being a part-time participant and part-time reporter, privately participant and publicly reporter, or publicly participant and secretly reporter. All these are practiced. All have their moral, personal, and scientific pitfalls. But the dialectic is never fully resolved, for to do good social observation one has to be close to people living their lives and must be himself living his life and must also report. The problem of maintaining good balance between these roles lies at the very heart of sociology, and indeed of all social science.

Each of the two disciplines, anthropology and sociology, which have made most use of field work, has its own history. In each, the field situation has tended to be different from that of the other. The ethnologist reported upon a whole community; the sociologist generally observed and reported only upon people of some segment, usually a poor and socially powerless one, of a community. In due time, it came about that some of the sociologists themselves came from odd and less-known corners of society or from minorities and began to report upon their own people to their new associates in the academic and larger society. This introduced a new element of distinction from the older ethnology. For the sociologist was now reporting upon observations made, not in the role of the stranger, but as a full member of the little world he reported on. He observed as a member of an in-group but, in the act of objectifying and reporting his experience, became of necessity a sort of outsider.

As one reads into the analyses and the documents included herein, he will see the meaning of this. For it comes out clearly, I believe, that the situations and circumstances in which field observation of human behavior is done are so various that no manual of detailed rules would serve; it is perhaps less clear, but equally true, that the basic problems are the same in all situations. It is the discovery of this likeness inside the shell of variety that is perhaps the greatest and most important step in learning to be an effective and versatile observer.

In the foregoing I have said nothing about the logic of field observation in social science. One reason I have not done so up to this point is that I wanted to emphasize that the departments of social science are as much historic institutions as logical divisions. Each one is the product either of social movements inside the academic world or of movements outside which later got into the academic world. While some of the departments have or claim a peculiar subject matter which sets them off from the others, this subject matter is perhaps more often a product of history, become convention and prerogative, than of pure logic. One might imagine a university in which there would be no divisions of subject matter except those dictated by clear differences of method. Economists would study all phenomena which could profitably be studied by the methods developed for analysis of the behavior of men playing the game of maximizing their share of scarce, but desired, goods. Some other branch would study all phenomena which yield well to analyses based upon skilled observation of power relations among men, and so on. I think it is obvious that this is not the situation at present. Each branch of social science appears to be some mixture of a concern with a basic logic or method with a somewhat monopolistic and jealous concern with some set of institutions or practical problems.

One should add that each, whatever its basic logic or method, has its favorite kinds of data. The historian loves to get his hands on a manuscript that no one has seen before. He wants to sit down in a quiet and musty corner of the archives and copy out parts of it by hand. He is preoccupied with manuscripts and prides himself on his skill in reading both the lines and what is between the lines. The political scientist shares this interest or preoccupation somewhat, with the variation that he especially loves a secret rather than merely rare document. The psychologist has, more than others engaged in the study of social behavior, set himself the model of the natural scientist making stylized observations in a prepared situation, that is, in a laboratory. The economist and some sociologists like to get their data already in quantitative form and in massive numbers. Their love is the manipulation of such data to create situations with a maximum of chance and then to discover departures from it.

Now there may be some relation between the number of possible fruitful kinds of data and ways of getting and handling them and the number of departments of social science in an American university, but I doubt it. We may discover in due time that there are only a few basic ways of getting human data and a few basic skills for analyzing them. While it may for a long time be true that the departments will be distinguished more by their preoccupations than by their method, conceived in terms of pure logic, it may also be that we can sort out these basic skills of observation and analysis and work on them irrespective of conventional disciplinary lines.

One of these areas of skill will be that of observing and recording the behavior of human beings "on the hoof." Men deposit some of their thoughts and actions in artifacts and documents which historians learn to read with consummate skill. Some of their actions yield to analysis of small items of behavior recorded in astronomical numbers of cases. But others, I am convinced, yield only to close observation at the time, observation sometimes of the passive bystander, sometimes of the active participant, sometimes of the active intervener, as in the case of the group experimenter and of the psychoanalyst who rends painful hidden memories from the unwilling patient. It is observation "on the hoof" that we refer to as field observation.

It is a method increasingly used by students of many modern institutions (unions, industries, hospitals, armies) as well as by students of communities, near or far from home. The outstanding peculiarity of this method is that the observer, in greater or less degree, is caught up in the very web of social interaction which he observes, analyzes, and reports. Even if he observes through a peephole, he plays a role: that of spy. And when he reports his observations made thus he becomes a kind of informer. If he observes in the role of a member of the group, he may be considered a traitor the moment he reports. Even the historian, who works upon documents, gets caught in a role problem when he reports, unless there is no person alive who might identify himself with the people or social group concerned. The hatred occasionally visited upon the debunking historian is visited almost daily upon the person who reports on the behavior of people he has lived among; and it is not so much the writing of the report, as the very act of thinking in such objective terms that disturbs the people observed. It is a violation of apparently shared secrets and sentiments. The reader will see that in the discussions and documents which follow we have all become very much occupied with the dimensions of this problem, of the on-going social and personal dilemmas of the man who observes and analyzes, more than is necessary for survival and good participation, the behavior of people about him and reports it to some audience.

The usefulness of field observation is not confined to one institution or aspect of life—religious conduct, economic, familial, political, or any other institutional aspect of behavior will yield in some measure to field observation. Insofar as it does, the observer, no matter what his formal field or academic fraternity, will share problems of skill, role, and ethic with all others who use the method. The aim of the project from which this book grew was not to sell this idea to people in sociology or in other fields, but to assemble what knowledge and insight we could on problems of learning and using the method of field observation, without limiting ourselves to any conventional confines.

If there is any sense in which field method is peculiarly sociological it is in this. If sociology is conceived as the science of social interaction and of the cultural and institutional results of interaction (which become factors conditioning future interaction), then field observation is applied sociology. Insofar as the field observer becomes a conscious observer and analyst of himself in the role of observer, he becomes also a pure sociologist. For the concepts which he will need for this observation of the observer are the very concepts needed for analysis of any social interaction. The very difficulties of carrying out field observation—the resistance of his subjects, the danger that his very success as a participant may later prevent him from full reporting, even the experience of getting thrown out of town—are facts to be analyzed sociologically. It was the realization of these points that made our little research group exclaim one day, almost as one man, "We are studying the sociology of sociology."

This has a peculiar corollary. The problem of learning to be a field observer is like the problem of learning to live in society. It is the problem of making enough good guesses from previous experience so that one can get into a social situation in which to get more knowledge and experience to enable him to make more good guesses to get into a better situation, ad infinitum.

The problem of any field observer is to learn how he, even he, can keep expanding this series as long as possible and in what situations he can do so. The part of theoretical analysis and the part of insightful experience, and the relation of the two to each other, are, in a sense, what we set out to discover.

FIFTY-ONE

Of Sociology and
the Interview:
Editorial Preface

Sociology has become the science of the interview, and that in two senses. In the first sense the interview has become the favored digging tool of a large army of sociologists. The several branches of social study are distinguished from one another perhaps more by their predilection for certain kinds of data and certain instruments for digging them up than by their logic. While the essential features of human society have probably varied within fairly narrow limits in all times and places where men lived, certain of these features can be more effectively observed in direct contact with living people. Others may perhaps be best seen through the eyes of men who left documents behind them. Sociologists have become mainly students of living people. Some, to be sure, do still study documents. Some observe people *in situ;* others experiment on them and look at them literally *in vitro.* But, by and large, the sociologist of North America, and in a slightly less degree in other countries has become an interviewer. The interview is his tool; his works bear the marks of it.

Interviews are of many kinds. Some sociologists like them standardized and so formulated that they can be "administered" to large groups of people. This can be done only among large homogeneous populations not

Reprinted from *American Journal of Sociology;* Vol. LXII, No. 2, Sept., 1956 (Mr. Mark Benney collaborated on this paper.) © 1956 by the University of Chicago.

507

too unlike the investigator himself in culture. Where languages are too diverse, where common values are too few, where the fear of talking to strangers is too great, there the interview based on a standardized questionnaire calling for a few standardized answers may not be applicable. Those who venture into such situations may have to invent new modes of interviewing. Some of the articles which follow deal with problems of large-scale standardized interviews; others tell of the peculiar problems of interviewing special kinds of people.

In the second sense sociology is the science of the interview in a more essential way. The subject matter of sociology is interaction. Conversation of verbal and other gestures is an almost constant activity of human beings. The main business of sociology is to gain systematic knowledge of social rhetoric; to gain the knowledge, we must become skilled in the rhetoric itself. Every conversation has its own balance of revelation and concealment of thoughts and intentions: only under very unusual circumstances is talk so completely expository that every word can be taken at face value. The model of such exposition is the exchange of information among scientists. Each is pledged to tell all he knows of the subject in terms whose meanings are strictly denoted. Every member of any society knows from early childhood a number of such model situations and the appropriate modes of rhetoric. He knows them so well, in fact, that he can improvise new ones and can play at the game of keeping others guessing just what rhetoric he is using. We mention these subtleties of social rhetoric and social interaction, not to spin out analysis of them, but to sharpen the point that the interview, as itself a form of social rhetoric, is not merely a tool of sociology but a part of its very subject matter. When one is learning about the interview, he is adding to sociological knowledge itself. Perhaps the essence of the method of any science is the application, in quest of new knowledge, of what is already known of that science. This is certainly true of sociology; what we learn of social interaction — of the modes of social rhetoric — we apply in getting new knowledge about the same subject.

But the interview is still more than tool and object of study. It is the art of sociological sociability, the game which we play for the pleasure of savoring its subtleties. It is our flirtation with life, our eternal affair, played hard and to win, but played with that detachment and amusement which give us, win or lose, the spirit to rise up and interview again and again.

The interview is, of course, merely one of the many ways in which two people talk to each other. There are other ways. About a year ago Miss Margaret Truman was employed on Ed Murrow's "Person to Person" television show to interview her parents in their home, and the event proved to be a notable exercise in multiple role-playing. As a daughter,

Miss Truman asked the kinds of questions that any daughter might ask of a parent: "Dad, how is the book coming?" As interviewer, she asked questions that bore the unmistakable stamp of the newspaperman: "So many people want to know what you do to relax, inasmuch as you don't fish, hunt, or play golf." And at the end of the interview she achieved a nice convergence of the two roles by asking, as interviewer, her parents' views about herself, as daughter. Now Miss Truman is by way of being both a professional daughter and a professional interviewer, and the happy idea that she should act in the one role in a situation and with people where the other role is conventionally to be expected takes us right to the center of our concern.

If we look at the variety of ways in which people in our culture meet together and talk, we will be struck not only by the range of expectations which subsume unique, particular encounters under a rubric of reciprocal roles but also by the different degrees of self-involvement that inform the playing of different roles. Much attention has been given to the range of intensity with which the individual plays his roles; much less attention has been paid to the degree of *expected* intensity. It is clear enough that along with more or less specific expectations of the appropriate behavior in a given role go other expectations about the degree of self-involvement. The general expectation is that Miss Truman should be more involved in the role of daughter than of interviewer; and certainly she managed to underline the family ties by very frequent use of the terms of address as "Dad" and "Mommie" and also by occasionally prefacing a question with the phrase, "Ed Murrow wanted me to ask. . . ." These differences of expected intensity are to some extent codified for us in such terms as "commandment," "law," "rule," "standard," "convention," "fashion." At the upper limits of intensity there is a total prescription of alternative roles — the priest must never be a lover, the citizen must never be a traitor: only minimal distinction is expected between the self and the role. At the lower limit there is still the expectation that, when roles conflict, the resolution shall favor one role rather than another — but, by their very semantics, such terms as "convention" or "fashion" operate in areas of life where ethical neutrality is acceptable and ambivalence frequent. Thus, Miss Truman could abandon the role of interviewer for that of daughter without our feeling that violence has been done to our ethos; she could not, if the two roles conflicted, abandon the role of daughter so easily.

The role of the interviewer, then, is one governed by conventions rather than by standards, rules, or laws; it is a role that is relatively lightly held, even by professionals, and may be abandoned in favor of certain alternative roles if the occasion arises. *What* alternative roles is another matter. The interview is a relatively new kind of encounter in the history of human relations, and the older models of encounter—parent-child, male-female, rich-poor, foolish-wise—carry role definitions much better articulated and more exigent. The interviewer will be constantly tempted, if the other party falls back on one of these older models, to reciprocate—tempted and excused. For, unlike most other encounters, the interview is a role-playing situation in which one person is much more an expert than the other, and, while the conventions governing the interviewer's behavior are already beginning, in some professional circles, to harden into standards, the conventions governing the informant's behavior are much less clearly articulated and known. Vidich and Bensman, discussing this aspect of the interview, give examples of the respondent's insecurity in his role: "In a difficult joint interview between a husband and wife, which required them to discuss certain problems, respondents would remind their spouses of failures to fulfill the instruction to 'discuss' with the remark that 'this is not what they wanted!' When couples failed to fulfill the instructions and saw that they had failed, they frequently apologized for their 'ignorance' or ineptitude."[1] Of course there is an enormous amount of preparatory socialization in the respondent role—in schools and jobs, through the mass media—and more and more of the potential respondents of the Western world are readied for the rap of the clipboard on the door. (In some places, perhaps, overreadied. There was a charming story in the London *News of the World* recently about a political canvasser who liked to demonstrate, on the backsides of young suburban mothers, how they could check the urge to delinquency in their offspring. During the ensuing prosecution it was suggested that the ladies had become, through their experiences with interviewers, so docile as subjects of experiments that they were surprised at nothing.) Probably the most intensive presocialization of respondents runs in roughly the social strata from which interviewers themselves are drawn—the middle, urban, higher-educated groups, while at the top and bottom—though for different reasons—the appropriate role of the informant is apparently much less known. At the moment it is enough to say that where the parties to an interview are unsure of their appropriate roles they are likely to have recourse to other, more firmly delineated social roles that will turn the encounter into one where they feel more at home.

Two conventions characterize most interviews and seem to give this particular mode of personal encounter its uniqueness: these are the conventions of *equality* and *comparability*.

The view that information obtained under stress is likely to be unreliable is not universal, even in our own culture, as "third degree" practices by the police and some popular techniques of cross-examination in the law courts

1. A Vidich and J. Bensman, "The Validity of Field Data," *Human Organization*, XIII, No. 1 (Spring, 1954), 20-27.

indicate. But in the research interview, at least — and we can regard this as archetypal — the assumption is general that information is the more valid the more freely given. Such an assumption stresses the voluntary character of the interview as a relationship freely and willingly entered into by the respondent; it suggests a certain promissory or contractual element. But if the interview is thought of as a kind of implicit contract between the two parties, it is obvious that the interviewer gains the respondent's time, attention, and whatever information he has to offer, but what the respondent gets is less apparent. A great many people enjoy being interviewed, almost regardless of subject, and one must assume, from the lack of tangible rewards offered, that the advantages must be totally subjective. Here Theodore Caplow's suggestion, in his article in this issue, that the interview profits as a communication device from the contrast it offers to conversation in less formal situations might satisfy us until further evidence is available: that by offering a program of discussion, and an assurance that information offered will not be challenged or resisted, self-expression is facilitated to an unusual degree and that this is inherently satisfying. In this sense, then, the interview is an understanding between the two parties that, in return for allowing the interviewer to direct their communication, the informant is assured that he will not meet with denial, contradiction, competition, or other harassment. As with all contractual relations, the fiction or convention of equality must govern the situation. Whatever actual inequalities of sex, status, intelligence, expertness, or physique exist between the parties should be muted. Interviewing-training consists very largely of making interviewers aware of the kinds of social inequalities with which respondents are likely to be concerned and of teaching them how to minimize them. This is most important, perhaps, if the respondent is likely to see himself as inferior in some respect to the interviewer, and certainly this has been the most closely studied aspect of interviewer effect.

But what happens when, as increasingly happens, a run-of-the-mill, middle-class interviewer encounters a member of some financial, intellectual, or political elite? Our own impression is that such respondents contrive to re-establish equality in the interview by addressing themselves subjectively, not to the actual interviewer, but to the study director or even his sponsor. The different subjective uses to which respondents put these ghostly figures is something that might very profitably be looked into; certainly, people of superior status are more aware of them, and make more use of them, than others.

Evidently such a view of the interview has much in common with Simmel's view of sociability. Both in the interview as seen here and in the sociable gathering as seen by Simmel the convention of equality is a formal necessity and is achieved by excluding from immediate awareness all those

attributes of the individual, subjective and objective, which make for inequalities in everyday life. But, as Simmel stresses, the objects of a sociable gathering can be achieved only within a given social stra-
tum—"sociability among members of very different social strata often is
inconsistent and painful."[2] The muting of minor social inequalities, such as
age, sex, wealth, erudition, and fame, can be accomplished only by the
physical elimination of the grosser subcultural differences. But the interview was designed to provide a bridge for communicating between the
social strata precisely of the kind that sociability cannot provide (if it could,
interviewing would be unnecessary). And this fact brings out another
important difference between the interview as practiced and the sociable
gathering as seen by Simmel—in the handling of affect. The identifications
which bring people together easily in sociable gatherings are primarily
established on an emotional basis, and, as Simmel stresses, any affective
expression which runs counter to these emotional bonds is suppressed: it
is, says Simmel, the essential function of *tact* "to draw the limits, which
result from the claims of others, of the individual's impulses, ego-stresses,
and intellectual and material desires."[3] The only emotional expression
tolerable in the sociable gathering is that which heightens the emotional
bonds already established within the group. Psychologically, however, exclusion from these shared affective responses constitutes social inequality;
and, if equality in the interview is to be established, it must at bottom be
achieved by the interviewer's encouraging and accepting the affect as well
as the information the respondent offers. (Hence the growing emphasis on
"rapport" in the technical manuals dealing with the interview.) The problem of establishing equality in the interview, then, depends on the expression rather than the suppression of affective responses, on some encouragement of the private, idiosyncratic, and subjective dimensions of at
least one of the personalities involved. True, the interview *tends* toward
the form of the sociable conversation, in that, once the interviewer has
been "cued" to the level of discourse a given respondent is capable of, and
has adapted himself to it, communication is expected to approximate that
which would take place between actual equals, so that the information
carried away is assumed to be such as a man might give when talking freely
to a friend. Thus students of the dynamics of interviewing find that there is
in general an early release of affect, followed by a more equable flow of
information.

Interviewing, then, is distinguished by the operations of the convention
that both parties to the encounter are equals, at least for the purposes and

2. Kurt Wolff (trans.), *The Sociology of Georg Simmel* (New York: Free Press, 1950),
p. 47.
   3. *Ibid.,* p. 45.

duration of the encounter. But there is another important characteristic of the interview which serves to differentiate it from other modes of human interaction — the convention of *comparability*. The first operates primarily for the advantage of the respondent; the second, for the advantage of the interviewer and his employers. They are not completely compatible conventions, and the latent conflict between them is always threatening to become manifest.

Regarded as an information-gathering tool, the interview is designed to minimize the local, concrete, immediate circumstances of the particular encounter — including the respective personalities of the participants — and to emphasize only those aspects that can be kept general enough and demonstrable enough to be counted. As an encounter between these two particular people the typical interview has no meaning; it is conceived in a framework of other, comparable meetings between other couples, each recorded in such fashion that elements of communication in common can be easily isolated from more idiosyncratic qualities. However vaguely this is conceived by the actual participants, it is the needs of the statistician rather than of the people involved directly that determine much, not only the content of communication but its form as well. Obviously, this convention conflicts with the psychological requirements for equality of affective interchange, and one can observe various attempts to resolve the problem from interviewing in groups to interviewing in depth. At its most obvious the convention of comparability produces the "standardized" interview, where the whole weight of the encounter is placed on the order and formulation of the questions asked and little freedom is permitted to the interviewer to adjust the statistician's needs to the particular encounter. The statistician, indeed, seldom uses *all* the material collected; few reports, apparently, make use of more than 30 or 40 per cent of the information collected. But less obtrusively it enters into almost all interviewing, even psychiatric interviewing, as the possibilities of statistical manipulation of "data" force themselves on the attention of research-minded practitioners. Here technological advances such as the tape recorder are hastening the process — directly, by making available for comparison transcripts of psychiatric interviews hitherto unobtainable and, indirectly, by exposing more clearly to colleagues those purely personal and private (or "distorting" and "biasing") observations and interpretations which the practitioner brings into the interview with him. The very displacement of the older words "session" or "consultation" by the modern word "interview," to describe what passes between the psychiatrist and his patient, is a semantic recognition of this spread of the convention of comparability.

All this amounts to a definition of the interview as a relationship between two people where both parties behave as though they are of equal status for its duration, whether or not this is actually so; and where, also, both behave as though their encounter had meaning only in relation to a good many other such encounters. Obviously, this is not an exhaustive definition of any interview; it leaves out any reference to the exchange and recording of information, to the probability that the parties involved are strangers, and to the transitory nature of the encounter and the relationship. In any formal definition of the interview these elements must have a place.

A relationship governed by the conventions just discussed can occur, it is clear, only in a particular cultural climate; and such a climate is a fairly new thing in the history of the human race. Anthropologists have long realized—if not always clearly— that the transitory interview, held with respondents who do not share their view of the encounter, is an unreliable source of information in itself. It is not until they have been in the society long enough to fit into one of its better-defined roles that they can "tap" a valid communication system and hear the kind of messages that the others in the culture hear. Equally, the climate which makes widespread interviewing possible in the West today is itself relatively novel. A century ago, when Mayhew pioneered in the survey by interviewing "some thousands of the humbler classes of society," the social distance between his readers and his subjects, though they largely lived in the same city, was such that he could best conceptualize his undertaking as an ethnological inquiry, seeking to establish that "we, like the Kaffirs, Fellahs and Finns, are surrounded by wandering hordes—the 'Sonquas' and the 'Fingoes' of this country." Mayhew was a newspaperman, and his survey was first published in a London newspaper. This fact serves to remind us that interviewing as we know it today was an invention of the mass-communications industry, and, as a mode of human encounter, has much the same boundaries. On the other hand, the interview has become something very like a medium of mass communication in its own right, and one, on the whole, with less frivolous and banal concerns than related media. One might even make the point that newspapers, movies, radio, and television have been encouraged to pursue their primrose paths by delegating to the survey researchers and their interviewers most of the more serious functions of social communication. If this is so, the interviewer has ousted the publicist by virtue of the convention of comparability, and the ideological and social shifts which have made it possible for individuals willingly to populate the statistician's cells become as worthy of study as, say, the spread of literacy.

We can trace the spread of this convention from the time it was a radical idea in the mind of Jeremy Bentham and a few of his disciples until it became a habit of thought of all but the very top and bottom segments of our society. In like fashion we trace the growth of the convention of equality from the ideas of John Locke and his disciples to its almost total permeation of the American scene. To chart such changes in the way people relate themselves to one another is the historian's job rather than the sociologist's, and it is one requiring volumes rather than pages. But even a brief review of the course of such changes will lead to a sharper sense of the novelty and significance of the interview as a mode of human relationship and will perhaps aid in assessing its limits and potentialities in the future.

FIFTY-TWO

The Gleichschaltung of the German Statistical Yearbook

"Racial Classification of People Who Married in 1938." In the summer of 1953, my eye fell by chance upon this heading of a table in the Statistical Yearbook of the German Reich for 1941–1942, the last published by the Nazi regime. From earlier work with German official statistics, I was practically certain that the pre-Nazi German had had a religion, but not a race. The statistical German was the opposite of the statistical American, who had a race but no religion. The accident of noticing this change of categories in the German census led me to ask a question: What changes did the statistician of the German Reich have to make in his official Yearbook when the Nazis came to power? Behind it lie more general questions for professional statisticians: How politically neutral is their work? To what extent are the very categories in which they report their data subject to political demands?

I do not know the answers to these general questions. But I did go through all of the German statistical yearbooks from the last one of the pre-Nazi Weimar republic, 1932, through the Nazi period, and including the first post-war volume, to see what changes of category and of reporting occurred along with the radical political changes. I don't know how deeply the Nazis dug into the private opinions of the Reich statistician, or whether Party people were put in his office to watch over him. I have only the internal evidence of the Statistical Yearbooks themselves. The last Weimar

Reprinted from *The American Statistician*, Vol. IX, No. 5, December, 1955.

516

volume, and all of the Nazi Yearbooks except the last are signed by one Dr. Reichardt of the Reich Statistical Office. The last Nazi volume, 1941–42, is signed Godlewski. Whether Dr. Reichardt simply reached the age of retirement about the end of 1940 or whether he finally turned out to be not sufficiently *gleichgeschaltet* (coordinated), I don't know. Many a man did try to get on with his work by making little compromises, only to find one day that it was impossible to continue and fatal to quit. I must add that I do not know what happened to Godlewski either; he certainly did not sign the first Yearbook of the new Bonn republic.

The Foreword to the last pre-Nazi Yearbook, 1932, is the exact, dull little statement one expects of a faithful public servant who is accustomed to going modestly on with his work while prime ministers and cabinets come and go. It contains no word about parties or government policies. It uses no political symbol. When, in November, 1933, Dr. Reichardt signed the next Yearbook, Hitler had been Reichschancellor for the better part of a year. The Foreword takes no notice of the change. It is the same little business-like statement about the contents of the book. In the next Foreword, 1934, however, Dr. Reichardt feels called upon to tell the reader that the Yearbook now contains a series of "German economic curves, showing the economic events since the taking over of power by the Nationalsocialist regime." In 1935, the mention becomes a plug, "In the many tables of the Yearbook there come to expression the powerful accomplishments made by the New State in all fields of folk and economic life in the three years since the taking over of power by the Nationalsocialist regime." He especially notes the great success of measures against unemployment. In passing he mentions some new family statistics, and tables on the Special Census of the Occupational and Social Distribution of *Glaubensjuden* (Jews by faith) and Foreigners.

From 1935 on, the Foreword always tells how many years it has been since the Nationalsocialists took power, and reports in more and more glowing terms the accomplishments of the New State. The statement is typically like this: "The Yearbook gives an accounting in sober, but eloquent figures of the measures taken by the New State in all fields of folk and economic life, and the results in population, economics and in cultural and political affairs." Dr. Reichardt even notes that the Yearbook has to be bigger because of the increased activity of the New State. From 1936 on, curves showing economic progress are put on the inside of the front cover where they are the first thing to be seen when one opens the book. In 1938 the flyleaf shows a map entitled "Folk and Space since the Assumption of Power." It shows how the empire has been expanded by the assimilation of Austria and Sudetenland. In 1939–40, a similar map shows most of Western Europe under German "protection." Under the map is a summary table showing the increase of territory and population accomplished by the New State. Dr. Reichardt tells us in his 1938 Foreword that the Yearbook now reports the Greater German Reich; he regrets that not many of the tables take account of the new territories, since comparable statistics do not yet exist. The last two books, done in war time, no longer bother to plug for the New State. A brief Foreword says that the Yearbook was produced under difficulties, "because the needs of the State and the Party require it." Readers are enjoined, under penalty, to keep copies in metal safes and to divulge the contents to no one not in government service.

The 1932 Yearbook shows the results of all Reichstag elections from 1919 to 1932, with the number of votes for each party. The most recent election, that of July 31, 1932, was reported in even greater detail. The 1933 book gives the same summary of past elections, and includes the detail of two new elections. One was the election of November, 1932, in which there was a considerable decline of the Nazi vote. In spite of that, Hindenburg had called upon Hitler to form a government. The other was the election of March, 1933, the only free election in the Hitler time; in it the Social-Democrats held their own, the Catholic Centre gained a little, and the Nazis gained tremendously. The Communists apparently contributed most to the Nazi increase, since they lost a million votes from November, before Hitler came in, to March, just after he came to power. But this is an aside. The Yearbook merely reports the figures. In 1934 and after, each Yearbook reports only the new-style Yes and No elections of the current year. I do not know whether Dr. Reichardt was told to stop reporting the elections of the late Weimar republic, or whether he gave it up for purely technical reasons. It would make no sense to try to compare the results of free elections in which a dozen or more parties struggled for slight gains in their popular vote and for more seats in parliament with those of the new style, high-pressure plebiscites in which the choice was to be for or against Hitler. Maybe Dr. Reichardt was not coordinated on this point; it was sufficient that the elections were coordinated.

But this Yearbook did not even bother to compare the Nazi elections with one another. Perhaps the Nazis missed a propaganda chance here; for it is quite an accomplishment to increase a party's vote from 43.9% of the total to 95.3% in the course of a few months, as did the Nazis between March and November, 1933. Of course, the percentage for the Fuehrer dropped back to 89.9% in August, 1934, but they soon got it up again. In 1936, 99.5% of all qualified voters did their duty, and 98.8% did it right by casting ballots "For the List and for the Fuehrer." There were by now so few negative votes that the statistical office simply lumped them together with the invalid ballots. After the great success in getting an expression of the people's will to follow the leader in 1936, there was no new plebiscite until the empire had expanded to take in more of the German folk. In April, 1938, the Austrians were allowed to show how devoted they were to the Fuehrer and how glad to be absorbed by the New State. The Sudeten Germans were given the same privilege in due time. After that there were no plebiscites. The war was on. But in the reporting of 1938 elections in the 1939 Yearbook a slight change was made. What had been called Austria in 1938 was now called "former Austria." One must remember that the German name for Austria means Eastern Empire, obviously not a fit name for a rather insignificant part of the all-inclusive eternal Greater German Empire.

Race, in the pre-Nazi Yearbooks, was a characteristic of stallions. The number of their registered services for the propagation of their respective races was faithfully recorded in the agricultural part of the book. Men, on the other hand, had religion. They were Christians of Protestant or Roman-Catholic confession, or they were Israelites. That took in most Germans; a handful of others were lumped together. The 1932 book showed how many of each of these categories had lived in various parts and in the whole of Germany in 1910 and in 1925. The only other tables of religion are those which show the religion of each partner in all marriages of the previous year. Religion is indirectly shown in the tables of membership in trade unions and professional organizations, for some such organizations were Catholic or Protestant. None was specifically Jewish. In the first Hitler Yearbook, 1933, the references to religion are exactly as before—with one exception. The trade unions had already been dissolved. The book listed the divisions of the new Labor Front, but regretted that membership figures were not yet available. They were not in the next book, or the one after that, or ever. Perhaps, since all workers belonged to the Labor Front by definition, it would have been silly to give figures; they would have been the same as the figures of people employed in each occupation and industry.

The expressions Jew, Jewess, and Jewish do not occur in the pre-Nazi books or in the first Hitler Yearbook, 1933. Some people were of Israelite religion; some men and women of Israelite religion were married to women and men of the same religion or of Protestant, Roman Catholic or other faiths. That was all. The 1934 Yearbook reports a new religious Census made in 1933, and compares the religious composition of the population of that year with that of 1925. The 1910 comparison was dropped. The same words are still used for the various religions. But in 1935, although the same figures and the same words were used, there is a whole new set of tables which tell us all about some people called "Glaubensjuden," of whom a special census had been taken on the 16th of June, 1933. They must be the same people who were formerly of Israelite religion, because there are exactly as many of them. But the change is more than one of name. The 1935 Yearbook picks these Glaubensjuden out for special attention not given people of other religions. We are shown what per cent Jews form of the population in all geographic divisions; how many of them live in cities of more than 100,000, more than 50,000 and so on. The Jewish populations of Berlin, Hamburg, Frankfurt, Breslau and a few other large cities are shown in a separate table. The places of birth of Jews are tabulated, also the number and per cent of them who are of German or foreign birth, and subjects of Germany or of other countries.

By this time, the Nuremberg laws had made a distinction between people who are subjects of Germany and those who are citizens. The Jews were subjects but could not be citizens. No such facts are presented for the population at large, or for Protestants or Catholics. It is clear that statistics on the Jew are of special interest to the government. We may fairly assume that the statistician had been told to prepare special data on Jews—and to change their names. The name Glaubensjuden (Jews by faith) is still one without racial connotation. Only in the tables on marriages and the religion of people who were born or who died in Prussia were there still people of Israelite religion. In fact, Israelites continued to be born, get married, and to die right down until 1939–40, while people called "Jews by faith" had occupations and lived in various places. In the 1939–40 Yearbook this name is dropped, and tables give us some new categories which take account of the finer distinctions of the Nuremberg laws: Jews, Jewish mixtures of the first degree and Jewish mixtures of the second degree in all parts of Germany, including Austria, for 1939. The same book still gives a table on the religion of the people, including Israelite. But in 1941–42, there is no longer an Israelite religion in German statistics. The religious categories are Protestant, Roman Catholic, Believers in God, and others. The Gleichschaltung of the statistics is complete. Jews are a race, not a religious group. German statistical segregation is also complete. Jews appear nowhere as simply another category of people in tables which include other Germans. There is one little exception: the good old Prussian vital statistics still show that people of Israelite religion are born and die. The Prussian civil servant is a stubborn fellow. He does his duty, come what may. Or maybe no one issued a new form for recording births and deaths in Prussia, and the officials just had to go on using the old ones.

Of all Israelite women married in 1930, one in eight married a Christian; of Israelite men, one in four married a Christian. From 1933 on, these proportions constantly decreased. In 1936, about one in fifty married out. The people of Germany were being *gleichgeschaltet*; but the statistical Yearbook stuck to its old form of reporting marriages by religion. Only in

1939–40 does racial reporting take the place of religious in marriage tables. There is in the book of that year a table showing the "Racial Classification of People Who Married in 1938." Marriage partners are now of five kinds: German-blooded, Jewish mixtures of the first degree, Jewish mixtures of the second degree, Jews and Jewesses, and persons of other foreign blood. Twenty-five German-blooded men married Jewesses, and thirty-three Jewish men married German-blooded women in that year. But these traitors to German blood were nearly all of foreign nationality; in 1939, no German-blooded subject of the Reich married a Jew or Jewess. Gleichschaltung both of marriage and marriage statistics was complete.

The Reichstatistician was prodded, I suspect, into setting up tables and graphs to show at a glance the progress of the New State's program of prosperity and territorial expansion. He never showed in a summary and graphic way the success of the program to rid the country and the folk of foreign (Jewish) blood. One has to dig the facts out from many tables. In 1910 there were 538,909 people of Israelite religion in the Reich; 564,379 in 1925; 499,682 in 1933. One can also figure it out that in 1939 there were 451,451 of the people called Jews, Jewish mixtures of the first degree and Jewish mixtures of the second degree in the new Greater Germany. The Nazi regime could have taken credit for most of the decrease of Jewish people between 1925 and 1933, and certainly they could claim as their own the whole decrease of 48,000 between 1933 and 1939. They could have made their success more impressive by reminding the reader that the new Germany of 1939 included new eastern territory in which many Jews had lived. They could have shown in a more prominent place the reduction in percentage of Jewish population. In 1910 and 1925 nearly one German in a hundred had been a Jew; in 1939, only about one in 190. The Yearbook could also have made a better story out of emigration. It reported only those emigrants who went overseas, and failed to tell how many of them were Jews rather than people of true German blood. This was corrected in later books; for the years 1937, 1938, and 1939 Jewish overseas emigrants are shown separately from others. Until then the total number of overseas emigrants per year had remained between 12,000 and 15,000 since before the Nazi time. Emigration overseas was 14,203 in 1937; 22,986 in 1938; 25,818 in 1939. One can see in a separate table that 7,155 of the emigrants in 1937 were Jews; 16,561 in 1938, and 22,706 in 1939. The reader has to figure out for himself that while in 1937 only half of the emigrants were Jews, over 90% of them were Jews in 1939. In still another table, the reader could learn that true Germans were actually coming home from overseas in greater number than they were leaving. In 1939, only 3,112 people not of Jewish blood emigrated overseas, while 10,455 came back to live or die under the New Order. The statistician could have put these things all together so that a person could follow with pride the purifying of his folk. But no; he reported it only bit by bit, grudgingly.

He did a little better for Prussia. Prussia, in its old-fashioned way, kept right on reporting births and deaths by religion, and persisted in considering that there was an Israelite religion—a fallacy that the New State had given up. If this kind of reporting had been done for all of Germany, one could have had an ideal record of the progress of the liquidation of the Jews. As it is, we do know from various tables that there were 370,348 Prussian Israelites in 1910; 404,446 in 1925; 361,826 Prussian Jews by faith in 1933; and 233,727 Jews, Jewish mixtures of the first and second degrees in the larger Prussia in 1939. Some measure of success is seen in the fact that actually one person in a hundred was a Jew in 1925 in Prussia, but only about half a person in a hundred in 1939. But how was the success achieved? Through encouraging emigration and the death rate? Or by discouraging the birth rate? One has to work hard to get some idea of the weights of these various methods. By using a lot of tables and making some assumptions of the kind that statisticians make, one can estimate that about 42,000 Prussian Jews emigrated overseas from 1933 to the end of August, 1939. As to the births, 2,100 children were born to Jewish mothers in Prussia in 1933, and about 100 to other mothers but of Jewish fathers. The births decreased steadily until 1939, when only 478 were born to Jewish mothers and less than fifty to other mothers and Jewish fathers. This was a good solid reduction of 75% in the number of Jews being produced by birth. But that is a slow method of liquidation. It depends too much upon the life-span. In the meantime, in spite of the smaller number of Jews left in Prussia, the death figure held up very well. In 1933, when there were 361,826 Jews in Prussia, 5,565 died. The number of deaths remained above 5,000 a year right along. In 1938, for instance, 5,632 died.

In 1939 the number of deaths weakened a little to 5,182. But since there were then only 233,727 Jews and mixtures left in Prussia, the death rate was more than holding its own. Just think of it: the Jewish population was down 128,099 in six years, a good 35%, without making a dent in the number of Jews who died every year! A pretty good record, all in all, when one remembers that the big campaign had not really started yet. But the statistician should have saved the reader all this trouble. He should have coordinated his statistics about this program of the New State, just as for others. I begin to think he wasn't really *gleichgeschaltet* at all. It is too late for him to make it good now. The 1941–42 Yearbook was the eighth and last put out by the 1,000-Year Reich.

To be sure, a new series of Yearbooks has been started. The first is out: Statistical Yearbook of the German Federal Republic, 1952. It looks a lot like the old ones. The Foreword, signed by one Dr. Gerhard Fuerst, is short and businesslike. He tells of the technical difficulties caused by loss of records and by changes in boundaries. A lot of the tables are devoted to the many refugees from the east. The New State of the Nazis, like the new eastern-zone Democratic German Republic, exported refugees. The new western Federal Republic of Germany receives refugees.

The new western statistical German has lost his race and got back his religion. Some of them even belong to "the Jewish religious community." Not many; just 17,116 as compared with 103,293 in the same territory in 1939. I am glad to say that the new statistician doesn't even try to tell us what happened to the others. I wish him well, and hope he will never have to face the problems of his immediate predecessors.

FIFTY-THREE

The Relation of Industrial to General Sociology

Herein I raise, for discussion by colleagues, some questions about the relation of the sociological study of industry to sociology in general. I touch also upon certain problems of the people who study industrial and other forms of work sociologically: the contingencies of their careers, their temptations, their sense of identification and colleagueship.

Sociology is not, in its logical essence, the study of the contemporary rather than of the past, of what is close rather than what is far away and exotic. Nor has it, by its logical nature, more to do with one set of institutions, one aspect of social life, or any specific content than with others. If a theory of society comes to be, it will be valid only insofar as it accounts for the societies of the past as well as of the present, for what is exotic to our culture as well as what is part of it, and insofar as it applies to one content, institution, and phase of life as well as to others. Sociology sets problems concerning social interaction, social organization, collective expression and action, social control, social change; concerning the socialization of the individual human, the formation of his self-conceptions and his goals, and so on.

Yet, in fact, sociology is very largely the contemporary social science; we collect our data from living people – by interviewing and by watching them, by participating and interacting with them. We do most of our work

Prepared for the Industrial Section, American Sociological Society, 1956.

Reprinted from *Sociology and Social Research*, Vol. 41, March – April, 1957, pp. 251-256. University of Southern California, Los Angeles, California.

in cultures very like our own. We work with some institutions and phases of life more than with others; with the family more than with business and governmental institutions; with the poor more than with the rich; with crime, with the slums, with "problems."

Part of our fate as a "here and now" social science is the expectation that we should tell the news about certain kinds of things. A sociological student of crime is expected not merely to formulate fruitful theories concerning the making and breaking of social rules, but to know about the trends in crime rates and the fashions in prison architecture and prison organization. He is even expected to know the personalities in the world of crime and correction. There appears to be, in our line of work, an eternal dialectic between the concrete goings on of the world about us and the abstract and generalized processes and concepts of a theoretically constructed society.

Here I make my first point in defense of industrial sociology. A good deal of industrial sociology is a reporting of the news of industrial management and organization and of labor relations and conflict in a given series of industries in a given time and place. What has that to do with the development of basic sociological theories?

To answer that brings us directly to the relation between so-called general sociology, or theoretical or systematic sociology, and the so-called applied or special kinds of sociology. It is true that a good sociological generalization is one only because it fits a great variety of social phenomena: let us say, monastic orders, vice rings, banks, and professional societies. But the generalization does not come from a social vacuum. It comes from the observation, description, and comparison of many actual organizations or situations where people are in interaction. Sociological generalizations come *from* the special or applied sociologies as well as being applied *to* them. Sometimes it is said that these special sociologies are fashions; true, they may be, but the motive which makes a man do his work gives no clue to the quality and validity of his product. Those of us who pursue industrial sociology, or any of the other special sociologies, should not yield an inch on the point that what we do is just as general as any other sociology. Whether it is general sociology or not depends not upon the subject matter, but upon the perspective, concepts, and methods which we bring to our work; and these, in turn, depend upon good communication between those who study one set of problems and institutions (law, industry, religion, or whatever) and those who study others.

But this defense does not dispose of the problem of generalization versus telling the news. If a person is to make good sociological generalizations, what he says in general terms must be true in the particular cases which he thus summarizes. He must be close to the facts and to the ongoing events.

Thus he must be able to tell at least some of the news about the kinds of institutions he is studying. In fact, I think it doubtful whether we will ever have fruitful contributors to general sociology—meaning to theories of broad application—who have not at some point in their careers been deeply involved in some one of the "special sociologies," whether race relations, criminology, industrial relations, or whatever else. How many of the special sociologies a man should get involved in during his career, and how often he should move from one to another, is another question.

There are dangers in the special sociologies, and—not to forget our assignment—especially in industrial sociology. One of them is the old danger of institutionalization, and of premature professionalization. The curriculum of college departments of sociology is the deposit of the special interests of our predecessors. The family, crime, social problems and disorganization, race and minority relations—these courses are in the curriculum because someone in the past was specially interested in them, not because someone concluded on the basis of some kind of evidence that these are the best subject matters on which to get youngsters to think sociologically and to learn sociological techniques of observation. They may be the best, but that is not why these are the backbone of the curriculum. We are apt to insist that our new special (industrial) sociology should be given a place in the undergraduate curriculum and that people should start early in their careers to identify themselves as industrial or some other special kind of sociologist. This may well overdevelop the identification of the young sociologist with his special sociology and with other people whom he comes to regard as rightful members of the industrial sociology fraternity. This can lead to a certain specialization of vocabulary and to other barriers against communication with the sociologists who study prisons, churches, families, leisure, public opinion, or what not. It may also lead industrial sociologists to develop so close an identification with industry that they fail to translate their problems and findings into such language as will make them part of the common stock of sociological concepts and knowledge.

An example is restriction of production. Some of the very best of sociological work in industry has had to do with productiveness. Neither the industrial sociologists nor people in other special sociologies have quite made the most of the problem and the findings by applying them to scholastic effort in high schools and colleges or to effort and accomplishment in churches, political parties and civic movements, or even in the kitchen. If a problem of industrial sociology is not so stated and studied that the method and findings can be applied to situations other than the industrial, it is not well stated even for industry.

Now for some remarks concerning the role and the career of the industrial sociologist himself. Before economics had been put through the neo-classical wringer, industrial institutions and labor relations were the academic property of economists, not of sociologists. Engineers now consider industry their professional domain. Accountants, specialists in administration and marketing, and others in schools of business are in a middle position; they study business and industry, but they also train young people for staff and line positions in them. Every kind of institution or enterprise we undertake to study is regarded by one or more professions as their special domain of knowledge and/or practice. Physicians not only practice medicine; they also teach it; they run hospitals; they write the histories of medicine; they, in large measure, determine public policy concerning matters of health. The professionals concerned with any such main concern as medicine or industry claim a broad mandate; they are jealous guardians of the operating philosophy of the enterprises in that field. They know the news and the low-down in terms sometimes sophisticated and esoteric, sometimes very practical and born of common sense. Often they have two languages, an esoteric one for an inner circle of colleagues and another for communication with laymen.

Whenever we sociologists ask or are asked to study some special set of enterprises—industries, hospitals, churches, even universities—we must define our relations with these people who have more intimate knowledge of and certainly much more power in the system of things than we do. They may have professional symbols of status more powerful than our own; they may have also stronger mysteries and charism both in their own eyes and in the eyes of others than has the sociologist. These are the people who control our access to the data we require, and who can set the terms of both our observation and our reporting. In industry the professionals—including line managers—may not enjoy an intellectual charism strong enough to make the sociologist feel inferior, but they command other status and personality characteristics which we may find difficult to handle. When the sociologist gets into hospitals, medical schools, and law schools, he meets people whose professional or even intellectual charism is not only equal to or greater than his own but who have as well a strongly developed and traditional mode of discourse and argument. They are likely to be a bit ethnocentric (with apologies to etymologists) and to consider their technical language the proper native language of the institution and all things pertaining thereto; our sociological language will sound alien and perhaps pretentious. Naturally, this tempts the humble sociologist to become a little doctor or a little lawyer, in the one case talking diagnostically and in the other being subtly drawn from the scientific into the legal style of argument over evidence. He is tempted to strengthen his position by shifting his identity, by taking members of the dominant group in the institutions he is studying as his "significant other" rather than taking his own professional colleagues. He may develop a slight case of "passing."

The problem of the sociologist in this situation is to develop knowledge of the insiders, to learn to understand them — their subculture, their philosophy, their problems, and their personalities — well enough to become acceptable to them as companion and as confidante and recipient of confidential knowledge, while also maintaining in its full strength and integrity the point of view and the professional identity which led to his being asked to do the research in the first place. This means, of course, keeping clear to himself and to these others at all times his role and the essential nature of the bargain between him and them. If the relationship does not get so close that one is tempted to break the bargain, to step out of the role, it is probably not a success. If William F. Whyte yielded to the temptation to help the Corner Boys a bit with getting out the vote, it means that he was a success as a field worker. If he had yielded more fully and too often, he would have ceased to be a sociologist. Hardly a good research person in medical schools escapes that crucial moment when the medical students egg him on to stick a needle into a patient's vein or to pronounce a diagnosis. There are, of course, degrees of sin — venial and mortal — in such cases; I suspect that all good industrial sociologists have sinned a bit now and then. Some have sinned their way into positions of industrial management. The problems of the social role and the research bargain of the industrial and other special sociologists are subtle and difficult; so much so that any manual which purports to tell what not to do would probably be artificial and superficial. But the good sociologist of industry must understand the problem. It is, after all, his business to be a master of the theory of social roles and the strains which both hold them together and threaten to destroy them; if he is to be a good research man, he will have to master the practice as well as the theory.

But, while he is being tempted by the very success of his relations with those in power in the institutions he is studying, our industrial sociologist will suffer cavil behind his back. His sociological colleagues will say that he is working for bad reactionary people who with his help are "manipulating" their poor employees. This will bother him, for who wants to be thought a traitor to his high calling as a sociologist? He may feel a little better if he learns that it is not considered "manipulation" to persuade white men to accept Negroes as co-workers or to tell a board of public health how to get people to let them put fluorine in the town's drinking water. Manipulating seems to mean persuading people to do things that are bad for them or things that are just plain bad, or perhaps things from which the persuader will get some personal advantage. In fact, the sociologist who will keep his research role and his research bargain clear will not often find himself working for the devil. If he has enough insight to make a good research bargain, he is hardly likely to be so stupid as to be taken in by the base motives of a villain.

Others of his colleagues will say he has gone off on a tangent, that he is departing from the true mission of the sociologist. His best answer to that will lie in what he contributes to method and to sociological theory as a result of his work. It need not be the less because the work was undertaken to solve a practical problem.

More troublesome may be the industrial sociologist's fear that he is embarking upon a career that will alienate him from the academic world without offering a firm footing in the world of industry, business, medicine, or whatever it is. There is no easy answer to this, except perhaps the proverb which warns us against carrying all our eggs in one basket. Good sociology is always a marginal phenomenon. We have to play a marginal role in the institutions we study. In a sense, our role in universities is marginal because, while there are institutions that are the proper domain of social workers, political scientists, lawyers, economists, educationalists, professors of business and theology and while even every anthropologist owns some tribe or other, the sociologist—as such—owns no institution, not even the family, but must intrude in all if he is to perform his intellectual and social mission. And it is this marginality that creates our intellectual, our ethical, even our career problems. Marginality, accepted in an adventurous spirit, is the making of a sociologist. The best way to get it and keep it is to do a certain amount of moving, not necessarily from one employer to another, but from one object of study to another. The facility with which we do move from one industry to another, or from industry to hospital, hospital to family, family to social agency, and so on, is one measure of our success both as theorists and as empirical observers.

FIFTY-FOUR

The Natural History of a
Research Project: French Canada

Robert Lamb has asked me to write something about the design of that research part[1] of which is reported in *French Canada in Transition*. His aim is to let it serve as a starting point for discussion of the several orders of social phenomena to which these sessions will be devoted, to wit: the individual, small groups, institutions (going concerns), and communities (social wholes). In telling of the course of the research, I will refer to things not done as well as to those done. I encourage you to comment upon omissions and shortcomings, the "might have beens" of this research. Will you, in doing so, remember that our aim is not so much to improve social research in French Canada, as to assess our knowledge and our methods of study generally.

The French Canada project was not, I must tell you, designed, if by

Reprinted by permission of the publisher from *Anthropologica*, N.S. Vol. V, No. 2, 1963.
1. This paper was prepared for discussion at the annual meeting of the Society for Applied Anthropology, held in the summer of 1952. Robert Lamb, who had planned the programme, died before the meeting was held.

No additions or corrections have been made to bring the paper up to date. There has been a terrific acceleration of both social change and social research since 1952. Some of my predictions of the 1930's are most certainly wrong. On one point, however, I was right. The big thing in French Canada continues to be urbanization and industrialization with their many consequences.

A paper-backed edition of *French Canada in Transition,* with a foreword by Nathan Keyfitz on recent demographic changes, was published by the University of Chicago Press, in 1963.

design one means a blue-print complete before the work was begun. It has been a growth of some twenty-five years. One might speak of it as a social movement, for eventually many people have been drawn into it. This memorandum will be a sort of natural history of this movement.

In the late 1920's, Carl A. Dawson began to study the process of settlement of the frontier, as seen in the growth and changes of a number of communities in the western provinces of Canada. Some of these communities were experiments in settling British urban workers on the land; many were created by people of Continental European origin; others, by sects who sought on the distant prairie a haven where they could practice a peculiar faith in peace and prosperity. Dawson had thus chosen as his own one of Canada's great problems.

He had just begun this work when in 1927, I joined him in the still new department of sociology at McGill University. (We two were the staff.) I had had no previous interest in Canadian problems, and but little knowledge of the country. In the several months between my appointment and my departure from Chicago for Montreal, I read a good deal about the French Canadians whom, I knew, were to be found in Montreal in large number. I decided to study the French Canadians simply because their presence seemed the most interesting thing about Montreal and that region. By so slight a joining of circumstances, I picked Canada's other great problem, that of the adjustment to each other of the two major ethnic groups. My choice complemented Dawson's. A few years later, the Rockefeller Foundation granted a sum of money to McGill University for social research. A committee decided to spend it on a study of a pressing problem of that time, unemployment. Dawson and I insisted that to understand unemployment, the basic pattern of employment in Canada must be understood, and that pattern was clearly ethnic. Our plan was not highly regarded by most of the committee, but since we had a plan and kept at it, eventually more of the money was spent on our studies than on others. Among them were monographs on various ethnic elements (including the British immigrants) in Canadian cities, as well as on the land; eventually, I got some students subsidized to study the division of labor between French and English in a number of industries, on the plea that this too was necessary to an understanding of unemployment.

The baggage I took with me from graduate school to Montreal included two conceptions of a people such as the French Canadians. They were: 1) that of an immigrant group in course of being assimilated, and 2) that of a national minority.

In the United States, sociologists had devoted much of their effort to study of European immigrants who had come to America more recently than themselves. From simple talk of loyalty and Americanization, some of the sociologists had gone on to seek a more general set of concepts for describing the changes which take place when diverse peoples meet in the same community (country or region). Robert E. Park adapted the socialization cycle of Simmel to this problem; contact was followed successively by conflict, accommodation and assimilation. Application of this set of concepts to the contact of peoples rested upon the assumption that one people was more ephemeral than the other, that one would disappear into the other. Although other Canadians knew well that the French Canadians were not an immigrant people, but a "charter member" group, I think that generally they thought that the French would, and ought eventually, to disappear; that the English Canadian group would and ought to outlast the French Canadians as an ethnic entity. A few studies appeared now and again on the number of French who spoke English, or who otherwise appeared to be abandoning their culture. Without going into why I think the measurement of change of individual cultural traits is a false way to study the relations between ethnic groups, I will simply say that for some reason I did not in fact accept this model of the assimilation cycle and resisted the desire of some of my students to proceed with studies on that model.

The second conception was that of a territorial national minority, such as one finds in Europe where a political boundary is shoved over in such a way as to leave some people in the wrong country. The people thus marooned may then seek to have the boundary put right so that their citizenship and ethnic identity will again correspond; or, if a whole people has been deprived of sovereignty, they may seek to found a new and separate state. The French Canadians were made into a people and a minority in precisely this way; but there was no movement among them to join France, and there appeared to be no major or persistent movement to seek political separation from Canada. They did show minority behavior in their insistence on a certain autonomy, and in their constant resistance to alleged encroachment on their rights. I found the national minority model of use, but as I read the voluminous literature, it appeared to me that political objectives, as such, were relatively unimportant to French Canadians. The most constant plaint was that French Canadians get less than their fair share of good positions, wealth and power in the economic and political institutions. The great battle cry, along with that for cultural autonomy, was *parity,*—a share in all positions commensurate with the French proportion in the population. But parity implied not separation, but integration into a larger whole. I find in my notes that I quite early came to the idea of studying just what the place of French and English was in the larger whole of which both are part, and especially of discovering the ethnic division of labor (or of economic function), both in its major outlines and in its subtleties.

In the course of following up this lead, I read a good deal on the establishment of industries in Quebec. That led to the labor movement. Now the Catholic Church had early tried to keep the French labor of Quebec out of unions, and especially out of unions which were "neutral" as to religion. A few good pieces of work had been done on the movement to organize Catholic labor syndicates. This led me to a literature I had known nothing of—that on the various attempts to establish a separate Catholic labor movement in various parts of Europe. A good deal of this literature dealt with the German Rhineland, where Protestant entrepreneurs from outside the region had brought heavy industry to utilize local resources and had mobilized local Catholic peasants as their labor force. Protestant labor leaders had followed the entrepreneurs to organize the local labor (exactly as in Quebec). As I followed up this case, I got more clearly into my mind the model of the region or community industrialized by outsiders, cultural aliens. The local region furnishes labor and/or raw materials and/or power. The newcomers furnish capital, enterprise and technical knowledge. In course of the development, the native non-industrial middle and/or upper class finds many of its functions usurped by the alien industrial leadership. In fact, the community now has two sets of leaders, one traditional and "spiritual," the other new, secular and technological. The strain between the two has many repercussions in politics and in local institutions. To rise in the new order of things requires new skills; but the educational institutions are geared to produce those qualities and skills valued in the pre-industrial regime. To re-tool the schools and universities for the new order quickly would require the calling in of even more cultural aliens. Similar dilemmas occur in other institutions: trade and labor organizations, local government, religious organizations, charities, and even in families and cliques. As I got into this it appeared to me there were essentially two kinds of industrial communities (or regions): 1) those in which by some social and economic chemistry local people themselves initiated the great changes of industrialization, eventually drawing a supply of labor from outside (this is the kind of situation to which the assimilation cycle concept may be applied with some reason); and 2) those to which industry is brought by outsiders who exploit local labor, and who undertake as many social changes as they think necessary for their purposes, within the limits of their power as counterbalanced by that of the local society. England and New England are of the first kind; the Rhineland and French Canada are of the second. Since the agents of social change in the Rhine country differed from the native people in religion but not in language, it seemed promising to examine this region so that I might better sort out the aspects due to ethnic difference from those due to the industrial invasion and to differences of religion. I did, in fact, spend more than a year in Germany digging up the story of industrialization there, and trying out with data of the German occupational and religious censuses various schemes of tabulation which I might use in analyzing the division of labor between French, English and others in Canada. The study of the Rhine case did indeed fix in my mind more clearly the model of a whole region undergoing that series of changes known as industrialization, with one ethnic element as the active, enterprising agent of change, and another in the position of having to adjust itself, although resisting them, to these changes.

When I got back to Montreal after the German excursion, I started a few students on the ethnic division of labor there. William Roy went to a number of industrial concerns and got the data which he worked up into tables showing the proportions of French and English among their employees of different kinds and ranks. From these tables we got several characteristic patterns. In heavy machine industries, a solid core of old-country British skilled workmen apparently could keep the French out of apprenticeships. In industries with mass production, and with great use of semi-skilled operators, the working force was almost completely French. Fiduciary functions were apparently kept closely in English hands, even including the faithful pensioners so often kept on as night watchmen. If there was need for extensive contact with the public, and especially the little people of the city and region, the French got their chance.

Stuart Jamieson worked on the professions, and found that not only were there marked differences in choice of profession as among French, English and Jewish, but that in the same profession each of the groups tended to practice in a certain way, the professionals of each group performing not only the peculiar services wanted by their own peoples but also some special part of the professional services of the larger system of which all were part. Thus French and Jewish lawyers tended to practice in small firms, while a very large majority of the English lawyers were gathered into a few huge firms. A leading figure in each such large firm was a member of the boards of a group of powerful corporations. Each such English firm had, however, one or two French members, apparently to act as liaison with French people and to plead before French judges. It thus became clear to me that it was much too simple merely to say that the French preferred certain occupations and the English preferred others, and that the English discriminated against French in appointing people to positions of authority in industry (although these things were doubtless true). One had to regard the whole thing as a system in which the interaction of the two peoples had brought about a division of function which was, in some points, quite subtle.

While we were working away on this line, I had some conversations with my close friend and associate, Robert Redfield, who had a crew working on a series of communities in Yucatan; he hoped to learn something of the change from what he called folk culture to urban civilization by studying simultaneously a series of communities each of which was assumed to present a point in this kind of change. It seemed to me that if we were to understand fully what was happening in metropolitan Montreal, we had to find a base line from which to gauge changes in French-Canadian culture and institutions. I began to think of a series of community studies with a village with no English people in or near it at one end, and with Montreal (where about one-fifth of all French Canadians live) at the other. Each community was to be picked for some special combination of the forces which might be at work on French Canadian institutions and mentality.

Somehow, in the midst of this, Horace Miner, an enterprising graduate student of anthropology at the University of Chicago, got himself a field fellowship to study the base-line rural community. After much search of statistics and maps a community — St. Denis de Kamouraska — was picked as being likely to show traditional French-Canadian institutions operating in full force. It was remote, but not back-woodsy or poor. This turned out to be an excellent choice, for it became clear that many of the traditional customs and practices depended on prosperity. A daughter of the house could not be kept at home spinning and weaving, on her own loom and with wool and flax from the family farm, unless the family land was plentiful and fertile. Farmers on back-country, poor and hilly farms had to go out to work in lumber-camps and their daughters had to go to towns to work, too; thus the common phenomenon of proud preservation of traditions by a prosperous peasantry after they are lost by the agricultural laboring class. Mr. Miner's work is published and well-known. A couple of years ago he spent a few weeks there and published some notes on change since his first study in the *American Journal of Sociology*.

It was our intention to study a series of rural communities, at various distances from the cities and from English people, with varying terrain and soil. The notion was that each kind of situation would tend to produce its own pattern of functional connections with the larger industrial and urban world outside. Léon Gérin, a French-Canadian sociologist who studied under LePlay, had done a series of rural communities some forty years earlier, and Raoul Blanchard, the French geographer, had given a basic description of the soil and terrain, modes of agriculture, and movements of populations. We used these works in tentative choice of kinds of communities to be studied. Some rather superficial studies of new northern settlements have been made since then, but no detailed studies to determine the flow of people and goods from country to city and from farm to industry, or the flow of fashion and other changes from city to country.

The middle term of the series was to be a small industrial city. Now there were many such in the province of Quebec. We worked over government and business statistics with great care before choosing the first town, which my wife and I were to study ourselves. In the north and on the mountainous fringes of Quebec are towns with pulp-mills, company towns where various non-ferrous ores are mined, and a few where colossal power developments have brought aluminum smelters (which require cheap power) far out into the back-woods of yesterday. In some of these the industry created the town. Some are seasonal; some hire men only, and so on. Since we wanted to see what effect the newer industry had on French-Canadian institutions, we chose as the starter a community in which those institutions had all been in existence well before industry came and in which there were local French families of a wide variety of occupations and of all the commoner social classes, and in which consequently there were French Canadians accustomed to the roles of political and economic leadership. The problem was not defined primarily in terms of English and industrial influence on, let us say, the language spoken by people, but in terms of the operating social structure. Again, as in the case of Miner's work, this study is published and may be seen.

It may perhaps be well to tell the plan of the book. In the foreword and first chapter I say some of the things I have enlarged upon in this memorandum. Then I described briefly the rural family and parish, for these are the cradle of the industrial labor force of the cities, and are the institutions which undergo change under the influence of industry and the English. After considering the larger series of industrial towns and cities, I go on to our chosen community. In order to understand the industrial town of today, it seemed to me that we had to know its past, the rise and decline of enterprises, institutions and families through more than a century. With this setting in the reader's mind, we took him directly to the division of labor, in an outside industry. In the case of industry, we were able to describe pretty exactly, I think, the division of labor, and to account for the details of it. Subsequent studies in other industries and cities have revealed very little deviation from these patterns.

In the section on non-industrial occupations I attempted to set up a scheme for analyzing what will happen in an inter-ethnic community to those service and business enterprises which are subject to daily small choices of customers and clients, rather than to the major policy choices of large executives. It seemed to me that one could posit that there are some services and goods wanted by both ethnic elements in identical form, while others are wanted by one more than by the other. Further one can suppose that there are some things which people insist on getting from people of their own kind, while they are relatively indifferent about the hands from which they get other things.

From there we go on to consideration of institutions, distinguishing those areas of life in which there is but one set of going concerns (institutions) operated by and for both elements of the population, and noting the changes brought about in them by industrializing, and the part played in them by French and English. Business, sports and government showed but a single set of institutions. In religion and education, there was almost complete separation of the two ethnic elements, but it turned out that the English as well as the French schools and churches had been profoundly affected by the new people of industry. The Catholic parishes and their auxiliary institutions have shown great modification to suit industrial and urban conditions.

In the later chapters we presented the less formal aspect of things; or perhaps, I should say the livelier side, for the French have a rich ceremonial calendar; informal social contacts, public gatherings, amusements and fashions. The book closes with reference to Montreal, the metropolis. It was our aim to continue with studies in Montreal, but I left Canada at this point.

There are some bad lacunae in the study and in the book. While we present some data concerning cliques in the chapter on Social Contacts, and have a good deal more in our field notes, we did not adequately analyze the operation of small and informal groups in the town and in the industries. I am reasonably sure that there were no inter-ethnic small groups to speak of in the industries, but we should have got the data on small-groups and informal understandings and controls. Our knowledge of informal organization of industry was confined to the upper levels of the hierarchy.

The analysis of the more intimate life of the masses of the people of the town is sketchy. The story of the working-class family,—the internal stresses and strains of such a family newly come from farm to town and factory,—is not more than touched upon. We did not get adequate case material on this point. In fact, what the family as a going concern is in Cantonville, what crises it meets in its ongoing life, we did not find out. M. Jean-Charles Falardeau of Université Laval, is in the midst of studying the families of a large working-class parish in Quebec City. He has already published one article on the contingencies and life-cycle of urban French-Canadian families. We still do not have adequate knowledge of the changes in consumption patterns of individuals and families of the various classes of urban French-Canadians. Such knowledge is necessary to an understanding of family objectives and of conflict between the family and its individual members.

Just before I left Montreal, I began to have some conversations with a psychiatrist who was analyzing some young people of the sophisticated classes of French Canadians. Although he had some rather ready clichés about them, he was really interested in learning the structure of French-Canadian personalities. I had run into a number of restless, uneasy French young men, who knew that they had been trained for a world that was passing, and that they had not the nerve to break away from their protective families far enough to start over and take the ego risks of a new kind of learning and a new kind of career; the contingency of being bred a gentleman a little too late had caught them. This aspect of the industrialization of this region has not been studied; the personality problems, the psychological risks. The most recent information I have shows that the French graduates of the French-Canadian engineering schools still tend to seek the cover of semi-bureaucratic jobs. Whether they do it before or after a rebuff or two in industry, before or after a minor failure, — I don't know. But the whole structure of the family, the church-controlled educational system, etc., as they operate to produce people geared to certain patterns of risk and security, with certain balances with respect to reaching out and travelling far as against digging in and staying near home, with certain capacities for aggressive interaction and for tolerating criticism, this should all be studied. And it should be studied by some combination of observing and analyzing personal careers with use of the devices now available for delving deep into the dreams and nightmares of people. The question may be this: Will the French-Canadian middle class personality ever gear into the interactional systems of industrial line organizations; or will they skirt the edges catching a slight hold only in certain liaison or staff positions which they hold precisely because they are French? In that case, it might be that if French-Canadians do rise in the line organization of industry they may be people of some new class created by industry itself. The story of the individual in French Canada, of the forming of his personality, and of his meeting the new big world as a series of career-crises demanding fateful decisions on his part, that has not been told either in my study or in any other.

The program for studying a whole series of industrial communities was not carried through. The great recent development in Quebec has been that of new towns around new industries in the far north. In such towns there is no established French middle class, no set of local businesses and institutions, around them is no established *habitant,* or farm-owning class. It might be argued that we should have studied a north-country boom town in the first place, but I still think it served our purpose better to start with a town in which the French-Canadian institutions and a French-Canadian society were in full operation before English people brought industry. Yet, the whole region will not be understood until someone takes a good look at what kinds of social and political structure grow up where the new industry with an English management builds a town with French labor, but no counter-balancing French social élite except the clergy.

Even on the rural front, the full variety of typical communities has not been studied. Aileen Ross of McGill University has done one good study of the social processes of ethnic succession on the frontier between French and English in the eastern townships of Quebec.

The third kind of community was to be metropolitan, Montreal. I had started there, and most of the work done by the few students I got interested (they were just beginning to flock my way when I left) was centered there. I carried some of the material to Chicago with me and with the aid of a research assistant whom I brought along — Margaret McDonald — a couple of articles got published on the ethnic division of labor. A few students came along and carried out small bits of work which fitted into the general scheme.[2]

The plan was to work out the whole scheme of division of labor with as much detail and subtlety as we could. It had already become clear that the Jewish people had to be drawn into the scheme. The fact that the English and French are so clearly marked off from each other, and that they have so many separate institutions made the Jews and Jewish institutions more visible than in many communities; they are a kind of third term in the local system. We also planned to watch changes in the larger institutional systems (philanthropy, education, etc.) of the French world in Montreal, and to see what kinds of connections might grow up between French and English institutions as the city grew.

My hypothesis concerning charitable institutions, for instance, was that the French would adopt the English institutional forms — raising money by city-wide campaigns, distribution of money and services by professional social workers, etc. — but that the French-Catholics and English-Protestants would continue to maintain fully separate systems of going-concerns in this field. The English Protestant institutions are those developed to replace, under urban and industrial conditions, the earlier parochial charitable institutions. It seemed almost inevitable that the French, finding their own parochial institutions inadequate to the new conditions, would follow the only available model. Aileen Ross has been studying further the English philanthropic structure, but I do not believe anyone is studying the further adaptation of the French. I do know that

2. Aileen Ross, for instance, found that the girls in the English Junior League were largely from very wealthy business and industrial families, while the girls of the corresponding French class were of landed, professional, and high-bureaucracy families, all much less wealthy than the English.

French and English are sharing some of the faculty of their schools of social work.

Some parts of the study as originally conceived are being carried out by Prof. Oswald Hall and his students. They are studying hospitals and one of his students, M. Jacques Brazeau, did a penetrating study of the career contingencies of French-Canadian physicians. This group and some other people are studying the inner organization of industries which have personnel of the two ethnic groups. (Incidentally, a little observation in a large company in Montreal suggested that the reason all their dietitians had nervous breakdowns in a few months after being hired was simply that they hired progressive English dietitians to feed French-Canadian pères de famille. Think of a compulsive English-speaking Protestant spinster dietitian trying to feed a bunch of hearty peasoupers!) They are also studying the induction of French and English recruits into the Canadian Army, with emphasis on small group formation as a factor in adjustment. But there is not quite, I think, a studied and persistent effort to build out the model of study of Montreal that we had thought of.

But a most interesting and unforeseen thing has happened. I had early concluded that the future of French Canada lay very much in the great national headquarters city, Montreal, and that Quebec City, the older and more purely French headquarters of French Canada, would have a minor role in the new industrial society. I visited down there occasionally, because it was picturesque and because I wanted statistics from provincial bureaux. But I did not take Quebec City seriously.

No sooner had I got settled in Chicago than I began, in one way or another, to meet people from Quebec City. Eventually I was invited down there for a semester as visiting professor at the Université Laval (I had never been invited in any way to the Université de Montréal, although I had tried to make contacts there). Laval had established a very live faculty of social sciences. I found there an active group of people engaged in a variety of movements of a "take the bull by the horns" spirit with respect to the industrialization of Quebec. A metropolicentric (sic) Montrealer, I knew almost nothing of the people or the movements in Quebec. Since then my contacts have been with the young social scientists of this faculty, nearly all of whom are continuing work on the economic and social changes accompanying industrialization of the province. I certainly did not create this group, nor did I design their research. Yet I have been a part of the movement of which they are also a part, and the general design worked out in course of my study has been, in general, followed out in their work. What interests me much more than the influence of this model on their work or on any one's work, is an incidental implication of some importance for applied social scientists. At a certain point in the history of Quebec, an outsider came there under circumstances which made it a most intriguing and natural thing to start study of the bi-ethnic community and region, and to turn that study toward the changes wrought by industrialization. I, the outsider, for a long time got little or no interest from English students of the region. The first to work with me on the problem was a new England boy, born of French-Canadian parents; he looked at the whole thing with interest but as from a slight distance; the next was a Western Canadian who looked on the whole world from a slight distance. This combination kept the work going for some time. Perhaps it was inevitable that, if the work was to be continued, it should be done by the French Canadians themselves, the people most affected by the changes. What good is a research design which does not include some reference to those who will execute it?

References

BLANCHARD, RAQUL

　　1936 Etudes Canadiennes, 2e série. I. La Région du Fleuve St. Laurent entre Québec et Montréal. *Revue de Geographie Alpine* 24:1–189.

　　1937 Etudes Canadiennes, 2e série. II. Les Laurentides, *ibid.,* 25: 1–210.

　　1938 Etudes Canadiennes, 2e série. III. Les Laurentides, *ibid.,* 26:1–183.

　　1935 L'Est du Canada-français, Montréal, Librairie Beauchemin.

BRAZEAU, JACQUES

　　1951 The French-Canadian Doctor in Montreal. Unpublished M.A. Thesis, McGill University.

DAWSON, CARL A.

　　1934 *The Settlement of the Peace River Country.* Toronto, Macmillan.

　　1936 *Group Settlement in the Canadian Prairies.* Toronto, Macmillan.

FALARDEAU, JEAN C. ed.

　　1953 *Essais sur le Quebec contemporain — Essays on Contemporary Quebec.* Symposium tenu à l'occasion du centenaire de l'Université Laval. Québec, Les Presses Universitaires Laval.

HUGHES, EVERETT C.

　　1933 The French-English Margin in Canada. *American Journal of Sociology* 39: 1-11.

　　1935 The Industrial Revolution and the Catholic Movement in Germany. *Social Forces* 14:286-292.

　　1938 Industry and the Rural System in Quebec. *Canadian Journal of Economics and Political Science* 4:341-349.

　　1943 *Programme de Recherches Sociales pour le Québec.* Québec, Université Laval.

　　1948 The Study of Ethnic Relations. *Dalhousie Review* 27:477-482.

　　1949 Queries Concerning Industry and Society Growing out of Study of Ethnic Relations in Industry. *American Sociological Review* 14: 211-220.

HUGHES, EVERETT C. AND MARGARET L. McDONALD
    1941 French and English in the Economic Structure of Montreal. *Canadian Journal of Economics and Political Science* 7:493-505.
JAMIESON, STUART M.
    1938 French and English in the Institutional Structure of Montreal. Unpublished, M.A. Thesis, McGill University.
REYNOLDS, LLOYD G.
    1935 *British Immigrant in Canada*. Toronto, Oxford.
ROSS, AILEEN D.
    1941 The French and English Social Elites of Montreal. Unpublished M.A. Thesis, University of Chicago.
    1950 Ethnic Relations and Social Structure. Unpublished Ph.D. Thesis, University of Chicago.
ROY, WILLIAM H.
    1941 The French-English Division of Labor in Quebec. Unpublished M.A. Thesis, McGill University.

FIFTY-FIVE

Robert E. Park

Sociology was a social movement before it was part of the academic establishment. In the joining of movement and establishment, which took place earlier at the University of Chicago, than in most universities, Robert E. Park was a central figure although not one of the founders. The road by which he got a place in the University of Chicago was unusual even in those days when few people who called themselves sociologists had any academic licence to do so.

Sometime about 1911 or 1912 William I. Thomas, professor of sociology at the University of Chicago, was invited to a conference on race relations to be held at the Tuskegee Institute in Alabama. Tuskegee was the "industrial school" for Negroes of which Booker T. Washington was the single-minded and popular head. Thomas himself had left the teaching of English at Oberlin College to study sociology, a new subject, at Chicago, a new university. He took a doctorate there in 1896 and stayed on. Thomas accepted the invitation to Tuskegee, expecting to remain for a couple of days. He stayed two weeks, walking the red clay roads in company with the brooding, infinitely curious and widely read Park, of whom he had never heard.

A little later, in 1914, Park—aged 50—went to the University of Chicago as professorial lecturer for a year with little salary and an understanding that under no circumstances would his appointment be renewed. He remained, became the central figure of the department and, for a time, of American sociology.

Born in Pennsylvania, but reared in Minnesota—then "the West"—Park

Reprinted by permission of *New Society,* the weekly review of the social sciences, London. *New Society,* December 31, 1964.

had gone to the University of Minnesota against the will of his father, builder of a successful business. After gaining a bachelor's degree in philosophy with John Dewey, "back East" at the University of Michigan, he became a newspaper reporter and in that capacity in the next few years walked the streets of New York, Chicago, Denver and Detroit. But he did more than report; he ruminated on the nature of man and society; he came to believe, with Dewey and others, that the key lay in communication (without an s) and public opinion. If only the reporting of events, large and small, were complete and the circulation of the news equally so, human progress would proceed apace.

Eventually his interest in public opinion and news brought him back to the university. He took an MA in psychology and philosophy at Harvard with Hugo Münsterberg, William James and Josiah Royce. It is said that James told him he was not bright enough to study philosophy. Park, indeed, always thought of himself as a slow man; the truth is that he was not easily satisfied with solutions to problems he thought fundamental. In 1899, at the age of 35, he went to Berlin, where he listened to Georg Simmel. It was his only formal instruction in sociology—instruction that influenced him and the course of American sociology deeply.

He went on to study at Strasbourg, with Windelband; there he met L. J. Henderson, a fellow American student, who became a noted biochemist, and who turned the attention of his Harvard colleagues to the sociological treatise of the Italian engineer and economist, Alfredo Pareto. In the late 1930s, I spent a lively day with Park and Henderson in northern Vermont. Henderson, a tremendous talker, allowed that his old friend Park was a good sociologist mainly because he had learned it for himself rather than from professionals, but maintained that all future good sociology would be done by scholars trained in the physical and biological sciences. Park, as usual, talked in his quiet, speculative—sometimes profane—way about ideas, ignoring Henderson's outrageous condescension. It was clear they liked and respected each other. The strands of the sociological movement have not been so separate as we often believe.

A Failure

Park followed Windelband to Heidelberg and there took a doctorate with a thesis described thus: *Masse und Publikum, eine methodologische und soziologische Untersuchung von Robert E. Park aus Watertown, South Dakota.* (The Crowd and the Public, a methodological and sociological investigation.) Park, then 40 years old, husband of an attractive woman who was also an artist, the father of four children, was sick—he said later—of the academic world, ashamed of the little book which was the only tangible product of seven years of postgraduate study and generally convinced that he was a failure. He came back to Boston, built a handsome house on a hill in Quincy (on a site so well chosen that his son, a Boston lawyer, can still look out over the city as well as his parents could 60 years ago) and became for one year an assistant (not assistant professor, he made it clear) in philosophy at Harvard. Here he continued briefly his connection with the Harvard pragmatists, William James and Josiah Royce.

The Harvard connection did not last. He was soon engaged by the Congo Reform Association, an arm of the Baptist Missionary Society, as a secretary; that is, as a press agent or public relations man. Again he was in the business of bringing about reform by telling the news. For *Everybody's Magazine,* foremost among the muck-raking organs, he wrote "A King in Business: King Leopold of Belgium, Autocrat of the Congo and International Broker," "The Terrible Story of the Congo" and "The Blood-Money of the Congo" in 1906 and 1907.

In course of this work, in which he was quickly somewhat disillusioned by the bickerings of missionaries, he met Booker Washington, who suggested that he should acquaint himself with the oppressed Negroes in North America before going to Africa. Thus Park became for about seven years publicity man to Booker T. Washington, the leading American Negro of that generation. In a conversation years afterwards, he said: "I was disgusted with what I had done in the university, and had come to the conclusion that I couldn't do anything first rate on my own account. I decided the best thing I could do was to attach myself to someone who was doing something first rate. Washington was not a brilliant man or an intellectual, but he seemed to me to be doing something real. So I went. I guess maybe I neglected my family during this period."

After seven years of travelling with and ghost writing for Mr. Washington, Park organized the conference to which he invited William I. Thomas. Thomas was just then in the midst of his great study of *The Polish Peasant in Europe and America,* with the aid of a young Pole, Florian Znaniecki. Into the five volumes of that work the authors put a deal of fact and theory concerning American social problems and institutions. It was but natural, for in American cities the masses of immigrants from other lands seemed if not to be the source, at least to aggravate every social problem.

When the social survey movement, best represented in England by Charles Booth's *The Life and Labour of the People of London,* came to America it became obvious that all that concerned poverty and slums also concerned recent immigrants and Negroes. American empirical sociology became study of immigrants, ethnic groups and what happens when several of them live in the same city, work in the same economy and are citizens of the same body politic. When Park joined Thomas, a man who knew the relations of Negroes with white Americans better than any social scientist in the country met the man who had done most to understand what happened to rural European immigrants and their institutions. They met in a new lively university, not too proud to admit a new branch of study, and in a city whose terrain—like London's—was so flat and uncomplicated that the forces that build cities could play themselves out in such a fashion that a map was also a systematic chart.

Perhaps it was Park's combination of German philosophical training with concern over the problems of American cities that led Albion W. Small, head professor of sociology at Chicago, to allow him to come even for a short time. For Small was two men: one of him wrote in a Germanic sort of way on the history of sociology and on its place among the disciplines; the other attacked the evils of capitalism and monopoly with such vigour that his style sometimes became almost lively. Indeed, he wrote a novel, so called, entitled *Between Eras from Capitalism to Democracy,* in which he told at boring length the horrendous stories of characters who can be identified only as Chicago tycoons and their coddled sons. At any rate the coming of Park gave new impetus to that combination of interest in social reform with earnest concern with theories of the nature of society which had characterized the department of sociology at the University of Chicago since its founding 20 years earlier.

Already at Chicago was Ernest W. Burgess, a long generation younger and I suppose one of the first sociologists not to have come in from some other occupation. Small, Thomas, Park, Burgess—these four men captured the energy and imagination of several generations of graduate students. Thomas was forced to leave the university not long after, and his place was taken by Ellsworth Faris, a man not always rated at his true value as social psychologist and teacher. Faris, as chairman, brought William F. Ogburn to the department in the 1920s just as Small was retired and as Park approached retirement. They were joined by several of their more brilliant students. Together they went through the years of the Great Depression, with many students at work on research financed by the New Deal.

As a sort of inaugural work, Park had written in 1915 "The City: Suggestions for the investigation of human behavior in the urban environment" for the *American Journal of Sociology.* It contained, in the germ, most of the studies of cities made by his students and others in the years following. Not long after its publication Small called the faculty of the several departments of social science together and proposed that they all work on a common project—the city—and that they start their work at home. With support from a foundation, this became in fact a programme. Historians, political scientists, economists, anthropologists, geographers and sociologists joined in. Park was the natural, if never the official, leader of this very energetic movement.

The first world war had broken the careers of many young Americans of religious and reforming bent. For a number of them who turned up in the department of sociology at Chicago, Park made an object of study and a new career out of what had been a personal problem or a crusade. Two, Frederic Thrasher and Clifford Shaw, probation officers, wrote *The Gang* and *The Natural History of a Delinquent Career,* ground-breaking monographs. Wirth, a social worker, became a sociologist and wrote *The Ghetto.* For the many monographs about the city, race relations, news and collective behaviour, Park wrote introductions; sometimes one must admit, to the book he had hoped the author would write, rather than to what he did write. If the incoming student did not bring a personal cause with him Park assigned him a problem about which he was to make his career. It mattered not to him whether the student was brilliant, so long as he would work on something of interest.

Thus the man who considered himself a failure at the age of 50 became the centre of a great movement of social investigation. His formal career at Chicago lasted 15 years, starting during the world war and ending at the onset of the Great Depression. But he did not stop with formal retirement. He travelled about the world, visiting former students and observing multi-racial societies. After that he settled down to teach at Fisk University, thus continuing his role as observer of and participant in Negro education until his death in 1944. He had only to come to the University of Chicago campus to bring a seminar into being for as long as he stayed. I do not remember that he ever, in that phase of his life, spoke of failure. Nor did he speak of any special achievement.

It was in the Chicago period, and following, that he did most of his sociological writing. With Ernest Burgess he prepared a set of readings to be used in teaching sociology; in 1921 they published them as *Introduction to the Science of Sociology.* It contained the readings, but it was also meant to be a treatise. It began with a long chapter on the relation of sociology to the other social sciences, and then developed, chapter by chapter, the concepts which Park considered necessary for the analysis of human social behaviour. He was also co-author of one and author of another of two books which grew out of the American concern over the loyalty of her immigrants: *Old World Traits Transplanted* (with H. A. Miller) and *The Immigrant Press and Its Control.*

He undertook, in the early 1920s, a study of the Asiatic immigrants, and their children, on the Pacific Coast. The only publication to issue from that undertaking was "East by West," a special number of *The Survey Graphic* containing poetry, portraits and personal documents of Chinese Americans, as well as a few general articles, including one by Park himself. From then on, he wrote a great many articles, and inspired others to write both articles, and monographs, and to assemble articles into symposia. The most famous of the latter was *The City,* which contained Park's own paper, one by Burgess on the natural areas of the city, and a bibliography on cities gathered by Louis Wirth. That little book was the manual and guide to sociological research on cities for a number of years.

Temptations

Park left no *magnum opus.* He regarded his writings as prolegomena to research which would result in a more systematic knowledge of human social life. If he was tempted to write a treatise, he was diverted from it by his interest in on-going social changes, in the events and problems of the day. If he was ever tempted to become an "expert" on some particular social problem, he was held back by his conviction that every event had a place somewhere in the universal human processes, that no situation can be understood until one finds in it those universal qualities which allow one to compare it with other situations — however near or distant in time, place and appearance.

But if there is no *magnum opus,* there is a large body of writing, mainly articles and his introductions to monographs written by his students and protégés. Nearly all of it is available in three volumes published some years after Park's death. *Race and Culture* contains the little known paper in which he introduced a concept — the marginal man — so well known that few think of its origin: "Human Migration and the Marginal Man." When that first volume of papers appeared I used it in a seminar of sociologists and anthropologists. A graduate student of anthropology, who had heard little of Park, reported that after reading a couple of the papers he wondered why that man Park had not footnoted his debts; then he noted the dates of original publication, and wondered why his favourite authors had not acknowledged *their* debt to Park.

The second volume, *Human Communities,* contains the paper on the city and Park's many papers on human ecology, a term and a branch of study he introduced into sociology. Park took from botanists the idea of a community of competing and mutually supporting organisms and applied it to human communities, making due allowance for the fact of human culture. Indeed, he tended to view cultures as in competition with one another or supporting one another in a kind of world-wide division of labour constantly altered by trade, migrations and conquests.

Into the third volume, *Society,* Professor J. Masuoka of Fisk University and I put the remaining papers. They turned out not to be a remnant, but a series of papers on the nature of society itself, on those lively forms of collective behaviour engaged in by enthusiastic or restless men either in last ditch defence of or determined attack upon an existing social order, and on the ways in which society may be studied. Posthumously collected and arranged papers are never quite "books;" they never arrange the thoughts of a man, as he would have arranged them. The way to read them is to dip in when one is interested in a problem, or an idea.

Park, man of wide experience, avid reader of poetry and fiction as well as of science and philosophy, recognized no academic line-fences in his choice of problems and methods. His inclination was towards realism, towards the study of wholes. He was interested in current goings on, but never content until he could put a news story into some universal theme of human interaction. Thus came the apparent anomaly, that the man who wanted to make sociology deal with the news was also the one who based his scheme on the work of the most abstract of all sociologists, Georg Simmel. He had no desire to form a system, yet he was primarily a systematic sociologist. His sources were whatever came to hand—Gilbert Murray, Bagehot, William James, Marx, Darwin, Walt Whitman.

The main thing to say about Park in NEW SOCIETY is that he was part of a great social movement for investigation of human society, great and small. One of the last remarks I heard him make was that there was no Negro problem in the United States, but a white problem. Not long before that he had shocked a young liberal political scientist by asking why there should be racial peace before there was racial justice.

FIFTY-SIX

The Academic Mind:
A Review

Lazarsfeld and his associates interviewed 2,451 teachers of social science concerning what went on in their minds, in their class-rooms, and in their colleges during the years made difficult by the activities of the late Senator Joseph McCarthy. They were carefully selected from among the teachers of social science in a sample of 165 of the some 900 accredited undergraduate colleges of the country. The results of the interviews are summarized, presented in easily read tables and charts, analyzed, and discussed in the first 265 pages of the book. The interview form and other technical information concerning the study are in appendices. One hundred pages are devoted to "Some Observations on the Interviewing," by David Riesman who, with Mark Benney, asked many of the respondents to comment on the interview itself, on the professional interviewers who "administered" it, and on the project. Riesman and Benney visited a number of colleges to learn more of the atmosphere in which the interviewing had been done and more of the reactions of respondents. They also talked to a number of the interviewers. The result is a book which contains not merely the report of the project, but a critique of its method

The Academic Mind, Social Scientists in a Time of Crisis. By PAUL F. LAZARSFELD and WAGNER THIELENS, JR. With a field report by DAVID RIESMAN, Glencoe, Ill.: Free Press, 1958. xiv, 460 pp.

Reprinted by permission of the publisher from the *American Sociological Review*, Vol. 24, No. 4, August, 1959. Copyright 1959, American Sociological Association.

and an assessment of the effect of the method upon the results obtained. It is a book with a built-in review.

This may be the wave of the future. Most people will probably agree, with Riesman, that the survey is a good one, in spite of certain weaknesses. But there have also been many reviews of the book in periodicals. Lionel Trilling in *The Griffin* (Vol. 7, No. 13, December, 1958) criticizes not so much the book as the craven professors who were so easily crushed by the pressures of the McCarthy time; he wonders why they were so crushable. Angus Campbell in *Science* (Vol. 129, No. 3340, 2 January, 1959) gives it a sober review, commenting not so much on the method as on the findings; he is disturbed by the concentration of the attack on the institutions of highest quality but heartened by the fact that the social scientists yielded less under pressure than he expected they would. There have been other reviewers. I suspect it may be the most reviewed book in social science since Kinsey—although certainly professors could not compete with sex as a topic of popular interest were it not for the "cold war" preoccupation with loyalty and the post-Sputnik wave of interest in education and in professors, of whom there are suddenly thought to be too few. And I suppose that Lazarsfeld and Riesman are the newsiest of the sociologists, anyway. At any rate, the book has been given so much attention in journals, both learned (*sic*) and intellectual (*sic*) that there is little to say that has not been said about the study and its method and about the problem and the people with which it deals.

I am in the peculiar position of having read Riesman's observations on the interviewing before I read the report itself. Also, I knew of the study ahead of time and expressed my belief then, as I do now, that it was a mistake to study only the social scientists. We are not alone in the colleges of the country. Our actions and thoughts occur in interaction with those of people in other fields; they may show what my colleague Peter Blau calls structural effects. Some teachers of English literature or classics are, in my experience, inclined to 19th century liberalism—which is to say, they are amateur liberals who cherish their freedom and defend it stubbornly—as contrasted with the quasi-professional and more modern liberalism of, say, the anthropologist or sociologist. I refer not to professional support of causes, but to the more subtle, implied "liberalism" that inheres in our very objects of study; if we study systems of race relations and compare them as they occur in different parts of the world, we imply an open-mindedness about the rightness of any of them. And such open-mindedness, in turn, implies a belief in the basic equality of the races. For we play with the notion that the underdog race might, under certain conditions, have been on top. Our very study implies always the attitude about everything that made Robert Musil's *Der Mann ohne Eigenschaften* so intriguing and got him into so much trouble: "It could have been otherwise." This is an intolerable and dangerous idea, in a world of conflicting social ideologies.

The peculiarity of the social scientist is not that there is a realm toward which he has this attitude, for all true academic people have this attitude toward some realm, but rather that we have this attitude toward social arrangements and sentiments. Our particular objective attitude demands an apparent neutrality toward those very problems where neutrality makes one appear a potential ally of the enemy. The social scientist, to the extent that he claims and acts upon a mandate to think that any social arrangement might be otherwise is the ultimate equalitarian, in that he can conceive the underdog being on top; the ultimate traitor, since he tries to understand the enemy and that seems to imply that he might have a case; and the ultimate conservative, in that he does not easily espouse new social doctrines. He is also the ultimate defender of academic freedom, this freedom being defined as the right to enough intellectual elbow room among sacred social arrangements to do his work. As the Catholic intellectual must have freedom to read the books on the Index of Prohibited Books, the social scientist must have freedom to entertain—at least for comparative and analytic purposes—all the forbidden thoughts.

Now this would seem to argue that the study should have confined itself to the social scientists. Theirs is certainly the moot case for academic freedom in an epoch when there is generally unquestioned freedom to question whether David wrote the Psalms, or Homer the *Iliad* (indeed, it is even respectable lately to suggest that he did), to study the relation of man to other species, the place of the earth in the universe, and the nature of matter. But if we are to understand the academic mind, as it relates to freedom of inquiry and teaching, we must understand the minds of all kinds of academic people and the influence of one kind upon another. Perhaps social scientists do not behave in the same way when they are a minority among teachers of engineering or theology. Perhaps teachers of engineering are influenced by the presence of a Harvard in the neighborhood.

Some subjects have won their battle for intellectual elbow room so long ago that people forget that other newer subjects have need of it. Moreover, some subjects need more elbow room than others. As a new field develops, those who study and teach it may seek new objects of emulation. When the sociologist begins to emulate the physicist he may out-physic the physicist in his opinions about both scientific method and other matters. "Hard" scientists may be softer-headed about some matters than teachers of "soft" subjects; the latter may be very tough in their logic and positively radical in their insistence on the right to deal objectively with any matter whatsoever. One of the men who did most to "harden" psychology in this country was positively soft-headed and muddle-headed in his thinking about people and society. If we are to gauge how the academic world will act in the face of full-scale attack from within and without, we must know a great deal more about the ways different kinds of academic minds act upon each other as their subjects develop and their places in academic institutions shift.

But I am not unhappy about this book. One cannot do everything at once, even with a generous grant from a foundation. The authors of this study used their resources to good advantage. They were working upon a timely matter and they got their work done and before the public more promptly than social scientists generally do. What they have learned may be of importance in preparing for other difficult years which may come at any time.

Just when I got to the pages which I thought the most important in the report, I found I was at the end. For it is at the very end that the authors develop the idea of "the effective scope" of both the individual academic man and of academic institutions. "It would be dangerous," they say, "to have the effective scope of the American college campus restricted again" (p. 265). This brought to my mind the whole natural history of American education enterprises. Many of the enterprises which now go by the name of college and university (and eventually any educational enterprise which has students older than high school youngsters changes its name, if it can, first to college and then to university) were founded for highly restricted purposes. Some of them were founded to train a ministry for a peculiar sect, but to do it without exposing young people to the dangers of the worldly and intellectual life. In the extreme case, students, staff, and trustees were all of the same sect. I know of none that refused worldly money, but certainly some were consistent enough not to seek it. In such cases the staff were primarily members of the group who founded the enterprise and were only incidentally, if at all, members of the secular academic fraternity and of those academic groups which cultivate a particular academic field. Their true colleagueship was denominational, regional, technical, ethnic, racial—depending upon the group which founded and maintained the enterprise. Normal schools, agricultural colleges, mechanics' institutes as well as sectarian and denominational colleges shared and may still share some of these characteristics. The effective scope—to use Lazarsfeld's term—of these institutions was limited by definition and by intent. Where such limitation existed, it was taken for granted that the administration, and the effective but particular lay body behind it, would keep the teaching in the college and the opinions and personal conduct of the teachers in line with the stated and limited purposes. Where the staff shared with equal enthusiasm these sentiments and purposes, one would expect little "apprehension"—just as the authors find little apprehension in Catholic colleges where purposes and the limits of freedom are pretty well known and accepted by the staff.

But what has been happening on a massive scale in this country in the last few decades is a progressive emancipation of many educational enterprises from their originally restricted purposes and scope. Nearly all of the sectarian and special-purpose institutions have taken on the outward form of four-year colleges and universities, give the conventional degrees, and seek accreditation. It is in part a case of social mobility of the groups which founded the institutions and in part a mobility of the people who teach in them. As a rule, those who teach in a college of traditionally restricted scope become emancipated more quickly than the laymen and administrators. The administrators, in the early phases of emancipation, are likely to continue to be drawn from the ranks of active leaders of the movement concerned, while the staff become progressively more academic and more inclined to find their colleagues in the academic world without reference to the sect or movement. This makes for one of the commonest kinds of strain in American educational institutions.

But one should not assume that all such educational enterprises go through the same sequence of changes in the course of being integrated into the "world." Certain religious sects—the Friends, Mennonites, the Brethren—have a broad and deep tolerance of dissenting views as part of their original faith. Sometimes their colleges are evidence of a beginning of return to conformity; there may be a phase of their development in which they have given up their other-worldly orientation for an other-directedness in which the significant other is some very limited and intolerant segment of the world. They may or may not later move on into the larger intellectual universe. Some embers of the original fire may kindle new flames from time to time in many of the enterprises which, growing out of religious or social movements, have substituted dreary new worldly restrictions for the old ones which came from within.

In the course of this process of emancipation or enlargement of scope, the institution may seek students in the open market, usually starting with those who live nearby. Eventually it will seek staff and money in the open market, very often while attempting to maintain a monopoly or at least a favored place in the competition for students, money, and other prerogatives from the original supporting body.

There is some evidence (we need some good empirical study of this matter) that we have a whole series of orbits in which academic people move, according to the point on the scale of emancipation which institutions and academic subjects have reached. There are regional orbits, teachers' college orbits, and, of course, there is a great national and international orbit in which the people of the leading institutions move.

I suggest that there are things about the American academic mind and about American academic freedom which would come more fully to light if we looked at the whole American academic system in this frame of reference — of movement from intentional restriction of effective scope or orbit to membership in some larger academic community. Some institutions are consciously seeking symbolic identification with the larger world, without quite knowing how to get it. Perhaps they seek it — as Freud says many people seek satisfaction of their libido — with limited goals. They don't want to go too far or too fast. The faculty may be willing, but the administration not; or, more often than is thought, the administration may be willing but the faculty — or some older coterie fearful of academic competition — may be "apprehensive" of too large an effective orbit — as seems the case in some small Southern Negro colleges.

In my own studies of professions and institutions I have used the terms "home-guard" and "itinerants" to distinguish the people of small, particular orbits from those of larger identifications and connections. Merton and Gouldner have been writing of "locals" and "cosmopolitans" in somewhat the same sense. Both refer to what Lazarsfeld and Thielens call "effective scope." Riesman, in his commentary on the interviewing, classifies institutions in a way that suggests a similar frame of reference. I strongly suspect that this discussion of effective scope, of the orbit in which the academic people and academic institutions move and have their being, will prove the most suggestive part of the report. I believe that what has been happening in the wonderously diverse — both as to specific aim and as to quality — American system (*sic*) of higher (*sic*) education is a movement from restricted effective scope toward that ultimate which has gone by the name *Universitas* since the Middle Ages.

The difficult years brought to a head by a McCarthy are simply one of the incidents in the long and painful dialectic between the particular and restricted and the more universal conceptions of education which has always characterized our system. The people who established our peculiar educational institutions were usually seeking progress along a particular line — toward Heaven, better crops, better schools, and what not. Progress, if persisted along a particular line for too long, may become regression and some measure of return to something more general may be called for. The latest particularism in American education is that of training people for particular occupations or specialties. The next fight for freedom in education may be that for freedom to choose one's prerequisites and to change one's mind about his career later than his freshman year. But I certainly agree with Lazarsfeld and Thielens about the danger of reducing the effective scope of our educational institutions. And I would like to see a whole series of studies—historical, legal, psychological, sociological—which would give us a better account than we have of the dialectic between restriction and universality in American education.

ly in the long first chapter, entitled "Considérations
ciales" ("General Considerations and Social Laws").
al notes are in German, I assume that he got the book
ving in Germany, that is, about the time when it was
udied in Germany from 1899 until he got his degree at
4. In his thesis, *Masse und Publikum (The Crowd and*
quite naturally refers repeatedly to Tarde's works on
lic, and imitation.[2] He refers once (p. 39) to Tarde's
psychological concepts and assumptions of the older eco-
s attempt to draw economics into the domain of social
a book entitled *Psychologie économique*. So far as I know,
gain referred to this work in print; nor did I ever, in twenty
ciation, hear him mention it. None of the forty references to
Introduction to the Science of Sociology[3] concerns the *Eco-*
nology. Park shared Tarde's interest in collective behavior and,
rote with admiration of his insights. He sometimes criticized his
ng of the concept of imitation. But he never spoke of him as his
s for the *Economic Psychology,* Park appears to have forgotten it
ly, as many doctoral candidates forget items in the bibliographies
dissertations. During the time of my acquaintance with him Park

ert E. Park, *Masse und Publikum* (Bern: Buchdrückerei Back & Grunau, 1904);
Sighele (*The Psychology of Sects*), J. Mark Baldwin (*Social and Ethical In-*
ations), and G. LeBon (*Psychology of Crowds*) are among the more frequently cited
s, in *Masse und Publikum*. In the *curriculum vitae* at the end of the book Park
wledges his debt to his teachers, Windelband, Münsterberg, John Dewey, Josiah Royce,
William James. He mentions the fact that he heard Simmel lecture for a semester in Berlin
99 – 1900 and refers to some of his work. There is nothing to suggest the very great
ence of Simmel upon Park's work. One must remember that only parts of Simmel's
iologie had then been published.
3. Robert E. Park and Ernest W. Burgess, *Introduction to the Science of Sociology*
hicago: University of Chicago Press, 1921).
In the "Index of Names" in the *Introduction to the Science of Sociology* Tarde is referred
o forty times, but no selection of his writing is used in the text. Simmel is mentioned
forty-three times, and nine passages from his writings are used. Park and Burgess were very
catholic in their references; they paid little attention to disciplinary boundaries and character-
istically referred directly to the works of a man rather than to secondary sources. Here are the
people most frequently referred to:
Thirty times or more: Darwin, Simmel, Tarde, Spencer
Twenty to twenty-nine times: Comte, Cooley, Durkheim, LeBon, Small, Sumner, W. I.
Thomas
Ten to nineteen times: Aristotle, J. Mark Baldwin, Bechterew, Bryce, Dewey, Havelock Ellis,
Freud, Gumplowicz, Hobbes, Hobhouse, William James, William McDougall, Sighele,
Adam Smith, Thorndike, Westermarck, Znaniecki
Park's major studies had been in philosophy, geography, economics and social psychology.
These interests are reflected in his use of sources. One must also remember that in 1921
professional sociologists were not as numerous as now; one was thus saved the temptation of
quoting none but members of the guild. But he need not have gone so far as to refer to George
Meredith, W. H. Hudson, and Émile Zola.

Tar

Gabriel Tarde, he of *Opinion and the Crowd* a
delivered a course of lectures on economic psych
France in the session of 1900-1901. He published
1902.[1] A copy of them, owned by Robert E. Park, s
study, noticed but unread, from shortly after Park
perhaps 1953 or 1954. I then, being interested in co
industry and human work, took them down and read parts
that, although Tarde was ahead of his time in defining t
industrial work and fatigue, he was even more so on those l
of sociologists, consumption and the use of leisure. I read a
the book, but not all. Nor, I believe, did Park, although he was a
reader of sociology, anthropology, philosophy, history, novel
newspapers, and comic strips. For his characteristic underlining o

Reprinted by permission of the publisher from *The American Journal of Sociology*
LXVI, No. 6, May 1961. Copyright 1961, University of Chicago Press.

1. *Psychologie économique* (2 vols.; Paris: Félix Alcan, 1902). The preliminary sec
contains a chapter on the general nature of society, one on "Value and the Social Sciences
which discusses the place of political economy among the social sciences, and one on th
history of economics in relation to psychology. Book I contains chapters on desire, belief,
needs, work, money and capital. Book II, entitled "Economic Opposition," has chapters on
price, struggle, crises and rhythms. Book III, entitled "Economic Adaptation," deals with the
economic imagination, property, exchange, association, and population.

558
passages is found or
générales et lois so
Since Park's margi
when he was stud
published. Park s
Heidelberg in 19
the Public), he
crowds, the pu
critique of the
nomics and hi
psychology in
Park never a
years of ass
Tarde in the
*nomic Psyc
at times, w
overwork
master. A
complete
of their

2. Ro
Scipio
terpret
author
ackno
and
in 1
infl
So

referred to Simmel and the American pragmatists, Dewey, Royce, and James, as his special mentors and to W. I. Thomas as a close friend and colleague from whom he had learned much.

This bit of intellectual biography raises an interesting question concerning the use of other people's work, and especially the works of our intellectual forebears, by sociologists. How do we choose, each of us, our sociological ancestors, and what use do we make of them? For our intellectual ancestors are numerous, and are more so unless limited by inbreeding, as are our biological ones, the further back we go. Most of us studied with one, two, or a few men; one of them is very likely to have adopted us as a sort of son and to have got in return something of a son's ambivalent combination of sentiments toward a successful father—love, pride, jealousy, resentment, loyalty, discipleship. But that man had ancestors, too. And, as one goes further back in his ancestry, choice from among them becomes more and more a symbolic act. The chosen ancestor himself becomes more and more a symbol of something we are or want to be, of some stream or system of thought with which we want our work identified. The others, not so chosen, are generally not even known to us; the more likely so because, as in human genealogies, names become numerous and are sometimes changed. An idea does not always keep the same name—especially in sociology.

But, in order to choose an ancestor to fit our case, we must simplify him. He must be reduced to a stereotype. It does not require great stretching of the facts to say that the history of sociology, as generally presented in encyclopedias and textbooks, in the classes and seminars which go by the name of "*the* theory course" or "*the* history course" (phrases which emphasize a strange divorcement of history and theory from our daily concern with empirical study), consist in the main of stereotyped sketches of a few arbitrarily chosen men and their work. If this statement contains a criticism, it does not imply that the opposite circumstance would be better. There is nothing so tiresome and fruitless as the compulsively exhaustive search for precursors and nagging criticism of men of creative mind who fail to footnote every possible source of their ideas. The latter fault, however, is not the common one among American sociologists. We tend rather to sketchy and stereotyped knowledge of sociologists of previous generations. We use that knowledge mainly to test graduate students; they learn the lesson well and use it, as they do their often farcical "knowledge" of a foreign language, only for examination purposes, or perhaps occasionally to win a point at one-upmanship (as I may be accused of doing now). The matter of language is related to our knowledge of past work, for much of it is in other languages, and we Americans, the world's linguistically most crippled of all people who claim to be scholars, are completely dependent upon the accidents of translation for whatever is written in other languages. Our publishing economy has not been inclined to publish foreign works either quickly or in full; and, even if it were a bit more profitable to publish translations, it is not likely that we will have in the future that supply of immigrants and refugees upon which we have largely relied in the past to do the hack work of translating.

However these things may be, it is the rule for a man to be known by some one concept, by some part of a theory, which has got attention and has become the sign called up when a student of sociology is asked to write a word suggested by the name Simmel, Weber, Durkheim, Spencer, or Comte. In such a test the student presented with the word "Tarde" would write "imitation."

He would, of course, be right. For Tarde not only wrote a book called *Les lois de l'imitation,* but he very much overworked the concept. It is, however, much less important in his way of thinking than are the concept "inter-psychologie" and its mate "inter-spirituel." On the first page of his *Psychologie économique* he defines society "as a web of interspiritual actions, of mental states acting upon each other . . . . Each interspiritual action," for its part, "consists in the relation of two living beings . . . one of which impresses the other, one speaks to the other who listens, one of whom, in a word, modifies the other mentally with or without reciprocity." Tarde's chief contention is that society is the result of mind working upon mind. Perhaps no sociologist, except perhaps Simmel (and Park, who adapted Simmel's work into his own), puts so much emphasis on the process and so little on the substantive results of social interaction. Indeed, what appears to be Tarde's last work is a utopian fantasy entitled *Fragment d'histoire future* in which, after a series of natural catastrophes destroys the earth as we know it but lets men live, there develops a society from which the distinctions of language, religion, region, and race and those of city and country are all gone, as are wealth and political power and the distinctions based upon them.[4] Man, being able to produce all the goods he can possibly want with no great effort and at the cost of but a fraction of his hours, and being freed of all social barriers, develops a purely interspiritual life, a life whose only disease is an intensity which sometimes causes people to destroy themselves. In this utopian world, the barriers to *conversation* being all gone, any idea becomes diffused quickly, its contagious power being gone only when it collides with another idea of greater truth and beauty. In the *Psychologie économique* itself there is a passage of almost equal fantasy in which Tarde speculates on the social effect of the world being spherical, rather than flat:

4. *Fragment d'histoire future* (Paris: A. Storck & Masson, 1904).

> If the earth were a plane surface . . . and not a sphere, the problems raised by the tendency to imitation, in every realm in indefinite progression would pose themselves in quite different ways and would bring other solutions. There would be peripheral states whose imitative radiation, whether in respect of political institutions, economic needs, products, mores, arts, etc., would press only in one direction, not in all, because of the limits of the earth, the impenetrable columns of Hercules, while the state at the center would enjoy the privilege of being able to radiate imitatively in all directions. . . . The central region of the earth would then be that which inevitably would serve as model in the long run to all the others and would be able to make its social forms spread gradually to all the world. But, the world being spherical, no natural advantage of this kind belongs to any state, since no point on a sphere can be considered central in relation to the other. There are other natural advantages, that, for example, of being in a more temperate zone, but this is shared by a number of states; they form a long broad band, not a point. . . . In sum, a flat earth would lead to increasing inequality among states and men; a round earth leads to increasing equality.[5]

There is plenty of evidence that Tarde was aware of the realities of political geography. These passages, and many others in his work, are important—as theoretical fantasy often is—because they bring a system of thought into clear relief. Tarde is preoccupied with the problems of the interaction of minds. The theoretically pure society would be that in which the conversation of minds would be uninhibited by all the barriers which now prevent the free movement of ideas from one mind to another:

> Given a group of minds in mental contact, if one of them conceives an idea, a new action, or one which appears new, and if this idea of action shows an appearance of truth or of superior utility, it will communicate itself to three, four, ten persons around; and each of them, in turn, will spread it around him, and so on until the limits of the group are reached . . . . This will at least be the tendency, although often stopped by obstacles or contradictory tendencies.[6]

In a footnote to that passage Tarde raises the question of the determination of the limits of the groups; he speaks of the multiplicity of *esprits de corps*–domestic, professional, national, political, religious—which limit the spread of ideas and action. This is, of course, very reminiscent of Simmel's discussion of the crossing of social circles (not then published, I believe), of Bayles' work on communications and power in small groups, of our present concept of the reference group, and of work on the spread of influence.

In the end, *conversation* for Tarde is a concept practically as broad as "interaction" is for Simmel. In some passages Tarde writes of conversation

5. *Psychologie économique*, I, 24. All translations here are my own.
6. *Ibid.*, p. 5.

in terms very like Mead's "conversation of gestures." In others, conversation becomes the great system of communication within a people and among peoples:

> If, among the actions from which opinion results, one seeks the most general and constant, one perceives easily that it is this elementary social relation, *conversation,* which has been most completely ignored by sociologists.[7]

That allegation would not be so true now as it was in 1901, for most sociology had been confined to grand treatments of society. Tarde, in that passage, goes on to plead for a complete history of conversation among all people, "a comparative conversation . . . almost on a par with comparative religion, comparative art, or even comparative industry, i.e., political economy." Perhaps he chose the wrong name for this great science of communication, for conversation ordinarily refers only to face-to-face talk. Nevertheless, he is, among pioneer sociologists, the one who thought of communication, of the influencing of minds by each other, as the central object of study and who worked out a set of basic concepts and problems to that end. They are not the concepts which have become current among students of communications; they are at once more direct and more poetic than the current concepts. In the *Psychologie économique* Tarde calls for the development of a *gloriometer* to measure notoriety and admiration, two of the great forces of society. Notoriety could be measured by finding out the number of people who have heard of a man or his actions. To measure admiration, one would have to find out not merely the number of admirers but also the intensity of their admiration and would have to take account of the "social weight" of the admirers.[8]

It is his preoccupation with the conversation of minds that leads Tarde to his extensive criticism of economics in the *Psychologie économique* and to his great emphasis on study of leisure. Of economists he makes the familiar complaints of the artificiality of their *homo oeconomicus.* He accuses the economists of having introduced into their work, sometimes consciously, sometimes unconsciously, the assumption that work is that human activity which is of greater value, leisure being merely a respite from work and preparation for more of it. They have not been completely consistent on this point, for they also seem to value such progress in production as will reduce the hours of labor. Here is how Tarde puts his case:

7. "Introduction," *L'opinion et la foule* (Paris: Félix Alcan, 1901).
8. *Psychologie économique,* I, 76 ff. One must not conclude from my discussion that Tarde's work did not have wide influence. A. Lawrence Lowell, in a passage of his *Public Opinion and Popular Government,* published in 1913 and quoted by Park and Burgess (*op., cit.,* pp. 826-29), refers to Tarde's discussion of the importance of intensity of belief in the spread of ideas.

We say that the economic life of man is composed not of work alone but of leisure, by their fêtes and their play, they unite themselves into a truly free is more important to consider, in one sense, than work; for leisure does not exist for work, but work for leisure. By their work men serve each other; by their leisure, by their fêtes and their play, they unite themselves into a truly free accord and they [*s'entreplaisent*] give one another truly social pleasure.[9]

He states clearly, although not in any sentence easy to quote, that leisure and the consumption of goods go together; and not merely in that goods are consumed in time of leisure but in that in leisure there occurs that conversation of minds out of which new wants develop. As leisure is increased, there arises the great problem of its distribution. The aristocratic solution was to give full leisure to a few people, while the others had little or none. In our times the leisure is divided among all, just as work is; everyone works more or less, but the hours of work are reduced for all. This solution, the more just and fraternal one, evidently is to Tarde's liking, but he insists that some people must have more leisure than others if we are to produce scientific discoveries and poetic beauties. A third solution would be that implied in economics: that leisure is bad and should be suppressed for all. Fortunately, Tarde says, the apostles of the virtues of labor do not draw this logical conclusion from their theories.[10]

Tarde expects that, given our solution of dividing leisure among all, there will be a wild growth of popular arts, just as there is a growth of weeds when ground is turned and not immediately planted. But that prospect pleases him. He believes that in America, where *machinofacture*[11] has gone furthest in giving every one free time, such a movement will show particular vigor. The wild growth of fantasy of mind will furnish the germ of industrial and aesthetic ideas.

Tarde does not claim to be the first to call attention to the necessity of studying leisure and consumption as an aspect of economics, but he correctly states that people who had done so did it in a spirit of homesickness for the rustic existence and for the virtues of the artisan. He is, I believe, the first to see leisure and the arts of consumption as integral parts of the economics of a growing and ever more urban world. His works breathe love of cities, of life that is more and more complicated, and a utopian faith that technological progress will free men of the material and traditional barriers to free social conversation. Race, class, nationality, religion are such barriers.

It is not the aim of this paper to prove any theory of Tarde's or to

9. *Psychologie économique*, I, 119 ff.
10. *Ibid.*, p. 121.
11. This is a word coined by Tarde to replace the (strictly speaking) obsolete *manu*facture. He would doubtless have loved the word *automation*, in spite of its slipped syllable.

promote any of what may appear his bizarre concepts. His theories bear looking at. His concepts are simply unpretentious combinations of words or syllables which say what he meant them to say. My aims are several. One is to convince readers that Tarde, although stereotyped as one who reduces all to imitation, was in fact a man of great scientific, literary, and human sophistication, who was preoccupied in a sensitive and rather prophetic way with the trends and issues of his time and with the problems of method of social science. Let me quote still another passage as evidence:

> The tendency to mathematize economic science and the tendency to psychologize it, far from being irreconcilables, ought rather, in my view, to support each other. In a statistics, reformed and better understood—in a statistics penetrated by interpsychological spirit, I see a possible and even an easy conciliation of these two apparently divergent tendencies.[12]

Another aim is to suggest that, if Tarde is so much richer in ideas than he is generally given credit for, the same may be true of others who have been given a place in the sentence-completion tests which we honor with the title, "Ph.D. examinations."

Finally, I would like to encourage discussion of the way in which we can use the work of such men. Most of them, as did Tarde, claimed by their writings a dual mandate for sociology. The one mandate was that of developing a general theory and method for study of human societies. The other was that of analyzing and commenting upon the societies in which they lived. Comte, Spencer, Bagehot, Simmel, Durkheim, Weber, Park—all were men who wrote in general terms, yet interlarded their work with quasi-empirical study of their own societies and with open or implied criticism of them.[13] These men, and others, vary in the proportion of their work given to general theory and methods as against that given to empirical study or comment on their own times or on some specific society. Some are more skillful in one part of their work, some in another.

If the work was done some time ago, we will generally find little profit in taking from it some particular hypothesis, concept, theory, or social comment which we test, in some way now thought appropriate, with a view to saying that Weber, Durkheim, Simmel, etc., or Tarde was right or wrong.

12. *Psychologie économique,* pp. 141-42.
13. Tarde gives us some lovely satire and criticism in *Fragment de l'histoire future.* In it he has someone in a time of the distant future discover an ancient document concerning a social experiment, based on the writings of the "ancient Herbert Spencer" in which cities were organized according to their professions. There was a city of sculptors, one of naturalists, mathematicians, even of psychologists, but none of philosophers. "It was impossible to establish and maintain a city of philosophers, mainly because of continual disturbances caused by the tribe of sociologists, the most unsociable of men" (p. 85). On the dual mandate see my paper, "The Dual Mandate of Social Science," *Canadian Journal of Economics and Political Science,* XXV (November, 1959), 401-10.

A great deal of time has, in my opinion, been wasted in taking the specific hypothesis of Durkheim on suicide, or some of those of Weber on protestantism or of Park on the marginal man or the race-relations cycle, and going through the exercise of proving those men wrong—as one obviously can. What one gets from such men, especially from those whose work was done before the more recent developments of empirical method, is a statement of general problems, a set of concepts, and sometimes some fruitful hypotheses and ideas with which to enrich one's own thinking and to suggest methods for solving the problems with which he is concerned.

If we read such men as Tarde—and encourage our students to do it—rather fully and in an imaginative mood, we may learn much. We may find that some of our pet notions have been stated or have been punctured by them (one is about as wounding to the ego as the other). We should not go to them for indisputable statement of fact or for petty hypotheses to test out as an exercise or as a way of getting an article into print. I am certain that any young sociologist will do better for his sociological imagination by reading some one or two classic sociologists fairly fully, and, if possible, in the original language, than by going through the usual course or two in which stereotyped figures are lined up in an alley and knocked down or in which a few, equally stereotyped, are canonized and others declared heretics.

As for Tarde, anyone who wants theoretical stimulation or even, in some degree, hypotheses concerning society considered as interaction of minds—or, correlatively, concerning the social processes involved in the use of leisure and in consumption generally—will be both amused and profited by reading a good deal of his work.[14] One might even try to find out why it was that he had no sociological sons, while Durkheim had so many. No one seems to have chosen Tarde as his sociological ancestor; I recommend him as at least an uncle who is generous with his ideas.

14. Tarde's *La Philosophie penale* ("Penal Philosophy") (Paris: Storck & Masson, 1890) is much better known than is his *Psychologie économique,* but I do not think that its basic theme is generally known. It is really a treatise on change from a society dominated by tradition to one in which fashions and other kinds of influence flow out from cities. It contains suggestive hypotheses on that problem. *L'opinion et la foule* is known, but the sections on *conversation* are not often referred to. Still another line of thought, related to that of the several things thus far mentioned, is to be found in a piece on various forms of organization in a collection known as *Essais et mélanges sociologiques* (Paris: Storck & Masson, 1895).

FIFTY-EIGHT

Teaching As Field Work

In October 1927 I went directly from graduate school at the University of Chicago to Montreal to teach sociology at McGill University, then quite firmly English in its language. Sociology was a new enterprise in Canada, in spite of the presence of Robert M. MacIver at the University of Toronto from 1911 until that very year. He himself writes, "I had not been able to introduce sociology at Toronto" (1968:96). I do not know what resistance there was to sociology at McGill; nor do I know who took the initiative to start the new department.

We were two in the McGill Department of Sociology. The other and senior member was Canadian to the bone, a native of Prince Edward Island (where 90 per cent of the brides were home-grown, and the bridegrooms were almost as native). That colleague, C. A. Dawson, was of that kind of Baptist bred in the Maritime Provinces of Canada and in the State of Maine, the breed that had staffed the University of Chicago.

Albion W. Small, founder of the first vigorous sociological enterprise in

This paper was the author's presidential address to the Eastern Sociological Society read on April 19, 1969, New York City. *The American Sociologist,* Vol. 5, No. 1, February, 1970. Reprinted by permission of the American Sociological Association.

Author's note: I did not begin this paper with the thought of making it any sort of formal contribution to the sociology of teaching. But as I thought about my own experience, and as I talked about it with Blanche Geer, Helen Hughes, and David Riesman (1968), there came to mind by free association the sources of some of my thoughts on teaching. Waller, with his sardonic remarks, who sat beside me in classes during my first year of graduate study, wrote the classic on interaction of teacher and pupil (Waller, 1932). Sumner's (1906) Chapter XIX, "Education, History" contains a basic statement on what we now call "student culture." Halbwachs (1959) has some telling paragraphs on the increasing age gap between teacher and pupil, and on the confusion of generations of pupils in the mind of the teacher. Blanche Geer (1967) has summed up a great deal of theory and insight in her article in the *Encyclopedia.*

the United States, was one of them, and—as was my colleague Dawson—an ordained Baptist minister. Small, an academic innovator in a new university, was one of the last wearers of the nineteenth-century conservative trimmed beard. Dawson, who had studied at Chicago with Small and with Robert E. Park, returned to Canada to carry the sociological gospel and to study migration to the Peace River valley in the Northwest. It was still the time when many countries were seeking to find new land to settle and cultivate.

I had hardly been in Canada before. I looked upon it as a field of observation. Teaching thus became for me, from the first moment, field observation. I learned about Canada from my students—doubly. I heard what they said and watched what they did; I heard their accents and their rhetoric. I also was sensitive to what they made of me, as an individual and as an American. The handful of graduate students—Canada's first graduate students of sociology—were about my age, some older, more a bit younger.

Where sociology is new, it is a second choice of those who choose to work at it. Those students had, most of them, started in divinity or social work. Sociology probably remains, like certain specialties in medicine, a second choice. The direction from which students come into sociology appears to have changed; that is itself a matter worth study. Near the end of that first academic year, a student in the introductory course came to ask if he could have an appointment with Professor Hughes. Evidently, he thought me a graduate assistant standing between him and some mysterious dignified character of that name. It is a favorite preoccupation of students to penetrate the teacher's mask and find out who he really is.

When, after twenty years of life, including four of college in Ohio, I had gone to organize English classes for immigrant workers in a Chicago steel mill, I found I could not be simply a Hughes and a preacher's son from Ross County; I could not even be just an American. I had to have some other origin. I had been declared an Englishman—indeed, by an Irishman, a bloody Englishman.

Now in Canada I became American in a special sense. A cousin of my Canadian mother-in-law had a Sunday tea to introduce my bride and me to her Montreal friends; it was evident that she took pride in telling people that I was to be teaching at "the college," but her crowning compliment was that although I was American, one would never know it. A few years later, when S. D. Clark, now of the University of Toronto, was interviewing Canadians about their attitudes to Americans, a few said that some of their best friends were Americans. This was my first experience of implicit criticism of my native identity and values. But it did not take long to learn that the Canadians themselves shared with me the smart of criticism by old-country English people. An English working-class student out in Canada on a divinity school fellowship showed in his expression, as well as in his words, his disgust at the North American habit of smearing our faces with butter as we vulgarly eat something we falsely call corn. But Montreal is good sweet-corn country, and the season runs late into October. That particular criticism only proved how benighted people could be. It cut deeper when an old-country professor of architecture spoke with disdain of the American practice, which he regretted to see copied in Canada, of working in the summer while attending university. How can a man be educated if he has to work the while? A strong voice at the neighboring table in the small faculty dining room was lifted up at that moment to remark that no man could be considered educated unless he had had the smell of cow manure on his hands. I felt reassured.

Within a few days, the World Series came on and dominated faculty conversation. In the following year, 1928, the U.S. presidential election campaign followed hard upon the World Series as a topic of conversation. It was soon clear that if Americans were ignorant about Canada, Canadians were not ignorant about the United States. The perceptible differences between Canadian English and American language and culture were not great, but they interested and continue to interest me; I learned early in my Canadian experience that slight differences may be more important than gross ones — important as symbols of identity.

But there was more to see: Montreal is in Quebec, the French province, although one could have taught at McGill many a long year without speaking a word of French. It took effort to have contact with the French world. Although North American was the prevailing brand of English in the university, no Canadian French was taught. To make sure of that, no French Canadian taught in the University. The teachers of English literature and language were all native Canadians or Americans. The teachers of French were all from France; not all were especially scholarly. English was taught as live; French as virgin, not to be touched. Teaching at McGill offered no opportunity for field observation of the French-Canadian language or culture; it did offer plenty of opportunity to study English Canadians' attitudes toward the French. In the course of eleven years, I had several very self-conscious French-Canadian students from whom I learned a good deal. My wife and I also engaged a student from the French University to tutor us in his language. He became a willing informant. We later settled in another town for a while to study French Canada. A good many years later I had the opportunity of learning about French Canada by teaching at Université Laval and living "French."

Before long in that first year, the McGill students wanted to know why we read so many U.S. publications. My colleague had warned me of this. I immediately went to the library and found a lot of books on social conditions in England. When the student objected to that, I suggested that together we should do Canadian sociology. This was, in fact, C.A. Dawson's idea more than mine. Students wrote reports on the communities in which they lived, on families they knew. Sometimes they wrote – or talked privately – about their backgrounds. A Jewish student, from the poorer northern quarter of Montreal, found in sociology support for his rejection of his bearded rabbi father's faith and practices. He once got a free shave in a department store where the new electric shaving machines were being demonstrated. It was on a day when no shaving was allowed in his father's house. The poor young man was seen by students he knew. He came to me to report, not his guilt at having deceived his father, but his shame at having been seen in a ridiculous situation by other students, and to seek understanding of his plight. Again the beard. Small's Van Dyke beard identified him as a dignified gentleman of his time. My father reports in his diary in 1901, "I went to the shop today and had my whiskers shaved off." He was keeping up with the times, at least in that respect. My Montreal student's father's beard identified him as a North End Orthodox Jew, not a well-to-do Westmount man. That student, now long a successful lawyer, may well be troubled, but I hope not shamed, by the beard of a son – a beard of the 1960's, new in its particular meaning, but old in that it is an identifying symbol. Three generations from beard to beard.

Another student, the son of a very successful Greek restaurant owner, reported a conflict between loyalty to sister and loyalty to father. The father put the son in charge of the daughter when they went to movies or college events. Was he disloyal in taking his sister only to the corner, and there turning her over to her date, coming back to get her later and deliver her innocently to the family? Those students – the rabbi's son and the Greek restaurant keeper's son – were in the course of being emancipated from the culture of their fathers. To them the sociology teacher was the person who could listen to their stories, not merely as one who hears confession of guilt turning to shame, but as one who would see their particular case in some broader perspective; their particular plight thus became part of the *comédie humaine* – and they themselves became part of a larger world.

But there were also respectable upper-middle-class Westmount Presbyterian daughters of Canada's establishment; they were of the first generation of their kind to attend college instead of merely getting finished by the Misses Edgar and Cramp (the names are real) before being introduced to society and married. During the Depression some of them got so emancipated from Calvinism that they sang with great glee a song about "Poisoning the Student Mind" with radical ideas; some became moderate Socialists; a few joined the Communists. For two who joined particular Communists in marriage their emancipation was at an end; they lived under orders. One of them wrote me a few years ago to say she had left "the church" and no longer had to report what everyone had said at social parties.

Back in Chicago, after eleven years of such field work in Canada, I found some students still in search of emancipation. A young woman of the Church of the Brethren, working for a master's degree in the teaching of social science, wrote that she had hidden a worldly hat in a hollow tree a mile down the road from the family farm so that she could put it on before she took the bus to the normal school in a city some distance from the rural community of the sect to which her family belonged. But some students who were more urban had other things to be emancipated from. One young woman, now these many years a competent teacher of sociology herself, had been brought up in a devoutly anarchist Utopian community in New Jersey, as unworldly as the Church of the Brethren, or the Mennonites. Indeed, more unworldly, for the Mennonites and Brethren believe in land and money, and exploit their austerity for material advantage. A young woman whose secondary education had been in private boarding schools on the East Coast got her first sight of lower-class ways while interviewing and working—and keeping a diary—in a low-grade industry. The Polish Catholic women with whom she worked wore their slips when taking showers at the end of the working shift. They could not be seen naked even by other women. But they talked freely and loudly about the probable sexual powers of men whom they saw going behind sheds for privacy down in the factory yard. For her, sociology was an expansion of her world, the learning of new ways and a new language, and even a new view of herself—for her fellow workers insisted on making her name her ethnic identity, which she had been accustomed to gloss over. It had happened to me in a steel mill in Chicago.

Many years later, I had a student at Brandeis who sold men's suits in the summer in a store of a chain for which his father was a buyer. People at Brandeis are often a little sensitive about the clothing business. But in a course on occupations, when we got around to interaction between customer, or client, and professional (or salesman), this young man told how sensitive one has to be in fitting coats on men. The salesman wants to make the suit fit, and to convince the customer that it does fit. So he pulls the jacket high and strokes neck, shoulders, and back close to the customer's body. But he must be quick to sense tightening and drawing away of customers who do not want any laying on of hands, for one reason or another. This case helps one understand why designers of dresses for women are, if they are, male homosexuals. Male males or male females would not do for most customers. The case brought to mind a study of the patients of osteopaths made by the late Harold McDowell. McDowell was the son of an osteopath. His thesis grew out of his, let us say, sympathetic emancipation from the osteopathic cult on which he had been fed. He found two kinds of patients at an osteopathic clinic. One group stoutly defended the osteopath as a specialist in ailments of joints and bones; the other liked the osteopath because the patient got his full attention, even a firm, exploring laying on of his hands. And this in turn reminded me of the almost magic reassurance of the touch of a bishop laying on his hands in confirmation. From there one goes on to think of the analyst who gets on with the business of encouraging the patient to peel off layer after layer that covers his unconscious by not touching, and not letting the patient even look at him during that delicate operation. All these are cases of interaction between professional and client, interaction that may be vocal and physical in various dimensions. Perhaps distant in one dimension, close in another. But distance there must always be, in some measure and in some dimension. Always there is also the question of how long it can endure. I have always wondered about the personal spiritual advisor or confessor; in the long run, I am sure there must be a second more episodic confessor to whom one confesses his thoughts about his permanent personal confessor.

In the course of years, many students—after some initial sense of shame about the occupations of their parents and of their part in it—have reported the stuff of which a nuanced frame of reference for professional-client relations can be constructed. If the frame of reference is to be applicable to the full range of human occupations, or exchanges of services, it must be based on free association, association, that is, untrammeled by restrictive definitions made in advance. Thus, if the teacher says in advance that he and his students will study only professional occupations, and then gives a definition, he cuts off free comparative association with occupations which do not clearly or by common consensus fall into that category. The student will then—and I speak from experience—either choose to study an occupation already considered prestigeful enough to merit the name "profession" in the narrow English sense, or he will undertake to prove that an occupation in which he has an interest is worthy, or nearly worthy, of the name. Thus is cultivated the common highbrow bias of excluding from comparative study by value-laden definition a part of the range of some order of social phenomena. David Riesman, commenting on these remarks, justly notes that the present generation of students is just as likely to limit observation—and the fullness of sociological learning—by excluding in advance anything that, in the past, has had prestige and high value. The student is more likely to start with the discothèque if he is to study something musical. The poor professor might be deceived, by the Greek roots of the name, into thinking that some sort of revival of ancient music was taking place. If he had already completely lost his hearing, he might continue to think so. Between them, students and teacher—some coming by the low road, some by the high—can bring into view a wide range of observations and thus find both the likenesses and distinctions required for full understanding of human activities.

One of the dimensions of any kind of work where there is interaction between the giver and the taker of goods or services is a set of definitions of the situation in which the interaction takes place, and of the role of each in it.

Part of the definition is preference for some kinds of takers rather than others. A student in the school of business administration at Chicago told this story. His father sold solid work clothes to industrial workers in Chicago. He had done so well that he sent his son to Yale for a B.A. and was now sending him to a graduate school of business to learn how to take over as his successor. The son found himself so upgraded that he could not bear to sell work clothes to steelworkers. He graduated from a willingness to sell whatever can be sold to a concern with the current fashion of clothes for men who went to Yale (not those who now go), and for customers who want fashion. He had joined and attended meetings of an organization interested in men's fashions. He had thus educated himself, with his father's help, out of the family business—out of its clientele, out of its line of goods, out of whatever colleagueship there is among dealers in stout clothes for steelworkers. He admired his father, however, and was ashamed that he could no longer be the father's business partner. When last seen, he was heading for a job in a company larger than his father's; thus from entrepreneur to bureaucrat in one generation.

Perhaps I have overplayed this matter of seeing the dimensions of the relations between giver and taker of services or goods through the eyes of students. I could have taken other matters. This one is prime for illustrating how teaching has been fieldwork. And are not teacher and student also professional and client? And future colleagues? Or future fellow citizens of whatever world will be?

Every student comes from some queer corner of American society, or Canadian, or some other. Each adds either a new dimension or a new case that has to be fitted into one's frame of reference—or perhaps requires a change in the frame to make place for the new information. Thus the teacher gets data and new ideas from the students, and the students are getting something. If a student is moved by what he hears in class from the teacher or from other students, or by what he reads, it is because he sees it as relevant to his own experience; at the same time, he sees his own experience as relevant to the subject, that is, to the experience of others. The whole becomes a more generalized, more abstract way of seeing society, one that can lead on to hypotheses and perhaps to refined methods of investigation (although there is naught so unrefined as premature refinement).

But one must ask under what conditions this kind of reciprocal learning can go on, what conditions of mind of the parties — teacher and student — and eventually also what condition of society. In American colleges of the time when I went to college and graduate school, and indeed through much of the period when I was teaching undergraduates and graduates (I have always taught both, and without any great distinction in my own mind), professors and students were often traveling in the same direction of emancipation. The professors had started earlier and had usually got further. They had started, as did Robert M. MacIver, "on the most northerly . . . of the Outer Hebrides" (1968:3); William I. Thomas, in a rural Virginia Methodist parsonage; Ernest Burgess, in a number of village parsonages; or Robert E. Park, in a Minnesota frontier town. Their rural, or at least provincial, and generally somewhat pious, upbringing had given them ambitions of almost typical Protestant ethic, without a very strong economic component. They wanted to be free of the restrictions of their background, but they were not alienated from it. They could comfortably go home for visits, although it was best not to stay long — not long enough, that is, for the joy of reunion to turn into the friction of difference between home and the world. One of my favorite graduate students is of Mormon family; she confesses to liking the collective warmth of sitting shoulder to shoulder in a great congregation of people all lifting up their voices in lusty song, as Mormons and Methodists do. She and I have this feeling in common, although neither of us subjects himself to the pressure for further participation that would come if we indulged that collective pleasure often. She has found other outlets for her love of collective activity and for the social idealism that is evidently part of her heritage.

But hers is not the reaction of the alienated; it is emancipation without alienation. That is something teacher and students can share. It makes a base for mutual learning and teaching; it allows a Lewis Killian, white Southerner who had never shaken the hand of a Negro, to become bosom friend in graduate school of a very black Samuel Adams (now a U.S. Ambassador) who had been protected all his life from dangerous white men by a school-teaching mother and a respectable gardener father in Texas. This was individual emancipation, enlargement of perspective for both of them; they became mutual informants and participant observers, each of the other's world and both of a new world of which they were becoming part. Oliver C. Cox, who wrote *Caste, Class and Race* (1948) a generation ago and has more recently written a foreword to Nathan Hare's *Black Anglo-Saxons* (1965), is not particularly fond of this sort of personal emancipation of individuals from the prejudices and practices of the society in which they were bred, yet he does not damn those who make the best of the world they live in. He would prefer a more collective solution of the problem of racial, and other, exploitation. Perhaps all of us of that earlier phase put too much faith in personal emancipation, in enlargement and humanizing of the mind by mutual observation and understanding, which we assumed would be followed by appropriate collective action. Sociology of the kind I have been talking of, taught by mutual field observation and penetration of each other's secrets of life, contains the assumption that men are equal, equal in their humanity. Only so is sociology, the analysis and comparison of human cultures and societies, possible.

This emancipation through expansion of one's world by penetration into and comparison with the world of other people and other cultures is not the only aspect of sociological imagination or the only activity of the sociological enterprise. Let no one get the idea that I think it is. But it is one great part of it, as it is of human life itself.

As higher education is now organized in most of the world, students are of a constant age while teachers individually get older. I am three and a half times as old as most undergraduates; graduate students are, I believe, getting younger. There is pressure on young people to pick their subjects and to complete their basic studies early. I am not sure of the latest developments in the age distribution of college and university teachers; the range is doubtless greater, whatever the distribution. No doubt someone will one day try to find the optimum chronological age difference between teacher and student. I will take no stock in their findings.

There would still remain the problems of historic change, of Zeitgeist, of the amount of common experience, and of the perspective through which teacher and students see their respective futures and the future of society. The difference in felt experience and in perspective appears to be great just now. Yet, now that I am teaching some Catholic undergraduates, I have the feeling that they are the American Protestants of thirty-five or forty years ago, although one of them has within the past few days expressed that deep pessimism with which this year's graduates view the day when they are no longer enrolled students. Most students I see are no longer being emancipated from anything. Their parents are so permissive that they ask the colleges to exert over the children a discipline that they themselves could not and would not exert. Yet if anyone should haul their children in to be disciplined, those same parents would join in the cry for amnesty and would hire lawyers to defend their young. They are, in short, *anxious* parents. The young appear to want action rather than observation. Many of them shy away from books: the book might be over thirty years old. In these few words I have already come close to stereotyping the young, as some of them stereotype those who are older. Stereotyping in this, as in other cases, is evidence of lack of communication and understanding.

The formula for understanding, for the teaching-learning relationship, is what we must discover. No doubt there are several formulae. It is fairly clear that the one that has prevailed in American sociology for several decades will not now work for many students. Part of the mood of many young people, and of Negro Americans, is that only they can understand themselves—that only black can teach black, that only the young can teach the young. Circumstances have led them to think that the experience of other kinds of people is not relevant to their lives, and that other people cannot understand them.

They appear to want learning and action to be brought closer together, to want more voice in the choice of subject matter, in the choice of teachers, and in the standards by which they are judged competent to leave school and begin to work. There are many issues involved in their demands—the demands of the young, of students, of the people who are, or want to be called, black. It is one of the by-products of the changes of structure and mood of our society that these and other kinds of people plead each other's cause and use the same rhetoric, that of colonialism.

I have no idea how many of the students of another day went to college seeking some sort of emancipation from family, religion, provincialism, or close ethnic group. It happened to many of them and many of them were glad. It was something for a high school pupil of my day to "go away" to college; to become a student, a word used only for those in college or university; and to become Hughes, or Mr. Hughes to all of his teachers and all but a handful of his fellows. But something has happened: college has become for many students the heavy hand that would take from them the considerable freedom of conduct, if not of thought, that they have had at home, the heavy hand of government, of the draft board, of wars that go on forever (and never ask me why), of business and industry, even of the systems of institutions in which professions are practiced. And if one is to have a job at all after college, he is very likely to have to have credentials that are imposed unilaterally by a bureaucratic professional organization. College has become a "must" for all who have, or whose parents have, middle-class lives or aspirations; it has become not an aspiration but a compulsive "right" to many whose position has been such that neither they nor their parents had, or ever understood, such aspiration.

The university has become the organ, for many of this generation, of repression rather than emancipation. My Uncle Si Hughes, the first Ph.D. in our family, became an organic chemist and went to teach and do research on government money at a land-grant college. For fifty years he studied the chemistry of fattening pigs and making cows produce more milk. He and his generation of nutrition chemists preached nutrition as the salvation not merely of the farmer but of the human race. Now the chemist may find himself on a government fellowship granted with the thought that he will learn how to defoliate Vietnam with a minimum of damage to beast and man.

To many students the university has become the agent of what students fear most, even of the things that appear likely to prevent them from having any future. And the professor has become either the innocent who is unaware of all this, or a conniving procurer to the lords of hell. That is, I suspect, what students mean when they say much that goes on is not relevant. The material taught is potentially as exciting as ever; an individual is still not really educated and mature until he becomes fully aware of his place in the world and frees himself from the very people who love him and give his life energies. The difference is that, in the given circumstances, the students see a greater danger than the very mild restrictions and provincialisms of the special circles in which they were brought up. It is even possible that they seek emancipation from permissiveness, or at least seek in university life and education a transition from whatever their earlier life may have been to manhood or womanhood in which they can use their technical and social talents and learning for goals for which they will be glad to submit to the discipline of their peers. If and when we can create a situation in which students and their teachers see the university and the world in such perspective, we can more fully realize the ideal of making the teaching of sociology a continuing joint field project of student and teacher, with support from the rest of the community.

References

Cox, Oliver C.
    1948. *Caste, Class and Race*. New York: Doubleday.
Geer, B.
    1967 "Teaching." *International Encyclopedia of the Social Sciences*, 15:560–565.
Halbwachs, Maurice
    1959 *Mémoire et Société*. Paris: Presses Universitaries de France.
Hare, Nathan
    1965 *The Black Anglo-Saxons* (with a critical introduction by Oliver C. Cox). New York: Marzani & Munsel.
MacIver, Robert M.
    1968 *As a Tale That Is Told*. Chicago: University of Chicago Press.
Riesman, David
    1968 *The Academic Revolution*. New York: Doubleday.
Sumner, William G.
    1906 *The Folkways*. Boston: Ginn.
Waller, Willard W.
    1932 *The Sociology of Teaching*. New York, Wiley.

Name Index

Subject Index